The Yearbook of Polar Law

The Yearbook of Polar Law

Editors-in-Chief
Gudmundur Alfredsson (*University of Akureyri, Iceland, and China University of Political Science and Law, Beijing*)
Julia Jabour (*Institute for Marine and Antarctic Studies, University of Tasmania, Australia*)
Timo Koivurova (*Arctic Centre, University of Lapland, Finland*)
Akiho Shibata (*Kobe University, Kobe, Japan*)

Editorial Board
Nigel Bankes (*University of Calgary, Canada, and the UiT – The Arctic University of Norway*)
Kees Bastmeijer (*Tilburg University, the Netherlands*)
Malgosia Fitzmaurice (*Queen Mary, University of London, United Kingdom*)
Kamrul Hossain (*Northern Institute for Environmental and Minority Law, Arctic Centre, University of Lapland, Finland*)
Marie Jacobsson (*Ministry for Foreign Affairs of Sweden and University of Lund*)
Arngrimur Johannsson (*Polar Law Institute, Akureyri, Iceland*)
Rachael Lorna Johnstone (*University of Akureyri, Iceland, and University of Greenland*)
David Leary (*University of Technology, Sydney, Australia*)
Natalia Loukacheva (*University of Northern British Columbia, Canada*)
Embla Eir Oddsdóttir (*Icelandic Arctic Cooperation Network*)
David VanderZwaag (*Dalhousie University, Canada*)
Laila Susanna Vars (*Norwegian National Human Rights Institution and the UN Expert Mechanism on the Rights of Indigenous Peoples*)
Lotta Viikari (*Faculty of Law, University of Lapland, Finland*)

Book Review Editor
Pirjo Kleemola-Juntunen (*Northern Institute for Environmental and Minority Law, Arctic Centre, University of Lapland, Finland*)

VOLUME 12

The titles published in this series are listed at *brill.com/pola*

The Yearbook of Polar Law

Volume 12, 2020

Edited by

Gudmundur Alfredsson
Julia Jabour
Timo Koivurova
Akiho Shibata

Special Editor for Volume 12

Julia Jabour

BRILL
NIJHOFF

LEIDEN | BOSTON

Typeface for the Latin, Greek, and Cyrillic scripts: "Brill". See and download: brill.com/brill-typeface.

ISSN 1876-8814
E-ISSN 2211-6427
ISBN 978-90-04-43637-4 (hardback)

Copyright 2021 by Koninklijke Brill NV, Leiden, The Netherlands.
Koninklijke Brill NV incorporates the imprints Brill, Brill Hes & De Graaf, Brill Nijhoff, Brill Rodopi, Brill Sense, Hotei Publishing, mentis Verlag, Verlag Ferdinand Schöningh and Wilhelm Fink Verlag.
All rights reserved. No part of this publication may be reproduced, translated, stored in a retrieval system, or transmitted in any form or by any means, electronic, mechanical, photocopying, recording or otherwise, without prior written permission from the publisher. Requests for re-use and/or translations must be addressed to Koninklijke Brill NV via brill.com or copyright.com.

This book is printed on acid-free paper and produced in a sustainable manner.

Contents

Preface   ix
    Gudmundur Alfredsson, Julia Jabour, Timo Koivurova and Akiho Shibata

Celebration of 60th Anniversary of Adoption of the Antarctic Treaty   1
    Sir Guy Green

The Fundamental Principles of Polar Law   5
    Ambassador Marie Jacobsson

Antarctic Law

Blue Ice, Meteorites, Fossil Penguins and Rare Minerals: The Case for Enhanced Protection of Antarctica's Unique Geoheritage – An International Legal Analysis   19
    David Leary

Biological Prospecting in Antarctica – A Solution-Based Approach to Regulating the Collection and Use of Antarctic Marine Biodiversity by Taking the BBNJ Process into Account   41
    Katharina Heinrich

Legal Issues concerning DROMLAN under the Antarctic Treaty System   61
    Osamu Inagaki

Legal Implications of China's Proposal for an Antarctic Specially Managed Area (ASMA) at Kunlun Station at Dome A   75
    Sakiko Hataya

An Overview of the Antarctic Treaty System and Applicable New Zealand Law   87
    Trevor Daya-Winterbottom

The *Déjà vu* System of International Trusteeship in Continental Antarctica: A Textual Analysis   108
    Xueping Li

Finding the 'Conservation' in the Convention on the Conservation of
Antarctic Marine Living Resources   132
    Lynda Goldsworthy

Compliance Evaluation and Sustainable Resource Management
in the CCAMLR   156
    Denzil Miller and Elise Murray

Challenges to Substantive Demilitarisation in the Antarctic Treaty Area   172
    Alan D. Hemmings

Arctic Law

Lessons from the Finland's Chairmanship of the Arctic Council: What Will
Happen with the Arctic Council and in General Arctic Governance   197
    Timo Koivurova

The Long Grass at the North Pole   210
    Andrew Serdy

New Russian Legislative Approaches and Navigational Rights within the
Northern Sea Route   228
    Jan Jakub Solski

Global Co-management and the Emergent Arctic: Opportunities for
Engagement and Collaboration between Arctic States, Indigenous
Permanent Participants, and Observers on the Arctic Council   251
    Barry S. Zellen

Some Icelandic Perspectives on the Agreement to Prevent Unregulated High
Seas Fisheries in the Central Arctic Ocean   268
    Jóhann Sigurjónsson

Prevalence of Soft Law in the Arctic   285
    Hema Nadarajah

From the Indian Ocean to the Arctic: What the Chagos Archipelago Advisory
Opinion Tells Us about Greenland   308
    Rachael Lorna Johnstone

Assessing Japan's Arctic Engagement during the ArCS Project
(2015–2020)   328
    Romain Chuffart, Sakiko Hataya, Osamu Inagaki, and Lindsay Arthur

The Polar Code and Telemedicine   349
    Johnny Grøneng Aase, Henrik Hyndøy, Agnar Tveten, Ingrid Hjulstad Johansen, Hege Imsen, Eirik Veum Wilhelmsen, Trude Duelien Skorge, Alfred Ingvar Halstensen, Arne Johan Ulven, Jon Magnus Haga

Indigenous Peoples' Rights

Corporate Behaviour towards the Upholding of Human Rights –
Exploring the Possibilities of Human Rights Impact Assessment in the
Sápmi Region   369
    Anna Petrétei

Communities' Reflections on Oil Companies' Corporate Social Responsibility
Activities in Utqiaġvik, Alaska   396
    Yu Cao

Polar Comparisons

Ethics of Observation in the Polar Regions   417
    Alexandra L. Carleton

Lessons from International Space Law: The Role of International Relations in
Governing Global Commons Regions   434
    Edythe E. Weeks

Book Reviews

Monica Tennberg, Hanna Lempinen and Susanna Pirnes (eds), *Resources, Social and Cultural Sustainabilities in the Arctic*   455
    Sohvi Kangasluoma

Stephen Allen, Nigel Bankes and Øyvind Ravna (eds), *The Rights of Indigenous Peoples in Marine Areas*   460
    Margherita Paola Poto and Apostolos Tsiouvalas

Nikolas Sellheim, *International Marine Mammal Law*   465
    Dele Raheem

Gunhild Hoogensen Gjørv, Marc Lanteigne and Horatio Sam-Aggrey (eds), *Routledge Handbook of Arctic Security*   472
    Saila Heinikoski

Gabriella Argüello, *Marine Pollution, Shipping Waste and International Law*   477
    Stefan Kirchner

Preface

Celebrating the 60th Anniversary of the Adoption of the Antarctic Treaty

The 12th Polar Law Symposium was held at the Institute for Marine and Antarctic Studies, University of Tasmania, Hobart, from 2–4 December 2019. A total of 110 participants from 15 countries attended the 3-day symposium and there were a number of post-event workshops engaging with the many topics that comprise the discipline(s) of polar law. The media showed good interest, covering the Antarctic Treaty anniversary event on 1 December, and the official Symposium opening the next day. Media interviews were conducted with six participants during the week.

The Governor of Tasmania, Her Excellency Professor the Honourable Kate Warner AC (herself a law professor) opened the Symposium and the Vice-Chancellor of the University of Tasmania, Professor Rufus Black, welcomed the participants back to Hobart, noting that the 7th Polar Law Symposium had been held there in 2014.

The December date was chosen for this event to coincide with the 60th anniversary of the adoption of the Antarctic Treaty on 1 December 1959. The serving Premier of Tasmania, the Honourable Will Hodgman, cut an Antarctic-shaped cake at the casual anniversary ceremony, and Tasmanian's Antarctic Ambassador, Sir Guy Green, gave an interesting historical and heart-felt account for why we need to protect this 'magnificently successful Treaty'. His presentation is reproduced in this volume.

Former Ambassador to Sweden, Mr Richard Rowe, give a personal account of his polar experiences and his optimism for the future. He was former Senior Legal Adviser in the Australian Department of Foreign Affairs and Trade (DFAT). During his long career with DFAT he was heavily engaged in Antarctic matters and attended many Antarctic meetings, including as Head of the Australian Delegation.

The anniversary event also served as the ice-breaker for the Symposium. The polar law community is small, very friendly and well-known to each other, and it was a great opportunity to renew old acquaintances and make new ones. However, the celebrations were marred by the death of Antarctic legend – Professor Denzil Miller AM – who died on Saturday, 30 November 2019.

Denzil Miller was a member of the 3-person organising committee for the 12th PLS and it was heartbreaking to carry on without him. He was Executive Secretary for the Commission for the Conservation of Antarctic Marine Living

Resources from 2002–2010 and on his retirement, chose to settle in Tasmania rather than return to South Africa. In October 2007, he was awarded the Duke of Edinburgh Conservation Medal for his contributions to Antarctic conservation and fisheries management and in 2011, he was made a member of the Order of Australia in recognition of his service to the conservation of Antarctic marine life. He was keenly involved in teaching at the Institute for Marine and Antarctic Studies, and was always a prolific author and sensitive mentor. His final paper, co-authored with Elise Murray, is published in this volume.

This volume contains a selection of papers presented in Hobart under the theme *The Fundamental Principles of Polar Law*. The diversity of subject matter is indicative of the way in which polar law has flourished since its inception. And it is pleasing to acknowledge the generous financial sponsorship which facilitated the attendance of so many early career researchers and graduates. Some of their papers are also published in this volume.

As we write this Preface, it is sad to note that the COVID-19 pandemic has forced the postponement of the physical meeting of the Polar Law Symposium scheduled for Kobe, Japan in November 2020. The event has been re-scheduled for around November 2021. In the meantime, the 13th PLS will be held as a Special Online Session for the first time in its history.

Gudmundur Alfredsson
Julia Jabour
Timo Koivurova
Akiho Shibata

Celebration of 60th Anniversary of Adoption of the Antarctic Treaty

Sir Guy Green*

On 5 April 1950, James Van Allen (the man after whom the Van Allen radiation belt is named) hosted a dinner in Silver Spring, Maryland in honour of the renowned physicist, Sydney Chapman. Over the port and cigars talk turned to the International Polar Years held in 1882 and 1932, which were themselves the successors to the great Magnetic Crusade of the 1840s. Lloyd Berkner, another physicist at the dinner, suggested that a third International Polar Year should be organised.

The idea was taken up and an IPY – later renamed the International Geophysical Year – was held in 1957/8. It was extraordinarily successful. The late Professor Pat Quilty describes it in a forthcoming book as marking the beginning of 'a new age of heroic learning'; 'It was,' he wrote, 'the most significant event in the human history of the Antarctic. It changed completely the role of science in the Antarctic and the way it is conducted.'

The scientific achievements of the IGY were matched by the powerful spirit of cooperation it engendered, upon which those involved wanted to capitalise. As Australian historian, Tom Griffiths, has observed, 'Politically the IGY was such a resounding success that it cried out to be continued and institutionalised.' Such was the momentum created by the IGY that – on the initiative of President Eisenhower – a series of meetings were held which culminated in agreement being reached upon the terms of the Antarctic Treaty.

Today we commemorate the day exactly 60 years ago when the Treaty was signed. It is certainly an occasion worthy of celebration.

The primary achievement of the Treaty was the resolution of the issue of who owns Antarctica – an issue which was the single greatest impediment to reaching agreement on a treaty. Seven countries had made formal territorial claims to Antarctica, some of them overlapping while others, including

---

* Tasmania's Honorary Antarctic Ambassador and former Governor of Tasmania. ggreo119@bigpond.net.au.

significantly the United States and the then Soviet Union, did not recognise any claims but reserved the right to make claims of their own.

It was a formidable task. Those negotiating the Treaty were confronted with decades of acts of possession on the ground or on the ice and a blizzard of diplomatic notes of all kinds which had passed between the parties supporting or disputing claims of sovereignty.

Of course all this could have been avoided had the claimants followed the lead given the British Secretary of State for the Colonies in a secret despatch he sent to Australia and New Zealand in which he grandly announced that 'HM Government have ... come to the conclusion that it is desirable that the whole of the Antarctic should ultimately be included within the British Empire.' That would indeed have provided a nice, uncomplicated solution but I rather doubt whether the other claimants would have seen it as an entirely satisfactory one.

As you know, the parties negotiating the Treaty eventually resolved this tangle of claims and counter claims by agreeing on a provision to the effect that the determination of all claims to territory and all objections to such claims were to be put on one side indefinitely and that the making of any new claims would not be recognised. In my view the pragmatism, readiness to compromise, mutual trust and shared commitment to doing whatever was necessary to create a workable treaty, which were manifested by that solution, epitomise the ethos which has characterised the Treaty ever since.

But the resolution of territorial issues was only one of the Antarctic Treaty's achievements. It has not only proved to be the world's most successful disarmament treaty but has also been instrumental in creating a distinct culture which it has managed to quarantine from the international affairs of the rest of the world. Compare the tension, distrust and conflict which have characterised much of military and political relations between the nations of the world since 1959, especially during the first 30 years of the Treaty which coincided with the Cold War, with the history of collaboration, mutual respect and productivity which have characterised the relationships between the parties to the Treaty during that time.

In addition, the Treaty has amply succeeded in realising the objective of ensuring, in the words of the Treaty 'freedom of scientific investigation in Antarctica and cooperation toward that end.'

And finally, the Treaty has been instrumental in ensuring the protection and beneficial use of the environment of an entire continent and its surrounding seas.

The Treaty has also shown itself to be a creative and resilient instrument. It was not overly prescriptive. It established fundamentals but also created a framework which allowed it to develop into the complex of protocols, measures and ways of doing things which has become known as the Antarctic Treaty system.

The Antarctic Treaty has been rightly characterised as the quintessential example of how science can be a tool of diplomacy. It certainly is that but it is more than that. It also created a precedent for how the world can better manage other assets or spaces, both terrestrial and extra-terrestrial, which should be recognised as not belonging to any one nation.

It is right that today we celebrate the Treaty and recognise the achievement of those who were responsible for bringing it into being and those who have made it work ever since. But we need to do more than merely commemorate the Treaty today, we need to defend it.

We need to remind ourselves that it was 60 years ago that the Treaty was signed. For many of the students and members of the wider community who are being introduced to Antarctica and the Treaty today, the signing of the Treaty is just history – for many not even their parents were born when the Treaty was signed. So it is important that we remind them of the significance of the Treaty and that today it is just as inspirational, vibrant and relevant as it was on the day it was signed.

We also need to be conscious of a more disturbing tendency. In some quarters it is becoming fashionable to view the Antarctic Treaty system and the principles upon which it is based with cynicism or scepticism and make dark pronouncements about its imminent demise. This may be because an increasingly politicised and sceptical world, where trust is a diminishing resource, is simply unable to accept that a civilised, principled regime like the Antarctic Treaty system can possibly exist.

But more seriously, the Treaty is also being attacked in order to serve other agendas which seek to reduce the role of the Treaty parties in the management of Antarctica as a first step to dismantling the Treaty altogether.

An especially egregious example appears in an editorial published in *Nature* last year. Adopting the fashionable phrase, it claims that the Antarctic Treaty is 'no longer fit for purpose.' The argument presented in support of that claim is seriously flawed. Amongst other things, it presents a version of the motives of the parties who engaged in the Treaty negotiations which can only be described as a travesty of history, trivialises the work of the 2018 Antarctic Treaty Consultative Meeting by selectively citing just a small part of its proceedings, confuses the nature of protocols to the Treaty with measures agreed upon at Antarctic Treaty Consultative Meetings, claims – with virtually no evidence – that unidentified 'strategic interests' are threatening to overtake Antarctic science, and concludes with the breathtaking non sequitur that the only solution to the crisis which the editorial has manufactured is to abandon the consensus rule without which, the author does not seem to appreciate, the Treaty would not have come into existence in the first place and which has been the key to its effectiveness ever since.

It is surprising to say the least to find such a partial, polemical piece published in a serious scientific journal, let alone *Nature*. But it cannot be dismissed. Even when they lack substance, views like that are gaining currency and are influential.

In short, we cannot afford to be complaisant about the Antarctic Treaty. We must keep Governments and the wider community aware of its importance and its continuing relevance and we must be prepared to promote and defend it.

But on the occasion of this anniversary today let us simply celebrate this magnificently successful Treaty and the inspirational role it continues to play even after 60 years and remind ourselves of the words of the geologist and polar explorer Laurence Gould: 'The Antarctic Treaty is indispensable to the world of science which knows no national or other political boundaries; but it is much more than that. I believe it is a document unique in history which may take its place alongside Magna Carta and other great symbols of man's quest for enlightenment and order.'

The Fundamental Principles of Polar Law

*Ambassador Marie Jacobsson**

Opening Remarks

The Honourable Sir Guy Green, Former Governor of Tasmania, Professor Rufus Black, Vice-Chancellor of the University of Tasmania,

I acknowledge the Aboriginal people of Tasmania as the traditional owners and custodians of the land on which we meet,

Polar Regions colleagues and friends, dear Julia, I would like to begin by thanking the organisers for inviting me to speak at this event. It is a great honour.

However, it is with great sadness that I will start by saying a few words about my friend, Professor Denzil Miller, who unexpectedly passed away two days ago.[1]

1   Introduction

Sixty years ago, on 1 December 1959, twelve men representing twelve States gathered in Washington DC to sign the Antarctic Treaty. The ceremony was the culmination of an intense period of formal diplomatic treaty negotiations, but also the crowning of a much longer period of informal discussions at diplomatic, political and scientific levels – all in a dramatically changing political landscape. These States negotiated against a background of security tensions that had intensified in the 1940s – when claims to sovereignty in Antarctica were a particularly fraught issue – through early attempts to settle the conflicts peacefully. Then came the Cold War and the arms race between the superpowers on Earth and in space, as well as a competition in science and technology. Despite this – or perhaps because of this – the 'primarily concerned States' involved managed to put their significant Antarctica interests aside in the best interests of mankind. Actually, in the best interests *also* of the 'primarily concerned States', I would like to add.

---

*   Ministry for Foreign Affairs, Sweden. Marie.Jacobsson@gov.se.
1   *A personal tribute to Professor Denzil Miller*, see pages 14 to 15 this volume.

During the same period, in the 1950s, the Cold War had tightened its grip over the Arctic region. Military and security interests dominated. At the same time, there was a military standoff since the superpowers and their allies had a common interest in ensuring that the tensions would not spiral out of control. The indigenous peoples of the Arctic had a challenging time. They were not part of the equation; their interests were either disregarded or deliberately set aside. Although the Arctic has no governance treaty to celebrate, tensions in the North remained under control, partly for political reasons, partly out of sheer luck.

Conflict management of the Antarctic was clearly different from that of the Arctic. But can we see any similarities? I believe we can, and it is those similarities that constitute the fundamental principles of polar law.

2   The Principles

I will focus on the fundamental principles of *international* law that stand out as particularly relevant with regard to the Polar regions. In my view, they are the following: sovereignty, conflict prevention, cooperation, peaceful use, sustainable management of fauna and flora and resources, environmental protection, the interest of the international community, and freedom of scientific research. We may label them '*fundamental principles of Polar law*'.

These legal principles are backed by political undertakings that are so intertwined with the legal principles and management of the Polar Regions that it is sometimes difficult to see what is *a legal* undertaking and what is *a political* undertaking. Let us take 'science as a tool of diplomacy and conflict prevention' as an example. This is not a legal principle *per se*, but without science and scientific cooperation as the 'common currency', we would not have had the Antarctic Treaty or the pattern of cooperation in the Arctic that we have today.

3   Sovereignty

The Polar regions were the last major areas of the world to be subject to national sovereignty and claims to sovereignty. The difference between the two Polar regions in this regard is well known. The Arctic region is subject to recognised sovereignty. There are hardly any areas with overlapping or disputed territorial claims. But the disputes relate to maritime claims *based* on sovereignty. Management of the Arctic land masses of the eight Arctic States rests on recognised sovereignty. These remote areas were discovered, occupied, annexed and administered. During this process, the indigenous peoples' use of the land was, generally speaking, disregarded. Sovereignty over maritime areas follows from sovereignty over land, as you all know. Hence, if maritime areas are beyond the sovereignty of the Arctic States or are not subject to their jurisdictional rights, they are a matter of international concern since both international waters and the Area are a global common *or* a common heritage of mankind, respectively.

The situation in the Antarctic is the opposite: seven States claim territorial sovereignty, with three of them claiming overlapping parts. There are also two recognised potential claimant States. The claims to sovereignty – or as the claimant states would say 'our sovereignty' – are recognised by a few States, but not generally. The Antarctic is often referred to as 'international space' or 'international common'. These two concepts must not to be confused with the legal concept of 'common heritage of mankind'. Antarctica is not, and will not become, a 'common heritage of mankind', even if attempts were made to label it as such in the 1980s. Many of the States that argued for this cause are now parties to the Antarctic Treaty.

The challenges facing both areas are the claims to maritime zones and continental shelves. Geographically speaking, such claims can emanate from *either* the continent of Antarctica *or* from areas north of Antarctica that stretch south towards the Antarctic.

Managing sovereignty is therefore the necessary starting point for any kind of inter-State conflict prevention or for handling existing conflicts in a peaceful manner. It does not matter if the territorial sovereignty is well demarcated and unchallenged *or* if the concerned States have decided to put their different views on sovereignty aside and cooperate to manage or protect the natural resources of the areas in question. If matters of sovereignty and jurisdiction are not addressed, the likelihood of a sustainable political solution is remote. Ownership of land, access to resources, area management – it all starts with the question: Who is the sovereign or who is the owner? Thus, an international law perspective always starts with the categorisation of the geographical area: is it a sovereign territory or an international space? Is it a condominium or a common heritage of mankind? Is it an area over which a particular state may claim sovereign rights and exclusive or partial jurisdiction?

Even if land masses and their adjacent water areas are recognised as part of a sovereign state, it does not necessarily mean a lack of legal challenges. The status of ice shelves was debated at an early stage, as were the extensive baselines drawn in the Arctic Ocean. The longer the baselines, the more coastal state control and the greater the risk of creeping jurisdiction. The status of both the North West Passage and the North East Passage is also discussed and challenged. These issues have not been solved through an international agreement; they remain in the hands of the coastal States, their neighbours, third States and the international community and, with respect to the Area, mankind as a whole.

In Antarctica, the sovereignty issue was 'solved' by the 'setting aside clause' in the Antarctic Treaty namely, Article IV. This brilliantly formulated provision preserves the legal rights and interests of claimant States, potential claimant States and non-claimant States alike. It also contains a formulation that aims to prevent acts or activities undertaken while the treaty is in force from being used at a later stage to buttress the claim as it stood at the time of the conclusion of the Antarctic Treaty.

The entire Antarctic Treaty System rests on Article IV. It has prevented the continent and Antarctic cooperation from being dragged into serious conflicts such at the Falkland/Malvinas war, or the boycott of South Africa during the apartheid regime. Article IV is repeatedly referred to at Commission for the Conservation of Antarctic Marine Living Resources (CCAMLR) meetings and other Treaty meetings. It is also referred to in external contexts, such as in submissions to the Commission on the Limits of the Continental Shelf (CLCS). The first submission of a claimant State (Australia, 2004) serves as a good example. Australia asked the Commission not to take action with regard to the information that related to the continental shelf appurtenant to Antarctica. Other Antarctic Treaty parties declared that they did not recognise claims of sovereignty over Antarctica. They did so with reference to Article IV, while at the same time expressing appreciation for Australia's request that the Commission not take action. Some States, including Sweden, did not make an official statement, considering that their view was already covered by Article IV. The way the States involved managed this may appear to have been straightforward and uncontroversial. It was not. But it bears evidence of the typical Antarctic Treaty ambition to find solutions that all Treaty parties can live with.

Conclusion: This is how the *geo-legal* (as opposed to *geopolitical*) situation looks in the Polar Regions, and this is why the *general principle of sovereignty is also a fundamental principle of Polar Law.*

4   Conflict Prevention and Cooperation

In the early 1950s, the Antarctic States (claimants and non-claimants) realised that the claims issue could lead to serious and possibly violent conflicts, and few were prepared to take the risk. Too much was at stake: military build-up, the arms race, the race for outer space, and tensions among the Latin American States and the European States are just a few examples. In 1955, the United

Kingdom filed the *Antarctica Case* at the International Court of Justice, but the case was removed from the Court's list since the Court found that it did not have any acceptance by Argentina to deal with the dispute.

In January 1956, the New Zealand Prime Minister, the former Labour leader of the opposition Walter Nash, proposed that Antarctica should be a UN Trusteeship. Nash also proposed the abandonment of claims in Antarctica. Allegedly inspired by Nash, India proposed in early 1956 that the question of Antarctica be included in the agenda of the United Nations General Assembly. According to an explanatory memorandum, the reason for the initiative was that India wanted all nations to affirm that the area will be utilized entirely for peaceful purposes and for the welfare of the whole world. Another objective was to secure the development of Antarctica's resources for peaceful purposes.

The Indian request was evidently due to the concern that Antarctica would be utilised for nuclear testing. There was no attempt to transfer the issue of territorial claims to the UN agenda; rather, the attempt was to secure the peaceful use of Antarctica, a concern that the United States tried to address by assuring that it had no intention of using Antarctica as a nuclear site. The claimant states were also clearly opposed to India's proposal, and Argentina and Chile argued that it would be contrary to Article 2, paragraph 7, of the UN Charter, namely that the UN was not authorised to *"intervene in matters which are essentially within the domestic jurisdiction of any state"* or require that Member States must *"submit such matters to settlement"* under the Charter. India's proposal was withdrawn later the same year.

This gave the parties engaged in the upcoming International Geophysical Year some respite, and they could build on the *'gentlemen's agreement'* among scientists (but with a blessing from the States). This laid the foundations of the renowned Article IV.

The Antarctic Treaty parties strengthened their political cooperation when they felt that the System was threatened from the outside in the 1980s. The Treaty parties' response to this was to become gradually more transparent and to further open up the System, for example by inviting more and more international and non-governmental organisations to attend and have a role at the meetings. Needless to say, the Antarctic Treaty is open for accession by any State.

Unlike cooperation on Antarctica, cooperation on Arctic issues took a long time to develop. Before the fall of the Berlin Wall and the subsequent dissolution of the Soviet Union, most attempts to cooperate or establish cooperative arrangements were viewed with suspicion. Given the security and military realities in the Arctic at the time, this was hardly surprising.

The only real cooperative consultation mechanism specifically addressing an Arctic issue was the 1973 Agreement on the Conservation of Polar Bears. Although the explicit aim of the Agreement was to protect the polar bear as a significant resource of the Arctic region, it also gave the five Arctic rim countries a chance to cooperate and proved to be an important legally binding security and confidence-building measure.

The next step in Arctic cooperation (*leaving aside the Comité Arctique*) was the establishment of the International Arctic Science Committee (IASC) – cooperation among scientists from the eight Arctic countries. The establishment of the IASC was a very delicate matter. Two issues were particularly sensitive: who would participate and be a member and the reluctance on the part of some states to establish a regional institution. States were certainly prompters behind the scientific academies that established the IASC. This is not remarkable: without the consent of states, scientific cooperation cannot take place. Physical participation and cooperation in international expeditions, and the exchange of scientific data and information all require a proper legal framework.

It took the fall of a wall in central Europe to lower the tensions and increase cooperation in the Arctic. Today, the situation is quite different. Arctic relations are, to a large degree, built on cooperation. The establishment of the Arctic Council has made it possible for the Arctic States and the indigenous peoples of the Arctic to develop cooperation on Arctic matters that was unthinkable during the Cold War. The Arctic structure remains in place and we must seriously hope that it will remain stable, despite challenges relating to differing views on climate change issues.

Cooperation is not defined in international law, and although cooperation does not in itself have a default *positive* effect, the *concept of cooperation* certainly has positive connotations. When States are encouraged to cooperate, they are obviously not supposed to cooperate to undermine the environment or the security situation.

Conclusion: The principle of conflict prevention and cooperation in the Polar Regions rests on the primary legal obligation of States to solve their disputes by peaceful and legal means.

5 Peaceful Use and Demilitarisation

The Antarctic Treaty clearly states that Antarctica '*shall be used for peaceful purposes only*'. Such a sweeping formulation has more of a political character than a legal character. Yet it is a binding *legal* rule. Compared with the United Nations Law of the Sea Convention (LOSC); purpose of the Convention is to '*promote the peaceful uses of the seas and oceans*'. Furthermore, the Convention reserves the high seas and the Area for *peaceful purposes*. These provisions are applicable in the Arctic and around Antarctica, but they have never prevented the Arctic from being used for military purposes. Peaceful purposes are not the same as non-military purposes – and the Antarctic Treaty bears evidence of this. Military personnel are allowed, but military activities are not. The Antarctic Treaty is even more specific. It prohibits any measures of a military nature, including the establishment of military bases. Most importantly, it sets up an inspection regime. This was a security policy mechanism and needs to be retained as such. Another type of inspection regime is set up through the Environmental Protocol. The different legal basis and objectives of these inspection regimes need to be kept in mind and preserved.

Unlike the Antarctic, the Arctic is not demilitarised except for the Svalbard area, as regulated under the Spitzbergen Treaty of 1920. The treaty makes it clear that the area falls under Norway's sovereignty. Norway's undertaking not to establish naval bases and not to construct fortifications is specific to Norway. It follows from the principle of sovereignty but in 1959 time was not ripe that other states cannot establish bases on Norwegian soil.

Conclusion: Both areas are subject to the basic legal principle of peaceful use, which does not necessarily imply demilitarisation obligations. Whereas the demilitarisation obligations embedded in the Antarctic Treaty stretch far beyond the treaty parties, the provisions regulating the demilitarised area in the Arctic, situated as it is within the sovereign territory of a State, are clearly more limited.

6   Sustainable Management of Fauna, Flora and Resources

Securing sustainable use of resources is part of the principle of conflict prevention which started with the protection of fauna and flora, seals, krill and fish in Antarctica and polar bears in the Arctic.

Environmental protection is partly embedded in the purpose of preserving the Antarctic for the benefit of all mankind, but time was not ripe to address *management* of natural resources. An indication of the need to do so is found in Article IX (f) of the Antarctic Treaty, which sets out as one of the objectives of the *Meeting of States Parties* (ATCM) *to recommend to their Governments 'measures in furtherance of the principles and objectives of the treaty, including measures regarding ... preservation and conservation of living resources in Antarctica.'*

It was a deliberate choice of the treaty negotiators not to address matters relating to natural resources at this stage of the discussions. It was too political. Resource matters had to be regulated gradually, starting with regulations on seals, marine living resources including fish and then minerals.

The starting point for multilateral cooperation in the Arctic was the opposite: protection of a natural resource was the very first step towards cooperation among Arctic States – or should I say the Arctic rim states. I am referring to the 1973 Agreement on the Conservation of Polar Bears. From this first step, we now have a pattern of regulatory treaties and national legislation irrespective of resource.

Conclusion: Sustainable management of resources is a fundamental principle of polar law.

7 Environmental Protection

The focus on conflict prevention and management of sovereignty was the obvious purpose of the Antarctic treaty. It is interesting to note that the 'environment' is not even mentioned in the Antarctic Treaty, whereas it was one of the main drivers of Arctic cooperation.

Environmental protection in the Arctic is, to a large extent, the responsibility of the sovereign Arctic States. But it is also the responsibility of those who use the region. In the Antarctic, it became the responsibility of those who were active on the continent. Later, the Antarctic Treaty Parties came under pressure from the international community – the United Nations and the environmental movement – and replaced the mineral regime with the Protocol on Environmental Protection (which became a crucial pillar of the Antarctic Treaty System).

The emerging international environmental regime for the Arctic is partly a result of cooperation in the Arctic Council.

Conclusion: Protection of the environment is another fundamental principle of polar law.

8 Recognition of the Interest of the International Community

Among the most important factors for the successful and sustainable management of the Polar regions is the recognition of the interest of the international community in both regions, as well as the international community's acceptance of the Antarctic Treaty System management of the area.

A considerable number of international conventions apply to both the Arctic and the Antarctic. Both are subject to international legal global regimes established by multilateral conventions such as the UN Law of the Sea Convention, the Convention on Biodiversity, the Convention on Migratory Species, ICAO, MARPOL, the Kyoto Protocol and the 2012 Doha Amendment to the Kyoto Protocol, the 2017 Paris Agreement under the UNFCCC, and, obviously also the entire body of human rights.

Environmental threats to the regions seldom come from local emissions; it has long been recognised that they come from sources outside the regions, and hence the need for third-party involvement in the process.

Conclusion: All activities in the Polar regions must be undertaken with the interest of the of the international community in mind.

9 Science

These legal principles are backed by political undertakings that are intertwined with the legal principles and management of the Polar Regions. I am thinking here of science as a tool of diplomacy and conflict prevention. The right to seek information and undertake scientific research is a fundamental principle of international law and particularly important in relation to the Polar Regions. Whereas the Antarctic Treaty is based on the idea of freedom of scientific research, science in the Arctic region may be subject to national and territorial legislation. The right to conduct marine scientific research is regulated under the LOSC.

Conclusion: Freedom of scientific research is a guiding legal principle in the Antarctic region, but subject to more stringent national and international regulations when conducted in the Arctic region.

10 Concluding Remarks

Two days ago, when Denzil and I were talking about the upcoming conference and his presentation with my presentation, he raised a very pertinent question: Of all the principles you refer to, which is the most important?

So Denzil, *here is my attempt to answer your question:*

As I see it, all the principles are interrelated. They are all part of the puzzle of managing the Polar Regions.

Most of the fundamental principles of polar law are rooted in the Charter of the United Nations, whose fundamental objective is to maintain international peace and security, to develop friendly relations among nations, and to achieve international cooperation. Members are therefore obliged to " settle their international disputes by peaceful means in such a manner that international peace and security, and justice, are not endangered. Human rights and the rights of indigenous peoples must always be respected.

Today, both the Arctic and the Antarctic are faced with a threat that goes far beyond sovereignty: the climate crisis.

Will the primarily concerned States and the international community as a whole focus on addressing the climate crisis *or* will they, in a worst-case scenario, allow the climate crisis to awaken dormant sovereignty conflicts?

I simply do not know.

Thank you.

11 A Personal Tribute to Professor Denzil Miller, Hobart, Tasmania

My friend Denzil picked me up at the airport when I arrived in Tasmania on 29 November. Later that day, he took me to his home for a wonderful, warm and charmingly chaotic dinner with almost all of his children and grandchildren, and his wonderful wife, Jenny, cheerful in the midst of it all.

After dinner, Denzil drove me back to my hotel. We talked all the way there and we still had more to say. The next morning, I was in touch with Jenny, sending her videos and photos from the previous evening.

A few hours later, Jenny called me to say that Denzil had had a heart attack and could not be saved.

Time stood still.

Denzil was my oldest Antarctic friend. I met him here in Hobart in 1986, during the negotiations on the Antarctic Mineral Resource Regime. He was part of the South African delegation and I was with the Swedish delegation. We got talking and a precious friendship was born.

Denzil also gave me my first krill, which I took back to Sweden. Not long after, I found myself having to convince the Swedish authorities that Denzil was a scientist, and that he was not a supporter of South Africa's apartheid politics. This was at a time when Sweden boycotted all cooperation with South Africa except for scientific cooperation. Denzil made it to Sweden for a marine science conference.

Denzil had a deep connection with the continent where he was raised, educated and embarked on a distinguished career. He was African, he said, and African soil was forever under his feet and in his hands.

Denzil drove me around the Cape Town region, showing me the places where he did his research on sea turtles. We went to the top of Table Mountain. We watched birds. He took me to the Cape of Good Hope. He introduced me to family and friends – and to African art. Here in Tasmania, he took me to Bruny

Island and Mount Field. We walked and talked and laughed a lot. We talked about everything: Antarctica and the Southern Ocean of course, but also politics, music, literature, our families.

Denzil's commitment to science was absolute, his rational thinking stimulating. He was always willing to share his knowledge and experience. He was a true humanitarian, humanist and intellectual.

He enjoyed every minute of his job with CCAMLR. He was looking forward to finishing his book on the history of the CCAMLR compliance regime. He was humbly proud to have become an Australian citizen, and to have been recognised by Australia and the international community for his contributions.

Several of his Antarctic friends and colleagues have been in touch with me, among them Ray Arnaudo from the US and Mike Richardson from the UK. Ray has written a beautiful poem, which goes like this:

> *I hear his chortle.*
> *I see his wistful smile.*
> *He loved,*
> *He worked,*
> *He laughed,*
> *He made his friends smile,*
> *Having had the good fortune*
> *To escape his Troubled Homeland*
> *And start a new life*
> *In the Land of*
> *The Eucalypts.*
> *His life work of*
> *Saving the Southern Seas*
> *Endures.*

Yes, Denzil, your life's work – and your memory – will live on.

Antarctic Law

Blue Ice, Meteorites, Fossil Penguins and Rare Minerals: The Case for Enhanced Protection of Antarctica's Unique Geoheritage – An International Legal Analysis

*David Leary**

Abstract

Its isolation and extreme climate means Antarctica is one of the world's richest regions for untouched geoheritage. The potential of mining in Antarctica is often talked of in public discourse as a future threat to Antarctica even though the prohibition on mining is absolute and is likely to stay so indefinitely. As such mining does not pose a realistic threat to Antarctica's geoheritage. The impacts of scientific research and tourism pose more pressing challenges to Antarctica's geoheritage. This paper considers emerging debates in the Antarctic Treaty System on the need for further protection of Antarctica's geoheritage. After considering the concept of geoheritage the paper considers key threats to Antarctic geoheritage. The role of Antarctic Specially Protected Area system in the protection of Antarctica's geoheritage is then considered as is the draft code of conduct on geosciences field research currently being developed within the Antarctic Treaty System. The final part of the paper then goes on to examine how the Antarctic Treaty system could in part draw on the experience of other international initiatives, including the frameworks associated with the UNESCO Global Geoparks movement in developing an Antarctic System for protection of geoheritage.

Keywords

Antarctic geoheritage – geoconservation – Antarctic Specially Protected Areas – meteorites

---

* Associate Professor, Faculty of Law, University of Technology Sydney, Australia. david.leary@uts.edu.au.

1 Introduction

> Planets, like people, have their own life history – they are born, they mature and die. For planets, as for people, each life history is unique: the time has come to recognise the uniqueness of the Earth.... Our history and the history of the Earth cannot be separated. Its origins are our origins, its history is our history and its future will be our future.... Just as an ancient tree retains the record of its life and growth, the Earth retains memories of the past inscribed both in its depths and on its surface, in the rocks and in the landscape, a record which can be read and translated.... We have always been aware of the need to preserve our memories – our cultural heritage. Now the time has come to protect our natural heritage. The past of the Earth is no less important than that of Man [sic]. It is time for us to learn to protect this Earth heritage, and by doing so learn about the past of the Earth, to learn to read this 'book', the record in the rocks and the landscape, which was mostly written before our advent.... Man [sic] and the Earth share a common heritage, of which we and our governments are but the custodians. Each and every human-being should understand that the slightest damage could lead to irreversible losses for the future. In undertaking any form of development, we should respect the singularity of this heritage.[1]

Scientific research in Antarctica has been very closely connected to the continent's geology from the beginning. The earliest of Antarctic explorers: Scott, Shackleton and Mawson were the first to identify minerals such as coal, copper, gold and silver in Antarctica.[2] Since then generations of geologists, geophysicists and other earth scientists have contributed to our understanding of the geology of Antarctica and more broadly to the major advances in science of the earth. The Antarctic rock record spans 3.5 billion years of history, nearly the entire history of earth's existence.[3] As a consequence, scientific research focussed on Antarctica's geology has contributed significantly to the

---

1 The European Association for the conservation of the geological heritage, *Digne-les-Bains Declaration of the Rights of the Memory of the Earth*, http://www.progeo.ngo/downloads/DIGNE_DECLARATION.pdf [accessed 17 January 2020].
2 Martijn Wilder, *Antarctica: An Economic History of the Last Continent* (Sydney: University of Sydney, 1992) 57.
3 Simon Harley, Ian Fitzsimmons and Yue Zhao, *Antarctica and supercontinent evolution: historical perspectives, recent advances and unresolved issues* (Perth: Geological Society Special Publications 383, 2013) 1–34, 1.

understanding of the origins and evolution of our planet and today continues to provide invaluable insights into our future as humanity attempts to tackle the challenge of climate change in the Anthropocene. Most notably scientific research in relation to Antarctica's geology including its fossil record was fundamental to the acceptance of the revolutionary scientific theory of continental drift.[4] The work of pioneering geologists in Antarctica indicated close correlations between the geology of the Transantarctic Mountains and those in Australia, southern Africa and India and were consistent with the possibility of the ancient super continent now known as Gondwanaland.[5]

Antarctica's geology is therefore incredibly valuable to understanding the history of scientific research in Antarctica, its contribution to science and the insights it may offer to science in the future.

While science itself lies at the heart of the sophisticated international governance mechanisms for Antarctica known as the Antarctic Treaty System, debates in relation to Antarctica's geology in international law have only focussed on the issue of whether mining should or should not be allowed in Antarctica. Since the entry into force of the Madrid Protocol to the Antarctic Treaty[6] in 1998 all activities relating to Antarctica's mineral resources, other than scientific research, have been banned.[7] Even if some state parties to the Madrid Protocol wanted to lift the ban on mining in Antarctica, it would be several decades before that could be possible. Under Article 25 of the Madrid Protocol, any party can request a conference be convened to review the operation of the Protocol. However, such a request cannot be made until the expiry of 50 years from the date of entry into force.[8] Even if a review conference were to be convened in or after 2048, the prohibition on Antarctic mining must continue until there is a binding legal regime in place to regulate mining. All states party to the existing Madrid Protocol would have to agree to the terms of the new regulatory regime which, given the current pro-environment stance of most countries in Antarctica, looks improbable.

This conclusion is re-enforced by both the 2016 Santiago Declaration on the Twenty Fifth Anniversary of the Signing of the Protocol on Environmental

---

4   Ibid, 4.
5   Ibid.
6   Protocol on Environmental Protection to the Antarctic Treaty, 30 International Legal Materials (1991): 1416 (hereinafter 'Madrid Protocol').
7   Ibid, article 7.
8   Ibid, article 25(2).

Protection to the Antarctic Treaty[9] and the 2019 Prague Declaration on the Occasion of the Sixtieth Anniversary of the Antarctic Treaty.[10] In Clause 3 of the 2016 Santiago Declaration, States reaffirmed 'their strong and unequivocal commitment' to the Madrid Protocol and its key principles including the prohibition 'on any activity relating to mineral resources, other than scientific research'.[11] A similar reaffirmation of these commitments was also given by State Parties in the 2019 Prague Declaration where state parties reaffirmed 'their commitment under the [Madrid Protocol] to the prohibition of any activity relating to mineral resources, other than scientific research'.[12]

The explicit obligations of states under the Madrid Protocol not to mine, and these two very recent reaffirmations of State's commitment to these obligations, put beyond doubt that Antarctica's geoheritage is protected against mining indefinitely. Although this of course will not prevent continuing ill-informed media speculation to the contrary.

However, beyond debates surrounding the prohibition on mining, there has been little consideration of whether or not the continent's unique geoheritage may be in need of protection from other threats in much the same way as Antarctica's unique biodiversity is subject to a range of protective measures. However, this situation is beginning to change and the need for Antarctica's geoheritage to receive greater protection is slowly emerging within the forums associated with the Antarctic Treaty System. This paper considers the emerging debate on the need for further protection of Antarctica's geological heritage. The paper begins by explaining key concepts central to these debates namely geodiversity and geoheritage and considers how Antarctica's geoheritage is under threat. It then goes on to highlight some key items of Antarctic geoheritage that have already been suggested as needing enhanced protection.

The paper then goes on to consider how the Antarctic Treaty System applies to Antarctica's geoheritage. This is followed by an examination of the emerging debates on protection of Antarctica's geoheritage within the Antarctic Treaty System. The final part of the paper then goes on to examine how international

---

9   Santiago Declaration on the Twenty Fifth Anniversary of the signing of the Protocol on Environmental Protection to the Antarctic Treaty, May 30, 2016, https://documents.ats.aq/ATCM39/ad/atcm39_ad003_e.pdf [accessed 17 January 2020] (hereinafter 'Santiago Declaration').
10 Prague Declaration on the Occasion of the Sixtieth Anniversary of the Antarctic Treaty, July 8, 2019, https://ats.aq/devAS/Meetings/Documents/87?tab=additional [accessed 17 January 2020] (hereinafter the 'Prague Declaration').
11 Santiago Declaration, clause 3.
12 Prague Declaration, clause 9.

experience outside the Antarctic Treaty System may be drawn on with a particular focus on the UNESCO Global Geoparks movement.

2 What Is Geoheritage and How Is under Threat in Antarctica?

The Geological Society of Australia has usefully defined geoheritage as

> globally, nationally, state wide, regional, to local features of geology ... that are intrinsically important sites or culturally important sites, that offer information or insights into the formation or evolution of the Earth, or into the history of science. or that can be used for research, teaching, or reference.[13]

In a similar way, the Scientific Committee on Antarctic Research (SCAR) in an information paper submitted to a meeting of the Committee on Environmental Protection (CEP) in 2016 defined geoheritage

> broadly speaking [as], the recognition and identification of geological, paleontological and geomorphological features that possess aesthetic, intrinsic or scientific and educational value, and that provide illustration of geological processes and insight into the formation and evolution of the Earth.[14]

In a recent detailed study of geoheritage and the related concept of geoconservation, Brocx has noted:

> Geoheritage and geoconservation are concepts concerned with the preservation of landforms, natural and artificial exposures of rocks and geological sites where geological features can be seen ... Globally, geoconservation has assumed importance because it has been recognised that Earth Systems are linked to the ongoing history of human development, providing the resources for development, and a sense of place, with aesthetic, historical, cultural, and religious values. In addition, Earth systems are the foundation of all ecological processes and part of the heritage of

---

13 Geological Society of Australia, Submission to the Heritage Strategy Team, Australian Heritage Strategy – Public Consultation, copy on file with the author.
14 Scientific Committee on Antarctic Research, *Antarctic Geoconservation: a review of current systems and practices* (2016) ATCM XXXIX IP 31, 3.

our sciences ... Once destroyed, the geoarchive of the Earth is lots to future generations with a loss of already discovered information and as yet undiscovered information.[15]

These values of geoheritage have also been identified in the Antarctic context. Hughes et al have highlighted that

> Antarctica's geodiversity is of fundamental importance to the environmental, scientific, wilderness and aesthetic values of the continent, and the pursuit of geological knowledge has had a strong influence on its historical values. For example, Captain Scott's doomed South Pole party of 1912 collected 16 kg of rocks including fossil leaves of *Glossopteris indicia*, which provided evidence that Antarctica was once part of the larger supercontinent of Gondwana. The spectacular nature and aesthetic qualities of Antarctica can be attributed in part to the landforms and geology of the region's ice free areas. However, the continent's scientific values are of primary importance and have provided knowledge on topics of global value, including plate tectonics and past climates. Therefore, it is essential that protection of Antarctica's geological features must accommodate access by scientists, application of research techniques and responsible removal of geological samples by researchers in the pursuit of scientific knowledge[16]

In essence geoheritage features have a value to science beyond just their historical value. They also offer insight into future scientific questions including climate change, the interaction between the biosphere and the geosphere, and the interaction between humans and the geosphere.[17] While many different justifications have been put forward for protecting and conserving geoheritage across the world, in the Antarctic context it is the scientific value of such sites that provides the primary justification for greater protection where such sites are threatened.

Threats to Antarctica's geoheritage come from two key activities: scientific research and tourism. This points to a key issue: the primary justification for

---

15 Margaret Brocx, *Geoheritage: from global perspectives to local principles for conservation and planning* (Perth: Western Australian Museum, 2008) 1.
16 Kevin Hughes et al, "Antarctic geoconservation: a review of current systems and practices," 43 (2) *Environmental Conservation* (2016): 1–12, 1.
17 J. Bradbury, "A preliminary Geoheritage Inventory of the Eastern Tasmania Terrance" (Unpublished Report to Parks and Wildlife Service Tasmania, 1993. Copy held on file by author) 1.

geoconservation is because such sites will be of value to science in the future, but it is scientific research at such sites which is one of main threats to their continued existence. In addition such sites may also be under threat from repeated visits by tourists. As Hughes et al[18] have identified, these activities are often concentrated in small areas and subject to repeated visits

> much of the human activity in Antarctica is limited to a small number of locations, predominately coastal, which are accessible by ship and thereby facilitate visitation by tourists and/or the establishment and maintenance of research stations by national operators ... Potential threats to geological features of environmental or scientific value might include oversampling of rare rocks, fossils and minerals for scientific purposes ... Rocks, meteorites, minerals and fossils may be vulnerable to unauthorised collection by tourists and national operator staff ... Inadvertent damage may be done to the scientific values of a location by movement of rocks and fossils out of their stratigraphical context; for example the movement of a surface fossil from one location to another may give false information of the presence of that fossil species in the geological record and even the age of the stratigraphic record.[19]

The movement of rocks and fossils will be of particular risk in areas subject to a high number of visits by tourists.[20] In addition, the construction of research stations and other facilities such as roads and runways for aircraft has also been identified as a possible threat to geoheritage.[21]

As noted above, calls for enhanced protection of geoheritage in the Antarctic context are largely driven by its value to science. Protection of Antarctica's geoheritage for its scientific values alone would be entirely consistent with Antarctica's status in international law as a unique place dedicated to "international cooperation in scientific investigation."[22] Freedom of scientific investigation and co-operation to that end is recognised explicitly by Article II of the Antarctic Treaty, but how can such freedom of scientific research be exercised in future if the object of that research (the local geology) is degraded? Preservation of Antarctica's geoheritage is therefore not only consistent with the commitment to science set out in the Antarctic Treaty, but on one

---

18   Hughes et al (n 16) 6.
19   Ibid.
20   Ibid.
21   Ibid, 7.
22   Antarctic Treaty, Adopted 1 December 1959, 402 United Nations Treaty Series 71, hereinafter the 'Antarctic Treaty', Preamble.

interpretation may form part of the broader commitment to science embodied in the whole fabric of the treaty.

Beyond the value of geoheritage to science noted above, as the earlier quote from Hughes et al[23] above highlights protection of geoheritage can also be justified on the basis of their wilderness and aesthetic values. The protection of Antarctica's wilderness values in addition to its scientific and aesthetic values are explicitly recognised by the Madrid Protocol. Article 3(1) of the Madrid Protocol provides

> The protection of the Antarctic environment and dependent and associated ecosystems and the intrinsic value of Antarctica, including its wilderness and aesthetic values as an area for the conduct of scientific research, in particular research essential to understanding the global environment, shall be fundamental considerations in the planning and conduct of all activities in the Antarctic Treaty area.[24]

Thus it can be argued that protection of Antarctica's geoheritage is consistent with both the foundational principle of freedom of Antarctic research in Antarctica and protection of its wilderness and aesthetic values.

3 How Is Geoheritage Protected under the Antarctic Treaty System?

Beyond these general principles justifying protection of Antarctica's geoheritage, specific provisions of the Madrid Protocol can and have been invoked to provide for its protection. Thus Article 3 of Annex V to the Madrid Protocol provides that any area may be designated as an Antarctic Specially Protected Area (ASPA) 'to protect outstanding environmental, scientific, historic, aesthetic or wilderness values, any combination of those values, or ongoing or planned scientific research'.[25] For present purposes it is worth noting that an ASPA can be designated for a range of different reasons including 'areas of particular interest to ongoing or planned scientific research'[26] and 'examples of outstanding geological, glaciological or geomorphological features'.[27]

Entry into an ASPA is strictly prohibited except in accordance with a permit issued by an appropriate authority approved by a State Party to the Madrid

---

23 Hughes et al (n 16) 1.
24 Madrid Protocol, article 3(1).
25 Madrid Protocol, Annex V, article 3.
26 Madrid Protocol, Annex V, article 3(2)(e).
27 Madrid Protocol, Annex V, article 3(2)(f).

Protocol. Any activities approved under such a permit must be consistent with the approved Management Plan in force from time to time for the relevant ASPA.

To date 26 ASPAs have been designated that have in part or in whole been created to protect specific geological features.[28] As at the date of writing, a further proposed ASPA relating to protection of geological heritage has been proposed but not yet designated. Table 1 below provides details of each of these ASPAs and highlights the specific geological features mentioned in the relevant Management Plan which the ASPA designation seeks to protect.

In addition, under Article 4 of Annex V of the Madrid Protocol an area may be designated as an Antarctic Specially Managed Area (ASMA) where activities are being conducted or may in the future be conducted, 'to assist in the planning and co-ordination of activities, avoid possible conflicts, improve cooperation between Parties or minimise environmental impacts'.[29] However, unlike ASPAs no permit is required to enter an ASMA.[30]

4 Debate on the Protection of Antarctica's Geoheritage within the Antarctic Treaty System

Debate on protection of Antarctica's geoheritage within the Antarctic Treaty System began in 2014 in the context of the Committee for Environmental Protection's (CEP) discussion of the ASPA system in Antarctica. At the CEP meeting in 2014 the United Kingdom circulated an Information Paper reviewing existing and proposed ASPA Management Plans and examining the level of protection afforded to geological features within the ASPA system.[31] This analysis in particular noted the description of geological features meriting protection was often 'unclear and lacked detail', provided 'imprecise' description of the location of such features and observed that 'geological features have not been protected within a systematic environmental-geographical framework'.[32] The information paper then provided an inventory of geological features identified as worthy of protection in the management plans of the current network of ASPAs.[33]

---

28 United Kingdom, *Antarctic Specially Protected Area protecting geological features: a review*, ATCM XXXVII, IP 22 (2014).
29 Madrid Protocol, Annex V, article 4(1).
30 Madrid Protocol, Annex V, article 4(3).
31 See United Kingdom (n 28).
32 Ibid, 4.
33 Ibid, 5–14.

TABLE 1   Geological features listed as values worthy of protection in the current network of ASPAs (United Kingdom 2014)[a]

ASPA	Geological features of value
ASPA 110: Lynch Island, South Orkney Islands.	Well-developed soils, possibly most advanced in Antarctica.
ASPA 115: Lagotellerie Island, Marguerite Bay, Graham Land.	Well-developed soils Fossiliferous rock types not commonly exposed.
ASPA 118: Summit of Mount Melbourne, Victoria Land.	Geothermally heated soils.
ASPA 119: Davis Valley and Forlidas Pond, Dufek Massif, Pensacola Mountains.	Geomorphological features and evidence of past glacial history (e.g. rare and unique types of moraines, erratics).
ASPA 120: Pointe-Geologie Archipelago, Terre Adélie	Structural geology and lithology of area.
ASPA 122: Arrival Heights, Hut Point Peninsula, Ross Island.	Soils and geomorphological features including sand-wedge polygons.
ASPA 123: Barwick and Balham Valleys, Southern Victoria Land.	Geomorphological features, including records of desert pavements, sand dunes, patterned ground, glacial and moraine features, streams, freshwater and saline lakes, valleys and high-altitude ice-free ground.
ASPA 125: Fildes Peninsula, King George Island.	Fossil remains. One of the areas in Antarctica of greatest paleontological interest, with fossil remains including vertebrate and invertebrate ichnites, and abundant flora with impressions of leaves and fronds, trunks, and pollen grains and spores.
ASPA 126: Byers Peninsula, Livingston Island, South Shetland Islands.	Jurassic and Cretaceous sedimentary and fossiliferous strata geomorphology considered of outstanding scientific value for study of the former link between Antarctica and other southern continents.

a   Note this table is adapted from Annex 1 of United Kingdom (n 28). The author acknowledges that much of the text of this table is reproduced verbatim from this source with some minor editing.

TABLE 1   Geological features listed as values worthy of protection (*cont.*)

ASPA	Geological features of value
ASPA 128: Western shore of Admiralty Bay, King George Island, South Shetland Islands.	Geomorphological features, volcanic rocks and fossil remains silicified wood fragments.
ASPA 130: 'Tramway Ridge', Mount Erebus, Ross Island.	Geothermally heated soils and associated gas emissions.
ASPA 132: Potter Peninsula, King George Island, (Isla 25 de Mayo), South Shetland Islands.	Geomorphological features, geological structures.
ASPA 135: North-east Bailey Peninsula, Budd Coast, Wilkes Land.	Glacial geomorphological features.
ASPA 136: Clark Peninsula, Budd Coast, Wilkes Land.	Glacial geomorphological features, soils.
ASPA 138: Linnaeus Terrace, Asgard Range, Victoria Land.	Physical weathering formations, trace fossils
ASPA 140: Parts of Deception Island, South Shetland Islands.	Geo-thermally heated soils and geothermally heated intertidal lagoon.
ASPA 143: Marine Plain, Mule Peninsula, Vestfold Hills, Princess Elizabeth Land.	Vertebrate fossil fauna, 8 m thick Pliocene marine sediments, periglacial and glacial features.
ASPA 147: Ablation Valley and Ganymede Heights, Alexander Island.	Only known rock exposure spanning the Jurassic–Cretaceous boundary in the Antarctic. Fossils and geomorphological features
ASPA 148: Mount Flora, Hope Bay, Antarctic Peninsula.	Rich fossil flora.
ASPA 149: Cape Shirreff and San Telmo Island, Livingston Island, South Shetland Islands.	Plant fossils.
ASPA 151: Lions Rump, King George Island, South Shetland Islands.	Fossils.
ASPA 165: Edmondson Point, Wood Bay, Ross Sea.	Geomorphological features. Fossil penguin colonies.
ASPA 168: Mount Harding, Grove Mountains, East Antarctica.	Geomorphological features Palaeo-soils microfossils.
ASPA 171: Narebski Point, Barton Peninsula, King George Island.	Use of the area for geological and geomorphological studies.

TABLE 1 Geological features listed as values worthy of protection (*cont.*)

ASPA	Geological features of value
ASPA 172: Lower Taylor Glacier and Blood Falls, Taylor Valley, McMurdo Dry Valleys, Victoria Land.	Subglacial marine salt deposit.
ASPA 173: Cape Washington and Silverfish Bay, Terra Nova Bay, Ross Sea.	Volcanic rock exposures.
Proposed ASPA XXX: Stornes, Larsemann Hills, Princess Elizabeth Land.	Type locality for three new minerals. A diverse suite of borosilicate minerals and phosphate minerals. Marine fossils.

In a Working Paper tabled at the same meeting, the United Kingdom, Argentina, Australia and Spain presented data to show that only six management plans relating to ASPAs 'listed geological and/or geomorphological features as the primary value for which the areas were designated with ASPA status'.[34] This represents only 8% of ASPAs in the entire ASPA network in Antarctica. The Working Paper therefore proposed that the CEP encourage

> Members and SCAR to identify outstanding geological features and consider requirements for their protection, including ASPA designation, use of zoning within ASMAs and/or the inclusion of specific considerations for protection in other developed management tools, such as the Site Guidelines for Visitors.[35]

In a separate Working Paper, Argentina focussed on threats posed to fossils in Antarctica.[36] The Argentinian document focussed in particular on the threats to Antarctica's rich fossil diversity posed by a lack of coordination between overlapping scientific research programs which interfered with each other, as well unauthorised fossil sampling and extraction.[37] Accordingly the Working Paper proposed the CEP issue a recommendation to the ATCM that:

---

[34] United Kingdom, Argentina, Australia and Spain, *The Antarctic Protected Area system: protection of outstanding geological features*, (2014) ATCM XXXVII WP 35, 5.
[35] Ibid.
[36] Argentina, *Contributions to the Protection of Fossils in Antarctica*, (2014) ATCM XXXVII WP 57.
[37] Ibid, 3.

- The parties ensure that research groups in charge of collecting or removing fossils have a permit issued by an Antarctic Treaty Member State's national competent authority, and that such groups keep said permit while working on the Antarctic continent;
- Tour operators cooperate for the purpose of verifying that researchers travelling by tourist aircrafts [sic] or vessels have the relevant permit granted by the competent authority of the Antarctic Treaty Member State to admit fossils as scientific load; and
- The parties share more information in order to provide broader access to scientific research conducted by all the Members and thus favour cooperation and avoid overlapping as regards fossil extraction.[38]

Both Working Papers and the Information Paper mentioned above featured in discussions at the CEP. But neither of the proposals put forward in the Working Papers were endorsed by the CEP. The CEP instead acknowledged 'the importance of guaranteeing protection' of Antarctica's 'geological and geomorphological values'.[39] Likewise, while it was clear many state parties acknowledged the importance of the protection of fossils in Antarctica, a number of members had reservations about adopting the Resolution proposed by Argentina.[40] While not endorsing either recommendation to the CEP, the CEP recognised that there were issues meriting further consideration and therefore included the 'protection of outstanding geological values' of Antarctica on its workplan.[41] The aim of this work was 'to consider further mechanisms for conservation and protection of outstanding geological values'.[42]

Subsequently SCAR established an Action Group on Geological Heritage and Geoconservation.[43] The terms of reference for the Action Group task it with developing a definition of 'geological heritage' and 'geoconservation'; developing 'criteria and principles for identifying and classifying feature of potential geo-heritage value within Antarctica'; formulating recommendations on development of a geo-heritage register; developing criteria for conserving geo-heritage sites; and the development of a strategy for 'global promotion

---

38   Argentina, Draft resolution-Protection of Fossils in Antarctica, Attachment A to Argentina, note 36, 5.
39   Antarctic Treaty Secretariat, *Final Report of the Thirty-seventh Antarctic Treaty Consultative Meeting – CEP XVII Report*, para 203.
40   Ibid, para 214.
41   SCAR Executive Committee Meeting 2019, Action Group on Geological Heritage and Geoconservation 2018–19, https://www.scar.org/library/scar-meeting-papers/scar-excom-2019-plovdiv-bulgaria/sub-group-reports-2019/5377-geoheritage-report-2019/ [accessed 17 January 2020], 1.
42   Ibid.
43   Ibid.

of geo-heritage values of the Antarctic through appropriate international forums'.[44]

In 2015 the CEP was provided with a further Working Paper by Argentina reporting on a survey it had undertaken on the assessment and authorisation approval processes of various States for the removal of fossils from Antarctica.[45] Only Australia, France, Germany, New Zealand, South Africa, the United Kingdom and the USA responded to the survey.[46] Despite this low response rate the survey concluded there is a diverse range of approaches by States in their approval processes for the removal of fossils from Antarctica.[47] Subsequent discussion of Argentina's Working Paper noted a number of possible responses to the emerging issue of protection of Antarctica's geoheritage, but agreed that further substantial action should await the completion of the ongoing work of the SCAR Action Group on Geological Heritage and Geoconservation.[48]

As at the date of writing of this paper, the work of the Action Group is ongoing. However, several notable developments are worth mentioning. Firstly, in accordance with its mandate in 2016 the Action Group produced an Information Paper which identified the key threats and existing mechanisms for protection of Antarctic geological values, which was tabled by SCAR at ATCM XXXIX.[49] In a separate paper submitted to the meeting of the CEP in 2016 SCAR identified an initial list of several important items of geoheritage in Antarctica that it suggested may need 'enhanced protection and/or special recognition'.[50] These include:

- outcrops containing rare or unique minerals (e.g. rare boron and phosphate minerals in ASPA 174 Stornes, Larsemann Hills, Princess Elizabeth Land);
- areas of blue ice where concentrations of meteorites are found (e.g. the Frontier Mountain blue ice field);
- ice-free areas or blue ice moraines that have unusually high potential to be used for cosmogenic dating (as has been done using geological material from the Heritage Range and Grove Mountains);

---

44 SCAR, *Approval of Action Group on Geological Heritage and Geo-conservation*, WP 36 EXCOM 2015, 3.
45 See Argentina, *Findings from ad hoc Surveys related to the protection of Fossils in Antarctica. Potential courses of action for further discussion*, ATCM XXXVIII (2015), WP 50.
46 Argentina, Ibid, 3.
47 Ibid.
48 Committee on Environmental Protection-CEP XVIII Report in Final Report of the Thirty-eight Antarctic Treaty Consultative Meeting, para 211.
49 See SCAR, Antarctic Geoconservation: a review of current systems and practices, (2016) ATCM XXXIX IP 31.
50 Ibid, 3.

- rare, unique or vulnerable glacial and/or geomorphological features (such as protected within ASPA 168 Mount Harding);
- representative sections of unique or particularly well-exposed stratigraphy (e.g. the Cretaceous–Paleogene boundary located within the James Ross Island group);
- unique or exceptional examples of rock structures (e.g. unconformities, folds, faults and intrusive relationships, e.g. Vestfold Hills, Prydz Bay; Finger Mountain, Transantarctic Mountains);
- locations where rare or unique fossils (including trace fossils) and fossil beds are found (e.g. ASPA 148 Mt Flora, ASPA 125 Fildes Peninsula, ASPA 143 Marine Plain; Miocene penguin fossil site, Fisher Massif, Prince Charles Mountains);
- the 'type locality' for a rock type, stratigraphic unit, fossil or mineral (the site where that particular feature is first described in the scientific literature);
- landforms such as raised beaches, patterned ground and unconsolidated soils of particular value, which may be vulnerable to relatively low levels of human impacts, including trampling (e.g. protected as a secondary value within ASPA 122 Arrival Heights, Hut Point Peninsula, Ross Island); and
- 'geo-cultural' sites, which are significant localities in the history of geosciences (e.g. Dallwitz Nunatak, Enderby Land, where the high temperature mineral assemblage, sapphirine + quartz, was first identified).[51]

To date no action has been taken to increase the protection for these sites as suggested by SCAR. As the work of both the Action Group and SCAR continues to evolve, it is still too early to see whether steps will be taken to protect individual sites.

In addition to this list identified by SCAR, I would suggest major sites for collection of meteorites in Antarctica should also be considered for enhanced protection. Recognition of Antarctica's geoheritage should include the large number of meteorites that have been found in Antarctica together with sites where they can be collected. Meteorites were first discovered in Antarctica by one of Douglas Mawson's field parties in 1912.[52] Large-scale collection of meteorites in Antarctica for scientific research purposes began with the International Geophysical Year in 1957 and since then most states active in scientific research in Antarctica have been collecting meteorites in Antarctica.

51　Ibid, 3–4.
52　Ralph Harvey, John Schutt, and Jim Karner, 'Fieldwork methods of the U.S. Antarctic search for meteorites program' in Kevin Righter, Catherine Corrigan, Timothy McCoy and Ralph Harvey, *35 Seasons of U.S. Antarctic Meteorites (1976–2010): A pictorial Guide to the Collection*, Special Publication 68, (Hoboken: John Wiley & Sons Inc, 2015) 23.

For example, the US research program has collected more than 20,000 meteorites in the course of scientific research.[53] While meteorite collection for scientific purposes is defensible, it is also acknowledged that an unregulated trade exists in meteorites found in Antarctica.[54] Some States have gone so far as to suggest that the unauthorised removal of meteorites from Antarctica constitutes a violation of Article 7 of the Madrid Protocol.[55]

Despite these concerns very little action has been taken by State parties to restrict the removal of meteorites from Antarctica. In 2001 the CEP passed Resolution 3(2001) stating:

> Concerned at loss to scientific research because of unrestricted Collection of meteorites in Antarctica;
>
> Urge parties to the Environmental Protocol to take such illegal or administrative steps as are necessary to preserve Antarctic meteorites so that they are collected and curated according to accepted scientific standards, and are made available for scientific purposes.[56]

It is worth noting that in debates at the CEP meeting in 2015 it was suggested that the removal of fossils from Antarctica could be dealt with under a similar resolution to that passed in relation to Antarctic meteorites.[57] Given doubts remain as to the effectiveness of the resolution passed in relation to meteorites it is doubtful if a similarly weak response in relation to the removal of fossils or geoheritage more broadly would be an adequate response.

While new measures to protect individual sites for their geoheritage values are in their infancy, the SCAR Action Group on Geological Heritage and Geoconservation has made considerable progress in developing a draft code of

---

53 Ibid, 23. For a detailed overview of the history of collection of meteorites in Antarctica see also Ralph Harvey, 'The origin and significance of Antarctic meteorites' *Chemie der Erde Geochemistry* 63 (2003): 93.

54 For examples see New Zealand, *Report to CEP IV on the question of collection of Antarctic meteorites by Private expeditions*, ATCM XXIV, IV CEP WP 9. A simple google search can locate examples of meteorites from Antarctica currently for sale online. See for example 'Meteorites-all about meteorites' http://www.meteorite.fr/en/forsale/ALH76009.htm [accessed 15 January 2020].

55 Antarctic Treaty Secretariat, *Final Report of the Twenty-fourth Antarctic Treaty Consultative Meeting* (2001), 74.

56 Resolution 3 (2001), CEP IV reproduced in Annex C, Antarctic Treaty Secretariat, *Final Report of the Twenty-fourth Antarctic Treaty Consultative Meeting*.

57 Committee on Environmental Protection – CEP XVIII Report in Antarctic Treaty Secretariat, *Final Report of the Thirty-eighth Antarctic Treaty Consultative Meeting*, para 212.

conduct on geosciences field research activities in Antarctica. A draft code of conduct was presented at the CEP meeting held in Prague in 2019.[58] The draft code 'provides recommendations on how scientists and associated personnel can undertake geological field activities while protecting Antarctic geological heritage for future generations'.[59]

Significantly the draft code refers to the Madrid Protocol and states explicitly that it 'complements the relevant sections of the protocol and provides guidance for researchers conducting land-based geological field research in the area of land and permanent ice south of latitude 60 degrees south'.[60]

The draft code of conduct contains a wide range of provisions dealing with geological field work in Antarctica likely to have an impact on Antarctica's geological heritage. Matters addressed include:
- planning of field work and assessment of potential environmental impact of proposed research;[61]
- requirements for permits prior to entering ASPAs;[62]
- consideration to possible co-ordination with other geologists to minimise environmental impacts and potential oversampling;[63]
- depositing of particularly rare specimens in geological repositories;[64]
- procedures for notifying SCAR and other relevant national and international bodies of the discovery of geological sites of particular interest or outstanding scientific value;[65]
- recommendations on handling of fossils which may be discovered in the field;[66]
- recommendations on handling meteorites discovered in the field including a specific reference to Resolution 3 (2001) mentioned above;[67]
- procedures for seeking approval to install instruments in the field;[68] and

---

58   See SCAR, *Draft Code of Conduct on Geosciences Field Research Activities in Antarctica*, ATCM XLII-CEP XXII (2019), IP 50.
59   See SCAR, *Draft Code of Conduct on Geosciences Field Research Activities in Antarctica*, ATCM XLII-CEP XXII (2019), IP 50, 1.
60   Ibid, 2.
61   Ibid.
62   Ibid.
63   Ibid, 3.
64   Ibid.
65   Ibid, 3.
66   Ibid, 5.
67   Ibid.
68   Ibid, 6.

– a series of recommendations on post-field work monitoring to ensure adequate geoconservation management.[69]

The current draft of the code of conduct has been developed with significant input from geoscientists active in scientific research in Antarctica. The CEP has welcomed the and it is likely that a final Version of the code of conduct will be presented at CEP XXIII in 2020.[70]

5   Experience Protecting Geoheritage outside Antarctica

Once finalised, and if implemented by scientists in the field, the code of conduct will provide a very detailed framework for the protection of Antarctica's geoheritage. It strikes a good balance between conservation of Antarctica's geoheritage and maintaining access to such sites for current and future generations of scientists. However, as noted above work is also underway to further refine how ASPA mechanisms can be utilised to better protect and manage Antarctica's geoheritage.

In developing further measures to protect Antarctica's geoheritage, States can draw on a wealth of experience in protecting geoheritage elsewhere in the world, including measures adopted under the auspices of the United Nations Educational, Scientific and Cultural Organisation (UNESCO). It is not suggested here that responsibility for managing Antarctica's geoheritage should pass to UNESCO. In the author's opinion nearly all environmental matters in Antarctica are best dealt with within the Antarctic Treaty System. Rather all that is suggested is that the UNESCO experience may be useful for Antarctic policy-makers to draw on in shaping an Antarctic response to the issue.

UNESCO has been the leading proponent of measures to protect geoheritage globally, both under the legal mechanisms provided for in the Convention Concerning the Protection of the World Cultural and Natural Heritage[71] and less formally through its UNESCO Geoparks program.[72]

The World Heritage Convention aims to establish 'an effective system of collective protection of the cultural and natural heritage of outstanding universal

---

69   Ibid.
70   CEP XXII Report contained in Antarctic Treaty Secretariat, *Final Report of the Forty-second Antarctic Treaty Consultative Meeting* (Preliminary version), para 68.
71   United Nations, Educational, Scientific and Cultural Organisation, Convention Concerning the Protection of the World Cultural and Natural Heritage, 16 November 1972, https://www.refworld.org/docid/4042287a4.html [accessed 20 January 2020] (hereinafter 'World Heritage Convention').
72   Brocx (n 15) 27–34.

value, organized on a permanent basis and in accordance with modern scientific methods'.[73] For the purposes of the World Heritage Convention "natural heritage" is defined as:

> natural features consisting of physical and biological formations or groups of such formations, which are of outstanding universal value from the aesthetic or scientific point of view;
>
> geological and physiographical formations and precisely delineated areas which constitute the habitat of threatened species of animals and plants of outstanding universal value from the point of view of science or conservation;
>
> natural sites or precisely delineated natural areas of outstanding universal value from the point of view of science, conservation or natural beauty.[74]

Pursuant to Article 4 of the World Heritage Convention, each State Party is under a duty to identify, protect, conserve, present and transmit such cultural and natural heritage on its territory to future generations.[75] State Parties are also required to take a range of 'effective and active measures' for the protection, conservation and presentation of the cultural and natural heritage situated on its territory.[76]

States nominate cultural and natural heritage for inclusion on the World Heritage List.[77] The final decision on the entry of nominated cultural or natural heritage on the list is taken by the World Heritage Committee.[78] Criteria for listing have been determined by the World Heritage Committee.[79] It has provided 10 criteria for determining whether or not a site nominated for listing is of 'outstanding universal character'. Of these, the following criteria are directly relevant to geoheritage:

(vii) [the area] contain[s] superlative natural phenomena or areas of exceptional natural beauty and aesthetic importance;

(viii) [it is of] outstanding examples representing major stages of earth's history, including the record of life, significant on-going geological

---

73 World Heritage Convention, Preamble.
74 World Heritage Convention, article 2.
75 World Heritage Convention, article 4.
76 World Heritage Convention, article 5.
77 World Heritage Convention, article 11.
78 World Heritage Convention, Article 11(2).
79 World Heritage Convention, Article 11(5).

processes in the development of landforms, or significant geomorphic or physiographic features[80]

As noted earlier in this paper, one of the issues under consideration by the SCAR Action Group on Geological Heritage and Geoconservation is the development of criteria and principles for identifying and classifying features of potential geoheritage value. Clearly a combination or one or both of these criteria developed by the World Heritage Committee may prove suitable as criteria in the Antarctic context.

In addition the UNESCO International Geoscience and Geoparks Programme is worth noting. Developed under national law and policy with assistance from UNESCO, UNESCO Global Geoparks are 'single, unified geographical areas where sites and landscapes of international geological significance are managed with a holistic concept of protection, education and sustainable development'.[81] To date governments have designated 147 UNESCO Global Geoparks in 41 countries.[82] Four features are said to be fundamental to a UNESCO Global Geopark: (1) Geoheritage must be of international value; (2) a Geopark is managed under national legislation including a role for all relevant stakeholders from the local population having regard to all social, economic and cultural interests of stakeholders; (3) The Geoparks must be visible to local communities and bring sustainable local economic development; and (4) be networked to stakeholders in other UNESCO Geoparks through the Global Geoparks Network.[83]

While not all of these features are necessarily relevant to Antarctica's geoheritage, the experience of the UNESCO Geoparks and Global Geoparks Network may provide a valuable source of information and experience for policy-makers in the Antarctic context as measures to protect Antarctica's geoheritage are developed. In that regard it is worth noting seven detailed criteria for designating a UNESCO Global Geopark have been developed.[84]

On many occasions UNESCO has also worked with a number of other organisations in relation to geoheritage. The work of these organisations also

---

80 United Nations Educational, Scientific and Cultural Organization, *Operational Guidelines for the Implementation of the World Heritage Convention*, WHC/19/01, https://whc.unesco.org/en/guidelines/> [accessed 21 November 2019].

81 UNESCO, 'UNESCO Geoparks', http://www.unesco.org/new/en/natural-sciences/environment/earth-sciences/unesco-global-geoparks/ [accessed 16 January 2020].

82 Ibid.

83 Ibid.

84 See Graeme Worboys, et al *Protected Area Governance and Management* (Canberra, ANU Press, 2015), https://press-files.anu.edu.au/downloads/press/p312491/pdf/book.pdf [accessed 20 January 2020], chapter 18.

provides valuable sources of information and experience. One of the most notable of these is the International Union for the Conservation of Nature (IUCN).[85] Of direct relevance to geoheritage is the work of the IUCN World Commission on Protected Areas (WCPA) and its Geoheritage Specialist Group which has expertise in all aspects of geodiversity in relation to protected areas and their management.[86] It has contributed this expertise to the development of a range of geoheritage projects including the IUCN's Protected Area Governance and Management Handbook[87] which devotes an entire chapter to geoconservation in protected areas.[88]

Beyond the IUCN there are also a range of other non-governmental organisations with a wealth of experience in the protection of geoheritage. These include organisations such as the European Association for the Conservation of the Geological Heritage (ProGEO), the international Union of Geological Sciences, the International Association of Geomorphologists and the European Union for Coastal Conservation.[89]

A detailed examination of the work of the IUCN and the other non-governmental organisations mentioned above is beyond the scope of this paper. However, they are mentioned to illustrate the wealth of global experience that exists for Antarctic policy-makers and States to draw upon.

6 Conclusion

Debate on the protection and conservation of geoheritage in Antarctica is emerging as an issue for consideration by Antarctic policy-makers and States. Much progress has been made in recent years. The development of a draft code of conduct for geosciences and ongoing consideration of the role of ASPAs in preserving geoheritage are positive and welcome developments. The value to

---

85 The IUCN describes itself as 'a membership Union composed of both government and civil society organisations. It harnesses the experience, resources and reach of its more than 1,300 member organisations and the input of more than 15,000 experts. This diversity and vast expertise makes IUCN the global authority on the status of the natural world and the measures needed to safeguard it.' See About the International Union for the Conservation of Nature (IUCN), https://www.iucn.org/about [accessed 17 January 2020].
86 See IUCN World Commission on Protected Areas, 'Geoheritage' https://www.iucn.org/commissions/world-commission-protected-areas/our-work/geoheritage [accessed 17 January 2020].
87 Worboys et al., above note 84.
88 See above note 84, Chapter 18.
89 For detailed examination of the work of these non-governmental organisations see Brocx, note 15 41–63.

science of Antarctica's geoheritage, as well as its other values, is clearly being recognised in current debates within the Antarctic Treaty System. It is still too early to know how robust the measures to protect geoheritage will be and whether they will include important components like meteorites. But with geoheritage, as with so many environmental issues before, again the Antarctic Treaty System reveals its agility in responding to new issues.

Biological Prospecting in Antarctica – A Solution-Based Approach to Regulating the Collection and Use of Antarctic Marine Biodiversity by Taking the BBNJ Process into Account

*Katharina Heinrich**

Abstract

Areas beyond national jurisdiction (ABNJ) are covering nearly two-thirds of the world's oceans and are rich in biological diversity. These also include the Polar Regions, where marine organisms adapted to extreme environments and led to increased scientific interest and activities, including bioprospecting activities. As a result, marine biodiversity is increasingly threatened. Thus, the Convention on Biodiversity (CBD) was established to ensure the conservation and sustainable use of biodiversity but left ABNJ and bioprospecting activities widely unregulated. In Antarctica, for instance, bioprospecting has raised concerns, and the matter has been discussed since 2002. As a result, the United Nations General Assembly (UNGA) Resolution 69/292 concluded the establishment of a new international legally binding instrument (ILBI) on the conservation and sustainable use of marine biological diversity for ABNJ. However, the inclusion of the Antarctic Treaty Area remains unclear. In light of the current BBNJ negotiations, the Antarctic Treaty Consultative Meeting (ATCM) only acknowledges the Antarctic Treaty System (ATS) as the appropriate framework to regulate these activities in Antarctica. Further, it seems to aim for regulation under the ATS, if at all. Therefore, this paper discusses a solution-based approach for possible regulation of the collection and use of Antarctic marine biodiversity. The negotiations and achievements of the current BBNJ process will be taken into account, as they might provide support for the regulation of these issues in Antarctica and the Southern Ocean.

---

* Independent researcher, former University of Akureyri Master of Polar Law student. katharina.heinrich1@gmx.net.

Keywords

biological prospecting – Antarctic Treaty System – areas beyond national jurisdiction – biodiversity conservation – biodiversity beyond national jurisdiction

1 Introduction

The Polar Oceans are among the most productive marine ecosystems on the Earth, supporting high biomasses of marine living resources. Nevertheless, only little is known about marine biodiversity, so that scientists believe that there are millions of unknown species in the oceans. Extreme environmental conditions in these regions restricted the accessibility to biodiversity to a great extent. However, technological advances and the warming of the oceans opened up previously inaccessible areas. In turn, the exploration of marine genetic resources, amongst others, was enabled to proliferate in Antarctica and on a global scale.

Marine bioprospecting activities, conducted in light of these new interests and possibilities, are the systematic exploration of valuable marine genetic resources (MGRS) in order to commercialise them in the pharmaceutical, biotechnological and cosmetic industries. These activities have increased considerably, and with its lack of regulation, bioprospecting has been one of the most controversial issues pertaining to environmental law for many years.[1] As the issues, regarding MGRS and related activities, have gained broad interest, legally binding instruments aiming for the conservation of the world's biodiversity, such as the Convention on Biological Diversity (CBD)[2] were established. The CBD, which entered into force in 1993, aims to promote the conservation and sustainable use of marine biodiversity, as well as the fair and equitable sharing of the benefits arising from the use of genetic resources. However, this Convention only covers areas within national jurisdiction and consequently leaves ABNJ widely unregulated. These areas also include Antarctica and its surrounding Southern Ocean, where bioprospecting activities present challenges to the parties of the ATS.

---

1 Maria Gluchowska-Wojcicka. 'Bioprospecting and Arctic Genetic Resources a Challenge for International Law' *XXXII Prawo Morskie* (2016):132. <https://journals.pan.pl/Content/93415/mainfile.pdf?handler=pdf> accessed 15.01.2020, 132.

2 Convention on Biological Diversity, opened for signature on 5 June 1992, 31 ILM (1992) (entered into force 29 December 1993) (hereafter CBD).

As the issues got more prevailing and human activities were increasingly threatening biodiversity in ABNJ, the UNGA decided to establish a new ILBI through its Resolution 69/292.[3] The new instrument will be established under the United Nations Convention on the Law of the Sea (UNCLOS)[4] and shall cover the conservation and sustainable use of marine biological diversity of ABNJ. However, due to its specific legal regime, it remains at this stage of the process unclear whether the instrument will include the AT area. Within the negotiation and preparation process, the General Assembly has reached out to the Antarctic Treaty Consultative Parties (ATCPs).[5] However, the Treaty Parties declined any further correspondence and cooperation with the BBNJ by stating in their response letter that 'the ATS is the appropriate framework to regulate the collection and sustainable use of Antarctic marine biodiversity.'[6] This statement marks the starting point of the research. The reaction of the ATCM, together with the current uncertainty whether the new instrument will include the AT area or not, has led to investigating other possibilities of regulation for the AT area and how this can be achieved. This paper outlines only one option for regulation of the matter under the ATS in detail, as the extent of this paper does not allow the exploration of further possibilities.

2   Biological Prospecting

Biological prospecting or bioprospecting[7] is described as the systematic exploration and use of biological material for commercially valuable genetic and biochemical resources,[8] and is a development in the scientific arena

---

3   United Nations General Assembly Resolution 69/292 'Development of an international legally binding instrument under the United Nations Convention on the Law of the Sea on the conservation and sustainable use of marine biological diversity of areas beyond national jurisdiction' A/RES/69/292 <https://sustainabledevelopment.un.org/index.php?page=view&type=111&nr=7897&menu=35> accessed 20.12.2019.
4   United Nations Convention on the Law of the Sea, 21 ILM (1982) 1261.
5   Antarctic Treaty Secretariat, Antarctic Treaty Consultative Meeting XL Report, Beijing, China (2017) accessed 15.12.2019. https://www.ats.aq/devAS/Info/FinalReports?lang=e, Item 9 para 172, 53.
6   Ibid. para 173:53.
7   Both terms will be used subsequently as synonyms for the activities of exploration, exploitation, and use of marine or terrestrial biodiversity.
8   Walter Reid, et al, 'Biodiversity Prospecting: Using Genetic Resources for Sustainable Development' World Resources Institute, Washington, DC (1993); Instituto Nacional de Biodervisidad, Santo Domingo de Heredia, Costa Rica; Rainforest Alliance, New York; African Centre for Technology Studies, Nairobi, Kenya.

that has been witnessed predominantly in the twentieth century.[9] Biological Prospecting can be divided into four phases: sampling; isolation and characterisation; development; and finally, the commercialisation of the product. Conducted in both terrestrial and marine environments,[10] it is a form of applied marine scientific research for commercial rather than purely academic research purposes.[11] Pharmaceutical, biotechnological, and cosmetic industries primarily use the resulting commercialised products.

Bioprospecting of land-living organisms is common. However, marine bioprospecting is a relatively new phenomenon[12] and has grown out of scientific and research capabilities.[13] By the early 2000s, about 15,000 natural products based on marine resources had been discovered.[14]

The increased access to MGRs simultaneously caused problems. Key issues regarding the access to MGRs in ABNJ pertain to the sharing of benefits resulting from the collection and use of marine biodiversity. One main concern is that developed countries have more financial and scientific capacities to access MGRs than developing countries. This concern, amongst others, is supported by a study that shows that BASF, a German chemical manufacturer, holds almost half of the patents related to MGRs.[15] Additionally, a recent analysis showed that out of 13,000 genetic sequences derived from 862 marine species, 98% of the patent sequences were registered in only ten countries. The USA, Germany, and Japan, the top three countries, are holding approximately 70% of the share.[16] This also results from the fact that access to MGRs,

---

9   Ann-Isabelle Guyomard, 'Ethics and bioprospecting in Antarctica', *Ethics Sci Environ Polit* 10 (2010):31–41, doi: 10.3354/esep00104, 31.
10 UNDP (2017) 'Bioprospecting' Financing Solutions for Sustainable Development UNDP. accessed 05.01.2020 http://www.undp.org/content/sdfinance/en/home/solutions/bioprospecting.html.
11 Alex Eassom, et al. 'Horizon scan of pressures on Biodiversity Beyond National Jurisdiction' (UNEP-WCMC, Cambridge, UK 2016), 15.
12 Marianne Synnes, 'Bioprospecting of organisms from the deep sea: scientific and environmental aspects' Clean Techn Environ Policy 9, 1 (2007):53–59. doi: 10.1007/s10098-006-0062-7, 53.
13 Alan D Hemmings and Michelle Rogan-Finnemore, 'The Issues posed by Bioprospecting in Antarctica.' In Antarctic Bioprospecting edited by Alan D Hemmings and Michelle Rogan-Finnemore, 234–244. (Christchurch: Gateway Antarctica Special Publication 2005). <https://www.researchgate.net/profile/Alan_Hemmings/publication/261996054_Antarctic_Bioprospecting/links/0a85e5363316c3e1000000/Antarctic-Bioprospecting.pdf> accessed 02.01.2020, 236.
14 See Synnes, note 12.
15 Robert Blasiak, et al., 'Corporate control and global governance of marine genetic resources' *Sci. Adv* 4, 6 (2018):1–7. DOI: 10.1126/sciadv.aar5237, 2.
16 Ibid.

especially those found in the deep seas, requires significant financial resources and well-advanced technology.[17] Consequently, the access to MGRs is highly uneven across nations, and the potential for their commercialisation currently rests in the hands of a few corporations and universities, primarily located in the world's most highly industrialised countries.[18]

Exclusive access to the potential economic benefits arising from bioprospecting activities and downstream development, especially commercialisation, is targeted through patents associated with MGRs. As a result, concerns regarding benefit sharing arise as the source country, or its indigenous people do not automatically benefit from the commercialisation of these products. Often, the products are based on techniques and resources that these communities have been using for centuries. Therefore, the CBD now guarantees and regulates the protection of indigenous people and their traditional knowledge (TK), specifically under Article 8(j) CBD.

In addition to that, the Nagoya Protocol establishes a regime for the fair and equitable sharing of resources related to the utilisation of genetic resources. Nonetheless, it only applies to territory within national jurisdiction, so that the access and use of MGRs in ABNJ remains unregulated.

An increasing interest in the search and sampling of biological material has been witnessed in Antarctica throughout the last decade. Additionally, bioprospecting activities have been discussed for almost two decades now. Nevertheless, the ATCPs have not decided on the regulation of these activities, and the regulatory framework for the collection and use of Antarctic MGRs, including bioprospecting activities, remains unregulated.[19] To give an insight into the issues the parties faced during the negotiations, the next part of the paper outlines the discussions on bioprospecting in the AT area that have taken place during the ATCMs.

3 Biological Prospecting in Antarctica and within the ATCM

Bioprospecting arose for the first time on the agenda of the ATCM in 2003. Since then, the issue has been debated extensively, and it was acknowledged

---

17 Marijo Vierros, et al, 'Who Owns the Ocean? Policy Issues Surrounding Marine Genetic Resources' *Limnology and Oceanography Bulletin*, 2 (2017):1–8. Doi: 10.1002/lob.10108, 3.
18 Ibid.
19 Roser Puig-Marcó, 'Access and benefit sharing of Antarctica's Biological Material' *Marine genomics* 17 (2014):73–78. doi: http://dx.doi.org/10.1016/j.margen.2014.04.008, 73.

that it is likely to raise more concerns in the future, especially in terms of legal and political issues.

The ATCM reports of the past 17 years show that the Meeting has developed a clear position on the matter of bioprospecting. In several ATCMs, the Meeting has made clear that only the ATS is acknowledged as the appropriate framework to regulate the sustainable collection and use of Antarctic marine biodiversity. On the occasion of the 40th ATCM in 2017, the Secretariat once again made clear that the ATS is the competent framework to regulate the conservation and sustainable use of Antarctic biodiversity. Therefore, a response letter was drafted in reply to a possible invitation to a forthcoming meeting in light of the BBNJ process.[20] In addition to that, the parties undertook extensive research in the form of Information and Working Papers and Intersessional Contact Groups. However, they have not been able to establish any regulation during the past 17 years.

The difficulties regarding bioprospecting activities are, to a large extent, based on the consensus approach that is incorporated in the ATS through Article IX(4) of the AT. According to this approach, all parties have to be in support of the decision or further procedure. This approach enables states with differing interests and views on a range of matters to come together and to cooperatively manage activities on the continent. Additionally, each consultative party possesses a veto power, which allows it to avoid discussions on any topic that could undermine its interests. Furthermore, the interests of the parties are strongly protected from being significantly compromised by the influence of other parties.[21] Hence, it can be said that the consensus approach provides durable protection of the claimants' interests within the ATS. This process, albeit its positive implications for the ATS, can result in adverse effects: such as in the process of negotiating the Liability Annex to the Environmental Protocol, which took almost 13 years.[22] This negative effect also applies to bioprospecting, as it has been discussed for 17 years without having reached a specific decision on its regulation.

In addition to that, the ATCM reports show that especially the definition of the term 'biological prospecting' and whether it shall be regulated as any

---

20 See ATCM XL Report, note 5, Item 9, para 173.
21 Ibid.
22 The Liability Annex to the Environmental Protocol (Annex VI to the Protocol in Environmental Protection) applies to environmental emergencies arising from authorised human activity. It regulates situations where an operator fails to take a prompt and effective response to environmental damage arising from its activities. In consequence, the operator is liable to pay the costs of approved response action taken by another party; see: Annex XI art 1 and 2.

other scientific research activity, is creating controversy amongst the ATCPS. Therefore, no official definition is provided until now, and only Resolution 7 from 2005[23] links bioprospecting to scientific research.

ASOC considered the regulation of bioprospecting, together with Antarctic tourism, as key challenges for the Consultative Parties. Additionally, various parties have acknowledged the need for regulation of these activities. After bioprospecting has been a long-standing item on the agenda of the ATCM, the Meeting acknowledged its complexity and finally included the matter in the Strategic Working Plan in 2018. This marks an essential step of the ATCM, and, in the authors' view, it might imply that the ATCM is slowly preparing to take further steps to address the issue of bioprospecting. It may be prepared to take the future lead for the regulation of the specifics of bioprospecting. However, the next step of the process is yet to be determined.

The BBNJ process itself, as well as the Antarctic legal framework regarding bioprospecting activities, will be outlined in the further part of this paper. Herewith, the value of the BBNJ process for the regulation under the ATS is targeted.

4 The BBNJ Process

ABNJ represent the largest environments on the planet and are comprised of the high seas (water column) and 'the area' (seabed) beyond the 200 nautical miles exclusive economic zones (EEZ) of a nation state. However, they are still the least understood, are an area of an increasing number of research activities, and, more importantly, are still lacking international protection.[24] Even though mechanisms for environmental protection in ABNJ, such as environmental impact assessments and area-based management tools, including marine protected areas, exist, an overarching framework for the conservation of marine biodiversity in ABNJ is missing. In short, the current international ocean governance framework is not sufficiently equipped to conserve and protect BBNJ.[25] Therefore, the UNGA adopted in 2006 a Resolution on Oceans

---

23   Resolution 7 (2005), ATCM Report XXVIII, p. 435 <https://ats.aq/devAS/Meetings/Measure/352> accessed 10.04.2020.
24   Elisabeth De Santo, et al, 'Protecting biodiversity in areas beyond national jurisdiction: An earth system governance perspective' *Earth System Governance*, 2 (2019). doi: https://doi.org/10.1016/j.esg.2019.100029, 2.
25   Muriel Rabone, et al, 'Access to Marine Genetic Resources (MGR): Raising Awareness of Best-Practice Through a New Agreement for Biodiversity Beyond National Jurisdiction (BBNJ)' *Front. Mar. Sci.* 6:520 (2019). doi: 10.3389/fmars.2019.00520, 2.

and the Law of the Sea[26] under which a working group was established on the conservation and sustainable use of marine biological diversity and genetic resources in ABNJ. After several meetings and substantive debates the BBNJ process led in 2015 to the development of an international, legally binding instrument,[27] which shall be established by 2020.

Subsequently, a Preparatory Committee (PrepCom) was created in order to provide recommendations for the creation of a draft text. These recommendations were delivered by the PrepCom in July 2017 and addressed the four key items that would be part of the 'package deal':[28] marine genetic resources (MGRS); area-based management tools (ABMTs), including marine protected areas (MPAS); environmental impact assessments (EIAS), as well as capacity building and technology transfer.[29] The new ILBI will be established under the UNCLOS and shall complement existing international agreements that regulate issues such as high seas fisheries, deep-sea mining, marine pollution, intellectual property rights, and biodiversity protection.[30] More importantly, it shall not undermine existing relevant legal instruments and frameworks, as well as relevant global, regional, and sectoral bodies.[31] The new ILBI will not contain any clear indication of the inclusion of the AT area and how the particular legal circumstances of this area will be recognised. However, with the repeated affirmation that the ATS is the appropriate framework to regulate the collection and use of MGRS in Antarctica, it seems like the ATCM is aiming to exclude the AT area from the scope of the new ILBI.[32] As this paper is referring to Antarctic biological prospecting activities, which are, along with marine scientific research, inextricably linked to MGRS, the focus will lie on the issue of MGRS within the BBNJ process.

---

26   United Nations General Assembly Resolution on the Law of the Sea (A/RES/61/222) adopted 20 December 2006.

27   United Nations General Assembly, Resolution 69/292 'Development of an international legally binding instrument under the United Nations Convention on the Law of the Sea on the conservation and sustainable use of marine biological diversity of areas beyond national jurisdiction' A/RES/69/292 <http://www.un.org/en/ga/search/view_doc.asp?symbol=A/RES/69/292> accessed 20.12.2019.

28   David Leary, 'Agreeing to disagree on what we have not agreed on: the current state of play of the BBNJ negotiations on the status of marine genetic resources in areas beyond national jurisdiction' *Marine Policy* 99 (2019):21–29, doi: http://doi.org/10.1016/j.marpol.2018.10.031, 21.

29   Elisabeth De Santo, 'Implementation challenges of area-based management tools (ABMTs) for biodiversity beyond national jurisdiction (BBNJ)' *Marine Policy* 97 (2018):34–48. https://doi.org/10.1016/j.marpol.2018.08.034, 34.

30   Ibid., 2.

31   UNGA, A/CONF.232/2020/3 'Revised draft text', Art. 4, 6.

32   See ATCM XL Report, note 5, Item 9, para 173.

In August 2019, the third Intergovernmental Conference (ICG) Session 'ICG-3' took place at the UN Headquarters, where more than 400 participants, including governments, international organisations, civil society and academia engaged in discussions to aim for the establishment of a new ILBI on the sustainable use of BBNJ.[33] For the first time, the delegates delved into textual negotiations based on a 'zero draft', which contained a treaty text.[34] This 'zero draft' includes 12 'parts' ranging from a preamble and general provisions, such as on the use of terms, to provisions on institutional arrangements, and the settlement of disputes.[35]

Amongst all negotiated items, MGRs are receiving the most attention during the negotiations[36] and the ICG-3 showed that there are still diverging views on various topics, in particular regarding MGRs. Consequently, the remaining uncertainties regarding the provisions on MGRs need to be discussed and solved in the fourth and last ICG, which will take place later this year.[37]

The ICG-3 made progress on several topics. Generally, the parties agreed that benefit-sharing modalities should be included in the ILBI. Further, it was agreed that non-monetary benefits should be referenced and that a definition of MGRs should be included in the new ILBI.[38]

One of the main disputes around MGRs is the definition of the access to MGRs. It is sure to say that the new ILBI will include a definition on the access to MGRs. However, no final definition was agreed upon during the ICG-3 and it is yet to be determined whether the definition should be subject to a permit or license, or if it should be open and free.[39] A reason for parties to argue against the regulation of the access to MGR in ABNJ is that it possibly could hinder marine scientific research and that it could lead to actors, such as developed states or companies from states with bigger capacities, profiting more than others.[40] Consequently, parties that fear not to be able to access and utilise MGRs originating from ABNJ, due to a lack of capacities, argue for the regulation of access

---

33 BBNJ-IGC-3FINAL 'Summary of the Third Session of the Intergovernmental Conference (IGC) on the Conservation and Sustainable Use of Marine Biodiversity of Areas Beyond National Jurisdiction: 19–30 August 2019' (2019) 25 Earth Negotiations Bulletin 218:2 <http://enb.iisd.org/oceans/bbnj/igc3/>, 2.
34 Ibid., 1.
35 Ibid., 21.
36 See Rabone et al., note 25, 2.
37 The fourth session of the ICG was postponed to a later, yet unclear, date due to the COVID-19 outbreak and following travel restrictions and lock-downs. The further evolvement of the situation will determine the date of the next session.
38 See BBNJ-IGC-3FINAL, note 33, 2.
39 Ibid., 2.
40 See Rabone et al., note 25, 7.

to MGRs and benefit-sharing. Differing views regarding access to MGRs are, to a large extent, connected to the political and economic interests of the respective state.[41] This refers, amongst others, to the fact that the access to MGRs is highly uneven across nations.[42] The inclusion of a provision on capacity building in the new ILBI shall solve the disparity between the states ensure the fair and equitable benefit sharing.

Furthermore, the provision on the application of the instrument still includes disagreements. At this point, it is still unclear whether the instrument will only include *in situ*[43] access to MGRs or, if also *ex situ*,[44] *in silico*,[45] and digital sequence information will be included in its application. Some parties argue that unlimited access is essential to guarantee the functioning of the research community.[46] This issue is again linked to the disparity between states regarding their capacity to access and use MGRs of ABNJ. By providing free access, these disparities can be overcome but are in consequence pertaining to the debate regarding the sharing of benefits arising from the collection and access of MGRs.

The equitable benefit sharing from the utilisation of MGRs in ABNJ has been another main topic of the discussion, which still needs to be considered in the next session of the ICG on the new ILBI. However, common ground has been found that a provision regarding the equitable benefit sharing needs to be included. This shall ensure the protection of the rights of developing countries. It needs to be ensured that developing countries, even though they might lack resources, have access to MGRs, and can utilise MGRs of ABNJ through the benefit-sharing mechanism.[47] Hitherto, it needs to be considered whether the provision on benefit-sharing of MGRs includes mandatory or voluntary benefit-sharing, as well as its modalities and triggers.[48]

In addition to that, it is still unclear whether intellectual property rights (IPRs) shall be included in the new IBLI, and if so, how.[49] The current draft of the new ILBI includes a provision on IPRs, which states that IPRs shall not be in conflict with the objectives of the agreement and shall not interfere

---

41   See BBNJ-IGC-3FINAL, note 33, 6.
42   Ibid., 4.
43   *In situ* means on site conservation.
44   *Ex situ* means off site conservation.
45   *In silico* means performed on computer or performed via computer simulation.
46   See Rabone et al., note 25, 2.
47   See BBNJ-IGC-3FINAL, note 33, 6.
48   Ibid., 2.
49   Ibid., 6.

with the benefit sharing and traceability of MGR's of ABNJ.[50] Furthermore, it is stated that they shall not be subject to patents unless the resources are modified by human intervention and result in a product that can be commercialised. However, the issue regarding IPRs of MGRs in ABNJ is that they are not clearly defined. The CBD is addressing the ownership of genetic resources but refers only to areas within national jurisdiction. The UNCLOS only designates mineral resources of the seabed (the Area) as the common heritage of mankind, whereby a benefit-sharing regime results but leaves the ownership of MGRs unresolved, as MGRs of ABNJ are at this moment not addressed.[51] Here the dichotomy of the Common Heritage of Mankind (CHM) principle and the freedom of the high seas comes into play. This has been part of the discussion from the very beginning on, and the states share widely differing views. In consequence, it is unclear at this point whether the CHM principle or the principle of the freedom of the high seas will apply. Throughout the discussion, a North-South divide is identifiable.[52] The G77 states and China, for example, argue for the application of the CHM principle, as it provides the legal foundation for the fair and suitable regime of conservation and sustainable use of marine biological diversity in ABNJ, including the benefit-sharing of MGRs. On the other hand, Iceland states that the CHM principle, according to Art 136 UNCLOS, applies to mineral resources beneath the seabed[53] and is consequently not applicable to renewable, biological resources on the seabed all in the water column beyond national jurisdiction.[54] In this regard, the principle of the freedom of the high seas would apply.

Generally, it can be said that it is more likely for developing countries to argue for the application of the CHM principle, as the high seas are global commons, and the resources need to be shared equitably among all states and therefore overcome disparities between the states. In contrast, states with the resources to exploit MGRs in the high seas would be more likely to argue that the ocean resources are subject to the freedom of the high seas, and consequently, no benefit-sharing mechanism arises. However, there are also parties pursuing the pragmatic approach, by which the progress of the negotiations is not dependent on the determination of the legal status of MGRs in ABNJ. In short, the principle that applies in regards to the collection and use of MGR from ABNJ is not a precondition for establishing relevant provisions

---

50 UNGA, A/CONF.232/2020/3 'Revised draft text', Art. 12(1), 11.
51 UNGA, A/CONF.232/2020/3 'Revised draft text', Art. 12(2), 12.
52 See Leary, note 28, 24.
53 UNCLOS, Art. 133.
54 See Leary, note 28, 24.

concerning the benefit-sharing issues of MGRs.[55] This again remains a matter that still needs to be discussed in the next ICG session later this year. The parties will need to consider the number of general principles that could be integrated into the agreement but might decide not to address the dichotomy of the CHM principle and the freedom of the high seas and thereby, follow the pragmatic approach.

The third session of the ICG on the establishment of the new ILBI has shown that the parties are on the right track. A draft text has been established, which has been thoroughly discussed by the parties. However, considerable disagreements on various issues under every key item were expressed. The draft text shows clearly the different issues, which are yet to be discussed, by using brackets for parts that are not final yet. These brackets indicate that there are two or more alternative options within a provision or that a 'no text' option was supported.[56] It shows that especially the topic of MGRs, including questions regarding the sharing of the benefits, is a complex issue for the state parties.

The next ICG-4 will convene later in the year 2020.[57] It remains to be seen if the parties will overcome these disagreements and will find compromises in order to achieve their goal to establish a coherent international legally binding instrument for the conservation of marine biodiversity in ABNJ.

The analysis of the BBNJ process, as well as the ATCM reports regarding bioprospecting activities, show that especially the definitions of the terms concerning the access of MGRs bear widely differing opinions. Further, the uncertainty of whether activities regarding MGRs in the AT area will be included in the new ILBI remains. Therefore, the paper aims to provide a solution-based approach to show that regulation of Antarctic bioprospecting activities could be achieved under the ATS. In the following, the Antarctic legal framework regarding Antarctic bioprospecting activities will be outlined. Further on, the proceedings of the BBNJ process, which can support this undertaking, will be taken into account.

5 The Antarctic Legal Framework on Bioprospecting Activities Regarding Antarctica

The Antarctic continent and all activities taking place in and around it are governed by its own legal regime: the ATS. The ATS is an international governance

---

55 Ibid.
56 UNGA, A/CONF.232/2020/3 'Revised draft text', 2.
57 See BBNJ-IGC-3 FINAL, note 33, 2.

arrangement, of which the basis is the AT.[58] It includes three subsequent treaties: Convention for the Conservation of Antarctic Seals (CCAS),[59] Convention on the Conservation of Antarctic Marine Living Resources (CCAMLR),[60] and Protocol on Environmental Protection to the Antarctic Treaty (Madrid Protocol).[61] In addition to that, the Convention on the Regulation of Antarctic Mineral Resource Activities (CRAMRA)[62] was established under the AT. However, it never entered into force and was replaced by the Madrid Protocol in 1991. This system aims to reinforce peace, freedom of scientific research, and international cooperation in which only regulated harvesting of marine living resources is allowed, and mineral resource activities are entirely banned.[63]

There are no specific regulations on MGRs contained within the Antarctic legal framework, and none of the different regulations are directly addressing biological prospecting. Yet, the matter was discussed in every ATCM since 2002 and led to recommendations enhancing the exchange of information regarding the utilisation of biological material.[64] More importantly, it has resulted in a Resolution declaring that the ATS is the appropriate framework for the management of the collection of biological material in the AT area. Resolution 9 (2009)[65] on the Collection of Antarctic Biological Material additionally declares that the Madrid Protocol and the CAMLR Convention address the environmental aspects of scientific research and the collection of biological material in the Antarctic region. Here a link to bioprospecting activities in the Antarctic legal framework is created. The ATCM also states that certain

---

58 Antarctic Treaty, opened for signature 1 December 1959, 402 UNTS 71 (entered into force 23 June 1961) (hereafter Antarctic Treaty/AT).
59 Convention for the Conservation of Antarctic Seals, opened for signature 1 June 1972, 11 ILM 251 (1972) (entered into force 11 March 1978) (hereafter CCAS).
60 Convention on the Conservation of Antarctic Marine Living Resources, opened for signature 20 May 1980, 19 ILM (1980) (entered into force 7 April 1982) (hereafter CCAMLR or CAMLR Convention).
61 Protocol on Environmental Protection to the Antarctic Treaty, opened for signature 4 October 1991, 30 ILM (1991) (entered into force 14 January 1998) (hereafter Protocol/Madrid Protocol).
62 Convention on the Regulation of Antarctic Mineral Resource Activities (CRAMRA) of 2 June 1988, 27 ILM 868, this treaty never entered into force.
63 Madrid Protocol, art 7.
64 Rene Lefeber, 'Marine Scientific Research in the Antarctic Treaty System.' In Law of the Sea and the Polar Regions: Interactions Between Global and Regional Regimes edited by Donald R Rothwell, Alex G Oude Elferink, Erik J Molenaar (Leiden: Martinus Nijhoff, 2013) 321–341, 326.
65 Resolution 9 (2009) on the Collection of Antarctic Biological Material, ATCM Report XXXII – CEP XII, Baltimore (adopted 17.04.2009) <https://www.ats.aq/devAS/Meetings/Measure/450> accessed 20.02.2020.

regulations can be linked to the collection and use of Antarctic marine biodiversity available under the ATS, such as articles II and III of the AT. These articles oblige the parties to respect the freedom of scientific investigation and to promote international cooperation, whereby information regarding scientific programs in Antarctica, scientific personnel, and scientific observations, as well as results, shall be shared.[66] Since bioprospecting activities in Antarctica can mostly be confined to the act of collecting and discovering biological resources, the activities are mainly of scientific research character, even though they might be collected for an ultimately commercial purpose.[67] Consequently, it can be stated that these AT articles do apply in the case of bioprospecting activities in Antarctica. Nevertheless, there are also regulations of the Madrid Protocol and the CAMLR Convention that apply regarding bioprospecting activities. The next part of the paper investigates the regulations regarding bioprospecting activities of the Madrid Protocol further and provides an outlook for a possible, more specific regulation for these activities.

6   The Madrid Protocol and the Regulation of Bioprospecting Activities

The ATS is a dynamic system, which allows the parties to incorporate new regulations if needed and thus can be modified through time.[68] Therefore, a regulation on the collection and use of Antarctic MGRs could be established under the Protocol on Environmental Protection. This paper, however, does not include any other possible regulation under the ATS due to its limited extent. A possible regulation under CCAMLR, for example, would need to be investigated further in an intensive research project. Moreover, it needs to be mentioned that this paper only touches briefly on the possibility of regulating bioprospecting activities under the Madrid Protocol. This is based on the fact that it merely aims to provide a solution-based approach to the general issue that the collection and use of Antarctic marine biodiversity, including bioprospecting activities, is currently unregulated. The exploration of the Madrid Protocol as a possible basis for regulation is hereby just a part of the process

---

66   Antarctic Treaty, arts I–III.
67   Dagmar Lohan and Sam Johnston, 'Bioprospecting in Antarctica' (UNU-IAS Report 17, 2005) accessed 16.12.2019. https://collections.unu.edu/eserv/UNU:3100/antarctic_biopros pecting_3.pdf, 17.
68   Julia Jabour-Green and Diane Nicol, 'Bioprospecting in Areas Outside National Jurisdiction: Antarctic and the Southern Ocean' *Melbourne Journal of International Law* 4, 76 (2003): 83.

towards fulfilling the original purpose of the paper. To be more specific, it shall be shown that the BBNJ negotiations can support the establishment of a regulation under the ATS profoundly and can lead to the regulation of these activities if decided so.

The idea to incorporate regulation on the sustainable use and collection of Antarctic marine biodiversity under the Protocol is based on the fact that the ATS does not have a comprehensive bioprospecting policy in general. However, the AT itself and its subsequent measures, such as the Madrid Protocol, contain few provisions that are relevant to this matter.[69] An interesting and innovative feature of the Protocol pertains to the fact that it neither modifies nor amends the AT but rather supplements it.[70]

The Protocol designates Antarctica as 'a natural reserve, devoted to peace and science'.[71] It places a moratorium on mineral exploration and reinforces the provisions of AT article III on cooperation in the planning and conduct of scientific activities and the sharing of information.[72] The heart of the Protocol lies with its article 7, which prohibits mineral resource activities and is also known as the mining ban. However, scientific research is exempt from the prohibition.[73] Therefore, it reiterates science as an essential and legitimate activity in Antarctica and designates Antarctica 'as an area for the conduct of scientific research'.[74] Under article 3(c) of the Protocol, it is stated that the parties shall 'ensure that the diversity of species, as well as the habitats essential to their existence, and balance of ecological systems existing within the AT area (are) maintained.' Moreover, even though bioprospecting does not present a current environmental concern, this article is to be considered in light of these activities. With that being said, no significant environmental concerns are arising from bioprospecting activities in Antarctica. However, cumulative minor adverse effects on the environment connected to these activities might arise, especially issues stemming from the *in situ* collection of Antarctic marine biodiversity. An example of such a negative effect would be the introduction of

---

69   Bernhard Herber, 'Bioprospecting in Antarctica: the search for a policy regime' *Polar Record* 42, 221:139–146. doi: 10.1017/S0032247406005158, 139.

70   Davor Vidas, 2000. 'Entry into Force of the Environmental Protocol and Implementation Issues: An Overview' In Implementing the Environmental Protection Regime for the Antarctic edited by Davor Vidas, 1–17. (Oslo: Fridtjof Nansen Institute: Springer Science and Business Media, 2000) 5.

71   Madrid Protocol, art.2.

72   See Herber, note 69.

73   Alan D. Hemmings, 'Does Bioprospecting risk moral hazard for science in the Antarctic Treaty System?' *Ethics in Science and Environmental Politics* 10 (2010):5–12. doi: 10.3354/esep00103, 8.

74   Madrid Protocol, art.3.

non-native species by the expedition ship that is building the base for the research expedition. The CO^2 emissions, which are generated by this expedition, would also need to be taken into account. While the activity of bioprospecting itself does not present a significant environmental impact, it should still be further observed in the future, because it might have the ability to cause adverse side effects on marine biodiversity.

The Madrid Protocol additionally requires that Environmental Impact Assessments (EIAS) need to be conducted prior to the exercise of all activities, including scientific research.[75] However, one issue of the Madrid Protocol is that it does not define scientific research, nor does the AT itself. Therefore, it is questionable whether biological prospecting activities fall under these regulations – this leaves room for interpretation. In the same vein, Hemmings, for example, points out that bioprospecting might be indistinguishable from conventional science but that others see it clearly as an industrial activity.[76] Yet, the resolutions on bioprospecting mentioned above state that bioprospecting shall be treated like any other scientific research activity and recall article 8 of the Protocol.[77] Due to the latter 'definition' provided in the Resolution, and the Madrid Protocol regulating these activities under the auspices of the AT, the Protocol seems to be the right instrument to regulate these activities further. Nonetheless, a specific definition of the term is required in the future. The collection and use of marine biodiversity is an extremely current matter, which needs to be kept on the agenda of international organisations dealing with biodiversity within and beyond national jurisdiction. For this reason, the ATCM also renewed the declaration of its position that the ATS is the appropriate framework to address bioprospecting issues within its area of application. By that, it shows that it is aware of the importance of the matter and will continue to examine biological prospecting activities with the support of the parties.

A further factor contributing to the issue's complex nature is the patchwork of different regulations that apply to the Antarctic continent and its surrounding ocean. This patchwork of different regulations also includes the UNCLOS, which applies to the world's oceans. Therefore, the ocean south of 60° S will be simultaneously regulated by the UNCLOS and the ATS, more specifically the CAMLR Convention, which applies to marine resources in the ocean area south of 60° S and to the area between that latitude and the Antarctic Convergence Zone. According to this view, it could be interpreted that the BBNJ, which will

---

75   Ibid. arts 3(c), 6(b), 8.
76   See Hemmings, note 73, 9.
77   Madrid Protocol art 8 regulates the requirement to undertake Environmental Impact Assessments prior to the exercise of all activities in the Antarctic environment.

be established under the UNCLOS, will apply to the ocean south of 60° S.[78] However, by reading the ATCM reports of the past 17 years, it becomes clear that the ATCM would not fully support that view, as they repeatedly stated in the past that the ATS is the appropriate framework to regulate the sustainable use and collection of Antarctic marine genetic resources. Yet, article 6 of the AT, which states that the Treaty shall not undermine any other global conventions, needs to be kept in mind as it affects the establishment process of new regulation on the collection and use of Antarctic marine biodiversity. The question is now the following: How does the ATCM establish a regulation under the ATS, which does not interfere with other international agreements, such as the new ILBI, and at the same time honours article 6 of the AT? This question is tackled in the following part of the paper.

7 A Solution-Based Approach for the Regulation of Antarctic Bioprospecting Activities

Until now, it has been shown that the ATS is providing only limited regulation regarding the sustainable use and collection of Antarctic marine biodiversity, including bioprospecting activities. Discussions on the need for extensive regulation and further research have lasted for almost two decades now without reaching any specific agreement. This has different reasons: the collection and use of MGRs at the international level, but also in Antarctica, is a highly complex issue that needs to be incorporated in a patchwork of various international and national regulations, agreements, and treaties. As a result of this, it additionally needs to be ensured that the new potential regulation does not contradict any pre-existing regulations. Another issue contributing to the complexity of the matter is that bioprospecting relates to natural resources, which in turn revolve around territorial claims in Antarctica. These represent an extremely sensitive matter within the ATS. Precisely this fact underlines the expertise and appropriateness of the ATS to regulate Antarctic bioprospecting activities. As a consequence, the paper argues for regulation under the AT, which incorporates these characteristics and ensures the sustainable collection and use of MGRs, as well as their fair and equitable benefit sharing.

A suitable basis for the regulation on the sustainable access and use of Antarctic marine biodiversity is the Protocol on Environmental Protection, as the Protocol already provides a basic regulation of scientific research in

---

78   Li Jinchang, 'New Relationship of the Antarctic Treaty System and the UNCLOS System: Coordination and Cooperation' *ASSEHR* 181 (2018):374–377, 374.

its article 3(1). Additionally, it serves as a supplementing regulation to the AT, which is designed around a core set of general environmental principles, with a series of Annexes that establish detailed rules and provisions. These annexes can be updated to accommodate changes in environmental management.[79] Therefore, an additional annex to the Protocol, for example, could be established.

Although the ATCPS acknowledge the need for regulation of bioprospecting issues, the lack of consensus between the ATCPS and the high complexity of the issue, have hindered the establishment of regulation under the ATS until today. Also, in an international sphere, the need for regulation of the collection and use of MGRs in ABNJ was acknowledged and has now, in contrary to the ATS, led to the BBNJ process. Here, too the state parties are facing difficulties resulting from widely differing opinions and views during the negotiations. This is based on the immense complexity of the topic. Despite these complexities, the negotiations have led to the creation and discussion of a 'zero draft'. The latter is a fundamental milestone for the proper development of the negotiations.[80] It shows that the parties of the BBNJ process are one step further than the ATCPs regarding the access and use of MGRs in ABNJ.

The establishment of the 'zero draft' has shown that the state parties are not too far away from reaching the primary goal of a new ILBI, and it seems within reach to finalise the instrument soon. However, the new ILBI leaves uncertainties regarding the AT area. The unique characteristics of the AT area will not be adequately represented if the new ILBI will not specify its application for this area. Therefore, it is suggested that the ATCM should use the present achievements of the BBNJ process and concentrate on a specific solution to regulate the access and use of Antarctic marine biodiversity. During the ICG session negotiating the new ILBI, the parties have agreed that, amongst others, a definition of MGRs and the benefit-sharing modalities will be included. This can support the establishment of a regulation under the ATS, as the instruments shall be harmonised and not contradict each other. The ATCPs, for example, could adopt the definition of MGRs from the new ILBI, once it is finalised, and if needed, adapt it to the characteristics of the AT area. It has been shown that during the BBNJ process and the ATCMs, the parties have faced similar issues, whereby the proceedings of the BBNJ process, which are further along, provide

---

79 Antarctic Treaty Secretariat (2016) '25 years of the Protocol on Environmental Protection to the Antarctic Treaty'. Accessed 15.04.2020. https://documents.ats.aq/atcm39/ww/atcm39_wwoo7_e.pdf, 8.
80 See BBNJ-IGC-3FINAL, note 33, 20.

a sound basis that can be used by the ATCPs. However, not all differences were settled, and the provisions of the zero draft need to be discussed further during the next ICG. Nonetheless, the basic framework has already been set up, and it is to be expected that for the next ICG, these differing opinions will be straightened out or will be put aside by including a broader provision on the discussed matter.

By taking the 'zero draft' or even the new ILBI into account, the specific needs and circumstances of activities relating to Antarctic MGRs can be considered appropriately. At the same time, the remaining uncertainty in the application of the new ILBI in the AT area, as well as a harmonisation with the new international agreement, is achieved.

8 Conclusion

This paper has highlighted that the collection and use of marine biodiversity in ABNJ are still widely unregulated. In consequence, the UNGA is establishing a new ILBI under the UNCLOS, which aims towards the conservation of marine biodiversity. However, the instruments' application incorporates problems and uncertainties, such as its application in the AT area. At the same time, the ATCM seems to strive for the regulation of these activities in Antarctica under the ATS, if at all. This uncertainty regarding the application of the instrument for the AT area, and its structure, if regulated under the ATS, leaves the question for the further procedure of the ATCPs.

Therefore, the author suggests using a solution-based approach. Through this approach, the focus lies on possible solutions instead of focusing solely on problems. The BBNJ process has already resulted in a draft treaty text, and the parties have been negotiating existing gaps thoroughly. Progress has been made regarding problems and differing views that came up during the negotiations, such as the provision on the access to MGRs or the benefit-sharing issues, for example. Therefore, it is suggested that the current BBNJ process and its zero draft shall be taken into account. This can be further supported if cooperation between the specialists participating in the BBNJ negotiations and the specialists of the ATCPs is established.

After almost two decades of negotiations on bioprospecting issues, the ATCPs finally need to act in order to regulate the sustainable collection and use of Antarctic marine genetic resources. Therefore, this paper has outlined the possibility of regulating these issues under the Protocol for Environmental Protection, as it already provides basic regulations that are relevant to the matter. In addition to that, the consideration of the current BBNJ process and its proceedings is suggested to support the establishment of such regulation. However, there is still capacity for intensive research on the sustainable collection and use of MGRS in ABNJ and their regulation, including bioprospecting activities in Antarctica. This is based on their immense complexity and the widely differing economic and political interests of state parties.

Legal Issues concerning DROMLAN under the Antarctic Treaty System

Osamu Inagaki*

Abstract

The purpose of this paper is to explore possible legal issues concerning the Dronning Maud Land Air Network (DROMLAN) under the Antarctic Treaty system. By examining the recent discussion concerning DROMLAN within the Antarctic Treaty Consultative Meeting (ATCM) and relevant State practice, this paper argues that States parties have difficulty in fully complying with the obligations of advanced notice under Article VII (5) of the Antarctic Treaty and Environmental Impact Assessment under Article VIII (2) of the Madrid Protocol for DROMLAN's operation. Finally, this paper suggests that good communication among relevant States parties and private actors is important for enhancing compliance with these obligations.

Keywords

DROMLAN – Antarctic Treaty – advanced notice – Madrid Protocol – EIA

1 Introduction

Currently air transport is vital for efficient research and for other human activities in Antarctica.[1] In fact, the States parties to the Antarctic Treaty have developed several air networks to and within Antarctica. According to the Council of Managers of National Antarctic Program (COMNAP), there are four regional

---

* Researcher, Polar Cooperation Research Centre (PCRC), Graduate School of International Cooperation Studies (GSICS), Kobe University, Japan. osamui@people.kobe-u.ac.jp.
1 For the overview of aviation activities in Antarctica, see COMNAP. 2019. Overview of Aviation Activity to Inform ATCM Discussion, Information Paper 2 submitted to the 42nd ATCM.

aviation 'hubs', namely the East Antarctica hub, the Dronning Maud Land hub, the Ross Sea hub and the West Antarctica/Peninsula hub.[2] This paper focuses on the air network between Cape Town and Dronning Maud Land (DML) which is called Dronning Maud Land Air Network (DROMLAN). DROMLAN is particularly notable in that it is well coordinated and operated by 11 national Antarctic programs that have research stations or research interest in the DML.

However, as will be described in detail later, issues concerning DROMLAN have recently been brought to the attention of the Antarctic Treaty Consultative Meeting (ATCM) by some consultative parties. These issues are particularly in relation to the obligations of advanced notice under Article VII (5) of the Antarctic Treaty[3] and of environmental impact assessment (EIA) under Article VIII (2) of the Protocol on Environmental Protection to the Antarctic Treaty[4] (Madrid Protocol). Considering this development, this paper aims to shed light on the legal issues concerning DROMLAN under the Antarctic Treaty system (ATS).

In order to achieve this objective, this paper first overviews the operation of DROMLAN and identifies its important characteristics. It then attempts to elucidate the legal issues concerning DROMLAN by examining two cases in which the issues concerning DROMLAN were discussed in the ATCM. The practice of relevant States parties is also discussed.

2 DROMLAN and Its Characteristics

This section seeks to overview the operation of DROMLAN and to identify its important characteristics.

2.1 Overview of DROMLAN[5]

DROMLAN is an international air network established by 11 national Antarctic programs that have stations or scientific interest in DML (Belgium, Finland,

---

2   Ibid, 9–10.
3   Antarctic Treaty, 1 December 1959, United Nations Treaty Series 402 (1962): 71.
4   Protocol on Environmental Protection to the Antarctic Treaty, 4 October 1991, United Nations Treaty Series 2941 (2019): 3.
5   For the basic information of DROMLAN, see Germany (2017) "DROMLAN-Dronning Maud Land Air Network" Information Paper 42 submitted to the 40th ATCM and H. Gernandt et al "Dronning Maud Land Air Network: A Decade of Internationally Co-ordinated Air Operations" in Proceeding of the COMNAP Symposium 2014, 59–70 available at <https://www.comnap.aq/documents/Symposium-Proceedings-final-16-February-2015.pdf> (accessed on 24 October 2020).

Germany, India, Japan, the Netherlands, Norway, Russia, South Africa, Sweden and the United Kingdom). DROMLAN was established during the COMNAP meeting in July 2002[6] and it became operative from the 2003–04 season. DROMLAN operations are based on its terms of reference originally adopted in 2003 and revised in 2010. These terms of reference are not publicly available.

The aim of DROMLAN is to facilitate inter-continental flights and intra-Antarctica flights. The inter-continental flights connect Cape Town, South Africa with two established gateway runways in Antarctica, namely the Novolazarevskaya runway[7] (hereinafter the Novo runway) managed by Russia and the Troll runway managed by Norway.

The aircraft used for the inter-continental flights from Cape Town to Novo runway are Iluyhsin-76, owned and operated by Vorga Dnepr Airline, a Russian private air company. From the 2002–03 season to the 2015–16 season, more than 150 round trip intercontinental flights were made.[8]

Intra-Antarctica flights, on the other hand, connect Novo runway or Troll runway with research stations located in the DML. The aircraft used for intra-Antarctica flights include Basler-BT67 and Twin Otter DHC-6/300 owned and operated by Kenn Borek Air, an air company based in Canada, and Basler-BT67 owned by Alfred Wegner Institute (AWI) and operated by Kenn Borek Air.

The users of DROMLAN are three categories.[9] The first comprises members of national Antarctic programs, who are considered priority users. The second category of users are members of government-funded scientific expeditions, but not organised by a national Antarctic program. The third category of DROMLAN users are non-governmental passengers, including private tourists. Non-governmental passengers can use the DROMLAN only if vacant seats are available. It is generally understood that the reason for allowing for non-governmental passengers is to reduce the cost for governmental passengers.[10] In the 2015–16 season, for example, DROMLAN service was used by 662 passengers of national Antarctic programs or government-funded scientific expeditions and 266 non-governmental passengers.[11]

---

6   Germany, ibid.
7   Novolazarevskaya Runway is located in 17 km Southwest of Novolazarevskaya Station, a Russian station.
8   See Germany, note 5, 7.
9   Ibid 3.
10 Russia. 2010. "Queen Maud Land – a new center of non-governmental activity in the Antarctic" Working Paper 61 submitted to the 33rd ATCM, 4.
11 See Germany, note 5, 6–7.

The administrative structure of DROMLAN includes a steering committee which is a decision-making body for policy and financial matters. The committee consists of one representative from each national Antarctic program and meets annually. It is important to note that these 11 national Antarctic programs outsource the operation of DROMLAN to Antarctic Logistics Centre International (ALCI), a Cape Town-based private company. ALCI is responsible for the overall operation of DROMLAN including travel arrangements for the members of National Antarctic Programs. ALCI charters the aircraft for inter-continental and intra-Antarctica flights from Vorga Dnepr Airline and Kenn Borek Air. Moreover, ALCI has its sister private company, The Antarctic Company (TAC), also based in Cape Town. TAC is responsible for the travel arrangement of non-governmental passengers, including private tourists, using DROMLAN's facilities.

2.2 Important Characteristics of DROMLAN

Based on the description of DROMLAN above, it is possible to detect two important characteristics of DROMLAN that seem to affect the implementation of obligations by the States parties to the ATS. These will be discussed later. The first important characteristic is that both governmental and private actors are involved in the operation of DROMLAN. As explained above, DROMLAN's operation is managed by ALCI and TAC, both South African private companies. The aircraft used for DROMLAN are owned and operated by two private air companies. Furthermore, the DROMLAN's facilities and service are used not only by governmental passengers but also by non-governmental passengers including private tourists.

The second characteristic is DROMLAN's multi-national character. In other words, various actors or facilities with various nationalities are involved in the operation of DROMLAN. For example, ALCI and TAC have South African nationality and the aircraft used for inter-continental flights and intra-Antarctica flights are registered in Russia and Canada. Novo runway is managed by Russia and Troll Runway is managed by Norway. Furthermore, the passengers of DROMLAN have different nationalities.

3 Legal Issues Concerning DROMLAN

This section seeks to explore legal issues concerning DROMLAN. First this section sketches out the relevant rules under the ATS and their subsequent development. It then attempts to elucidate legal issues concerning DROMLAN by examining two cases dealt with in the ATCM and the practice of relevant States parties regarding the obligation of advanced notice. Finally, this section examines the possible causes for this legal issue and offers some solutions.

3.1 Relevant Rules under the ATS and Their Development

As mentioned earlier, the issues concerning DROMLAN have been discussed in the ATCM, particularly in relation to Article VII (5) of Antarctic Treaty and Article VIII (2) of the Madrid Protocol. Article VII (5) of the Antarctic Treaty provides that:

> 5. Each Contracting Party shall, at the time when the present Treaty enters into force for it, inform the other Contracting Parties, and thereafter shall give them notice in advance, of
> (a) all expeditions to and within Antarctica, on the part of its ships or nationals, and all expeditions to Antarctica organized in or proceeding from its territory;
> (b) all stations in Antarctica occupied by its nationals; and
> (c) any military personnel or equipment intended to be introduced by it into Antarctica subject to the conditions prescribed in paragraph 2 of Article I of the present Treaty.

This article requires the parties to give advanced notice of certain information on their expeditions, stations and military personnel and equipment in Antarctica. This obligation of advanced notice was originally introduced to make the inspection system under Article VII effective.[12] Since the 2008–09 season, the States parties have been required to give notice under this paragraph through Electronic Information Exchange System (EIES), instead of through diplomatic channels.[13]

Under this paragraph, specifically sub-paragraph (a), it is assumed that every single State having 'expeditions' defined by this paragraph shall give notice of them. The wording '*all* expeditions' in this paragraph supports this interpretation. Thus, there might be a case where multiple States give notice over a single expedition. This overlap of advanced notices can happen when the expeditions involves multiple States parties (multi-national character).[14]

---

12   Sir Arthur Watts, International Law and the Antarctic Treaty System (Cambridge Grotius Publication Limited, 1992), 171.
13   Decision 5 (2008) Electronic Information Exchange System: Start of operations, ATCM XXXI – CEP XI, Kyiv. The notices given under this paragraph are available at website of the Antarctic Treaty Secretariat <https://www.ats.aq/e/exchange-requirements.html>.
14   Kees Bastmeijer, The Antarctic Environmental Protocol and Its Domestic Legal Implementation. (The Hague London New York: Kluwer Law International, 2003), 121.

The scope of the information to be notified under this paragraph has been subsequently expanded and elaborated by number of Measures and Decisions adopted by the ATCM.[15] Among them, two important developments are relevant. First, the term 'expeditions' in Article VII (5) (a) came to be interpreted to include non-governmental expeditions including those of private tourists.[16] Second, even though the text of Article VII (5) does not explicitly refer to aircraft activities, this paragraph came to be considered to cover expeditions using aircraft as well.[17] Thus, theoretically, it is argued that based on these two subsequent developments, Article VII (5) now comprehensively covers DROMLAN operations that transport governmental passengers as well as private tourists involved in non-governmental flight activities. In fact, according to the latest decision on information exchange, the States parties are required to give advanced notice of aircraft activities of non-governmental expeditions.[18]

Although Article VII (5) is a purely procedural obligation, this provision is referred to several more substantive provisions in the Madrid Protocol.[19] Among them Protocol Article VIII (2) is particularly relevant. It provides that:

> 2. Each Party shall ensure that the assessment procedures set out in Annex I are applied in the planning processes leading to decisions about any activities undertaken in the Antarctic Treaty area pursuant to scientific research programmes, tourism and all other governmental and non-governmental activities in the Antarctic Treaty area for which advance notice is required under Article VII (5) of the Antarctic Treaty, including associated logistic support activities.

---

15 For recent discussion as to the scope of Article VII (5) in the ATCM, see Philippe Gautier, "The Exercise of Jurisdiction over Activities in Antarctica: A New Challenge for the Antarctic System," in Law of the Sea, From Grotius to the International Tribunal for the Law of the Sea, ed. Lilian del Castillo (Leiden/Boston: Brill Nijhoff, 2015), 200–204.

16 See, for example, Recommendation VI-7 (1970) Regulation of Antarctic Tourism, ATCM VI, Tokyo, para 2; Recommendation VIII-6 (1975) Standard format for exchange of information, ATCM VIII, Oslo, Annex. See also, Akiho Shibata, "The Antarctic Treaty System: Its Foundation and Evolution" Jurist 1409 (2010): 90 (in Japanese).

17 As early as Recommendation I-6 adopted at the 1st ATCM (Canberra, 1961) refers to aircraft as information to be notified.

18 Decision 7 (2019) Reviewing Requirements for Exchanging Information on Non-Governmental Expeditions, ATCM XLII-CEP XXII, Prague, Annex 1.1.2.C.

19 See, Article III (4), Article VIII (2) and Article XV (1) (a) of the Madrid Protocol and Article I of Annex VI to the Madrid Protocol.

This Article obliges States parties to ensure that EIA procedures[20] are applied for governmental and non-governmental activities in the Antarctic Treaty area for which advance notice is required under Article VII (5) of the Antarctic Treaty. At the level of domestic law, these EIA procedures are closely linked with the permit system for activities planned in the Antarctic, even though the latter procedure is not explicitly obliged to be applied under the Madrid Protocol.[21]

Article VIII (4) provides that:

> [w]here activities are planned jointly by more than one Party, the Parties involved shall nominate one of their number to coordinate the implementation of the environmental impact assessment procedures set out in Annex I.

Thus, unlike the obligation of advanced notice under Article VII (5) of the Antarctic Treaty, it is NOT assumed under Article VIII of the Madrid Protocol that all the relevant States parties that are jointly planning activities shall individually ensure EIA for those activities. Rather, this article allows States parties to apply just one EIA for an activity that is planned by more than one States jointly.[22]

3.2   Case Study (1): Operation of Passenger Terminal by ALCI

There are two recent cases where the issues concerning DROMLAN were discussed in the ATCM, especially in relation to the obligations of advanced notice and EIA. The first case is related to the operation of passenger terminal at

---

20   The EIA procedures provided by Annex I of the Madrid Protocol are as follows: If a proposed activity are determined as having less than a minor and transitory impact, the activity may proceed. If the activity is determined as likely to have a minor and transitory impact, then an Initial Environmental Evaluation (IEE) shall be prepared. If the IEE indicates that the activity is likely to have more than a minor and transitory impact, a Comprehensive Environmental Evaluation (CEE) shall be prepared. The draft CEE shall be circulated to all parties and the Committee for Environmental Protection (CEP) before the ATCM considers it. Any decision on whether and how the proposed activity proceed shall be based on the final CEE that shall address the comments made by the parties.

21   William Bush "Means and Methods of Implementation of Antarctic Environmental Regimes and National Environmental Instruments: An Exercise of Comparison," in Implementing the Environmental Protection Regime for the Antarctic ed. Davor Vidas (the Netherlands: Kluwer Academic Publishers, 2000), 34.

22   Professor Kees Bastmeijer observes that Article VIII (4) is applied not only to governmental expeditions but also to non-governmental expeditions that fall under the jurisdiction of two and more contracting parties. See, Bastmeijer, note 14, 174–5.

Novo runway by ALCI and tourism activities by TAC at Novo runway. Norway brought this case to the 33rd ATCM in 2010 as a result of its inspections in DML under Article VII of the Antarctic Treaty in February 2009. In this inspection, the Norwegian inspection team visited Novo runway area where ALCI operates a seasonal passenger terminal consisting of tents and containers to accommodate stopover passengers during the summer season.

In the inspection report, Norway first observed that there was a lack of clarity regarding the ownership and responsibility for operation of the passenger terminal.[23] The report found that although ALCI was a South African company and worked closely with the South African government, it had not yet obtained an official permit from South African authorities because of the absence of a domestic permitting system. The report also revealed that while ALCI thought that it was Russia that was responsible for EIA and the authorization of its activities, the Russian Arctic Expedition (RAE) maintained that 'the activity of the ALCI Company is carried out beyond the legal framework which applies to RAE, and that RAE does not bear any responsibility'.[24] Therefore, the report found that '[a]s far as the inspection team can discern, neither Russian nor South African authorities have notified the ALCI-activity as activity organized out from their country in accordance with current exchange of information requirements under the Antarctic Treaty'.[25] Norway further reported that during the inspection ALCI did not provide the inspection team with an EIA for the operation of the passenger terminal.[26]

In addition to the operation of the passenger terminal, Norway pointed to the issue of non-governmental tourism activities at Novo runway arranged by The Antarctic Company (TAC), a South African sister company of ALCI. In this regard, the inspection report found that TAC had organized and operated non-governmental expeditions using the DROMLAN aircraft.[27] The report observed that '[a]s far as the inspection team can discern TAC has not notified its activity and/or submitted an environmental impact assessment according to the provisions of the Environmental Protocol to South-African authorities'.[28] It was also noted that the TAC was waiting for a South African permitting system to be in place. In the conclusion of the inspection report, while recognizing the clear logistical benefits of a passenger terminal at novo runway, Norway

---

23 Report of the Norwegian Antarctic Inspection under Article VII of the Antarctic Treaty (February 2009).
24 Ibid, 29.
25 Ibid.
26 Ibid, 31.
27 Ibid, 33.
28 Ibid.

pointed out that the responsibility to undertake permitting and notification of the activities at Novo runway was unclear. Thus, it recommended that 'all involved parties clarify their responsibilities and obligations'.[29]

This inspection report was submitted to the 33rd ATCM and 13th CEP in 2010 where Norway stated that 'the operations at Novo runway/ALCI Airbase provide a platform for unregulated tourism to Dronning Maud Land'.[30]

At that ATCM, Russia also submitted a Working Paper on DROMLAN activities. In the paper, Russia admitted that while it had conducted an EIA for ice airfield operations and inter-continental flight activities, the EIA did not cover the impact of governmental and non-governmental passengers at Novo runway.[31] Russia stated that to address this gap ALCI planned to prepare a separate EIA for the activities at Novo runway.

Again, in 2012, Russia submitted an Information Paper on the operation of DROMLAN to the 35th ATCM, in which Russia observed that ALCI is a South African private company and, therefore, it is subject to South African domestic law. Russia emphasised that the ALCI had already completed its own EIA for the passenger terminal even though South Africa had not yet developed the domestic procedures for regulating its individuals and legal entities in the Antarctic.[32]

In this case, neither Russia nor South Africa gave advanced notice of the operation of the passenger terminal and tourism activities at Novo runway. In addition, EIA seems not to have been undertaken for either activities. Although the direct cause of these failures was the absence of domestic procedure in South Africa, a lack of coordination between South Africa and Russia in implementing the obligations seems to have also been an important factor for these failures. This case indicates that relevant States parties had difficulty in complying with the obligations of advanced notice under Article VII (5) of the Antarctic Treaty and of EIA under Article VIII (2) for DROMLAN activities.

3.3 Case Study (2): Construction of Perseus Runway

The second case concerns the construction by ALCI of a new blue ice runway – the so-called Perseus Runway – near the Belgium Princess Elisabeth Station. This runway is intended to be the third gateway runway for inter-continental

---

29 Ibid, 34.
30 Final Report of the Thirty-third Antarctic Treaty Consultative Meeting Punta del Este, Uruguay 3–14 May 2010, 84 para 388.
31 See Russia, note 10.
32 Russia. 2012. Activity of the international air program DROMLAN and its interaction with non-governmental activity in the Antarctic, Information Paper 72 submitted to the 35th ATCM.

flight for DROMLAN operations. At the DROMLAN meeting in May 2015, ALCI indicated their intention to submit an EIA for construction of the runway to the next ATCM in June 2015. However, at the 39th ATCM in May and June 2016, Belgium reported that ALCI had not yet submitted the EIA.[33] After discussion, the ATCM accepted Belgium and Norway's offer to make further inquiries about the construction of a new runway.[34]

Belgium and Norway reported the result of their inquiry to the 40th ATCM in 2017. They found that ALCI is the operator in charge of construction of the runway and that 'plans for construction of the blue ice runway did commence before an IEE/CEE was submitted to an appropriate authority'.[35] Belgium and Norway further pointed out that although Russia made an EIA for a test flight conducted to the Perseus Runway in January 2015, the EIA covered only the flight activity and not the construction of the runway. Finally the two countries recommended that '[w]hen there are multiple Parties and private entities involved it is especially important that all parties are clear on what procedures need to be followed, and who is in charge of reporting activities to the appropriate authorities, and that all formalities are in order prior to commencing any work'.[36]

In response to this report, Russia gave the following explanation at the 40th ATCM in 2017. ALCI prepared an EIA for the construction of the runway, but it failed to obtain a permit from South African government because of the lack of relevant domestic legislation in South Africa. Thus, a new company named ALCI Nord was established in St. Petersburg and ALCI Nord submitted the EIA to Russian authorities to obtain a permit. Russian authorities subsequently issued a permit to ALCI Nord for the construction and operation of the blue ice runway.[37] After discussion, the ATCM noted that 'the EIA process needs to be conducted prior to projects commencing, in accordance with the Environment Protocol, and that there should be good communication between stakeholder Parties during the review process'.[38] The ATCM further stressed that such

---

33   Final Report of the Thirty-ninth Antarctic Treaty Consultative Meeting, Santiago, Chile 23 May–1 June 2016, 78 para 277. See also Belgium. 2016. Developing a Blue Ice Runway at Romnoes in Dronning Maud Land, Information Paper 56 submitted to the 39th ATCM.

34   Final Report of the Thirty-ninth Antarctic Treaty Consultative Meeting, Santiago, Chile 23 May–1 June 2016, 80 para 282.

35   Belgium and Norway. 2017. Blue Ice Runway by Romnæsfjellet, Information Paper 66, submitted to the 40th ATCM, 3.

36   Ibid, 4.

37   Russia. 2017. On use of the blue ice area in the vicinity of Romnaes Mount as a reserve airstrip, Information Paper submitted to the 40th ATCM.

38   Final Report of the Fortieth Antarctic Treaty Consultative Meeting, Beijing, China 22 May–1 June 2017, 106 para 390.

communication was particularly important in case of the activities involving multiple parties and private entities. In the 41st ATCM in 2018, Russia reported that Perseus Runway became operative from the 2017–18 season.[39]

It appears that the direct reason behind this non-compliance with Protocol obligations was also the lack of South African domestic procedure. Thus, Russia finally undertook the responsibility to prepare an EIA for the construction of the runway, by creating a new company in its territory. However, more fundamentally, the miscommunication between South Africa and Russia in implementing the obligation of the EIA seems to have prevented the application of EIA in advance of the activity taking place.

3.4   State Practice of Advanced Notice under Article VII (5)

These two case studies reveal the difficulties that States parties have in complying with the obligations of advanced notice under Article VII (5) of the Antarctic Treaty. The practice of advanced notice regarding DROMLAN is further explored in this sub-section. As mentioned above, nowadays advanced notice of activities is given through EIES by the States parties and they are publicly available at the Antarctic Treaty Secretariat website.[40] This paper explores the practice of five relevant DROMLAN member States (South Africa, Russia, Canada, Japan and Germany) by examining their pre-season information (advanced notice) from the 2008–09 season to the 2018–19 season.[41]

South Africa: As mentioned above, DROMLAN's operator companies, namely the ALCI and TAC are based in South Africa. In addition, DROMLAN's inter-continental flights proceed from Cape Town. However, from the 2008–09 season to the 2013–14 season, South Africa did not give advanced notice of the DROMLAN activities. It was since the 2014–15 season that South Africa has given notice of several non-governmental expeditions operated by TAC, though it was not clear whether all these non-governmental expeditions used DROMLAN's aircraft and facilities. These non-governmental expeditions include the World Marathon Challenge[42] (since 2017–18) and the transportation

---

39 Russia. 2018. Preparation for putting into operation the Perseus Runway in the vicinity of the Romnaes Mount (Queen Maud Land), Information Paper 143 submitted to the 41st ATCM.
40 These notices are available at <https://www.ats.aq/devAS/InformationExchange/ArchivedInformation?lang=e> (accessed on 29 January 2020).
41 It should be noted that there are several seasons in several countries which lack the information. For example, there is no information for South Africa in the 2009–10 season and for Russia in the 2008–09 and 2014–15 seasons.
42 For World Marathon Challenge, see its website <https://worldmarathonchallenge.com/> (accessed on 29 January 2020).

of NHK (Japan Broadcasting Corporation) staff in the 2016–17 season. Moreover, in the 2016–17 and 2017–18 seasons, South Africa also gave notice of the activities of aircraft, including Ilyushin and Basler operated by ALCI as non-governmental expeditions.

Russia: DROMLANS's Ilyushin-76 is registered in Russia and the Novo runway is managed by Russia. Since the 2008–09 season, Russia has given notice of Ilyushin-76 flights as national expeditions. It should be noted that Russia has also given notice of the activities involving the Basler BT-67, a Canada-registered aircraft.

Canada: As noted above, the aircraft for intra-Antarctic flights such as the Basler and Twin Otter are registered in Canada. However, Canada has not notified the participation of its aircraft except for the 2014–15 season at which time Canada gave notice of aircraft activities operated by Kenn Borek Air for logistical support of DROMLAN.

Japan: Japan is a user state of DROMLAN. In the 2008–09 and 2009–10 seasons, Japan notified the use of Ilyushin-76DT, Twin Otter, and Basler BT-67 as national expeditions. It seems that members of the Japanese Antarctic Research Expedition (JARE) took these DROMLAN flights. However, since the 2010–11 season, Japan has not given pre-season (advanced) notice of the use of DROMLAN.

Germany: Germany is also a user state of DROMLAN. Germany gave notice of governmental use of Ilyushin-76 and Basler BT-67 in the 2008–09 and 2009–10 seasons. Additionally, in the 2013–14, 2014–15 and 2016–17 seasons, Germany notified non-governmental use of the DROMLAN flights. Since the 2015–16 season, Germany has included the transportation of personnel by DROMLAN as a part of the information on Stations.

Since the actual data on the use of DROMLAN service by these five States is not publicly available, it is difficult to accurately verify whether the relevant States parties fully comply with the obligation of advanced notice under Article VII (5) of the Antarctic Treaty. However, the general feature of State practice is that States give notice of DROMLAN's operation sporadically and inconsistently. Only Russia constantly gives notice of DROMLAN's aircraft. Moreover, as noted above, it is assumed under Article VII (5) that every single State having 'expeditions' as defined by this paragraph shall give notice of them. In view of these considerations, it is questionable that all relevant States parties have fully complied with the obligation of advanced notice for DROMLAN's operation.

3.5 Examination: Causes of and Prescriptions for the Compliance Issue

The above information reveals that there is an issue of compliance with the obligations of advanced notice and EIA under the ATS for DROMLAN's operation.

For enhancing compliance with these obligations, it would be beneficial to explore the possible causes of this issue. In my view, this issue of compliance could ultimately be derived from the two key characteristics of DROMLAN, namely involvement of private actors and multi-national character.

First, the operation of DROMLAN involves various private operators, such as ALCI, TAC, and others. When private actors are involved in activities as operators, relevant States parties are required to effectively regulate these private actors. In other words, they have to effectively ensure the application of EIA for the proposed activities before the private actors start the activities. Thus, if States parties are not capable of regulating their private entities, it will leave a loophole enabling unregulated activities by private actors, as was the case of South Africa that did not have domestic authorisation procedure. Furthermore, there might be also the possibility that the activities of the private operator are not regulated if one relevant State party believes that the private operator's activities are being regulated by another State party.[43]

Second, and more importantly, DROMLAN has a multi-national character. This character pluralises the States parties that are obliged to give notice under Article VII (5). For example, for an inter-continental flight of Ilyushin-76 from Cape Town to Novo runway, it is possible that up to four categories of States are obliged to give notice of that flight: (1) the State of registry of Ilyushin-76 (Russia); (2) the State in whose territory the expedition is organized (varies); (3) the State from whose territory the expedition proceeds (South Africa) and (4) the States of the passengers' nationalities (also varies). As noted above, it is assumed under Article VII (5) that each of these States shall give notice of the flight individually. However, the pragmatic understanding shared by the States parties seems to be rather that it is legally acceptable if only one of the relevant States gives advanced notice of the flight.[44] Thus, again, there could be the case where no State gives notice if each relevant States assumes that another State is responsible.

How can we enhance compliance with the obligations of advanced notice and EIA? In this regard, it should be recalled that the 40th ATCM emphasised the importance of good communication between relevant States parties and the private operators involved in the project.[45] This communication between relevant stakeholders can contribute to enhancing compliance in two ways.

---

43   Belgium pointed to this possibility in its information paper, see note 33.
44   It might be worth examining whether this shared understanding constitutes 'subsequent practice in the application of the treaty which establishes the agreement of the parties regarding its interpretation' in the sense of paragraph 3(b) of Article 31 of the Vienna Convention on the Law of Treaties.
45   See supra note 38 above.

First, the communication allows States parties to know the activities planned by the private operators in advance of their commencement. Second, the communication also allows relevant States parties to clarify and coordinate the allocation of responsibility for regulating the activities of private operators.

4   Concluding Remarks

This paper has explored legal issues concerning DROMLAN. This paper shows that while DROMLAN has contributed to efficient operation of the Antarctic research, the States parties to the Antarctic Treaty system have difficulties in fully complying with the obligations of advanced notice and EIA for DROMLAN operations. In the 60 years since the signing of the Antarctic Treaty, the transport and logistics systems for Antarctica have become significantly complex, involving multiple States and private operators. Logistic collaboration, such as exemplified by DROMLAN, is undoubtedly beneficial to scientific research in the Antarctic and should certainly be encouraged; however, at the same time, so should transparency of human activities[46] and environmental protection in the Antarctic be ensured. Thus, ultimately, the case of DROMLAN identifies the challenge of improving compliance with the obligations of advanced notice and EIA for the modern complex transport and logistics systems in the Antarctic. The first step in overcoming this challenge is to ensure good communication between the relevant States and private operators.

---

46   Professor Akiho Shibata observes that Article VII (5) has played a role in ensuring the transparency of the activities in the Antarctic Treaty area. See, Akiho Shibata "Domestic Implementation of Antarctic Environmental Liability Annex: Issues for Japan," in Aspects of International Law Studies: Achievements and Prospects ed. Junichi Etō (Shinzansha, 2015), 658 and 663 (in Japanese).

Legal Implications of China's Proposal for an Antarctic Specially Managed Area (ASMA) at Kunlun Station at Dome A

Sakiko Hataya*

Abstract

Built in 2009, Kunlun Station, China's third Antarctic research station, is located in the Dome A region. In 2013, during the 36th Antarctic Treaty Consultative Meeting (ATCM), China proposed the establishment of a new Antarctic Specially Managed Area (ASMA) within Dome A and prepared a draft management plan for it. Yet, several ATCM members questioned China's motives for designating Dome A as a new ASMA, and, as a result, no consensus could be reached. *Surprisingly however, the Chinese ASMA proposal spurred a new impulse to introduce guidelines for the designation of ASMAs.* This paper explores the legal implications of China's proposal for an ASMA at Kunlun Station in Dome A and, in particular, focuses on the new legal developments that followed.

Keywords

Proposal – Antarctic Specially Managed Area (ASMA) – Chinese Kunlun Station at Dome A

1 Introduction

Since 2013, China has been seeking to establish an Antarctic Specially Managed Area (ASMA) around its Kunlun Station in the vicinity of Dome A,

---

* PhD Candidate, Graduate School of International Cooperation Studies, Kobe University, Kobe, Japan. 166i032i@stu.kobe-u.ac.jp.

the highest ice feature in Antarctica. This proposal aroused much controversy at the Antarctic Treaty Consultative Meeting (ATCM) and, as of 2019, no consensus has been reached on the proposal. The media and some scholars have interpreted China's proposal as a manoeuvre for a sovereign claim with clear potential implications.[1] However, this is not strictly a political issue. At root, the controversy really results from doubt about whether China's proposal satisfies the substantive rules of the Protocol on Environmental Protection to the Antarctic Treaty, Annex V, Art. 4. This paper first explores the legal dynamics of China's ASMA proposal for Dome A against the ASMA system itself. Considering the findings made in this regard, this paper suggests that China's proposal highlights the need to create new ASMA guidelines.

A second section lays out the contextual and factual background of Kunlun Station and Dome A as well as an analysis of the reasons behind China's proposal to designate the area as an ASMA. Section 3 illustrates the controversy within the Committee for Environmental Protection (CEP) and the ATCM, unpacking the reasons why several members questioned China's justification for applying for ASMA designation. Section 4 lays out the legal framework around ASMAs and evaluates the practices of existing ASMAs in light of this framework. Section 5 presents a comparative analysis of stations with similar features to Kunlun Station. Lastly, Section 6 discusses how the ASMA system could be improved and the potential implications of China's proposal on the evolution of the system.

2   Basic Information about Kunlun Station at Dome A

Built in 2009, Kunlun Station is China's third research station. It is located in the Dome A region of the hinterland of East Antarctica's plateau and situated in the middle of the ice divide of the East Antarctic Ice Sheet, near the center of East Antarctica. Its geographical position is 80°25′01″S, 77°06′58″E, and it is approximately 4000 meters above sea level. Since Dome A is a remote area, it is difficult to access and as a result, no conflicting uses or activities have

---

1   Anne-Marie Brady, "China's Expanding Antarctic Interests: Implications for New Zealand," Small States and the New Security Environment (SSANSE), University of Canterbury. Commissioned by Small States and the New Security Environment (SSANSE) Project Policy Brief (2017). <https://www.canterbury.ac.nz/media/documents/research/China%27s-expanding-Antarctic-interests.pdf> (accessed 14 June 2020).

occurred in this region. Kunlun station is used only in the summer and comprises some 250 square meters of living and working space, accommodating up to 25 research and logistics personnel. The station is home to projects such as astronomical research, meteorological observation, radar sounding and ice coring.

Dome A is one of the best locations on Earth to carry out astronomical observation, more specifically, it's extremely thin and stable atmosphere, very dry air, absence of pollution, and low background radiation make it an ideal site for conducting astronomical research. In January 2012, the first of three remotely steerable 50-centimetres Antarctic Survey Telescopes was installed at Kunlun to study extra-terrestrial activities,[2] and China emphasised that such scientific endeavors needed to be protected from any disturbances.[3] It seems that this is one of the reasons why China wants to designate the region as an ASMA.

3 Controversy within the CEP and ATCM (2013-2019)

China introduced a draft management plan for a new ASMA at Dome A in 2013, describing its scientific, environmental, and logistical values. China stated that its proposal was based not on the premise that more than one party would be using the site, but on a precautionary approach based on the assumption that future interest and activities in the region were likely to occur.[4] Additionally, China mentioned specific values to be protected and stated that 'the building of Kunlun Station can provide key support for further scientific research and all kinds of scientific activities by China and other countries in Dome A area and the broader surrounding areas'.[5] Thus, China wanted to protect its facility from the disturbances that such activities may bring about.

However, there was controversy about China's proposal within the CEP and ATCM, with several members questioning the justification of China's

---

2 Jean de Pomereu, 'China's research programmes at Kunlun Station', *Science Poles* (2012, November). <http://www.sciencepoles.org/article/china-research-programmes-at-kunlun-station> (accessed 17 February 2020).
3 Final Report of the Committee for Environmental Protection, CEP XXI, 2018, para. 161. All CEP and ATCM Final Reports are available from https://ats.aq/devAS/Info/FinalReports?lang=e.
4 Final Report of the Antarctic Treaty Consultative Meeting, ATCM XXXVI, 2013, para 127.
5 China, 'Proposal for a new Antarctic Specially Managed Area at Chinese Antarctic Kunlun Station, Dome A', ATCM XXXVI, Working Paper 8, 5.

application for an ASMA and suggesting that China's proposal might be premature since international science programs and other activities have not yet been conducted at Dome A; that is, there are currently no overlapping activities from multiple operators in the area. Moreover, the United Kingdom questioned whether China's proposal aligned with the purposes of ASMAs as defined by Annex 5 of the Environmental Protocol, with the principal objectives of avoiding conflict and improving collaboration between different users of an area. The Russian Federation and Norway also questioned the threats that China may pose to this remote area, and Germany questioned the advantages of designating an ASMA in such a remote region with a low level of biodiversity.[6] Further discussion among members continues today and no consensus on the ASMA proposal has been reached.

With its proposal not accepted, China has, since 2018, been expressing an intention to develop a Code of Conduct to serve as a first step for managing activities at Dome A in order to protect its scientific values.[7] More specifically, China argued that the site needed to be protected from disturbances so that two more telescopes could be established there to study extra-terrestrial activities.[8] Several parties have responded by noting such practical guidance has been a defined requirement for other national programs; however, China's Code of Conduct has not yet been approved.

4 ASMAs in the Antarctic Treaty System: Legal Requirements

As Hughes and Grant posit: 'the development of area protection within Antarctica started when the Agreed Measures for the Conservation of Antarctic Fauna and Flora were agreed to in 1964, which were established to designate Antarctic Specially Protected Areas (ASPAs) to preserve the area's "unique natural ecological system"'.[9] The Protocol on Environmental Protection to the Antarctic Treaty, also known as the Madrid Protocol, gives the ASMA a legal identity in Annex V, Art. 4, which also provides guidelines for designating ASMAs. More specifically, Art. 4 states that

---

6 CEP XVI Final Report 2013, para 120.
7 CEP XX Final Report 2017, para 108.
8 CEP XXI Final Report 2018, para 161.
9 Kevin A. Hughes and Susie M. Grant, 'The spatial distribution of Antarctica's protected areas: A product of pragmatism, geopolitics or conservation need?', *Environmental Science & Policy*, 72 (2017) 42–43.

any area, including any marine area, where activities are being conducted or may in the future be conducted, may be designated as an Antarctic Specially Managed Area to assist in the planning and co-ordination of activities, avoid possible conflicts, improve cooperation between Parties or minimize environmental impacts.[10]

ASMAs have come into existence since 2004, with the first being designated in Admiralty Bay on King George Island. The most recent ASMA was designated in 2008. Currently there are seven AMSAs in the Antarctic, detailed in Table 1 below.

TABLE 1

	Name	Proponent	Year of establishment
ASMA 1	Admiralty Bay, King George Island	Brazil, Poland, Ecuador, Peru, USA	2005
ASMA 2	McMurdo Dry Valleys, Southern Victoria Land	New Zealand, USA	2004
ASMA 3*	Cape Denison, Commonwealth Bay, George V Land, East Antarctica	Australia	2004
ASMA 4	Deception Island	Argentina, Chile, Norway, Spain, UK, USA	2005
ASMA 5	Amundsen-Scott South Pole Station, South Pole	USA	2007
ASMA 6	Larsemann Hills, East Antarctica	Australia, China, India, Romania, Russian Federation	2007
ASMA 7	Southwest Anvers Island and Palmer Basin	USA	2008

* Revoked by Measure 9 in 2014

---

10 Annex V to the Protocol on Environmental Protection to the Antarctic Treaty Area Protection and Management, Art. 4. ASMAs require a management plan, but no permit is required to enter an ASMA, distinguishing them from Antarctic Specially Protected Areas (ASPAs).

Comparative studies into existing ASMAs reveal that they have common features. ASMA 2, ASMA 4, ASMA 5, ASMA 6, and ASMA 7 are all relatively accessible, even for tourists, and multiple stations and research programs already existed at these sites before applications were made to designate them as ASMAs.

An analysis of these examples shows that, before proposing an ASMA, potential conflicting activities need to be clearly identified and actual conflicts need to have already occurred in the area where an ASMA is proposed. For example, in the ASMA Designation and Management Plan for Admiralty Bay at King George Island (ASMA 1), 'diverse human activities, which [were] continuously growing and becoming more complex' had already been identified and moreover, 'over the last 30 years, more stations were settled and have grown in area, and visitors increased in numbers per year, from a few hundred to over 3,000. Better planning and co-ordination of existing and future activities will help to avoid or reduce the risk of mutual interference and minimize environmental impacts'. This information makes it clear that human beings were already quite active in the area, and so, the question of how to manage that impact was raised. The following should be noted:

> Five parties: Poland, Brazil, United States, Peru and Ecuador have active research programmes in the area. Poland and Brazil operate two all-year round stations (Poland: Henryk Arctowski Station at Thomas Point; and Brazil: Comandante Ferraz Antarctic Station at Keller Peninsula). Peru and United States operate two summer stations (Peru: Machu Picchu at Crepin Point; USA: Copacabana at Llano Point). Ecuador has a refuge at Hennequin Point. There are several small removable and permanent installations elsewhere.[11]

The management plan for ASMA 1 clearly shows that several stations and many visitors were already present in the area before the proposal was made. The logic behind the request to designate the area as an ASMA was thus evident, that is, ASMAs should be established to 'manage potential or actual conflicts of interest between different activities, including science, logistics and tourism'[12] and to 'avoid possible conflicts, improve cooperation between

---

11 ATCM Final Report, Measure 2 (2006) Antarctic Specially Managed Area: Designation and Management Plan: Admiralty Bay, King George Island, 169.
12 Ibid, 172.

Parties or minimize environmental impacts'.[13] The proposal thus satisfied the guidelines set out in Annex V, Art. 4 of the Madrid Protocol.

Moreover, it is helpful to note that the management plan for ASMA 1 clearly outlined the following plans for coordination to prevent conflicts:

> Parties that have active research programmes within the Area should establish an international Admiralty Bay Management Group, which will hold regular meetings (at a convenient time) to:
> - review the functioning and implementation of the Management Plan
> - facilitate communication between those working in or visiting the Area;
> - monitor the Area to investigate possible sources of environment impact including cumulative impacts;
> - promote the dissemination of information on this Management Plan to all parties operating in the Area, and all other visitors to the Area;
> - maintain a record of activities in the Area;
> - provide the name and address of their co-ordinator.[14]

This coordination, by clearly explaining how potential conflicts would be diffused in the area, strengthened the case for designating the area an ASMA.

Notably, proposals for the seven ASMAs listed above were not met with any controversy; therefore, it is obvious that the Kunlun case is unique. It is also helpful to recall here that China's proposal focused on current and future pressures to the scientific and environmental values of Dome A, and China has pointed out that some ASMAs were also proposed by single members, such as ASMA 3 (by Australia) and ASMAs 5 and 7 (by the United States). In short, China expressed that the Committee had previously accepted a range of approaches to ASMA designation.[15]

5   Contrastive Study between Kunlun Station and Other Stations

Kunlun Station shares some similarities with Japan's Dome Fuji Station. Thus, they serve as good candidates for a contrastive case study. In 1995, the Japanese

---

13 See Protocol on Environmental Protection, note 10.
14 ATCM Final Report, Measure 2, note 11, 172.
15 CEP XIX Final Report, 2016, para 144.

Antarctic Research Expedition established Dome Fuji as a new inland station at 77°19′01″S, 39°42′12″E, 1000 kilometres inland on the Antarctic Continent. Dome Fuji (Dome F) is 3810 metres above sea level and is one of the significant domes on the Antarctic ice sheet. The climate conditions around Dome F are similar to those at Kunlun: the conditions are harsh and the temperatures are extremely low, with annual average air temperature at −54°C, making it difficult to access. The main activities at Fuji are deep ice drilling and atmospheric observation.[16] In recent years, it has become widely known that the high-altitude environment of inland Antarctica is suitable for astronomical observation,[17] and thus, the Japanese astronomy community has identified the station as a potential candidate for a future astronomical observatory, with one author, Kazuyuki Shiraishi remarking that 'in the future, astronomical research will be a high priority at Dome Fuji Station'.[18] Japan's ambition triggered China's desire, discussed above, to establish two more telescopes at Kunlun Station for astronomical observation.[19] It is notable, however, that Japan has not asked to designate Dome F as an ASMA.

Meanwhile, the United States' Amundsen-Scott Station (ASMA 5), located on the polar plateau near the geographic South Pole at 90° S, was designated as an ASMA in 2007. It is the only station in the area. The station can hold 150 personnel in summer and is a relatively large station. The Area is located in a region of high scientific value – the South Pole Station facilitates exceptional scientific research with extensive international collaboration. Before the United States submitted its proposal for an ASMA, the area was already home to scientific programs being carried out by different nations,[20] and tourists had already begun to visit the area (beginning in 2006), with around 190 arriving per year. These two factors together – that is, scientific programs run by different nations in one region and a fair number of tourists – suggested that conflicting activities might occur in the region. This justified the application for ASMA designation to prevent conflicts among activities, including areas for different scientific research, science support activities, and non-governmental

---

16   Kazuyuki Shiraishi, 'Dome Fuji Station in East Antarctica and the Japanese Antarctic Research Expedition', in M.G. Burton et al., (eds.) *Astrophysics from Antarctica Proceedings IAU Symposium*, no. 288 (2012) 161–168. <http://articles.adsabs.harvard.edu/cgi-bin/nph-iarticle_query?bibcode=2013IAUS..288..161S&db_key=AST&page_ind=0&plate_select=NO&data_type=GIF&type=SCREEN_GIF&classic=YES> (accessed 3 February 2020) 161.
17   Ibid, 167.
18   See Shiraishi, note 16, 167.
19   See CEP XXI Final Report, note 8, para 161.
20   ATCM XXX Final Report, Measure 2 (2007) Management Plan for Antarctic Specially Managed Area No. 5 AMUNDSEN-SCOTT SOUTH POLE STATION, SOUTH POLE, 77.

activities, and to promote coordination for future activities, including coordination with tour operators.[21] An ASMA proposal was, therefore, submitted by the United States. Moreover, the United States notably performed field visits and conducted interviews with United States Antarctic Program (USAP) participants before submitting their proposal. In addition, after the ASMA proposal in 2005, the United States incorporated feedback from Australia, the United Kingdom, and the International Association of Antarctica Tour Operators (IAATO) into their management plan.[22]

These practices suggest that, although ASMA 5 was proposed solely by the United States (similar to China's proposal), the conditions on the ground that underpin these proposals are very different: the area that became ASMA 5 was home to very clear potential conflicts, and the applicant conducted preliminary assessment procedures for its proposal.

6   ASMA Guidelines: Legal Developments in Light of the Kunlun Case

Under the regime of the Protocol, an ASPA designation constitutes the central instrument because of its outstanding values under the Antarctic Treaty,[23] and in particular, the 'Guidelines for implementation of the Framework for Protected Areas set forth in Art. 3, Annex V of the Environmental Protocol' adopted in 2002. Importantly, these guidelines specifically mention ASPAs and clearly state that 'ASMAs are not considered' therein.[24]

However, some legal developments did occur after China began considering proposing an ASMA for the area around Kunlun station. The need to create ASMA guidelines was mentioned at the 2010 CEP meeting, and a workshop was held in 2011, with special attention paid to clarifying the proposal procedure and defining objectives under Annex V, Art. 4. However, during the workshop no major controversies or inquiries was raised by any of the participants. After China's proposal for the ASMA at Dome A in 2013, the CEP Chair reported

---

21   Ibid, 78.
22   United States, Update on the Draft Management Plan for ASMA? Amundsen-Scott South Pole Station, South Pole, ATCM XXIX, 2006, Information Paper 55, 2.
23   Kees Bastmeijer and Steven van Hengel, 'The Role of the Protected Area Concept in Protecting the World's Largest Natural Reserve: Antarctica', *Utrecht Law Review*, 5:1 (June 2009) 73.
24   ATCM XII Final Report, Resolution 1 (2000), Annex F Guidelines for implementation of the Framework for Protected Areas set forth in Article 3, Annex V of the Environmental Protocol, 103.

that the Committee had agreed that the Subsidiary Group on Management Plans (SGMP) should address the need for guidance material for establishing ASMAs and preparing and reviewing ASMA management plans in the intersessional period.[25] Subsequently, the SGMP advised the CEP of the need to develop guidelines for determining whether an area should be designated as an ASMA, prepare a document similar to the 'Guide to the Preparation of Management plans for Antarctic Specially Protected Areas,' and consider pre-consultation procedures before ASMA designations.[26] The SGMP members also assessed commonalities and differences between existing ASMAs. This assessment was used as a starting point for the development of guidelines. However, the SGMP also expected challenges. First, the SGMP pointed out that the preliminary assessment of potential ASMAs was unclear; it was difficult to understand the process and considerations behind the assessment. Moreover, the SGMP also pointed out that the involvement of stakeholders in the assessment process was unclear,[27] so the appropriateness of the ASMA designation process should also be explicitly clarified in the guidelines.

Regarding the actual or potential conflicts in use, the guidelines clearly mention the requirement for the recognition of ASMA designation, namely that a region must exhibit a 'duplication of activities'. As the fruit of the discussion, the 2017 guidelines – 'Guidance for assessing an area for a potential Antarctic Specially Managed Area designation' and 'Guidelines for implementation of the Framework for Protected Areas set forth in Art. 3, Annex V of the Environmental Protocol' – contain two main features worth noting: the guidelines clearly state that the designation of an ASMA requires: 1) a consensus of all Antarctic Treaty Consultative Parties (ATCPs), and 2) that this consensus derives from the appropriate process governed by explicitly and systematically formulated procedural standards.[28]

In light of these findings, the guidelines were reviewed. Potential recommendations to strengthen the overall ASMA system are put forth in the analysis below:

---

25 ATCM XXXVII Final Report, 2014, para 130.
26 Norway, Subsidiary Group on Management Plans – Report on 2014/15 Intersessional Work, ATCM XXXVIII, 2015, Working Paper 15, 3.
27 Norway, Subsidiary Group on Management Plans – Report on 2015/16 Intersessional Work, ATCM XXXIX, 2016, Working Paper 31, 1–6.
28 ATCM XL Final Report, Resolution 1 (2017) Annex B Guidelines for the Preparation of ASMA Management Plans, 309–312.

Aims of the Management Plan
- establishment of an ASMA Management Group to facilitate and ensure effective communication among those working in or visiting the Area;
- provision of a forum to resolve any actual or potential conflicts in use and to help minimize the duplication of activities;
- dissemination of information on the Area, in particular on the activities occurring and the management measures that apply within the Area;
- maintenance of a record of activities and, where practical, impacts in the Area and the development of strategies to detect and address cumulative impacts;
- review of past, existing, and future activities and evaluation of the effectiveness of management measures, potentially through site visits; and
- data collection to further support, gain further knowledge and detect any ongoing changes to the values of the Area.[29]

Special attention should also be paid to references to any actual or potential conflicts, for example, when the guidelines mention the need for the area to experience a 'duplication of activities' or when they emphasise the importance of cooperation with other parties.[30]

7 Conclusion: Lessons Learned from China's Proposal for an ASMA at Dome A

China's proposal for an ASMA at Dome A has led to discussions about guidelines for designating ASMAs and legal developments on the designation of ASMAs. This paper reviewed these developments by looking into the 2017 guidelines and clarifying the procedural rules for ASMA designation. Prior to these developments, no clear guidelines existed for the designation of an ASMA, unlike the designation of an ASPA, which already had clear guidelines. To be sure, since ASMA guidelines, including guidelines on procedural rules, have now been clarified, it is also important to ensure that any ASMA proposal accords with the substantive rules provided in Annex V, Art. 4 of the Protocol on Environmental Protection to the Antarctic Treaty.

---

29   ATCM XL Final Report, Resolution 1 (2017) Annex B Guidelines for the Preparation of ASMA Management Plans, 303.
30   Ibid.

While China has been trying to follow the designation process that existing ASMAs have followed, its ASMA proposal does not satisfy the substantive rules laid out in Annex V, Art. 4: its proposed management plan fails to prove that there will be sufficient actual or potential conflicts in the area. Accordingly, to justify its proposal, China must clarify the anticipated use conflicts. Contrary to the key requirements that this paper spotlights for ASMA designation, there are no duplicate activities occurring at Dome A.

However, since it is now widely known that the high-altitude environment of inland Antarctica is suitable for astronomical observation, international interests may indeed intensify the activity in Dome A in the future. If this were to happen materially, it would then be reasonable for China to review this issue and propose an ASMA to resolve real and potential conflicts of use and activities so as to meet the requirements of Annex V, Art. 4.

An Overview of the Antarctic Treaty System and Applicable New Zealand Law

*Trevor Daya-Winterbottom**

Abstract

The Antarctic Treaty 1959 has now been in place for 60 years and is regarded by informed commentators as one of the most successful multi-party international treaty systems. This paper provides an opportunity to look back and take stock of previous success, and more importantly, an opportunity to assess the future prospects of the treaty system. New Zealand has played a key role in the Antarctic Treaty system and has had a long involvement with Antarctica since accepting the transfer of sovereignty over the Ross Dependency in 1923. This paper therefore focuses on the effectiveness of the Antarctic Treaty system through a New Zealand lens.

Keywords

Antarctica – future prospects – New Zealand

1   Introduction

Antarctica is unique in public international law. Claimed by seven states but recognised by none as sovereign territory, the governance of the continent rests on the 'without prejudice' clause in Article IV of the Antarctic Treaty 1959.[1] This device preserves the rights of claimants from potential competition while ensuring that other states are generally free to pursue activities without permission. This fragile compromise paradoxically provides stability

---

* FRSA FRGS, Associate Professor, Faculty of Law, University of Waikato. trevor.daya-winterbottom@waikato.ac.nz.
1 James Crawford, *Brownlie's Principles of Public International Law* (8th edn, Oxford University Press, 2012) 252.

for both scientific and tourist activities and the Antarctic governance system, and illustrates both the potential weakness of the international arrangements that underpin these activities and their possibilities for future dynamic legal development.

While Article IV does not extinguish the territorial claims to Antarctica, the claims are suspended indefinitely because the Treaty does not provide for termination. Decision-making is by consensus via the annual consultative meeting but only the original parties (claimants) and other parties closely associated with substantial scientific research in the continent and surrounding seas are allowed to participate.[2]

The primary objectives of the Antarctic Treaty system are maintaining peace and security and promoting scientific research. Nuclear weapons are prohibited and military action is limited to peaceful purposes. The regime applies generally south of 60° S while reserving high seas rights for all states. These aspects of the system are illustrated by the 'liberal' inspection provisions that allow parties to nominate observers who are given complete freedom of access across the continent at all times, by the implicit designation of the continent as the last *terra nullius* terrestrial area on the planet.[3] Notwithstanding these positive aspects of the regime, future problems abound in the shape of:

> Whaling disputes, continental shelf claims, prospecting for offshore hydrocarbon resources, and the effects of climate change ...[4]

Other commentators also identify 'the need to integrate oceans management across a range of sectors and institutions' as a future challenge facing Antarctica.[5]

To address these matters, the original Treaty regime is supplemented by the Convention for the Conservation of Antarctic Seals 1972 (CCAS), the Convention on the Conservation of Antarctic Marine Living Resources 1980 (CCAMLR), and the Protocol on Environmental Protection to the Antarctic Treaty 1991 (Madrid Protocol).

Somewhat surprisingly, the Antarctic Treaty system does not provide a comprehensive or omnibus definition of the Antarctic environment. The common denominator is that 'dependent and associated ecosystems' clearly form part

---

2   Malcolm N Shaw, *International Law* (8th edn, Cambridge University Press, 2017) 399.
3   See Crawford, note 1, 346.
4   Ibid.
5   Karen N Scott and David L VanderZwaag, 'Polar Oceans and Law of the Sea' in Donald R Rothwell and others (eds) *The Oxford Handbook of the Law of the Sea* (Oxford University Press, 2015), 750.

of the environment under the various instruments. For example, CCAMLR governs 'the complex of relationships of marine living resources with each other and with their physical environment', while the Convention on the Regulation of Antarctic Mineral Resource Activities 1988 (CRAMRA) in terms of environmental damage (while not in force) pertains to 'any impact on the living or non-living components of that environment or those ecosystems, including harm to atmospheric, marine or terrestrial life', and the Madrid Protocol also relates to 'the intrinsic value of Antarctica, including its wilderness and aesthetic values'.[6] Additionally, for the purposes of 'protection' the Madrid Protocol designates the continent as a Special Conservation Area, and acknowledges the 'intrinsic value' and 'wilderness and aesthetic values' of Antarctica.[7] The regime protects Antarctica 'in the interests of mankind as a whole'.[8]

In particular, the strict controls put in place by CRAMRA (while now of largely historic interest as noted below) reflect both the divergent interests of the parties and the controversial nature of mineral exploitation. No mineral exploitation can take place under CRAMRA without approval from a committee established under the auspices of the Antarctic Mineral Resources Commission (AMRC) for the relevant area that can set binding regulations regarding (inter alia) environmental matters. The AMRC (assisted by a Scientific, Technical and Environmental Advisory Committee) has wide powers to determine what areas may be opened up for mineral exploitation, what regulations should apply to safeguard environmental protection, to ensure that environmental impact assessment occurs, and to keep mineral exploitation activities under review.[9] This model is similar to the International Seabed Authority.

However, CRAMRA has not entered into force as a result of opposition by Australia and France, and the Madrid Protocol that designates Antarctica as natural reserve and bans mineral exploitation for a period of 50 years has effectively superseded the arrangements described above.[10] Under the Protocol, management is vested in the Committee for Environmental Protection that operates under the aegis of the Conference of Parties and thus requires unanimous decision-making. These arrangements can be viewed as a type of

---

6   Patricia Birnie and Alan Boyle, *International Law & The Environment* (2nd edn, Oxford University Press, 2002) 4; Philippe Sands and Jaqueline Peel, *Principles of International Environmental Law* (4th edn, Cambridge University Press, 2018) 15.
7   Ibid, Birnie and Boyle, 46; Ibid Sands and Peel, 635.
8   Ibid, Birnie and Boyle, 144.
9   Ibid, Birnie and Boyle, 213; Sands and Peel, note 6, 637–638.
10 New Zealand is a signatory to CRAMRA (25 November 1988). But CRAMRA has not been ratified by any one of the 19 signatories, and is not expected to enter into force.

environmental 'trusteeship' that overcomes the problem of state control of resources.[11]

The CCAS continues the theme of environmental protection and imposes restrictions on the numbers, species, gender, and location of seals that can be taken or killed annually. It also regulates hunting methods and establishes breeding and scientific reserves. Detailed provisions are included regarding the exchange of scientific information via annual reports prepared by the parties that are submitted to the Scientific Committee on Antarctic Research (SCAR).[12]

The Madrid Protocol also establishes a sophisticated dispute settlement process under the Antarctic Treaty. In particular, it provides for compulsory arbitration where conciliation and negotiation attempts have been exhausted. The arbitration process is novel and also provides for third parties to be involved in the process where they have a legal interest that could be 'substantially' affected by the arbitral award.[13] Alternatively, parties can accept the jurisdiction of the International Court of Justice.

Beyond that, Article 8 and Annex I of the Protocol make detailed provision for environmental impact assessment of activities. These arrangements are described below in the context of the Antarctica (Environmental Protection) Act 1994. Annex III of the Protocol prohibits waste disposal onto ice-free areas, and generally requires all other solid and liquid waste generated in Antarctic base camps to be stored prior to removal from the continent by the generator.[14] Additionally, Annexes IV, V, and VI of the Protocol respectively impose obligations on flagged ships of the parties consistent with MARPOL, provide for management plans to be prepared regarding the designated Antarctic Specially Protected Areas and the Antarctic Specially Managed Areas that prohibit or restrict or manage activities in these areas, and address liability arising from environmental emergencies by requiring the parties to take preventive measures to reduce risk (including having contingency plans in place for prompt clean-up and remediation) and imposing strict liability to repay costs incurred by other parties.[15]

As noted above, the ecosystem-based approach in CCAMLR is dynamic and innovative. For example, the CCAMLR preamble emphasises the need to protect both the terrestrial continent and the surrounding marine environment

---

11 See Birnie and Boyle, note 6, 214; Shaw, note 2, 400; Sands and Peel, note 6, 637–638.
12 See Sands and Peel, note 6, 635. New Zealand has signed, but has not ratified CCAS.
13 See Birnie and Boyle, note 6, 229.
14 See Sands and Peel, note 6, 618.
15 See Sands and Peel, note 6, 641–642.

as an integrated ecosystem (based on increased scientific knowledge), and the substantive treaty provisions build on this complex web of relationships and extend protection to all living resources within the marine areas including birds.[16] The Madrid Protocol provides a mechanism for applying the Convention on Biological Diversity 1992 (CBD) across the Antarctic environment.[17] Notwithstanding the fact that the CCAMLR preamble references environmental protection as the 'prime responsibility' of the parties and the fact that the Commission is given legal personality under Article VII and has the power to prepare conservation measures under Article IX, the parties have been unable to agree on any conservation measures regarding migratory species and biodiversity due the need for consensus (Article XII) and the provision made for objections (Article IX). As a result, compliance with the CBD has been left for the parties to pursue outside the Antarctic Treaty system.[18]

While CCAMLR enables the 'rational use' of resources, any harvesting is required to be carried out in accordance with ecological principles that are designed to avoid population reduction and maintain stable population levels by ensuring that natural annual recruitment levels are (in particular) maintained. This approach is radically different from other management approaches (e.g. maximum sustainable yield), but nevertheless encounters practical difficulties in terms of implementation because the CCAMLR institutions (i.e. the Commission and the Scientific Committee) currently only meet annually and fishing interests frequently override ecological interests. This interaction makes it difficult for science-based decision-making to prevail, and fishing by third party states has (in particular) been difficult to control.[19]

The concept of environmental trusteeship noted in relation to the CRAMRA regime above brings into sharp focus the legal issues associated with common areas or common resources where 'collaboration is required because they lie beyond the jurisdiction of individual states'.[20] Absent collaboration, 'all states' would otherwise 'have access to the commons', and 'no state' would be 'legally in a position to impose a particular approach to their use or protection'.[21]

Overall, the Antarctic Treaty system presents a novel response to these issues of state responsibility, including, for example: the designation of Antarctica

---

16   See Birnie and Boyle, note 6, 601; Sands and Peel, note 6, 635–637.
17   Ibid, Birnie and Boyle, 601.
18   Ibid, 606–607; Sands and Peel, note 6, 635–637.
19   See Birnie and Boyle, note 6, 552–553.
20   Jutta Brunee, 'Common Areas, Common Heritage, and Common Concern' in Daniel Bodansky, Jutta Brunee, and Ellen Hey (eds) *The Oxford Handbook of International Environmental Law* (Oxford University Press, 2007) 554.
21   Ibid.

'exclusively for peaceful and scientific uses'; the interlocking instruments within the Treaty system and their focus on an ecosystem approach that embraces both 'the Antarctic continent and associated marine ecosystems'; the focus in CCAMLR and the Madrid Protocol on 'safeguarding the interests of humankind rather than merely those of the treaty parties'; the moratorium on all mineral resource activities, in particular, 'the sweeping nature of the restriction that it places on the open access normally associated with common property'; and the attempts made to establish an 'innovative environmental liability regime' (e.g. the provisions made in CRAMRA for the 'restoration or compensation of damage to ecosystems').[22] However, notwithstanding the strong emphasis within the Antarctic Treaty system on the concept of 'trusteeship' for the benefit of 'humankind', this approach remains distinctively different from the common heritage of mankind promoted via the United Nations Convention on the Law of the Sea 1982 (Article 136) in relation to the management of the deep seabed.[23]

Some commentators have, however, observed that international governance systems for common areas or common resources (including Antarctica) are sometimes justified by the fact that 'economic exploitation of these areas was not yet feasible due to lack of appropriate technology'.[24]

Despite this economic justification for the Antarctic Treaty system, trusteeship has been a common theme since 1945. For example, placing Antarctica under the supervision of the United Nations Trusteeship Council (normally reserved for former colonies in transition toward independence) was mooted in 1947 but rejected because the Trusteeship system 'applied only to people not to penguins'.[25] Other scholars have argued that environmental trusteeship is required to regulate non-state actors because the international treaty regimes 'lack overarching objectives, are full of loopholes and have virtually no effect in preventing continued degradation', and because there is 'no functioning governance of the global commons'.[26] As a result, they have proposed the estab-

---

22 Ibid, 561.
23 Carina Costa de Olivera and Sandrine Maljean-Dubois, 'The contribution that the concept of global public goods can make to the conservation of marine resources' in Ed Couzens et al (eds) *Protecting Forest and Marine Biodiversity: The Role of Law* (Edward Elgar Publishing, 2017) 305–307.
24 Klaus Bosselmann, *Earth Governance: Trusteeship of the Global Commons* (Edward Elgar Publishing, 2015) 72.
25 Peter J Beck, *The International Politics of Antarctica* (Croom Helm, 1986) 271; Bosselmann, note 24, 231–232.
26 Ibid, 245.

lishment of a 'World Environment Organization' or UN Trusteeship Council to govern common areas including Antarctica.[27]

The concept of trusteeship has also been suggested given the 'glaring misfit' between sovereign authority and the inability of states to govern common areas beyond national jurisdiction.[28] Several factors may encourage states to become trustees: First, using trusteeship to define community interests, political ambitions, and the right to 'freely dispose of natural wealth and resources';[29] second, viewing states 'as agents for humanity as a whole' in order to legitimise the exercise of sovereignty over common areas or common resources;[30] and third, basing the power to exclude others from access to common areas or common resources on property concepts that included a moral dimension to exercise such powers for the benefit of humankind.[31] Beyond that, viewing states as trustees can result in more effective national implementation of international law obligations.[32] But some institutional oversight of state exercise of trusteeship functions is considered appropriate to avoid 'democratic failure' by ensuring that states are subject to more than merely 'minimal obligations'.[33]

The Antarctic Treaty system (notwithstanding the strengths noted above) will nevertheless rely in part on the national implementation of international law. For example[34]

> legislative implementation of a state's international obligations performs a 'delegated normativity' function, conditioning not only state but also non-state actors' behaviour.

This paper will therefore consider next the vertical implementation of the Antarctic Treaty system via New Zealand statute law.

27　Peter H Sand, 'The Concept of Public Trusteeship in the Transboundary Governance of Biodiversity' in Louis J Kotze and Thilo Marauhn (eds) *Transboundary Governance of Biodiversity* (Brill, 2014) 51–52; Bosselmann, note 24, 251–252.
28　Eyal Benvenisti, 'Sovereigns as Trustees for Humanity: On the Accountability of States to Foreign Stakeholders' (2013) 107 (2) *AJIL* 295, 301; Bosselmann, note 24, 169.
29　Ibid, Benvenisti; Ibid, Bosselmann, 175.
30　Ibid, Benvenisti; Ibid, Bosselmann, 175–176.
31　See Benvenisti, note 28, 308–310; Bosselmann, note 24, 176.
32　Ibid, Benvenisti, 316; Ibid, Bosselmann, 179.
33　Ibid, Benvenisti 300, 303; Ibid, Bosselmann, 202.
34　Catherine Redgwell, "National Implementation" in Daniel Bodansky, Jutta Brunee, and Ellen Hey (eds) *The Oxford Handbook of International Environmental Law* (Oxford University Press, 2007) 929.

2   New Zealand: Antarctic Governance

New Zealand has enjoyed a long period of engagement with Antarctica.[35] According to Maori tradition, the Polynesian chief, Ui Te Rangiora, was the first person to see the icebergs of Antarctica during a voyage from New Zealand across the Southern Ocean in 650 AD,[36] and archaeological evidence has been found of Maori settlement (reputedly) from that time on the Antipodes Islands and later Maori settlements from the 13th and 14th centuries on the Auckland Islands.[37] In modern times, the New Zealand whaler Tuati (alias John Sac) was part of the United States Exploring Expedition to the Southern Ocean led by Captain Charles Wilkes during the period 1838–1842 and was reputed to be the first New Zealander to sight the west coast of Antarctica in 1840, while Alexander von Tunzelmann became the first recorded New Zealander to land on the Antarctic continent in 1895 as part of a Norwegian whaling and sealing voyage.[38] During the first half of the 20th century a number of New Zealanders were members of the Antarctic expeditions led by Captain Robert Falcon Scott, Sir Ernest Shackleton, Douglas Mawson, and Richard Byrd,[39] and Dunedin and Lyttelton became established as gateway ports to the Antarctic. However, the most intensive period of New Zealand activity in the Antarctic was 1955–1958 as a result of the Commonwealth Trans-Antarctic Expedition (that saw Sir Edmund Hillary reach the South Pole overland by tractor in 1958), the focus on the International Geophysical Year 1957–1958, and the opening of Scott Base in 1957.[40]

---

35   Antarctica is defined by s 2(1) of the *Antarctica Act 1960* as 'the area south of 60⁰ south latitude, including all ice shelves in that area'.

36   Encyclopaedia Britannica, Antarctica History, https://www.britannica.com/place/Antarctica/History#ref390155, accessed 07 July 2020.

37   GL Pearce, 'Nga-Iwi-O-Aotea', *Te Ao Hou The Maori Magazine* (No 59, June 1967) 43; Atholl Anderson, "Subpolar settlement in South Polynesia", *Antiquity Magazine* (Volume 79, Issue 306, December 2005), 791. The first modern recorded discoveries of Antarctica were the sightings by Fabian Gottleib von Bellingshausen and Mikhail Lazarev (27 January 1820), Edward Bransfield and William Smith (30 January 1820), and Nathaniel Palmer (17 November 1820).

38   See Encyclopaedia Britannica, note 36.

39   Discovery Expedition 1901–1904 (Scott); Nimrod Expedition 1908–1909 (Shackleton); Australasian Antarctic Expedition 1911–1914 (Mawson); Endurance Expedition 1914–1917 (Shackleton); British, Australian and New Zealand Antarctic Research Expedition 1929–1931 (Mawson); Byrd Antarctic Expedition (BEA2) 1933–1935 (Byrd); www.history.govt.nz.

40   See Encyclopaedia Britannica, note 36.

The Order in Council made by King George V on 30 July 1923 defined the Ross Dependency as that part of His Majesty's Dominions in the Antarctic seas which comprises all the islands and territories between the 160th degree of east longitude and the 150th degree of west longitude which are situated south of the 60th degree of south latitude.[41] The decision by the New Zealand Government to accept the offer of the transfer of sovereignty to the Ross Dependency from the United Kingdom was made 'on behalf of the Empire as a whole, and not specially in the interests of New Zealand'.[42]

Pursuant to the British Settlements Act 1887 that enabled the Sovereign to establish the governance arrangements for any British settlement, the Order in Council appointed the Governor-General of New Zealand for the time being as the Governor of the Ross Dependency,[43] and empowered the Governor to make such laws as may be required 'for the peace, order, and good government' of the Dependency (subject to any instructions received from any Ministers of the Crown) and authorised the Governor to grant and dispose of any lands within the Dependency.[44]

Subsequently, Viscount Jellicoe (the newly appointed Governor) made the *Ross Dependency Regulations* 1923. They provided that all New Zealand laws in force on 14 November 1923 should apply within the Ross Dependency insofar as they were applicable to the conditions of the Dependency, and that any statutes enacted subsequently by the New Zealand legislature should 'as far as applicable' have the same force and effect within the Dependency unless disallowed or modified by the Governor.[45] Thus any New Zealand statutes enacted after 14 November 1923 will only be law within the Ross Dependency where they expressly provide for such extraterritorial effect. Increasingly, the

---

41   Order in Council Providing for Government of Ross Dependency 1923 (Gazette 1923, vol II, No 63 (16 August) p2211) cl I. The Dependency was discovered by Captain James Clark Ross in 1841 who explored and named the Ross Sea, Victoria Land, Mount Erebus, Mount Terror, the Great Ice Barrier (now known as the Ross Ice Shelf), and McMurdo Sound, and subsequently visited New Zealand.

42   Sir Francis Bell, Attorney-General, New Zealand Parliamentary Debates 202 (15 August 1923), 81.

43   Order in Council Providing for Government of Ross Dependency 1923 (Gazette 1923, vol II, No 63 (16 August) p2211) cl II.

44   Order in Council Providing for Government of Ross Dependency 1923 (Gazette 1923, vol II, No 63 (16 August) p2211) cl IV, cl V.

45   The Governor also made the *Ross Dependency Whaling Regulations* 1926 and 1929 to prohibit whaling operations within the boundaries of the Ross Dependency unless expressly allowed by licence, but no whaling licences were issued under the regulations.

New Zealand Parliament has legislated for the Ross Dependency after becoming a party to the Antarctic Treaty on 1 November 1960.

Section 2(1) of the *Territorial Sea, Contiguous Zone, and Exclusive Economic Zone Act* 1977 defines New Zealand as including the Ross Dependency, except for the purposes of part 2 that established the exclusive economic zone (EEZ) of New Zealand. Accordingly, the provisions in part 1 of the statute that establish the 12nm territorial sea of New Zealand and beyond that the 12nm contiguous zone of New Zealand also apply to the Ross Dependency and establish these zones in the waters around the Dependency. Subsequently, the legal status of the Ross Dependency as part of the realm of New Zealand was confirmed in 1983 when the Letters Patent Constituting the Office of Governor-General of New Zealand were updated and replaced.[46] The Ross Dependency is defined as including 'all islands and ice shelves with the Dependency, and the continental shelf of the Dependency'.[47] Accordingly, there is a potential discrepancy between these legal provisions that on the one hand include the continental shelf, but on the other hand fail to include the Dependency within the New Zealand EEZ.

2.1 New Zealand's Criminal Jurisdiction in Antarctica

The *Antarctica Act* 1960 extends New Zealand criminal jurisdiction to offences committed in the Ross Dependency by any person, or in any other part of Antarctica by New Zealand citizens or permanent residents (except while on board any ship or aircraft).[48] Criminal offences committed in other parts of Antarctica by observers or exchanged scientists (who are New Zealand citizens) are deemed to have been committed in New Zealand, and the New Zealand courts have jurisdiction regarding such offences.[49] Civil and criminal jurisdiction over observers or exchanged scientists (who are foreign nationals of any contracting party to the Antarctic Treaty) is restricted regardless of whether any act or omission was done in the Ross Dependency or elsewhere in Antarctica, and the New Zealand courts have no jurisdiction over such persons unless jurisdiction is waived by the other contracting party.[50]

---

46 Letters Patent Constituting the Office of Governor-General of New Zealand (SR 1983/225), cl 1(e). The realm of New Zealand also comprises the Cook Islands, Niue, and Tokelau.
47 *Antarctica (Environmental Protection) Act* 1994, s 7(1).
48 *Antarctica Act* 1960, s 3.
49 Ibid, s 4.
50 Ibid, s 5.

2.2 Antarctic Marine Living Resources Act 1981

The *Antarctic Marine Living Resources Act* 1981 was enacted to give effect to CCAMLR. The statute restricts the taking of marine organisms (whether dead or alive) and requires permits to be obtained from the Minister of Fisheries. When deciding a permit application, the Minister must have regard to the objectives and principles of CCAMLR, and the need to conserve marine organisms in accordance with CCAMLR. The Minister may attach such conditions as he or she thinks fit, including conditions that restrict what may be taken, the quantum that may be taken, where it may be taken from, the period when it may be taken, and the purposes for which it may be taken.[51]

Provision is made for criminal offences and penalties (fines up to NZ$250,000), and a defence of prior authorisation under New Zealand or foreign law is available.[52] Leaving traps or substances where they may harm marine organisms is also an offence (subject to fines of up to NZ$100,000), and provision is made for defences in circumstances of stress or emergency, or in cases where the act or omission was unavoidable and allowed by the permit or was necessary to prevent damage to equipment.[53]

2.3 Antarctica (Environmental Protection) Act 1994

The *Antarctica (Environmental Protection) Act* 1994 was enacted to give effect to New Zealand's international obligations under the Madrid Protocol. In particular, it: prohibits mineral resource activities; provides for environmental impact assessments; includes measures for the conservation of fauna and flora and protected areas; provides for waste disposal; and provides for the application of the *Maritime Transport Act* 1994 regarding marine pollution. Prospecting, exploration and mining of mineral resources is prohibited throughout Antarctica, its ice shelves, the islands south of 60 degrees south latitude, and the adjacent continental shelf.[54] Any person who contravenes this prohibition commits an offence, and on conviction may be sentenced to up to two years' imprisonment or a fine of up to NZ$200,000. Additionally, New Zealand citizens and corporations also commit an offence when they carry out mineral resource activities elsewhere in Antarctica; and foreign nationals, who are members of official expeditions, and New Zealand citizens and permanent

---

51 *Antarctic Marine Living Resources Act* 1981, s 5.
52 Ibid, s 7.
53 Ibid, s 13.
54 *Antarctica (Environmental Protection) Act* 1994, s 11, s 14.

residents on board any ship or aircraft supporting an official expedition, may also commit offences under this provision.[55]

The statute provides for a hierarchy of environmental evaluation regarding any proposed activities in Antarctica. A preliminary environmental evaluation is required to assess whether the proposed activity is likely to have less than minor or transitory impacts on the Antarctic environment. The evaluation must include: a description of the proposed activity; a statement about the anticipated environmental effects; whether another contracting party to the Antarctic Treaty has applied or is applying the environmental assessment procedures under the Protocol for the activity; New Zealand-based contact details for the application; the number of likely persons on any expedition; and the date and place of departure for Antarctica. Where the Minister of Foreign Affairs and Trade considers that any effects are likely to be less than minor or transitory, he or she must notify the applicant that the proposed activity may be carried out.[56]

An initial environmental evaluation is also required unless the Minister has determined that any effects will be less than minor or transitory, or the applicant proceeds to prepare a comprehensive environmental evaluation.[57] The initial environmental assessment is required to include sufficient detail to enable an assessment of the scale and significance of any potential effects on the Antarctic environment.[58] Where the Minister considers (after reviewing any comprehensive evaluation) that any effects are likely to be less than minor or transitory, he or she must notify the applicant that the proposed activity may be carried out subject to any directions made about the activity (which may include conditions, monitoring requirements or payment of a compliance bond).[59] A draft comprehensive environmental evaluation is required where the applicant proceeds directly to prepare that evaluation, or where the Minister considers that the proposed activity is likely to have more than a minor or transitory effect on the Antarctic environment.[60]

Where a draft comprehensive environmental evaluation is required, it will be prepared in greater detail to cover the matters listed in Article 3(2) of Annex I to the Madrid Protocol, including consideration of alternatives, cumulative effects and accident responses.[61] Consultation is also required with

---

55 Ibid, s 12, s 13.
56 Ibid, s 17.
57 Ibid, s 18(1).
58 Ibid, s 18(2).
59 Ibid, s 18(3), s 10(1).
60 Ibid, s 18(4), s 19(1).
61 Ibid, s 19(2).

the parties to the Madrid Protocol and the Committee for Environmental Protection established under Article 11 of the Madrid Protocol, together with public notification in New Zealand.[62]

A final comprehensive environmental evaluation may be required: on the advice of the Committee for Environmental Protection, after the draft has been considered by the Consultative Meeting under Article IX of the Antarctic Treaty; or by the Minister where he or she thinks that there is unreasonable delay by the Consultative Meeting in considering the draft.[63] The final comprehensive environmental evaluation must address, and include summaries of, any comments received as a result of the consultation process.[64] After considering the final comprehensive environmental evaluation, the Minister is required to notify the applicant as to whether the proposed activity may be carried out, including any directions about the activity.[65]

Permits are required for: carrying out activities in any Antarctic Specially Protected Area;[66] removing any part of a Historic Site or Historic Monument;[67] taking any native birds or mammals in Antarctica;[68] removing or damaging native plants in Antarctica in a way that may significantly affect their local distribution or abundance;[69] and introducing non-indigenous animals, plants or microorganisms into Antarctica.[70] These activities are generally prohibited without a permit, and provision is made for offences and penalties in the event of any non-compliance (for example, sentences of up to six months' imprisonment or fines of up to NZ$100,000 may be imposed).[71] Generally, waste disposal in Antarctica is unlawful.[72]

The *Antarctica (Environmental Protection) Act 1994* was amended by the *Antarctica (Environmental Protection: Liability Annex) Amendment Act 2012* to give effect to Annex VI to the Madrid Protocol regarding liability arising from environmental emergencies. But these amendments are not currently in force. An Order in Council is required to be made by the Governor-General setting the date for the commencement of these provisions.

---

62 Ibid, s 19(3).
63 Ibid, s 20(1).
64 Ibid, s 20(2).
65 Ibid, s 20(3), s 10.
66 Ibid, s 27(1), s 28(1)(a), s 30.
67 Ibid, s 27(2), s 27(3).
68 Ibid, s 28(1)(b), s 31.
69 Ibid, s 28(1)(c), s 31.
70 Ibid, s 28(1)(e), s 28(2), s 31.
71 Ibid, s 33.
72 Ibid, s 34, s 35, s 36, s 37.

2.4 Other Relevant Statutes

New Zealand has enacted a broad range of extraterritorial statutory provisions that apply to the Ross Dependency.

For example, tourism is regulated by the need for visas or permits to enter the Ross Dependency and tourists are required to pay a levy to contribute to the costs of conserving the unique Antarctic environment. Under the *Immigration (Visa, Entry Permission, and Related Matters) Regulations* 2010 members of scientific programmes or expeditions under the auspices of a Contracting Party to the Antarctic Treaty (or any person associated with such a programme or expeditions) are, however, exempted from the international visitor conservation and tourism levy,[73] and are entitled to the waiver of any transit visa requirement or the requirement for a visa permitting travel to New Zealand (where a temporary entry class visa is sought).[74] Such persons are deemed to have been granted entry permission and hold a temporary visa where they enter the Ross Dependency from a foreign country (including where they subsequently travel to another part of New Zealand).[75]

The *Marine Mammals Protection Act* 1978 also has very broad territorial and extraterritorial application. It applies to acts and omissions that occur anywhere within New Zealand or within New Zealand waters,[76] acts and omissions that occur on any New Zealand ship or aircraft wherever it may be, and to acts and omissions carried out by New Zealand citizens wherever the person may be.[77] Under the statute, holding marine mammals (e.g. seals, whales, dolphins, and porpoises)[78] in captivity or taking them from their natural habitat (whether alive or dead) is prohibited, unless a permit is obtained from the Minister of Conservation.[79] However, these provisions do not derogate from the provisions in part 4 of the *Antarctica (Environmental Protection) Act* 1994 (that gives effect to Annexes II and V of the Madrid Protocol), or the *Ross*

---

73   *Immigration (Visa, Entry Permission, and Related Matters) Regulations* 2010, s 26AAD(2)(e); *Customs and Excise (Border Processing Levy) Order* 2015, cl 11; *Biosecurity (Border Processing Levy) Order 2015*, cl 9.
74   Ibid, Immigration Regulations, sch 1, cl 6; sch 2, cl 3.
75   Ibid, sch 3, cl 11, cl 12.
76   New Zealand fisheries waters are defined by s 2(1) of the *Fisheries Act* 1996 as including all waters in the exclusive economic zone, all waters in the territorial sea, all internal waters, and all other fresh or estuarine waters where indigenous and acclimatised aquatic fauna and flora are found.
77   *Marine Mammals Protection Act* 1978, s 1.
78   Ibid, s 2(1).
79   Ibid, s 4.

Dependency Whaling Regulations 1929 (that prohibit whaling operations within the boundaries of the Ross Dependency unless expressly allowed by licence).[80]

Beyond that, the functions of the Department of Conservation under s 6(c)(ii) of the *Conservation Act* 1987 also include promoting the benefits to present and future generations of the conservation of the natural and historic resources of New Zealand's sub-Antarctic islands (subject to the provisions of the Conservation Act 1987), and of the Ross Dependency and Antarctica generally (consistent with all relevant international agreements).

3 Antarctic Science

The principal functions of the New Zealand Antarctic Institute include developing, managing, and executing New Zealand activities in Antarctica, the Southern Ocean, and the Ross Dependency in particular; maintaining and enhancing New Zealand Antarctic research; and cooperating with similar institutions and organisations within New Zealand and internationally.[81] The Institute is required under s 6 of the *New Zealand Antarctic Institute Act* 1996 to carry out its functions in a manner that is (*inter alia*) consistent with New Zealand's international obligations, and in particular with 'the need to conserve the intrinsic values of Antarctica and the Southern Ocean' and 'active and responsible stewardship of the Ross Dependency for the benefit of present and future generations of New Zealanders'.

In particular, the New Zealand Strategy for the Future Management of the Marine Living Resources and Biodiversity of the Ross Sea (2006) seeks to balance 'well managed sustainable harvesting' with 'marine protection to safeguard the long-term ecological viability of marine systems and protect Antarctic marine biological diversity and areas potentially vulnerable to human impacts'.[82] These objectives are to be achieved by: increasing marine research and ecosystem monitoring; improving fisheries management by establishing a catch allocation mechanism, and by permanently codifying non-catch and environmentally focused conservation measures; promoting the establishment of a high seas marine protected area; combating illegal

---

80   *Marine Mammals Protection Act* 1978, s 20.
81   *New Zealand Antarctic Institute Act* 1996, s 5.
82   New Zealand Foreign Affairs and Trade, Ross Sea MPA Documents, https://www.mfat.govt.nz/en/environment/antarctica/ross-sea-mpa-documents/. (accessed 06 July 2020).

unreported and unregulated fishing; and improving the effectiveness of the Antarctic Treaty system.[83]

The Antarctica Science Platform is currently funded by an appropriation of $36,549,000 during the period 1 July 2019 to 30 June 2024.[84]

3.1   Marine Protected Areas

New Zealand has also been committed to establishing a marine protected area (MPA) in the Ross Sea that balances marine protection, sustainable fishing and opportunities to pursue scientific research. Together with the United States, New Zealand presented a joint proposal to the meeting of the CCAMLR Commission in Hobart in 2012. The proposal was science-based and sought to protect a range of ecosystems and habitats. Following subsequent discussions at meetings of the Commission during 2013, the Commission adopted the Ross Sea MPA in 2016. This decision signalled a move from regulation over access to advancing conservation by establishing (what was then) the world's largest MPA covering 2,060,000 km², of which 1,120,000 km² is fully protected.[85] The MPA designation will remain in place for a period of 35 years from 1 December 2017.

The MPA covers one of the world's most biologically diverse and pristine natural areas and provides a home to (*inter alia*) 30% of all Adélie penguins, 30% of Antarctic petrels, 25% of all Emperor penguins, 50% of Ross Sea killer whales, and 50% of South Pacific Weddell seals, and protects critical habitats and foraging areas for these species. Overall, the MPA strikes a balance between environmental protection, sustainable fishing, and scientific research.

To meet these general objectives the MPA comprises three zones: the General Protection Zone (GPA) where no commercial fishing is allowed; the Special Research Zone (SRZ) where limited krill and toothfish fishing is allowed for research purposes; and the Krill Research Zone (KRZ) where controlled fishing for krill is allowed for research purposes.

The objectives of the MPA will be assessed by the Commission every 10 years to ensure that it continues to provide effective protection.[86] However, the MPA does not satisfy the IUCN definition of a marine protected area because the designation (35 years) is not permanent.

---

83   Ibid.
84   *Appropriation (2019/20 Estimates) Act* 2019, s 7, sch 2.
85   Julia Jabour and Danielle Smith, 'The Ross Sea region marine protected area: can it be successfully managed?' *Ocean Yearbook* 32 (2018) 190. Subsequently, the Cook Islands Parliament enacted the *Marae Moana Act* 2017 that establishes the Marae Moana multiple-use MPA covering the whole Cook Island's exclusive economic zone (1,976,000 km²).
86   See MFAT, note 82.

While the designation of the Ross Sea MPA is clearly significant, it should be considered in the context of the desire by CCAMLR to establish a representative system of MPAs in the Southern Ocean. Current proposed MPAs (at the time of writing) include: the Western Antarctic Peninsula MPA proposed by Argentina and Chile in 2018, the East Antarctica MPA (950,000 km²) proposed by Australia, France, and the European Union in 2011; and the Weddell Sea MPA (2,000,000 km²) proposed by the European Union and Germany in 2016 (including the 58 km² Bouvet Island MPA designated by Norway in 1971). There are currently no proposals to establish MPAs in the Amundsen and Bellingshausen seas. Beyond that, existing CCAMLR MPAs designated by Antarctic Treaty consultative parties include: the South Georgia and South Sandwich Islands MPA (1,070,000 km²) designated by the United Kingdom in 2012 (but contested by Argentina), the Weddell Sea MPA (2,000,000 km²) proposed by the European Union and Germany in 2016 (including the 58 km² Bouvet Island MPA designated by Norway in 1971), the Prince Edward Islands MPA (180,000 km²) designated by South Africa in 2013, the Crozet Islands and Kerguelen Islands MPA (1,140,000 km²) designated by France in 2017, and the Heard Island and McDonald Islands MPA (71,000 km²) designated by Australia as a World Heritage Site in 1997 and subsequently expanded in 2014. The first MPA was designated around the South Orkney Islands (94,000 km²) in the Western Antarctic Peninsula domain in 2009. The overall picture is therefore one of gradually expanding protection of the fragile Southern Ocean environment via the CCAMLR negotiation process.[87]

4   Whaling, Sovereignty, Hydrocarbon Resources, and Climate Change

New Zealand has enacted a broad range of legislation to give normative effect to the Antarctic Treaty system. In particular, these statutes will have an effect on the behaviour of non-state actors. There is however no standard approach in these statutes regarding how natural and juridical persons should be bound by these obligations. Accordingly, adopting a uniform approach whereby all New Zealand citizens, permanent residents, and registered aircraft, companies, and ships are bound by these obligations (regardless of whether any acts or omissions are carried out within the Ross Dependency or Antarctica

---

[87] Pew Trusts, A network of marine protected areas in the southern Ocean, https://www.pewtrusts.org/en/research-and-analysis/fact-sheets/2017/04/a-network-of-marine-protected-areas-in-the-southern-ocean, accessed 07 July 2020.

generally) would be sensible in terms of ensuring that activities within New Zealand's jurisdiction or control do not cause damage to the environment.[88]

Prohibiting whaling has been a feature of the Ross Dependency legal regime since 1926. New Zealand's continued focus (together with Australia) on whaling in the Southern Ocean is not therefore surprising. For example, the decision of the International Court of Justice (ICJ) in *Whaling in the Antarctic (Australia v Japan: New Zealand intervening)*,[89] focused on the legality of Japan's whaling programme in the Southern Ocean (JARPA II). Australia contended that JARPA II was unlawful and in breach of the provisions of the International Convention on the Regulation of Whaling 1946, and sought orders that Japan should cease the programme. New Zealand's intervention was limited to presenting its views on the interpretation of the Convention. In particular, the proceedings centred on Article VIII(1) of the Convention that allows the killing of whales for the purposes of scientific research under a special permit issued by a State party. Absent the issue of a valid permit under Article VIII, whaling is generally prohibited under the Convention. A key submission made by New Zealand in its written observations was whether Article VIII was a 'self-judging' provision to be determined solely by the State party concerned, or whether it should be determined objectively. The ICJ agreed with the position maintained by New Zealand, and recorded in the concession made by Japan during the oral proceedings that:[90]

> the test ... [is] whether a State's decision is objectively reasonable, or 'supported by coherent reasoning and respectable scientific evidence and ... in this sense, objectively justifiable'.

Overall, the position adopted by New Zealand provided the catalyst for the ICJ to explore what the appropriate standard of review should be in relation to the exercise of discretionary powers. The judgment marks a transition from *Wednesbury* irrationality review to a much narrower margin of appreciation for decision-makers where the Court's objective view of the decision becomes paramount. This finding is important because it provides a handle to depart from deference in (potentially) all cases. Beyond that, the separate opinion of Judge Xue also clarified the standard of expert evidence required to support

---

88   Rio Declaration on Environment and Development 1992, Principle 2, https://www.un.org/en/development/desa/population/migration/generalassembly/docs/globalcompact/A_CONF.151_26_Vol.I_Declaration.pdf, accessed 07 July 2020.

89   International Court of Justice, ICJ Reports 2014, https://www.icj-cij.org/en/case/148, 226, accessed 07 July 2020.

90   Ibid, 253–254.

discretionary decision-making by importing the 'best evidence' rule.[91] But the New Zealand concern with whaling discloses an anomaly in that while New Zealand actively protects marine mammals (including seals) by statute, it has not to date ratified the CCAS despite the significant population of South Pacific Weddell seals within the Ross Sea MPA.

4.1 Trusteeship for the Benefit of Humankind

These broad interests in Antarctica and the Southern Ocean are consistent with the theme of trusteeship for the benefit of humankind that is explicit in the Antarctic Treaty system and is reflected in the growing body of scholarly literature about the nature of sovereignty noted above. New Zealand's acceptance of the transferred claim to the Ross Dependency in 1923 also reflects these broad themes of trusteeship. This approach was also reflected in the New Zealand position at the Washington Conference in 1959 where the Prime Minister, Walter Nash, stated in the context of discussions about surrendering territorial claims that he would 'have wished to see the conference agree on more imaginative and a more adventurous approach to the problems arising from claims to sovereignty in Antarctica.[92] Against this background, extraterritorial legislation for the Ross Dependency (as a constituent part of the realm of New Zealand) and establishing maritime zones under UNCLOS are consistent with the concept of the 'sovereign as trustee'[93] rather than advancing national populism.[94]

The extension of the sovereign right to legislate leads to the question of whether New Zealand should go further (like Australia) and establish a 200 nm EEZ adjacent to the Ross Dependency. It also leads to a secondary question as to whether New Zealand should designate marine protected areas across the whole EEZ around its sub-Antarctic islands in order to enhance environmental protection in the region. While this would be consistent with the approach adopted by the Cook Islands Parliament (and the designation of the Ross Sea MPA), this would require consultation with Maori given their historic connections with these islands and special purpose legislation to establish marine

---

91 For further discussion regarding the standard of review applied by the ICJ see: Trevor Daya-Winterbottom, "No deference", *The New Zealand Law Journal* (2017) 351–355.

92 Malcolm Templeton, *A wise adventure: New Zealand in Antarctica 1920–60* (Victoria University Press, Wellington, 2000), 265.

93 See Benvenisti, note 28, 295.

94 Roger Eatwell and Matthew Goodwin, *National Populism: The Revolt Against Liberal Democracy* (Pelican Books, 2018).

reserves beyond the territorial sea.[95] Additionally, this issue brings into play the indigenous concept of *kaitiakitanga* or the exercise of guardianship or stewardship in relation to natural or physical resources that has provided a basis for giving legal personality to geographic features (e.g. mountains and rivers),[96] and that could provide a (further) normative basis for translating New Zealand sovereignty into trusteeship in relation to its marine and Antarctic interests.

Establishing an EEZ adjacent to the Ross Dependency would also be consistent with New Zealand's policy position against offshore hydrocarbon prospecting and the prohibition on mineral resource activities in the *Antarctica (Environmental Protection) Act* 1994. However, addressing the effects of climate change is more complex. For example, despite the success in *Thomson v Minister for Climate Change Issues*[97] where the New Zealand High Court held that the publication of a new assessment report by the International Panel on Climate Change required the Minister to consider whether existing greenhouse gas emissions targets should be reviewed, and that the effect of climate change on Tokelau (another constituent part of the realm of New Zealand) was also a mandatory consideration that would be relevant in relation to New Zealand's approach to climate change, these matters have subsequently been downgraded to become merely permissive considerations and the ability to seek *certiorari* or *mandamus* via judicial review have been removed.[98] Additionally, unlike in Tokelau, there has been no announcement by the Minister to bring the Ross Dependency into the United Nations Framework Convention on Climate Change 1992 or the Paris Agreement 2015,[99] notwithstanding the fact that Antarctica (like Tokelau) forms part of the realm of New Zealand.

---

95 Ben France-Hudson, 'The Kermadec/Rangitahua Ocean Sanctuary: Expropriation-free but a breach of good faith', *Resource Management Theory & Practice* [2016] 55.

96 *Resource Management Act* 1991, s 2(1), s 7(a); Rachael Harris, 'A legal identity for Te Urewera: The changing face of co-governance in the central North Island' *Resource Management Theory & Practice* [2015] 148; Trevor Daya-Winterbottom, 'Personality and representation in environmental law' *NZLJ* [2018] 130.

97 Thomson v Minister for Climate Change Issues [2018] 2 *NZLR* 160.

98 *Climate Change Response Act* 2002, s 5ZM, s 5ZN (as amended by *Climate Change Response (Zero Carbon) Amendment Act* 2019.

99 Hon James Shaw, "Global climate change agreement extended to Tokelau" (14 November 2017), https://www.beehive.govt.nz/release/global-climate-change-agreement-extended-tokelau, accessed 07 July 2020.

5 Conclusions

Generally, the Antarctic Treaty system has enriched the development of international law, has encouraged domestic transposition of the Antarctic Treaty obligations, and the relative success in establishing an Antarctic MPA is encouraging. However, guardianship or stewardship concepts (as a foundation for the sovereign as trustee) could provide a catalyst for broader conceptions of more extensive MPA designations in Antarctic marine zones, provide links to indigenous knowledge, enhance cooperation with stakeholders more widely, and overcome some of the problems currently inherent in Antarctic governance. But real commitments outside Antarctica to end fossil fuel exploration and development, set meaningful climate change targets, and allow public scrutiny via judicial review are required to protect the fragile continent.

Acknowledgement

The research for this paper was funded by a grant from the New Zealand Law Foundation.

The *Déjà vu* System of International Trusteeship in Continental Antarctica: A Textual Analysis

*Xueping Li**

Abstract

In the name of environmental protection, the Antarctic Treaty Consultative Meeting seems to have borrowed the paradigm of international trusteeship of the United Nations for managing the Antarctic land-based protected areas. By comparing and analysing the critical questions highly concerned, this paper offers preliminary thoughts on the development and refinement of the conception of land-based protected areas as a déjà vu system of international trusteeship and its surrounding legal applications and implications in continental Antarctica, and challenges the direction followed by this system in protecting Antarctic intrinsic values in legal discourse.

1 Introduction

Antarctica is the only continent whose sovereignty is undetermined to date. In 1961 when the Antarctic Treaty came into force, the territorial claims and disputes over the continent were shelved and suspended. In order to regulate the international involvement in the Antarctic environment, States Parties to the Antarctic Treaty adopted the agreed measures for the protection of Antarctic flora and fauna at the third Antarctic Treaty Consultative Meeting (ATCM) in 1964, proposing for the first time the establishment of Specially Protected Areas in continental Antarctica. In 1972, the proposal of 'a special area of scientific interest' was added. In 1991, areas addressing tourism, historic relics, marine resource research and usage were further proposed.[1] So far, there are as many as nine categories of Antarctic Specially Protected Areas with different

---

*   Professor of International Law, School of Law, Wuhan University, Wuhan, China. lixueping@whu.edu.cn.
1   Annex V to the Protocol on Environmental Protection to the Antarctic Treaty (1991): article 3(2). Adopted 4 October 1991, entered into force 3 October 1992.

contents and objectives, which play a positive role in protecting many specific values in Antarctica.

However, in this paper, Antarctic protected areas refer to those specific land-based places with irregular boundaries designated according to the relevant instruments, in particular Annex V to the Protocol on Environmental Protection to the Antarctic Treaty (hereinafter 'the Environmental Protocol') and in particular the Revised Guide to the Presentation of Working Papers Containing Proposals for Antarctic Specially Protected Areas, Antarctic Specially Managed Areas or Historic Sites and Monuments adopted by the ATCM.[2] They include the Antarctic Specially Protected Areas (ASPA), the Antarctic Specially Managed Areas (ASMA) and the Antarctic Historic Sites & Monuments (HSM). To date, there are 74 ASPAs, seven ASMAs and 28 HSMs (hereinafter with a joint name 'the Areas').[3] These numbers are potentially increasing because such information may be modified according to the ATCM annual discussions and final decisions on the proposals summited by the Antarctic Treaty Consultative Parties (ATCPs). By the Antarctic Treaty, the Environmental Protocol and its Annex V, and the relevant guides or guidelines, the legal system of Antarctic land-based protected areas of a wider context has been set up for protecting the intrinsic values of continental Antarctica, including its wilderness and aesthetic values and its value as an area for the conduct of scientific research, which are reasonable and essential elements for proposing Areas.

The Areas have been a matter of practice with the ATCPs' management plans approved by the ATCM. But the continental Antarctica is not *terra nullius* since the Antarctic Treaty has legally defined it as a land for international peaceful use and for the interest of all mankind.[4] In this case, is the ATCM, the highest authority for Antarctic affairs, operating a system of international trusteeship by way of approving ATCPs to establish Areas in Antarctica? If the Areas could be somehow defined as trust ones, what is the essential difference from that under the Charter of the United Nations (UN)? What is the intrinsic nature of the ATCM decisions on the establishment of those Areas? Do these decisions have legal binding force for both the ATCM and the ATCPs of the Areas? Can ATCPs aggrandise their authorised power beyond those in defined and approved plans for managing the Areas in case of emergencies? Since

---

2 This Resolution put the three kinds of land-based protected areas together. See Revised Guide to the Presentation of Working Papers Containing Proposals for Antarctic Specially Protected Areas, Antarctic Specially Managed Areas or Historic Sites and Monuments, Resolution 5 (2016) – ATCM XXXIX – CEP XIX, Santiago (2016).
3 Antarctic Treaty Secretariat, Antarctic Protected Area Database https://www.ats.aq/devph/en/apa-database/search#apa-results [accessed 12 November 2019].
4 Antarctic Treaty. Adopted 1 December 1959, entered into force 23 June 1961, article 1.

any protection is a process full of activities and actions, what is the destination of managing the Areas in the case of lacking definite periods of time and clear legal status for the common heritage of mankind in Antarctica? Has a new system of international trusteeship been established in the continental Antarctica? Can the management of these Areas be developed over time into preemption under international law for the purpose of independently dealing with the matters there? In order to reply these critical questions, this paper will trace the origin, the process, the result and the subsequent influence of the international trusteeship system, and offer preliminary thoughts on the development and refinement of the concept of the Areas in Antarctica and the surrounding legal applications and implications in regulating the Areas in Antarctica.

2   A Review on the UN System of International Trusteeship

"International trusteeship" is tightly connected with the mandate of colonies in the name of protection and progress of the colonies after wars.[5] But it was until the aftermath of the First World War (WWI) when the mandatory system was established for 'a single overwhelming, powerful group of nations who shall be the trustee of the peace of the world' under the League of Nations.[6] This is the prototype of the subsequent international trusteeship designed almost at the end of the Second World War (WWII).

The San Francisco Conference, held in May 1945, was of great significance for the post-war world order. The United States came up with series of draft policies to reform the system of colonialism. The main contents are as follows: First, specific and detailed plans and steps should be made for the colonial territories in order to achieve their autonomy and independence as soon as possible; second, there should be a specific timetable for gradual acquisition of independence by those colonies that already had the capacity for self-government or independence; and third, it should be ensured that all over the world within the scope of colonies in the political, economic, cultural, diplomatic and other aspects of equality through international trusteeship make colonies in a group under the supervision and management of international

---

5 Philip Towle, *Democracy and Peacekeeping: Negotiations and Debates, 1815–1973* (London and New York: Routledge, 2000) 12–15.
6 Patrick O. Cohrs, *The Unfinished Peace after World War I: America, Britain and Stabilization of Europe, 1919–1932* (Cambridge: Cambridge University Press, 2008) 35.

security and for custody of colonial independence schedule.[7] Those policies were very much influential to the UN Charter with the involvement of the determined and codified colonial problems. Thus, came into being the UN System of International Trusteeship instead of that of mandate of the League of Nations.

The UN System of International Trusteeship is a new solution on the colonial problem in the new era. It advocates the collective stewardship on the mandatory territories (which have all become trust territories under the authority of United Nations) that have not yet been granted autonomy for temporary administration under the supervision of the United Nations, 'as may be placed thereunder by means of trusteeship agreements'.[8] The principles and procedures upon which the International Trusteeship System are set out in Chapters XII and XIII of the UN Charter. According to articles 76 and 77, the trustee States shall assume the civil and military responsibilities of the trust territories (or non-self-governing territories), which would gain its independence in conditions of political, economic, social and educational advancement and progress.[9]

As the international program to deal with colonial problems, both systems reflected the characteristics of international relations at the time after World Wars, and they both played an inestimable role in progressing decolonisation by means of protection and promotion of colonies. However, they both have great differences in historical background, legal basis and territorial limits. The Mandate System of the League inherited and developed the experiences of the predecessors, while the UN System of International Trusteeship has a key innovation in the composition and characteristics of the supervisory mechanism besides a close historical origin and background with the Mandate System. It was deeply impressive that, in the whole process of formulating the UN System of International Trusteeship, the Great Powers borrowed the relevant policies of the League with the protection of the trust territories prevailing. In the meantime, the UN Trusteeship Council inherited, evolved and developed the supervisory approaches and function over the mandatory territories of the League of Nations,[10] and became a UN major political organ where the five

---

7   Harry S Truman, *Memoirs by Harry S. Truman* (New York: Konecky, 1995) 108.
8   Charter of the United Nations. Adopted 26 June 1945, entered into force 24 October 1945. United Nations Treaty Series 1 (1945): XII, article 77 (1). For example, the Approval of Trusteeship Agreements (Tanganyika), A/RES/63(I) (1946), para 6.
9   See in detail https://www.un.org/dppa/decolonization/en/nsgt [accessed 10 August 2019].
10 The Trusteeship Council suspended its operations on 1 November 1994, a month after the independence of Palau, the last remaining United Nations trust territory. By a resolution adopted on 25 May 1994, the Council amended its rules of procedure to drop the

permanent members of the Security Council – China, France, the Soviet Union (the Russian Federation in 1991), the United Kingdom and the United States – 'shall designate one specially qualified person to represent it therein'.[11]

It is believed that effective ways to avoid war(s) are to internationalise the colonial problem by carrying out a kind of international management on all colonies, and to move them towards self-governance or independence by promoting the political, economic, educational and social progress of those trust territories. Such idea and practice were supported by major Great Powers, such as the United States and the Soviet Union, as well as other countries with rich colonial experience, and turned into the prelude to the movement of decolonisation after the WWII. 'It would add greatly to the value of the discussions of the Trusteeship Council if the non-administering members were to include among their representatives a number of persons of experience specially qualified to discuss these problems.'[12] Therefore, article 87(d) of the UN Charter provides that the functions of the Trusteeship Council are to be carried out 'in conformity with the terms of the Trusteeship Agreements'. All the Trusteeship Agreements provide that the administering authority concerned 'shall be responsible for the peace, order, good government and local defense' of the trust territory and that, for these purposes, 'the administering authority shall have full powers of legislation, administration and jurisdiction' in the trust territory subject to the provisions of the UN Charter and of this Agreement.[13]

It is very curious that a *déjà vu* mode with like design and requirements of the UN System of International Trusteeship appears in the case of Antarctic land-based protected areas. Dramatically, the provisions of the UN Charter for international trusteeship under the Great Powers are substituted by those of Antarctic Treaty system for international protection under the ATCPs, and the Trusteeship Agreements between the UN Trusteeship Council and the trustee States by the decisions between the ATCM and the ATCPs. If say that the UN Trusteeship System still has the ideal of pursuing development and independence of the trust territories, the legal character, effect and impacts of the ongoing Antarctic Areas are indeed worth studying. The rules, regulations and even guidelines adopted by the ATCM on establishing, administering

---

obligation to meet annually and agreed to meet as occasion required – by its decision or the decision of its President, or at the request of a majority of its members or the General Assembly or the Security Council.

11   See UN Charter, note 8, XII, article 86 (2).
12   J Fletcher-Cooke, 'Some Reflections on the International Trusteeship System, with Particular Reference to Its Impact on the Governments and Peoples of the Trust Territories' *International Organization* 422–430 [1959], DOI: 10.1017/S0020818300009048.
13   See UN Charter, note 8, XII, article 84.

and regulating the Areas have seemingly developed, in no small measure, a new system of international trusteeship on the basis of experience and lessons learned from the predecessors discussed above.

3 Homogeneity of the System of International Trusteeship in Continental Antarctica

Antarctica is a continent with an area of about 14 million square kilometers, covered by ice and snow all year round, but it is not a desert of life. The diverse Antarctic communities of penguins, skuas, krill, Antarctic cods, seals and whales thrive here in a unique polar ecosystem. Looking back at the 200 years of human Antarctic expedition, the ancestors have left many historical legends for the coming generations. However, the increasing human activities in continental Antarctica have brought unprecedented threats and even damages to the Antarctic environment. For the sake of future survival and common good of mankind, the ATCM declared Antarctica a natural reserve in 1991 by the adoption of the Environmental Protocol and its Annexes and further established a number of Areas for protecting various legitimate values.

3.1 *What Are the Objects of Designating the Areas?*

In terms of its textual requirements, article IX of the Antarctic Treaty can be referred as a 'negotiation clause', which advocates negotiations in the ATCM on all matters in Antarctica. The specific items for negotiation include measures regarding 'preservation and conservation of living resources in Antarctica' as regulated in article IX(f). But it is very essential to make sure what living resources are in Antarctica, who has the responsibility to preserve and conserve these living resources and how they preserve and conserve these living resources.

Negotiations continued. As the only authority, the ATCM has the power to adopt and the responsibility to carry out the results of negotiations. 'Bearing in mind the special legal and political status of Antarctica and the special responsibility of the ATCPs to ensure that all activities in Antarctica are consistent with the purposes and principles of the Antarctic Treaty', as stipulated in article 10 of the Environmental Protocol, the ATCM shall 'define in accordance with the provisions of this Protocol, the general policy for the comprehensive protection of the Antarctic environment and dependent and associated ecosystems'. The ATCPs 'convinced of the need to enhance the protection of the Antarctic environment and dependent and associated ecosystems', and committed themselves 'to the comprehensive protection of the Antarctic environment and dependent and associated ecosystems and hereby designate Antarctica as a natural reserve, devoted to peace and science'.[14] Therefore, it is certain that 'preservation and conservation of living resources in Antarctica' in article IX of the Antarctic Treaty has been textually evolved into 'the comprehensive protection of the Antarctic environment and dependent and associated ecosystems' in the Environmental Protocol and its Annexes, and definitely implies inseparability and non-partition of the natural reserve in Antarctica.[15]

Moreover, Annex V provides a legal basis for the establishment of specially protected and managed areas within the overall 'natural reserve'.[16] It clearly sets up rules and regulations for the Areas and their management plans for the purpose to preserve and conserve the dependent and associated ecosystems in Antarctica.

'Area' geographically means a particular region of indefinite boundary, usually serving some special purpose or distinguished by its people or culture or geography, therefore 'area' is a real material content always relating to the demarcation or partition of a land that have clear boundary, including natural, cultural and economic elements. In this very sense, the Areas imply the demarcation or partition of the whole land in Antarctica, thus the designation of various Areas seems to be contrary to the requirement of 'comprehensive protection of the Antarctic environment and dependent and associated ecosystems' or that of 'a natural reserve'. As for a 'Management Plan' for these protected areas, Annex V at its very beginning defines it as a plan to manage the activities and protect the special value or values, like outstanding environmental, scientific, historic, aesthetic or wilderness values, in the Areas.[17] Further, the ASMA may include those where activities pose risks of mutual interference or cumulative environmental impacts, and sites or monuments of recognised historic value (historic sites, monuments, artefacts and other historic remains in Antarctica), which are legally included as part of 'any area'.[18] At this point, the preservation and conservation of living resources advocated by the Antarctic Treaty has evolved into the protection of 'dependent and associated ecosystems' which in turn has been split into various Areas respectively

---

14 See the Environmental Protocol, note 1.
15 Julia Jabour, 'Biological Prospecting: The Ethics of Exclusive Reward from Antarctic Activity' *Ethics in Science and Environmental Politics*, 10 (2010): 20.
16 Guide to the Preparation of Management Plans for Antarctic Specially Protected Areas, Resolution 2 (2011) – Annex (2011): 2.
17 See the Environmental Protocol, note 1, Annex V.
18 Guidelines for the Designation and Protection of Historic Sites and Monuments, Resolution 3 (2009) – ATCM XXXII – CEP XII, Baltimore.

proposed by different ATCPs for the protection of special value or values in the sense of demarcation of the whole land in Antarctica.

In essence, the designation procedure, as regulated in article 6 of Annex V, is a process of splitting up the dependent and associated ecosystems in Antarctica. Apparently, Annex V defines nine primary reasons for designation.[19] They also illustrate nine kinds of land-based protected areas with specific articulated standards, including their wilderness and aesthetic values and their values as areas for the conduct of scientific research and for a better understanding of global climate change.

In addition, these reasons or standards are fundamental for any ATCP to draft its proposal for a land-based protected area. This situation is similar to the proposed purposes or aims of the UN Charter for trusteeship system, such as: (1) for further international peace and security; (2) to promote the political, economic, social, and educational advancement of the inhabitants of the trust territories ... as may be provided by the terms of each trusteeship agreement; (3) to encourage respect for human rights and for fundamental freedoms for all; (4) to ensure equal treatment in social, economic, and commercial matters for all Members of the United Nations.[20]

In continental Antarctica, 'inhabitants' mainly refer to the local animals, and 'human rights' can be changed to the rights of Antarctic local animals. In a further sense, the Areas defined by the ATCPs' proposals discussed and determined by the ATCM are also very similar to trust territories determined by the trusteeship agreements concluded under the authority of the United Nations, just as the UN Charter demands that 'there may be designated, in any trusteeship agreement, a strategic area or areas which may include part or all of the trust territory to which the agreement applies', and 'such agreement or agreements shall govern the numbers and types of forces, their degree of readiness and general location, and the nature of the facilities and assistance to be provided'.[21]

3.2 Why Is 'Territory' Not Used in Designating the Areas?

Though the ATCM is convinced that the development of a comprehensive regime for the protection of the Antarctic environment and dependent and associated ecosystems is in the interest of mankind as a whole, it designed the rules and regulations for protected areas in striking features.[22]

---

19   See Antarctic Treaty Secretariat, note 3.
20   See UN Charter, note 8, XII, article 73.
21   Ibid, articles 82 and 43.
22   See the Environmental Protocol, note 1, Preface.

Annex V and its relevant instruments adopted by the ATCM avoid sensitive terms in proposing and designating the Areas by 'areas' instead of 'territories'. 'Territory' in international law refers to specific parts of the earth's surface, including the land, rivers, lakes, inland seas and territorial seas as well as their beds, subsoil and airspace under the jurisdiction of a sovereign state, and UN Charter recognises the exclusive jurisdiction of the sovereign state within its territory.[23] In 1959 when the Antarctic Treaty was going to be concluded, seven countries (Argentina, Australia, Chile, France, New Zealand, Norway, and the United Kingdom) maintained their territorial claims in Antarctica, but the United States and most other countries did not recognise those claims.[24] In order to prevent conflicts between themselves in Antarctica, those States have put territorial issues into the Antarctic Treaty with the commitment that whatever happened 'during the validity of this Treaty, any conduct or activity should not constitute a claim in Antarctica which denied the creation of any territorial sovereignty and sovereign rights in Antarctica'.[25]

Such a provision forms the core of the Antarctic Treaty and safeguards the positions of three groups of states which are Parties to the Treaty: those that had previously asserted rights of or claims to territorial sovereignty in Antarctica, those that consider themselves as having a basis of claim to territorial sovereignty in Antarctica, and those that do not recognise any other state's right of or claim or basis of claim to territorial sovereignty in Antarctica.[26] The same article, however, goes on to provide that "no new claim, or enlargement of an existing claim, to territorial sovereignty in Antarctica shall be asserted while the present Treaty is in force".[27] Though some scholars argued that the Antarctic Treaty has a transitory character and article IV imposes only a moratorium on claims and thus the definite regulation of this issue is not its purpose, it is difficult to deny that the Antarctic Treaty did not regulate the issue of sovereignty, resource allocation or that it insufficiently regulates issues of jurisdiction.[28] The intention of the States Parties to settle definitely the other essential issues of using the Antarctic territory clearly follow from the preamble of the Antarctic Treaty (e.g. 'recognising that it is in the interest

---

23 See UN Charter, note 8, XII, article 2(7).
24 Up to now, both the United States and Russia still maintain a basis to claim territory in Antarctica. See https://www.state.gov/key-topics-office-of-ocean-and-polar-affairs/antarctic/ [accessed 31 August 2019].
25 See Antarctic Treaty, note 4, article 4(2).
26 Wei Menghua and Guo Kun (eds.), *Politics and Law in Antarctica*, (Beijing: Law Press, 1989): 140.
27 See Antarctic Treaty, note 4, article 4(2).
28 Anna Wyrozumska, 'Antarctic Treaty as a Customary Law' *The Polish Y.B. Int'l L.* 19 (1991–1992) 232.

of all mankind that Antarctica shall continue forever to be used exclusively for peaceful purposes'). The ATCM in its newly adopted Prague Declaration (2019) unanimously reaffirmed the importance of the contribution made by the Antarctic Treaty, and by article IV in particular, to ensuring the continuance of international harmony in Antarctica.[29]

3.3 What Is the Procedure of Legally Designating an Area?

Annex V specifies that any Party to the Antarctic Treaty, the Environmental Committee, the Scientific Committee on Antarctic Research (SCAR) or the Commission for the Conservation of Antarctic Marine Living Resources (CCAMLR) may propose an area for designation as an ASPA by submitting a proposed Management Plan to the ATCM.[30] Any party shall first design its proposed Management Plan with supporting documentation for a protected area in very detail, including 10 necessary requirements like the sufficient size and the values of special protection or management, before tabling to the Environmental Committee, the SCAR and CCAMLR for scientific analysis. After evaluating the comments provided by the SCAR and CCAMLR as appropriate, the Environmental Committee shall formulate and provide its advice on the operation and further elaboration of the Area system to the ATCM (art. 12.g of the Protocol). Then, the ATCM shall negotiate it and adopt a decision or recommendation with the one-country-one-vote principle according to article IX (1) of the Antarctic Treaty and the proposed timetable for such issues.

This procedure under the ATCM is very similar to that of the UN Trusteeship System. The ATCM, like the UN General Assembly, shall discuss the proposed Management Plans for all Areas not designated as strategic purpose, including the approval of the terms of the proposals and of their alteration or amendment.[31] The Environmental Committee operating under the authority of the ATCM, very like the Trusteeship Council under that of the General Assembly, shall assist the ATCM in carrying out these functions.[32] The UN Trusteeship Council, the professional organ for dealing with trust territories,

---

29   Prague Declaration on the Occasion of the Sixtieth Anniversary of the Antarctic Treaty. (2019): para 2. Adopted 8 July 2019.
30   See the Environmental Protocol, note 1, Annex V article 5.
31   Under the UN Trusteeship System, there are strategic and non-strategic areas for being trust territories which shall be exercised respectively by the Security Council and the General Assembly. See UN Charter note 8, XII, articles 83 and 85.
32   In addition, the Special Political and Decolonization Committee (the Fourth Committee) considers agenda items allocated to it by the UN General Assembly and prepares recommendations and draft resolutions and decisions for submission to the General Assembly plenary. See https://www.un.org/dppa/decolonization/en/fourth-committee [accessed 6 November 2019].

'shall formulate a questionnaire on the political, economic, social, and educational advancement of the inhabitants of each trust territory, and the administering authority for each trust territory within the competence of the General Assembly shall make an annual report to the General Assembly upon the basis of such questionnaire'. In the case of a questionnaire, it is easily found in Guidelines for Implementation of the Framework for Protected Areas Set Forth in article 3, Annex V of the Environmental Protocol. Even the lists of questions under both procedures are largely formatted and can be fine-tuned in response to specific situation. The UN Trusteeship Council shall, when appropriate, avail itself of the assistance of the Economic and Social Council and of the specialised agencies in regard to matters with which they are respectively concerned,[33] while the Environmental Committee shall inquiry technological issues from the SCAR and CCAMLR in order to assist the ATCM in discussing to make decisions and review on the Management Plans and their implementation.

Such discussions give most careful consideration and due regard is paid to the fact that they represent the collective views of the ATCM and embody all the moral force that implies. The ATCM examines the proposed Management Plans in consultation with the relevant States Parties and making decisions on the Plans. But the final responsibility for deciding whether to implement them is, and must remain, the administering authorities of the relevant Parties. As for implementing rules of the Plans, the Annex V states that each Party shall appoint an appropriate authority to issue permits to enter and engage in activities within an Area in accordance with the requirements of the Management Plan relating to that Area, and each Party shall require a permit-holder to carry a copy of the permit while in the Area concerned. In addition, it asks the general requirements on publicity and exchange of information for those Areas (arts. 9 and 10 of the Annex V). In fact, it is much easier for States Parties to obtain the affirmative decision on their proposed Plans from the ATCM if compared with that in the UN Trusteeship System. The exact rationale is that the former is the outcome of a collective decision-making probably hitting the interest of all Parties who will certainly have opportunities to present their Plans being discussed in the ATCM while the latter demands a mutual agreement on a territory to be placed under the Trusteeship System between States directly concerned, including the mandatory Power in the case of territories held under the trusteeship of the Great Powers of the United Nations.[34]

---

33   See UN Charter, note 8, XII, article 91.
34   See UN Charter, note 8, XII, article 79.

The discussions of the ATCM on a proposed Management Plan generally result in one of the two cases: a decision to adopt the Plan, and a recommendation to revise the Plan. In fact, the second case would be nothing more than a delay of the discussion, as it might be the case for all the ATCPs, since the potential consensus for decision-making supports the interest of all of them for their proposed Plans. In the first case, however, the questions arise: what is the intrinsic nature of the decisions which are generally attached to the annual final report of the ATCM? Does the ATCM agree a Management Plan as a trusteeship contract or agreement between itself and the ATCP concerned? How does the ATCM learn whether the activities or actions of the relevant ATCP administering the Areas are in conformity with the terms of the approved Plans? The answers to these questions will reflect the heterogeneity of the system of international trusteeship in continental Antarctica.

4 Heterogeneity of the System of International Trusteeship in Continental Antarctica

For the purpose of peace, security and environmental protection, the Antarctic Treaty system (ATS) does not exclude the application of relevant international treaties to which States Parties have negotiated and acceded. At the same time, it also recognises the status and role of customary international rules and general principles of law in order to carry out the arrangement of the obligations preceding the rights, such as the principle of state independence and equality, of international treaties superior to domestic law, of the later law superior to the former, and of the special law superior to the general.

Correlatedly, the arrangement of the obligations of ATCPs going first within the system of Areas is analogue to that of the UN trusteeship system on trustee States who have or assume responsibilities for the administration of territories whose peoples have not yet attained a full measure of self-government recognise the principle that the interests of the inhabitants of these territories are paramount, and accept as a sacred trust the obligation to promote to the utmost, within the system of international peace and security ..., the well-being of the inhabitants of these territories.[35]

---

35   See UN Charter, note 8, XII, article 73.

The difference between the obligations of the two systems lies in the dynamic issues involved. Comparatively, the trust agreements under the UN system are more difficult to revise and the dynamic that existed here goes towards a more independent trust territory, so the trustee issues should be gradually reduced with the all-round development of trust territory, while the dynamic of Areas demands constant changes and adjustments by way of enlargement and extension of the areas and protection. In this case, the principle of obligation-priority in Antarctica will be eroded and ruined by these dynamic issues. The original reasons for designation of Areas were extended and elaborated by various revision of the proposed management plans with necessary changes to be contained so that the areas fit into the wider context of the Area system for protecting valuable targets. However, without knowing exactly the who, whom, what, when, where, why and how of protecting, other matters such as access, management, jurisdiction or benefit-sharing in the Antarctic context cannot be clarified. In the meantime, the onus remains with individual Treaty signatories to provide rules and guidelines, for their own activities undertaking protecting anywhere in the Antarctic. Quite likely, these rules and guidelines, in the name of permits, will be no different to those applicable to Antarctic activities generally there.[36]

Although there are no indigenous people in continental Antarctica and Antarctica is not *terra nullius* under the Antarctic Treaty, which means that managing the Areas is not for an independent purpose but for the meaning of protection itself. For example, Taylor Rookery (67°27'S; 60°51'E, Map A) is designated to protect the largest known colony of emperor penguins located entirely on land. The site was originally designated as Specially Protected Area No.1 through Recommendation IV-I (1966) after a proposal by Australia, and the Management Plan for the Area was adopted under Recommendation XVII-2 (1992). In accordance with Decision 1 (2002) the site was redesignated and renumbered as ASPA No. 101 and the revised Management Plan were adopted under Measure 2 (2005) and Measure 1 (2010).[37] Another example is Lagotellerie Island (67°53'20"S; 67°25'30"W) whose primary reason for the designation as an ASPA is 'to protect environmental values, and primarily the terrestrial flora and fauna but also the avifauna within the Area'.[38] In the name of pro-

---

36 See Jabour, note 15, 20.
37 Management Plan for Antarctic Specially Protected Area No. 101, Taylor Rookery, Mac. Robertson Land, Measure 1 (2015), ATCM XXXVIII Final Report (2015).
38 Management Plan for ASPA No 115 – Lagotellerie Island, Marguerite Bay, Graham Land, Measure 4 (2017), ATCM XL Final Report (2017).

tection, however, any area as stated in Annex 5 could be dynamic if there are legitimate reasons addressing the theme of the protection by way of alteration, amendment or revision of the Management Plans, which means that 'the Plans shall be updated as necessary' for their own.[39] Though within the UN Trusteeship System the General Assembly shall exercise the approval of the terms of the trusteeship agreements and of their alteration or amendment, the dissimilarity lies in promoting the independence of trust territories.[40]

It should be noticed that there is no deadline but a dynamic period for the management on these Areas. Article 6.3 of Annex 5 states that 'designation ... shall be for an indefinite period unless the Management Plan provides otherwise'. Resolution 3 (2008) recommended that the Environmental Domains Analysis for the Antarctic Continent, be used as a dynamic model for the identification of ASPA within the systematic environmental-geographical framework referred to in article 3(2) of Annex V of the Protocol. Resolution 3 (2017) recommends to the Governments of States Parties that the revised Antarctic Conservation Biogeographic Regions annexed to this Resolution ("ACBRs Version 2") be used in conjunction with the Environmental Domains Analysis and other tools agreed within the Antarctic Treaty system to support activities relevant to the interests of the Parties, including as a dynamic model for the identification of areas that could be designated as Antarctic Specially Protected Areas within the systematic environmental-geographical framework referred to in paragraph 2 of article 3 of Annex V to the Protocol on Environmental Protection to the Antarctic Treaty.[41]

Under such authoritative permits, the period of time can be, and are determined by relevant Parties as designated for an indefinite period in all their management plans. This, of course, satisfies the provisions of the Protocol, its Annex V and the relevant Guidelines which imply that there are no standards which must be attained before an Area can graduate to independence.[42] The Guidelines ask questions on Duration/Time Period of the Areas like 'Can the area be protected for a time period that allows full achievement of management objectives?' or 'Are there some seasonal periods when parts of the

---

39 See the Environmental Protocol, note 1, Annex V article 6(3).
40 See UN Charter, note 8, XII, article 85.
41 Revised Antarctic Conservation Biogeographic Regions, Resolution 3 (2017) – ATCM XL – CEP XX, Beijing, adopted 1 June 2017.
42 Guidelines for Implementation of the Framework for Protected Areas Set Forth in Article 3, Annex V of the Environmental Protocol provides 'quality criteria' with a checklist of questions to evaluate or assess further whether an area deserves special protection or not.

area or species in it are not vulnerable to human activity?', but the answers to them must be individually independent. Compared with the references in articles of the UN Charter for 'the political, economic, social and educational advancement of the inhabitants of the trust territories' and to 'their progressive development towards self-government or independence as may be appropriate', there are no desiderata but intrinsic values in Antarctica. These values have never been specifically catalogued but comprehensively given possibly because of the mutual realisation between States Parties that an agreement on universal standards to be attained could never be reached within the ATCM by way of consensus, the egalitarianism in decision-making.

Another probable tendency is that various restrictions will be created by the ATCPs of the Areas. A classical statement for this can be seen in all Management Plans like 'entry into the Area is prohibited except in accordance with a Permit issued by an appropriate national authority' as designated under article 7 of Annex V of the Protocol on Environmental Protection to the Antarctic Treaty. 'Permit' means a formal permission in writing issued by an appropriate authority.[43] Conditions for issuing a permit to enter an Area are regulated by the Party itself, probably including general permit conditions, access to and movement within or over the area, activities which are or may be conducted within the area, including restrictions on installation and location of field camps, on materials and organisms which may be brought into the Area, and on disposal of waste and measures that may be necessary to continue to meet the aims of the Management Plan. For general permit conditions, it is issued only for compelling scientific reasons that cannot be served elsewhere, particularly for scientific study of the avifauna and ecosystem of the area, or for essential management purposes consistent with plan objectives, such as inspection, management or review.[44] And more notably, the permit conditions are more stringent based on the revisions of the Management Plans. A permit, like a licensing, is in effect full of restrictive measures. Even restrictions may happen in assessing the degree of human interference in an Area, since the Guidelines defines an Area that has not experienced local human-induced change and is protected from it because of isolation may have higher quality wilderness values and might be more valuable as an undisturbed reference

---

43 See the Environmental Protocol, note 1, Annex V article 1(b).
44 Management Plan for Antarctic Specially Protected Area No. 108, Measure 1 (2018), ATCM XLI Final Report (2018).

area than a less natural area.[45] To a large extent, these restrictions, whether legitimate or disguised, have the connotation of administration, control, intervention and jurisdiction by the authorities of the Parties of those Areas, which are the terms frequently appearing in the name of sovereignty and often have to do with the exercise of sovereignty. Such situation exceeds the scope of UN System of International trusteeship, and the management plan, unlike the trusteeship agreement, is not going towards to the independence or self-determination of the Areas. Therefore, it is possibly predictable that the legal effect of the Areas may have chances to become *de facto* territory, or permanent trust territory in nature, which is very close to preoccupation or preemption under international law.

As regulated in the Protocol and its Annex V, the objectives or aims of protected areas should be for the various public interests of mankind, for example, the aims of Management Plan of Taylor Rookery (ASPA 101)[46] and those of the Management at Lagotellerie Island (ASPA 115).[47] These "case by case" aims reflect that the reputation of Areas, in terms of "local" public good, tends to vary according to the degree of accuracy and objectivity attained. They are always decisive for continuous management of these areas. This element of continuity has been reinforced by the fact that the ATCPs have tended to make comparatively long-term management as representatives and advisers, and as a result that there has grown up an indefinable *"esprit de corps"* among those who have been associated with the work of the Areas during the past years in the ATCM.

However, to whom to be responsible for the results of the Areas is not clear under the ATCM System of Protected Areas. After the Areas were claimed in the ATCM, the relevant Parties have the right to modify the original management plan with the change of the environmental situation in the Areas according to their five-year reports.[48] In the case of no clarified authoritative line to follow for reviewing and evaluating this work, few suggestions could be put forward for improving the existing situation in the Areas. It is unlike the UN Trusteeship System where direct contact between the inhabitants and the Trusteeship Council may be considered under three heads: written

---

45   Guidelines for Implementation of the Framework for Protected Areas Set forth in Article 3, Annex V of the Environmental Protocol, Resolution 1 (2000) Annex, SATCM XII Final Report (2000): Part II.

46   Management Plan for Antarctic Specially Protected Area No. 101, Measure 1 (2015), ATCM XXXVIII Final Report (2015).

47   Management Plan for Antarctic Specially Protected Area No. 108, Measure 1 (2018), ATCM XLI Final Report (2018).

48   The Environmental Protocol, note 1, Annex V article 6(3).

petitions, oral petitions, and visiting missions.[49] Even under the UN Charter, the Trusteeship Council is authorised to examine and discuss reports from the administering authority of the trustee State on the political, economic, social and educational advancement of the peoples of trust territories and, in consultation with the administering authority, to examine petitions from and undertake periodic and other special missions to trust territories. It cannot be deniable that self-evaluation is a best way to persistently keep the Areas by States Parties under the ATCM System, but the recommendations and conclusions on the Areas are their own concern even if their self-made reports are required to describe the conditions prevailing in Areas to be accurate, factual, objective, and comprehensive.[50]

The rules and regulations of Areas are largely independent within the ATS. They are full of information about conditions prevailing in the Areas, which shall be available at all times to States Parties of the Antarctic Treaty. Every government, like every other man-made organisation, including the ATCM itself, has an element of inertia in its make-up and working procedure. The administering authorities of the Areas are no exception to this rule. Therefore, it is good for States Parties of the Areas to be queried and criticised, provided that the criticism is informed, objective, and disinterested.

The principle to "form a sacred trust of civilisation" is obviously here, and there is no change of practicing it in continental Antarctica if only considering the objective fact, except that the characters of the Areas must differ according to geographical situation, environmental conditions and other circumstances. Even if the subject in Areas and make slight changes on request, the article 22 of the League of Nations, concluded a century ago, may be still applicable, let alone the potential impact of the system of UN Trusteeship on that of the ATCM Areas. The best method of giving practical effect to this principle is that the tutelage (i.e. the proposed management plan implies responsibility for preservation and conservation) of such Areas should be entrusted to States Parties who by reason of their scientific capability, financial strength, experience of expedition and geographical position can undertake the responsibility, and that the tutelage should be exercised by them as trusteeship on behalf of the ATCM and for the common good of mankind.

---

49 Although the direct impact of the trusteeship system on the inhabitants may appear to be slight, it does exist. Occasion when there is direct contact between the inhabitants of the trust territories and the Trusteeship Council occurs when the Council's missions visit the territories, and as a general rule each trust territory is visited once every 5 years.

50 Guidelines: A Prior Assessment Process for the Designation of ASPA and ASMAs, Appendix 4 CEP XX Report (2017).

TABLE 1 Comparison between the Systems of UN Trusteeship and ATCM Land-based Protected Areas

No.	Item Name	UN Trusteeship system	ATCM Land-based protected areas system
1	Legal Basis	Chapter XII and XIII of UN Charter	Annex V to the Environmental Protocol
2	Authority	UN Trusteeship Council	ATCM
3	Subsidiary Organs	4th Committee of the General Assembly	CEP and SCAR
4	Management Ground	Trusteeship Agreements	Management Plan
5	Objectives	peace and security	environment
6	Parties Concerned	colonies and administering States	ATCPS
7	Responsibility	protection and promotion	protection
8	Supervision	UN Trusteeship Council	Not clear
9	Aims of Review	evaluation and reform	revise the Plan
10	Communication	bidirectional	monodirectional
11	Expiration	till the day of independence	indefinite
12	Destination	independence of a trust territory	not clarified

5   A Déjà vu System of International Trusteeship with Antarctic Characteristics

The ATCM System of Areas is the result of evolution of politics and law centering on Antarctic environment by way of adopting measures, decisions and resolutions under the ATCM and Environmental Committee. It also reflects the work of the SCAR and CCAMLR on all aspects of science and technology. 'Protected areas provide a higher level of protection for specific values beyond that achieved by other forms of planning and management measures under the Protocol. These areas are designated within geographically defined limits and are managed to achieve specific protection aims and objectives.'[51] The

---

51   Guidelines for Implementation of the Framework for Protected Areas Set Forth in Article 3, Annex V of the Environmental Protocol, Resolution 1 (2000) Annex, SATCM XII Final Report (2000): Part I.

whole complex of protection seemingly creates a system of international trusteeship with Antarctic characteristics.

Firstly, this system demands all States Parties to maintain peace in good faith in Antarctica. In the maintenance of peace in Antarctica, States Parties cannot block the influence of the UN Charter. The UN System of International Trusteeship is designed to solve the postwar colonial issues and thus avoids colonial disputes between Great Powers, while the system in Antarctica has begun with the demands of peace stemmed from the Antarctic Treaty by regulating that the States Parties shall make their due efforts under the UN Charter to ensure that no activities undertaken in Antarctica are contrary to the principles or purposes of itself. By this way, these rules bear the nature of coerciveness and the meaning of axiom for peace in Antarctica.

Peace is the very foundation of all relations of nations. Under the Antarctic Treaty system, Antarctica should be used for peaceful purposes only, and for this purpose, there shall be prohibited, *inter alia*, any measures of a military nature, such as the establishment of military bases and fortifications, the carrying out of military maneuvers, as well as the testing of any type of weapons,[52] and any nuclear explosions in Antarctica and the disposal there of radioactive waste material shall be prohibited.[53] In addition, the Antarctic Treaty shelves the most sensitive issue by not denying the territorial claims of the States concerned at the time of concluding the Treaty, but states that no acts or activities taking place while the Treaty is in force shall constitute a basis for asserting, supporting or denying a claim to territorial sovereignty in Antarctica or create any rights of sovereignty in Antarctica, and no new claim or enlargement of an existing claim, to territorial sovereignty in Antarctica shall be asserted while the present Treaty is in force.[54]

If taking the nuke-free issue alone, the International Court of Justice (ICJ), in dealing with the case of *Australia v. French Nuclear Tests* in 1973, closely supported Australia's view: Any radioactive material stored on the territory of Australia have potential risk to its people, and may cause any irreparable damage. Any impact of the French nuclear tests on marine resources or environmental conditions can never be eliminated and cannot be remedied by

---

52 See Antarctic Treaty, note 4, article 1.
53 On this occasion, the Antarctic Treaty system does not exclude the application of the rules established under the international treaties or conventions to Antarctica which the States Parties concluded. See also Antarctic Treaty, note 4, article 5.
54 Ibid, article 4.

the payment of any damages.[55] In 1974, the ICJ again pointed: 'As the United Nations Scientific Committee on the Effects of Atomic Radiation has recorded in its successive reports to the General Assembly, the testing of nuclear devices in the atmosphere has entailed the release into the atmosphere and the consequent dissipation, in varying degrees throughout the world, of measurable quantities of radio-active matter'.[56] The ICJ conclusions cautions that all States Parties shall be responsible for denuclearisation in Antarctica for the sake of regional peace.

Secondly, this system exerts the obligation on States Parties to undertake international cooperation in Antarctic environmental protection. At the constitutional level, the Antarctic Treaty states that in order to promote international cooperation in scientific investigation in Antarctica, information regarding plans for scientific programs in Antarctica shall be exchanged to permit maximum economy and efficiency of operations, and scientific observations and results from Antarctica shall be exchanged and made freely available(art. 3). It further requires that 'all areas of Antarctica, including all stations, installations and equipment within those areas, and all ships and aircraft at points of discharging or embarking cargoes or personnel in Antarctica, shall be open at all times to inspection by any observers'.[57] Annex V of the Environmental Protocol, identifying the Areas within a systematic environmental-geographical framework, demands exchange of information between States Parties including any significant change or damage to any Areas and the contravention of the provisions of the approved Management Plan as well.[58] These requirements for close international exchange and cooperation are preciously particular in comparison with the UN System of International Trusteeship. To this point, it is safe to conclude that the obligation in the ATCM System of Areas is overwhelmingly superior. However, does this mean that this *déjà vu* system of international trusteeship in Antarctica is obligation-based or obligatory orientation?

Thirdly, this system has laid a solid foundation for other ATCM legal texts by following the arrangement of the obligations preceding the rights of States Parties. The obligations under the ATCM System of Areas are regulated to all States Parties but not imposed against any State Party, and in return to ensure their rights in the Areas. Though specific provisions of the Environmental

---

55 Nuclear Tests (Australia v. France), Interim Protection, Order of 22 June, I.C.J. Reports (1973): 99.
56 Nuclear Tests (New Zealand v. France), Judgment, I.C.J. Reports (1974): 461–465.
57 See Antarctic Treaty, note 4, article 7 (4).
58 See the Environmental Protocol, note 1, Annex V article 10.

Protocol and its Annex V and the Guidelines clearly define the rights of States Parties in the Areas, for the most part undertaking their obligations should go before enjoying their rights. This idiosyncratic trend has been fully demonstrated by the provisions of the Antarctic Treaty already for 60 years.

It is interesting to figure out why the ATCM made such an arrangement of obligatory orientation for the System of Areas. First, Antarctica is very far away from the residential continents with high altitude in average and changing heavy weather, these natural geographical restrictions require that any Party to organise and conduct its activities must fully estimate the unexpected difficulties and emergencies in Antarctica. It needs not only the peaceful regional environment but also good-will cooperation with other States Parties to achieve its Antarctic activities. Second, Antarctica is covered with heavy snow and thick ice that implies its very nature of fragility, and it is strongly necessary for States Parties to protect the Antarctic environment and associated ecosystems. Third, this arrangement conforms to the social basis of international legal relations between States Parties in Antarctica. The mutual challenges confronted by States Parties in Antarctica are closely related to the survival and destiny of mankind, so it fully reflects the nature of international community which necessitates cooperation in good faith as described many times in the Antarctic Treaty system.

This arrangement has brought forth a series of legal consequences, and in turn, makes itself much unique with the nature of *jus cogens* in the system of Antarctic land-based protected areas. At the ATCM level, measures, decisions and resolutions of varying effectiveness constitute a legal system governing the Areas particularly bearing the nature of the obligations preceding the rights of States Parties. At the national level, States Parties take this arrangement into their Antarctic legislation by way of transformation or incorporation, highlighting its impact on the domestic legal systems in despite of certain changes. There may be cognitive divergencies and varied demands between States Parties on certain specific matters of the Areas, but there has been so far no principled dispute arising from the violation of relevant obligations in practice.

Fourthly, this system has been the highlighted legal topic of protection under the Antarctic Treaty system. Comparatively, the security protection of trust territories was a key issue in the United Nations trusteeship system, but the Antarctic Treaty system pays the highest attention to environmental protection by setting a legal system of land-based protected areas with a series of relevant documents. They were legally designed for protection from human activities in Antarctica, and the choice of those areas location nearby the

ATCPs scientific investigation stations can largely reflect this claim.[59] Though many management plans did not clearly indicate which was the priority of conservation and scientific investigation, a major purpose of scientific investigation is destined to facilitate the protection of Antarctic aesthetic and wilderness values just by checking its required conditions on licensing, access and exchange of information. Compared with other Antarctic issues, the topic of land-based protected areas is sufficiently discussed, legally advanced and practically mature under the Antarctic Treaty system.

Yet for all that, this system remains problematic in a strict legal sense: is it a form of colonialism as opposed to decolonisation? Though 'colonialism is not best understood primarily as a political or economic relationship that is legitimised or justified through ideologies of racism or progress' and 'its discoveries and trespasses are imagined energised through signs, metaphors and narratives',[60] this déjà vu system can be likely taken as a sign of white colonisation in continental Antarctica. The ATCM system of land-based protected areas, we might say, has a constitutive interest in trusteeship. It is in part an act of remembrance and maintenance of international trusteeship on colonies. It revisits the colonial past in order to recover the dead weight of colonialism: to retrieve its shapes and to keep the living bodies they so imperfectly summon to presence. But it is also an act of opposition. It reveals the continuing impositions and exactions of colonialism in order to subvert them: to examine them, disavow them, and dispel them. Postcolonial critique must not only counter amnesiac histories of colonialism but also stage 'a return of the repressed' to resist the seductions of nostalgic histories of colonialism.[61]

6 Concluding Remarks

The UN System of International Trusteeship is in any case a success. It has fulfilled its main goals in promoting the advancement of the inhabitants of trust territories and their progressive development towards self-government or political independence, either as separate States or by joining neighboring independent countries. However, the UN's decolonisation successes across the

---

59   Kevin Hughes and SM Grant, 'The Spatial Distribution of Antarctica's Protected Areas: A Product of Pragmatism, Geopolitics or Conservation Need?' *Environmental Science & Policy* 72 (2017) 41–51.

60   Nicholas Thomas, *Colonialism's Culture: Anthropology, Travel and Government* (Oxford: Polity Press, 1994) 10.

61   Derek Gregory, *The Colonial Present: Afghanistan, Palestine, Iraq* (Oxford: Blackwell Publishing, 2004) 45.

decades can inspire us today in an opposite way.[62] In continental Antarctica, a *déjà vu* system of international trusteeship, named the ATCM System of Land-based Protected Areas, is in development in the name of protecting Antarctic environment and associated ecosystems. This will further raise the attention of States Parties on the identification of the Areas and may trigger a new wave of declaration with approved management plans on the Areas. Even though the Environmental Protocol and its Annex V and relevant guidelines provide an essential basis for the Areas network, it is questionable whether those Areas in partition can guarantee the dependent and associated ecosystems in Antarctica since the tendency of the Areas is likely to flow from its progressive disintegration of the whole continent. It is also doubtful whether this was ever foreseen, or intended, by the architects of the Antarctic System of Land-based Protected Areas.

In terms of the Antarctic Treaty system, any land-based protected area cannot be endowed with political expectations that go beyond its instrumental value of environmental protection. This is much different from that of the UN System of International Trusteeship which encourages and assists the political independence of trust territories according to the UN Charter and related agreements. Although the sensitivity of Antarctic territory is always there when proposing, negotiating and establishing the land-based protected areas, the value of those areas has been highly affirmative in protecting Antarctic environment in a whole sense. Considering the constraints of natural conditions in the continental Antarctica, even the *pro forma* trusteeship under the authority of the ATCM necessitates a sense of responsibility to any land-based protected area involved.[63]

Public interest in international law is likely to wax and wane with changes in geopolitical power. In Antarctica, the reviews of the Antarctic Treaty have been challenging by time and contemporary international relations are increasingly measured by national interests. This complicated situation has led to a resurgence of territorial claims and potential disputes in Antarctica. In order to strengthen their substantial presence in Antarctica, States Parties have expanded and built more shelters for various activities which are helpful to propose the Areas. Even though the ATCM is a high centralisation of decision-making on Antarctic affairs, sovereignty is still transgression rather

---

62   UN Secretary-General at the Special Committee on Decolonization 21 February 2019, https://www.un.org/dppa/decolonization/en [accessed 12 November 2019].
63   W Roger Lewis, 'Great Britain and International Trusteeship' *African Studies Bulletin*, 4 (1964) 35.

than suspension under the Antarctic System of Land-based Protected Areas.[64] The centralisation of the ATCM and the transgression of sovereignty can impact on each other and thereout influence the ATCM System of the Areas. We cannot make calculable predictions on the development of this déjà vu system of international trusteeship with Antarctic characteristics, but we are starting to worry about the future of the continental Antarctica by way of designating various Areas which have been interpreted, by law and in practice, into protecting outstanding environmental, scientific, historic, aesthetic or wilderness values, any combination of those values, and ongoing or planned scientific research.

64   Noemi Gal-Or, 'Suspending Sovereignty Reassessing the Interlocking of Occupation, Failed and Fragile State, Responsibility to Protect, and International Trusteeship (Lessons from Lebanon)' *Israel Law Review*, 1 & 2 (2008) 303–304.

Finding the 'Conservation' in the Convention on the Conservation of Antarctic Marine Living Resources

*Lynda Goldsworthy**

Abstract

The Convention on the Conservation of Antarctic Marine Living Resources (CCAMLR) was adopted in the 1980s amid concerns of a growth in unregulated fishing in the region. The Convention's objective – 'the conservation of Antarctic marine living resources' – reflects the negotiators' intention for CCAMLR's responsibilities to extend beyond fisheries responsibilities to the conservation of all species and marine ecosystems in the Convention's area. The intention of CCAMLR's objective has generated significant debate throughout CCAMLR's 39 years of operation, and there appears to be no common agreed understanding. A review of management measures adopted by the Commission is one method for considering how the Commission has approached delivering its objective. This paper reviews management measures in force from 1982 to 2019 and concludes that, while CCAMLR has made significant advances regarding the delivery of ecosystem-based and precautionary fisheries management, it has generated significantly fewer management measures that might stand independently of fisheries management or extend to species or habitats not directly impacted by fishing operations.

Keywords

CCAMLR – conservation – fisheries management – marine ecosystems – Antarctic protection

---

* PhD candidate, Institute for Marine and Antarctic Studies, University of Tasmania, Hobart, Tasmania, Australia. Lynda.goldsworthy@utas.edu.au.

1 Introduction

The Convention for CAMLR was negotiated by the Consultative Parties to the Antarctic Treaty (ATCPs) in the late 1970s in response to an increasing interest in fishing in the Southern Ocean, and increasing awareness of the broader impacts of fishing on marine ecosystems. There were particular concerns about the impact of unregulated harvesting of Antarctic krill, a keystone species in Antarctic ecosystems and pivotal to the recovery of severely depleted whale species and stocks. CCAMLR entered into force in 1982. It is an independent agreement but also an integral part of the Antarctic Treaty (AT) system. The Commission currently has 26 Members, including the EU and 10 acceding States.

The CCAMLR area covers 10 per cent of the global oceans and its boundary is based on ecological rather than administrative or 'political' boundaries. The boundary is defined in Article 1 of the Convention:

> This Convention applies to the Antarctic marine living resources of the area south of 60° South latitude and to the Antarctic marine living resources of the area between that latitude and the Antarctic Convergence which form part of the Antarctic marine ecosystem.[1]

The boundary thus extends beyond the Antarctic Treaty boundary in some places (the latter extends to latitude 60° South) and reflects a biophysical boundary between ecosystems to both the south and the north.

Current fishing activities target four species: Patagonian toothfish (*Dissostichus eleginoides*), Antarctic toothfish (*Dissostichus mawsoni*), Mackerel icefish (*Champsocephalus gunnari*) and Antarctic krill (*Euphausia superba*). Table 1 outlines notifications by vessel per fishery for 2019, subdivided into exploratory and established fisheries.[2] See Figure 5 for locations of management units.

---

1 CCAMLR, *Convention on the Conservation of Antarctic Marine Living Resources* (CAMLR Convention). Article 1. https://www.ccamlr.org/en/organisation/camlr-convention-text. Map of CAMLR Convention Area with Statistical Areas, Subareas and Divisions can be downloaded at https://www.ccamlr.org/en/data/online-gis. A 13MB high-resolution jpg file is available on request (accessed 01 July 2020).

2 Exploratory fisheries are described by CCAMLR in Conservation Measure (CM) 21-02 as 'a fishery previously classified as a "new fishery", as defined by CM 21-01', and 'shall continue to be classified as such until sufficient information is available'. CM 21-01 describes a new fishery as 'a fishery on a species using a particular fishing method in a statistical subarea or divisions for which (i) information on distribution, abundance, demography, potential yield and stock identity from comprehensive research/surveys or exploratory fishing have not been submitted to CCAMLR; or (ii) catch and effort data have never been submitted to CCAMLR;

TABLE 1   Members undertaking directed fishing in 2018/2019 Antarctic fisheries excluding catches below 5 tonnes

Area	Patagonian toothfish (*D. eleginoides*)	Antarctic toothfish (*D. mawsoni*)	Mackerel icefish (*C. gunnari*)	Antarctic krill (*E. superba*)
48.1			Chile	Chile China Korea Norway Ukraine
48.2		Ukraine		Chile China Korea Norway Ukraine
48.3	Chile NZ UK Uruguay			Chile China Korea Norway
48.4	NZ UK	NZ UK		
48.5				
48.6		Japan South Africa		
58.4.1		Australia France Spain		
58.4.2		Australia France		China
58.4.3a				
58.4.3b				
58.4.4a				
58.4.4b				

or (iii) catch and effort data from the two most recent seasons in which fishing have not been submitted to CCAMLR'. CCAMLR does not include a definition of an established fishery; all existing fisheries prior to the adoption of CM 21-01 and CM 21-02 are considered to be established fisheries.

TABLE 1   Members undertaking directed fishing in 2018/2019 (cont.)

Area	Patagonian toothfish (*D. eleginoides*)	Antarctic toothfish (*D. mawsoni*)	Mackerel icefish (*C. gunnari*)	Antarctic krill (*E. superba*)
58.5.1	France			
58.5.2	Australia		Australia	
58.6	France			
58.7	South Africa			
88.1		Australia Korea NZ Russia Spain UK Ukraine		
88.2		Australia NZ UK Ukraine Uruguay		
88.3				

Sources: https://www.ccamlr.org/en/sc-camlr-38/bg/01-rev-1 and https://www.ccamlr.org/en/ccamlr-38, available on request from CCAMLR Secretariat), accessed 30 November 2019

The current Patagonian toothfish and icefish fisheries are close to being fully exploited according to the CCAMLR harvest rules for the maintenance of these stocks. All current Antarctic toothfish are classified as exploratory fisheries, and thus require research to support any expansion. Several fisheries that operated in the past have been closed following severe depletion resulting from unregulated harvesting prior to the adoption of the Convention. In 2019 there were 13 licensed fisheries targeting toothfish in Areas 48, 58 and 88, including seven exploratory fisheries,[3] fisheries targeting Mackerel icefish in subarea 48.3 and Area 58.5.2, and krill fisheries in Subareas 48.1–48.4. Krill catches in

---

3   CCAMLR website, accessed 18 November 2019, https://www.ccamlr.org/en/fisheries/toothfish-fisheries.

2019 were the highest since the early 1990s (381,922 tonnes), although they remained below the precautionary trigger level of 620,000 tonnes for Area 48, established in 2007.

The Commission inherited a number of unregulated fisheries, several of which were heavily fished. Initial management efforts were focused on fisheries around South Georgia and Kerguelen, where the biomass of marbled rock cod (*Notothenia rossii*) in both areas was estimated at less than 10 per cent of the pre-fishing biomass at the time.[4] While marbled rock cod had been heavily fished in other South Atlantic grounds within the Convention area, there were insufficient data in these areas to determine the status of fished stocks.

The Commission introduced its first catch limit on a fishery in 1987 – Mackerel icefish (*Champsocephalus gunnari*) around South Georgia – and by 1991, catch limits were expected for all approved fisheries. However, these fisheries were closed in the 1990s following severe depletion of stocks from unregulated fishing conducted through the 1970s and 1980s, and were reopened in 2000 with highly precautionary catch limits based on biannual surveys and confirmation of sufficient stock availability. A small established fishery for Mackerel icefish currently operates in Areas 48.3 and 58.5.2. Figure 1 shows catches of Mackerel icefish between 1970 and 2018.

Figure 2 reports catch totals for Patagonian toothfish (*Dissostichus eleginoides*) for 1977–2018, and Figure 3 shows catches for Antarctic toothfish (*Dissostichus mawsoni*) for 1981–2018.

Krill fishing is currently conducted in Subareas 48.1 to 48.4. The fishery is currently constrained by highly precautionary catch limits while additional management measures are being developed. These additional management measures are particularly important given the role krill plays in the Antarctic marine food web, and the apparent susceptibility of this species to rapid environmental changes. Figure 4 illustrates catches since 1970.

CCAMLR has also adopted two Marine Protected Areas (MPAS), several sites for the study of predator–prey relationships – CCAMLR Ecosystem Monitoring Program (CEMP) sites – and one Special Area for Scientific Study (SASS) for the study of recently exposed areas following the rapid retreat of ice shelves. It has protected four Vulnerable Marine Ecosystem areas (VMES) and registered over 70 VME-risk areas, most in areas currently closed to fishing activity, the status of which are pending Scientific Committee review. It has also

---

4 Report of the Third meeting of the CAMLR Commission (Hobart, Australia, 3–14 September, 1984) paras 7.11 and 7.15.

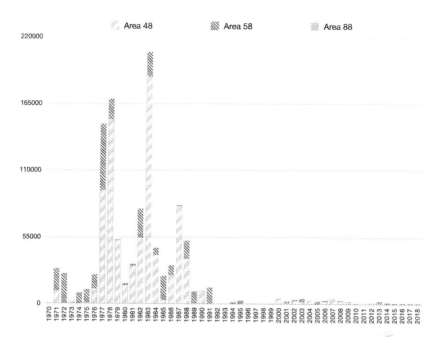

FIGURE 1　Catch of Mackerel icefish (*Champsocephalus gunnari*) 1970–2018
SOURCE: HTTPS://WWW.CCAMLR.ORG/EN/FISHERIES/ICEFISH-FISHERIES

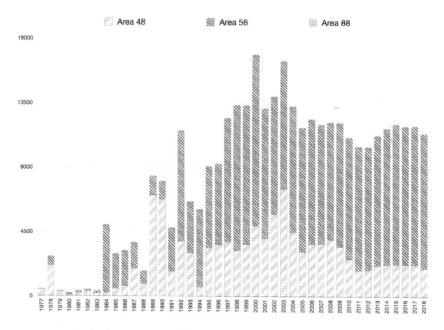

FIGURE 2　Catch of Patagonian toothfish (*Dissostichus eleginoides*) 1977–2018
SOURCE: HTTPS://WWW.CCAMLR.ORG/EN/FISHERIES/
TOOTHFISH-FISHERIES

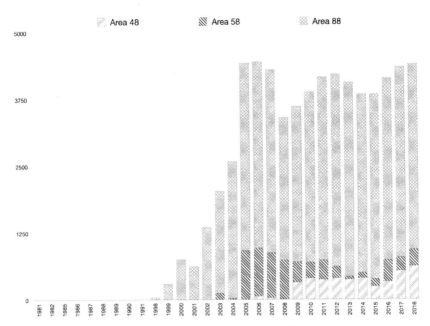

FIGURE 3   Catch of Antarctic toothfish (*Dissostichus mawsoni*) 1981–2018
SOURCE: HTTPS://WWW.CCAMLR.ORG/EN/FISHERIES/TOOTHFISH-FISHERIES

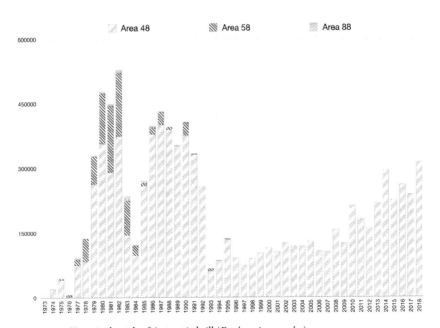

FIGURE 4   Historical catch of Antarctic krill (*Euphausia superba*)
SOURCE: HTTPS://WWW.CCAMLR.ORG/EN/FISHERIES/KRILL

FIGURE 5   Areas set aside for biodiversity protection or scientific research
SOURCE: HTTPS://WWW.CCAMLR.ORG/EN/DATA/INVENTORY

acknowledged Antarctic Treaty-gazetted Antarctic Specially Protected Areas (ASPAS) and Antarctic Specially Managed Areas (ASMAS) located within the CCAMLR area. All these areas are illustrated in Figure 5.

2   Relationship to the Antarctic Treaty

Article IX(f) of the Antarctic Treaty established the means by which Antarctic Treaty parties could develop the CAMLR Convention:

> for the purposes of [*inter alia*] formulating and considering ... measures in furtherance of the principles and objectives of the Treaty, including ... preservation and conservation of living resources in Antarctica.[5]

The public record of the negotiations suggests that the intention was not a fisheries exploitation regime but rather a regime for ensuring that any harvesting

---

5   Antarctic Treaty, Article IX(f). https://www.ats.aq/e/antarctictreaty.html.

that does occur does not adversely affect the Southern Ocean ecosystem and environment. Hofman, a member of the US CCAMLR negotiation team, states that:

> The intent of the Objective of the Convention was to ensure that harvesting and associated activities do not adversely affect the ecological relationships among all biological components of the Antarctic marine ecosystem(s).[6]

The CAMLR Convention includes references to the Antarctic Treaty (AT) in its Preamble and in Articles III, IV, V, IX.5, XV.3 and XXIII. These references establish a strong legal linkage to the Antarctic Treaty and highlight the intention for CCAMLR to be part of the system of Antarctic Treaties and to adhere to Antarctic Treaty principles of peace, demilitarisation, scientific cooperation and maintenance of the special conservation nature of the region. The Convention also explicitly requires all CAMLR Commission Members, irrespective of whether they are members of the AT, to acknowledge the special conservation nature of the region embedded in the AT and its instruments.

3   The Convention's objective

The objective of the Convention, spelt out in Article II,[7] is 'the conservation of Antarctic marine living resources', other than whales and seals covered by other regimes.[8] Article II.2 clarifies that 'conservation' includes 'rational use'.[9] Article II.3 then sets out the constraints on any harvesting and associated activities that may be approved, as: maintaining harvested populations at levels that ensure their stable recruitment; maintaining ecological relationships between harvested, dependent and related populations of Antarctic marine living resources (AMLR); and preventing or minimising the risk of irreversible change in the marine ecosystem over a two–three decade time period. Thus, while the objective explicitly allows for the harvesting of resources, such activity is constrained by a set of preconditions also spelt out in the objective,

---

6   R Hofman, 'The intent of Article II of the CAMLR Convention' (CCAMLR 2015; ASOC, Hobart, 2015).
7   CAMLR Convention. Article II.1. https://www.ccamlr.org/en/organisation/camlr-convention-text.
8   CAMLR Convention, Article IV.
9   CAMLR Convention, Article II.2.

and there are also many species within its mandate that are not harvested or harvestable.

A key point separating CCAMLR from standard regional fisheries regimes is that not all Members have a singular focus on harvesting and some Members do not or have never undertaken fisheries activities.[10]

There are also many differences between the CCAMLR and Regional Fisheries Management Organisations (RFMOs), bodies with explicit and singular responsibility for fisheries management. As noted above, Antarctic Treaty responsibilities are embedded in the Convention, the mandate of the Convention is broader than that of targeted fisheries, and the conservation standard for the application of ecosystem-based and precautionary fisheries management is embedded in the Convention itself rather than negotiated and adopted by Members.

In addition, CCAMLR does not assume an automatic right to fish and requires fisheries notifications to be considered and agreed against scientific constraints and information. There are three means through which fishing activity is constrained by the Convention: where the principles of conservation articulated in the objective cannot be met (Article II.3); when areas are set aside for the purposes of ecosystem conservation (Article IX.2(g)); and when areas are set aside for scientific study (Article IX.2(g)). Furthermore, the Commission may refuse a fishing proposal if it considers the scientific basis for harvest is not sufficiently developed.

The interpretation of the objective has generated many hours of discussion within CCAMLR meetings since its early years. Initial discussions focused on the practical implementation of measures to deliver Article II.3, the threat of illegal, unreported and unregulated (IUU) fishing activity and the relationship with adjacent national jurisdictions and other regional bodies. However, by the early 2000s, a range of views on the interpretation of the objective began to emerge[11] and an item dedicated to this issue has remained on the Commission's agenda since without a clearly agreed common understanding being stated.

---

10   Members who have never undertaken fishing activity in the Southern Ocean are Belgium, Brazil, India, Italy, Netherlands and Sweden.
11   Report of the Twenty-first Meeting of the Commission for the Conservation of Antarctic Marine Living Resources 21 October–1 November 2002. (Hobart, Australia: CCAMLR, 2002) paragraphs 15.1–17.

The Commission's approach to the application of responsible and precautionary fisheries management has been extensively studied.[12,13,14] This paper takes a different approach. It uses an assessment of management measures adopted by CCAMLR, known as Conservation Measures (CMs), to gain insights into how CCAMLR has practically interpreted its objective. CMs are the primary vehicle by which CCAMLR addresses and implements its objective and are legally binding on its Members.

In this context, if the Commission considers CCAMLR to be a conservation regime that extends beyond the role of fisheries management, management decisions would extend to the ecological maintenance of all Antarctic marine living resources, beyond those fished or directly impacted by fishing. Some examples might include:
- consideration of biodiversity and science values prior to the approval of fishing proposals;
- prior consideration of impacts of all human activities, including fishing;
- the designation of areas for protection of biodiversity;
- the identification and protection of unique, vulnerable and rare ecosystems separate to or not dependent on fisheries interests;
- designation of species needing specific protection;
- scientific study and review of the conservation needs of species beyond harvested and might-be-harvested species;
- regular review of the assumptions behind precautionary and ecosystem-based fisheries decisions; and
- clearly articulated justification of the assumptions made when fishery activity is given priority.

The Commission has adopted CMs every year since its third meeting in 1984. Each year, it amends, rescinds and adopts new measures. As of December 2019, CCAMLR had 69 Conservation Measures (CMs) in force, 21 hortatory resolutions,

---

12 Andrew J Constable, WK de la Mare, DJ Agnew, I Everson, and DGM Miller, 'Managing fisheries to conserve the Antarctic marine ecosystem: practical implementation of the Convention on the Conservation of Antarctic Marine Living Resources (CCAMLR)' *ICES Journal of Marine Science / Journal du Conseil* 57:3 (June 2000): 778. https://login.ezproxy.utas.edu.au/login?url=http://search.ebscohost.com/login.aspx?direct=true&db=edb&AN=44591724&site=eds-live.

13 Karl-Herman Kock, 'Understanding CCAMLR's approach to management' (Hobart: CCAMLR 2000).

14 DGM Miller, EN Sabourenkov and DC Ramm, 'Managing Antarctic marine living resources: the CCAMLR approach', *The International Journal of Marine and Coastal Law* 19:3 (2004) https://doi.org/10.1163/1571808042886075, https://login.ezproxy.utas.edu.au/login?url=http://search.ebscohost.com/login.aspx?direct=true&db=edswst&AN=edswst.891878&site=eds-live.

and policies or procedures covering Cooperation with non-contracting parties, Inspection, Scientific observation, and Compliance evaluation.

This paper does not review whether the Conservation Measures have achieved what they were intended to do or whether this is enough to deliver the objective.

4 Research approach

This paper reviews all Conservation Measures in force for each year from 1984 to 2019, when 69 CMs were operating. These were first tabulated against the CCAMLR categories adopted in 2002,[15] as outlined in Table 2. The CCAMLR categories give little clue as to the extent of conservation afforded by each CM, however, other than for those allocated to the 'Protected areas' category. CMs were thus reviewed to assess their level of conservation, according to the categories set out in Table 3.

TABLE 2   CCAMLR categories of Conservation Measures

Category	Subcategory	CCAMLR code
Compliance		10
General fishery measures	General fisheries matters; Notifications; Gear regulations; Data reporting; Research and experiments; Minimisation of incidental mortality; Environmental protection.	20; 21; 22; 23; 24; 25; 26
Fisheries regulations	Fisheries regulations; General measures; Fishing seasons, closed areas and prohibition of fishing; bycatch limits.	30; 31; 32; 33
	Finfish fisheries: Toothfish; Icefish; Other finfish.	40; 41; 42; 43
	Crustacean fisheries; Krill; Crab.	50; 51; 52
	Mollusc fisheries; Squid.	60; 61
Protected areas		91

SOURCE: CCAMLR WEBSITE: HTTPS://WWW.CCAMLR.ORG/EN/CONSERVATION-AND-MANAGEMENT/BROWSE-CONSERVATION-MEASURES (ACCESSED 18 NOVEMBER 2019)

---

15   CMs adopted prior to 2002 have been allocated to a CCAMLR category based on their purpose.

TABLE 3   Categorisation according to level of conservation afforded

Category	Description	Example	Associated CCAMLR category
Conservation independent of fisheries management (CIF)	CMs that explicitly address broad conservation issues not specifically related to fishing activity; that can exist independent of fishing activity or fisheries measures.	– Area protections of VMEs – Protection of representative examples of biodiversity – Areas set aside for scientific studies dedicated to understanding Antarctic marine ecosystems – Maintenance of ocean health, such as prohibition on dumping and marine debris clean-up – Protection of threatened, endangered or locally significant species and their foraging areas – Assessment of broad conservation values prior to agreement of proposed activity.	No specific category. Examples found in General fisheries measures and Protected areas categories.
Extended conservation through fishery measures (CTFM)	CMs that apply prohibitions or restrictions to fishing activity for the purpose of general protection of species or habitat.	– Prohibition of gear types – Prohibition of directed fishing on species.	No specific category. Examples found in General fisheries measures.
Minimisation of impact during fishing operations (EBFM)	CMs that aim to minimise impact of fishing on other species or habitats during fishing operations.	– Avoidance of incidental mortality – By catch limits or prohibitions – Closures of areas where insufficient information is available – Move-on rules when particular habitats are encountered.	General fishery measures. Fishing regulations.

TABLE 3 Categorisation according to level of conservation afforded (*cont.*)

Category	Description	Example	Associated CCAMLR category
Recovery of depleted species (DSR)	CMs that aim to facilitate recovery of depleted species, including where insufficient data exists to allay concerns about status of fished species.	– Prohibitions on fishing specific species – Closure of areas to fishing of specific species – Recovery programs.	Fishing regulations.
Fisheries management (FM)	CMs that are explicitly oriented to facilitate directed fishery.	– Regulations for new and exploratory fisheries – Gear usage – Catch limits – Data-reporting requirements.	General fishery measures. Fishing regulations.
Science supporting fisheries management (SCI-FM)	CMs that facilitate understanding of ecosystem-based fishing operations.	– Research to improve understanding of stock status, to identify dependent and related species or to identify and manage impact of fishing.	No specific category. Examples found in General fisheries measures.
Scientific programs beyond fisheries management (SCI-IFM)	CMs that aim to facilitate understanding of broad marine environment.	– Study of ocean habitats beyond or independent of fishing activity – Studies to assist the understanding of global issues – Studies of climate change impacts on habitat.	No specific category. Examples found in General fisheries measures and Protected areas categories.
Antarctic Treaty obligations (ATO)	CMs that specifically address an Antarctic Treaty obligation.	– Protection of Antarctic Treaty-designated protected areas – Cooperation with the ATS – Promotion of AT values.	No specific category. Example found in Protected area category.

5 Results

Figure 6 illustrates the number of Conservation Measures adopted each year since CCAMLR was established. In recent years, the number of CMs in force on an annual basis has been consistently around 65–70.

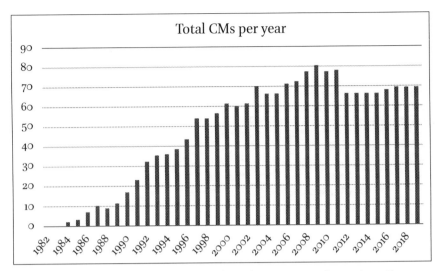

FIGURE 6   Number of CMs in force per year, drawn from CCAMLR website at https://www.ccamlr.org/en/publications/past-conservation-measures

Figure 7 categorises the CMs according to the four general CCAMLR categories: Compliance (Comp), General fisheries measures (GFM), Fisheries regulations (FR) and Protected areas (PA).

Most CMs relate to the management of harvesting activities. These measures include restrictions and limitations on fishing activities across gear types, areas and seasons, measures to reduce the impact of fishing on other species and the environment, and requirements to assess the size and health of targeted populations and associated species.

Compliance measures have been adopted since the mid-1990s and now total 10. Many of these measures were developed to address IUU fishing activity. More recently, CCAMLR has adopted a compliance evaluation procedure that is applied on an annual basis. All the compliance measures relate to management of fisheries activities, including schemes to promote compliance by non-contracting parties. While this is not surprising, compliance could equally apply to broader measures extending beyond fisheries management, such as compliance with Marine Protected Areas or cooperation with the Antarctic Treaty.

CCAMLR Members have only adopted one CM relating to their obligations to the Antarctic Treaty: CM 91-02, which is listed in the 'Protected area' category. This CM aims to ensure that fishing vessels are aware of the location and management plans of Antarctic Treaty-designated Antarctic Specially

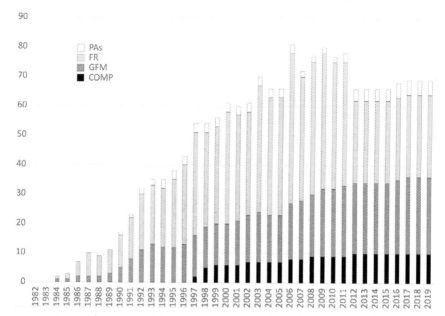

FIGURE 7   CMs by CCAMLR Category in force per year, drawn from CCAMLR website at https://www.ccamlr.org/en/publications/past-conservation-measures

Protected Areas (ASPAS) or Antarctic Specially Managed Areas (ASMAS), and can avoid these areas if so required.

The first CM allocated to the CCAMLR 'Protected area' category was adopted in 1990, and concerned procedures for the management of CCAMLR Ecosystem Monitoring Program (CEMP) sites to facilitate the scientific study of predator–prey relationships in the krill ecosystem. Other CMs relating to facilitation of scientific study are allocated to the 'Research and experiments' subcategory under 'General fishery matters', including CM 24-04 (2017) 'Establishing time-limited Special Areas for Scientific Study in newly exposed marine areas following ice-shelf retreat or collapse in statistical Subareas 48.1, 48.5 and 88.3', which might logically be grouped in the same category as CEMP sites. There are currently five CMs allocated to the PA category.

Figure 8 identifies fishery-related CMs against the total number of CMs in force each year, divided into general fisheries measures, general fisheries regulations and measures governing specific fisheries.

As might be expected, given the number of fisheries operating in any one year and the requirement to implement ecosystem-based fisheries management, there are significant numbers of fishery-related CMs adopted each year.

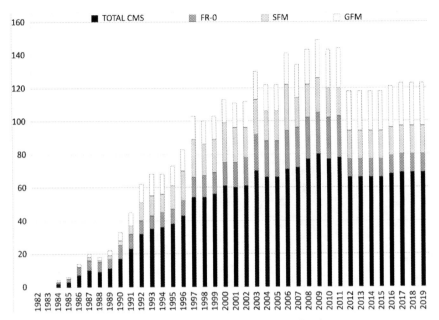

FIGURE 8   Fishery-related CMs (according to CCAMLR category) in force per year, drawn from CCAMLR website at https://www.ccamlr.org/en/publications/past-conservation-measures

The CCAMLR categorisation of CMs does not readily provide an understanding of the level of conservation intended by any CM. It fails to highlight those CMs with a primary fisheries focus that also include some level of protection for non-target species, habitats and depleted species. Figure 9 illustrates the number of CMs listed in CCAMLR's 'General fishery matters' category that contribute to the conservation of species or habitats beyond those impacted by specific fishing operations (conservation through fishery measure or CTFM), the number of CMs per year dedicated to depleted species recovery (DSR),[16] those that facilitate or designate PAs and those that facilitate broad scientific programs.[17] However, deeper analysis shows that few CMs fit these categories.

Article 11.3b mandates efforts to facilitate the recovery of species depleted by fishing activity. The Commission prohibited directed fishing of marbled

---

16   The decline in CMs dedicated to depleted species recovery in 2012 relates to a consolidation of those CMs rather than an indication of significant recovery or lack of interest.

17   Two CMs designed to trial line weighting for seabird conservation have been excluded as they are explicitly related to the avoidance of seabird mortality during fisheries operations. CMs relating to the CEMP have been included as these contribute to broader understanding of Southern Ocean marine ecosystems beyond their potential use for fisheries management.

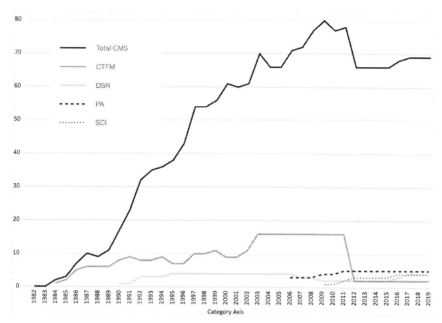

FIGURE 9   CMs facilitating conservation or scientific programs beyond fisheries operation, drawn from CCAMLR website at https://www.ccamlr.org/en/publications/past-conservation-measures

rock cod (*Notothenia rossii*) in Subarea 48.3 from 1985 and in Subarea 48.1 and 48.2 from 1986 following evidence of severe depletion of this stock. Between 1986 and 1998, five further CMs were adopted prohibiting the directed fishing of various species. Between 2002 and 2011 a further seven CMs designed to facilitate the recovery of heavily depleted species were adopted. In 2012, the Commission consolidated these measures into a single CM, 32-02. This measure is updated as required. In 1997, CCAMLR also adopted a CM providing a general prohibition of directed fishing of *Dissostichus* species except in accordance with specific CMs, and it is annually updated.

Excluding depleted species recovery measures, which are designed to facilitate the recovery of species severely depleted by fishing activities, over the life of CCAMLR only 15 CMs fit into the category of facilitating conservation or scientific activity beyond fisheries operations. These are listed in Table 4, and 13 of them are currently in force. Generally, they facilitate or set aside areas to where non-fishing related scientific study may be conducted or for protection of specific examples of habitat. The Seal Islands CEMP site (91-03) was rescinded in 2006 as no activity was occurring on the site, and the Shirreff CEMP site (91-02) was reallocated at ASPA 149 and is currently listed in 91-02/Annex A. CM 91-02

TABLE 4 CMs facilitating conservation or scientific activity beyond fisheries operations

CM	Description	CCAMLR category	Conservation category	Can exist without fisheries?	Years in force
22-04	Deep-sea gillnet prohibition	GFM	CTFM		2006–present
22-05	Restrictions on Bottom Trawl gear in high seas	GFM	CTFM		2006–present
22-08	Prohibition of *Dissostichus* spp. <550 m	GFM	CTFM		2009–present
22-09	Protection of registered Vulnerable Marine Ecosystems	GFM	PA	yes	2011–present
24-01	Application of measures to research	GFM	SCI	yes	1992–present
24-04	Time-limited Special Areas for science	GFM	SCI-PA	yes	2016–present
24-05	Research fishing under 24-01	GFM	SCI		2017–present
32-18	Prohibition of directed fishing of sharks	FR	CTFM		2006–present
91-01	General procedure for CCAMLR Ecosystem Monitoring Program (CEMP) site protection	PA	SCI-PA	yes	2000–present
91-02	Cape Shirreff CEMP site	PA	SCI-PA	yes	2000–2008*
91-03	Seal Islands CEMP site	PA	SCI-PA	yes	2000–2006
91-02 (2012)	Antarctic Specially Protected Areas (ASPAs) and Antarctic Specially Managed Areas (ASMAs) designated by the Antarctic Treaty	PA	PA-ATO	yes	2012–present
91-03 (2009)	South Orkney Islands southern shelf Marine Protected Area	PA	PA	yes	2009–present
91-04	General framework for development of Marine Protected Areas	PA	PA	yes	2011–present
91-05	Ross Sea region Marine Protected Areas	PA	PA	yes	2016–present

* 2009: 91-02; 2012: ASPA 149

Key
ATO: Antarctic Treaty obligation
CTFM: Conservation through fishing measure
FR: Fishing regulations
GFM: General fisheries measures
PA: Protected area
SCI: Facilitation of science
SCI-PA: Area set aside for science

was reallocated to 'Protection of the values of Antarctic Specially Managed and Protected Areas' in 2012, and CM 91-03 was reallocated to 'Protection of the South Orkney Islands southern shelf' in 2009. CM 22-08, relating to protection of registered VMEs, currently lists four VMEs; as of December 2019, 75 VME-risk areas are listed on the VME registry maintained by the CCAMLR Secretariat.[18] These areas remain closed to fisheries until the Commission determines appropriate management advice based on recommendations of the Scientific Committee. Of these 13 CMs, eight could exist independently of fishing activities.

CCAMLR has implemented many CMs designed to facilitate ecosystem-based fisheries management, in line with Article II.3. Most fisheries-specific CMs illustrate an intent to apply Article II.3.a to ensure maintenance of targeted stocks at the agreed levels, and to apply Article II.3.b to species and habitats directly affected by the fishing operation, through bycatch limitations, measures to minimise incidental mortality of seabirds and marine mammals, and measures to avoid vulnerable benthic habitats.

All current CMs dedicated to managing specific fisheries:
- specify catch limits for the target species;
- include requirements for avoiding the incidental mortality of seabirds (and marine mammals where relevant);
- prohibit the discharge of plastics, oil or fuel products;
- restrict dumping of garbage, poultry, offal, food waste and sewage; and
- require measures to be taken to avoid incidental mortality of seabirds and/or mammals.

All fisheries have some level of mandated observer coverage. Finfish fisheries have mandated bycatch limits. All exploratory fisheries must also undertake a tagging or research plan, and exploratory finfish fisheries must also adhere to restrictions relating to bottom fishing activities.

Figure 10 shows the uptake of these requirements from the early years, when CMs for specific fisheries focused on catch limits for the targeted species.

6 Discussion

CCAMLR's conservation objective is firmly and clearly stated in Article II. While this objective has provided the foundation for the Commission's work for many years, the absence of a clear and common understanding of the intent of Article II provides a serious challenge to implementing the objective.

---

18 https://www.ccamlr.org/en/document/data/ccamlr-vme-registry (accessed 01 July 2020).

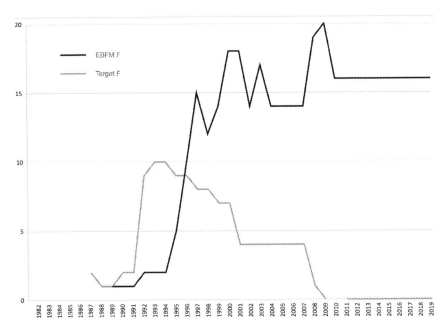

FIGURE 10   Inclusion of ecosystem-based management elements in specific fisheries CMs

Different perspectives on interpreting the Convention' objective have played out in CCAMLR meetings for many years, and are reflected in the types of decisions that readily gain agreement.

While most fisheries-specific CMs illustrate an intent to be precautionary in applying Article 11.3.a to ensure maintenance of targeted stocks at the agreed levels, and in applying Article 11.3.b to bycatch and the incidental catch of seabirds, marine mammals and vulnerable benthic species, the rules vary according to the fishery. Some of the bycatch levels do not appear to be explicitly based on a scientific justification or the results of stock assessments. The incidental mortality measures appear to assume that some level of mortality is acceptable, without a clear scientific justification of why this is so. In terms of the application of Article 11.3.c, some effort has been directed to establishing restrictions on habitats known to include long-lived vulnerable benthic species. However, what initially appears to be a conservation-oriented measure related to the protection of vulnerable marine ecosystems (VMES), established under CM 22-09, has been developed primarily from fisheries data rather than any systematic or independent survey (the VMEs identified in 58.4.1 derived from an Australian marine science voyage). The categorisation of this CM in 'General fishery matters' rather than the 'Protected areas' category further suggests that VMEs are viewed more as an impediment to fishing rather than having an intrinsic value.

There appears to be no cumulative impact CMs for the consequences of fishing in general, no studies into the effectiveness of the benthic protections CMs, and adopting CMs designed to protect habitat outside of or independently of existing or planned fishing activity has been difficult.

A detailed review of the three MPA-specific measures indicates that only one is not explicitly linked to rational use concerns or fisheries data,[19] although it does allow research fishing.[20] The South Orkney Islands southern shelf MPA and the Ross Sea region MPA were designated as part of the system of Marine Protected Areas (MPAs) agreed by the Commission in alignment with objectives outlined at the 2002 World Summit on Sustainable Development (WSSD), and for the purposes of biodiversity protection. CM 91-05, the Ross Sea MPA, and CM 91-04, 'General framework for the establishment of CCAMLR Marine Protected Areas,' both make explicit reference to rational use,[21,22] maintaining fisheries access[23] and research fishing[24] within the MPA itself. This has resulted in an expectation in the discussions of further proposals that fishing interests must be considered when proposing an MPA, both in terms of the location and boundary of the proposed MPA, and fisheries access within the MPA itself. This is problematic when areas of high fishing interest overlap with highly productive ecosystems that are also strong candidates for MPA designation. Such areas are clearly one element of a network of marine protected areas which aims to set aside representative examples of habitat.

The recent 2019 Commission meeting saw no agreement to any proposal that might pause or exclude fishing activity now and into the future, including proposals for the extension of Time-Limited Special Areas for Scientific Study. This meeting also saw a lack of consensus around future MPA designation and little agreement on the research and monitoring plans proposed for the two existing MPAs. No MPA has been established that prioritises or is fully consistent with biodiversity protection in the region.

---

19 CCAMLR. Schedule of conservation measures in force 2019/20. CM 91-03 (2009). https://www.ccamlr.org/en/document/conservation-and-management/schedule-conservation-measures-force-2019/20 Protection of the South Orkney Islands southern shelf was adopted to provide additional protection to this area 'in order to provide a scientific reference area, and to conserve important predator foraging areas and representative examples of pelagic and benthic bioregions'.
20 CCAMLR Schedule. CM 24-05 authorises 'Fishing for research purposes' to include the collection of data from fishing vessels to contribute to an understanding of harvestable/harvested stocks and their relationships with associated or dependent species.
21 CCAMLR Schedule. CM 91-04 paragraph 2.
22 CCAMLR Schedule. CM 91-05 Preambular paragraph 2.
23 CCAMLR Schedule. CM 91-05 Preambular paragraph 13.
24 CCAMLR Schedule. CM 91-05 paragraph 6.

The extremely slow, if not stalled, process for designating areas to ensure that representative, vulnerable and rare or unique habitats are maintained or protected is counter to CCAMLR's conservation objective. A review of the effectiveness of the CCAMLR's approach to designating and managing vulnerable marine ecosystems (VMEs), and to considering the many identified VME-risk areas, is well overdue. There are no designated protected species – and no systematic process for the identification and designation of such species with the exception of CM 32-18, which prohibits directed fishing of sharks except for research purposes.

More broadly, there is an absence of a strategic or overarching Convention-wide approach as recommended by the second Performance Review,[25] including consideration of broad conservation objectives when considering fishery proposals or the study of conservation needs of species outside those that are harvestable. There are differing views on the value of, or necessity for, addressing uncertainties associated with impacts of climate change on fishery management.

7 Conclusion

There are many further steps needed to assess the effectiveness of the CCAMLR CMs, including: taking the CMs as whole rather than individually; evaluating whether the existing CMs have delivered their intentions; and examining whether additional broad conservation measures are needed. Notwithstanding these caveats, three questions arise as a result of the analysis presented in this paper:

1. Can CCAMLR claim to be a conservation regime if it is only able to deliver fisheries management, albeit best-practice fisheries management?
2. Is minimisation of fishing impact sufficient to meet the objective requirements without regular assessment of that impact?
3. Can CCAMLR deliver the broader conservation aspects of its objective, given divergent views of that objective and an apparent inability to deal with the risks and uncertainties associated with a rapidly changing physical environment?

The research presented in this paper shows that, while CCAMLR has made some significant advances, particularly with respect to delivery of responsible fisheries management, it has made significantly less progress in delivering

---

25 Second Performance Review of CCAMLR – Final Report of the Panel, CCAMLR-XXXVI/01–31 August 2017, 13. https://www.ccamlr.org/en/system/files/e-cc-xxxvi-01-w-cp.pdf.

broader conservation-based measures. One possible outcome is that, despite CCAMLR's commitment to its conservation-based objective and its precautionary ecosystem-based approach, a more singular focus on fisheries management emerges.

Acknowledgements

I would like to thank Professor Marcus Haward, IMAS, UTAS, and Dr Dirk Welsford, AAD, for their helpful insights, and Ms Jill Taylor for her invaluable assistance in editing the paper.

Compliance Evaluation and Sustainable Resource Management in the CCAMLR

Denzil Miller and Elise Murray*

Abstract

Regional fisheries organisations globally are feeling the impacts of non-compliant behaviour by both contracting and non-contracting parties. Non-compliance arising from activities such as illegal, unreported and unregulated fishing, or failures by flag states to appropriately report the activities of their vessels, has resulted in damage to the environment and damage to the performance of regional fisheries management organisations themselves. As a result, many of these organisations are adopting and implementing a relatively new mechanism to tackle non-compliance: the compliance evaluation procedure. This article demonstrates that by adopting a compliance evaluation procedure, regional fisheries organisations are better placed to identify and address non-compliance in an effort to improve compliance with their conservation measures. It analyses in detail the procedure adopted by one particular organisation, the Commission for the Conservation of Antarctic Marine Living Resources (CCAMLR), to suggest that implementation of their procedure has improved transparency, accountability and enforcement. It is argued that the CCAMLR compliance evaluation procedure represents a model for other polar and high seas areas to promote sustainable, and responsible, fishing practices globally.

Keywords

CCAMLR – compliance evaluation – global fishing crisis – responsible fisheries

---

* Sadly, Dr Denzil Miller passed away in November 2019 prior to this article being considered by the Yearbook of Polar Law. He was a close friend and mentor of Dr Elise Murray, co-author. Of particular relevance to this article, Dr Miller served two, four-year terms as Executive Secretary of the CCAMLR from 2002–2010 and was a respected and well-loved academic in the field. This article is dedicated to his memory. Elise Murray is Lecturer in Law, Law Faculty, University of Tasmania, Australia. eliseannemurray@gmail.com.

1   Introduction

Compliance evaluation procedures (CEPs) have recently emerged as an important tool for regional fisheries organisations to identify and address non-compliance by both contracting and non-contracting parties. The Commission for the Conservation of Antarctic Marine Living Resources (CCAMLR) was one of the first of these organisations to introduce a CEP, hereafter referred to as the CCEP, and is a strong example of how the introduction of these processes can encourage regional fisheries organisations more generally to reflect on their performance. It was not until 2006 that CCAMLR formally considered developing a compliance evaluation process,[1] the CCEP, to improve the application of its conservation measures.

Following its inception in 1982, the CCAMLR developed a conservation, fisheries management, ecosystem and biodiversity protection framework consistent with the Convention's objective.[2] The CCAMLR has a unique approach to fisheries regulation which stems from its inception as a 'conservation' organisation, rather than a regional fisheries management organisation (RFMO) *per se*. Article II of the 1980 Convention on the Conservation of Antarctic Marine Living Resources (CAMLR Convention) provides that the CCAMLR will adopt an ecosystem-based approach to managing marine living resources south of the Antarctic Polar Front.[3,4]

This article evaluates the effectiveness of the CCEP over the first five years of its operation, and considers the future of this procedure in light of growing global demand for transparency and accountability in the fisheries sector. The article argues that the CCEP has improved accountability, transparency and,

---

[1] CCAMLR-XXX, 2011. Report of the Thirtieth Meeting of the Commission (CCAMLR-XXX), paragraph 8.7. Hobart, CCAMLR, https://www.ccamlr.org/en/system/files/e-cc-xxx.pdf (accessed 1 September 2019).

[2] Article II.1, states the Convention's objective as 'the conservation of Antarctic marine living resources'. In its broadest sense, this objective aims to conserve, including rational use of, Antarctic marine living resources south of the Antarctic Polar Front (Antarctic Convergence) (c.±45°S) through precautionary and ecosystem-based management. See CCAMLR, Basic Documents, https://www.ccamlr.org/en/system/files/e-basic-docs-dec-2018_6.pdf (accessed 1 September 2019).

[3] Ibid. CAMLR Convention Article 1.4 defines the Convention Area's the northern boundary as the 'Antarctic Convergence' or Antarctic Polar Front as currently known. In this paper, the 'Convention Area' will be referenced as such, or as the 'CCAMLR Area'.

[4] Established by the CAMLR Convention Contracting Parties (CPs) under Convention Article VII.1, the Commission's membership conditions are elaborated in Article VII.2. A CCAMLR CP that is a signatory to the Convention in conformity with paragraph 1 of Article XXIX is eligible to become a CCAMLR Member on fulfilling the conditions of Article VII.1.

ultimately, enforcement of CCAMLR conservation measures by encouraging an ongoing dialogue on the topic of compliance within the organisation.

First, the article introduces the CCAMLR system of management and explains how the system functions within the context of global fisheries. Next, the article examines the evolution of the CCEP as a mechanism to mitigate the challenges posed by non-compliance with conservation measures of the CCAMLR and to encourage open and frank discussion on internal instances of non-compliance. The article concludes that the CCEP is a critical tool if we are to achieve sustainable fisheries in high seas areas. It encourages the global adoption of consistent and coordinated compliance evaluation between and amongst RFMOs more generally. The CCEP provides a model for other polar and high seas areas and that increased adoption of CEPs by RFMOs may offer a way forward to promote sustainable, and responsible, fishing practices globally.

2   The CCAMLR Management Approach

Covering just over 70% of the earth's surface, the oceans are crucial to the important geochemical processes regulating world climate and sustaining planetary life.[5] They are also fundamentally important to the global economy,[6] with about 40% of the world's human population living within 100 kms of the coast.[7] This figure is expected to rise to more than 60% by 2020[8] and to 75% by 2050, with tens of millions of people depending on fishing as a protein source.[9,10]

---

5   Pew Environment Group, 2010. Protecting Life in the Sea. Pew Environment Group, Washington DC, https://www.pewtrusts.org/-/media/legacy/uploadedfiles/peg/publications/report/protectinglifeintheseapdf.pdf (accessed 4 June 2019).

6   World Bank Group, 2017. The Potential of the Blue Economy. Washington DC, The World Bank, https://openknowledge.worldbank.org/bitstream/handle/10986/26843/115545.pdf?sequence=1&isAllowed=y (Accessed: 4 June 2019). United Nations, 2016. The First Global Integrated Marine Assessment: World Ocean Assessment I, Group of Experts of the Regular Process. New York. https://www.un.org/regularprocess/content/first-world-ocean-assessment (accessed 12 August 2019).

7   United Nations, 2017. Factsheet: People and Oceans. In: The Ocean Conference, 5 to 9 June, 2017. New York, United Nations, https://www.un.org/sustainabledevelopment/wp-content/uploads/2017/05/Ocean-fact-sheet-package.pdf (accessed: 2 August 2019).

8   UNEP, 2007. GEO$_4$ Global Environment Outlook. Environment for Development, https://na.unep.net/atlas/datlas/sites/default/files/GEO-4_Report_Full_en.pdf, 23, s 23 (accessed 6 June 2019).

9   World Bank Group, note 6.

10 In 2010, the United Nations estimated that fish provided more that 2.9 billion people with at least 15% of their average per capita animal protein intake. In 2014 an estimated 58.6

With global fish production currently approaching sustainable limits,[11] around 90% of the world's fish stocks are being fully fished, or are overfished. Nonetheless, the FAO forecasts a 17% fishery production increase by 2025, with aquaculture providing a larger contribution than at present. Despite the obvious importance of the oceans to humanity,[12] as well as global environmental health,[13] it has only been recently acknowledged that the world's oceans are not effectively managed.[14,15] For many years, increasing and unrestrained human activity has impacted the global marine environment in fundamental, and possibly irreversible, ways.[16]

Straddling and highly migratory fish stocks have been heavily exploited, particularly in areas where sustainable management remains a serious challenge and when such stocks spend significant time in international waters outside sovereign Exclusive Economic Zones (EEZ) or Fishing Zones (FZS).[17] Of nearly

---

million people were directly engaged in producing fish, either by fishing or aquaculture. Most of the approximately 35 million people engaged in such fishing in 2010 operated at a small (i.e. local) scale, or were artisanal fishers, predominantly operating in coastal and inland waters. See UN, https://www.un.org/depts/los/convention_agreements/review conf/FishStocks_EN_A.pdf (accessed: 10 August 2019).

11   Manuel Barange (FAO Fisheries Director) 2016 has noted that 'There is an absolute limit to what we can extract from the sea and it is possibly very close to current production levels'. See *The Guardian*, https://www.theguardian.com/environment/2016/jul/07/global-fish-production-approaching-sustainable-limit-un-warns (accessed: 4 June 2019).

12   Ibid. Barange has also indicated that it is 'quite momentous' to have attained recent fish production levels, since 'In the struggle to make sure that we have enough food to feed more than nine billion people by 2050, any source of nutrients and micro-nutrients is welcome'.

13   European Marine Board (2013). Linking Oceans and Human Health: A Strategic Research Priority for Europe. Position Paper 19. Ostend, European Marine Board, http://marineboard.eu/publication/linking-oceans-and-human-health-strategic-research-priority-europe (accessed 4 June 2019).

14   Pew, note 5; Tundi S Agardy, 'Casting Off the Chains that Bind Us to Ineffective Ocean Management: The Way Forward' *Ocean Yearbook*, 22 (2008): 1–17.

15   Daniel Pauly and D Zeller, 'Catch reconstructions reveal that global marine fisheries catches are higher than required and declining' *Nature Communication*, 7 (2016): 10244, https://www.nature.com/articles/ncomms10244.pdf?proof=true&draft=journal (accessed 15 June 2019).

16   CL Griffiths et al., 'Impacts on human activities of marine life in the Benguela: A historical overview' *Oceanography and Marine Biology: An Annual Review*, 42 (2004): 303–392, https://www.researchgate.net/publication/261706175_Impacts_of_human_activities_on_marine_animal_life_in_the_Benguela_A_historical_overview (accessed 15 June 2019).

17   T Bjørndal and S Martin, 'The Relevance of Bioeconomic Modelling to RFMO Resources: Regional Fisheries Management Organizations' Technical Study No 3, Chatham House, London (2007), https://www.chathamhouse.org/sites/default/files/public/Research/Energy,%20Environment%20and%20Development/rfmotech3.pdf (accessed: 11 June 2019).

600 species groups monitored by the FAO, only 23% are not fully exploited or are overexploited.[18]

All conservation measures adopted by the CCAMLR are required to be based on 'the best scientific evidence available'.[19] In addition, catch monitoring and harvested stock sustainability assessment are key CCAMLR priorities,[20] and socio-ecological values are also critical considerations. This approach is in line with the Antarctic Treaty System's (ATS)[21] political and diplomatic benefits which have served as global enablers of the Treaty's ideals for close to 60 years.

These ideals aim to preserve Antarctica as an international zone of peace, cooperation, and science,[22] with the ATS becoming the home of significant, and precedent-setting, environmental protection, resource conservation and rational exploitation initiatives.[23] As an important ATS institution, CCAMLR's implementation of conservation measures provides a sturdy foundation for marine conservation and biodiversity protection in the Convention Area.

The Antarctic krill (*Euphausia superba*) fishery's vast potential and ecological importance[24] require effective compliance enforcement to meet Convention Article II objectives. Fisheries trends in the CCAMLR Area have varied over the years, with krill catches even being dominant prior to the Convention's entry into force in 1982. Although slightly affected by the 2008 Global

---

18 FAO, *The State of World Fisheries and Aquaculture, 2018*, http://www.fao.org/3/i9540EN/i9540en.pdf, (accessed 13 August 2019).

19 CAMLR Convention Article IX.1.(f). CCAMLR Resolution XXVIII.10 in CCAMLR Schedule of Conservation Measures in Force 2018/19, 322 pp. Unless otherwise stipulated, all CMs cited is this paper are based on the current (2018/19) version of CCAMLR Conservation Measures in Force, https://www.ccamlr.org/en/document/publications/schedule-conservation-measures-force-2018/19 (accessed 11 July 2019).

20 CAMLR Convention Article IX.1.(b).

21 The ATS is a complex array of international arrangements with the expressed purpose of regulating relations among States in the Antarctic. The 1988 Convention on the Regulation of Antarctic Mineral Resource Activities was signed in Wellington but never ratified. See Tina Tin, et al. 'Setting the Scene: Human Activities, Environmental Impacts and Governance Arrangements in Antarctica'. In *Antarctic Futures*, T Tin, D Liggett, PT Maher and M Lamers (eds) (Dordrecht: Springer Science 2013) pp. 1–24.

22 John R Dudeney and DWH Walton, 'Leadership in politics and science within the Antarctic Treaty' *Polar Research* 31 (2012): 11075, 1–9, https://www.tandfonline.com/doi/pdf/10.3402/polar.v31i0.11075 (accessed 2 June 2019).

23 See Tin, et al., note 21.

24 SL Hill, et al., 'Is current management of the Antarctic krill fishery in the Atlantic sector of the Southern Ocean precautionary?' *CCAMLR Science*, 23 (2016): 31–51, https://www.ccamlr.org/en/publications/science_journal/ccamlr-science-volume-23/31%E2%80%9351 (accessed 1 June 2019).

Financial Crisis, krill catches have exhibited a steadily increasing trend following the 2005/06 deployment of Norwegian pumping technology that improves krill catch quality.[25] In the CCAMLR Area, Antarctic krill catches increased substantially over the past 5–10 years to around 306,000 tonnes in the 2017/18 season; a level last experienced in the mid-1980s.

CCAMLR's experiences from the mid-1990s with the negative consequences of illegal, unreported and unregulated (IUU)[26] fishing for Toothfish (*Dissostichus* spp.) are particularly noteworthy. However in the 2017/18 season, catches of highly prized Toothfish totalled just below 17,000 tonnes, a situation particularly attributable to effective and robust CMs countering IUU fishing in the Convention Area.[27] Nonetheless, IUU fishing continues to challenge CCAMLR in meeting Article 11.3.(a) conservation principles,[28] and in ensuring that CCAMLR-sanctioned fisheries continue to be sustainable.[29] Overall, the need for robust CM compliance is crucial, despite CCAMLR having achieved considerable success in combating Toothfish IUU fishing.[30]

2.1 *CCAMLR Compliance Enforcement*

Monitoring, control and surveillance (MCS) provides for effective implementation of fisheries enforcement to ensure compliance with fisheries policy,

---

25 Denzil GM Miller, 'Managing Harvests of Marine Life'. In: *Exploring the Last Continent*, Daniela Liggett, B Storey, Y Cook and V Meduna (eds) (Heidelberg: Springer, 2015) 429–461, https://link.springer.com/chapter/10.1007/978-3-319-18947-5_21 (accessed 12 August 2019).

26 Rachel Baird credits CCAMLR as the first organisation to formally recognize the problem of non-compliant fishers and to coin the phrase 'IUU fishing'. See Rachel Baird, 'Illegal, Unreported and Unregulated fishing: An analysis of the legal, economic and historical factors relevant to its development and persistence' *Melbourne Journal of International Law* 5 (2004): 36 and Rachel Baird, *Aspects of Illegal, Unreported and Unregulated fishing in the Southern Ocean* (Dordrecht: Springer, 2006).

27 See Denzil Miller and NM Slicer, 'CCAMLR and Antarctic Conservation: The leader to follow'. In: SM Garcia, J Rice and AT Charles (eds) *Governance for Fisheries and Marine Conservation: Interactions and Co-Evolution* (Oxford: Wiley-Blackwell, 2014) 253–270.

28 See Baird, 2006, note 26.

29 Denzil GM Miller, N Slicer and EN Sabourenkov, 'IUU fishing in Antarctic Waters: CCAMLR actions and regulations'. In: Davor Vidas (ed) *Law, Technology and Science for Oceans in Globalisation* (Leiden: Martinus Nijhoff, 2010) 175–196.

30 H Österblom, Ö Bodin, UR Sumaila, and AJ Press, 'Reducing illegal fishing in the Southern Ocean: A global effort' *Solutions* 4 (2015): 72–79, https://www.thesolutionsjournal.com/article/reducing-illegal-fishing-in-the-southern-ocean-a-global-effort/ (accessed 1 June 2019).

standards and laws.[31,32] Being able to evaluate compliance success and failure is vital to determining whether management measures are effective, or whether modification and/or redevelopment is required. Monitoring and evaluation are also crucial for identifying systemic non-compliance where common elements link vessel identity, vessel control, non-compliance deterrence, non-compliance sanction(s) and a need for cooperation from non-Contracting Parties (NCPS).

Globally, effective compliance enforcement promotes responsible fishing to maintain long-term sustainable[33] fisheries.[34] For CCAMLR, a primary objective is to minimise negative effects from direct, and/or indirect, effects of harvesting on the Antarctic marine ecosystem as a whole, recognising that effective compliance enforcement through MCS ensures that CMS are effective and complied with.[35,36]

In addressing compliance enforcement, various CAMLR Convention Articles require that Contracting Parties (CPS):[37]

(a) operate harmoniously and cooperatively,
(b) comply with general principles and CMS,
(c) ensure compliance by third parties, and
(d) deal with compliance breaches.

---

31 EA Clark, 'Compliance Enforcement in Regional Fisheries Management Organisations to which Australia is Party', Master of Laws Thesis, University of Tasmania, 2011, https://eprints.utas.edu.au/12423/1/Final_Thesis.pdf (accessed 14 May 2019).

32 PE Bergh and S Davies, *A Fishery Manager's Guidebook* (Second Edition) (Rome: FAO, 2009) Chapter 14: Fishery, Monitoring, Control and Surveillance, 373–403, http://www.fao.org/3/i0053e/i0053e.pdf (accessed 6 June 2019).

33 In this paper, the term 'sustainable' is used to indicate the maintenance of a particular property, quality or entity, at a rate or level that does not compromise that property, quality or entity's ability to meet its own, or other future needs. According to the Brundtland report, sustainable development is defined as 'development that meets the needs of the present without compromising the ability of future generations to meet their own needs'. See Brundtland Report, https://www.are.admin.ch/are/en/home/sustainable-development/international-cooperation/2030agenda/un-_-milestones-in-sustainable-development/1987--brundtland-report.html (accessed 13 August 2019).

34 FAO, 1995, 'Code of Conduct for Responsible Fisheries', http://www.fao.org/3/v9878e/v9878e00.htm (accessed 13 May 2019).

35 Davor Vidas, 'IUU Fishing or IUU Operations? Some Observations on Diagnosis and Current Treatment' In: DD Caron and HN Scheiber (eds). *Bringing New Laws to Ocean Waters* (Leiden, Brill 2004) 1–20.

36 See Miller, et al., note 29.

37 Under Article XXIX, Contracting Parties comprise all signatories of, or acceding parties to, the Convention, with Commission Members having fulfilled Article VII.2 requirements. See CCAMLR Basic Documents, note 2.

They include, *inter alia*, Articles X (third parties and CM integrity), XI (harmonization with adjacent jurisdictions), XX (information), XXI (compliance), XXII (third party compliance), XXIV (observation and inspection), and XXV (dispute settlement). In effect, the Convention's compliance-focused provisions guide how CCAMLR undertakes policing, monitoring and CM application to meet Convention objectives.

Since 2002, the Standing Committee on Implementation and Compliance (SCIC),[38] previously the Standing Committee on Observation and Inspection (SCOI), has overseen development of CCAMLR's compliance-enforcement regime and the provision of relevant advice to the Commission. Its compliance evaluation process has been extensively summarised by Miller and Murray.[39]

It is noteworthy that CCAMLR's management and conservation practices compare favourably with global best-practice in applying the PA and EBM approaches to fisheries management, as well as in the systematic provision of objective scientific advice drawn from the best scientific evidence available.[40,41] CCAMLR has made strides towards meeting international standards in this regard, but an obvious black mark persists for efforts addressing attendant complexities explicitly accounting for ecosystem considerations in management decisions.[42]

Nonetheless, CCAMLR has demonstrated significant progress in satisfying the conservation and management requirements[43] identified by the international

---

38 Standing Committee on Implementation and Compliance (SCIC), 2002. Terms of Reference and Organisation of Work, https://www.ccamlr.org/en/document/publications/standing-committee-implementation-and-compliance-scic (accessed 10 June 2019).

39 Denzil Miller and Elise Murray, 'The CCAMLR Compliance Evaluation Procedure' *Australian Journal of Maritime & Ocean Affairs* 11 (2019) 1–36, https://www.tandfonline.com/doi/abs/10.1080/18366503.2018.1540168 (accessed 11 July 2019).

40 Anna Willock and M Lack, 'Follow the Leader: Learning from Experience and Best Practice in Regional Fisheries Management Organizations' (Gland: WWF/TRAFFIC, 2006), https://www.bmis-bycatch.org/system/files/zotero_attachments/library_1/JET97P5W%20-%20traffic_pub_fisheries3.pdf (accessed 10 June 2019). See also Miller and Slicer, note 27, Table 18.3.

41 M Mooney-Seus and AA Rosenberg, Regional Fisheries Management Organizations Progress in Adopting the Precautionary Approach and Ecosystem-Based Management: Recommended Best Practices for Regional Fisheries Management Organizations, Technical Study No. 1 (London: Chatham House, 2007), https://www.chathamhouse.org/sites/default/files/public/Research/Energy,%20Environment%20and%20Development/rfmotech1.pdf (accessed 11 June 2019).

42 See Miller and Slicer, note 27.

43 Andrew Constable, 'Lessons from CCAMLR on the implementation of the ecosystem approach to managing fisheries' *Fish and Fisheries* 12 (2011): 138–151, https://doi.org/10.1111/j.1467-2979.2011.00410.x, https://onlinelibrary.wiley.com/doi/abs/10.1111/j.1467-2979.2011.00410.x (accessed 11 June 2019).

community at large.[44] In this regard, the organisation has come a long way in developing guidelines for sustainable management practices, as well as in providing baselines against which future changes may be compared.[45]

3   The Evolution of the CCAMLR Compliance Evaluation Procedure

CCAMLR's institutional enforcement regime relies on individual Flag State control and CP actions to ensure compliance. Specifically, CPs are obligated to implement CMs under Convention Article IX, particularly Article IX.6. To optimise compliance enforcement, CMs may also include provisions to address burden-sharing. This may result in joint enforcement action, as well as CP resource-sharing (e.g. vessels, at-sea inspection capabilities, information).[46] The CCAMLR System of Inspection[47] is a notable example of such activities.

Concerns over meeting compliance enforcement needs led to CCAMLR's 2008 adoption of terms of reference (TORs) for an intersessional Working Group (WG) on the Development of a CCAMLR Compliance Evaluation Procedure (WG-DOCEP).[48] These TORs extended the remit of an existing intersessional Working Group at the time.[49] Following the inaugural DOCEP

---

44   Michael Lodge, et al., Recommended Best Practices for Regional Fisheries Management Organizations: Report of an independent panel to develop a model for improved governance by Regional Fisheries Management Organizations (London: Chatham House, 2007), https://www.oecd.org/sd-roundtable/papersandpublications/39374297.pdf (accessed 11 June 2019). See also C Mora, et al., 'Management effectiveness of the world's marine fisheries' PLoS Biol., 7 (2009): 1–11, https://pdfs.semanticscholar.org/f569/700e643 75df8b2ca0ef038b8f998351f1570.pdf (accessed 11 June 2010).

45   See Miller and Slicer, note 27.

46   See CCAMLR Basic Documents, note 2, Part 9.

47   CCAMLR, Compliance, https://www.ccamlr.org/en/compliance/conformit%C3%A9 (accessed 1 June 2019).

48   CCAMLR, 2008. Report of the Twenty-Eighth Meeting of the Commission (CCAMLR-XXVIII). CCAMLR, Hobart. Paper, CCAMLR-XXVIII/44 – Proposed Work Programme for the Development of a Compliance Evaluation Procedure Working Group, https://www.ccamlr.org/en/system/files/e-cc-xxvii.pdf (accessed 10 July 2019).

49   Set up in 2006, this group considered compliance elements identified by the CCAMLR Secretariat (Papers CCAMLR-XXV/37 and SCIC-06/10). These included the development of compliance evaluation criteria and a standardised evaluation procedure model for use in consistent evaluation of vessel compliance with CMs in force. CCAMLR-XXV, 2006. Report of the Twenty-Fifth Meeting of the Commission (CCAMLR-XXV). CCAMLR, Hobart, https://www.ccamlr.org/en/system/files/e-cc-xxv.pdf (accessed: 4 June 2019), para. 7.30.

Workshop in 2009, CCAMLR became the first regional marine management organisation to formally address compliance evaluation.[50]

The approach aimed to detect and rate CM compliance breakdowns generally, as well as potential ecosystem impact(s)[51] where possible.[52] This not only gave SCIC responsibility for providing general compliance advice to the Commission, but also responsibility for overseeing the CCAMLR Compliance Evaluation Procedure's (CCEP) development.

CCAMLR CPs are responsible for ensuring their vessels act in accordance with CMs in force (CAMLR Convention Article XXI.1). They are also obligated to take appropriate measures to ensure that this happens. Consequently, CPs are also required to ensure that CCAMLR is informed of any measures taken, "including the imposition of sanctions for violations".[53] With Convention Article XXII.1 requiring CPs to make sure that "no one engages in any activity contrary to the Convention objective in a manner consistent with the United Nations Charter", a CP is also required to "notify CCAMLR of any such activity which comes to its attention" (Article XXII.2).

CAMLR Convention Article XXII provisions may be more broadly applied to target vessels and nationals engaged in IUU fishing activities contrary to CCAMLR CMs. In effect, CCAMLR can act collectively to bring non-compliance with its CMs to the attention of the State(s) concerned and, if these persist, are not rectified or acted upon, individual CCAMLR Members may adopt appropriate, international law consistent measures to counter perceived threat(s) to the Convention objective.[54]

---

50 CCAMLR-XXX, 2011. Report of the Thirtieth Meeting of the Commission (CCAMLR-XXX). Hobart, CCAMLR. paragraph 8.7. At: https://www.ccamlr.org/en/system/files/e-cc-xxx.pdf and CM 10-10 at https://www.ccamlr.org/en/document/conservation-and-management/schedule-conservation-measures-force-2012/13-season. (Both documents accessed: 10 July 2019).

51 CCAMLR-XXIX, 2010. Report of the Twenty-Ninth Meeting of the Commission (CCAMLR-XXIX). CCAMLR, Hobart, Annex 6, para. 2.42. At: https://www.ccamlr.org/en/ccamlr-xxix. (Accessed: 10 July 2019).

52 See Miller and Murray, note 39.

53 CAMLR Convention Article XXI.2.

54 Such actions include bilateral and/or diplomatic demarches, as well as collective CCAMLR actions such as CMs and Resolutions ('Res.') targeting IUU fishing (e.g. Res. 25/XXV, 32/XXIX) and non-compliance generally (CMs 10-06, 10-07 and 10-10; Res. 35/XXXIV). The Policy to Enhance Cooperation between CCAMLR and Non-Contracting Parties is another key CCAMLR initiative in this regard.

Both the Inter-Ministerial High Seas Task Force[55] and 2016 UNFSA Review Conference[56] emphasise the key role played by unsatisfactory Flag State performance in allowing IUU fishing to take place. The Conference[57] in particular noted the need to promote:

> the implementation of the Voluntary Guidelines for Flag State Performance as a valuable tool for strengthening compliance by flag States with their duties and obligations, and urge all flag States to implement the Guidelines as soon as possible, including, as a first step, by carrying out a voluntary assessment

This invocation reinforced obligations regarding flagged vessels set out in the 1993 FAO Compliance Agreement[58] and other relevant international instruments.[59] For CCAMLR, the question became: How can CP compliance with CMs be evaluated?

Drawing on Western Central Pacific Fisheries Commission (WCPFC) Licensing Obligations and International Commission for the Conservation of Atlantic Tuna (ICCAT) Trade Reporting, CCAMLR made a case for more detailed analyses of its unique compliance purview.[60] To standardise future

---

55 OECD, 'Closing the Net: Stopping illegal fishing on the high seas. Summary Proposals of the Ministerially-Led Task Force on IUU Fishing on the High Seas'. United Kingdom Department for Environment, Food and Rural Affairs and the Department for International Development (DFID), London 2006, https://www.oecd.org/sd-roundtable/papersandpublications/39375316.pdf (accessed 30 June 2019).

56 United Nations, 'Report of the Resumed Review Conference on the Agreement for the Implementation of the Provisions of the United Nations Convention on the Law of the Sea of 10 December 1982 relating to the Conservation and Management of Straddling Fish Stocks and Highly Migratory Fish Stocks', Division for Ocean Affairs and the Law of the Sea, New York, A/CONF.210/2016,: https://undocs.org/A/CONF.210/2016/5 (accessed 10 July 2019).

57 Ibid, Section C, para. 2 (a).

58 The 1993 Agreement to Promote Compliance with International Conservation and Management Measures by Fishing Vessels on the High Seas (FAO Compliance Agreement) was unanimously approved at the 27th Session of the FAO Conference of that year. It entered into force on 24 April 2003, http://www.fao.org/fileadmin/user_upload/legal/docs/012t-e.pdf (accessed 30 April 2018).

59 Internationally, the 2015 FAO Voluntary Guidelines for Flag State Performance took an important step forward in scoping the Guidelines' application and providing performance assessment criteria against which to evaluate Flag State performance, could be evaluated, especially in relation to IUU fishing and implementing Flag State responsibilities, http://www.fao.org/3/a-i4577t.pdf (accessed 10 June 2018).

60 CCAMLR, 2009. Assessing compliance performance of CCAMLR Contracting Parties. Paper DOCEP-09/4, p. 3. Appendix II of the Report of the Workshop for the Development of a Compliance Evaluation Procedure (DOCEP), Annex 6 of CCAMLR-XXVIII, Hobart, https://www.ccamlr.org/en/ccamlr-xxviii (accessed 11 June 2018).

analyses of 11 RFMOs, including itself, CCAMLR proposed a targeted and in-depth analyses of its compliance needs.[61] It recognised that such an assessment should be objectively formulated and procedurally standardised to provide an institution-wide view of CCAMLR's compliance performance and underpin development of institutional best-practices. However, a comprehensive comparison of CCAMLR compliance measures with other identified RFMOs remains outstanding, despite the CCEP's development remaining as a CCAMLR priority.[62]

Recognising that risk and compliance are inclusive for any compliance evaluation, a 2009 CCAMLR Workshop proposed a compliance procedure model.[63] In the model, scientific observers were seen to play an important role in providing relevant ancillary information to the CCEP process.[64] A non-compliance, risk severity matrix was also constructed and substantially adapted to provide non-compliance assignations for perceived impacts on the Antarctic marine ecosystem, as well as on harvested, dependent and related species as per Convention Article II.3.[65]

Following the CCEP's formal adoption in 2012, SCIC extensively debated and trialled various processes before the current procedures were settled.[66] These focused on the CCEP's implementation of consistent and cost-effective actions to address the compliance performance elements proposed by the 2009 Workshop.

Adoption of CM 10-10 in 2012 officially launched the CCEP, while subsequent modification of the CM in 2016 and 2017 merged DOCEP-identified compliance categories and actions. The 2017 CM 10-10 revision addressed:

(a) assignation of compliance status (particularly specific categories);
(b) procedures for determining further Member action;
(c) reaching consensus on issues involving individual Members, and
(d) methods for CCEP improvement to avoid future problems like those encountered when the 2017 CCAMLR Compliance Report was not agreed as China could not accept its non-compliance rating for CM 10-04.[67]

This resulted in paragraph 1(iii) of CM 10-10 being modified in 2018 to make it mandatory for a Member to propose a preliminary compliance status when

---

61 Ibid.
62 Miller and Murray, note 39.
63 See CCAMLR, note 60, Annex 6 of CCAMLR-XXVIII.
64 Ibid.
65 Ibid. See also Miller and Murray, note 39.
66 CCAMLR, Compliance Evaluation Procedure, https://www.ccamlr.org/en/compliance/compliance-evaluation-procedure (accessed 11 June 2019).
67 See Miller and Murray, note 39. CCAMLR-XXXVI, 2017. Report of the Thirty-Sixth Meeting of the Commission (CCAMLR-XXXVI). Hobart, CCAMLR, https://www.ccamlr.org/en/system/files/e-cc-xxxvi_0.pdf, paragraphs 3.23 to 3.26 (accessed 10 July 2019).

responding to its Draft Compliance Report.[68] Other difficulties encountered, and associated solutions developed during the CCEP's evolution have been elaborated elsewhere,[69] along with associated key events since 2012.

4 Compliance by CCAMLR Contracting Parties

The effects of CCAMLR CMS will be short-lived if they cannot rely on long-term cooperation between, and the joint political will of, all CCAMLR CPs. Voluntary compliance has only recently evolved into a fisheries compliance-enforcement tool,[70] but it requires further development. As the CAMLR Convention Area is remote and predominantly comprises the high seas,[71] this complicates efforts to achieve voluntary compliance. However, under UNCLOS Article 116, the right to fish is moderated by the requirement that States cooperate in taking, and supporting, measures necessary for the conservation of high seas living resources.

To this extent CCAMLR's consensus-based decision-making could be strengthened, especially if CMs are agreed before their entry into force and are consequently supported in the absence of any substantive objection to

---

68 See paragraph 9.17 in CCAMLR, 2018. Report of the Thirty-Seventh Meeting of the Commission (CCAMLR-XXXVII). Hobart, CCAMLR. At: https://www.ccamlr.org/en/system/files/e-cc-xxxvii.pdf. (Accessed: 10 July 2019).

69 See CCAMLR Compliance Evaluation Procedure, note 66; O Urrutia, 'The Compliance Assessment Process of the Commission for the Conservation of Antarctic Marine Living Resources: Current Problems and Proposals for Improvement', *Antarctic Affairs*, V (2018) 57–74 http://www.agendaantartica.org/agendaen/journal.html (accessed 14 June 2019). A full summary of the DOCEP process based on the CCAMLR official record is available from the authors on request.

70 Elise Clark, 'The Duty of States to Cooperate in International Marine Capture Fisheries Law', *Antarctic and Southern Oceans Law and Policy Occasional Papers*, 13 (2009) 46–63; Elise Clark, 'Strengthening Regional Fisheries Management: An Analysis of the Duty to Cooperate' *New Zealand Journal of Public and International Law* 9 (2011), 223–246, https://www.academia.edu/478222/Strengthening_Regional_Fisheries_Management_an_Analysis_of_the_Duty_to_Cooperate?auto=download (accessed 15 July 2019); Coastal Resources Center, Hεn Mpoano Policy Brief No. 3, 'Integrating Policy Compliance with Effective Enforcement of Fisheries Regulations'. USAID Integrated Coastal and Fisheries Governance Program for the Western Region of Ghana. Narragansett, RI: Coastal Resources Center, University of Rhode Island, 2013, http://www.crc.uri.edu/download/GH2009COM005ib3_.pdf (accessed 19 July 2018).

71 This classification is consistent with Part VII, Section 2 of the 1982 United Nations Convention on the Law of the Sea (UNCLOS), https://www.un.org/depts/los/convention_agreements/texts/unclos/unclos_e.pdf (accessed 1 June 2019).

their initial promulgation.[72] This has important implications for the CCEP's implementation when 'push back' on non-compliant events results in a lack of agreement on non-compliance ratings within SCIC. On occasion, such circumstances have provoked seemingly self-serving explanations from China, Russia, South Africa, Uruguay and other SCIC Members, with a consequent lack of consensus on a particular CCEP-evaluated compliance status.[73]

With potential capacity issues at play in addressing collective compliance problems, a perception of unilaterality by a CCAMLR coalition of the willing runs the risk of the CCEP being perceived as lacking legitimacy. This could result in concern for a process intended to improve compliance within the CCAMLR Area, where the Area is being managed for a collective good.[74] It could also pose a significant risk of being labelled trade protectionism. An obviously comparable example is the Shrimp-Turtle Case, where the World Trade Organisation's (WTO) Appellate Body stressed that measures addressing international environmental problems are more appropriately agreed by a multilateral rather than a unilateral process;[75] the exact solution CCAMLR seeks through its consensus-based decision-making regime.

Other complications to the challenges posed by CP non-compliance include the Convention Area's size and remoteness.[76] These considerations not only result in challenging financial costs (e.g. for at-sea inspections and sophisticated surveillance strategies), they complicate effective application of Flag State jurisdiction where capacity disparities, cost-efficiency needs and jurisdictional determinants are likely to impact MCS execution. Despite such concerns, it is

---

72 Jacque Turner, J Jabour and DGM Miller, 'Consensus or Not Consensus: That is the CCAMLR Question', *Ocean Yearbook*, 22 (2008): 117–157.
73 See Miller and Murray, note 39.
74 See Urrutia, note 69.
75 RW Parker, 'The Use and Abuse of Trade Leverage to Protect the Global Commons: What We Can Learn from the Tuna-Dolphin Conflict' *Georgetown International Environmental Law Review*, 12 (1999), https://opencommons.uconn.edu/cgi/viewcontent.cgi?article=1036&context=law_papers (accessed 14 June 2019); L Guruswamy, 'The Annihilation of Sea Turtles: WTO Organization Intransigence and U.S. Equivocation' *Environmental Law Reporter* 30 (2000) 10261, https://scholar.law.colorado.edu/cgi/viewcontent.cgi?referer=https://www.google.com.au/&httpsredir=1&article=2210&context=articles (accessed 14 June 2019).
76 CCAMLR IUU catch estimates may be regarded as sub-global, or regional estimates, that are not applicable to all fisheries or ocean areas since they focus on 'far seas' IUU fishing, often by CCAMLR NCPs, which overlaps with other geographical areas and high seas fisheries in some cases. Furthermore, IUU catch estimation for different areas is often different and uses non-comparable methodologies. Poseidon review of studies estimating IUU fishing and the methodologies used. FAO, Rome: 103 (2016) http://www.fao.org/3/bl765e/BL765E.pdf (accessed 23 July 2019).

suggested that the CCEP has notably improved CCAMLR's compliance regime. The current process promotes institutional transparency to allow CPs a fair opportunity to respond to non-compliant incidents and for CCAMLR to adopt a range of responses to CM issues, including necessary improvements enhancing technical operability.[77]

Consequently, it is suggested that CM compliance remains central to meeting the CCAMLR Convention's objective. The CCEP offers a fair and equitable way to achieve institution-wide compliance, where due weight is afforded fairness along with CCAMLR fishery values and sustainability needs.[78] However there remains a need to standardise the adoption and implementation of CEPs between and amongst RFMOs globally, particularly in regards to the type of non-compliance being assessed and/or compared.

Some RFMOs have undertaken a review of their CEPs or equivalent; for example the WCPFC has recently reviewed its Compliance Monitoring Scheme (CMS).[79] While it cannot be stated with certainty that the CCEP has substantially contributed to increased compliance with the CMS of the CCAMLR,[80] there is no doubt that the CCEP offers a significant step forward for CCAMLR as a mature RFMO-like management organisation.

In this regard, the CCEP could serve as a model from which other RFMOs may draw information and experience. This may prove useful in developing global standards to augment compliance evaluation as a crucial, best-practice management tool for the sustainable fisheries management 'toolbox'.

5 Conclusion

The UN has long recognised that global "environmental problems are greater than the sum of those in each country".[81] The world must transcend national

---

[77] CCAMLR-XXXIII, 2014, Report of the Thirty-Third Meeting of the Commission. Hobart, CCAMLR. Australia, paras 3.5 to 3.6. At: https://www.ccamlr.org/en/system/files/e-cc-xxxiii.pdf. (Accessed: 15 July 2019).

[78] Miller and Murray, note 39.

[79] WCPFC, Final Report from the Independent Review Panel to Review the Compliance Monitoring Scheme, 2018, https://www.wcpfc.int/doc/final-report-independent-panel-review-compliance-monitoring-scheme-0 (accessed 16 July 2018).

[80] Miller and Murray, note 39.

[81] United Nations, *Our Common Future: Report of the World Commission on the Environment and Development* (New York: United Nations, 1987) Chapter 10 – Managing the Commons. UNGA Document A/42/427, http://www.ask-force.org/web/Sustainability/Brundtland-Our-Common-Future-1987-2008.pdf (accessed 16 June 2019).

self-interest to embrace the collective interests of human survival.[82] It has been demonstrated that the introduction of the CCEP, and similar procedures, can encourage voluntary compliance and evoke the collective interests of the organisation. However it has also been shown that RFMOs more generally must adopt a coordinated and consistent approach to the CCEP so that a more holistic approach to the global fisheries crisis might emerge.

Based on the evaluation undertaken, it is concluded that the CCEP offers a useful model for developing compliance evaluation regimes. More broadly, it is concluded that enhancing fisheries compliance via the increased adoption of CCEP-like processes by RFMOs globally would improve fishery resilience and provide valuable input into a globally co-ordinated fishery governance regime.[83]

The CCEP process offers a useful precedent for considering what might be achieved by other similar organisations. The additional risks of non-compliance and unsustainable fishing practises would thus add to such concerns, particularly in light of the important role that seafood and common-access fisheries are likely to play in future global food security.[84] As we strive for common understanding, considerably more effort must be directed at adaptive compliance evaluation to attain the best possible societal outcomes and minimise potential conflict(s).[85] Ongoing academic discourse is critical if we are to achieve an effective, common and universal framework to underpin compliance evaluation globally.

---

82   Ibid. See Statement by Canadian Minister of Environment in UN, 1987.

83   JS Barkin and ER DeSombre, 'Do we need a global fisheries management organization?' *Journal Environmental Studies and Sciences* 3 (2013): 232–242; JS Barkin and ER DeSombre, *Saving global fisheries: reducing fishing capacity to promote sustainability* (Cambridge, Massachusetts: The MIT Press, 2013).

84   FAO, *Oceans and sustainable development: Integration of the three dimensions of sustainable development, namely environmental, social and economic*. FAO Contribution to Part 1 of the Report of the Secretary-General on Oceans and the Law of the Sea. Submitted Pursuant to General Assembly Draft Resolution A/69/L.29 (Rome: FAO, 2015) https://www.un.org/depts/los/general_assembly/contributions_2015/FAO.pdf (accessed 9 July 2019).

85   MF Schupp, et al., 'Towards a Common Understanding of Ocean Multi-Use' *Frontiers in Marine Science*, 6 (2019): 1–12, https://www.frontiersin.org/articles/10.3389/fmars.2019.00165/full (accessed 17 July 2019).

Challenges to Substantive Demilitarisation in the Antarctic Treaty Area

*Alan D. Hemmings**

Abstract

The demilitarisation provisions of the 1959 Antarctic Treaty are limited and contingent. Critically, a functional gap is enabled within the key Article 1, which both prohibits 'measures of a military nature' and sanctions the use of military personnel and equipment in pursuit of 'peaceful purposes'. None of the key terms and concepts are defined. With increasing focus on and in the Antarctic Treaty Area on interstate competition around resource access and regime control, and in particular the rapidly increasing geopolitical struggle between 'the West' and China both globally and within the Antarctic, and the transformation of what military activity actually entails, the existing demilitarisation principles are now inadequate. The failure to update these in the 60 years since the Antarctic Treaty was adopted, the lack of confidence that the historic Antarctic Treaty model of regional governance can itself manage the struggle, and indications over recent years that some states are even increasing the level of military entanglement with their Antarctic programmes, suggest it is now timely to reassess and respond to the case for substantive demilitarisation in the Antarctic Treaty Area.

Keywords

Antarctica – Antarctic Treaty System – demilitarisation – military – revolution in military affairs

---

* Polar Specialist and Adjunct Associate Professor, Gateway Antarctica Centre for Antarctic Studies and Research, University of Canterbury, Christchurch, New Zealand. Email: aland hemmings@xtra.co.nz.

1   Introduction – Antarctic Demilitarisation

It is a reasonable question to ask why anyone would see any need for, and purpose in, a discussion of demilitarisation in the Antarctic in the year 2020. The topic was, surely, resolved 60 years ago,[1] in and by the Antarctic Treaty;[2] since when we have seen the continuation of peaceful, collegial interstate relations there – involving, moreover, expansion into an Antarctic Treaty *system* (ATS) – despite all the ups and downs of wider international relations over this period. On this analysis, if even intense contestation (sometimes violent) elsewhere between the states party to the Antarctic Treaty has not unhinged the principles,[3] if 'measures of a military nature' have not obviously occurred within the Antarctic Treaty Area, and 'peaceful purpose(s)'[4] obtain, demilitarisation is intact and all is well. The aspiration that Antarctica 'not become the scene or object of international discord' is achieved,[5] and the ATS can moreover justify itself as one of the 'Regional Arrangements' maintaining 'international peace and security' anticipated in the Charter of the United Nations.[6]

This picture has something to be said for it. The Antarctic has indeed been peaceful and free of military confrontation, and it remains the only substantial area on the globe where inter-state warfare, or butchery amongst humanity more generally, has not occurred. But the picture has been framed in particular ways. First is the question to what extent the happy situation of the Antarctic – in demilitarisation terms – is in fact due to the Antarctic Treaty, if we consider demilitarisation strictly, rather than in the context in which it is used *in relation to* the Antarctic Treaty (noting that the word itself does not appear therein). Second, is the nature of the relationship between peaceful purpose and military agency, where a boundary ambiguity is employed. This is seen clearly in Article 1 of the Treaty, where the first paragraph is prohibitive and the second paragraph permissive of military agency: certain measures of a military *nature* are prohibited but military *personnel* or *equipment* may be used.[7]

---

1   For a sense of the thinking around demilitarisation in both polar regions by the late 1950s, see the seminal paper by Robert D Hayton, 'Polar Problems and International Law' *American Journal of International Law* 52 (1958) 746–765.
2   Antarctic Treaty, 1 December 1959, 402 UNTS 71.
3   Recalling perhaps, the bon mot attributed to Napoleon that 'Principles are fine, they don't commit you to anything', Roberto Calasso, *The Ruin of Kasch* (Translated by Richard Dixon) (New York, Farrar Straus and Giroux, 2018), 19.
4   Antarctic Treaty, Preamble – 1st and 4th recitals, Art I.1 and I.2., Art IX.1.a.
5   Ibid, Preamble.
6   Charter of the United Nations, 26 June 1945, 892 UNTS 119, at Chapter VIII.
7   Antarctic Treaty, Art I.1: 'Antarctica shall be used for peaceful purposes only. There shall be prohibited, inter alia, any measure of a military nature, such as the establishment of military

The legitimating principle is scientific research 'or any other peaceful purpose', but without either of these being defined in the Treaty and each having quite fuzzy edges, understanding quite where the boundaries are for the principle is difficult. So, one may have scientific research that is for military purposes, and one can rationalise military action as directed to peaceful purposes (the key doctrine of 'deterrence' is after all, in a manner predicated on such).[8] How these considerations can be disaggregated in practice in Antarctica has not always been clear.[9] Nor, generally, has anyone really cared to examine the reality of military engagement with national presence in the Antarctic Treaty Area. It is arguable that, enabled by the ambiguities of the legal obligations in the Treaty and a reasonably relaxed view of state practice on the part of other Antarctic states, we have seen over many decades the testing of military systems, the deployment of dual use communications and positioning systems, military training, military-utility research, and extension of command areas into the Antarctic.[10] Third, in a formal sense the Antarctic Treaty's area of application, particularly when it comes to consideration of the maritime domain and airspace, is limited. As a consequence, it has never been in breach of that Treaty to sail military vessels across or under Antarctic waters,[11] or overfly the area.[12] So, in terms of actual operational capabilities, the Antarctic Treaty de-

---

bases and fortifications, the carrying out of military manoeuvres, as well as the testing of any type of weapon'; Art 1.2: 'The present Treaty shall not prevent the use of military personnel or equipment for scientific research or for any other peaceful purpose'.

8 See e.g. Michael J Mazarr (2018) 'Understanding Deterrence' *Perspective* PE-295-RC, Rand Corporation https://www.rand.org/content/dam/rand/pubs/perspectives/PE200/PE295/RAND_PE295.pdf (accessed 1 June 2020).

9 See Alan D Hemmings, 'Is Antarctica Demilitarised?' in *Antarctica's Future: Continuity or Change?* edited by RA Herr, HR Hall and MG Haward, (Hobart, Australian Institute of International Affairs, 1990), 225–241.

10 On the last, see Klaus Dodds and Alan D Hemmings, 'The United States 2002 Unified Command Plan: Antarctica and the areas of responsibility of military commanders' *Polar Record* 44 (2008) 173–177.

11 Antarctic Treaty, Art VI '.... Nothing in the present Treaty shall prejudice or in any way affect the rights, *or the exercise of the rights*, of any State under international law with regard to the high seas within that area' (emphasis added).

12 The 'Open Skies' aspiration of the Eisenhower administration is reflected in Antarctic Treaty, Art VII.4 'Aerial observation may be carried out at any time over any or all areas of Antarctica by any of the Contracting Parties having the right to designate observers'. A general Treaty on Open Skies was adopted 24 March 1992 and entered into force 1 January 2002, https://www.osce.org/library/14127?download=true. At the time of writing the US proposes withdrawal: see Reuters (2020) 'US Pulls Out of Open Skies Treaty, Trump's Latest Treaty Withdrawal', The New York Times 21 May. https://www.nytimes.com/reuters/2020/05/21/world/europe/21reuters-usa-russia-openskies.html?searchResultPosition=3 (accessed 1 June 2020).

militarisation has been largely without prejudice to whatever military activities states may actually wish to undertake aerially, in space or the maritime domain around Antarctica,[13] and in relation to such activities as signals intelligence. One might include these putative gaps in coverage of the Antarctic Treaty to a broader suite that I have referred to elsewhere as part of 'the deep structural hollowness of the ATS'.[14]

Nevertheless, on the basis of the Treaty itself, and state practice since its adoption, a reasonable assessment is that some degree of demilitarisation (and hereafter I use that term to capture the whole basket of concerns around 'peaceful purposes', 'measures of a military nature' and the functioning of the 'inspection' rights)[15] of Antarctica has occurred. But, as with the situation around nuclear explosions and radioactive waste disposal,[16] this is contingent.

2   Framing Demilitarisation

A key early framing of the demilitarisation achieved through the Antarctic Treaty is found in the Address of Welcome to the First Antarctic Treaty Consultative Meeting by Australian Prime Minister Robert Menzies:

> The first of these [three major principles] is that this region is not to be regarded as a region in which preparations for war or conflict can be engaged in. It would not, perhaps, be grammatically accurate to say that it is demilitarized, because it has never been militarized; but it is to be non-militarized, and this is of tremendous importance because if, in this great area of the world, and with the modern development of weapons of destruction, you could have a conflict, or preparation for conflict, a new horror would be added to the world.[17]

---

13   But see the discussion (including reference to Antarctica) around 'limitation of use of the sea to peaceful purposes' and whether this limits or excludes military activity, in Francesco Francioni, 'Peacetime use of Force, Military Activities, and the New Law of the Sea', *Cornell International Law Journal* 18 (1985) 203–226, 222.
14   Alan D Hemmings, 'The Hollowing of Antarctic Governance' in *Science and Geopolitics of the White World: Arctic-Antarctic-Himalaya* edited by Prem Shanker Goel, Rasik Ravindra and Sulagna Chattopadhyay (Cham, Springer, 2017) 17–31, 20.
15   Inspection is considered in detail below.
16   Antarctic Treaty, Art v where these are prohibited unless and until a general international agreement is concluded.
17   Robert Menzies, 'Address of welcome on the occasion of the opening of the First Antarctic Treaty Consultative Meeting by the Prime Minister and Minister of State for External Affairs in Australia, the Right Honourable R.G. Menzies, C.H., Q.C., M.P., 10 July 1961' in

Menzies puts it starkly: the issue is to prevent 'preparations for war or conflict'. This is not phrasing that one finds in the Treaty itself; but it was, at the height of the Cold War and just 15 years after the end of the Second World War, the underlying hope of the states which had negotiated the Antarctic Treaty, and a key purpose of that Treaty. The assessment of the Antarctic Treaty by the specialist arms control bureau within the US State Department of State is that:

> The Antarctic Treaty, the earliest of the post-World War II arms limitation agreements, has significance both in itself and as a precedent. It demilitarized the Antarctic Continent and provided for its cooperative exploration and future use. It has been cited as an example of nations exercising foresight and working in concert to prevent conflict before it develops. Based on the premise that to exclude armaments is easier than to eliminate or control them once they have been introduced, the treaty served as a model, in its approach and even in its specific provisions, for later 'non-armament' treaties – the treaties that excluded nuclear weapons from outer space, from Latin America, and from the seabed.[18]

The statement that the Antarctic Treaty is 'the earliest of the post-World War II arms limitation agreements', takes us to another construction of demilitarisation, through the concept of a 'nuclear weapon free zone' (NWFZ). In formal terms, five NWFZs are usually identified.[19] However four further instruments (including the Antarctic Treaty) also ban deployment of nuclear weapons,[20] and are accordingly generally rolled into the series of international demilitarisation agreements, or an even wider of alleged 'Demilitarised Zones'.[21] It is

---

    Report of the First Consultative Meeting, (Canberra: Commonwealth Government Printer, 1961) 17.

18   Bureau of Arms Control, Verification and Compliance, US Department of State, 'Antarctic Treaty' https://2009-2017.state.gov/t/avc/trty/193967.htm (accessed 1 June 2020).

19   1967 Treaty of Tlatelolco; 1985 Treaty of Rarotonga; 1995 Treaty of Bangkok; 1996 Treaty of Pelindaba and the 2006 Treaty of Semipalatinsk. See Arms Control Association Fact Sheet 'Nuclear-Weapon-Free-Zones (NWFZ) at a Glance' https://www.armscontrol.org/factsheets/nwfz (accessed 1 June 2020).

20   The others are: Treaty on Principles Governing the Activities of States in the Exploration and Use of Outer Space, including the Moon and Other Celestial Bodies (Outer Space Treaty), 27 January 1967, 610 UNTS 205 at Art. IV; 1971 Treaty on the Prohibition of the Emplacement of Nuclear Weapons and other Weapons of Mass Destruction on the Seabed and the Ocean Floor and in the Subsoil thereof (the Seabed Arms Control Treaty), 11 February 1971, 955 UNTS 13678; 1992 Law of Mongolia on its Nuclear-Weapon-Free Status https://media.nti.org/documents/law_of_mongolia.pdf (accessed 1 June 2020).

21   In relation to the latter, see e.g. the Wikipedia entry at https://en.wikipedia.org/wiki/Demilitarized_zone (accessed 1 June 2020).

from characterisations that the idea that the Antarctic had been demilitarised took wing in the wider public imagination. This framing remains the public one to this day.

Within the specialist polar legal literature, this broad conception of the demilitarisation of Antarctica was also generally accepted. Arthur Watts opened a chapter entitled 'Non-Militarisation and Non-Nuclearisation' by saying: 'It is often forgotten that the Antarctic Treaty is a significant treaty providing for the demilitarisation of an extensive area – in fact, of course, of a whole continent'.[22] Similarly, Jeffrey Myhre:

> The Antarctic Treaty of 1959 is a most remarkable agreement. At the height of the Cold War, the Treaty bound the US and the USSR to demilitarization of the entire continent, to ban nuclear testing in the region, and to allow on-site inspection of their respective facilities.[23]

However, more recently such general statements appear less frequently. In part this may be an artefact of a switch in focus, with grand systems narratives superseded by more narrowly targeted analyses of environmental rather than strategic issues. Whatever the reason, contemporary legal scholars seem inclined to disaggregate the components of demilitarisation within the Antarctic Treaty, trace the containment of conflict to the Treaty as a whole, or (particularly) its Article IV, and not use the word 'demilitarisation'. Thus, Ben Saul and Tim Stephens, in the introduction to their collection of Antarctic instruments,[24] merely state that one of the three main elements of the Treaty is that it:

> establishes that Antarctica is to be used exclusively for peaceful purposes, and prohibits the deployment of military forces in Antarctica unless used for scientific research or other peaceful purposes. A right to inspect others' scientific bases has, however, been little used.[25]

Donald Rothwell takes Art IV, rather than any of the demilitarisation elements in the Treaty, as the significant factor containing 'tensions amongst some parties, such as those between Argentina and the United Kingdom during the 1982

---

22 Arthur Watts, *International Law and the Antarctic Treaty System*, (Cambridge: Grotius, (1992) 205.
23 Jeffrey D Myhre, *The Antarctic Treaty System: Politics, Law, and Diplomacy*, (New York: Routledge, (1986) 23.
24 Ben Saul and Tim Stephens, *Antarctica in International Law*, (Oxford: Hart, 2015).
25 Ibid. at ix.

Falklands War'.[26] Saul and Stephens with Rothwell are of course essentially making an historic assessment of the Treaty. James Crawford is evidently considering the near-past, present and future when he itemises the 'significant challenges to the Antarctic treaty system' as '[w]haling disputes, continental shelf claims, prospecting for offshore hydrocarbon resources, and the effects of climate change'.[27] Significant contemporary challenges to be sure, but again no focus on demilitarisation *per se*.[28] A similar focus on resource and environmental issues informs Crawford's thinking elsewhere.[29]

Having grounded the elements of demilitarisation in the Antarctic Treaty and briefly canvassed its historic and more recent framing, consideration shifts to the present time and the challenges that are at the heart of this article.

3 Substantive Concerns about Antarctic Demilitarisation Today

In 2020, the concerns can be seen to fall into one or more of four classes, across which there are obviously some synergisms:

i. Concern that the structural limitations of demilitarisation under the Antarctic Treaty pose less and less of an impediment to real-world measures of a military nature, even if fully complied with. This reflects both the historically partial coverage of things military in the Treaty,[30] and the profound and massive transformation of the conception and nature of military activities and purposes over the now more than 60 years since the drafting of the Treaty. The latter has been magnified and accelerated as a result of what has been termed the 'Revolution in Military Affairs'.[31]

ii. Concern that the historically permissive nature of the ATS[32] may not provide adequate confidence (to either participants or external observers)

---

26   Donald R Rothwell, 'Dispute Settlement under the Antarctic Treaty System' *Max Planck Encyclopedias of International Law* [June 2018] – paragraph 28.
27   James Crawford (2012) *Brownlie's Principles of Public International Law* (8th Edn) Oxford University Press, Oxford, 346.
28   He may, of course, like others, consider demilitarisation as essentially 'done and dusted'.
29   See for example, James Crawford, *Chance, Order Change: The Course of International Law*, (The Hague Academy of International Law, 2014), paragraphs 651, 655.
30   See discussion above.
31   See discussion in Michael O'Hanlon (2018) *A Retrospective on the So-Called Revolution in Military Affairs, 2000–2020*, Washington DC, Brookings Institution https://www.brookings.edu/wp-content/uploads/2018/09/FP_20181217_defense_advances_pt1.pdf (accessed 1 June 2020).
32   Alan D Hemmings, 'The philosophy of law in the Antarctic' in *Philosophies of Polar Law* edited by Dawid Bunikowski and Alan D. Hemmings, (London: Routledge, 2020)

that non-compliance with supposed duties and obligations, including demilitarisation (below quite significant thresholds), will be detected, challenged, let alone stopped;[33]

iii. Concern that we have entered a rather different period in the framing of Antarctic interests and futures to that of the Cold-War period when the Antarctic Treaty was codified, and during which it operated in a relatively (and perhaps retrospectively) stable or predictable global context. This concern posits a materially different context between a period when the prime global protagonists (the United States and the Soviet Union, with their respective satellites) jointly entered into regime-building precisely to contain their regional contestation, and a period (now) when the prime global protagonists (the United States and China) are contesting within a regime that was not built around, or to restrain, their particular global or regional contestation. The regional contestation is now also more acute because technology has enabled activities and aspirations in Antarctica that were all but impossible in the first decades of the Antarctic Treaty. Moreover, the historic Antarctic exceptionalism that guided behaviour and institutions has been largely disabled.[34] On this thinking, the 'West vs China' is materially different to the 'West vs USSR'; and

iv. Concern that as a result – and perhaps particularly the concerns noted at iii. – there is evidence that challenges within the Antarctic Treaty Area are now increasingly being framed in conventional strategic competition terms, requiring (or at least rationalising) conventional strategic responses, including even military contingency planning. In short, that there has been a decay of the *sui generis* framing of Antarctica,[35] which whilst it never entirely decoupled Antarctica from global geopolitics, saw events in Antarctica responded to in particular and distinct ways. These transformations, and what they may auger for the future conduct of inter-state

---

13–29, 22.

33 Observing that, through the entire history of the ATS there has been no recourse to the dispute settlement provisions provided at Article XI of the Antarctic Treaty, Article XXV of CCAMLR (Convention on the Conservation of Antarctic Marine Living Resources, 20 May 1980, 1329 UNTS 47) and Article 18 of the Madrid Protocol (Protocol on Environmental Protection to the Antarctic Treaty, 4 October 1991, 2941 UNTS 3). There are no explicit dispute settlement provisions in the Convention for the Conservation of Antarctic Seals (1 June 1972, 1080 UNTS 175).

34 See Alan D Hemmings 'From the New Geopolitics of Resources to Nanotechnology: Emerging Challenges of Globalism in Antarctica' *The Yearbook of Polar Law* 1 (2009) 55–72, at 62–64.

35 See Hemmings, note 32, 23.

relations in Antarctica, seem – at least to the present author – to be matters of some moment.

4 Military Activities That Are Currently Not Viewed as Breaches of the Antarctic Treaty

In light of the careful itemisation of the coverage of the demilitarisation principles in parts 1 and 2 above, here we consider some current activities in the Antarctic Treaty Area which on any common-sense understanding of the concept are plainly military activities, whatever else they might be in terms of the permissive understandings under that Treaty and the emergence, and dramatic expansion, of the construct of 'dual-use' goods, technologies or activities since the drafting of the Treaty.[36] The instances adduced here are simply examples. There is no attempt to provide a comprehensive inventory of current military activities across the states which are parties to one or more of the instruments of the ATS. There has been an attempt to select examples that reveal the diversity of these activities; and some contextual remarks are made around each example. The purpose here is not to allege illegality or impropriety *per se*, nor to stigmatise particular states. It is to illustrate the sorts of military activities which are conducted – and in one of the cases, not actually conducted but hypothesised – within the contemporary Antarctic geopolitical space, without seemingly either being in breach of the demilitarisation principles or inciting any sort of general questioning or anxiety. If this can be explained by a conservative reading of the black-letter obligations in the Antarctic Treaty, it still appears to present a paradox given the wider declaratory and (most particularly) wider public understanding of a demilitarised Antarctic.

4.1 *Extending Military Command Areas into Antarctica (United States)*

'Command and Control' (C2) is a key component of US military doctrine,[37] and part of its substructure are the geographic Combatant Commands which

---

[36] A succinct, if broad, definition of dual-use is provided by New Zealand's Ministry of Foreign Affairs and Trade, 'Dual-use goods are goods and technologies developed for commercial purposes, but which may be used either as military components or for the development or production of military systems or weapons of mass destruction' https://www.mfat.govt.nz/en/trade/brokering-weapons-and-dual-use-items-for-military-use/what-is-controlled/ (accessed 1 June 2020).

[37] 'C2 enhances the commander's ability to make sound and timely decisions and successfully execute them. Unity of effort over complex operations is made possible through decentralized execution of centralized, overarching plans or via mission command. Unity of command is strengthened through adherence to the following C2 tenets: clearly defined authorities, roles, and relationships; mission command; information management and

are assigned a diverse range of responsibilities.[38] As previously discussed by Dodds and Hemmings,[39] the largest US Combatant Command, Pacific Command, now Indo-Pacific Command (USINDOPACOM)[40] includes the entire Antarctic Continent within its geographical area of responsibility. Two other Commands, Africa Command (USAFRICOM) and Southern Command (USSOUTHCOM) extend to the coastline of the Antarctic continent, and so include islands and maritime area within the Antarctic Treaty Area.[41]

Is this not a rather profound militarisation of the notionally demilitarised Antarctic Treaty Area, even if some of the activities within the area are in support of science and the US national Antarctic programme? The issue here is not that assets from a military command are employed in Antarctica – that is plainly covered by Article 1.2 of the Antarctic Treaty – but that USINDOPACOM (and USAFRICOM and USSOUTHCOM to lesser extents) formally include the Antarctic Treaty Area in what are manifestly wider military C2 contexts.

4.2 Declaring That One's Strategic Missiles Can Evade Detection and Interception by Flying over the Antarctic (Russian Federation)

The development of Russian military technology formed a part of President Putin's address to the Federal Assembly on 1 March 2018.[42] Remarkably, President Putin proudly spruiked two cutting edge missile developments which allowed the weapons to fly very long distances, including (as the visual displays showed) over the Antarctic. How feasible these claims are, and if they are feasible how close to operational deployment these weapons are, is not clear – but that is not the issue of significance here. The focal issue here is the leader of a key Antarctic state boasting about his missiles being able to overfly the Antarctic:

> Voevoda's range is 11,000 km while Sarmat has practically no range restrictions. As the video clips show, it can attack targets both via the North

---

knowledge sharing; communication; timely decision making; coordination mechanisms; battle rhythm discipline; responsive, dependable, and interoperable support systems; situational awareness; and mutual trust', Joint Chiefs of Staff, *Doctrine for the Armed Forces of the United States* at xxiii. https://www.jcs.mil/Portals/36/Documents/Doctrine/pubs/jp1_ch1.pdf?ver=2019-02-11-174350-967 (accessed 1 June 2020).

38 Ibid, III-8.
39 See Dodds and Hemmings, note 10.
40 See https://www.pacom.mil/About-USINDOPACOM/USPACOM-Area-of-Responsibility/ (accessed 1 June 2020).
41 See the map 'The World with Commanders' Areas of Responsibility', 2011 https://archive.defense.gov/news/UCP_2011_Map4.pdf (accessed 1 June 2020).
42 English transcript available at http://en.kremlin.ru/events/president/news/56957 (accessed 1 June 2020).

and South poles. Sarmat is a formidable missile and, owing to its characteristics, is untroubled by even the most advanced missile defence.[43]

In late 2017, Russia successfully launched its latest nuclear-powered missile at the Central training ground. During its flight, the nuclear-powered engine reached its design capacity and provided the necessary propulsion. Now that the missile launch and ground tests were successful, we can begin developing a completely new type of weapon, a strategic nuclear weapons system with a nuclear-powered missile. Roll the video, please. You can see how the missile bypasses interceptors. As the range is unlimited, the missile can manoeuvre for as long as necessary. [Putin later refers to this weapon as the 'global range cruise missile'.][44]

To be clear, this is not a case of missiles actually being flown over the Antarctic, far less an incident involving weapons being fired into or from the Antarctic – which, we may hope, would be clearly recognised as a breach of the Antarctic Treaty's demilitarisation principles. Of course, an eventuality entailing the sort of high-end military action in which these, nuclear armed, weapons are actually used would have presented us with rather graver international circumstances than 'merely' a breach of the Antarctic Treaty – and in that case we should, realistically, be quibbling over a side-issue. But is it not fundamentally at odds with any sensible conception of Antarctica as a demilitarised space to have the leader of a key Antarctic state stating and visualising a capacity to send nuclear-armed missiles over Antarctica, en route to their destination somewhere else. Putting some rather obvious issues to one side, it was not even necessary – the missiles could have been modelled flying over similar stupendous distances across open ocean, for the purposes of the presentation. Whatever else it tells one, it says clearly that nobody involved in planning this extravaganza had seriously considered the Antarctic as a demilitarised place, and the 'atmospherics' around violating that idea.

4.3 Using High End Military Capabilities to Support Routine National Antarctic Programme Activities (Australia)

The Royal Australian Airforce (RAAF) operates eight Boeing C-17A Globemaster III, the first acquired in 2006, the last in 2015.[45] The aircraft was

---

43 https://www.youtube.com/watch?v=srapMvLKdms Video simulation at 1.33.40 shows missile flying over what seems to be the Antarctic (accessed 1 June 2020).
44 Ibid. Video simulation at 1.36.32 shows missile flying over the Antarctic Peninsula.
45 RAAF, 'C-17A Globemaster III' https://www.airforce.gov.au/technology/aircraft/air-mobility/c-17a-globemaster-iii (accessed 1 June 2020).

first used by the RAAF to support Antarctic operations in 2015,[46] although it has been used by the US to support Antarctic operations out of Christchurch since 1999. Most RAAF flights have been to and from the Wilkins ice runway near Casey station.

However, in September 2017, the RAAF started a series of cargo air drops,[47] in what seems to be a new departure in the use of the military within the Australian Antarctic programme. Enabling this was a complicated (and presumably rather expensive) military operation, with the flight out and back being 10,000 km. It involved the C-17 flying from Avalon airport near Geelong in the state of Victoria, being refuelled by an RAAF KC-30A Multi-Role Tanker 'about half-way through the mission, high above the Southern Ocean', and dropping various supplies near Davis Station.[48] The inflight refuelling occurred three hours into the outbound flight and 'RAAF Flight Lieutenant Justin McFadden, who captained the C-17A, said it was the first time Australia has conducted air-to-air refuelling over the sub-Antarctic region'.[49] In 2020, what are termed 'precision airdrops' near Casey Station have been employed using two new parachute systems – one a guided conventional parachute, the other using a 'low cost' and potentially disposable parachute.[50] It appears that this is the first use of precision-guided drops in Antarctica.

There is no doubt that the technology, and the footage of the Antarctic operations publicly available, is impressive. It allows not only drops near stations, but deep field support. As somebody who did two winters in the Antarctic and commanded a station, I can understand the appeal that the arrival of fresh food and other supplies (to say nothing of the excitement) will have for those on stations or in deep field. But, what we are seeing here plainly also has some fairly

---

46 'RAAF operates c-17 Proof of Concept Flights to Antarctica' Australian Aviation, 22 November 2015 https://australianaviation.com.au/2015/11/raaf-operates-c-17-proof-of-concept-flights-to-antarctica/ (accessed 1 June 2020).

47 Karolina Prokopovič (2017) 'RAAF C-17A Completes Antarctic Cargo Air Drop' Aviation Voice, 21 September https://aviationvoice.com/raaf-c-17a-completes-antarctic-cargo-air-drop-2-201709211216/; Australian Antarctic Division 'Airdrop ensures Australia's Antarctic runway opens on schedule' 21 September 2018 https://www.antarctica.gov.au/news/2018/airdrop-ensures-australias-antarctic-runway-opens-on-schedule/ (accessed 1 June 2020).

48 'C-17 non-stop paradrop in Antarctica' Contact 25 September 2017 https://www.contactairlandandsea.com/2017/09/25/globemaster-paradrops-in-antarctica/ (accessed 1 June 2020).

49 Ibid. On the basis of this statement, the refuelling was not carried out within the Antarctic Treaty Area.

50 'Australia lands precision Antarctic airdrop' 29 January 2020 https://www.youtube.com/watch?v=TgXyYgXDBao; 'B-Roll – RAAF C-17A airdrop to Antarctica' 30 January 2020 https://www.youtube.com/watch?v=1qWFZwnd8Vo (accessed 1 June 2020).

clear geopolitical and military purposes. In relation to the former, Australia has been developing capacities in response to what it sees as challenges within what it calls the Australian Antarctic Territory, and particularly in relation to China. These matters have been considered elsewhere.[51]

The military purpose here seems inescapable. Within a few years of acquiring the last of its eight C-17s, the RAAF was deploying them to support Australians in Antarctica, first for landings at the Wilkins airstrip, subsequently involving inflight refuelling from another military aircraft and extremely sophisticated (and evolving) parachute drop technologies. It is unlikely that the Australian Antarctic Division met the costs of these operations. Whilst these operations have been over Antarctica, in all general respects they could be any military operation anywhere in the world, and the activity has, whatever else it is, obvious training and capacity-building value for the RAAF. Media reports in 2019 suggested that the Australian Defence Force were interested in 'implementing dual-use capabilities where we can',[52] and the C-17 Antarctic deployments seem consistent with that. But, howsoever one interprets that report, in relation to the air operations itemised above, consider the likely framing and response in Australia and the wider Western Antarctic community if it had not been RAAF C-17s doing this but Chinese People's Liberation Army Air Force Y-20s.

4.4 *Obtaining Military Capabilities Designed for Use in Antarctica (New Zealand)*

Unlike many other Antarctic states, the New Zealand Antarctic agency – Antarctica New Zealand – does not have any aircraft or vessels of its own to resupply its Antarctic station (Scott Base). New Zealand's own logistic support has depended upon the Royal New Zealand Air Force C-130s (and historically – but not recently – upon ships of the Royal New Zealand Navy). This is not sufficient to provide autonomous Antarctic support for its Antarctic programme. New Zealand (NZ) Antarctic logistics is, accordingly, heavily dependent upon the United States' air and sea support. With the US main station at McMurdo being next to Scott Base, and with most US logistics in support of its own programme operating via Christchurch, NZ has essentially piggy-backed on arrangements primarily focussed on sustaining the United States own Antarctic

---

51 See, inter alia, Alan D Hemmings, 'Subglacial nationalisms' in *Anthropocene Antarctica* edited by Elizabeth Leane and Jeffrey McGee, (London: Routledge, 2020) 33–55 at 44–45.
52 Jackson Gothe-Snape, 'Defence wants to roll out military tech in Antarctica despite ban on military activity' *ABC News*, 20 August 2019, https://www.abc.net.au/news/2019-08-19/australia-antarctica-military-dual-use-technology/11427226?nw=0 (accessed 1 June 2020).

operations. The relationship is eased somewhat by the conception of a shared Antarctic pool provided by US, NZ and Italian aircraft, but the US is by far the largest contributor and the dominant partner. The US support system is overwhelmingly provided through the use of military equipment (aircraft from the US Air National Guard and US Air Force; icebreaker and transport ship support from the US Coastguard and US Navy). In geopolitical terms, NZ is faced with three sensitive issues:

a. That as a claimant to what it calls the Ross Dependency it hosts and depends upon a state that does not recognise NZ's claim (quite aside from, and prior to, the constraints of Article IV of the Antarctic Treaty) and maintains vastly greater activity levels in the claimed area than NZ is ever likely to be able to match.

b. That in operational terms it must manage a client-relationship with the US National Science Foundation and other agencies involved in the US programme, from a position of relative weakness. If NZ can contribute something that might ease the asymmetry, it seeks to do so.

c. That as a consequence of a broader (and non-Antarctic) NZ policy – namely the basket of issues around nuclear-free NZ in the 1980s, which saw the country substantially removed from the hitherto critical ANZUS relationship with the US and ended much of the military cooperation between the two states.[53] New Zealand has continued a tight military to military relationship in two main areas – intelligence cooperation through the 'Five-Eyes' arrangements;[54] and logistic cooperation in support of US and NZ Antarctic operations.

The Royal New Zealand Navy's new tanker,[55] HMNZS *Aotearoa*,[56] is the largest vessel in the navy. Its most striking feature is that it is ice strengthened to Polar Class Level 6. Although NZ is an original signatory to the 1920 Spitsbergen Treaty,[57] NZ government agencies do not conduct military or civilian activities in the Arctic. The vessel will thus be likely to only encounter polar conditions in the Antarctic. Indeed, official documents identify the vessel's purpose, beyond

---

53 For a review by a former senior NZ official, see Gerald Hensley, *Friendly Fire: Nuclear Politics and the Collapse of ANZUS, 1984–1987* (Auckland: Auckland University Press, 2013).
54 See, e.g. Robert G. Patman 'New Zealand–US Relations in the Trump Era and Beyond' in *Small States and the Changing Global Order: New Zealand Faces the Future* edited by Anne-Marie Brady, (Cham: Springer, 2019) 111–126 at 120–121.
55 The RNZN assigns it to the Class 'Auxiliary Oiler Replenishment'.
56 See Factsheet at http://navy.mil.nz/downloads/pdf/rnzn-fleet-today/hmnzs-aotearoa-fact sheet-web.pdf (accessed 1 June 2020).
57 Treaty Concerning the Archipelago of Spitsbergen, 9 February 1920, 2 LNTS 8.

general fleet support anywhere,[58] in terms of 'Southern Ocean monitoring and Antarctic operations including the resupply of McMurdo Station and Scott Base',[59] and providing 'an opportunity to incorporate ice-strengthening and winterisation features to the new ship, enabling it to support New Zealand's continued civilian presence in Antarctica through a contribution to the Joint Logistics Pool. *Aotearoa* will be able to deliver specialised Antarctic fuel, and transport containerised scientific material and supplies to McMurdo Sound'.[60]

A tanker is not of itself a weapon as (say) a destroyer is, but it is a critical force enabler and multiplier in military systems. When it is operated by a military agency such as a navy, it presents many of the same issues that Antarctic use of other military assets – such as the Australian C-17 case noted previously – such as training, testing, signalling capabilities to potential competitors or adversaries and thereby contributing to deterrence. One may adduce various mitigating circumstances, such as the fact that NZ is not ordinarily seen as a belligerent military entity, may be too small to sensibly justify possessing a 'Coastguard' service to which vessels could be assigned to more clearly detach them from conventional military services. But, HMNZS *Aotearoa* is not the only navy ship to have Antarctic purposes built into its specifications at ordering. The two Protector Class Offshore Patrol Vessels (OPV), HMNZS *Wellington* and HMNZS *Otago* which entered into service in 2010 are:

> designed for maritime surveillance, supply and support, and patrol missions around New Zealand's 15,000-kilometre coast, the Southern Ocean and into the Pacific. Their hulls are strengthened, which enables them to enter southern waters where ice may be encountered.[61]
>
> The OPVs are designed to undertake patrols in the southern ocean where ice may be encountered. The ship is not designed as an icebreaker or to enter Antarctic ice packs but has a strengthened hull that enables her to enter southern waters where ice may be encountered. The ship

---

58 The NZ Ministry of Defence argues that HMNZS *Aotearoa* is at the heart of wider 'Maritime Sustainability Capability project' https://www.defence.govt.nz/what-we-do/delivering-defence-capability/defence-capability-projects/maritime-sustainment-capability/ (accessed 1 June 2020).
59 See Factsheet, note 56.
60 See NZ Ministry of Defence, note 58.
61 Ministry of Defence 'Southern Ocean Patrol Vessel' https://www.defence.govt.nz/what-we-do/delivering-defence-capability/defence-capability-projects/southern-ocean-patrol-vessel/ (accessed 1 June 2020).

CHALLENGES TO SUBSTANTIVE DEMILITARISATION IN THE ATA 187

also has the range and other cold-climate capability to undertake operations in the freezing conditions of the southern oceans.[62]

For the tiny RNZN to have three of its vessels designed to operate in Antarctic waters surely says something about NZ's assessment of future needs and intentions. Whilst the activities for which these vessels are tagged are entirely consistent – as with Australia's C-17 activities – with Article 1.2 of the Antarctic Treaty, some other functions are also being served.

4.5   *Dual-Use Capabilities and Facilities* (*Numerous States*)

The classic critique of the limitations in the demilitarisation of the Antarctic Treaty Area focusses on dual-use technologies that are (variously) permanently sited in Antarctica. These include: satellite-based positioning system such as the US 'Global Positioning System' (GPS); the Russian 'Global Navigation Satellite System' (GLONASS) and China's 'BeiDou Navigation Satellite System' (BDS);[63] satellite-based imaging systems such as France's 'Satellite Pour l'Observation de la Terre' (SPOT); Arctic and Antarctic conjugate point satellite ground stations such as those operated by Norway in Svalbard and Dronning Maud Land;[64] and even secondary uses of the equipment in Antarctica contributing to the Comprehensive Test Ban Monitoring Sites.[65] I do not wish to explore these issues further here, beyond noting that aside the selective accusations about the real purpose of *others'* facilities in the media and by particular scholars, there has been no robust demonstration that these activities are, in general or particular, in breach of the existing demilitarisation principles of the Antarctic Treaty. Particularly in relation to positioning systems, these technologies are now so pervasive and widely embedded in everyday use across the world that it seems very difficult indeed to see how their use in the Antarctic could now be successfully disaggregated into notionally 'military' and 'civilian' usages. If that assessment is correct, then we may have an example of

---

62   Royal New Zealand Navy 'HMNZS *Otago* – P148 our navy's offshore patrol vessel', http://navy.mil.nz/downloads/pdf/rnzn-fleet-today/hmnzs-otago-factsheet-web.pdf (accessed 1 June 2020). Note that the vessel is shown in this document in open pack in the Antarctic.
63   See Anne-Marie Brady, 'China's Expanding Antarctic Interests: Implications for New Zealand', *SSANSE Policy Brief* 2, 3 June 2017), https://www.canterbury.ac.nz/media/documents/research/China's-expanding-Antarctic-interests.pdf (accessed 1 June 2020).
64   Bard Wormdal, *The Satellite War*, Privately published by the author (2011) ISBN 9781479187072.
65   The global sites, including in Antarctica, can be seen in the interactive map available at the Comprehensive Nuclear Test Ban Treaty Organisation site https://www.ctbto.org/map/ (accessed 1 June 2020).

the temporal transformation in acceptability that was proposed in relation to military-utility research.[66]

Before concluding, something needs to be said about a key policing mechanism in the demilitarisation principles, inspection.

5 Inspections

Article VII is intended to 'promote the objectives and ensure the observance of the provisions of the present Treaty'.[67] Its substantive reach is itemised in paragraphs three, four and five:

> 3. All areas of Antarctica, including all stations, installations and equipment within those areas, and all ships and aircraft at points of discharging or embarking cargoes or personnel in Antarctica, shall be open at all times to inspection by any observers designated in accordance with paragraph 1 of this Article.
> 4. Aerial observation may be carried out at any time over any or all areas of Antarctica by any of the Contracting Parties having the right to designate observers.
> 5. Each Contracting Party shall, at the time when the present Treaty enters into force for it, inform the other Contracting Parties, and thereafter shall give them notice in advance, of
>
> a) all expeditions to and within Antarctica, on the part of its ships or nationals, and all expeditions to Antarctica organized in or proceeding from its territory;
> b) all stations in Antarctica occupied by its nationals; and
> c) any military personnel or equipment intended to be introduced by it into Antarctica subject to the conditions prescribed in paragraph 2 of Article I of the present Treaty.

There have been 327 station inspections, plus 30 of ships (most are tourist vessels, some are support or research ships of national Antarctic programmes, but none are naval or coastguard ships).[68] The station inspections have been un-

---

66   See Hemmings, note 9, 237.
67   Antarctic Treaty, Art. VII.1.
68   Secretariat of the Antarctic Treaty, 'Inspections Database' https://www.ats.aq/devAS/Ats/InspectionsDatabase?lang=e (accessed 10 May 2020). Note that because the Antarctic Treaty Consultative Meeting (ATCM) was cancelled in 2020 due to the COVID-19 pandemic, the database only shows inspections reported up to the 2019 ATCM.

even; some stations have never been inspected, but six have been inspected 10 or more times.[69] Inspection of the stations of the three greatest global powers (as would be assessed today) has been relatively high,[70] but again not consistent in coverage.[71] Contemporary inspections are complicated by the fact that the Madrid Protocol also mandates inspections to ensure compliance with environmental duties,[72] and any inspection is now an amalgam based on these two quite different mandates.

The picture that emerges in relation to the inspection regime is that, in terms of the Article VII inspections at least, it has been under-utilised, patchy and may anyway be predicated on rather traditional on-site protocols. Overflight inspections seem not to have been conducted. It is not clear that traditional Article VII inspections are likely to find breaches of the demilitarisation principles. If the revolution in military affairs is factored into the assessment, it may be that we are missing the key contemporary manifestations of any military activity. If we wish to gain traction here, perhaps a rather different sort of inspection from that anticipated and codified in the late 1950s may now be necessary.

6 The Current Challenges

The foregoing issues – an historically limited formal demilitarisation under the Antarctic Treaty which has not undergone any further development during the succeeding 60 years; a profound transformation of the nature of the military project generally; the increasing complexity of inter-state relations in Antarctica; the technological enabling of resource activities there; and a changing world order – suggest that the idea of a demilitarised Antarctic may be under challenge. What are the primary current challenges to the idea of the Antarctic as a demilitarised space on the planet?

Above all, in my estimation, is the geopolitical anxiety precipitated by the manifestly fast-changing global power re-ordering. Almost independently of what the end-result of this process may be, states, and opinion leaders within those states, fear the very fact of change in what they frame as the previously

---

69 Ferraz (Brazil) 10, Great Wall (China) 12, King Sejong (Republic of Korea) 12, Arctowski (Poland) 11, Bellingshausen (USSR/Russian Federation) 15, Artigas (Uruguay) 12 – all on the relatively accessible King George Island in the South Shetlands group.
70 USA (4 stations) 19, USSR/Russian Federation (12 stations) 37, China (3 stations) 15 inspections.
71 Four of 12 USSR/Russian Federation stations, and 1 of 3 Chinese stations have never been inspected.
72 Madrid Protocol, Art. 14.

stable and predictable Antarctic regional norms and architecture. Suddenly Antarctic hegemony (US) or claimant position, or Western norms within the Antarctic are supposedly under challenge. It is not all about China, but it is largely about China. At least for the moment, because the nature of the anxiety may suggest that it could also apply to any *other* fast emerging great power – so India, Brazil, South Africa, Indonesia and others might elicit the same in time. If that is the case, and it cannot be sensibly explored further here,[73] it may speak to a more systemic anxiety at the heart of the current Antarctic regime.

Whatever the actual situation, it is the rise of China that those anxious about a range of transformations most frequently frame as the central event. Apparently, it is China that is going to destabilise the ATS, that 'really' wants to open the Antarctic up to mining, whose protected area proposals (most notably the ASMA proposal for Dome-A)[74] are materially about territorial acquisition and/or control, and which state is going to trash the place environmentally. It is China that is 'spending-big' on stations, ships and science in Antarctica. One does not have to be an apologist for China to note that so many of the things it is accused of doing in Antarctica are precisely the same things that other states have done and may still aspire to do. Even if one can share genuine concerns about Chinese behaviour, whether in general or in relation to specific acts, avoiding hypocrisy in policy responses in the Antarctic would seem sensible.

The anxiety in relation to the Antarctic displays any number of paradoxes. In a regime specifically (and seemingly successfully) crafted to contain the great geopolitical confrontation of the Cold War, there seems no confidence that those approaches – suitably modified and updated – offer any sort of architecture and norms for managing the supposed new confrontation. If one remembers that the ATS managed to navigate quite profound periods of confrontation between the US and Soviet led blocs (amongst many, the Vietnam and previous Afghan wars), it does seem remarkable that we now have so little confidence in it. A variation on this is that when it comes to China, in distinction to the West's approach to the Soviet Union (and perhaps contrariwise), there is a tendency to import perceptions of Chinese behaviour elsewhere into the Antarctic evaluation. China as the usual suspect, with little willingness to view any of its Antarctic actions as benign or neutral so long as egregious behaviour can be identified elsewhere in the world. The historic *modus operandi*

---

[73] But under development in Alan D Hemmings, Timo Koivurova and Sanna Kopra 'Anxiety and the Antarctic Legal Order'.

[74] For a summary account, see Nengye Liu, 'The heights of China's ambition in Antarctica' *The Interpreter*, 11 July 2019, https://www.lowyinstitute.org/the-interpreter/heights-china-s-ambition-antarctica (accessed 1 June 2020).

of the ATS was that Antarctica was functionally *decoupled* from general interstate relations to some extent. Never entirely of course, but if one can use that expression used in relation to opera, it was considered helpful to 'willingly suspend disbelief'. What mattered within Antarctic fora was how the state in question signalled and behaved in relation to the *Antarctic*.

That these verities are not (seemingly) seen to hold in relation to China in the Antarctic may in part explain the apparent recourse to traditional strategic management tools – attempts to contain China through bloc solidarity, freezing regime development (so that new norms cannot emerge), and even military contingency planning. The 'military-activities-that-are-not-breaches' scoped above look awfully like 'tooling-up', just in case. Are there examples of China doing the same? There may be, although I have not found any – or I should have cited them. However, perhaps a still largely centrally planned and formally communist system is so unitary that it can achieve its purposes more seamlessly than Western states where civilian–military divides are more evident.

This 'tooling' up is facilitated and legitimised through Article 1.2 of the Antarctic Treaty. This is the 'worm-hole' through which a militarisation of Antarctica can progress. Whatever its historic justification – and in the late 1950s probably only the military had the technology and training to provide much of the necessary Antarctic support and infrastructure – the case is weaker now. Elsewhere in the world, extremely complex logistical activities (think mining, hydrocarbon extraction and transport, much high-end oceanographic research) are conducted entirely within the civil sector. Why has this not been the case in Antarctica; why are the military still so heavily involved? Well, twenty years ago, with the ending of the Cold War and the adoption of the Madrid Protocol, there was a demonstrable reduction in military engagement in the Antarctic programmes of a number of states; not total, but substantial. New Zealand and the US, whilst continuing their employment of the military in the provision of inter-continental air support (but even here there were some changes),[75] moved from helicopters operated by their militaries to civilian contractors.[76] The Australian Antarctic Division took over the tasks delivered by the Australian Army's 'ANARE Detachment' in 1994.[77] The more recent increase in military engagement in both the Australian and NZ programmes is

---

75   In the case of the US, this involved the US Air National Guard taking over from the US Navy as the operators of the LC-130 fleet in 1999.
76   In the case of the US, from the 1996/97 and for New Zealand, from the 1999/20 season.
77   Mike Cecil (2006) 'Remember when …. We sent amphibious trucks to the Antarctic?' On Target, November https://web.archive.org/web/20081201193633/http://www.defence.gov.au/dmo/news/ontarget/nov06/rw.cfm (accessed 3 June 2020).

thus a reversal of that post-Cold War policy. It reflects too an increasing acceptance and exploitation of the concept of dual-use – or at least it does if *we* are doing it. The Antarctic is not isolated from norms and trends elsewhere, and we see renewed enthusiasm for military 'solutions' both globally and in the Arctic. For those states that operate in both polar regions, 'leakage' of practice and hardware that is usable in both may therefore be an additional accelerant.

7   Conclusion – What Can We Do about This?

Analysis of a problem does not necessarily entail an obligation to provide a solution. However, the analysis here plainly indicates that the present author believes there is a problem that requires response, if we are (in the words in the Preamble to the Antarctic Treaty) to ensure that Antarctica is 'used exclusively for peaceful purposes and … not become the scene or object of international discord'. Recognising that the nature and mechanism of such a response will, if it occurs at all, be a complex diplomatic process (and who, looking at global political leadership in 2020 can be sanguine about outcomes), I conclude by offering some proposals for action.

First, we need to again talk about 'security' issues within ATCMs and other formal and informal fora of the ATS. The sense that these issues were satisfactorily and finally resolved back in the 1950s during the negotiation of the Antarctic Treaty (and adequately covered in that Treaty) is, frankly, ridiculous. Much has changed in the world since then, and particularly in relation to military doctrine and practice. Integral to such a discourse is some serious effort to clarify, agree and codify what 'measures of a military nature' are today. From such a process we would then be in a far more robust position to characterise and operationalise what 'demilitarisation' would require today. Doing this need not necessarily entail a renegotiation of the Antarctic Treaty (a contingency that some, opposed to updating our understandings of military measures and demilitarisation, may well flag as too risky). The new understandings could be codified in a legally binding Measure – or if that proved impossible, through a hortatory Resolution – adopted by consensus at an ATCM.[78]

The actual practice of inspections conducted in furtherance of the historic Antarctic Treaty Article VII warrants attention (the practice in relation to Madrid Protocol Article 14 inspections is more robust and need not be

---

78   The tripartite decision making system was codified in Decision 1 (1995) 'Measures, Decisions and Resolutions' https://www.ats.aq/devAS/Meetings/Measure/221 (accessed 1 June 2020).

affected). If we have clarified our security constructs, that will of itself provide new guidance for what inspections should look for. Updating the mechanism of inspections may also be required. Site visits will no doubt continue, but a much more robust inspection regime would be provided by overflights and satellite surveillance. To give just one instance – the remarkable fact that China's Kunlun station has been the focus of particular anxiety in some quarters, yet has not been subject to an inspection, may be explained away by its geographical remoteness and difficulty of access (although other, equally remote, plateau stations operated by great powers have been inspected) could be readily addressed by aerial or satellite overflight. As noted above, there seem to have been no declared overflight inspections in Antarctica. One presumes that there has been satellite surveillance,[79] but this has not been formally reported through the Antarctic Treaty if it has. In light of the Trump administration's repudiation of the Treaty on Open Skies it may not be the best time to propose it, but a formalised Antarctic overflight inspection agreement and reporting of satellite surveillance would be a useful development of the Antarctic inspection regime.

Dual-use equipment, facilities and activities pose very real challenges to Antarctic demilitarisation, but they also present challenges of patrolling. With time, the relative benefit of 'dual-use technology' (if we use that term to capture the whole basket of issues) may shift from a preponderant benefit to military users to a wider civilian utility. A questioner sensibly asked when an earlier version of this paper was presented at the 12th Polar Law Symposium, 'how does one address dual-use when it is so pervasive?' My sense is that it would be useful to require transparency and reporting through a development of the existing advance notice obligations under Paragraph 5 of Article VII of the Antarctic Treaty. This would enable other states to interrogate the usage, and if necessary object to its continuation – if necessary, invoking the dispute settlement provisions. But, beyond this, I think we need to see states exercising a self-denying ordinance and not use advanced military systems to support *routine* national operations in Antarctica. The case for calling upon such military capabilities *in extremis*, in response to emergencies or entirely unforeseen events need not be contested. This is, basically, an argument for a case of *compelling need* being made before use of such capabilities, rather than the currently emerging pattern of normalising anything on grounds of convenience.

If we wish to substantively remove concern about what states are actually up to or doing at their stations, there is surely a case for seriously engaging with

---

79   See Alan Boyd, 'Cold war chill settles over Antarctica' *Asia Times*, 7 March 2019, https://asiatimes.com/2019/03/cold-war-chill-settles-over-antarctica/ (accessed 1 June 2020).

the idea of international stations and other joint facilities.[80] The concern here is to encourage demilitarisation, but such a project also promises benefits for the conduct of science, the reduction of environmental impact, and economic and opportunity cost (perhaps more acute with depressed economies 'post' COVID-19).[81]

Finally, might we benefit from a wider reassessment of the modus operandi of the ATS? The technical engagement model of ATS operation, which has since the adoption of the Madrid Protocol seen progressively less and less attention to substantive policy-making and political visualisation of the Antarctic, may be a problem. My view is that we would be better placed if we saw that technical engagement as an adjunct to, and not a substitute for, diplomacy. The Antarctic remains an intensely contested geopolitical space, and there is nothing about it that will of itself ensure that we do not do what we have done everywhere else as a result of contestation.

Acknowledgements

An earlier version of this paper was presented at the 12th Polar Law Symposium in Hobart in December 2019. I thank the organiser of that symposium, Julia Jabour, for the opportunity to participate in that meeting, for her sterling work in organizing it, and for enabling me to present this more refined paper in The Yearbook of Polar Law edited by her. I also thank the participants in the Hobart symposium for helpful comments on the oral presentation there, which I hope has improved the subsequent development of the case here. Of course, none of these people are responsible for the analysis and positions adopted here, for which (and for any errors or oversights therein) the author remains solely responsible.

---

80   Alan D Hemmings, 'Why did we get an International Space Station before an International Antarctic Station?' *The Polar Journal* 1 (2011) 5–16; Alan D Hemmings, 'International Antarctic Stations' in *Antarctic Resolution* edited by Giulia Foscari, (Baden: Lars Müller Publishers, in press 2021).
81   Alan D Hemmings and Bob Frame, 'Antarctica's Latest Challenge: Coronavirus' in Ibid.

Arctic Law

Lessons from the Finland's Chairmanship of the Arctic Council: What Will Happen with the Arctic Council and in General Arctic Governance

*Timo Koivurova**

1   Introduction**

For a long time, many of us observing Arctic affairs have been using the term 'Rovaniemi Arctic spirit'[1] when we refer to Arctic international cooperation. It aims to capture the sentiment that it is in this region that Arctic states can foster peace and international cooperation, even if there are tensions between their overall relations. The name derives from the fact that Arctic intergovernmental cooperation between the eight Arctic states commenced in Rovaniemi with the signing of the Arctic Environmental Protection Strategy.[2] This Rovaniemi Arctic spirit is now in danger.

The 2019 Rovaniemi ministerial meeting that ended the Finnish chairmanship of the Council was the first ministerial meeting in which the Arctic states could not sign onto a joint declaration, mainly because US did not want to have any mention of climate change, the biggest threat to the region. Moreover, just before the ministerial meeting, the Secretary of State of the United States, Mike Pompeo, wanted to give an open presentation on the US's views of Arctic cooperation, and Pompeo aired out his concerns towards military threats posed by China and Russia in the Arctic region. Because of these developments, this article asks what will be the future of the Arctic Council, given that climate

---

* Research Professor, Director of Arctic Centre, University of Lapland, Rovaniemi, Finland. timo.koivurova@ulapland.fi.
** This paper is based on the presentation by author in the 12th Polar Law Symposium in Hobart, Tasmania, on 1 December 2019. Some parts of this paper have been shortly argued in a blog post in Polar Connection, "Is this the End of the Arctic Council and Arctic Governance as we know it?", at http://polarconnection.org/arctic-council-governance-timo-koivurova/.
1 The term derives from the start of the inter-governmental cooperation between the eight Arctic states, when they signed the Arctic Environmental Protection Strategy in 1991 in the city of Rovaniemi, Finland. The AEPS was merged into the Canadian initiative the Arctic Council in 1996.
2 See Arctic Environmental Protection Strategy, 14 January 1991, 30 ILM 1624.

change work is so big portion of what the Council does. As the Arctic Council is part and parcel of general international governance of the region, it is also important to ponder whether the Arctic can be kept as a region of low tension. The statements by the US national leadership have placed a question mark as to whether we can keep the cooperative Arctic spirit as the predominant mode of Arctic international cooperation.

The article progresses in the following way. First, it is important to briefly review how the Arctic Council and its climate change work have evolved to a more ambitious direction in few most recent years. Thereafter, the focus will be on Finland's Arctic Council chairmanship. Two periods will be examined: first, the time during which Finland prepared its chairmanship programme (2015 to 2017) and when the country served as the chair of the Council (2017 to 2019).[3] Closer scrutiny will be on what happened during the Rovaniemi ministerial meeting, and why. After reviewing these developments, it is possible to provide tentative responses to the main questions of what will happen with the Arctic Council and Arctic governance in general. These will be dealt with in the concluding section of the article.

The article is based on the insights the author had during the Finnish chairmanship of the Arctic Council between 2017 and 2019. I was leading a consortium that provided knowledge and information briefings to the various ministries that were in charge of implementing Finland's Arctic Council chairmanship, and also served as a Finnish delegate in both Fairbanks and Rovaniemi ministerial meetings.[4] I also served as a co-lead, together with Saara Tervaniemi, Saami Council representative, in one of Arctic Council's Sustainable Development Working Group's expert committees, that of Social, Economic and Cultural Expert Group (SECEG).[5] In addition, I have carried semi-structured interviews with all the key ministry persons who were in charge of implementing the Finland's Arctic Council and Arctic Economic Council chairmanships.[6]

---

3   My own experience stems from the Finnish chairmanship of the Arctic Council between 2017 and 2019. Not only did I play multiple roles in implementing that chairmanship, but also I interviewed all the key civil servants and diplomats who were in charge of various aspects of the Finnish chairmanship.

4   The author was also a chair of the so-called Arctic Council host committee, which consisted of various stakeholders in Lapland who wanted to provide information and showcase their products outside the official meetings of the Council that took place in Lapland.

5   See more at https://www.sdwg.org/expert-groups/social-economic-and-cultural-expert-group/ (accessed 1 July 2020).

6   The interviewees were asked to outline what were the goals at the start, how the work was progressing, what were the problematic areas, and how do they evaluate that the goals set at the beginning were achieved.

2 Evolution of the Arctic Council

In few recent years, the Arctic Council has developed to be a more ambitious inter-governmental governance forum. This has been manifested in various ways. Institutionally, the Council has gotten stronger. In 2013, the permanent secretariat of the Arctic Council commenced its work in Tromsø Norway.[7] The Council has also revised many of its internal rules to accommodate increased interest in the Council's work. Particularly important was that the Council was able to adopt criteria as to how applications for observer status can be evaluated. In recent years, the number of observers, also major non-Arctic states (such as China) has increased. Currently there are 39 observers in the Council, with European Union enjoying an observer-in-principle status.[8] It is also significant that it is only two last ministerial meetings in which the foreign ministers of the Arctic states have participated, which tells about the growing importance of the Council. The Council has also commenced work on its first ever long-term strategy, work that continues now in Icelandic chairmanship.

The Arctic Council has also facilitated the negotiations of legally binding agreements between the eight Arctic states. These have been the 2011 search and rescue agreement,[9] 2013 oil spills agreement[10] and 2017 international science agreement.[11] This has been done via the task-forces of the Council. In addition, the Council has catalysed independent international forums between the Arctic states that can assist the Council in its work, the most recent of these

---

7 See further info at https://arctic-council.org/index.php/en/about-us/arctic-council/the-arctic-council-secretariat (accessed 1 July 2020).

8 See more at https://arctic-council.org/index.php/en/about-us/arctic-council/observers (accessed 1 July 2020). The European Union's observer application has been received by the Council but no decision has not yet been taken, meaning that EU is treated like any other observer in the Council, even if it is not formally an observer. The reason for this status for the EU is that Russia has objected to giving the EU the status of an observer, but the Council has not made a negative decision on the matter.

9 Agreement on Cooperation on Aeronautical and Maritime Search and Rescue in the Arctic (signed 2011), can be downloaded at https://oaarchive.arctic-council.org/handle/11374/531 (accessed 1 July 2020).

10 Agreement on Cooperation on Marine Oil Pollution Preparedness and Response in the Arctic (signed 2013), can be downloaded at https://oaarchive.arctic-council.org/handle/11374/529 (accessed 1 July 2020).

11 Agreement on Enhancing International Arctic Scientific Cooperation (signed 2017), can be downloaded at this site https://oaarchive.arctic-council.org/handle/11374/1916 (accessed 1 July 2020).

being the Arctic Economic Council,[12] the Arctic Coast-Guard Forum[13] and the Arctic Offshore Regulators forum.[14]

2.1 Evolution of the Council's Climate Change Work

The clear shift in Council's emphasis as regards climate change took place when the Arctic Climate Impact Assessment (ACIA) was undertaken between 1998 to 2004. This ground-breaking large-scale assessment of climate change (and ozone layer depletion) that assessed the speed at which climate change progresses in the Arctic as well as what consequences are already visible in the region.[15] ACIA established the Arctic as an early warning of climate change, since the region warms twice the rate as compared to global average and has a significant impact on the work agenda of the Arctic Council.

Since climate change is the main driver of long-term changes in the region, it is directly or indirectly included in most projects under the Council. Yet, the Council has also increasingly had projects on climate change. It has conducted climate science projects after the ACIA, such as the Snow, Water, Ice and Permafrost in the Arctic (SWIPA) assessment[16] and various types of adaptation to climate change consequences in the region projects.[17] Importantly, the framework programme on black carbon and methane also commits Arctic states and few observer states to reduce those short-lived climate forcers, so the Council is therefore engaged with climate mitigation.[18]

3 Finland's Arctic Council Chairmanship

Finland's previous Arctic Council chairmanship was from 2000 to 2002[19] and the country prepared intensively for the 2017–2019 chairmanship, given that now the Council is clearly a much more ambitious international governance forum than at the beginning of 2000.

---

12   See https://arcticeconomiccouncil.com/ (accessed 1 July 2020).
13   See https://www.arcticcoastguardforum.com/ (accessed 1 July 2020).
14   See https://oaarchive.arctic-council.org/handle/11374/1729 (accessed 1 July 2020).
15   See https://acia.amap.no/ (accessed 1 July 2020).
16   See https://swipa.amap.no/ (accessed 1 July 2020).
17   For instance, Adaptation Actions for a Changing Arctic, at https://arctic-council.org/index.php/en/our-work2/8-news-and-events/193-adaptation-actions-for-a-changing-arctic (accessed 1 July 2020).
18   See https://arctic-council.org/index.php/en/expert-groups/339-egbcm (accessed 1 July 2020).
19   See the programme for the Finnish chairmanship for the 2000 to 2002, see https://oaarchive.arctic-council.org/handle/11374/1781 (accessed 1 July 2020).

3.1 Preparing the Chairmanship Programme

Finland prepared its chairmanship programme during the United States chairmanship (2015–2017)). Foreign ministry's Arctic officials commenced this process already in 2015 and there were many discussions in Finland and abroad much before its first presentation. With the good practice established by the previous chairs, Finland consulted with all the other member states about its proposed priorities. Yet, Finland also organized a joint meeting with the permanent participants, which apparently was the first time that all the Permanent Participants were able to comment on the chairmanship priorities. Finnish Sami parliament was also consulted, even if that body does not have a seat in the Arctic Council. This shows how carefully the Arctic officials in the foreign ministry wanted to have the country's priorities discussed and agreed upon much ahead of the start of the chairmanship. The chairmanship programme was effectively presented already in Portland SAO meeting in October 2016 and remained virtually unchanged till the ministerial meeting in 2017.[20]

Finland's chairmanship programme very much reflected the ambitious Obama-era priorities of the US chairmanship: along with other goals, we expressed our willingness to implement the Paris climate agreement and the UN Sustainable Development Goals (UN SDGs) via the Arctic Council. Four other 'national' priorities are: environment, education, meteorology and connectivity. These are national priorities in a very limited manner as being a chair of an inter-governmental forum means that first and foremost the chair state is expected to deliver on the objectives of the forum. Finland's four goals are well developed since they both serve in reaching the objectives of the Arctic Council but serve also to consolidate the expertise of Finland in those areas within which Finland already has a strong expertise. The idea behind this is that Finland can become a leader (or one of them) in certain aspects of Arctic expertise.[21]

Yet, the first challenge was already around the corner. It was not Hillary Clinton who was elected as the President of the United States, but Donald Trump, whose priorities were diametrically opposed to those of the Obama

---

[20] Timo Koivurova, "Finland's chairmanship program for the Arctic: Setting priorities", in *The Arctic in Word Affairs: A North Pacific Dialogue on Building Capacity for a Sustainable Arctic in a Changing Global Order* 2017 North Pacific Arctic Conference Proceedings. RW Corell, JD Kim, YH Kim, & OR Young, (eds.) (Busan: Korea Maritime Institute, 2017), 47–54 (KMI/EWC Series on the Arctic in World Affairs, Vol. 7).a.

[21] Timo Koivurova, "How science can influence the way Finland's chairmanship in the Arctic Council is advanced", in Ibid; Timo Koivurova, "Perspective from Finland 2018", in Ibid, 73–79.

administration. Trump had openly undermined both the Paris climate agreement and multilateral frameworks in general in his campaign.

So, when the Fairbanks ministerial meeting of 11 May 2017 drew near, we found ourselves in a very tricky situation: our chairmanship programme was built on those multilateral frameworks that the Trump administration was thought to oppose. During the Spring of 2017 there were many debates as to what will happen with the Finland's chosen priorities, especially those of implementing Paris climate agreement and the SDG's via the Arctic Council.

And this did manifest itself in the Fairbanks ministerial meeting. When we, in the Finnish delegation, made our way to Fairbanks, we heard that the then Secretary of State Rex Tillerson had challenged the Fairbanks declaration. This caused a lot of uproar, and diplomats from all the other seven Arctic Council member states were busy trying to convince Tillerson and his aides that the declaration is acceptable. Finally, Tillerson did accept the declaration, and it was ultimately signed, but he did mention in the final plenary that the Trump administration had not yet made up its mind about whether or not to stay in the Paris climate agreement.[22] The good side, from the viewpoint of the Finns, was this: we could commence our chairmanship programme with our stated priorities.

3.2   *Implementing the Chairmanship*

The initial stages of the chairmanship were fairly problem-free but gradually the imprint of the Trump administration started to manifest itself. The US had a very ambitious Arctic Council chairmanship 2015–2017 and had, for example, commenced two initiatives to make the Council a more ambitious and strategic forum: to establish a Marine Commission within the Arctic Council to consolidate the marine policy of the Arctic waters and to adopt the first ever long-term strategy for the Council. Finland, hence, was tasked with completing these projects as the next chair, but unfortunately was unable to finalise either. The United States, which commenced the Marine Commission work, was also one country that was now against establishing the Commission.[23] The long-term strategy work continued until the final stages of Finland's chairmanship, but there were several reasons why it could not be adopted. Sadly, one of these reasons was that we did not want to have a first-ever long-term strategy for the Council that would not mention climate change.

---

22   And, as we now know, they have announced their withdrawal from the Paris climate agreement.
23   Interview with Anita Mäkinen from the Finnish Transport Safety Agency, who was one of the co-leads of this work (16 April 2019).

Finland was also leading the expert group on black carbon and methane, which became a visible activity during our chairmanship, given that our President was actively discussing the issue of black carbon with both Presidents Putin and Trump. Unfortunately, by the end of the work, the US did not accept anymore the collective goal that was agreed in the Fairbanks declaration for black carbon reduction: 25–33% reduction by 2025 from their 2013 emission levels. Furthermore, the US did not perceive the work in this expert group as climate change mitigation but as related to curtailing air pollution, and was generally against referring to multilateral frameworks in this work. Russia, on its part, had difficulties in delivering information to the expert group.[24]

In my own work as the chair of Social, Economic and Cultural Expert Group, an expert group under the Arctic Council's Sustainable Development Working Group (SDWG), the problem turned out to be the UN Sustainable Development Goals (SDG). When I presented our work to the SDWG, at first the US representative said that I can talk of UN SDGs in general, but not of the individual goals of the UN SDGs. Then, in the February 2019 SDWG meeting, the US representative asked me not to refer anymore to the UN SDGs at all.

On the other hand, Finland's own "national" priorities advanced well. All these various four priorities were developed via different ways. Education priority was advanced via the SDWG project on "Teacher Education for Diversity and Equality in the Arctic"[25] and conclusions from this project were endorsed by the SDWG.[26] This work is also continuing under the University of the Arctic's thematic network in this area. The Finnish Chairmanship's meteorology priority has led to the first and second Arctic Meteorology Summits and was able to advance both meteorological cooperation between the eight Arctic states and also integrating this joint work to assist the various areas of action in the working-groups of the Arctic Council.[27] The priority on connectivity is advancing primarily through the Task Force on Improved Connectivity in the Arctic (TFICA) and the task-force was able to achieve its aims to "compare

---

24 Interview with Mikael Hilden from the Finnish Environment Institute who chaired the expert group during the Finland's chairmanship (25 April 2019).

25 More information on the project can be accessed at http://www.sdwg.org/activities/sdwg-projects-2017-2019/teacher-education-for-diversity-and-equality-in-the-arctic/ (accessed 1 July 2020).

26 Interview with Dr. Tuija Turunen from the university of Lapland, who led the project during the Finland's chairmanship (18 April 2019). See also Meeting Summary Sustainable Development Working Group (SDWG), Kemi, Finland, 04–06 February 2019, at https://oaarchive.arctic-council.org/bitstream/handle/11374/2335/SAOFI204_2019_RUKA_InfoDoc12_SDWG_Chairs-Summary.pdf?sequence=1&isAllowed=y (accessed 1 July 2020).

27 Interview with Johanna Ekman from the Finnish Meteorological Institute (FMI) who was a key person advancing this from the FMI (23 April 2019).

the needs of those who live, operate, and work in the Arctic with available infrastructure, and work with the telecommunications industry and the Arctic Economic Council to encourage the creation of required infrastructure with an eye toward pan-Arctic solutions".[28] Finland's most concrete contribution to advancing its environmental protection priority was the SDWG project "Good Practice Recommendations for Environmental Impact Assessment and Public Participation in the Arctic", which aims at "providing Arctic-specific recommendations that can be applied in the vulnerable and changing Arctic environment, taking into account the indigenous peoples and other inhabitants living there".[29] These were accepted to enable better EIA's in Arctic conditions and also received international recognition from the International Association of Impact Assessment.[30]

Overall, when the Rovaniemi ministerial meeting approached, most of us knew that the Trump administration's values and priorities had started to influence the work of the Arctic Council, but it is also equally clear that we could not foresee what was ahead of us. The US challenge to the work of the Arctic Council had been visible but it was not systematic. Most work in the Council was still going forward relatively well, especially the achievement of our national priorities.

3.3   Rovaniemi Ministerial Meeting

The Rovaniemi ministerial meeting received an unexpected start. Surprisingly, the Secretary of State Mike Pompeo wanted to give an unscheduled presentation on 6 May, just before the actual ministerial meeting in the same hockey arena where the ministerial meeting would take place the next day. Most of us who were invited to hear this speech were also surprised about its aggressive tone. Pompeo aired out the Trump administration's concerns towards both China and Russia. He perceived that China's behaviour needs to be carefully monitored because, according to him, China will likely be as dubious an actor in the Arctic as it has been elsewhere in the world. He also argued that China is already a military threat in the Arctic and will only be more so in the future. For Pompeo, Russia also poses a threat, given that it has militarised its Arctic regions and has enacted an illegal decree to impede navigation along the

---

[28]   Interview with Marjukka Vihavainen-Pitkänen from the Ministry of Transport and Communications, who served as the co-chair of the Task-Force (23 April 2019).

[29]   Interview with Päivi Karvinen from the Ministry for the Environment, who was one of the leads of the project (24 April 2019), see https://www.sdwg.org/activities/sdwg-projects-2017-2019/arctic-eia/ (accessed 1 July 2020).

[30]   See https://arcticeconomiccouncil.com/globalpress-release-award-of-the-international-association-for-impact-assessment-iaia-to-arctic-eia-project/ (accessed 1 July 2020).

Northern Sea Route. The tone of his speech was aggressive, and he advanced the Arctic not as a place for peaceful cooperation but one of strategic competition. These views have been confirmed by the then national security adviser Bolton[31] and President Trump himself.[32]

There were many problems that Finland's chairmanship faced during the actual Rovaniemi ministerial meeting ending the Finnish chairmanship. The preparation of the declaration, as usual, was commenced much before the ministerial meeting. During the weekend before the ministerial (6–7 May 2019), the Senior Arctic Officials (SAOs) were able to remove most of the bracketed sentences, and by Sunday, 5 May 2019, the declaration was acceptable to all the eight Arctic states.[33]

Yet, gradually over that weekend, the US delegation leadership was overtaken by high-level officials from the US State Department. For this reason, few hours after the declaration had been accepted, the US informed that it no longer consents to the declaration, and it proposed its own draft for a declaration, which lacked any references to climate change. This was a vast surprise to other delegations, given that much of the Arctic Council's work deals directly or indirectly with climate change, and the other states signalled their disapproval of the US proposal. On Monday, the foreign ministers convened in the Arktikum building in Rovaniemi for a dinner, which was the final opportunity for Finland to bridge these two opposing views. Yet, the US was adamant in not having climate change mentioned in the declaration, and the other delegations were equally clear that climate change needs to be mentioned. Hence,

---

31 See e.g. https://www.arctictoday.com/with-coast-guard-commencement-speech-bolton-pushes-the-trump-administrations-newly-aggressive-arctic-stance/ (accessed 1 July 2020).
32 Yet, during the visit by the President of Finland with President Trump in Washington DC in October 2019 the two issued a joint statement whereby they confirmed the status of the region as low-tension. They for instance stated that "The United States and Finland, as members of the Arctic Council, want to maintain the Arctic as a region of cooperation and low tension. Security, sustainable development, environmental protection, the well-being of the people living in the Arctic, and cooperation in this important region are essential to us. Arctic governance, guided by applicable international law, is the responsibility of Arctic nations, particularly through the Arctic Council". See https://www.whitehouse.gov/briefings-statements/joint-statement-president-united-states-president-republic-finland/ (accessed 1 July 2020). Yet, Trump also emphasised that the Arctic should be governed by Arctic states and referred also to freedom of navigation operations in the region. Hence, both the issues that Pompeo identified before the Rovaniemi ministerial meeting were also implicitly included by what Trump said, see https://www.arctictoday.com/trump-niinisto-remarks-show-two-different-visions-of-the-arctic/ (accessed 1 July 2020).
33 Interview with the chair of Senior Arctic Officials, Aleksi Härkönen from the Ministry for Foreign Affairs (13 May 2019).

Finnish diplomats needed to acknowledge that, realistically, no signed declaration could be achieved.

This started a busy period of coming up with a solution on how to save the Rovaniemi ministerial meeting and continue the work of the Arctic Council. Finland's solution was based on the already existing declaration and was twofold: signing a joint statement by all the eight Arctic states, which welcomed the Icelandic chairmanship and its chairmanship programme and contained preambular type of language, and a statement by the chair (foreign minister of Finland) as to what was agreed in the meeting and what was not, underlining that the others placed a lot of emphasis on climate change and the US objected (phrased in a way that 'most of us agreed').

Yet, this was not the end of the challenge from the US viewpoint. The US delegation was also not ready to adopt the SAO report as it contained a lot of references to climate change, and it asked Finland to remove it from the agenda of the plenary. Why is this report so important? It contained the working plans of all six working-groups of the Arctic Council and also the budget of the Council secretariat. Finland took a conscious risk and placed it on the agenda of the ministerial meeting, just before the signing of the joint ministerial statement, thinking that the US would not dare to challenge the consensus in this formal meeting. This strategy proved successful, and the US did not object to the SAO report in the plenary of the ministerial.

4 What Will Happen with the Arctic Council?

These events lead to serious questions. Was there a real challenge to the further functioning of the Arctic Council? No. The US did welcome the short signed ministerial statement, in which the Icelandic chairmanship and chairmanship programme were approved. Yet, it did object to the acceptance of the SAO report, which was meant to guarantee the continuation of work-plans of the working-groups and secure the budget for the Arctic Council secretariat. This was a real challenge since no one was able to tell at the time how we could continue the work of the working-groups, as normally these are authorised by a signed declaration and now they were not. This needs to be kept in mind, even if ultimately the SAO report was accepted, with the daring strategy from the Finnish chairmanship.

Why did the ministerial meeting then become such a dramatic event? As I already mentioned, there were some signs of Trump administration priorities starting to influence the views and behaviour of few US officials during the

Finnish chairmanship. Yet, clearly the bigger challenge came from the fact that the US delegation leadership changed just before the ministerial, which then led to greater challenges in the ministerial meeting. It did seem that this new leadership was not much aware of what the Arctic Council does, which then, in part, led to significant problems in keeping the Arctic Council going.

What will happen with the Arctic Council? Perhaps it can continue as before, now that all the important documents have been adopted by the Rovaniemi ministerial. The first signs from the Icelandic chairmanship are bright, things are moving well, but so they were even at the beginning of the Finnish chairmanship. Yet, now that we know that US officials were implementing the Trump agenda during the Finnish chairmanship and that the US did not accept climate change even mentioned during the ministerial meeting, it is difficult to maintain that nothing has changed (at least until the end of Trump presidency). It is a fact that the Trump administration is against exactly those climate change and multilateral frameworks that are at the core of how the Arctic Council functions.

What will be important is who will be nominated as the next SAO of the US, as currently there is an interim SAO. It is not even sure that a regular SAO will be nominated, but if this does take place and if this person is close to Trump administration (as one can suspect), this nomination would have a wider impact on the functioning of the Arctic Council. This is because it is the SAOs that co-ordinate all the work within the Arctic Council. It is also important to highlight the importance of the results of the next Presidential elections in the US in November 2020. If a Democrat wins, it is likely that the functioning of the Arctic Council will be restored to normal, indicating how much the current challenge to the Arctic Council and Arctic governance is related to Trump himself.

If Trump wins the re-election, it seems quite likely that the Council will also change. It is difficult to foresee that if Trump gets another four years continuation for his Presidency, climate change work in the Arctic Council could continue. In this scenario, it is more likely that the Council gradually focuses more on traditional environmental protection and sustainable development, with a heavy tilt towards advancing economic opportunities in the region.

What will then happen with the climate change work of the Council? It is my belief that this will continue in other international cooperation forums that are plentiful in the Arctic, science and university organisations but also in other intergovernmental forums where the US is not a member, such as the Nordic Council or the Barents Euro-Arctic Council. If climate change work will be scaled down from the Arctic Council, how would the other member states react to this. I do think that, in this scenario, other Arctic Council member states would see it more important to continue Council cooperation than pulling out of it because of obstacles to continue climate change work.

5   What Will Happen with Arctic International Governance?

What about the future direction of Arctic international governance in general? After all, the Arctic Council is only part and parcel of the larger governance framework of the region. For long, we have been defining the Arctic as an exceptional area, a region to which the general tensions of the major powers will mostly not extend. This has been a longstanding policy of all Arctic states – to keep the Arctic outside these tensions and build collaborative structures to advance sustainable development in the region. A good example of this is the Ukraine controversy and conflict. All the other Arctic Council member states participated in sanctions against Russia, and Russia counter-sanctioned. Yet, this did not prevent the Arctic and other actors from building further international cooperation – the Arctic Council functioned fine, and produced a new legally binding agreement on scientific cooperation in 2017; the Polar Code entered force in 2017; and the Central Arctic Ocean Fisheries agreement was signed in 2018.

Yet, now we have an Arctic Council member state, USA, which openly challenges Russia and wants to fight its global "war" with China also in the Arctic, as shown by the Pompeo speech in Rovaniemi. The US also denies the existence of climate change, even if it clearly is the biggest threat to the future of the Arctic and forms a main part of the work that the Arctic collaborative arrangements focus on. It is because of this change in the geopolitical situation that, at the last Arctic Circle, the Prime Ministers of Finland and Iceland were discussing whether we should include hard security issues in the agenda of the Arctic Council – and at least the Icelandic premier seemed to be of that opinion.[34] In general, discussion has increased on the need to have hard security issues being discussed in the Arctic Council or in some other forum.

The US tries to portray the Arctic as a place for strategic competition, which works against the image most of us have had of the region – that of being a place for peace and international cooperation. Mostly the US has moved forward with heavy words, rather than actions, and we have to see how serious the Trump administration is in its Arctic actions. But words also matter. The

---

34   See https://www.highnorthnews.com/en/why-finland-and-iceland-want-security-politics-arctic-council (accessed 1 July 2020).

world's only superpower can create realities simply by re-stating what is happening in the Arctic, in its own view, however wrongly it would capture the reality of the region. If this were to become the perceived reality of the region, we may still have international cooperation and the Arctic Council functioning in the region, but their relative importance would diminish.

6   Concluding Words

It is, hence, difficult to conclude in any other way than to say that there are grave uncertainties as to how the Arctic Council and Arctic international governance in general will develop. We know that the Arctic Council and Arctic governance will continue to face serious challenges as long as Trump remains the President of the United States. The framework of Arctic governance will be put into a test of resilience – how can climate change work continue when the US does not even want to have that term in a declaration, or wants to portray the region as a place for strategic competition?

Will we, 10 years from now, recall that it was the Rovaniemi Arctic Council ministerial meeting where we lost the Rovaniemi Arctic spirit that was triggered in that very same town with the conclusion of the AEPS. Those of us who deeply care about the Arctic Council and the future of the Arctic should be aware of what is happening and should do our utmost to speak for the values the Arctic Council represents.

The Long Grass at the North Pole

Andrew Serdy*

Abstract

Though legally no more significant than any other point in the Arctic Ocean, into which State's continental shelf the geographic North Pole will ultimately fall is politically charged for the three States involved – Canada, Denmark (Greenland) and Russia – that have submitted to the Commission on the Limits of the Continental Shelf outer limits within which the Pole falls. The 2014 Danish submission, for an area extending beyond the equidistance line with Canada, was in that sense paradoxically helpful to Canada, as Denmark, with the northernmost land territory, is by definition closest to the Pole, which must therefore lie on its side of any such line drawn between itself and any other State; thus Denmark gave cover to Canada which needed to take a similar approach to define its continental shelf entitlement as including the North Pole. Boundaries will eventually have to be delimited, but as it likely to be 20 years before the Commission examines the last of the submissions, the three States have ample pretext to postpone this step until then, a solution likely to suit them all.

Keywords

North Pole – Continental Shelf – UNCLOS (United Nations Convention on the Law of the Sea) – Commission on the Limits of the Continental Shelf – Canada – Denmark – Russia

1 Introduction

Different topics and specialisations within public international law capture the public imagination at different times, and while the three United Nations

---

* School of Law, University of Southampton, United Kingdom, A.L.Serdy@soton.ac.uk; originally presented as a paper of the same title at the 12th Polar Law Symposium, Institute for Marine and Antarctic Studies, Hobart, 2 December 2019. The author thanks an anonymous reviewer for helpful comments.

Conferences on the Law of the Sea attracted the attention of many legal scholars, making for a healthy subdiscipline, for around a quarter of a century, after the product of the last such conference, the United Nations Convention on the Law of the Sea[1] (UNCLOS) was adopted, the law of the sea became decidedly unfashionable. Notwithstanding its initially uncertain prospects for entry into force, most casual observers would have assumed that, with that momentous step, the main problems were now resolved and all that was left were uninteresting matters of technical detail. If that reason for the ensuing relative obscurity of the law of the sea is an oversimplification, its return to prominence in 2007 was also due to a widespread misunderstanding. The placement of a titanium flag on the seabed at the geographic North Pole by a group of Russian researchers triggered an avalanche of ill-informed speculation about a geopolitically fuelled race for resources that, in the fevered imagination of some in the media, might even lead to inter-State conflict. The reality is much more mundane: the Russian research was being carried out in response to recommendations of the Commission on the Limits of the Continental Shelf (CLCS) created by Article 76 and Annex II to UNCLOS, reacting to the inadequacies of the evidence underlying the submission as to the outer limits of the Russian continental shelf made to it in December 2001 by Russia pursuant to paragraph 8 of Article 76.[2] Moreover, thanks to Article 137, paragraph 1 of UNCLOS[3] the placement of a flag on the deep seabed is no more legally significant than that of an American flag on the moon by United States (US) astronauts,[4] in other words what was occurring was simply a stage in an orderly process governed by UNCLOS.

From a legal perspective, the North Pole has no particular significance either at the surface or on the seabed; it is simply a point in the middle of an ocean

---

1 Montego Bay, 10 December 1982, 1833 UNTS 3.
2 The continental shelf as defined in Art 76(1) of UNCLOS may in certain parts of the world extend beyond 200 nautical miles from the baseline, and where this is the case, the status of the superjacent water column as high seas is not affected, per UNCLOS Art 78, while by Art 77(1) and (2) the seabed and subsoil and its resources are under the sovereign rights of the coastal State. See generally J Mossop, *The Continental Shelf Beyond 200 Nautical Miles: Rights and Responsibilities* (Oxford University Press, 2016).
3 This provides as follows:
   "No State shall claim or exercise sovereignty or sovereign rights over any part of the Area [beyond national jurisdiction, i.e. the continental shelf] or its resources, nor shall any State or natural or juridical person appropriate any part thereof. No such claim or exercise of sovereignty or sovereign rights nor such appropriation shall be recognized."
4 Treaty on Principles Governing the Activities of States in the Exploration and Use of Outer Space, including the Moon and Other Celestial Bodies (London, Moscow and Washington DC, 27 January 1967; 610 UNTS 205), in particular Art II, whereby "Outer space, including the moon and other celestial bodies, is not subject to national appropriation by claim of sovereignty, by means of use or occupation, or by any other means."

governed, like all other oceans, by the law of the sea, and which is unusual only because it is ice-covered – and even that may not be the case in summer for much longer. What salience it has is thus purely political, amplified through interest on the part of the media in which State may ultimately attain jurisdiction of some kind over the Pole, a matter which, because conflict is always more newsworthy than cooperation, they naturally tend to assume – wrongly, as will be demonstrated below – must necessarily be to the exclusion of all other States, so raising the stakes and hence the tension too. In reality, nothing legally untoward has so far occurred, nor is it likely to in the foreseeable future. That said, the differing perspectives and potential rights of the most immediately affected States are well worth exploring. The next section identifies those States, a subset of those with Arctic Ocean coastlines. This is followed by section 3, which canvasses the possible fates that the submissions to the CLCS of those States may meet, after which section 4 ponders and answers in the affirmative the question whether these States can delimit what they assume to be their overlapping entitlements without waiting for the outcome of the CLCS process. In section 5 an intelligent precedent for managing the legal risk posed by this inversion of the logical order is considered, before section 6 weighs the relative costs and benefits of compromise solutions. The paper concludes (section 7) with a tentative prediction that the line of least resistance for the States concerned will hold the greatest attraction for them: they can take shelter behind the long-running CLCS process which drains the urgency out of the delimitation of their respective entitlements, so that no significant steps towards either this or the delineation of the outer limits of more than one of those areas should be expected in the short and medium term.

2   Overlapping Continental Shelf Entitlements over the North Pole

Five States have Arctic Ocean frontages – Canada, Denmark (in respect of Greenland), Norway, Russia and the US – but the North Pole potentially falls within the continental shelf of only three of these coastal States. The Pole is located more than 200 nautical miles from the nearest land, Cape Morris Jesup at the northernmost tip of Greenland, and thus any State believing that its continental shelf as defined in Article 76 of UNCLOS may reach as far as the Pole will need to make a submission to the CLCS under paragraph 8; this needs to be done within ten years of the entry into force of UNCLOS for the relevant State.,[5] The US is not at present affected by this condition because

---

5   See UNCLOS, note 1, Annex II, Art 4.

it is not yet party to UNCLOS; for each of the other four Arctic Ocean coastal States, UNCLOS entered into force on different dates, and not all of them made their submissions to the CLCS within ten years of the respective dates, a matter considered further below.[6]

Submissions of outer limits seaward of the North Pole have now been made to the CLCS under Article 76 by Russia (in 2001, with a revised submission in 2015[7] responding to recommendations from the CLCS in 2002 that called for that step,[8] Denmark in respect of Greenland (in 2014, the fifth submission by that State,[9] after others in 2009 for an area north of the Faroe Islands, 2010 for the Faroe-Rockall Plateau, 2012 for the area south of Greenland and 2013 for an area north-east of Greenland[10]) and Canada (in 2019).[11] Had it adhered to its original intention, Canada would have made its entire submission in 2013,

---

6   By Art 308(2), UNCLOS entered into force "[f]or each State ratifying or acceding to this Convention after the deposit of the sixtieth instrument of ratification or accession ... on the thirtieth day following" the deposit of its own such instrument.

7   For the executive summary see "Partial Revised Submission of the Russian Federation to the Commission on the Limits of the Continental Shelf in respect of the Continental Shelf of the Russian Federation in the Arctic Ocean[,] Executive Summary[,] 2015" (hereinafter Russian Executive Summary), https://www.un.org/Depts/los/clcs_new/submissions_files/rus01_rev15/2015_08_03_Exec_Summary_English.pdf (accessed 6 May 2020).

8   UN doc A/57/57/Add.1 (8 October 2002), Oceans and the law of the sea[:] Report of the Secretary-General[:] Addendum, at 10 (paragraph 41). Although the nature of the shortcomings in the original submission were not made public in this document, the introduction to the executive summary of the revised submission, note 7, at 5, itself revealed them to be that the Scientific and Technical Guidelines of the CLCS had not been followed, and that the CLCS was not persuaded by the materials provided in the submission that the Lomonosov Ridge could be considered a submarine elevation within the meaning of Art 76(6); nor, according to the then current state of scientific knowledge, could the Alpha-Mendeleev Ridge Complex be so considered. See also TL McDorman, "A Note on the Commission on the Limits of the Continental Shelf and the Submission of the Russian Federation", in DD Caron and HN Scheiber (eds), *Bringing New Law to Ocean Waters* (Leiden/Boston: Martinus Nijhoff, 2004), 467–481.

9   For the executive summary see "Partial Submission of the Government of the Kingdom of Denmark together with the Government of Greenland to the Commission on the Limits of the Continental Shelf[:] The Northern Continental Shelf of Greenland[,] Executive Summary" (hereinafter Danish Executive Summary), https://www.un.org/Depts/los/clcs_new/submissions_files/dnk76_14/dnk2014_es.pdf (accessed 6 May 2020).

10   Executive summaries of each of these are accessible via the CLCS webpage, https://www.un.org/depts/los/clcs_new/commission_submissions.htm (accessed 25 January 2020).

11   For the executive summary see "Partial Submission of Canada to the Commission on the Limits of the Continental Shelf regarding its continental shelf in the Arctic Ocean [,] Executive Summary" (hereinafter Canadian Executive Summary), https://www.un.org/Depts/los/clcs_new/submissions_files/can1_84_2019/CDA_ARC_ES_EN_secured.pdf (accessed 6 May 2020).

but at a late stage the Arctic Ocean portion was excised and preliminary information as envisaged by SPLOS/183 was substituted for it.[12] According to contemporary media reports, this was because the area encompassed by the outer limit prepared by Canadian officials did not include the North Pole, a state of affairs that was evidently politically unacceptable to the government of the day.[13]

For the other two States, any continental shelf entitlement ends well short of the North Pole. The Norwegian submission was for an outer limit whose northernmost turning point was between 85° and 86° N, and this was endorsed by the recommendations issued to Norway in 2009 by the CLCS.[14] For the US, the boundary in its 1990 treaty with Russia[15] runs due "north along the 168°58′37″ W meridian through the Bering Strait and Chukchi Sea into the Arctic Ocean as far as permitted under international law". This formulation assumes that the entitlement stops short of the Pole, possibly because the meridian in question meets the line of equidistance between the nearest points on the baselines of the US on one hand and Canada on the other far south of the North Pole.[16] Although there is no rule requiring continental shelves to be delimited

---

12 See "Preliminary Information concerning the outer limits of the continental shelf of Canada in the Arctic Ocean", https://www.un.org/depts/los/clcs_new/submissions_files/preliminary/can_pi_en.pdf (accessed 10 February 2020). On SPLOS/183 see note 22 below and accompanying text.

13 See e.g. "Canada makes territorial claim for North Pole", *The Toronto Star*, 9 December 2013, http://www.thestar.com/news/queenspark/2013/12/09/canada_makes_territorial_claim_for_north_pole.html (accessed 10 February 2020). The last paragraph of Canada's preliminary information, note 12, is consistent with this: "Canada notes that a substantial amount of the necessary scientific, technical and legal work for the submission of information in respect of continental shelf areas in the Arctic Ocean has been accomplished, and Canada is currently continuing its work on this part of the submission. Canada intends to make a partial submission in respect of areas in the Arctic Ocean at an appropriate date that may depend, among other things, on the acquisition of additional data." This careful phrasing stops short of affirming that additional data were actually needed.

14 Summary of the Recommendations of the Commission on the Limits of the Continental Shelf in regard to the Submission made by Norway in respect of Areas in the Arctic Ocean, the Barents Sea and the Norwegian Sea on 27 November 2006, https://www.un.org/depts/los/clcs_new/submissions_files/nor06/nor_rec_summ.pdf (accessed 25 January 2020). A note on the cover page indicates that this document is "based on excerpts of the [full] Recommendations", which are not public, but excludes information "of confidential or proprietary nature."

15 Agreement between the United States and the Union of Soviet Socialist Republics on the Maritime Boundary (Washington, 1 June 1990), not yet in force, reprinted in (1990) 29 *International Legal Materials* 941. The Agreement is being applied provisionally pending its entry into force, pursuant to an exchange of notes appended to the agreement: AG Oude Elferink, "The 1990 USSR-USA Maritime Boundary Agreement", 6 (1991) *International Journal of Estuarine and Coastal Law* 41, 46.

16 See the map in JS Baker and M Byers, "Crossed Lines: The Curious Case of the Beaufort Sea Maritime Boundary Dispute", 43 (2012) *Ocean Development & International Law* 70, 73.

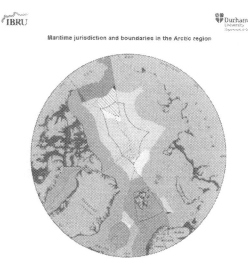

FIGURE 1
IBRU (Durham University) consolidated map of Arctic Ocean submissions including equidistance lines (dashed) but omitting legend

along the equidistance line either within or beyond 200 nautical miles, so that it cannot be excluded that a future treaty boundary with Canada will be somewhat more favourable to the US than that,[17] nevertheless it is hard to imagine that the difference would be so great as to permit a much closer approach to the North Pole. Hence it can be confidently concluded that the US, like Norway, is not among the Arctic Ocean coastal States into whose continental shelf the Pole may potentially fall.

The situation thus far described is clearly illustrated by the map published by the International Boundaries Research Unit at the University of Durham reproduced in Figure 1.[18] This leaves, however, the question of what effect, if any, the failure of some of the submitting States to comply strictly with the 10-year rule in Article 4 of Annex II has.

A comparison between the dates of deposit and dates of the submissions[19] reveals that the Russian and Danish submissions were on time (entry into force for Russia 16 November 1994, original submission on 20 December 2001; entry into force for Denmark 15 January 2005, submission 15 December 2014), but Norway's was a few months late (entry into force 2 July 1996, submission

17 It could also, of course, be less favourable.
18 Downloaded on 6 May 2020 from http://www.durham.ac.uk/ibru/resources/arctic in compliance with the conditions imposed for this.
19 See respectively the chronological list on a webpage maintained by the UN Secretariat's Division for Ocean Affairs and the Law of the Sea, https://www.un.org/depts/los/reference_files/chronological_lists_of_ratifications.htm#The%20United%20Nations%20Convention%20on%20the%20Law%20of%20the%20Sea (accessed 25 January 2020), and the CLCS webpage, note 10.

27 November 2006), while Canada's first submission in respect of its Atlantic Ocean frontage was lodged with a day to spare, but the Arctic Ocean portion of its submission did not follow until several years later (entry into force 7 December 2003, submissions 6 December 2013 (Atlantic) and 23 May 2019 (Arctic)).

For Norway this does not matter, because it has fully delimited its boundaries beyond 200 nautical miles from its baselines with both of its neighbours, Denmark and Russia,[20] and because its entitlement under the rules of paragraphs 4 to 7 of Article 76 does not extend as far as the North Pole, as explained above: it can thus safely rely on the decision of the States Parties in 2001 which deemed the ten years to have begun running on 13 May 1999 for any State for which UNCLOS had by then already entered into force.[21] This is so even though a meeting of the States Parties has no competence to amend UNCLOS or its annexes; Articles 312 and 313 provide other processes for this which do not involve any such collective decision. It is submitted that the decision is best understood as functioning as a mutual waiver of rights flowing from non-adherence to the ten-year rule among all States that were party to UNCLOS at the time it was made, which includes Russia, or which had become party by the time of a subsequent States Parties decision in 2008 which referred to and built on the earlier decision;[22] this includes Denmark. Canada's position is more complex because, although it met the condition in the 2008 decision supported by Denmark, Norway and Russia, its other neighbour the US remains a non-party and may, should it eventually accede to UNCLOS, argue that it is not bound by the 2001 and 2008 decisions precisely because the text of UNCLOS remains unamended. Because the US is also extremely unlikely to have a continental shelf entitlement stretching as far as the North

---

20 Agreed Minutes on the Delimitation of the Continental Shelf beyond 200 Nautical Miles between the Faroe Islands, Iceland and Norway in the Southern Part of the Banana Hole of the Northeast Atlantic (New York, 20 September 2006), https://www.regjeringen.no/en/dokumenter/Agreed-Minutes/id446839 (accessed 10 February 2020); Treaty between the Russian Federation and the Kingdom of Norway concerning maritime delimitation and cooperation in the Barents Sea and the Arctic Ocean (Murmansk, 15 September 2010), 2791 UNTS 3.

21 UN doc SPLOS/72, Decision regarding the date of commencement of the ten-year period for making submissions to the Commission on the Limits of the Continental Shelf set out in article 4 of Annex II to the United Nations Convention on the Law of the Sea (29 May 2001).

22 Recorded in UN doc SPLOS/183, Decision regarding the workload of the Commission on the Limits of the Continental Shelf and the ability of States, particularly developing States, to fulfil the requirements of article 4 of Annex II to the Convention, as well as the decision contained in SPLOS/72, paragraph (a) (20 June 2008).

Pole, however, the effect of this may be limited to rendering it in Canada's interests to finalise the outstanding maritime boundary delimitation with the US before, rather than after, the US accedes to UNCLOS; at the time of writing there is no indication that either of these is likely to happen any time soon.

3 Consideration by the CLCS of the Three Submissions with Outer Limits Seaward of the North Pole

The culling exercise undertaken in the previous section has reduced from five to three the number of States into whose continental shelf the North Pole may ultimately fall: Canada, Denmark and Russia. There are several reasons, however, why that number could fall further, in theory all the way to zero, although that most extreme of scenarios remains unlikely.

As already noted, since the North Pole is more than 200 nautical miles from the nearest land, in order to come within the continental shelf of any of the three remaining States, at least one of them will need to obtain recommendations to that effect from the CLCS under Article 76, paragraph 8 of UNCLOS. The final sentence of that paragraph makes limits established "on the basis of" those recommendations "final and binding" *erga omnes partes*,[23] subject however to delimitation of any entitlements that overlap, as provided in paragraph 10.[24] There is no guarantee that this condition will be met, although the reason why it might not be met for any one or more of the States is a scientific rather than a legal matter, beyond the scope of this paper; suffice it to observe in this respect that, for the North Pole in particular, the scientific cases for all three submissions depend on demonstrating the geological and/or geomorphological continuity of the transoceanic Lomonosov Ridge with the land territory of the submitting States, Russia from one end of the ridge and Denmark and Canada from the other. Some commentators have doubted whether this can be shown for one or more of the States, but the decision is for the CLCS alone, as the final arbiter on scientific matters within its expertise. The author at any rate is not competent to venture an opinion on how likely such doubts

---

23   The English text and four of the five other authentic language texts are ambiguous as to who is bound, but the Russian text translates as "binding for all" and this authoritatively resolves the ambiguity in the other languages too by virtue of Art 33 of the Vienna Convention on the Law of Treaties (Vienna, 23 May 1969; 1155 UNTS 371).

24   NB: thanks to paragraph 10, the CLCS process mandated by paragraph 8 is not a race – each submission is considered entirely on its own merits without prejudice to the others, so a State derives no advantage from securing the first positive recommendation, as this does not eliminate, or give it priority over, the others.

are to be resolved in any given State's favour. To date, when the CLCS has not been satisfied that outer limits submitted to it by a State are in conformity with the formulae laid down in paragraphs 4 to 7 of Article 76, its recommendations say so; usually it also suggests (and the submitting State under Annex II, Article 8 in any event has the right to make) a "revised or new submission". This indeed is what happened to the original Russian submission of 2001,[25] which is why the further submission of 2015 became necessary. Another possibility is that the submitting State may conclude from the recommendations that its chances of ever persuading the CLCS of the merits of its scientific case are remote, and decide to accept those recommendations for an outer limit closer to land,[26] or even confine itself to the default minimum 200 miles of continental shelf to which paragraph 1 entitles it.[27]

What follows from negative recommendations of this type depends on how many of the three remaining States receive them. If this happens for all three submissions, then the North Pole is not in any State's continental shelf, but instead is part of the seabed beyond national jurisdiction where mineral rights are administered by the International Seabed Authority (ISA) under Part XI of UNCLOS and its 1994 implementing agreement.[28] If it happens for two of the submissions, then the result is equally simple: the North Pole becomes part of the continental shelf of the remaining sole successful submitting State, as there is then no overlap of entitlements to delimit. By contrast, should it happen for either only one of the submissions, or none, then the North Pole falls within the primary continental shelf entitlements of two or three States respectively, and a delimitation becomes necessary to resolve their overlap.

At the time of writing, the Russian submission is under examination by a subcommission, which will draft recommendations for the full Commission

---

25 See note 8 and accompanying text.
26 In practice the submitting State modifies its submitted outer limit to one that its interactions with the CLCS leads it to believe the latter will accept, as happened, e.g., in the case of Suriname; see "Summary of Recommendations of the Commission on the Limits of the Continental Shelf in regard to the Submission made by Suriname on 5 December 2008", https://www.un.org/depts/los/clcs_new/submissions_files/sur08/sur08_summary_recommendations.pdf (accessed 10 February 2020), at 6, where Figure 2 is captioned "Extended Continental Shelf of Suriname as proposed by Suriname in its letter of 17 March 2011 and agreed by the Commission".
27 The only instance to date of a recommendation against any extension at all of the continental shelf beyond 200 miles is that made to the United Kingdom in respect of Ascension Island, obtainable via the CLCS webpage, note 10.
28 Agreement on the Implementation of Part XI of the United Nations Convention on the Law of the Sea of 10 December 1982 (New York, 28 July 1994; 1836 UNTS 3).

to adopt or amend by two-thirds majority.[29] As a new or revised submission, it went automatically to the head of the queue as submission 1b, pursuant to the Rules of Procedure of the CLCS.[30] The Danish submission is well back in the queue, as submission number 76 (with 35 submissions ahead of it at the end of 2019, by the author's calculation), while the Canadian submission is even further behind at number 84 (44th in the queue). At the current rate of progress, the latter two are unlikely to be reached before the mid-2030s, so it is not until then that it will become apparent whether delimitation is even necessary. This is not to say, though, that a delimitation is absolutely precluded before then, as is examined in the next section.

4   An Alternative: Reversing the Order of the Foregoing Stages to Start with Delimitation of Overlapping Continental Shelves of Those States That Can Reach the North Pole

When two (or sometimes more) opposite or adjacent States both (or all) consider that they may be able to satisfy the CLCS of their individual entitlements to a continental shelf beyond 200 nautical miles from the baseline, they face a collective sequencing problem: should delineation or delimitation occur first?

The logical order is to go through the Article 76 process first to establish the primary entitlements, as the purpose of delimitation is to resolve any overlap between them.[31] This also serves to avoid the risk, if States A and B first delimit a boundary between their putative continental shelf entitlements, that it may transpire through the recommendations of the CLCS that no such overlap in fact exists. Should that eventuate, it complicates the situation considerably. If State A is in fact not entitled to some part of the area on its side of the negotiated boundary, one possible consequence would then be that this part reverts to the ISA acting on behalf of the human race as a whole.[32] On the other hand, it may well also be that State B feels emboldened to demand the

---

29   See Arts 5 and 6 of Annex II to UNCLOS, note 2, and the most recent statement by the Chair of the CLCS: UN doc CLCS/51/1 (13 December 2019), Progress of work in the Commission on the Limits of the Continental Shelf[:] Statement by the Chair, at 2–3 (paragraphs 4–7).

30   UN doc CLCS/40/Rev.1 (17 April 2008), Rules of Procedure of the Commission on the Limits of the Continental Shelf; see also the CLCS webpage, note 10, on which the submissions are numbered in order of receipt in the first column.

31   As noted succinctly by the International Tribunal for the Law of the Sea (ITLOS) in *Delimitation of the maritime boundary in the Bay of Bengal (Bangladesh/Myanmar), Judgment*, ITLOS Reports 2012, 4 at 105 (paragraph 397), "Delimitation presupposes an area of overlapping entitlements."

32   See UNCLOS, note 1, Art 137(2).

termination or reopening of the treaty on the ground of fundamental change of circumstances as set out in Article 62 of the Vienna Convention on the Law of Treaties (VCLT), so as to gain so much of the area in question as falls within its own pre-delimitation entitlement. The common interest in keeping boundary treaties and thus the boundaries themselves in being led to this becoming an exception to the rule in Article 62, and there is nothing in the text of the relevant provision, subparagraph 2(a), to indicate that this applies any less than to boundaries delimiting zones in which the coastal State has sovereign rights rather than full sovereignty, namely the exclusive economic zone and continental shelf, than to land and territorial sea boundaries. Yet it is not necessarily for this reason that B's claim would meet resistance, as it is just as arguable that the situation is instead one of a shared mistake, which has its own rule in Article 48. On its face this is no more promising for State B, despite the absence of any exception for boundary treaties, since an error under which one of the parties to a treaty is labouring is a ground for invalidating the treaty only if that error "relates to a fact or situation which was assumed by that State to exist at the time when the treaty was concluded and formed an essential basis of its consent to be bound" by it,[33] and does not apply "if the State in question contributed by its own conduct to the error or if the circumstances were such as to put that State on notice of a possible error."[34] While in this situation B will probably not have contributed to A's error, making the first limb of the exception inapplicable, even so, the overall circumstance is that, by anticipating the recommendations of the CLCS, the parties are taking a joint legal gamble with their eyes open, and it is not obvious what excuse either party might have for failing to appreciate the inherent risks of that step. In other words both States are put on notice of the possibility that scrutiny of their submissions by the CLCS will expose any error on which either of them rests.

A more practical solution may be for State A to continue managing the area as its continental shelf using the entitlement of State B, though this only works if the CLCS has found State B to have such an entitlement, and depends on State B being willing to do State A this substantial political favour, which may in turn depend on how close their bilateral relations are, or failing that to extract from State A some suitable *quid pro quo*. While any third State C may argue that under Article 34 of the VCLT it is not bound by any treaty giving effect to the arrangement between A and B,[35] and although it would have had

---

[33] VCLT, note 23, Art 48(1).
[34] Ibid, Art 48(2).
[35] This provision codifies the customary international law principle *pacta tertiis nec nocent nec prosunt* (literally "agreements neither harm nor benefit third persons"), by which only those States that are parties to a treaty are bound by its rules.

to respect B's exclusive rights in the area, it need not respect A's, this is not necessarily conclusive – A could counter that these are in fact B's rights that it is exercising by delegation against all other comers.

All that said, there is nothing in law to stop States delimiting their continental shelf boundaries beyond 200 nautical miles in advance of making their respective submissions to the CLCS, and a relatively recent survey[36] showed around 15 treaties doing just that, not backed by any recommendation from the CLCS. The non-prejudice rule in Article 76, paragraph 10 of UNCLOS supports this, as it covers existing delimitations just as much as future ones, except where States purport to divide among themselves an area more than 200 miles from either of them over which neither in fact has any continental shelf entitlement. As the *Bay of Bengal* case showed in 2012, international courts and tribunals, once hesitant,[37] are also now willing to delimit continental shelf boundaries beyond 200 miles, and there have now been three such cases.[38] This should not be surprising, as the courts are simply defining a boundary for the area beyond 200 miles that the parties could have drawn for themselves had they been able to reach agreement on where to draw it.

5 A Way of Managing the Risk: the "Nordic Solution"

Two non-treaty instruments between Denmark and Iceland of 2006[39] and 2013,[40] with Norway also a party to the earlier of these (in which the Danish territories were the Faroe Islands and Greenland respectively) took account of the risk by specifying in advance an adjustment of the boundary in these

---

36 BM Magnússon, "Outer Continental Shelf Boundary Agreements" 62 (2013) *International and Comparative Law Quarterly* 345.
37 *Delimitation of maritime areas between Canada and France*, (1992) XXI Reports of International Arbitral Awards 265 at 292–293 (paragraphs 77–82); *Territorial and Maritime Dispute between Nicaragua and Honduras in the Caribbean Sea (Nicaragua v. Honduras)*, Judgment, ICJ Reports 2007, p. 659 at 759 (paragraph 319): "any claim of continental shelf rights beyond 200 miles must be in accordance with Article 76 of UNCLOS and reviewed by the Commission on the Limits of the Continental Shelf established thereunder."
38 *Bay of Bengal Case*, note 31, decided by ITLOS in 2012; the award of the arbitral tribunal formed under Annex VII to UNCLOS in Bay of Bengal Maritime Boundary Arbitration between Bangladesh and India, Award of 7 July 2014, http://www.pca-cpa.org/showpage .asp?pag_id=1376; *Delimitation of the maritime boundary in the Atlantic Ocean (Ghana/Côte d'Ivoire)*, Judgment, ITLOS Reports 2017, 4 (delivered by a Special Chamber of ITLOS).
39 Agreed Minutes, note 20.
40 Agreed Minutes on the Delimitation of the Continental Shelf beyond 200 Nautical Miles between Greenland and Iceland in the Irminger Sea (Reykjavík and Copenhagen, 16 January 2013), https://www.stjornarradid.is/media/utanrikisraduneyti-media/media/thjodrettarmal/Agreed-Minutes-og-vidaukar.pdf (accessed 10 February 2020).

circumstances. This is wise, as it is likely to be easier for States to reach agreement on such matters before any submissions are made, when the risks of disappointment at the hands of the CLCS are roughly symmetrical unless both sides know that one side's scientific case is significantly weaker than the other's, whereas once the subcommission has begun interacting with the submitting State, and especially once recommendations are actually delivered to it, asymmetries will inevitably arise if the outcome is to set up the situation between A and B described above. The 2006 instrument showed its worth in 2009, when CLCS recommendations to Norway denied its entitlement to a small part of the area enclosed within Norway's submitted outer limit,[41] although the adjustment mechanism did not need to be activated, because the recommendation still left to Norway the whole of the area on its own side of the boundary, so it had no need to make a new or revised submission even if it disagreed with those recommendations, as it no longer had anything to gain by doing so.

6   Potential Compromises

The natural tendency for any government faced with a politically sensitive negotiation over a single objectively trivial point in the ocean is to delay dealing with it for as long as it can, in the hope that the passage of time may either see the problem resolve itself or reduce its significance. Rationally or not, the continental shelf at the North Pole has become such an issue. All three States that have made submissions to the CLCS have differing reasons of their own for wanting the Pole within their continental shelf. For Canada, the Pole itself seems to carry inordinate political significance, if the media reports are correct in attributing the exclusion of the Arctic Ocean frontage from Canada's 2013 submission to the non-inclusion of the North Pole in the area landward of the outer limit prepared by officials.[42] Russia's motivation rests on a legal policy preference, traceable to its advocacy since the 1920s of the "sector theory" in the Arctic,[43] by which undiscovered land should, instead of being subject to claim by occupation, simply be deemed to belong to the coastal State into whose sector it falls, each sector being a roughly triangular area bounded

---

41   Summary of the Recommendations, note 14, 29 (text) and 32 (map).
42   See note 13.
43   Decree of the Central Executive Committee of the Union of Soviet Socialist Republics (15 April 1926); for an English translation see WE Butler, *International Straits of the World: Vol. 1, Northeast Arctic Passage* (Alphen aan den Rijn: Sijthoff & Noordhoff, 1978), 72.

by the Arctic Ocean coast of the State and meridians from the easternmost and westernmost points of its land territory on the coast, which by definition meet at the Pole. As its original submission of 2001 and its boundaries with the United States[44] and more recently Norway[45] show, it has similarly long supported delimiting maritime boundaries along meridians, and has more or less achieved this. If the State's UNCLOS Article 76 entitlement extends beyond the meridian, however, then the coastal State is disadvantaging itself by limiting itself to that line, and thus in the 2015 revised submission, as seen in Figure 2, the outer limit no longer just passes through the North Pole, but deviates around it on what from Russia's perspective is the far side, so that the Pole is now within, rather than at the edge of, the Russian continental shelf. Denmark has kept a low profile, perhaps because it has the clearest claim: thanks to having the closest land territory, if boundaries were drawn on the most common basis used in maritime delimitation, lines of equidistance from the nearest points of the land territory of each relevant State, the Pole would fall within its continental shelf, as long as it can establish a primary entitlement to the satisfaction of the CLCS. The much larger area encompassed by the limits submitted by Denmark is shown in Figure 3.

If the States concerned are willing to compromise, there may be an obvious way to do so, but it carries costs that one or more of them may view as too high for the time being. Precisely because the Pole is a point rather than a line or area, it can serve as a vertex where two or three areas of continental shelf under the jurisdiction of the rival States meet, as was implicitly assumed in Russia's now superseded 2001 submission. That is, each pair of States would agree to delimit their boundary along a line running through the North Pole. Assuming that all three submissions eventually clear the CLCS hurdle, this would probably suit Canada and Russia which would be net gainers by comparison with a strict equidistance solution, but not Denmark, which would be the net loser despite having the smallest Arctic Ocean continental shelf of the three if the division were based purely on equidistance, so it would need to be offered some kind of compensation to induce its agreement to this solution.

It is not immediately obvious what sort of compensation Russia might be willing to offer, but since there is no requirement that it be something related to the law of the sea, it could be found in any aspect of the two States' bilateral relationship if the political will exists. For Canada, on the other hand, there are two readily imaginable possibilities: one is simply to balance the shift

---

44   See Agreement, n 15 and accompanying text.
45   See 2010 treaty, note 20.

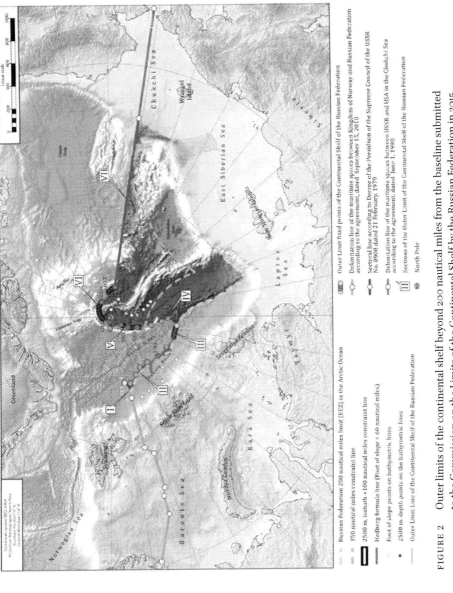

FIGURE 2   Outer limits of the continental shelf beyond 200 nautical miles from the baseline submitted to the Commission on the Limits of the Continental Shelf by the Russian Federation in 2015, cropped, from Russian Executive Summary, note 9, 23.

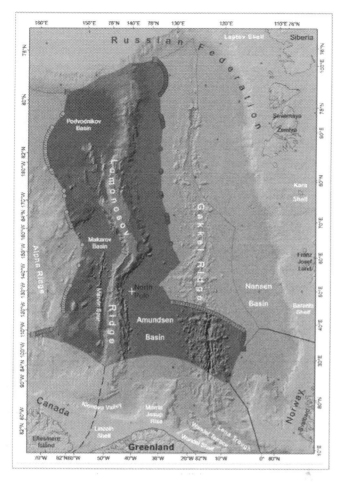

FIGURE 3 Outer limits of the continental shelf north of Greenland beyond 200 nautical miles from the baseline submitted to the Commission on the Limits of the Continental Shelf by Denmark in 2014, cropped, in Danish Executive Summary, note 9, 8.

away from the equidistance line in Canada's favour in the vicinity of the Pole with a shift in Denmark's favour closer to land, easily done in a lateral situation as opposed to one between States facing each other across an ocean, as in the Denmark-Russia pairing. Another would be for Canada to concede to Denmark the hitherto disputed title to Hans Island.[46] Should the reader be

---

46 For the background to this dispute see e.g. M Byers, *Who Owns the Arctic? Understanding Sovereignty Disputes in the North* (Vancouver: Douglas & McIntyre, 2009), 22–30.

tempted to object that the latter concession would be equally politically unthinkable for any Canadian government in the foreseeable future, the author, taking no position on this, would merely observe that, in view of the negligible objective value of Hans Island to either claimant, any refusal to contemplate this suggestion would only reinforce even more starkly the relative unimportance of the North Pole. If so, however, then it follows from this that the Pole should never be allowed to become a factor in the delimitation at all – this at any rate would have been the author's suggestion as an outsider; while it is not possible to escape entirely the need to humour States' political sensibilities, nonetheless it would be desirable to avoid exacerbating situations where issues acquire importance *ex nihilo* solely because of a vicious cycle in which political and media circles spur each other on and succeed in persuading each other that there must after all be something to them.

7   Conclusion: Prediction and Paradox

Although the author is not usually given to making predictions on international legal issues, he is prepared to chance his arm on this occasion. Because the UNCLOS Article 76 process is likely to take another 20 years to move to completion, if not more, there is no pressing need to do anything until at least two of Canada, Denmark and Russia secure positive recommendations from the CLCS, hence the most probable outcome in the short and medium term is that all three submitting States will find it easier to leave the delimitation pending until then, as only Russia's revised submission of 2015 is likely to receive recommendations in or not long after 2020.[47]

This leads to a striking counterintuitive implication of the 2014 Danish Submission. Denmark's expansive submitted outer limit runs well beyond the equidistance line with Canada, which might normally be seen as unhelpful *vis-à-vis* a neighbour with which there will be a lateral delimitation, as Greenland and the northernmost Canadian islands are both in essence detached parts of the North American continent, and only rarely would one expect to encounter a lateral discontinuity, whether geological or morphological, marked enough to warrant placing a boundary along it rather than using the equidistance line. Instead of criticising it as an unjustified attempt to encroach on what should be Canada's shelf, however, objective observers and perhaps Canada itself would see that in fact this did Canada a substantial favour, by legitimating a similar

---

47   This reckons without any delay caused by the COVID-19 crisis should one or more sessions of the CLCS, which meets at UN headquarters in New York, need to be postponed or cancelled.

counter-encroaching approach from Canada as the next step in order to reach the North Pole, as duly occurred with its 2019 submission, as seen in Figure 4. If it is not too bold an inference that officials on all sides would be pleased to be able to leave the problem for their successors to solve, those in Canada and Denmark may thereby have found what is perhaps the only way of meeting the conflicting demands of their present political masters, while waiting and hoping that among those who come after them there will eventually be some who prove less difficult to please.

FIGURE 4   Outer limits of the continental shelf in the Arctic Ocean beyond 200 nautical miles from the baseline submitted to the Commission on the Limits of the Continental Shelf by Canada in 2019, cropped, in Canadian Executive Summary, note 13, 16.

New Russian Legislative Approaches and Navigational Rights within the Northern Sea Route

*Jan Jakub Solski**

Abstract

The regulation of foreign navigation in the Northern Sea Route (NSR) has been dominated by the rules of international law applicable to merchant ships only. Neither the domestic set of rules of navigation on the NSR, based on Article 234 of UNCLOS nor the Polar Code applies to State-owned vessels. While the application of Article 234 has so far let Russia evade discussion on the navigational rights, one can expect an increasing spotlight on this issue.

In response to the recent crossing of the NSR by a French warship, as well as the voices from the United States indicating similar plans, Russia has signalled the intention to adopt more stringent rules for passage of warships, potentially including the requirement of prior notification and pilotage.

The aim of the paper is twofold. First, examine the navigational rights as applicable in the NSR. As such, the paper will discuss historical State practice and relevant international law to demonstrate, among other things, that the enclosure with straight baselines preserved innocent passage in all Russian Arctic straits. Second, examine the international legality of prior notification and pilotage in the context of the applicable navigational rights on the NSR.

---

* Norwegian Centre for the Law of the Sea, UiT – the Arctic University of Norway, Tromsø, Norway. jan.solski@uit.no.

1   **Introduction**[1]

In September 2018, the French Navy's new offshore support and assistance vessel, the *Rhône (A603)*, transited the Northeast Passage (NEP),[2] starting in Tromsø, Norway on 1 September and ending in Dutch Harbor, Alaska on 17 September.[3] There is little explicit information available as to whether the vessel coordinated its plans with Russian authorities beforehand, but Russian sources refer to the voyage as conducted 'without warning'.[4] The vessel navigated independently,[5] without icebreaker assistance or pilotage, although the Russian news agency Interfax informs that it was 'monitored' by the radio intelligence equipment of the Northern and Pacific fleets in their areas of responsibility in the Russian Arctic.[6]

---

1   This paper draws from the earlier work of the author, specifically JJ Solski, "Navigational rights of warships through the Northern Sea Route (NSR) – all bark and no bite?", The JCLOS Blog 2019, https://site.uit.no/nclos/2019/05/31/navigational-rights-of-warships-through-the-northern-sea-route-nsr-all-bark-and-no-bite/ (accessed 2 January 2020); and JJ Solski, "Russia" in RC Beckman, T Henriksen, KD Kraabel, EJ Molenaar and JA Roach, *Governance of Arctic Shipping: Balancing Rights and Interests of Arctic States and User States* (Brill Nijhoff 2017).
2   The notion of the NSR (Severnyi Morskoj Put') was conceptualised in the early years of the Soviet Union to assist the northern delivery of goods into the Soviet Arctic settlements and shipping the resources out of the Arctic, and to a lesser degree as a trans-Arctic passage between Soviet ports. The latter objective relates closely to the vision behind the international concept of the Northeast Passage (NEP) as an Arctic corridor linking Atlantic and Pacific ports. The two notions developed somewhat independently alongside one another, and without clear specification regarding what exactly each entailed. Since 1932, Soviet and Russian legislation has included a few different and, until 2012, imprecise definitions of the NSR. See Section 2 below for the currently applicable and clear definition of the NSR.
3   Atle Staalesen, "Izvestia: This is what awaits foreign military vessels on Northern Sea Route", The Barents Observer, 7 March 2019, https://thebarentsobserver.com/en/security/2019/03/izvestia-what-awaits-foreign-military-vessels-northern-sea-route (accessed 21 January 2020).
4   Aleksej Kozachenko, Bogdan Stepovoj, Jel'nar Bajnazarov, "Holodnaja volna: inostrancam sozdali pravila prohoda Sevmorputi: Voennym korabljam i sudam pridetsja uvedomit' Rossiju o svoih planah za 45 sutok", Izvestya, 6 March 2019, https://iz.ru/852943/aleksei-kozachenko-bogdan-stepovoi-elnar-bainazarov/kholodnaia-volna-inostrantcam-sozdali-pravila-prokhoda-sevmorputi (accessed 21 January 2020).
5   AFP, "Arctique: le passage Nord-Est franchi pour la première fois par la Marine", Franceinfo, 2 October 2018, https://france3-regions.francetvinfo.fr/bretagne/finistere/brest/arctique-passage-nord-est-franchi-premiere-fois-marine-1551014.html (accessed 21 January 2020).
6   Interfax, "Korabl NATO vpervye proshel Severnym morskim putem", 2 October 2018, https://www.interfax.ru/world/631532 (accessed 21 January 2020).

Over the past years, different signals have been coming from another NATO member State, the United States,[7] indicating the US objections and concerns regarding Russia's NSR regulatory scheme, and, more recently, its readiness to take concrete action by transiting the Russian Arctic with surface vessels as part of the US Freedom of Navigation Program.[8]

In November 2018, Mikhail Mizintsev, the Head of the Russian National Defense Management Center pledged that by the start of the 2019 navigational season foreign warships would only be able to navigate the NSR following prior notification.[9] According to his statement, new legislative developments were supposed to fill the legal vacuum regarding the use of the NSR. In March 2019, a Draft Resolution of the Government of Russia was published on the website of the Government.[10]

The draft legislation, prepared by the Russian Ministry of Defense, targets foreign warships and other vessels operated by a State and used on non-commercial service to the extent that they exercise the right of innocent passage in the territorial sea of the NSR. The draft would require:

> The flag State to submit a notification concerning the planned passage through the territorial sea of the Russian Federation in the NSR no later than 45 days before the start of the proposed passage;
>
> The ship to use the service of mandatory ice pilotage in the territorial sea and internal waters of the NSR; and
>
> The ship to use icebreaker assistance in the territorial sea and internal waters of the NSR if necessary.

---

[7] United States of America, Diplomatic Note from the United States to Russia regarding the NSR (29 May 2015) reproduced in CarrieLyn D Guymon (ed), *Digest Of United States Practice In International Law* 2015, 526, https://2009-2017.state.gov/documents/organization/258206.pdf (accessed 21 January 2020).

[8] David Auerswald, "Now is not the time for a FONOP in the Arctic", War on the Rocks, Texas National Security Review, 11 October 2019, https://warontherocks.com/2019/10/now-is-not-the-time-for-a-fonop-in-the-arctic/ (accessed 21 January 2019).

[9] Interfax, "S 2019 goda voennye korabli smogut khodit po Sevmorputi tolko uvedomiv RF", 30 November 2018, https://www.interfax.ru/russia/640154 (accessed 21 January 2020).

[10] Draft Resolution of the Government of Russia on Amendments to the Resolution of the Government of Russia No. 1102, 2 October 1999, "On the rules of navigation and presence of foreign warships and other state-owned ships operated for non-commercial purposes in the territorial sea, internal waters, on naval bases, and bases for stationing warships in seaports of the Russian Federation", https://regulation.gov.ru/projects#npa=89000 (accessed 21 January 2020).

Besides, the draft proposes that foreign warships exercising innocent passage 'must have the necessary ice construction, observe special precautionary measures and comply with the requirements relating to the safety of navigation and protection of the marine environment from pollution from ships (as applicable to the waters of the Northern Sea Route)'.

Ironically, the recent tension over the applicable regime of navigation through the NSR has arguably arisen, at least in part, due to the liberalisation of Russian legislation on navigation there. The 2012 Federal Law[11] introduced into the 1999 Merchant Shipping Code[12] Article 5.1, entitled 'navigation in the water area of the NSR'. This provision became central to the legal regime of the NSR. It provides, among other things, the definition of the NSR and calls for the adoption of rules of navigation. In as much as the 2013 Rules of Navigation in the NSR (2013 Rules)[13] are legally based on Article 5.1(2), other provisions of the 1999 Merchant Shipping Code limit their scope of application *ratio personae*. Pursuant to Article 1, the 1999 Merchant Shipping Code applies only to relations arising from merchant shipping; Article 3(2) explicitly excludes its application to State-owned vessels.

The decision to anchor the 2013 Rules in the 1999 Merchant Shipping Code, thus rendering the 2013 Rules applicable only to commercial ships, deserves appreciation as a departure from the earlier policy of non-discrimination between commercial and State-owned vessels. The 1990 Regulations[14] applied to all ships, which was inconsistent with Article 236 of the United Nations Convention on the Law of the Sea (UNCLOS).[15] According to Article 236, the provisions of UNCLOS regarding the protection and preservation of the marine environment 'do not apply to any warship, naval auxiliary, other vessels

---

11 Federal Law on Amendments to Specific Legislative Acts of the Russian Federation Concerning the State Regulation of Merchant Shipping in the Water Area of the NSR, 28 July 2012, No. 132 FZ, Sobranie zakonodatel'stva Rossiyskoy Federatsii 30 July 2012 No. 31 p. 4321 (2012 Federal Law).

12 The Merchant Shipping Code of the Russian Federation), 30 April 1999, No. 81 FZ, Sobranie zakonodatel'stva Rossiyskoy Federatsii 3 May 1999 No. 18 p. 2207 (1999 Merchant Shipping Code).

13 Rules of Navigation in the Water Area of the Northern Sea Route, as approved by the order of the Ministry of Transport of Russia, 17 January 2013 № 7, registered by the Ministry of Justice 2 April 2013 No. 28120 (2013 Rules).

14 The 1990 Regulations for Navigation on the Seaways of the Northern Sea Route, approved on 14 September 1990), published on 18 June 1991 in 29 Izveshcheniya Moreplavatelyam (1990 Regulations).

15 DR Brubaker, *Environmental Protection of Arctic Waters – Specific Focus the Russian Northern Sea Route* (Doctoral Thesis, University of Stockholm 2002): 299–300.

or aircraft owned or operated by a State and used, for the time being, only on government non-commercial service'. A flag State is required to adopt appropriate measures not impairing the operational capabilities of such vessels to ensure that they act in a manner consistent with the Convention, but only so far as is reasonable and practicable. Furthermore, it follows from Article 30 of UNCLOS that warships are required to comply with laws and regulations of the coastal State concerning passage through the territorial sea, but other than that, Article 32 reaffirms the immunity of warships and other government ships operated for non-commercial purposes. A joint interpretation of the three provisions suggests that sovereign immune vessels may be obliged to comply with laws and regulations of a coastal State as long as they are lawful, i.e., permissible in the territorial sea, and applicable, i. e., not regarding the protection and preservation of the marine environment.

This leads to the main question this article aims to address, namely, what are the applicable navigational rights in the NSR, and where exactly do they apply? In Russia, there exists a particular discourse, as reflected in academic writings and statements by politicians, which creates the impression that the NSR is a national asset because of the sacrifices made to develop it.[16] This perception seems to have laid the groundwork for the determination of the NSR as a 'historically developed national transport line of communication of the Russian Federation'.[17] Yet, the geographical scope and substantive extent of coastal State jurisdiction, as well as concomitant navigational rights and freedoms within the NSR, are determined by international law.

In practice, Russia's measures with the official purpose of ensuring maritime safety and environmental protection in the Arctic, broadly associated with Article 234, blurred the distinction between a right and privilege. The recent developments in Russian State practice, such as the recognition for the distinction between merchant and sovereign immune vessels, and the clarification of the international legal basis for the 2013 Rules,[18] have been helpful to isolate the question of the applicability of navigational rights from the

---

16 See JJ Solski, "New developments in Russian regulation of Navigation on the Northern sea route" 1 *Arctic Review on Law and Politics* 90 (2013): 103–107.

17 Currently included in Article 14 of the Federal Law On the internal sea waters, territorial sea and contiguous zone of the Russian Federation), 31 July 1998, No. 155-FZ, Sobranie zakonodatel'stva Rossiyskoy Federatsii 3 August 1998 No. 31 p. 3833 (1998 Federal Law on the IWTSCZ).

18 The clarification that the 2013 Rules are "adopted and enforced by the Russian Federation in accordance with Article 234 of UNCLOS" came from the Ministry of Transport of the Russian Federation, Federal Agency for Sea and Inland Water Transport, Administration of the NSR, 'Notification No. 77', 20 September 2013, http://www.nsra.ru/files/zayavka/20130920143952ref%20A%20S.pdf (accessed 21 January 2020).

overshadowing effect that jurisdiction exercised pursuant to Article 234 might have. This issue is not only of fundamental and current relevance for sovereign immune vessels. After all, the powers enshrined in Article 234 depend on the specific characteristics of the physical environment. This article will not deal with the question of Article 234's (in-) applicability in the areas that no longer qualify as 'ice-covered' for most of the year because of climate change, but one should be mindful of such possibility.

The remainder of the paper is structured as follows. Section 2 briefly presents the current legal status of the NSR. Section 3 gives an overview of Russia's relevant historical practice to support the conclusions on its effects on navigational rights in Section 4. Section 5 deals with prior notification and pilotage under the international law of the sea. The paper ends with conclusions in Section 6.

2 The Northern Sea Route

Article 5.1 of the 1999 Merchant Shipping Code defines the NSR as:

> [A] water area adjoining the northern coast of the Russian Federation, including internal sea waters, territorial sea, contiguous zone and exclusive economic zone of the Russian Federation, and limited in the East by the line delimiting the sea areas with the United States of America and by the parallel of the Dezhnev Cape in the Bering Strait; in the West, by the meridian of the Cape Zhelanie to the Novaya Zemlya archipelago, by the east coastal line of the Novaya Zemlya archipelago and the western limits of the Matochkin Shar, Kara Gates, Yugorski Shar Straits.

As such, Russian legislation recognises that the NSR consists of internal waters, territorial sea, contiguous zone, and exclusive economic zone (EEZ).[19] Moreover, it is not controversial or disputable that under international law, other States within the NSR enjoy the right of innocent passage in the territorial sea and the freedom of navigation in the EEZ. A somewhat more controversial issue arises concerning the applicable navigational rights through different

---

19 Notably, under this new definition the NSR does not extend beyond 200 nm from Russia's baselines. This is quite an important novelty, since the 1990 Regulations were ambiguous concerning the northern limits of the NSR. See Solski, note 16, 95–96 for a discussion on this matter.

straits enclosed within straight baselines in the 1985 Decree on Baselines.[20] These include the following straits: Matochkin Shar, Kara Gates and Yugorskii Shar connecting the Barents Sea with the Kara Sea; the Vilkitsky, Shokalsky, Red Army and Yungshturm Straits connecting the Kara and Laptev Seas; the Dimitri Laptev and Sannikov Straits connecting the Laptev and East Siberian Seas. The Long Strait, which connects the East Siberian and the Chukchi Seas, has not been enclosed with a straight baseline.

Assuming, but only for the sake of argument, that Russian straight baselines are valid, the legal status of waters landward of baselines is that of internal waters. Under the law of the sea, there are three possible scenarios regarding the applicable navigational rights in these waters. The first one is that no right of navigation exists,[21] the second one that innocent passage has been preserved, the third one that at least some of these straits are subject to the right of transit passage.[22]

The following sections aim to analyse Russia's historical practice and its effect on the status of waters, as well as the existence of navigational rights.

---

20   Russia, The USSR Council of Ministers, Decree of 15 January 1985, http://www.un.org/Depts/los/LEGISLATIONANDTREATIES/PDFFILES/RUS_1985_Declaration.pdf (accessed 21 January 2020) (1985 Decree on Baselines).

21   Russian international law authors seldom discuss this question, but when they do, that is the position they take. Note that VV Gavrilov, "Legal Status of the Northern Sea Route and Legislation of the Russian Federation: A Note" (2015) 46 *Ocean Development and International Law* 256: 260 asserts, "(accessed w)ith respect to those areas of the NSR that are within the internal waters of Russia, the area is under the complete sovereignty of the Russian Federation". V Golitsyn, "The Legal Regime of the Arctic" in DJ Attard (general ed), M Fitzmaurice, Norman A Martinez Gutierrez (eds), *The IMLI Manual on International Maritime Law: Volume I: The Law of the Sea* (Oxford University Press 2014): 471–472 states that the position of the USSR at the time of the adoption of the 1985 Decree on Baselines was that none of the straits had been used for international navigation and the right of innocent passage was not preserved. More recently, P Gudev, "The Northern Sea Route: a National or an International Transportation Corridor?", Russian International Affairs Council, 24 September 2018, concludes his analysis of the exchange of notes between the USSR and the United States in the 1960s, as well as the 1985 Decree on Baselines with the observation that the latter 'made it possible to declare the Vilkitsky, Shokalsky, Laptev, Sannikov and Kara Straits historical internal waters of the USSR'.

22   This is a position taken by the United States, see 2015 US Diplomatic Note to Russia, note 7 "to the extent that the Northern Sea Route scheme continues the view of the Russian Federation that certain straits used for international navigation in the Northern Sea Route are internal waters of the Russian Federation, the United States renews its previous objections to that characterization."

3 Overview of Russia's Historical 'Tools and Claims' Affecting 'Control' over the NSR

3.1 Russia's de Facto *Control of Navigation in the* NSR

The primary obstacle hindering the NEP from becoming of genuine significance for global maritime trade has been the presence of ice, remoteness, and otherwise challenging navigational conditions. The Arctic has been used for navigation for centuries, although not so in the form of transits between ports in the Atlantic and Pacific Oceans.

Furthermore, Soviet and Russian practice over nearly ninety years of the existence of the NSR has been guided by the objective of keeping the Arctic straits for national use, and under national control. When offers were made to foreigners to use the NSR, the first in 1967, repeated by Gorbachev in 1987, and set out in the 1990 Regulations, it was presupposed that the coastal State remained in charge of the route's administration and that the users would pay for the services provided.[23]

Moreover, during the Soviet era, foreign merchant vessels could effectively only operate in the NSR under charter with Soviet trade organisations.[24] Coastal trade between ports – cabotage – was under the 1929 Merchant Shipping Code of the USSR,[25] and later the 1968 Merchant Shipping Code of the USSR,[26] reserved only for Soviet vessels.[27] While both the 1929 Merchant Shipping Code and the 1968 Merchant Shipping Code distinguished between 'small'[28] and 'large'[29] cabotage, both types of transport were allowed for Soviet vessels only. As such, navigation between the port of Saint Petersburg and Vladivostok would still be considered cabotage, despite the ship would have to pass many different seas.

In essence, if a foreign commercial ship were to navigate through the NEP, its initial port or the port of destination would have to be a foreign port.

---

23 See Solski, note 1, 180.
24 WE Butler, Northeast Arctic Passage (Sijthoff & Noordhoff 1978): 61.
25 Article 71 of the Merchant Shipping Code of the USSR), 14 June 1929, Sobraniye zakonov SSSR, 1929, No. 41, p. 366.
26 Article 2 of the Merchant Shipping Code of the USSR), 17 September 1968, Vedomosti VS SSSR, 1968, No. 39, p. 351.
27 Butler, note 24: 98–99.
28 In principle, small cabotage referred to transport between ports of one sea. However, the Arctic Ocean and the White Sea were regarded as one sea; as such, navigation between all Soviet Arctic ports would qualify as "small" cabotage, regardless of the fact, that such navigation could pass through up to five different seas: the White, Barents, Kara, Laptev, East Siberian and Chukchi Seas.
29 Large cabotage would denote transport between Soviet ports in different seas.

Besides, most Soviet Arctic ports were closed to foreign vessels at different times.[30] Therefore, as the right of cabotage between Soviet ports was restricted to Soviet ships, and navigation without the use of Soviet icebreakers was unlikely, there was little incentive for foreign companies to engage in shipping through these waters in a way that would challenge Soviet legislation. Both natural conditions and the official approach were not conducive to the international use of the NSR.

The number of foreign-flagged vessels traversing the entire NEP demonstrates this reality. The few occurrences of foreign ships transiting the NEP include the voyage by the *Vega* in 1878–79, or later the *Maud* in 1918–19, both taking place before the official commencement of the NSR's development, and before the USSR came to be. Against this background, Franckx describes the 1991 trip of the *Astrolabe* – not only allowed by the Russian authorities but also conducted with their active participation – as the first circumnavigation of the Eurasian continent by a Western ship since the early 1920s.[31] As such, the NSR has not been utilised by foreign ships, warships, and commercial ships, until its 'official opening' in 1991, or more precisely the navigational season of 2010 – the first one that featured the international use of the NSR for commercial purposes, preceded by the exploratory voyages of the *MV Beluga Fraternity* and the *MV Beluga Foresight* in 2009.[32] Since then, all voyages were conducted with the explicit permission of the Russian authorities, granted within the frameworks set up first by the 1990 Regulations, and later by the 2013 Rules. In this regard, the circumnavigation of the entire NEP by the Rhône (A603) without Russian coordination appears remarkable.

It is, therefore, evident that the NSR has remained under the control of the USSR/Russia for decades. Adding to the physical environment and the practical effect of cabotage laws, the policy was successful due to other tools and practices targeting ships in the lateral passage as well. This article systematises

---

30   GN Semanov, "Legal and Environmental Evaluation of Selected Routes along the Northern Sea Route" in CL Ragner (ed), *The 21st Century – Turning Point* (Springer 2000): 98, refers to only the port of Igarka that would normally be open for foreign vessels, but the list of open ports in the Russian Arctic was updated annually.

31   E Franckx, "The Soviet Maritime Arctic, Summer 1991: A Western Account" (1992) 1 *Journal of Transnational Law and Policy* 131:141. One may also take note of the somewhat exceptional trip of the German auxiliary cruiser the *Komet* in 1940, conducted with the approval of the USSR and with use of its icebreakers, during World War II.

32   E Franckx and L Boone, "New Developments in the Arctic: Protecting the Marine Environment from Increased Shipping" in MH Nordquist, JN Moore, AHA Soons and Hak-So Kim (eds), *The Law of the Sea Convention: US Accession and Globalization* (Martinus Nijhoff Publishers 2012): 188–190.

these three pillars as follows. The first related to the controversial Soviet policy regarding the problematic interpretation of innocent passage. The second involved the adoption of straight baselines. The third, predominant one, has been based on measures with the official purpose of ensuring maritime safety and environmental protection.

3.2 Territorial Sea and Innocent Passage in the Arctic: Early Perspectives

Once the USSR established a 12 nm belt of territorial sea for the first time in the 1960 Statute,[33] its Article 15 qualified the right of innocent passage by the requirement that '(...) passage shall be considered innocent if the vessel follows a customary navigational course or a course recommended by competent agencies (...)'.[34] It is important to note that the 1958 TSCZ Convention did not include any such qualification for the innocence of passage.[35]

However, the lack of recognition of the right of innocent passage for warships in the 1960 Statute was more controversial.[36] Article 16 provided for a procedure of authorisation,[37] specified by a requirement on warships to seek at least 30 days in advance and obtain prior authorisation to pass the territorial sea.

This requirement was consistent with the Soviet position for which they sought international recognition unsuccessfully during UNCLOS II in 1960.[38] The USSR attached a reservation to its instrument of ratification of the 1958 TSCZ Convention,[39] which stipulated that the USSR interpreted international law in a manner such that a coastal State had a right to establish an authorisation procedure for the passage of foreign warships through its territorial sea.[40] Although the USSR openly reserved its rights, the reservation appears to have

---

33 Statute on the Protection of the State Border of the USSR), 5 August 1960, Vedomosti vs RSFSR, 1960, No. 31 (1960 Statute).
34 Ibid.
35 See Article 14 of the Convention on the Territorial Sea and the Contiguous Zone (adopted 29 April 1958, entered into force 10 September 1964) 526 UNTS 205 (1958 TSCZ Convention).
36 See, generally, E Franckx, "Innocent Passage of Warships: Recent Developments in US-Soviet Relations" (1990) 14 (6) *Marine Policy* 484.
37 Article 16 of the 1960 Statute.
38 For example, Franckx, note 36, 485.
39 The USSR ratified the 1958 TSCZ Convention after UNCLOS II on 22 November 1960.
40 D Pharand, "Soviet Union Warns United States against Use of Northeast Passage" (1968) 62 (4) *American Journal of International Law* 927: 933.

been contrary to the object and purpose of the 1958 TSCZ Convention, and thus unlawful.[41]

The 1982 Law on State Boundary of the USSR (1982 Law)[42] introduced a change in the Soviet approach to innocent passage. An improvement was that Article 13 of the 1982 Law provided for a right of innocent passage for both merchant vessels and warships. However, the legislation continued the qualification of innocent passage of merchant ships by insisting that the vessels follow the 'customary navigational course or a course recommended by competent agencies'.[43]

To implement the 1982 Law, the 1983 Rules[44] set out a specific procedure for the exercise of innocent passage by warships. Article 12 of the 1983 Rules permits the innocent passage of warships by using lanes, customarily used for international navigation.

Further, Article 12 of the 1983 Rules listed existing traffic separation schemes in the Baltic Sea, the Sea of Okhotsk and the Sea of Japan. The omission of the Arctic stirred questions on the policy of the USSR on the innocent passage of warships in the Arctic.[45] It was not clear whether the list was intended to be exhaustive, meaning that innocent passage was not allowed elsewhere; or, as an alternative, that in areas not mentioned, the usual international rules applied.[46]

The Black Sea incident in 1988 made it clear that the USSR favored the former interpretation. The US Navy sent ships to the Black Sea in 1986 and in 1988 to navigate in the territorial sea south of the Crimean Peninsula.[47] In response to the second incident, the USSR provided an explicit position, favoring a restrictive interpretation of Article 12 of the 1983 Rules.[48] From this, one can infer

---

41 Ibid, 934.
42 Law on State Boundary of the USSR, adopted 24 November 1982, Vedomosti VS SSSR, 1982, No. 48, p. 891 (1982 Law).
43 Article 13 of the 1982 Law.
44 Russia, 1983 Rules Concerning Navigation and Sojourn of Foreign War Vessels in the Territorial Waters of the USSR, the Internal Waters of the USSR and Ports of the USSR, 34 Notices to Mariners, 42–47.
45 See, for instance, E. Franckx, "Non-Soviet Shipping in the Northeast Passage, and the Legal Status of Proliv Vil'kitskogo" (1988) 24 (151) *Polar Record* 269: 272–273.
46 Ibid.
47 E Franckx, Maritime Claims in the Arctic: Canadian and Russian Perspectives (Martinus Nijhoff Publishers 1993): 165–166.
48 Franckx, note 47: 166, reproduces the communication of the USSR that reads: "(…) According to existing Soviet rules, foreign warships only enjoy such right (accessed innocent passage) in places where sea lanes for international navigation are established (…)".

that the USSR intended to allow innocent passage of warships in some parts of its territorial sea.[49]

However, as this position explicitly addressed the innocent passage of warships, it did little to clarify the enigmatic qualification of innocent passage of merchant ships. It is possible that the USSR would have indicated that there was no customary navigational course through its Arctic straits, and as such, innocent passage would not be recognised. Yet when an occasion to do so arose, when the US Coast Guard's vessels intended to cross the Vilkitsky Strait in August 1967, the USSR chose not to argue that the right of innocent passage did not apply. The Soviets successfully discouraged the vessel from proceeding, but the emphasis was made on the requirement of prior authorisation for warships, and not on the non-applicability of innocent passage in the Vilkitsky Strait.[50] If the USSR had chosen to argue that innocent passage did not apply, this would have been inconsistent with the 1958 TSCZ Convention, which recognises the right of innocent passage with no qualification as to the historical exercise of the right. Likely, other States would not have accepted such an assertion.

The Soviet stance on the application of innocent passage for merchant vessels in the Arctic straits overlapping with the territorial sea until 1985 was never tested. When the *Astrolabe* navigated the NSR in 1991, the legal regime for navigation in the NSR was based on the other two pillars of Soviet/Russian practice: straight baselines and the requirement of prior authorisation under the 1990 Regulations.

Crucially, in 1989, the United States and the USSR reached a compromise with the 1989 USSR-USA Joint Statement, including the Uniform Interpretation of Norms of International Law Governing Innocent Passage. This marked a change in the Soviet approach to innocent passage, recognising its application in the territorial sea regardless of the adoption of sea lanes, TSSs or the existence of a 'customary navigational course'.[51]

---

49   Ibid.
50   Russia, "Aide Memoire from the Soviet Ministry of Foreign Affairs to the American Embassy Moscow", American Embassy Moscow telegram 754, 24 August 1967, as reproduced in JA Roach and RW Smith, *Excessive Maritime Claims* (3rd edn, Martinus Nijhoff Publishers 2012): 315.
51   Paragraphs 2 and 5 of the Union of Soviet Socialist Republics – United States of America: Joint Statement with attached uniform Interpretation of Rules of International Law governing Innocent Passage (23 September 1989) (1989) 28 *International Legal Materials* 1444 (1989 USSR-USA Joint Statement).

3.3 Do Russian Straight Baselines Delineate Historic Waters in Any of the NSR Straits?

It seems likely that the only valid argument supporting the view that the waters in straits had been considered internal waters before the establishment of straight baselines would be that Russia has successfully made a historic waters claim in respect of them. The 1985 Decree, includes the only list of historic waters claims explicitly made by Russia in the Arctic. It refers to only three areas: the White Sea, the waters of Cheshskaya Bay, and only one bay located within the NSR – the Baidaratskaya Bay, as waters 'historically belonging to the USSR, internal waters'.[52]

Admittedly, in 1964 the USSR explicitly referred to the Laptev and Sannikov Straits as 'historically belonging to the USSR'. In response to the intention of the US vessel *Burton Island* to traverse the Dmitry Laptev and Sannikov Straits in 1964, the Soviet Ministry of Foreign Affairs presented the Aide Memoire to the USA, which stipulated that the Dmitry Laptev and Sannikov Straits belong historically to the Soviet Union. The relevant passage reads:

> It should also be kept in mind that the northern seaway route at some points goes through Soviet territorial and internal waters. Specifically, this concerns all straits running west and east in the Karsky Sea. In as much as they are overlapped two-fold by Soviet territorial waters, as well as the Dmitry Laptev and Sannikov Straits, which unite the Laptev and Eastern Siberian Seas and belong historically to the Soviet Union. Not one of these stated straits, as is known, serves for international navigation.[53]

The assertion that the Sannikov and Dmitry Laptev Straits 'belong historically to the USSR' did not specify whether this meant internal waters or the territorial sea. The note refers to the concepts of 'territorial waters' and 'internal waters' in parallel. As the former notion is not traditionally used in the law of the sea, it is helpful to see that Article 3 of the 1960 Statute used the concept of the territorial waters to denote the territorial sea.[54]

The Soviet authorities deemed the *Burton Island* a military vessel, and thus, subject to the requirement of prior authorisation in both the territorial sea and

---

52   The 1985 Decree.
53   JA Roach and RW Smith, *Excessive Maritime Claims* (3rd edn, Martinus Nijhoff Publishers 2012): 312–313.
54   The 1960 Statute.

the internal waters under Article 16 of the 1960 Statute in force at that time. Hence, the Soviets didn't need to specify at what parts of the NSR were the territorial sea and at what parts were internal waters. The lack of decisiveness of the USSR perhaps indicates that it could not find sufficient legal support for an internal waters claim concerning these straits.

If the USSR believed these straits had been historically overlapped with internal waters, this should have been affirmed when the opportunity arose, namely in the 1985 Decree. As such, the categorisation of the waters in the Laptev and Sannikov Straits cannot be considered to reflect a clear and consistent intent to claim waters as historic internal waters.

Other Russian Arctic straits, including the traditional chokepoint, the Vilkitsky Strait, have never been the subject of a formal and, of course, *a fortiori* successful claim to historic internal waters.

3.4 *Maritime Safety and Environmental Protection*

The third pillar of Soviet/Russian practice, with the practical effect of asserting control over Arctic navigation involved invoking coastal State jurisdiction to ensure maritime safety and environmental protection – associated with Article 234 of UNCLOS.

The first specific enactment to ensure maritime safety was the mandatory icebreaker assistance and pilotage requirements established for the Vilkitsky and Shokalsky Straits in 1965.[55] In 1972, these requirements were extended to the Dmitry Laptev and Sannikov Straits.[56] The 1985 Soviet Notices to Mariners included the same requirements, applicable to all vessels within these four straits.[57] Later, mandatory icebreaker assistance and pilotage requirements in these straits were included in Item 7.4 of the 1990 Regulations. Notably, the 2013 Rules do not include such a requirement.

The first document where the USSR asserted special rights to regulate navigation in the entire NSR was the 1971 Statute on the NSR Administration. The Statute laid out a broad framework for the operation of the ANSR, enumerated its tasks and prerogatives, as well as mandated the ANSR to establish

---

[55] Franckx, note 47, at 156 refers to the Notices to Mariners, 1965, No 31, p. 10.
[56] Butler, note 24, 174, reproduces the text of the Procedure for Navigation of Vessels in the Vilkitsky, Shokalsky, Dmitry Laptev and Sannikov Straits, Notices to Mariners 1972, Number 20.
[57] Franckx, note 47: 180–181.

rules for navigation along the NSR[58] – a task only completed by the Ministry of Merchant Marine of the USSR twenty years later.[59]

In light of the general nature of the 1971 Statute on the NSR Administration, it would be a strain to attribute it to any endorsement of claims to sovereignty or jurisdiction.[60] It is, however, evident that the Statute constituted a marked shift towards the increased emphasis of the USSR on particular conditions of Arctic navigation, which required new approaches to ensure maritime safety and prevent vessel-source pollution. This led the USSR to endorse the idea behind Article 234 during UNCLOS III that took place in 1973–1982.

The first formal exercise of the jurisdiction to prescribe mandatory icebreaker assistance and pilotage requirements beyond the territorial sea only took place after the adoption of UNCLOS. Under Item 7.4 of the 1990 Regulations, the Marine Operation Headquarters[61] obtained the mandate to prescribe mandatory icebreaker assistance and pilotage requirements within the entire geographical scope of the NSR, if necessary in light of navigational conditions.[62]

However, the legislative reform leading to the adoption of the 2013 Rules liberalised the regime of icebreaker assistance and pilotage. Items 10.6 and 23 of the 2013 Rules stipulate that the information on the necessity of icebreaker assistance be provided in the permission granted by the ANSR. Mandatory icebreaker assistance and pilotage requirements only arise under specific circumstances, but the ship owner is required to send an application anyway.

A significant feature of the mandatory icebreaker assistance and pilotage requirements in straits was that to comply with the requirements and pass through the straits, a formal request for assistance had to be made to the USSR. The effect in Soviet/Russian law of the failure to request assistance was that the proposed passage was an unauthorised passage of the vessel. This procedure avoided the necessity to defend the questionable Soviet legal posture on innocent passage.

Likewise, the enactment of the 1990 Regulations, the first instrument setting out detailed conditions for the use of the NSR by foreign ships, can be viewed

---

58 Article 3 (h) of the Decree On the Confirmation of the Statute of the Administration of the Northern Sea Route Attached to the Ministry of the Maritime Fleet, 16 September 1971, Sobraniye Postanovleniy Soveta Ministrov SSSR No. 17, p. 124 (1971 Statute on the NSR Administration).
59 The 1990 Regulations.
60 See discussion in Franckx note 47: 160–161.
61 The Marine Operation Headquarters were under Item 1.7 of the 1990 Regulations defined as special navigational services of the Murmansk and Far East Shipping Companies, directly performing ice operations on the Northern Sea Route, under the general co-ordination by the Administration.
62 Item 7.4 of the 1990 Regulations.

as having the effect of 'opening' the NSR, but at the same time, the right to enter and navigate on the NSR has been conditioned on prior authorisation.[63] While, in principle, other States enjoy rights and freedoms of navigation through the different maritime zones within the NSR, the USSR/Russia has assumed the discretion to determine whether a vessel is fit to enter and navigate the NSR. This has allowed the USSR/Russia to evade the question of other States' navigational rights through straits. As explained by Kolodkin, Markov and Ushakov, any vessel accepted for 'guiding' along the NSR automatically 'receives the right of passage' through all its areas lying on the vessel's itinerary, including internal waters and territorial sea.[64]

This pillar of State practice has become of paramount significance for Russia's policy to control the NSR. The evolution of Soviet legislation to protect the fragile Arctic environment corresponded with a similar shift in international law. Soviet practice contributed, in part, to the development of international law, namely Article 234. Besides, the focus on the practical aspects of ensuring maritime safety and environmental protection has allowed Russia to deflect attention from the contentious issue of the navigational rights in the straits of the NSR. Otherwise, this pillar of Soviet/Russian State practice did not affect the applicability of navigational rights in the NSR. Instead, these measures should be seen as attaching conditions to the exercise of navigational rights.

4   The Effects of Russian State Practice on Navigational Rights

The reliance on all these different tools and claims, in addition to the extreme conditions for Arctic navigation, have allowed the USSR/Russia to exercise *de facto* control over the NSR. What effect have all these claims and practices had on navigational rights and freedoms of other States under international law? In other words, what is the relevance of the situation *de facto* for the situation *de jure*?

---

63   Item 2 of the 1990 Regulations. Also under Item 2 of the 2013 Rules, there is a requirement to obtain permission to enter and navigate the NSR. This requirement applies in the whole 'water area' of the NSR, encompassing internal waters, territorial sea and the EEZ.
64   AL Kolodkin, V Yu. Markov and AP Ushakov, "Legal Regime of Navigation in the Russian Arctic", International Northern Sea Route Programme Working Paper 94–1997: 38.

4.1 Does Innocent Passage Apply in Russian Arctic Straits?

Having established that internal waters within straits enclosed by straight baselines do not constitute historic waters, the question remains whether they are subject to the right of innocent passage. Two issues can affect the answer.

The first relates to straight baselines adopted before UNCLOS entered into force. The question is whether such baselines qualify as established 'in accordance with the method set forth in article 7'.[65] The second relates to the argument of the non-applicability of the right of innocent passage in a strait overlapped with the territorial sea, but not having been used for international navigation without the consent of the coastal State. These two issues are addressed in order.

Regarding the specific situation of the Russian Arctic straits, it is not necessary to solve the temporal complication created by the adoption of baselines before UNCLOS entered into force. When the USSR established straight baselines in the Arctic in 1985, it was party to the 1958 TSCZ Convention and bound by its Article 5(2). Therefore, the right of innocent passage was unaffected by the designation of straight baselines surrounding relevant Russian archipelagos in the Arctic (Novaya Zemlya, Severnaya Zemlya, Novosybirskie Ostrova).

The second limitation relates to the applicability of the right of innocent passage in straits where the right of innocent passage was not previously used without the USSR/Russia's consent. Under the 1958 TSCZ Convention, the right of innocent passage applies anywhere in the territorial sea, including straits, regardless of whether they are used for international navigation.[66] Article 8(2) of UNCLOS repeats Article 5(2) of the 1958 TSCZ Convention,[67] with minor adjustments necessary to reflect the developments in the law of the sea. As a result, both these provisions preserve innocent passage without the need for previous acceptance, acknowledgment or use.[68]

---

65 Article 8(2) of UNCLOS.
66 Article 16(3) and 16(4) of the 1958 TSCZ Convention.
67 Notably, during the preparation for the 1958 TSCZ Convention, the draft, available in the Report of the ILC covering the work of its eighth session, 23 April–4 July 1956, Document A/3159, included Article 5(3), which would have preserved innocent passage in areas enclosed by new straight baselines only where the waters had normally been used by international traffic. The inclusion of this additional criterion was not successful, however.
68 International Law Association (ILA), Baselines under the International Law of the Sea, Final Report 2018, https://www.ila-hq.org/images/ILA/DraftReports/DraftReport_Baselines.pdf (accessed 21 January 2020). As observed by K Trümpler, "Article 8" in A Proelss (ed), *United Nations Convention on the Law of the Sea, A Commentary* (CH Beck, Hart, Nomos 2017): 96, the applicability of the right of innocent passage under Article 8(2)

In summary, for navigation, it does not matter whether the Russian Arctic baselines are consistent with international law. The right of innocent passage under international law applied in all Russian Arctic straits, and it continues to apply there, despite Russia's current claim that internal waters cover them.

4.2 Does Transit Passage Apply in Russian Arctic Straits?

Turning to the question of whether Russian Arctic straits can qualify as 'straits used for international navigation' with the corresponding right of transit passage, this section first addresses the geographical and then the functional criterion.

Concerning the geographical criterion, an essential factor is the location of Russian Arctic baselines. The Barents, Kara, Laptev and East Siberian Seas are all overlapped with different maritime zones, including the EEZ and high seas. All straits mentioned above serve as a link between different seas (Barents, Kara, Laptev, East Siberian Seas), and the respective parts of Russian EEZ within these seas. This condition appears to satisfy the geographical criterion in the process of determining if a strait is a 'strait used for international navigation', as per the understanding of Part III of UNCLOS.

Concerning the functional criterion, the situation is slightly more complicated. The international use of the NSR, including its straits, had not started until 2010.[69] Brubaker, writing in 2001, concluded that Russian Arctic straits could be considered 'non-international'.[70] The following section will highlight three points suggesting that sufficient 'international use' may accumulate to the point where the status of specific straits could be altered.

First, under international law, the right of innocent passage has applied in all Russian Arctic straits, regardless of the status of the waters overlapping them, and irrespective of the actual exercise of the right. Russia's current practice, i.e., the use of straight baselines does not rebut the presumption that innocent passage has been preserved.

Second, as the Russian requirement to obtain permission applies in the vast area of the NSR, encompassing different maritime zones,[71] it is not specific enough to rebut the presumption that innocent passage applies within

---

appears in practice to render the status of waters enclosed by 'fresh' straight baselines to be more akin to the territorial sea than to internal waters proper.

69 Franckx and Boone note 32: 188–190.
70 DR Brubaker, "Straits of the Russian Arctic" (2001) 32 (3) *Ocean Development and International Law* 263: 271.
71 See note 63 above.

the straits.[72] Therefore, even if one assumes for the sake of argument that Article 234 supports the requirement of prior authorisation,[73] it cannot serve as an argument to prevent transit passage from materialising. Russia may always claim full sovereignty over specific waters, clarifying at some point that innocent passage does not apply there, but the current permit scheme does not amount to such a claim. Besides, the political cost of such an action would be high, given the clarity about the relevant rules of the international law of the sea.

Third, there is a question of 'use', and whether different modes of navigation, independent or with icebreaker assistance, would amount to one. Crucially, Russian Arctic straits are generally navigable with or without icebreaker assistance, depending on the ship's ice class and the navigational conditions. Moreover, although Russian legislation reserves icebreaker assistance to Russian icebreakers only, since the adoption of the current 2013 Rules, Russian legislation has allowed independent navigation, and many ships have availed themselves of this opportunity.

As such, current Russia's practice is unlikely to impede the process of an emerging regime of transit passage. It is thus reasonable to expect that independent navigation through straits will eventually contribute to the fulfillment of the functional criterion of use for international navigation. In any event, Russia has been marketing the NSR as an attractive alternative to other routes. If this aspiration materialises, at some point Russia will have to recognise the applicability of transit passage. At this moment, one can conclude that the applicability of transit passage in the Russian Arctic straits is *in statu nascendi.*

5 The Law of the Sea on Mandatory Prior Notification and Pilotage for Warships in Lateral Innocent Passage

Innocent passage applies in all Russian Arctic straits, and there are no special rules of international law, other than Article 234, that would grant additional

---

72   If one assumes that the requirement to obtain permission to enter and navigate the NSR does not affect the applicability of innocent passage in the territorial sea within the NSR, why would it affect the applicability of innocent passage in internal waters within the NSR?

73   After all, this appears to be the best argument for Russia to maintain the authorization-based order of the NSR in place, see note 18 for evidence of Russia's practice. The discussion whether Article 234 allows for prior authorization lies beyond the focus of this article. Note, however, that in JJ Solski, *Russian Coastal State Jurisdiction over Commercial vessels navigating the Northern Sea Route,* (PhD Thesis UiT the Arctic University of Norway 2019): 387–389 the author argues otherwise.

jurisdiction to Russia to regulate navigation in the NSR. Russia cannot rely on Article 234 to regulate the passage of sovereign immune vessels, and therefore, the proposed regulations can be assessed in light of the generally applicable law of the sea, in the same way as elsewhere in the world. This section briefly discusses prior notification and pilotage.

Prior notification has long divided States. Regardless of numerous attempts to address the issue, the question of whether a coastal State has the right to require prior notification from high-risk vessels, such as warships or merchant ships carrying hazardous or noxious materials, including hazardous waste or radioactive materials, remains contentious. Churchill accurately notes that UNCLOS is 'arguably unclear or ambiguous about whether a coastal State may require prior notification of the passage of ships carrying hazardous cargoes through its territorial sea as part of its powers under Article 21'.[74]

When acceding to or ratifying UNCLOS, many States decided to attach declarations expressing their views on prior notification. Bangladesh, China, Ecuador, Egypt, Malta, Montenegro, Serbia all issued declarations under Article 310 in which they claim the right to require prior notification from some categories of ships.

On the other hand, some States felt the need to declare their opposition to the prior notification as incompatible with the right of innocent passage. These States included Germany, Italy, the Netherlands, and the UK. In a similar vein, the USA and the Soviet Union rejected the requirement of prior notification concerning innocent passage of all ships, including warships, regardless of cargo, armament or means of propulsion. Paragraph 2 of the 1989 USSR-USA Joint Statement reads:

> All ships, including warships, regardless of cargo, armament or means of propulsion, enjoy the right of innocent passage through the territorial sea in accordance with international law, for which neither prior notification nor authorization is required.

These clear statements of position indicate that some States feel strongly about prior notification, arguing either for or against the right of a coastal State to require it. Moreover, Russia has taken a clear position in this debate, which helped protect its flag State interests.

Pilotage involves the deployment of an experienced officer, usually on board, to guide the ship through exceptionally challenging waters. The crux

---

74 RR Churchill, "The Impact of State Practice on the Jurisdictional Framework Contained in the LOS Convention" in AG Oude Elferink (ed), *Stability and Change in the Law of the Sea: The Role of the LOS Convention* (Martinus Nijhoff Publishers 2005).

of the measure lies in the ability of the pilot to share her/his navigational experience in the areas where such experience is vital for the safety of navigation. Traditionally, pilotage has been associated with ports and internal waters, where it can be made mandatory based on the port or coastal State's sovereignty. Some States have, however, adopted pilotage seaward of their internal waters.

Although pilotage is considered as one of the oldest means of facilitating navigation, international legal instruments have approached it with remarkable reserve. UNCLOS does not explicitly address pilotage in any of the provisions. Neither does SOLAS, despite its Chapter V entitled 'Safety of Navigation', where pilotage could arguably fit well. It is thus notable that even though States have long recognised the benefits of pilotage, including mandatory pilotage schemes, for the safety of navigation, the international community has not yet come to terms with how to specify the parameters of the international legal regime governing pilotage. Moreover, State practice shows that while compulsory pilotage can instigate much controversy for merchant ships exercising the right of innocent passage, it is much more contested for vessels enjoying sovereign immunity. Here one can recall US protests against a Finnish requirement to use pilot service when navigating in Finnish territorial waters, as well as US protests against similar requirements attempted by Italy in the Strait of Messina.[75] Furthermore, the introduction of a compulsory pilotage scheme in the territorial sea in the Great Barrier Reef by Australia was successful pursuant to the recognition by the IMO that the waters in question required the services of a pilot to ensure safe passage. This was crucial for the appreciation that Australia's action did not hamper innocent passage.[76] Norway has so far adopted the requirement of compulsory pilotage only within some parts of internal waters around Svalbard.[77] These examples show that it is unlikely lawful for the coastal State to adopt compulsory pilotage for merchant ships exercising innocent passage unilaterally. The endorsement of the IMO, although providing no specific legal basis for the measure, helps to dispel doubts about proposed compulsory pilotage in the territorial sea. In instances where States proceeded unilaterally, other States are known to have protested against such a course of action. Also, the relevant legislation of both Australia and Norway

---

75 Roach and Smith. note 53, 231.
76 DR Rothwell, "Compulsory Pilotage and the Law of the Sea: Lessons learned from the Torres Strait", ANU College of Law Research Paper No. 12–06: 10.
77 This follows from the official information by the Norwegian Coastal Administration, published at <http://www.kystverket.no/en/EN_Maritime-Services/Pilot-Exemption-Certificate/PEC---Pilotage-Service-in-Svalbard/> (accessed 21 January 2020). Also, Norway has not adopted compulsory pilotage in other parts of the territorial sea.

exempts warships and other government vessels not employed on commercial service, which is consistent with UNCLOS.

6 Conclusions

The analysis of Russian State practice from a historical perspective allows the following conclusions. In pursuit of the general objective to exert control over the NSR, the USSR/Russia deployed different tools and claims. These were not part of a coordinated strategy but rather a result of opportunism and international legal developments. As such, they were characterised by a careful *prima facie* reliance on the international law of the sea. The application of international legal instruments with relevance for the NSR was, usually, subject to specific deviations. These deviations were not accidental since the omissions or additions in domestic legislation implementing international law allowed for a gradual increase in the geographic scope and substantive extent of coastal State jurisdiction.

Yet the USSR/Russia never endorsed broad sovereignty-related theories regarding the regime of navigation, such as the application of the sector theory to marine expanses, or broad historic claims, both of which were advocated for by Soviet academics. Arctic baselines drawn in 1985 confirmed that vast expanses of the Kara, Laptev and East Siberian Seas were comprised by the high seas, and the 200 nm EEZ that followed. Moreover, the right of innocent passage applies in all Russian Arctic straits because they were comprised of the territorial sea before their enclosure with straight baselines.

To be sure, the USSR had a choice not to ratify UNCLOS and claim sovereignty over its Arctic sector. However, this course of action likely would not have benefited or advanced Soviet interests. Even specifically concerning the Arctic, the USSR/Russia walked out of UNCLOS III with Article 234, as well as the procedure to obtain recognition for sovereign rights over a sizeable continental shelf. It is doubtful that Russia would ever have been able to garner international recognition for claims having a similar effect in the Arctic had it not joined UNCLOS, not to mention all the other rights and freedoms that the USSR secured outside the Arctic.

The liberalisation of the legal regime of navigation in the NSR can only partially be explained by the effort to make the NSR attractive for international use. Another part of the equation is respect for the international law of the sea. In this context, it is not entirely surprising that the gradual clarification of the Russian position can sometimes backfire, leaving challenging gaps, such as the question of the navigational regime for sovereign immune vessels. It is difficult to predict how determined Russia is to adopt new regulations for the innocent passage of ships enjoying sovereign immunity within the NSR. At the time of writing, nine months have already passed since the draft legislation was published for consultations.

The impression is that the primary purpose of the draft is to send a strong political signal to deter further challenge to Russia's somewhat ambiguous claims. Even without having been signed, the draft received much publicity in Russian and foreign media, at times even creating a wrong impression that it has entered into force.[78] Here one can also recall the statement by the Chief of the General Staff of the Armed Forces of the Russian Federation Valery Gerasimov, who at the meeting with foreign military attaches said

> [O]ur Armed Forces can fully ensure the safety of navigation in the waters of the Northern Sea Route, and therefore there is no need to find warships of other countries in this sea corridor.[79]

In any event, the adoption of such regulations would undoubtedly be very controversial and unlikely to garner international recognition. Russia may amend its current legislation, but even then, the question would remain about enforcement.

Acknowledgements

Research for this article has been supported by the Norruss Pluss programme of the Research Council of Norway through the research project Regulating Shipping in Russian Arctic Waters: Between International Law, National Interests and Geopolitics, project. No. 287576.

I thank my PhD supervisors Professor Erik Jaap Molenaar and Professor Erik Franckx, as well as Professor Ted L. McDorman, for all the helpful comments and suggestions.

---

78 The media – here it is not necessary to refer to examples of sub-optimal reports or diagnose why they came about – were quick to pick up a story without due verification of facts, which would require an understanding of the Russian language and the legislative process in that country.

79 O Vozhyeva, "Eksperty otsenili vozmozhnost' voyennogo konflikta v Arktike", 18 December 2019, MKRU, https://www.mk.ru/politics/2019/12/18/eksperty-ocenili-vozmozhnost-voennogo-konflikta-v-arktike.html (accessed 21 January 2020).

Global Co-management and the Emergent Arctic: Opportunities for Engagement and Collaboration between Arctic States, Indigenous Permanent Participants, and Observers on the Arctic Council

Barry S. Zellen*

Abstract

Successful collaboration between the indigenous peoples and the sovereign states of Arctic North America has helped to stabilise the Arctic region, fostering meaningful indigenous participation in the governance of their homeland, the introduction of new institutions of self-governance at the municipal, tribal and territorial levels, and successful diplomatic collaborations at the international level through the Arctic Council. This stability and the reciprocal and increasingly balanced relationship between sovereign states and indigenous stakeholders has yielded a widely recognised spirit of international collaboration often referred to as Arctic exceptionalism. With competition in the Arctic between states on the rise, the multitude of co-management systems and the multi-level, inter-governmental and inter-organisational relationships they have nurtured across the region will help to neutralise new threats to 'Arctic Exceptionalism' posed by intensifying inter-state tensions.

1 Introduction: Westphalian State Competition in a Co-managed Arctic – Moderating Conflict and Fostering Collaboration

While the post-Cold War Arctic has been marked by a spirit of collaboration between multiple levels of stakeholders, whether indigenous peoples, states, or transnational organisations, this collaboration has taken root at a unique historical moment. This unique moment is defined as much by the dramatic

---

* Center for Arctic Study and Policy (CASP) at the U.S. Coast Guard Academy (USCGA), and a 2020 Fulbright Scholar at the Polar Law Centre at the University of Akureyri. Barry.S.Zellen@uscga.edu.

decline in international tension and inter-bloc state rivalry that followed the end of the Cold War and the largely peaceful breakup of the Soviet Union into independent states as by the historic reconciliation between tribe and state in the Arctic region, especially Arctic North America, after the nearly half-century long process of land claims negotiation, structural innovation, political devolution, and implementation of co-management systems across the entirety of Arctic North America. Throughout this transformation in its political geography, the region has been buffered from external stressors by the remoteness and harshness of Arctic climate and geography. Thus, the state of Arctic exceptionalism may not be an inherent 'default' condition of Arctic international relations but one that has arisen in lockstep with its historical and strategic context, and one that can evaporate as historical trends and the strategic environment transform. Add to this the many complexities of the Arctic's geophysical transformation catalysed by climate change, which may introduce myriad stressors to disrupt the Arctic calm, one may reasonably look to the future with new caution and concern.

A comparative look at U.S. Arctic strategy during the post-Cold War period shows a continuous, unbroken chain of official documents committed to collaborative, multilateral Arctic engagement, in partnership with Arctic indigenous peoples and states. These include Russia, with which the U.S. directly aligned its interests at the May 28, 2008 Arctic Ocean Conference in Ilulissat, Greenland – as reflected in the Ilulissat Declaration uniting the interests of the Arctic 5 (A5) littoral states and embracing the Law of the Sea Convention (LOSC) as the guiding mechanism for Arctic Ocean management. This collaborative embrace was evident as far back as the Clinton Administration's Arctic policy (as articulated by Presidential Decision Directive/NSC-26 issued on 9 June 1994) as well as the G.W. Bush Administration's policy update, as articulated in National Security Presidential Directive (NSPD-66) on 9 January 2009, and again in the Obama Administration's National Strategy for the Arctic Region (NSAR) issued on 10 May 2013.

Over two decades spanning the collapse of the Soviet Union and re-emergence of a sovereign Russian state, and the eruption of the Global War on Terror, and well into the acceleration of a polar thaw, regardless of ruling political party, American Arctic strategy remained at heart collaborative and multilateral. But in the years that followed the release of NSAR, global interest in the Arctic has greatly intensified, and in response the Arctic Council opened its doors to a wide range of non-Arctic states as official observers of the Council, with indirect opportunities to participate through partnership with Arctic Council members. The increased complexity of world politics, and in particular, of Arctic international relations, and the assertion of interests in and through the Arctic by non-Arctic states, combined with a strategic re-assessment of Russian military ambitions in world politics, began to shake the very foundations of Arctic exceptionalism.

This precipitated a re-assessment of American strategic policy with regard to the Arctic region, and a questioning of the very foundation of Arctic exceptionalism. This became evident in the December 2016 Report to Congress on Strategy to Protect United States National Security Interests in the Arctic Region, and has again been reflected by the updated United States Coast Guard Arctic Strategic Outlook, released in April 2019, where dual concerns with both Russia's and China's Arctic ambitions contrast with the collaborative spirit that infused preceding strategy documents. Importantly, Arctic collaboration and cooperation is still a guiding principle, but it is framed in prudence more by alliance cooperation and joint military partnerships than by any presumed universality of an inherent Arctic cooperation. The cooperative foundation undergirding Arctic exceptionalism for more than a generation has been shaken, but so far it has withstood these new competitive pressures. Enduring structural changes to Arctic governance, particularly the rise of co-management as a paradigm for joint governance between natives and the state, has much to do with the durability of Arctic exceptionalism amidst the recent rise in Westphalian state competition across the Arctic region.

2 Arctic Indigenous Empowerment and Tribal Engagement – Beyond the Point of No Return

Since the state and its colonial proxies first began to encroach upon their homelands centuries ago, Natives of Arctic and Subarctic North America have endeavored to assert and defend their Aboriginal rights and cultural traditions, and to preserve as much of their autonomy as they could. As Natives learned more about the many systems and structures of governance that were exported from distant colonial centers in Europe, from the commercial trading posts and early global networks they were part of, to the largely democratic constitutional polities that would eventually take root in their homelands, they found many new ways to reassert, and increasingly, restore, their autonomy – through diplomacy, protracted (sometimes multi-decade and multi-generational) negotiations, and various forms of political protest and engagement. In the Eurasian Arctic, a greater demographic upheaval by settlers would initially limit gains by Natives in restoring their rights and reasserting autonomy – but through international Native diplomacy by regional Native organisations like the Inuit Circumpolar Conference (later renamed the Inuit Circumpolar Council), and later through their status as Permanent Participants on the Arctic Council, Natives from the more settled regions of the Eurasian Arctic would join in the movement toward the collaborative and inclusive vision of Native self-governance that took shape in Arctic North America a generation earlier, transforming what began as a regional movement into a veritable circumpolar (and increasingly global) movement for the restoration of Native rights.

The scale of this movement and the support for its goals from most member states on the Arctic Council, many of which view Native constitutional integration as an efficient, elegant and inexpensive solution to their mutual problem of sovereign legitimacy in the Arctic, contributed to both the domestic social peace as well as circumpolar international peace – and the resulting calm became known as Arctic exceptionalism.[1] Its relative tranquility, with its balanced relationship between indigenous and state interests and institutions, owes much to the domestic reconciliation of tribe and state that has taken place during this historic and exemplary period of northward state expansion. This contrasts sharply with elsewhere in the world, from further south in the Americas to the bitterly contested colonial expansions in Africa and Asia. There, the modern state collided more forcefully (and with greater kinetic energy) with the interests and sovereign aspirations of hundreds of indigenous empires, nations, and tribes, from the late 15th century onward – the result of which was a long legacy of annihilatory warfare, genocide, forced migrations, and coercive assimilation policies as states expanded onto indigenously self-governing lands. This resulted in the general extinguishment of indigenous identity even as tribes heroically fought back against the expanding state, even if inevitably losing to the state's superior military power.[2]

---

[1] Lassi Heininen, 'Arctic Geopolitics from Classical to Critical Approach: Importance of Immaterial Factors' (2018) 11 *Geography, Environment, Sustainability* 171–186; Juha Käpylä and Harri Mikkola 'On Arctic Exceptionalism: Critical Reflections in the Light of the Arctic Sunrise Case and the Crisis in Ukraine' Finnish Institute of International Affairs, FIIA Working Paper 85 (April 2015), available online at https://www.fiia.fi/wp-content/uploads/2017/01/wp85.pdf (accessed 21 January 2020).

[2] Time–Life Books, *The Way of the Warrior* (New York: Time–Life Books, 1993); Tzvetan Todorov, *The Conquest of America: The Question of the Other* (Norman, OK: University of Oklahoma Press, 1982); Robert M Utley and Wilcomb E Washburn, *The American Heritage History of the Indian Wars* (New York: American Heritage Publishing, 1977).

3 Northward State Expansion: from Colonisation to Collaborative Arctic Governance

In the Far North of the North American continent, stretching from the Aleutians in the west to Greenland in the east, sovereign states (with their concentrated military–industrial powers) collided with indigenous peoples and polities much later in history – with economic contact through corporate proxies such as chartered companies operating on behalf of distant sovereigns coming to dominate the process of colonisation from the first Arctic voyages of the 16th century onward.[3] By the time the presence of the rapidly modernising state began to be felt in the Arctic, its methods for asserting political control began to soften, with hard military power (as embraced by the Russians in their initial conquest of the Aleutians and consequent displacement of its peoples), shifting to softer power, with economic integration, enhanced by treaty and autonomy negotiations, largely replacing conquest for the final integration of Arctic territories into the American, Canadian and Danish polities.[4] With this softer expansion marked less by muscular conquest and more by a gradual hybridisation of economic structures to integrate subsistence practices with market dynamics, northern Natives did not feel compelled to engage the state frontally by force but began to see state expansion more symbiotically.[5] Sovereignty, security, and survival across the Arctic region would require accommodation, rather than confrontation, from both sides.

In 1867, America purchased Alaska from Russia, and with the purchase gained title to the Russian–American Company's broad assertion of sovereignty over Alaska's interior tribes – even in the more remote and northern territories, where the Russians never settled.[6] Most Americans believed Secretary of State William H. Seward, the architect of the deal, had been unwise to have

---

3   Georg Hartwig, The Polar and Tropical Worlds (Springfield, MA: C.A. Nichols and Company, 1874); John R Bockstoce, *Furs and Frontiers in the Far North: The Contest Among Native and Foreign Nations for the Bering Strait Fur Trade* (New Haven: Yale University Press, 2009).

4   Hannes Gerhardt, 'The Inuit and Sovereignty: The Case of the Inuit Circumpolar Conference and Greenland' (2011) 14 *Politik* 1; Oran R Young, *Creating Regimes: Arctic Accords and International Governance* (Ithaca: Cornell University Press, 1998); Barry Scott Zellen, *Breaking The Ice: From Land Claims to Tribal Sovereignty in the Arctic* (Lanham, MD: Lexington Books, 2008).

5   Carina Keskitalo and Mark Nuttall, 'Globalization of the Arctic' in Joan Nymand Larsen, Øyvind Paasche and Birgitta Evengård (eds) *The New Arctic* (Springer, New York, 2015), 175–187; John W. Heaton, "Athabascan Village Stores: Subsistence Shopping in Interior Alaska, 1850–1950," *Western Historical Quarterly* 43, No. 2 (Summer 2012), 133–155.

6   Alan Boraas and Aaron Leggett, "Dena'ina Resistance to Russian Hegemony, Late Eighteenth and Nineteenth Centuries: Cook Inlet, Alaska," *Ethnohistory* 60, No. 3 (2013), 485–504.

spent $7 million on these frozen acres, dubbing the new territory 'Seward's Ice Box' or 'Seward's Folly.'[7] Great Britain, and later Canada, similarly acquired their way to sovereign expansion, first through the purchase of Rupert's Land (funded with a £300,000 loan from Britain, after Parliament's 1868 approval of the Rupert's Land Act, and agreed to by the newly established Dominion of Canada, which coveted its territories – providing the Hudson's Bay Company (HBC) with a variety of land and tax benefits in exchange for accepting the Deed of Surrender). And later by entering into a series of Numbered Treaties, nation-to-nation peace accords pledging friendship and alliance with the Natives of Canada's new territories (who, like their brethren in Alaska, had not been consulted by either the Crown or HBC during the negotiations that preceded Canada's accession of Rupert's Land).

Thus, largely through negotiation, the new territories of the far northwest of North America entered into southern control without, by and large, recourse to war (in marked contrast to the armed conquest of the southwest frontier during America's long series of campaigns known in their collectivity as the Indian Wars) – with rare exceptions to this pacific expansion including the Métis rebellion from 1871 through 1885, perhaps the greatest indigenous threat the young dominion would ever face.[8] In Greenland, the era of colonisation has yet to fully come to an end, with the predominantly Inuit island of Greenland still governed as a semi-autonomous peripheral region under the sovereignty of the Kingdom of Denmark, though the role and structure of the Royal Greenland Trading Department has greatly modernised (much like that of the HBC), shedding its quasi-sovereign powers as Home Rule governance, and more recently (after the 2008 referendum), Self-Rule governance, increasingly re-empowered Greenlanders.[9]

Because economic integration of Arctic North America preceded political integration into the constitutional fabric of the state, and this subsequent political integration was achieved largely without war, the preferred tools for

---

7   See Bockstoce, note 3; Lee A. Farrow, Lee A. Seward's Folly: A New Look at the Alaska Purchase (Anchorage: University of Alaska Press, 2016).
8   Geoffrey York and Loreen Pindera, *People of the Pines: The Warriors and the Legacy of Oka* (Boston: Little, Brown, 1991). More recently, in Canada's densely populated southern corridor, there have been recurrent but highly localised and mostly symbolic armed uprisings, such as that which embroiled Oka, Quebec in 1990, and which escalated to the very threshold of civil war with the seizure of the Mercier Bridge connecting Montreal to the Southern Townships, a months-long siege of a contemporary North American metropolis by an armed tribal movement of the type seen elsewhere in the world, but which has generally been the exception in contemporary North America.
9   Hannes Gerhardt, "The Inuit and Sovereignty: The Case of the Inuit Circumpolar Conference and Greenland." *Politik* 14, No. 1 (2011).

reconciling the interests of tribe and state have remained predominantly nonviolent, modeled on transactional treaty and purchase processes, with multiyear treaty negotiations helping to bring structural balance to the many other material asymmetries – such as economic and military power – that differentiated the indigenous tribes from the modern states that would ultimately assert formal sovereign claims to the Arctic.

4 War Comes to the Arctic: Militarisation, Modernisation, and Native Engagement

While the expansion of the modern state into the North did not require frontier warfare as experienced elsewhere in colonial expansion (from Asia to Africa, and including most of the Americas below the tree line), modern warfare nonetheless did have a significant impact on the evolving relationship between Natives and the modern state. This was most dramatically illustrated in June 1942 when Japan bombed Dutch Harbor and invaded the islands of Attu and Kiska in the Western Aleutians. With Japan's forcible resettlement of the surviving Aleuts from Attu to Hokkaido for the remainder of the war, Alaska Natives quickly recognised that they too faced grave danger, and the crucible of war would help to tighten the bond between Alaska's indigenous peoples and the rapidly expanding modern state, which mobilised for war by building new airstrips, surging manpower, and cutting the Alaska Highway across 1,400 miles of northern wilderness in 1942.[10]

While this rapid mobilisation would create many stresses and strains on the long-isolated Native population, including the painful odyssey of the remaining Aleut population as it was evacuated outside the war zone to camps in Alaska's southeast (suffering significant losses to their population from the strains of displacement and internment), the wartime experience would in other ways help bring Natives and settlers closer together. This was evident in the formation of the Alaska Eskimo Scouts in 1942, the famed 'Tundra Army' organised by Major Marvin 'Muktuk' Marston, which would later become the Alaska Territorial Guard, with its thousands of volunteers representing over 100 Aleut, Athabaskan, Inupiaq, Haida, Tlingit, Tsimshian, Yupik, and non-native communities.[11] In the high North Atlantic, the dual impact of

---

10   Fern Chandonnet, *Alaska at War, 1941–1945: The Forgotten War Remembered* (Anchorage: Alaska at War Committee, 1995).
11   Marvin "Muktuk" Marston, *Men of the Tundra: Eskimos at War* (New York: October House, 1969).

the Battle of the Atlantic, and America's defense of Greenland and maritime Canada, would similarly bring modern state power into remote and traditional Inuit territories in Labrador, Baffin Island, and Greenland. Later, during the Cold War, the massive DEW (Distant Early Warning) Line Project and integration of the isolated Arctic coast into North America's air defense would have a similarly transformative impact, extending modern state power deeper into the homeland of the Inuit.

5   Land Claims, Economic Integration, and Cultural Preservation: Striking a Balance

Native participation in the defense of Alaska would provide a powerful unifying force, stimulating the movement for Native rights as the dynamic social transformation of the U.S. Civil Rights movement flowed north into Alaska, culminating in the historic 1971 passage of the Alaska Native Claims Settlement Act (ANCSA), the pioneering land treaty transferring 44 million acres of land title and $1 billion in compensation to Alaska natives, a model embraced and later enhanced as Inuit land claims were negotiated across the entire North American Arctic, with Inuit gaining title to nearly one-tenth of their traditional land base, and new co-management structures enabling a joint approach to managing natural resources, land access, and economic development.[12]

By the time the Inuvialuit of Canada's Western Arctic settled their land claim in 1984, based on their Agreement-in-Principle (AiP) negotiated in 1978, they had greatly advanced the land claims model, favoring the many Native traditions that ANCSA had, in its original form, overlooked, and departing from ANCSA, allowing subsistence activities unhindered. This, in turn, inspired the U.S. federal government to finally address, and in essence federalise, subsistence in its 1980 Alaska National Interest Lands Conservation Act (ANILCA).[13] The revised model, integrating economic modernisation and native corporate development with resource co-management and subsistence, has remained largely intact in subsequent comprehensive land claims, from Nunavut to Nunatsiavut to the east, and in the many Dene and Yukon First Nation settlement areas to the south of the Inuit homeland, showing great endurance as a model for northern development from which there has been no retreat.

---

12   Barry Scott Zellen, Breaking The Ice: From Land Claims to Tribal Sovereignty in the Arctic (Lanham, MD: Lexington Books, 2008).
13   Ibid.

While augmented with new tools for achieving increasing levels of self-governance, the land claims treaty structure continues to embrace collaborative (and adaptive) co-management of lands and resources, and to balance the inherent tensions between market economies and traditional subsistence. And, while constitutionally distinct, the steady evolution from Home Rule to Self-Rule in Greenland mirrors the achievements of Natives in Alaska and the Canadian Arctic, leveraging the long and enduring foundation of economic integration to assert and achieve political gains, and to strengthen the role of Natives in governing their homeland.

The range of governing institutions has, as a result of this complex jurisdictional landscape of Arctic North America, proliferated in form and in number: At the municipal level of government, there is the North Slope Borough in Alaska, a vast municipality that sustains itself through property taxation of the Prudhoe Bay oil facilities, a borough larger in size than the state of Massachusetts that governs a population of just 9,800 – with hundreds of millions of dollars in property taxes to build world-class infrastructure and provide modern government services in a region that had historically lacked such essentials as schools and hospitals.[14] At the territorial level, there is the vast Nunavut Territory, governing one-fifth of Canada's landmass, creating through the peaceful secession of the Eastern Arctic from the old Northwest Territories, and home to some 40,000 people, almost entirely Inuit, scattered across 28 villages in an area larger than Europe – and a source of much of Canada's future natural resource wealth and strategic waterways.[15] And at the tribal/indigenous level, there is the Inuit government of Nunatsiavut in northern Labrador, which has a unique Inuit constitution that governs its 2,500 Inuit residents living in six villages in a traditional manner, rejecting a public governance model

---

14   Native American Rights Fund (NARF), "'The Fifth Disaster': The Colonization of the North Slope of Alaska," NARF Newsletter (Boulder: NARF, 1975), 1–14, 47; Native American Rights Fund (NARF), "1988 Amendments Provide Stop-Gap Protection for Native Land and Corporations," NARF Newsletter (Boulder: NARF, 1988), 1–5.

15   Hannes Gerhardt, "The Inuit and Sovereignty: The Case of the Inuit Circumpolar Conference and Greenland," *Politik* 14, No. 1 (2011). On the complexity of the wildlife management decision-making process under Article 5 of the Nunavut Land Claim Agreement, see Nicholas Lunn et al., "Polar Bear Management in Canada, 2005–2008," in *Polar Bears: Proceedings of the 15th Working Meeting of the IUCN/SSC Polar Bear Specialist Group*, 29 June–3 July 2009, Copenhagen, Denmark, Occasional Paper of the IUCN Species Survival Commission No. 43, Martyn E. Obbard, Gregory W. Thiemann, Elizabeth Peacock, Terry D. DeBruyn, eds. (Gland, Switzerland: IUCN, 2009). For a similar illustration of the complexity in the Inuvialuit Settlement Region, see the Wildlife Management Advisory Council – North Slope (WMAC – NS) figure at https://wmacns.ca/about-us/co-management/.

in favor of one more distinctively tribal in nature (owing to the demographic predominance of non-Natives in Newfoundland and Labrador, making a public model inherently risky there in contrast to Nunavut, which enjoys Inuit demographic predominance). Together, the whole of Arctic North America presents us with a fascinating contemporary realm of settled land claims, dynamically evolving systems of indigenous and regional governance, indigenous and collaborative international diplomacy, and flexible balancing of subsistence culture with economic modernisation and development, blending two worlds, one traditional, one contemporary.

The northern tranquility that distinguishes today's Arctic region from so many other parts of the globe, and which has led many to affirm their faith in the existence of a state of Arctic exceptionalism predisposed to international cooperation, owes much then to the domestic reconciliation of tribe and state that has taken place during this historic and exemplary period of northward state expansion into Arctic North America. This iterative reconciliation process between tribe and state has dialectically catapulted the region beyond its earlier dichotomous categorisation as either a northern 'frontier' or 'homeland,'[16] so that in synthesis it has evolved to become both frontier *and* homeland, and in this symbiotic fusion to emerge as something altogether new. The end result has been a distinctive, hybrid level of analysis that owes its legitimacy, historic endurance, and pacific international environment to both tribe and state, and whose 'sovereign duality'[17] brings order to a land that might otherwise collapse into partisan conflict as seen in other tribally governed regions of the world. The reason why sovereign duality brings order to the Arctic is its mutuality of commitment to the development of hybrid systems of joint governance systems that universally embrace the principle of co-management while defining the specific terms of co-management locally.

The subsequent post-land claims proliferation of co-management boards across Arctic North America, and the limited geographical reach of each board (centered upon a single indigenous polity), has created a complex new map of the Arctic which requires granular knowledge to successfully navigate. This granularity presents significant challenges to government and business entities, with successful co-management depending upon both a good faith commitment to a mutually beneficial partnership between tribe and state, a

---

16 Thomas R. Berger, *Northern Frontier, Northern Homeland: The Report of the Mackenzie Valley Pipeline Inquiry*. Ottawa: J. Lorimer in association with Pub. Centre, Supply and Services Canada, 1977.

17 Barry Scott Zellen, *Breaking The Ice: From Land Claims to Tribal Sovereignty in the Arctic* (Lanham, MD: Lexington Books, 2008).

detailed knowledge of the human terrain that is no less nuanced, nor less strategically important, than that of the most hotly contested zones of insurgency to any counterinsurgency strategist.

6 Co-management and the Complexity of Post-land Claims Arctic Governance

Thierry Rodon and Aude Therrien describe the land claims process and the consequent institutional development of co-management boards for jointly governing indigenous homelands as a complex governance arrangement necessitated by the demands for multilevel governance in the Arctic.[18] Despite complaints from numerous political and business leaders on the resulting 'Balkanisation' of decision-making in the post-land claims Arctic and ongoing efforts to streamline this process through regional integration, Native leaders have to a large measure defended their gains and protected existing co-management structures, with their intensely localised geography, particularly in the ethnically diverse NWT and Yukon.

In Nunavut, which is ethnically unified by its overwhelming Inuit majority population, concern is less with a Balkanised decision-making landscape of the sort that has emerged in the more western territories of the Canadian North and in Alaska, and more with the Government of Canada's lackluster commitment to land claims implementation, and what Inuit perceived to be a half-hearted commitment to co-management in Ottawa. As a result, Arctic North America's lands, waters and resources remain governed by a continent-wide patchwork of co-management boards that is, by its very nature, institutionally complex.[19]

This complexity is highlighted in Mark Nuttall's insightful research on the co-management of Arctic oil and gas resources in Alaska and the Western Arctic,[20] and Claudia Notzke's pioneering research on resource co-management across Canada,[21] which chronicles both the proliferation and

---

18   Thierry Rodon and Aude Therrien, "Resource Development and Land Claims Settlement in the Canadian Arctic: Multilevel Governance, Subsidiarity and Streamlining," in *2015 Arctic Yearbook: Arctic Governance and Governing*, Lassi Heininen, Heather Exner-Pirot, and Joel Plouffe, eds. (Akureyri: Northern Research Forum, 2015), 119–131.
19   Ibid.
20   Mark Nuttall, "Aboriginal Participation, Consultation, and Canada's Mackenzie Gas Project." *Energy & Environment*, 19:5 (2008), 617–634.
21   Claudia Notzke, "A New Perspective in Aboriginal Natural Resource Management: Co-management," *Geoforum* 26:2 (May 1995), 187–209.

increasing saliency of co-management as a governing principle for natural resource management, even in regions without settled land claims. Indeed, so well-suited is co-management to resource-rich frontier regions, it has been decoupled from the land claims process, finding its way into resource-rich parts of Canada's settled southern provinces where competing claims to the land have precluded successful negotiation of land claims, becoming a salient micro-level of analysis independent of land claims settlement – as evident in the emergence of 'strategic co-management' systems designed for 'cooperative environmental management' of natural resource-rich area, yielding stand-alone co-management bodies in areas of southern Canada without settled land claims.[22]

Derek Armitage et al.'s 2011 study of co-management in the Canadian Arctic demonstrates how co-management provides a mechanism for both Natives and governments to learn how to be adaptive amidst 'uncertainty and environmental change,' and thus to benefit from social learning for developing adaptive capacity for resolving complex challenges collaboratively, resulting in new levels of knowledge co-production that successfully synthesise indigenous and western approaches – introducing a 'collaborative process to bring together a plurality of knowledge sources' that both reconciles asymmetries in power and overcomes the many complexities of multilevel governance.[23]

7 The Globalisation of Co-management

Armitage's earlier 2007 volume, co-edited with Fikret Berkes and Nancy Doubleday, *Adaptive Co-Management: Collaboration, Learning and Multi-Level Governance*,[24] illustrates the globalisation and universalisation of co-management far beyond the Arctic region. Its case studies include northern examples of co-management from Alaska, Yukon, NWT and Nunavut as might be expected, as well as case studies of co-management in places as diverse as Vancouver Island, Southern Ontario and Atlantic Canada in Canada's southern provinces; in addition to Wisconsin in the United States; Belize, Barbados, and Granada in the Central America/Caribbean region; and Sweden in Europe.

Indeed, co-management has truly gone global. Former Yukon Premier Tony Penikett has observed that Native treaties in Canada are themselves 'inherently

---

22 Ibid.
23 Derek Armitage, Fikret Berkes and Nancy Doubleday, eds., *Adaptive Co-Management: Collaboration, Learning and Multi-Level Governance* (Vancouver: UBC Press, 2007).
24 Ibid.

international because natives are transnational,' even if governments in North America still view Natives as 'domesticated' components of their constitutional polities. To Penikett, land claims treaties and the many co-management structures they yielded are 'remarkable nation-building achievements,' helping to offset earlier colonial-era treaties and the 'historic failures of colonising states to respect their treaty promises.'[25] Looking to the future, as the polar thaw drives continuing Arctic globalisation, and non-Arctic states show increasing interest in Arctic lands, waters and resources, the strategic center of mass for engaging in Arctic enterprises of all sorts will be the myriad co-management structures that define the post-land claims political topography of Arctic North America.

Just as co-management strives to institutionalise the dynamic balancing of competing traditional and modern values, and of tribal and state powers, it could establish a foundation for the diplomatic balancing of Arctic interests and non-Arctic interests alike. Co-management can thus form a vital nexus at the very heart of Arctic globalisation. Co-management introduces a collaborative decision-making process that is at heart adaptive, and as such is well suited to the arrival of new actors on the Arctic stage with values, interests, and capabilities that may differ profoundly from their local, regional and indigenous counterparts. Just as co-management has successfully (but not always frictionlessly) negotiated an equilibrium between contending traditional and contemporary values, and between tribal and state interests, it could serve not only as a metaphor, but an institutional foundation, for the management of the emergent state competition gathering steam in the Arctic.

8   Co-management, Collaborative Governance and the Challenge of Increased State Competition in the Arctic

Recent updates to U.S. Arctic strategy and policy documents noted in the first section of this paper reflect the widening perception in policy circles of the emergence (and in the case of Russia, re-emergence) of competing interests in the Arctic, a region hitherto widely perceived to be a definitive sea of calm at the top of the world. These tensions leapt forth from the pages of policy and strategy documents to diplomatic ripples on the world stage at the May 2019 Arctic Council Ministerial in Rovaniemi, Finland. But even there, public comments from the U.S. Secretary of State on the return of Westphalian state

---

25   Tony Penikett, "An Unfinished Journey: Arctic Indigenous Rights, Lands, and Jurisdiction?" *Seattle University Law Review* 37:4 (2014), 1127–1156.

competition to the Arctic made outside the Council chambers for the benefit of both his domestic audience as well as for news headlines to convey the newly re-articulated U.S. position on a more competitive Arctic domain, did not prevent the Secretary's continued collaboration with fellow Council members behind closed doors during the very same Council session.

And while the Ministerial did not conclude with a consensus statement, as has long been the tradition for such meetings at their conclusion, this had more to do with new disagreements within the Council on both the causal origins and global nature (which had previously enjoyed consensus on the Council) of a polar thaw that nonetheless remains universally accepted on the Council than with the external strategic environment of Arctic international affairs. Indeed, widely quoted comments by the U.S. Secretary State rejecting China's claim of a special 'Near-Arctic' status and calling for a transparent, rules-based order in the Arctic have been warmly (if more discreetly) embraced by several other Council members. Internal divisions within the Council membership, such as those between the Arctic Five (A5) and three other Council member states which flared up a decade ago, or the potential rift between Russia and the other seven member states after Russia's Crimea annexation, were potentially more divisive, and thus a far graver threat to the Council's collaborative dynamic, and yet the Council's collaborative dynamic has held.

Because the Council is so deeply collaborative at its core, with its three categories of participants (members, permanent participants, and observers – including both state and non-state entities) finding many opportunities to work together on the Council's many substantive working groups tackling the region's many challenges in a collaborative manner regardless of formal powers within the Council itself, like any collaborative governing body, disagreements are quite natural, and can be resolved through ongoing discussion. After all, the Arctic is the one front during the Cold War that remained free of armed conflict, and was recognised not only by the indigenous Inuit as a natural zone of peace, but also by the premier of the Soviet Union itself for this very same virtue. As more and more states from outside the Arctic region join the Council as observers, new and diverse interests in the Arctic will find a voice in these discussions, and transform what was an easier dialogue between fellow Arctic states with a common heritage and shared geopolitical frontier into a more dynamic, complex and at times more difficult conversation.

But a conversation it will be, and it is at this table where old Arctic powers like America and Russia found common ground for nearly a quarter century in spite of the previous three quarters of a century marked largely by rivalry, suggesting that the introduction of new voices, from non-Arctic states with increasing interest in Arctic economic opportunities, will not jeopardise the underlying spirit of collaboration that has guided the Council since its inception. Indeed, the Council emerged through a process of multi-level and multilateral co-management – between tribes, local governments, state and territorial governments, national governments, economic interests and environmental interests, both within and across borders. The Council, with its unique and evolving structure bringing indigenous permanent participants with the founding member states together, joined by observers (both state and non-state that increase in number and diversity over time), is well designed for the inclusion of new voices, particularly competing voices. After all, it was the moderation of competing voices between tribal and settler interests that, through the land claims process, transformed Arctic governance into a meaningfully collaborative process that in many cases successfully balances those voices, finding consensus despite the many asymmetries of the actors involved. The Council is thus firmly rooted in collaboration, bringing co-management to the global stage.

9 Conclusion: The Return of Westphalian State Competition – New Arctic Tensions and Rivalries

The depth of commitment to Arctic collaboration has thus far not been meaningfully undermined or threatened by a renewal of Westphalian state competition, since state rivalry, amidst the post-Cold War calm that has led many to perceive an inherent state of Arctic exceptionalism, has truly never gone away. It's just the conflicts that have existed between the Arctic states have been successfully counterbalanced by a mutuality of collaborative values with deep historical roots reaching back long before the Council itself was formed. The United States and Canada embrace this collaboration while disagreeing, as friends and neighbors, on many issues including their joint boundary in the petroleum-rich Beaufort Sea, and the legal status of the Northwest Passage – neither a trivial matter. Norway and Russia likewise have found many reasons to cooperate, even with one firmly embedded in the NATO alliance and the other long NATO's principal adversary. Within the Council, there have been many tensions before, including those between the littoral Arctic states with shores along the Arctic basin (A5) and the three other Arctic states that brought Russia together with four NATO members in alignment against another NATO member and two non-NATO Arctic states in 2008. A mutual commitment to collaboration does not simply erase the existence of competing national interests; it just manages this competition within a structure defined by mutual commitment to collaboration rather than conflict. This is borne of the Council's foundation in co-management, which itself managed the competing interests of tribe and state.

So even as new stakeholders come to the Council as observer states, such as the economically powerful maritime trading states of East Asia – China, Korea, Japan and Singapore – its underlying spirit of collaboration will more than likely continue to illuminate its path forward. The opportunity for the Arctic to continue as a zone of international peace and cooperation, as long hoped by so many Arctic stakeholders for so long, remains strong – so long as the many stakeholders in the Arctic continue to work collaboratively, and work diligently to align their interests as much as is possible, and to recognise when it is not that other common values and mutual interests contextualise and thus moderate these differences when they exist.

There is always the specter of the re-emergence of a new Arctic Cold War should such a collaboration prove incompatible with the future actions of the many states vying for Arctic influence and involvement, whether Arctic states or not. But this would likely happen only if the consensus underlying the Council since its formation is broken by events external to the Arctic (such as war breaking out elsewhere in the world). This was the case in World War II, where states external to the Arctic through their military aggression in northern lands and waters brought war into this otherwise pacific realm. Even then, the pressures of war brought the northern nations closer together than ever in their joint effort at mutual defense and national survival, despite vast ideological distance between them.

Whether the path forward is continued exceptionalism, or a collapse in the peaceful Arctic order, thus depends much on the willingness of new Arctic stakeholders to uphold the collaborative commitments embraced by the Arctic states and the indigenous peoples of the Arctic who established trust and cooperation through the creation of joint-governing mechanisms, such as the many co-management regimes established after indigenous land claims were settled across Arctic North America. An interesting barometer of this will be whether the new Arctic stakeholders engage respectfully with the co-management system. While the Arctic Council's member states and indigenous permanent participants reflect, to a large measure, the original parties to the co-management process that took root in Arctic North America after land claims were settled, recent years have witnessed a proliferation in the number of observer states that now participate in Council meetings and on its working groups from well outside the Arctic, including the industrialised maritime states of Asia with domestic markets hungry for natural resources, shipping companies that can benefit from emergent Arctic sea lanes, and the technological solutions needed for Arctic resource and infrastructure development.

There is much potential for North–South partnerships as Arctic globalisation continues, with technology and innovation from outside the region fostering future growth; but in order to proceed, knowledge of and respect for these many localised systems of co-management is essential.

By embracing co-management, and navigating the complex administrative landscape of the post-land claims Arctic with humility and respect, non-Arctic states will find enthusiastic partners in villages from one end of the Arctic to the other, and through the mutuality of collaboration, enjoy the reciprocity of what Jamie Snook, Ashlee Cunsolo, and Aaron Dale have called the 'shared space' of co-management.[26] This will build trust, and smooth relations not only with native communities and local levels of governance, but also with the national agencies and departments that participate equally in the co-management process. But it is important to remember that Arctic co-management has been around for nearly half a century, and that local stakeholders are deeply committed to the co-management process and the reconciliation of competing interests through mutual respect. They not only sit at the table, they built the table at which they sit, having negotiated for many years, sometimes decades, in an historic process of re-empowerment of indigenous peoples across the Arctic. Just as non-Arctic observers at the Arctic Council sit around the table but not at it, a place at the co-management table is earned through embracing this very same commitment to trust and mutual respect. Remembering this can unlock unimagined opportunities for mutual gain and prosperity across the Arctic region. Forgetting this, however, could result in a missed opportunity of equal magnitude, and plant the seeds for what could become a new Cold War at the top of the world.

Acknowledgements

The author is the Class of 1965 Arctic Scholar at the Center for Arctic Study and Policy (CASP) at the US Coast Guard Academy (USCGA), and a 2020 Fulbright Scholar at the Polar Law Centre at the University of Akureyri. The views expressed in this paper are the author's own, and do not reflect the policies or views of any other organisation, government or agency.

---

[26] Jamie Snook, Ashlee Cunsolo, and Aaron Dale, "A Conceptual Representation of the 'Shared Space' of Co-management Reseasrch, Recommendations, Actions, and Decision-making." *Northern Public Affairs* (July 2018): 52–56.

Some Icelandic Perspectives on the Agreement to Prevent Unregulated High Seas Fisheries in the Central Arctic Ocean

*Jóhann Sigurjónsson**

Abstract

This paper reflects on several aspects of the Agreement to Prevent Unregulated High Seas Fisheries in the Central Arctic Ocean from the standpoint of Iceland, prior to, during and at the conclusion of the negotiations of the Agreement in late 2017. Particular reference is made to UNCLOS and coastal State interests, status of knowledge on the fish stocks and the importance of scientific cooperation which the Agreement facilitates.

During the years 2008–2015, the so-called Arctic Five consulted on cooperation in Arctic matters including future management of fisheries in the central Arctic Ocean. These rather exclusive cooperative efforts were criticised by Iceland and other States that felt these matters were to be dealt with in a broader international context. It seems evident that Iceland's desire to become a full participant in the process during the subsequent years was both based on legal arguments as well as fair and natural geopolitical reasons. Iceland became a participant in the negotiations in December 2015.

The final version of the Agreement is a fully fledged platform for coordinating scientific research and it even allows for interim management measures until future

---

* The author of this paper was Special Envoy on Ocean Affairs, Ministry for Foreign Affairs of Iceland 2016–2019 and served as Head of Delegation of Iceland during the negotiations on the Agreement to Prevent Unregulated High Seas Fisheries in the Central Arctic Ocean. johann.sigurjonsson@utn.is.

During 1998–2016 he served as Director General of Iceland's Marine Research Institute. The views expressed in this paper are personal to the author and do not necessarily represent those of the Government of Iceland. The author wants to thank Mr Arnór Snæbjörnsson and Mr Stefán Ásmundsson, the Ministry of Industries and Innovation of Iceland, Dr Matthías G Pálsson, Mr Árni Þór Sigurðsson and Mr Jörundur Valtýsson, Ministry for Foreign Affairs of Iceland, and Dr Snjólaug Árnadóttir, University of Iceland, and an anonymous reviewer, who kindly read over the manuscript and made useful suggestions for improvements.

regional management framework is in place. In essence, the Agreement can be taken as a regional fisheries management arrangement (RFMA), since most elements of relevance are incorporated in accordance with the 1995 UN Fish Stocks Agreement.

The opening of the central Arctic Ocean for fishing is not likely to take place in the nearest future, although the development of sea ice retreat is currently faster than earlier anticipated. While the Agreement is today regarded as being historic due to its precautionary approach, future may prove that it was a timely arrangement in a fast-moving world with dramatic changes taking place in the Arctic Ocean.

1   Introduction

In 2008, five Arctic States, i.e. Canada, the Kingdom of Denmark (on behalf of Greenland), the Kingdom of Norway, the Russian Federation, and the United States of America, signed in Ilulissat, Greenland, a Declaration[1] to strengthen cooperation in Arctic Ocean matters. The close cooperation of the same five States (called the 'Arctic Five') was further expanded in July 2015 with a more focused Declaration regarding 'the implementation of interim measures to prevent unregulated fishing in the high seas portion of the central Arctic Ocean'.[2]

The 2008 Declaration was rather general with respect to the Arctic marine environment and the inhabitants of the high north. However, it stipulated the 1982 UN Convention on the Law of the Sea ('UNCLOS')[3] as the general legal framework for all aspects of ocean activities, the delineation of the outer limits of the continental shelf, the protection of the marine environment, including ice-covered areas, freedom of navigation, marine scientific research, and other uses of the sea. At that time, it was of concern to Iceland, Sweden and

---

1   2008 Ilulissat Declaration, adopted by the Arctic Ocean Conference in Ilulissat in Greenland on 28 May 2008, https://cil.nus.edu.sg/wp-content/uploads/2017/07/2008-Ilulissat-Declaration.pdf (accessed 15 December 2018).
2   Declaration Concerning the Prevention of Unregulated High Seas Fishing in the Central Arctic Ocean, adopted by Canada, the Kingdom of Denmark, the Kingdom of Norway, the Russian Federation and the United States of America in Oslo 16 July 2015, https://oceanconservancy.org/wp-content/uploads/2017/04/declaration-on-arctic-fisheries-16-july-2015-1.pdf (accessed 15 December 2018); Alf Håkon Hoel, "The 5+5 Process in Arctic Fisheries", in Robert W Corell, Jong Deog Kim, Yoon Hyung Kim and Oran R Young (eds), *The Arctic in World Affairs – A North Pacific Dialogue on Arctic Futures: Emerging Issues and Policy Responses* (Busan, Republic of Korea: Korea Maritime Institute; Honolulu: East-West Center 2016), 127, 131–132.
3   United Nations Convention on the Law of the Sea (adopted 10 December 1982, entered into force 16 November 1994), 1833 UNTS 3.

Finland,[4] all members of the Arctic Council, that these matters were handled by this non-institutional Arctic Five, matters that were more suited to be dealt with under the Arctic Council umbrella. It was the firm view of Iceland, that all Arctic coastal States should be at the table where the dramatic changes of ocean conditions and ice coverage in the Arctic Ocean were being discussed.

Notwithstanding the immediate interests of the Arctic Five in this connection, the Declaration of July 2015 was relevant to all States with a stake in UNCLOS and its implementation agreement, the 1995 UN Fish Stocks Agreement,[5] as well as States with coastal zones adjacent to the central Arctic Ocean. Therefore, it was even more important that the process be open and inclusive instead of rather closed and exclusive as it appeared to those not participating. Iceland therefore welcomed becoming a part of the negotiation process in late 2015.

This paper is written to reflect on several aspects of the Agreement to Prevent Unregulated High Seas Fisheries in the Central Arctic Ocean ('the Central Arctic Ocean Fisheries Agreement' or 'the Agreement')[6] from the standpoint of Iceland, prior to, during the negotiations 2015–2017, and after their conclusion. Particular reference is made to UNCLOS and coastal State interests, as well as the importance of scientific elements and organisational structure for scientific cooperation, which the Agreement facilitates.

2 Points for Consideration while Negotiating the Central Arctic Ocean Fisheries Agreement

The Central Arctic Ocean Fisheries Agreement is exceptional in many ways. It is precautionary in the sense that it is negotiated before it is urgently needed

---

4 Betsy Baker, "The Developing Regional Regime for the Maritime Arctic", in Erik J Molenaar, Alex G Oude Elferink, and Donald R Rothwell (eds), *The Law of the Sea and the Polar Regions – Interactions between Global and Regional Regimes* (Martinus Nijhoff Publishers 2013), 35, 37; Hugi Ólafsson, "Commentaries", in Oran R Young, Jong Deog Kim and Yoon Hyung Kim (eds), *The Arctic in World Affairs – A North Pacific Dialogue on the Arctic in the Wider World* (Korea Maritime Institute and East-West Center 2015), 48,55; Njord Wegge, "The emerging politics of the Arctic Ocean. Future management of the living marine resources" (2015) 51 *Marine Policy*, 331, 335.
5 Agreement for the Implementation of the Provisions of the United Nations Convention on the Law of the Sea of 10 December 1982 relating to the Conservation and Management of Straddling Fish Stocks and Highly Migratory Fish Stocks (adopted 4 August 1995, entered into force 11 December 2001), 2167 UNTS 3.
6 Agreement to Prevent Unregulated High Seas Fisheries in the Central Arctic Ocean (adopted 30 November 2017).

from the conservation point of view and before any commercial harvest of the fish resources has commenced, and without potential conflicts among interested parties having had time to develop into unresolved disputes. Here, science and precaution are the key elements to safeguard the resources. In historic sense, it is noteworthy that with the conclusion of this Agreement, the last high seas pocket, i.e. the last ocean area beyond the 200 nautical miles limits of States in the high north, has been 'closed' with a legal instrument that meets the requirements of UNCLOS and the 1995 UN Fish Stocks Agreement.

2.1 *Participating States*

In essence, the Declaration of the Arctic Five of July 2015[7] included commitments by the States concerned for cautious, science-based approach towards utilisation of fish stocks in the central Arctic Ocean.[8] Such approach was in line with Iceland's general policy towards sustainable management of living resources of the sea. However, adopting management measures, where not all stakeholders are included, is hardly in the spirit of current international management practices, where cooperation is part of the rights and obligations of States as well reflected in the 1995 UN Fish Stocks Agreement. This was firmly indicated by the Icelandic authorities as early as in the year 2008 and as late as 2015,[9] i.e. before Iceland enjoyed the invitation to the central Arctic Ocean fisheries negotiations in December 2015 along with the three Asian States, China, Japan and South Korea, in addition to the European Union.

In 2011, the Icelandic Parliament's (named Alþingi) Resolution on Iceland's Arctic Policy[10] outlined the general policy in a changing Arctic, where, among other things, Iceland's special status as a coastal State in the area, in legal, economic, ecological and geographic sense, was stressed and where the point was made that the Arctic needed to be defined with the above in mind but also in light of political and security aspects as opposed to a narrow geographical definition. Furthermore, the international legal right of Iceland was stressed, where binding agreements of cooperation as well as close cooperation of Iceland with its closest neighbours, the Faroe Islands and Greenland, was

---

7   Declaration Concerning the Prevention of Unregulated High Seas Fishing in the Central Arctic Ocean, note 2.
8   See Hoel, note 2.
9   Hugi Ólafsson, note 4; Ministry for Foreign Affairs of Iceland, Press Release of 23 July 2015, https://www.government.is/news/article/?newsid=981727d5-fb94-11e7-9423-005056 bc4d74 (accessed 15 December 2018).
10 Þingsályktun um stefnu Íslands í málefnum norðurslóða, 2011, https://www.althingi.is/altext/139/s/1148.html (accessed 16 December 2018).

highlighted. Economic growth with science-based sustainable utilisation of natural resources is a key element of the policy.

In July 2015, the Ministry for Foreign Affairs communicated an official response of the Icelandic Government to the Declaration signed in Oslo a week earlier by the five States. It was stressed 'that all parties are on equal footing in order to ensure efficiency and strengthen the basis of collaboration on fishing in international waters, including the Arctic Ocean'.[11] As perhaps the Arctic State with the single most dependence on fisheries for its economy, it was considered natural that Iceland contributed with scientific knowledge and fishing experience to consultations on future cooperation in this field as climate change may open up new fishing possibilities in the central Arctic Ocean. Iceland further pointed out the importance of regional collaboration on solid scientific basis, taking into account that Iceland takes active part in the North-East Atlantic Fisheries Commission (NEAFC), which currently has a Convention Area that partly covers the central Arctic Ocean,[12] and plays an active role in the cooperative work of the International Council for the Exploration of the Sea (ICES). Iceland also stressed its longstanding contribution to the development of the law of the sea, including as one of the founding Parties of UNCLOS and the 1995 UN Fish Stocks Agreement which provide the legal framework for fishing in international waters. Iceland claimed that despite its repeated request to be included as an active participant during the consultations and preparations of the Declaration, this had not been accepted by the Arctic Five.

Finally, Iceland made the important point[13] that participation in the consultations of these five States had, rightly, not been conditional on them having an exclusive economic zone (EEZ) adjacent to the high seas portion of the central Arctic Ocean as neither Norway nor the Faroe Islands met such condition. Iceland stressed that it had the same rights and duties to take full part in discussions on the future development of fishing in international waters in the central Arctic Ocean. To exclude Iceland and other relevant States from the consultations was considered to go against the important element of inclusiveness when consulting on the emerging issues in the central Arctic Ocean, where one questioned what determines which State is a coastal State in this context. It was further pointed out that the Declaration by the five States is non-binding under international law, is not made under the auspices of or in

---

11   Ministry for Foreign Affairs of Iceland, Press Release, note 9.
12   Ibid; Erik J Molenaar, "Arctic Fisheries Management", in Erik J Molenaar, Alex G Oude Elferink, and Donald R Rothwell (eds), *The Law of the Sea and the Polar Regions – Interactions between Global and Regional Regimes* (Martinus Nijhoff Publishers 2013), 243, 251.
13   See Ministry for Foreign Affairs of Iceland, Press Release, note 9.

the name of any international organisation or arrangement and is thus not legally binding on any State.

This final point relates to the fundamental disagreement that exists between Norway and most other Parties to the Treaty of Spitzbergen of 1920, where Norway holds the view that the equal access of all Parties to the Treaty to fish does not apply outside the 12-nautical-mile territorial sea.[14] This question will be briefly touched upon here below. However, the use of the term 'coastal State' or 'Arctic Ocean coastal States' caused some controversy and perhaps deserves some mentioning here, since it was referred to when defining who were legitimate participants in the consultations.

On the one hand, one would regard the geographic location with respect to the international waters, which means States having national waters adjacent to the high seas portion in question. Here, obviously, Canada, Denmark (Greenland), the Russian Federation and the United States would rank as coastal States, but not Norway in the view of many States that have reservations with respect to the said interpretation of the Treaty of Spitzbergen. Certainly, Iceland does not have such geographic adjacency to the high seas portion of the central Arctic Ocean. However, if considering such definition with respect to straddling and highly migratory fish stocks, i.e. stocks occurring in the high seas as well as within the EEZ of a state, all the Arctic Five stand as coastal States.

States can also argue[15] that they have a 'real interest' in the resources in the high seas, e.g. history of exploitation, and would thus have full status as participating States according to article 8 of the 1995 UN Fish Stocks Agreement. A real interest could also arise if a fish stock straddles a State's EEZ and the high seas beyond and potentially stocks currently occurring either in the North Pacific or the North Atlantic can in the future migrate into the central Arctic Ocean high seas and thereby establish a real interest of the States in question.

However, in this context, while there is no universal definition of either the 'Arctic', the 'Arctic Ocean' or the 'marine Arctic', a broad definition used by CAFF, the Arctic Council Working Group on Conservation of Arctic Flora and

---

14 See Molenaar, note 12, 250; Erik J Molenaar, "Status and Reform of International Arctic Fisheries Law", in Elizabeth Tedsen, Sandra Cavalieri, R Andreas Kraemer (eds), *Arctic Marine Governance* (Springer, Heidelberg 2014), 103, 113; Robin Churchill and Geir Ulfstein, "The Disputed Maritime Zones around Svalbard", in Myron H Nordquist, Tomas H Heidar and John Norton Moore (eds), *Changes in the Arctic Environment and the Law of the Sea* (Leiden: Martinus Nijhoff Publishers 2010), 551–593.

15 See Njord Wegge, note 4.

Fauna, certainly includes Iceland as an Arctic country[16] and as such the country has various coastal States interests in the Arctic.

One may speculate why the exclusive approach of the Arctic Five was applied and persisted for such a prolonged period of time, to the discontent of Iceland and some other parties. One explanation is offered by Martin Breum, a Danish journalist specialising in Arctic affairs who referred to two Danish specialists at the Royal Danish Defence College and their published paper,[17] as he considered this question when publishing an article on the occasion of the ten years anniversary of the Ilulissat Declaration.[18] He dwelled on one event that may have influenced this development, namely when the Russian Federation in 2007 placed a flag on the polar ocean floor. His conclusion reads as follows: 'Out of sheer mistrust in the Arctic Council's ability to act swiftly in the eye of the Russian flag-planting, the Danish government in effect invented a new international institution, since known as A5 or the Arctic Five. This procedure secured the speedy adoption of the Ilulissat Declaration, but it also added to a lack of clarity in the Arctic.'[19]

Breum opines that this mechanism avoided unnecessary conflicts related to the 'flag-planting' and proved to be a practical solution for the five States to come together for more general geopolitical purposes until the dissatisfaction of other parties that later became part of the 5+5 process required an opening up of the process.[20]

2.2 The Agreement Area

During the negotiations on the Agreement, the general understanding was that the area under consideration was the central bit of the Arctic Ocean beyond 200 nautical miles off the coasts of Greenland, Canada, the United States and the Russian Federation, and 200 nautical miles to the north of Spitzbergen, encompassing an area equalling some 2.8 million km² or approximately the size of the Mediterranean Sea. This was well reflected in the media at the time

---

16   See Molenaar, note 12, 245.
17   Jon Rahbek-Clemmensen and Gry Thomasen, "Learning from the Ilulissat Initiative: State Power, Institutional Legitimacy, and Governance in the Arctic Ocean 2007–18" (Centre for Military Studies, University of Copenhagen 2018), https://cms.polsci.ku.dk/publikationer/learning-from-the-ilulissat-iniative/download/CMS_Rapport_2018_1_-_Learning_from_the_Ilulissat_initiative.pdf (accessed 16 December 2018).
18   Martin Breum, "Analysis: Ilulissat Two, Why Greenland and Denmark are inviting Arctic governments back this May" (*High North News* 2018) https://www.highnorthnews.com/nb/analysis-ilulissat-two-why-greenland-and-denmark-are-inviting-arctic-governments-back-may (accessed 16 December 2018).
19   Ibid.
20   Ibid.

of adoption of the July 2015 Declaration and during the following period of negotiations between the ten parties. However, there were some difficulties among the delegations to find the exact descriptive wording to define the area. The final text, appearing in Article 1 of the Agreement ('Use of Terms'), reads as follows:

> Agreement Area means the single high seas portion of the central Arctic Ocean that is surrounded by waters within which Canada, the Kingdom of Denmark in respect of Greenland, the Kingdom of Norway, the Russian Federation and the United States of America exercise fisheries jurisdiction.

Iceland made the point that it was fundamental that all parties shared the same understanding of the area in question and preferred to make no reference to the legal status of the area, e.g. by referring to jurisdiction or EEZ, but rather to describe the area in terms of distance from land masses. Otherwise, parties might, e.g. because of different interpretation of the Treaty of Spitzbergen of 1920, have different understanding of the geographical scope of the Agreement. Such ambiguous text was to be avoided. Iceland filed an explanatory note on this matter during the process for ratification of the Agreement, where it is underlined that this provision is without prejudice to the position of Iceland with respect to the rights and obligation of the High Contracting Parties to the Treaty of Spitzbergen of 1920, and that any exercise of fisheries jurisdiction by Norway within the maritime area around Svalbard is subject to the limitations of that Treaty.

As mentioned above, the negotiated Agreement Area had to recognise that part of the central Arctic Ocean was already covered by the NEAFC Convention. This recognition appears in one of the preambular paragraphs and is underscored in Article 14 of the Agreement, where Parties recognise that they will continue to be bound by their obligations under relevant international law despite the new Agreement. How this will work in the future is not certain at this point in time, but probably it will imply cooperative efforts between NEAFC and one or more regional fisheries management organisations or arrangements (RFMOS or RFMAS).

2.3 General Principles behind International Fisheries Management

One of the concerns of several delegations at the outset of the 10 party negotiations was the importance of managing all fishery resources, within and outside States' EEZs, in accordance with international law, particularly UNCLOS and the 1995 UN Fish Stock Agreement. Although a declaration with constructive sentiments in this spirit is perhaps made with good intentions, management measures stipulated in a declaration by a selected number of States without a formal framework for cooperation of all stakeholders may undermine the implementation of the current international legal framework. During the negotiations, Iceland preferred firm commitments in terms of a legally binding agreement where the necessary 'ingredients' of proper modern fisheries cooperative management are secured as a step towards establishment of a future RFMO or RFMA. A major concern was that a simple declaration might function as a *de facto* 'moratorium' rather than an interim step towards a dynamic international sustainable harvest regime. The 16 year time frame from the entry into force to the termination of the Agreement, unless all Parties desire its continuation, is therefore an important factor.[21] The Agreement is intended to be a step towards regional science-based management of the sustainable utilisation of the area's living marine resources and is not intended to bring about a long-term closure of commercial fisheries.

In Iceland's view, as a State with a long history of sustainable harvest of fish stocks, it was important that if and when the resources can be sustainably harvested, this shall be possible under such an international management scheme. This sentiment is well fostered in Article 5(c)(i) of the Agreement,[22] where the conditions are outlined as to 'whether to commence negotiations to establish one or more additional regional or subregional fisheries management organisations or arrangements for managing fishing in the Agreement Area'. During the negotiations, this was referred to as the 'RFMO trigger' and an integral part of a step-wise process that one envisaged could take place with more scientific knowledge and provided that fish stocks will develop towards sustainable harvest levels as time passes. This is in line with article 8(2) of the 1995 UN Fish Stocks Agreement that provides for any State to take the initiative 'without delay' and when needed and reads as follows: 'consultations may be initiated at the request of any interested State with a view to establish appropriate arrangements to ensure conservation and management of the stocks'.

In accordance with modern fisheries management and international law, the Agreement includes important scientific elements in Articles 3 to 5,[23] which promote scientific activities that can cast further light on the situation of fish stocks and the marine environment in the Agreement Area. The

---

21 Agreement to Prevent Unregulated High Seas Fisheries in the Central Arctic Ocean, note 6, Article 13.
22 Ibid, Article 5(c)(i).
23 See Agreement to Prevent Unregulated High Seas Fisheries in the Central Arctic Ocean, note 6.

Agreement also provides for the formal establishment of a scientific forum, the Joint Program of Scientific Research and Monitoring, to organise and facilitate collection and exchange of scientific information with the same aim. The science-based management is the natural basis for the precautionary approach that States lend full support through the Agreement and puts precaution on fishing in the area until the situation is better known. In Article 5(d) of the Agreement exploratory fishery is outlined,[24] including restrictions on the scope of such activities and the requirement to exchange results of them as part of the overall aim of strengthening the common knowledge base.

During the negotiations, different views were expressed on the decision-making process, particularly voting. Should all Parties have the same status when it comes to taking decisions? Iceland felt that the States closest to the resource might be candidates to have a strong saying in decision-making, while granting the right to 'veto' decisions to some States but not others did not seem to be a useful future set-up. Therefore, Iceland supported the consensus requirement for all decisions on substance as it finally appears in Article 6 of the Agreement.[25]

3   Some Scientific Findings and the Importance of Science in Future Management of the Fish Resources

In Iceland's view, as a responsible fisheries nation, it was important that if and when the resources can be sustainably harvested, this should be possible under a science-based international management scheme. The dramatic changes in ocean conditions in the central Arctic Ocean are well known and current predictions demonstrate that a new ocean with potential future possibilities may be appearing. We are in the fortunate situation to consider future mechanisms to safeguard sustainability in the area before any commercial fishing is taking place there, but knowing that the conditions can change quickly when ice retreats. Therefore, it is essential to gather information on the status of the stocks and base all decisions on best available science.

3.1   *Central Arctic Ocean Fish Stocks: Some Scientific Findings*

Prior to and during the ten party consultations, five formal meetings of scientific experts took place in the years 2011–2017,[26] focusing on fish stocks in the

---

24   Ibid, Article 5(d).
25   Ibid, Article 6.
26   See Hoel, note 2.

central Arctic Ocean, first with participation of representatives of the Arctic Five only, i.e. Canada, the Kingdom of Denmark on behalf of Greenland, the United States, the Russian Federation and Norway. Later the other Parties to the Central Arctic Ocean Fisheries Agreement, the European Union, China, Iceland, Japan and South Korea, also participated in those meetings. Also participating were representatives of international science bodies, such as ICES (focusing primarily on the science of the North Atlantic Ocean), PICES (the Pacific counterpart) and relevant Arctic Council Working Groups, i.e. PAME (Protection of the Arctic Marine Environment Working Group) and CAFF.

At the first scientific meeting in 2011, the experts made an initial review of available information on the situation in the central Arctic Ocean with respect to changes in the ecosystem and in particular the fish stocks. The meeting[27] concluded that, 'within the Arctic, current information on distribution and abundance of concentrations of these species, uncertainty in the ecosystem effects of fishing, and the technical and logistical challenges of conducting fishing operations in remote regions all suggest that commercial fisheries are not likely to emerge in the short term'. However, it was stressed that there is limited scientific knowledge available on the high seas in the Arctic and that there is a strong need to establish baseline data.

At the third meeting in 2015, the main focus was to generate an inventory of Arctic research and monitoring programs,[28] an important exercise, as well as analysing and reporting on status and gaps of knowledge in the central Arctic Ocean. It clearly demonstrated that much information is missing with respect to habitats and ecosystems. In particular, quantitative biomass estimates are lacking for fish stocks that are likely targets for future harvest. Quantifiable survey data for modelling and baseline data for future monitoring are much needed to assess the role of the fish stocks in the Arctic marine ecosystem.

At the 4th meeting of the scientific experts in 2016, a synthesis of current knowledge was completed,[29] revealing some twelve species of fish now known from the high seas area in the central Arctic Ocean, while more than 300 fish

---

27 Report of a Meeting of Scientific Experts on Fish Stocks in the Arctic Ocean (Arctic Fisheries Workshop, Anchorage, Alaska, June 15–17, 2011), https://www.afsc.noaa.gov/Arctic_fish_stocks_third_meeting/First%20Meeting%20Sci%20Experts%20Arctic%20Fisheries%2030%20Aug%202011.pdf (accessed 17 December 2018).

28 Final Report: Third Meeting of Scientific Experts on Fish Stocks in the Central Arctic Ocean (July 2015), https://www.afsc.noaa.gov/Arctic_fish_stocks_third_meeting/meeting_reports/3rd_Arctic_Fish_Final_Report_10_July_2015_final.pdf (accessed 17 December 2018).

29 Final Report of the Fourth Meeting of Scientific Experts on Fish Stocks in the Central Arctic Ocean (January 2017), https://www.afsc.noaa.gov/Arctic_fish_stocks_fourth_meeting/pdfs/FourthFiSCAOreportfinalJan26_2017.pdf (accessed 17 December 2018).

species are known in waters adjacent to the high seas. Of these twelve species there are three potential commercial species, i.e. the Greenland halibut (*Reinhardtius hippoglossoides*) and two cod-like species, Arctic cod (*Arctogadus glacialis*) and polar cod (*Boreogadus saida*). The problem of limited sampling was highlighted, and it seems evident that the number of high seas fish species is likely to increase with more sampling. And, again, it was concluded 'that fish densities of commercial interest are not likely to occur in the high seas in the near future'.

While the meetings of fisheries experts focused on the likely situation in the central Arctic Ocean, a number of studies have evaluated more broadly the possibilities of expanding fish stocks into the Arctic waters as warming up continues, not the least based on past and present observations in the North-east Atlantic and North Pacific Oceans.[30]

Hollowed *et al.* (2013)[31] studied the potential movements of fish stocks from the sub-Arctic to the Arctic Ocean, where the potential for expansion or movement into the Arctic was qualitatively ranked (low potential, potential, high potential). It is predicted that the Arctic Ocean will become ice-free during the summer season in coming decades, and when this happens new areas will open up for plankton production. This may lead to new feeding areas for fish stocks. Five species were considered as potential candidate species to move to or expand in the high Arctic. These were Greenland halibut, Atlanto Scandian herring (*Clupea harengus*), capelin (*Mallotus villosus*), yellowfin sole (*Limanda aspera*) and Alaska plaice (*Pleuronectes quadrituberculatus*). These species were believed to exhibit life history characteristics that allow them to survive in challenging environmental conditions that will continue to prevail in the

---

30 ACIA, *Arctic Climate Impact Assessment* (Cambridge University Press 2005); Hjálmar Vilhjálmsson, et al, "Fisheries and aquaculture", in *Arctic Climate Impact Assessment Report* (Cambridge University Press 2005), 691–780; Molenaar, note 12, 244; Anne Babcock Hollowed, Benjamin Planque, Harald Loeng, "Potential Movement of Fish and Shellfish Stocks from the sub-Arctic to the Arctic Ocean" (2013), 22 (5) *Fisheries Oceanography*, 355–370; Verena M Trenkel, et al., "Comparative ecology of widely distributed pelagic fish species in the North Atlantic: implications for modelling climate and fisheries impacts" (2014), 129 *Progress in Oceanography*, 219–243; Hoel, note 2, 133–134; Jóhann Sigurjónsson, "Changes in the Distribution and Migration of Fish Stocks in the Northeast Atlantic Ocean due to Climate Variations", in Myron H Nordquist, John Norton Moore and Ronán Long (eds), *Challenges of the Changing Arctic – Continental Shelf, Navigation, and Fisheries* (Center for Oceans Law and Policy, vol. 19, Brill Nijhoff, Leiden and Boston 2016), 407–428; Tore Haug, et al., "Future harvest of living resources in the Arctic Ocean north of the Nordic and Barents Seas: A review of possibilities and constraints" (2017), 188 *Fisheries Research*, 38–57.

31 See Hollowed, Planque and Loeng, note 30.

north under changing climate conditions on the basis of several significant life history factors.

The same study identified, based on similar life history methodology, Beaked redfish (*Sebastes mentella*), Greenland shark (*Somniosus microcephalus*), Arctic skate (*Amblyraja hyperborea*), polar cod (*Boreogadus saida*), and Bering flounder (*Hippoglossoides robustus*) as high potentials for movement to Arctic shelf seas. This qualitative assessment of potentials for demersal fish stocks reveals what dictates and restricts their scope of survivorship, but it also becomes clear that none of these species, perhaps with the exception of the redfish (*Sebastes spp.*) stocks, will provide substantial additional yields in terms of biomass.

Trenkel et al. (2014)[32] and Sigurjónsson (2016)[33] discussed the so-called pelagic complex in the Northeast Atlantic Ocean, the temperate/boreal Atlanto-Scandian herring, blue whiting (*Micromesistius poutassou*) and mackerel (*Scomber scombrus*) stocks, as well as the northernmore capelin stock. These large pelagic stocks have during the past decade expanded their distribution northwards and are likely candidates to invade the northern and Arctic seas under continued warm water conditions. An important reason is the fact that these stocks are not restricted to continental shelves compared to the demersal stocks, although reproduction and feeding may depend on conditions and productivity in the shelf areas. In that sense, they are more likely to be subject to commercial fishery in substantial quantities in the future than the demersal stocks. However, Haug et al. (2017),[34] after considering oceanographic conditions, bottom topography of the Arctic Ocean, continued low productivity and the dependence of both demersal and pelagic stocks on shelf areas in the Barents Sea part of the Arctic Ocean, concluded that in the coming 10–20 years large commercial harvest in the high north is not a likely scenario.

It is important to keep in mind that, although global rise in temperature is likely to continue, the amplitude in natural variations in ocean conditions can counteract these global changes to such a degree that certain areas, such as off Iceland, may still undergo periodic cooling of the ocean temperature, rather than continued steady warm conditions.[35] However, the conditions at the North Pole will most likely undergo a dramatic rise in temperature and reduced ice coverage, i.e. huge shifts in environmental conditions, making predictions difficult. Therefore, rapid changes in fish stocks in the area as these changes

---

32   See Trenkel et al., note 30.
33   See Sigurjónsson, note 30.
34   See Haug et al., note 30.
35   See ACIA, note 30.

occur in even not too distant future cannot be ruled out and are perhaps beyond the scope of what we can predict. This applies not least when we keep in mind the fast-moving pelagic fish stocks that often respond extremely quickly to environmental changes, as has been the case, for example, with North Atlantic herring and mackerel stocks during the last 50 years or so.[36] Therefore, it is very important that States have developed a management framework that can address abrupt future changes in environmental conditions and fish stock abundance that may take place sooner than we even anticipate today.

3.2   *The Joint Program of Scientific Research and Monitoring*

As outlined above, science-based management is the fundamental approach for rational harvesting of fish stocks and thus the sole basis of all management measures implemented both nationally and in international cooperation. Therefore, Iceland and some other delegations put much emphasis on securing a proper mechanism to deal with scientific matters among the participating States. This applied both to the framework for cooperative aspects of gathering the necessary scientific information and also the mechanism to evaluate collectively scientific information to underpin responsible management decisions.

Article 4 of the Agreement provides for the establishment of a Joint Program of Scientific Research and Monitoring ('Joint Program'). It describes its role in scientific and advisory activities, scientific meetings, and sharing and handling of data with the overall 'goal of increasing knowledge of the living marine resources of the central Arctic Ocean and the ecosystems in which they occur', and with the particular aim of 'determining whether fish stocks might exist in the Agreement Area now or in the future that could be harvested on a sustainable basis and the possible impacts of such fisheries …'. Furthermore, Article 4 stipulates the importance of evaluating information as changes occur or new information becomes available by determining that Parties shall hold joint scientific meetings 'at least every two years' and 'at least two months in advance of the meetings of the Parties' in order to secure full availability of latest information for the decision makers.

There were lengthy discussions among the Parties as to whether the Joint Program was to be directly linked to an international scientific body for overseeing the scientific activities, organising cooperation and providing scientific advice. It was the view of the Icelandic delegation and some other delegations that, for practical reasons, ICES would be an appropriate platform to make use of in this context. This would both secure a good scientific basis as well as

---

36   See Sigurjónsson, note 30.

minimising duplication of efforts. ICES, established in 1902, has active scientific cooperation, is a forum for scientific debate and a mechanism for generating scientific advice on status of fish stocks and the marine environment.[37] The organisation involves thousands of scientists specialised in the marine field, including Arctic waters,[38] and has in recent decades expanded its geographic scope of activity, including by direct linkage with PICES in the Pacific and by attaining an observer status at the UN General Assembly[39] in 2018. States and organisations worldwide are welcome to become members of ICES following a defined application procedure. Undoubtedly, ICES and PICES will play a role in the scientific work under the Agreement in the future, but the final text keeps this question open so as not to preclude any potential means of scientific input from other organisations and States as the implementation of the Agreement develops.

Article 5 of the Agreement[40] calls upon the Parties to take actions, including conservation and other management actions, based on scientific information, primarily on the basis of the Joint Programme, but also all other relevant sources of information. It specifically calls for evaluation as to whether the distribution, migration and abundance of fish in the Agreement Area would support a sustainable commercial fishery and, on that basis, to determine, *inter alia*, whether to commence negotiations to establish one or more additional RFMO/As. Finally, the Parties to the Agreement are committed to establish conservation and management measures for exploratory fishing in the Agreement Area, which may give important scientific input to decision-making in the future if well conducted and coordinated by the Parties.

The aforementioned Articles 4 and 5 are the core of the Agreement. At the fifth and last meeting of scientific experts, the ten negotiating parties had requested the experts[41] to focus on basic information that is of fundamental importance for the future work of the Joint Program. This included, firstly, a

---

37 The International Council for the Exploration of the Sea (ICES), "Who we are", http://ices.dk/explore-us/who-we-are/Pages/Who-we-are.aspx (accessed 17 December 2018).

38 ICES, "Arctic research", http://ices.dk/explore-us/Action%20Areas/Pages/Arctic.aspx, accessed 17 December 2018; ICES, "Arctic Fisheries Working Group" (Chair: Daniel Howell, ACOM), http://ices.dk/community/groups/Pages/AFWG.aspx (accessed 17 December 2018).

39 ICES, "ICES becomes an observer to the United Nations General Assembly" (2 November 2018), http://ices.dk/news-and-events/news-archive/news/Pages/ICES_becomes_UN_observer.aspx (accessed 17 December 2018).

40 See Agreement to Prevent Unregulated High Seas Fisheries in the Central Arctic Ocean, note 6.

41 Final Report of the Fifth Meeting of Scientific Experts on Fish Stocks in the Central Arctic Ocean (2018), https://www.afsc.noaa.gov/Arctic_fish_stocks_fifth_meeting/pdfs/Final_report_of_the_5th_FiSCAO_meeting.pdf (accessed 17 December 2018).

short-term mapping program to acquire some basic information on fish stocks in the Agreement Area and, secondly, starting the design of a future resource and environment monitoring program, including assessing what is required in terms of man-power, ship-time and other resources. Finally, this included outlining how to collect and share data.

In light of the obvious lack of coordinated scientific efforts and to add to the limited knowledge of the opening of the central Arctic Ocean, the Agreement and the Joint Program – when properly in place – will be the coordinating platform called for by scientists[42] to avoid mistakes due to lack of knowledge in management of the resources in this vulnerable ocean area.

4   Concluding Remarks

Iceland's desire to become a full participant in the consultations on high seas fisheries in the central Arctic Ocean was based both on legal arguments as well as fair and natural geopolitical reasons. Iceland therefore much welcomed to participate in the ten party negotiations that were finalised on 30 November 2017 with a draft agreement and formally concluded with the signing of the Central Arctic Ocean Fisheries Agreement in Ilulissat, Greenland, on 3 October 2018. During the negotiations, serious efforts were devoted to securing that management measures to be implemented in the central Arctic Ocean will become more than a *de facto* moratorium, and to ensuring that they do not undermine and are in accordance with international law, including UNCLOS and the 1995 UN Fish Stocks Agreement. This was well materialised with the new Agreement.

The Agreement is a fully fletched platform for coordinating conduct of scientific research by interested Parties and the necessary mechanism for generating scientific advice on sustainable harvest, including responsible mechanism for managing exploratory fishing and collecting, handling and sharing scientific data. Furthermore, it provides the road towards future organisational arrangements when needed and establishes interim management measures until such arrangements are in place. In essence, the Agreement can probably qualify as a regional fisheries management arrangement, RFMA, since most elements of relevance have been incorporated in the Agreement, including

---

42   Thomas I Van Pelt, Henry P Huntington, Olga V Romanenko and Franz J Mueter, "The missing middle: Central Arctic Ocean gaps in fishery research and science coordination" (2017), 85 *Marine Policy*, 79–86.

the rights and obligations of Parties in accordance with the 1995 UN Fish Stocks Agreement.[43]

The opening of the central Arctic Ocean for fishing is not likely to take place in the nearest future according to the latest assessments of scientific experts, although the development of the sea ice retreat is currently faster than was earlier anticipated. This may in turn, however, generate environmental conditions for migrating fish stocks that can form basis for sustainable commercial harvest in coming years. While the Central Arctic Ocean Fisheries Agreement is today regarded as being historic due to its cautious approach, where the sentiment certainly is to base fisheries management on best available scientific information with precaution as the guiding principle, the future may prove that it was a timely arrangement in a fast-moving world with dramatic changes taking place in the Arctic Ocean.

---

43   See 1995 UN Fish Stocks Agreement, note 5, article 10; Molenaar, note 12, 245, see note 8 therein.

Prevalence of Soft Law in the Arctic

*Hema Nadarajah**

Abstract

Soft law has been observed to be increasing within the frontiers – regions and issue-areas that extend beyond national jurisdiction, and where governance substantively integrates scientific and technological knowledge. The often-used assumption for the prevalence of such instruments has been the uncertainty of scientific knowledge. This paper takes this facile analysis further by examining the dynamic changes to the number and diversity of state and non-state actors as well as their relative influence. Using a revised definition of soft law which encompasses both binding and non-binding forms, this article shows that this has not been the case. Through analysis of the legal framework within which the region is governed and a mixed methodology drawing from the fields of international relations and international law, this research confirms that soft law is prevalent within the Arctic and that it is an outcome of domestic politics, as well as geopolitical tensions among the relevant states.

Keywords

soft law – Arctic – international relations – international law – diplomacy

1 Introduction

> [T]hus the belief in an ice-free north-east and north-west passage to the wealth of Cathay or of India, first propounded towards the close of the 15th century, cropped up again and again, only to be again and again refuted[1]

---

* University of British Columbia. hema.nadarajah@gmail.com.
1 Fridtjof Nansen, *Farthest North* (Macmillan and Co., 1897), 5.

This belief that Fridtjof Nansen writes of in 1897 is one that is fast becoming a reality in the face of increasingly warming temperatures in the Arctic. Alongside these changes, interests from non-Arctic states and non-state actors are also mounting as the region's resources and trade routes are becoming more commercially accessible. In a large part, these biophysical changes have necessitated a science-based decision-making approach to the region's governance, whether on issues pertaining to territorial claims or on the management of fisheries resources.[2]

Several scholars have argued that a legal structure comprising of soft law is preferred due to the uncertainty in scientific knowledge and the pace at which this knowledge is developed.[3] This paper takes this simplified analysis further by examining the dynamic processes leading to the negotiation and conclusion of a sub-set of binding and non-binding soft instruments as well as their relative implications on the region's governance, in order to investigate other underlying reasons for soft law's prevalence in the Arctic. However, before examining why states are increasingly choosing to opt for soft law instruments in the Arctic, this article first addresses claims made within the International Relations literature on the increasing number of soft law instruments.[4] By analysing a small sample of soft law instruments within the auspices of the Arctic Council, it aims to understand why states negotiate and conclude legal instruments that are softer than the often-assumed to be superior alternative of hard law.

2 The Argument in Brief

While the realm of Arctic law is fundamentally grounded by hard treaties such as United Nations Convention on the Law of the Sea (UNCLOS), it is the

---

2   NB: Cooperation over the management of fisheries takes places the Central Arctic Ocean, the Barents Sea, Bering Seas as well as the North-East and North Atlantics, where science-based quotas are used.

3   Andrew Guzman, "The Design of International Agreements", *European Journal of International Law* 579 (2005); Sumudu Atapattu, "'International Environmental Law and Soft Law': A New Direction or a Contradiction?," in *Non-State Actors, Soft Law, and Protective Regimes: From the Margins* (Cambridge University Press, 2012), 200–226; Timothy Meyer "Shifting Sands: Power, Uncertainty and the Form of International Legal Cooperation", *European Journal of International Law* 27(1) (2016): 161–185.

4   John J Kirton and MJ Trebilcock, *Hard Choices, Soft Law: Voluntary Standards in Global Trade, Environment, and Social Governance* (Routledge, 2016), 4; Atapattu, note 3, 212; Dinah Shelton, "Soft Law", in *Routledge Handbook of International Law*, ed. by David Armstrong, (London: Routledge, 2008), 14.

soft law instruments that have animated it in the absence of harder treaty making efforts, yielding considerable research on soft law and the Arctic.[5] Adding to the existing research, this article makes two important and unique contributions to this literature by conducting its inquiry within the context of soft law's prevalence. First, the very definition of soft law is argued to include both binding and non-binding variants. The former is referred to in this article as a "soft treaty". This revised definition is in contrast to the existing soft law-Arctic literature which refers to soft law as encompassing solely non-binding forms. It then uses this updated definition to examine just how prevalent soft law is in the region and finds that soft law is far more pervasive than previously assumed.

I have argued elsewhere[6] that there are a number of reasons as to why states sometimes conclude soft law and soft treaties rather than hard treaties. These reasons, readily evident in the Arctic, are drawn from observations as well as an analysis of legal documents. They include: papering over otherwise irreconcilable differences; coordinating behavior during periods of mutual suspicion; building towards the conclusion of a hard treaty or the development of customary international law; promoting the role and influence of epistemic communities; enabling governments to be seen by their citizens to be doing something, even if they are not; and avoiding constitutional constraints.

It should be noted that the definition of soft law utilised in this article is based on an "ex ante negotiation perspective" – whereby States are able to conclude an instrument that may take on a number of possible characteristics rendering the instrument as non-binding soft law, soft treaty or hard treaty.[7] From an ex post perspective, courts may take on a binary perspective as to whether an instrument is simply binding versus non-binding. This is not to say that there are no ex poste variations to the consequences of a soft versus hard treaty. However, in order to set some methodological boundaries to this research, this article will be solely focused on the negotiation processes leading up to the conclusion of the respective instruments examined in greater detail in the subsequent sections.

---

5 Camille Escudé, "The Strength of Flexibility: The Arctic Council in the Arctic Norm-Setting Process," *Arctic Yearbook* (2016): 48–60; Md Waliul Hasanat, *Soft-law Cooperation in International Law: The Arctic Council's Efforts to Address Climate Change* (Lapland University Press, 2012).

6 Michael Byers and Hema Nadarajah, "Soft Treaties" (9640 words, in peer-review) (n.d.) (available from author on request).

7 Gregory C Shaffer and Mark A Pollack, "Hard v. Soft Law: Alternatives, Complements, and Antagonists in International Governance," *Minnesota Law Review* 94(3) (2010), 716.

Before delving into soft law's prevalence in the Arctic the soft law framework this article utilises to categorise written international law in the Arctic will first be introduced. Following which, existing written legal instruments will be classified accordingly, and a sub-set of non-binding and binding soft law instruments will be extrapolated and examined in-depth to understand the dynamics of the ex-ante processes leading to the negotiation and conclusion of each instrument. The implications of such instruments will then be examined within the Arctic Council context before concluding this article.

3 Conceptualising Soft Law

3.1 *Soft Law Finding Its Place within the Sources of International Law*

International law instruments seek to formalise cooperation among states and to constrain their behaviour. This is done with a range of instruments of varying degrees of legalisation. The five primary "sources of international law", according to Article 38.1 of the International Court of Justice (ICJ) Statute, are:

a. "international conventions, whether general or particular, establishing rules expressly recognized by the contesting states;
b. international custom, as evidence of a general practice accepted as law;
c. the general principles of law recognized by civilized nations;
d. subject to the provisions of Article 59, judicial decisions and the teachings of the most highly qualified publicists of the various nations, as subsidiary means for the determination of rules of law."[8]

In recent decades, parallel to these sources, international law has grown to include a new category – soft law. The use of these formal sources of international law – treaties, customary international law, and general principles – are argued to have been "unable to create an adequate international response to the rapid devastation of various aspects of the earth's environment", leading to calls for a more nuanced distinction within these formal sources as they fail to provide "a sufficient framework for cooperation and collective environmental action".[9] Soft law has been identified as a way to fill this normative gap within international environmental protection.[10] Over time, soft law came to be viewed as a

---

8   Statute of the International Court of Justice. 33 UNTS 993 (1945): article 38.1.
9   Krista Singleton-Cambage, "International Legal Sources and Global Environmental Crisis: The Inadequacy of Principles, Treaties, and Custom," *ILSA Journal of International and Comparative Law* 2(1) (1995), 172; Fabián Augusto Cárdenas Castañeda, "A Call for Rethinking the Sources of International Law: Soft Law and the Other Side of the Coin," *Anuario Mexicano de Derecho Internacional*, 13(13) (2013): 355–403.
10 Ibid, Singleton-Cambage (1995).

substitute and, at times, a complement of legally-binding international law, also known as 'hard law' – usually in the form of treaties and customary law.[11]

Within the literature, written international law has been differentiated in several ways. The first approach describes *a spectrum* ranging from hard law in the form of legally binding treaties, to soft law in the form of resolutions and declarations.[12] A second approach differentiates written agreements in *a binary* manner, i.e. binding and non-binding, with the former being hard law and the latter being soft law.[13] Third, there are *sceptics* such as Jan Klabbers, who agree that international law is binary in nature but argue that labelling soft law as "law" is both unnecessary and problematic.[14] Kal Raustiala, in criticising the conceptual coherence of soft law, similarly argues that "there is no such thing as soft law" and that instead, international documents should be categorised as either contracts (legally binding) or pledges (non-legally binding).[15] Prosper Weil has gone so far as to warn that soft law instruments could have destabilising consequences for the effectiveness of international law as well as the international system as a whole.[16] However, none of these means of differentiation (or non-differentiation) have achieved consensus support within the disciplines of international relations or international law.[17] Moreover,

---

11   John J Kirton and MJ Trebilcock, *Hard Choices, Soft Law: Voluntary Standards in Global Trade, Environment, and Social Governance*, (1st Edn, Aldershot, England, Routledge; 2004).

12   Kennneth Abbott and Duncan Snidal, "Hard and Soft Law in International Governance," *International Organization* 54(3) (2000): 421–56; Cárdenas Castañeda (2013); Christine Chinkin, "The Challenge of Soft Law: Development and Change in International Law," *The International and Comparative Law Quarterly* 38 (4) (1989): 850–866; Andrew Guzman and Timothy Meyer, "International Soft Law," *Journal of Legal Analysis* 2 (1) (2010):171–224; Ilhami Alkan Olsson, "Four Competing Approaches to International Soft Law" *Scandinavian Studies Review* 58 (2013): 177–196; Shaffer and Pollack (2010).

13   Arif Ahmed and Md Jahid Mustofa, "Role of Soft Law in Environmental Protection: An Overview," *Global Journal of Politics and Law Research* 4(2) (2016): 1–18; Atapattu (2012); László Blutman, "In the trap of a legal metaphor: International soft law," *International and Comparative Law Quarterly* 59(3) (2010): 605–624; Shelton, note 4.

14   Jan Klabbers, "The Redundancy of Soft Law," *Nordic Journal of International Law* 65(2) (1996):167–182.

15   Kal Raustiala, "Form and substance in international agreements," *The American Journal of International Law* 99(3) (2005): 586.

16   Prosper Weil, "Towards Relative Normativity in International Law?" *The American Journal of International Law* 77(3) (1983):413–442.

17   Jaye Ellis, "Shades of grey: Soft law and the Validity of Public International Law," *Leiden Journal of International Law* 25(2) (2012):313–334; Timo Koivurova and Leena Heinämäki, "The Participation of Indigenous Peoples in International Norm-Making in the Arctic," *Polar Record* 42 (2) (2006): 101–109.

different scholars have quite differing views as to the role, effectiveness, and consequences of soft law for the international political system.

4 Categorising Written International Law

This research broadens the examination of soft law in the international system via the definition upon which it bases its analysis on. Soft law is used to refer to written legal instruments, other than hard treaties, that exist in either binding or non-binding forms. Non-binding soft law can exist in various forms, such as declarations, recommendations, resolutions, and official ministerial statements.[18] As for binding soft law, Abbott, Snidal, Chinkin, and Olsson have all identified that formally binding instruments are not always "hard" in terms of their obligation, precision, and delegation.[19] Exploring this phenomenon further, Abbott, Snidal, Keohane, Moravcsik, and Slaughter contended that the "legalization of international norms, agreements, and regimes" further depends on the variability of each of the aforementioned dimensions.[20] Steven Freeland likewise identified that soft law can be found in the form of weaker provisions in binding treaties, although for the purposes of his research, he examined soft law solely as found in non-binding instruments.[21]

Abbott and Snidal's definition of soft law, which forms the cornerstone of the topic in international relations, is fairly broad.[22] Soft law is argued to encompass any instrument that deviates from hard law with respect to the dimensions of obligation, precision, and delegation. It is also distinguished from political arrangements where legalisation is absent. This leaves us with a rather large number of instruments that can be classified as soft law and fails to account for the full range of implications of 'soft' governance within the international system. Defining non-binding soft law to encompass a lower degree of precision, as Abbott and Snidal do, implies that such instruments contain vague provisions relative to binding instruments.

Figure 1 below illustrates the definitional framework this article uses. The spectrum indicates the degree to which a written international legal instrument is binding on its parties.

18 See Olsson, note 12; Shelton, note 4.
19 See Abbott and Snidal, note 12; Chinkin, note 12; Edward T. Canuel, "The four arctic law pillars: A legal framework" *Georgetown Journal of International Law* 46(3) (2015); Olsson, note 12.
20 See Abbott and Snidal, note 12; Chinkin, note 12; Olsson, note 12.
21 Steven Freeland, "For Better or for Worse? The Use of 'Soft Law' Within the International Legal Regulation of Outer Space," *Annals of Air and Space Law* 36 (2011): 409–445.
22 See Abbott and Snidal, note 12.

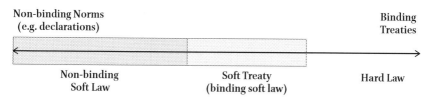

FIGURE 1   Spectrum of written international law with the shaded segments representing the focus of my analysis

Dinah Shelton's widely cited definition of soft law will be used in this article for the category of *non-binding soft law*.[23] Shelton defines soft law as non-legally binding instruments that may take the forms of 'normative texts not adopted in treaty form that are addressed to the international community as a whole or to the entire membership of the adopting institution or organization' such as the ASEAN Joint Statement on Climate Change to the UNFCCC Conference of the Parties[24] or as declarations, recommendations, resolutions, and other writings meant to 'supervise state compliance with treaty obligations'.[25]

In contrast to existing definitions of written international law, particularly those that find soft law to lie somewhere along a spectrum,[26] non-binding soft law here is not defined to be less permissive, redundant or ambiguous than its binding counterpart. States may be more willing to adopt mandatory language in non-binding instruments precisely because they are not legally bound to them, which may help to explain the mandatory language in, for example, the 1948 Universal Declaration of Human Rights.[27] Such a definition may also lead one to assume that non-binding soft law instruments are benign and "residual", possibly causing states to be lenient in their negotiation.[28] Demonstrated later in this article, such an assumption may be inaccurate. The negotiations leading to the 2019 non-binding ministerial declaration by Arctic Council member states is such a case in point. The United States was opposed to the inclusion of any reference to climate change, and the other seven countries refused to

---

23   See Shelton, note 4.
24   ASEAN. "ASEAN Joint Statement on Climate Change to the 25th Session of the Conference of the Parties to the United Nations Framework Convention on Climate Change (UNFCCC)," (2019) https://asean.org/storage/2019/11/2-ASEAN-Joint-Statement-on-Climate-Change-to-the-UNFCCC-COP-25.pdf [9 January 2020].
25   See Shelton, note 4, 72; UN COPUOUS 2018.
26   See Abbott and Snidal, note 12.
27   Michèle Olivier, "The Relevance of 'Soft Law' as a Source of International Human Rights," *The Comparative and International Law Journal of Southern Africa* 35, no. 3 (2002): 289–307.
28   Eric Posner and Jacob Gersen, "Soft Law", *University of Chicago Public Law & Legal Theory Working Paper No. 213* (2008), 45.

concede. This first-ever failure to adopt an Arctic Council ministerial declaration demonstrates that the language and content of some soft law instruments are hard-fought, and that states do consider them important.[29]

Some treaties are, in their entirety, properly categorised as 'soft' rather than 'hard' law. '*Soft treaty*' is defined as a binding instrument containing some combination of permissive language, ambiguity, and redundancy that leaves it devoid of mandatory, clear, and new obligations.[30] Placed on the spectrum in figure 1, soft treaties would thus fall between non-binding soft law and binding hard treaties.

Language within a treaty can be either mandatory or permissive. Words such as 'shall' and 'must' carry mandatory force, while 'should' signals that a provision is permissive; a recommendation rather than a requirement.[31] However, the existence of mandatory or permissive language does not determine whether the instrument itself is binding or non-binding.[32]

As a result of human error, especially during negotiations involving complex issues, divergent interests, and tight time constraints, ambiguity can find its way into international agreements. Ambiguity may also be unavoidable when crafting general rules that will later be applied to subsequent instruments and situations, each composed of its own specific set of facts.[33] This is evident in broadly encompassing Conventions and subsequent Protocols that may be more specific. Examples of such forms of ambiguity include the 1992 UN Framework Convention on Climate Change and the 2005 Kyoto Protocol.

However, ambiguous language is often deliberately included in international legal instruments for a number of reasons. Such 'constructive ambiguity' is defined by GR Berridge, Alan James, and Lorna Lloyd as 'the deliberate use of ambiguous language in a sensitive issue in order to advance some political purpose'.[34] Legal instruments where language could have been more

---

29   Anne Gearan, Carol Morello, and John Hudson, "Trump administration pushed to strip mention of climate change from Arctic policy statement," May 2, 2019, https://www.washingtonpost.com/politics/trump-administration-pushed-to-strip-mention-of-climate-change-from-arctic-policy-statement/2019/05/02/1dabcd5e-6c4a-11e9-8f44-e8d8bb1df986_story.html (accessed 8 June 2019).

30   See Byers and Nadarajah, note 6.

31   Lavanya Rajamani, "The 2015 Paris Agreement: Interplay between Hard, Soft and Non-obligations," *Journal of Environmental Law 28* (2) (2016): 337–58.

32   See Shelton, note 4, 73.

33   Michael Byers, "Still Agreeing to Disagree: International Security and Constructive Ambiguity." *Journal on the use of Force and International Law* (2020): 1–24.

34   Geoff Berridge and Lorna Lloyd, *The Palgrave Macmillan Dictionary of Diplomacy* (Palgrave Macmillan, 2012), 73. Berridge and Lloyd explain that constructive ambiguity is also known as "fudging"; see also Byers, note 33.

precise is argued to be a result of the political rather than the legal aspect of negotiations.[35] Such ambiguity is an indicator of the negotiators' position and as such reflects 'good rather than bad drafting'.[36] Such deliberately ambiguous language where provisions could entail different meanings to each Party, came to be diplomatic trademarks of Henry Kissinger and Abba Eban.[37] Aside from bringing negotiation deadlocks to a closure particularly when consensus is required, such constructive ambiguity may also be desirable because of the associated lowered transaction costs associated with a shorter negotiation process as well as the flexibility that ambiguity provides in foreign policy.[38]

Some treaties do nothing more than repeat obligations from pre-existing treaties that are already binding on the negotiating states. This phenomenon is readily apparent in the Arctic, where the obligations from several global treaties have been recast in new regional instruments such as the Agreement on Cooperation on Aeronautical and Maritime Search and Rescue.[39] By redundancy, I mean provisions that repeat hard law commitments that were already binding on all the negotiating parties. It is also important to note that the focus is on the substantive provisions of treaties and not their preambles, the provisions of which are almost always permissive, ambiguous, or redundant. Yet as the next section of this article will illustrate, softness across the substantive provisions of a treaty, while less frequent, is also widespread.

While this article is focused on soft law, there lies a need for *hard law* to be defined clearly in order to better situate the former within the spectrum of written legal instruments. The reverse of the elements that this research uses to describe soft treaties – permissive language, ambiguity, and redundancy – could constitute a new list of the attributes, not just of hard treaties, but of hard law generally. These attributes could be expressed as: mandatory language, clarity, and novelty. Hard law broadly encompasses written international legal instruments, that may take the form of treaties, agreements, conventions, as well as customary international laws.

---

35 See Byers, note 33; Kyung-Bok Son and Tae-Jin Lee, "The Trends and Constructive Ambiguity in International Agreements on Intellectual Property and Pharmaceutical Affairs: Implications for Domestic Legislations in Low- and Middle-Income Countries," *Global Public Health* 13, no. 9 (2018): 1169–1178.

36 See Byers, note 33; Berridge and Lloyd, note 34, 73.

37 Itay Fischhendler, "When Ambiguity in Treaty Design Becomes Destructive: A Study of Transboundary Water" *Global Environmental Politics* 8, no. 1 (2008): 111.

38 See Ibid, 111–112 for an extended discussion on the benefits and costs of constructive ambiguity; Son and Lee, note 35.

39 See Byers, note 33.

5 Establishing Prevalence of Soft Law in the Arctic

Utilising the definitions outlined in the earlier section, Table 1 below illustrates a categorisation of hard and soft treaties, and non-binding soft law instruments governing the Arctic. In populating Table 1, each binding instrument was closely examined for characteristics of soft treaty – permissiveness, ambiguity, and redundancy. Extrapolated from this list, Section 5 examines two soft treaties and two non-binding instruments, all four of which were negotiated within the auspices of the Arctic Council.

5.1 Trends in Prevalence

TABLE 1   A categorisation of hard and soft treaties, and non-binding soft law instruments governing the Arctic

Year	Int'l organisation/ members	Binding/ Non-binding	Legal instrument	Type of instrument
1920	Multilateral[a]	Binding	Svalbard Treaty	Hard
1973	Arctic Five[b]	Binding	Agreement on the Conservation of Polar Bears	Hard
1982	UN	Binding	UN Convention on the Law of the Sea	Hard
1987	UN	Binding	Montreal Protocol on Substances that Deplete the Ozone Layer	Hard
1991	Arctic Countries[c]	Non-Binding	Arctic Environmental Protection Strategy	Soft
1992	UN	Binding	UN Framework Convention on Climate Change (UNFCCC)	Hard

a   There is a total of 43 member states that have signed the Svalbard Treaty, which recognises Norway's sovereignty over the Svalbard and also providing signatories rights to commercial activity over the archipelago. The member states are: Afghanistan, Albania, Argentina, Australia, Belgium, Bulgaria, Canada, Chile, Denmark, the Dominican Republic, Egypt, Estonia, Finland, France, Greece, India, Iceland, Italy, Japan, China, Latvia, Lithuania, Monaco, the Netherlands, New Zealand, North Korea, Norway, Poland, Portugal, Romania, Russia, Saudi Arabia, Spain, the UK, Switzerland, Sweden, South Africa, South Korea, Czech Republic, Germany, Hungary, the USA, Venezuela, Austria.
b   Canada, Denmark, Norway, the then-Soviet Union, and the United States.
c   The Arctic Countries constitute the countries that would later form the Arctic Council Member States: Canada, Denmark, Finland, Iceland, Norway, Sweden, Union of Soviet Socialist Republics, USA.

TABLE 1   A categorisation of hard and soft treaties, and non-binding soft law instruments (cont.)

Year	Int'l organisation/ members	Binding/ Non-binding	Legal instrument	Type of instrument
1993	Barents-Euro Arctic Council	Non-Binding	Kirkenes Declaration	Soft
1993	Barents-Euro Arctic Council	Non-Binding	Terms of Reference	Soft
1994	Northern Forum	Non-Binding	Tromsø Declaration	Soft
1994	Northern Forum	Non-Binding	Rovaniemi Code of Conduct	Soft
1996	Arctic Council	Non-Binding	Declaration on the Establishment of the Arctic Council (Ottawa Declaration)	Soft
1998	Arctic Council	Non-Binding	Rule of Procedure	Soft
2000	Arctic Council	Non-Binding	Barrow Declaration	Soft
2001	UN	Binding	Stockholm Convention on Persistent Organic Pollutants	Hard
2002	Arctic Council	Non-Binding	Inari Declaration	Soft
2004	Arctic Council	Non-Binding	Reykjavik Declaration	Soft
2004	Arctic Council	Non-Binding	Arctic Climate Impact Assessment	Soft
2006	Arctic Council	Non-Binding	Salekhard Declaration	Soft
2008	Arctic 5	Non-Binding	Ilulissat declaration	Soft
2009	Arctic Council	Non-Binding	Tromsø Declaration	Soft
2011	Arctic Council	Non-Binding	Nuuk Declaration	Soft
2011	Arctic Council[d]	Binding	Agreement on Cooperation on Aeronautical and Maritime Search and Rescue	Soft Treaty
2013	UN	Binding	Minamata Convention on Mercury	Hard
2013	Arctic Council	Non-Binding	Kiruna Declaration	Soft
2013	Arctic Council	Binding	Agreement on Cooperation on Marine Oil Pollution Preparedness and Response in the Arctic	Soft Treaty

d   Each of the soft treaties was negotiated "under umbrella of" the Arctic Council, as such they were technically, negotiated and concluded outside of the Arctic Council by the same eight states.

TABLE 1 A categorisation of hard and soft treaties, and non-binding soft law instruments (cont.)

Year	Int'l organisation/ members	Binding/ Non-binding	Legal instrument	Type of instrument
2015	International Maritime Organization (IMO)	Binding	Polar Code	Hard
2015	Arctic Council	Non-Binding	Iqaluit Declaration	Soft
2017	Arctic Council	Non-Binding	Fairbanks Declaration	Soft
2017	Arctic Council	Binding	Agreement on Enhancing International Scientific Cooperation	Soft Treaty
2018	China, Japan, and South Korea[e]	Non-Binding	Joint Statement the Third Trilateral High-Level Dialogue on the Arctic	Soft
2018	Arctic Five+Five[f]	Binding	Agreement to Prevent Unregulated Commercial Fishing on the High Seas of the Central Arctic Ocean	Hard
2019	Arctic Council	Non-Binding	Joint Ministerial Statement	Soft

e China, Japan, and South Korea held the annual Trilateral High-level dialogue in Shanghai on June 8, 2018 to reiterate their recognition of the Arctic being "an important platform for deepening and broadening cooperation on the Arctic among the three countries" (Joint Statement 2018: Art 11).

f Arctic Five+Five refers to the five coastal Arctic Ocean states (Canada, Denmark, Norway, the Russian Federation, and the US) and five other major fishing non-Arctic actors (China, the EU, Iceland, Japan, and South Korea).

6   Prevalence of Soft Law in the Arctic: a Closer Look

6.1   *Declaration on the Establishment of the Arctic Council*

In 1987, the then General Secretary of the Soviet Union, Mikhail Gorbachev, delivered a historic speech in Murmansk that is often credited with igniting regional cooperation in the Arctic and leading to the establishment of the Arctic Council less than a decade later.[40] The Arctic Council is a 'high level forum',

---

40   Timo Koivurova, "Increasing Relevance of Treaties: The Case of the Arctic." *AJIL Unbound* 108 (2014): 52–56.

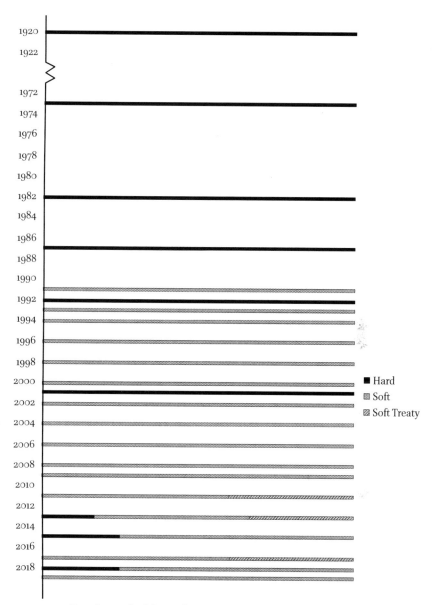

FIGURE 2   Prevalence of soft law in the Arctic

the foundation of which was the previously established Arctic Environmental Protection Strategy (AEPS). In 1996, Arctic states adopted the non-binding soft law instrument entitled the Declaration on the Establishment of the Arctic Council ('Ottawa Declaration'). The work of the AEPS – programs such as the Arctic Monitoring and Assessment Program, Conservation of Arctic Flora

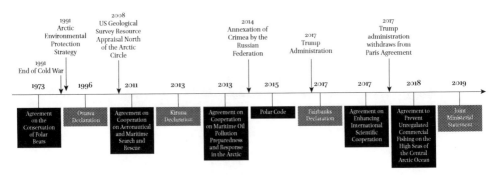

FIGURE 3   Selected international law instruments and key events in the Arctic

and Fauna, Protection of the Arctic Marine Environment, and Emergency Prevention, Preparedness and Response – was then integrated into the Arctic Council over two years.[41] These four programs would later form the Arctic Council's Working Groups alongside the Sustainable Development Working Group and Arctic Contaminants Action Program.

The Ottawa Declaration is the first of eleven non-binding soft law instruments agreed biennially on the basis of consensus by the eight 'Arctic States'.[42] The exception to these 'ministerial declarations' occurred in 2019 at Rovaniemi, Finland, which will be discussed in detail later in this section. Chairmanship of the Arctic Council is held for two years by each member state, on a rotating basis. With the handover of preceding to the incoming Chair, a declaration summing up the accomplishments over the past two years as well as the future work to be carried out is outlined in these ministerial declarations. While non-binding, these declarations carry political weight and significance. Reaching consensus on the agenda for the next two years legitimises the work of the previous two years, including findings and recommendations by the working groups, as well as all the work that follows, including, to some significant degree, the results of that work in the form of scientific findings and recommendations such as the Arctic Climate Impact Assessment.

6.2   *Agreement on Cooperation on Maritime Oil Pollution Preparedness and Response in the Arctic*

Two years after the conclusion of the Agreement on Cooperation on Aeronautical and Maritime Search and Rescue in the Arctic (SAR), the eight Arctic states concluded the 2013 Agreement on Cooperation on Maritime Oil

---

41   Ottawa Declaration, Art. 1(b).
42   Ottawa Declaration, Art. 2.

Pollution Preparedness and Response in the Arctic ('Arctic Oil Spill Response Agreement'). Both the SAR and Arctic Oil Spill Response agreements are being implemented by the Arctic Council's Working Group on Emergency Prevention, Preparedness, and Response (EPPR).

The stated goal of this second binding instrument to emerge from negotiations conducted among the eight Arctic Council member states is to 'strengthen cooperation, coordination and mutual assistance among the Parties on oil pollution preparedness and response in the Arctic in order to protect the marine environment from pollution by oil.'[43] However, the Arctic Oil Spill Response Agreement fails to create any new obligations.[44] This is because by previously ratifying the 1990 Convention on Oil Pollution Preparedness, Response and Cooperation (OPRC), a treaty negotiated within the framework of the International Maritime Organization, all eight Arctic states had already made the same commitments.[45]

This instrument reiterated obligations made in the OPRC without adding any new ones.[46] These obligations include: Parties having to institute measures for dealing with pollution incidents, such as 'the stockpiling of oil spill equipment, the development of clean-up plans, and the holding of exercises'.[47] In the event of a spill, Parties are required to cooperate by means such as providing equipment when requested by another party. This requirement, however, is a 'soft' provision concealed within what may seem like a hard provision. Article 8(3) of the Agreement states that 'The Parties shall cooperate and provide assistance, which may include advisory services, technical support, equipment or personnel'.[48] The requirement to provide assistance while mandatory is not in any way specific. While this Agreement is part of a 'broader regime'[49] it is nevertheless the first legal instrument that is focused on oil spill response within the Arctic. This reiterates the Arctic states' commitment in addressing

---

43 Agreement on Cooperation on Marine Oil Pollution Preparedness and Response in the Arctic 2013, Art. 1.
44 Michael Byers and Mark Stoller. "What Small Teeth You Have," *European Union's Arctic Portal* (2013) https://www.arcticinfo.eu/en/features/76-what-small-teeth-you-have (accessed 10 January 2020).
45 International Convention on Oil Pollution Preparedness, Response and Cooperation 1990; Ibid, Byers and Stoller.
46 See Byers, note 33.
47 Ibid.
48 Agreement on Cooperation on Marine Oil Pollution Preparedness and Response in the Arctic 2013, Art. 8(3).
49 Svein Vigeland Rottem, "A Note on the Arctic Council Agreements," *Ocean Development & International Law* 46, no. 1 (2015): 50–59.

the issue regionally and as such is more likely a 'symbol of Arctic cooperation than a practical mechanism'.[50]

6.3   *2017 Agreement on Enhancing International Scientific Cooperation*

In May 2017, the eight Arctic Council member states signed the Agreement on Enhancing International Arctic Scientific Cooperation. The Agreement was a product of the Scientific Cooperation Task Force which had its first meeting in 2013. Like the previous two binding agreements, the 2011 SAR Agreement and the 2013 Arctic Oil Spill Response Agreement, the latest Agreement – although technically a treaty – does not create new obligations. Unlike the preceding agreements, this Agreement does not have a specific Arctic Council working group tasked with its follow-up.[51] In its preamble, the Agreement reiterates existing scientific cooperation practices undertaken by various inter-governmental and non-governmental organisations, such as the World Meteorological Organization and the International Arctic Science Committee. In its substantive sections, the Agreement defines 'scientific activities' in a very loose manner. It also uses qualifying terms such as 'shall, where appropriate', 'best efforts', 'may continue', and 'shall facilitate' throughout.[52]

The sole substantively specific section of the Agreement is that of the 'Identified Geographic Areas' listed in Annex I. These areas correspond with the territories and maritime zones of the parties and are therefore redundant.[53] Apart from this, Article 17 calls for cooperation with non-Parties to the Agreement, but only at the 'discretion' of the Parties. Nothing in agreement legally requires cooperation between the Arctic member states or with non-parties such as the thirteen observer states of the Arctic Council. The Agreement, therefore, fails to add new obligations to an already existing practice of scientific research cooperation in the region. The implementation of the Agreement itself is rather vague as outlined in Article 10 of the instrument which states that activities and obligations under the Agreement are applicable only if they do not violate the laws, rules, regulations, and even procedures and policies of the respective Parties and in Article 11(2) which states that implementation 'shall be subject to the availability of relevant resources'.[54] This allows Parties a great degree of leeway and discretion in enforcing the Agreement. Furthermore, it in no way incentivises or even binds the Parties to alter existing domestic arrangements

---

50   Ibid, 55.
51   Malgorzata Smieszek, "The Agreement on Enhancing International Arctic Scientific Cooperation: From Paper to Practice" *Arctic Yearbook* (2017), 3.
52   Ibid., Arts. 3–7, and 17.
53   Agreement on Enhancing International Scientific Cooperation 2017, Annex 1.
54   Agreement on Enhancing International Scientific Cooperation, Art. 10.

to enforce the Agreement. Last but not least, the dispute settlement provision in the Agreement allows for direct negotiation only, without an alternative mechanism being provided for when direct negotiation fails.[55] Why, then, did the Arctic Council members negotiate a binding instrument, if the activities and obligations of these parties are to be conducted at their discretion and based on existing practices

While the Agreement lacks specific and obligatory language, it does reiterate the importance of science-based decision making as well as that of the need to facilitate cooperation in the region. To some degree, this signals the intent of the Arctic countries to maintain the Arctic as a region of peaceful co-operation. It also consolidates pre-existing commitments and provides greater political attention and importance to these matters.

The Agreement has already been credited with propelling diplomatic interests and reaffirming common interests.[56] A 'soft' instrument such as this can indeed formally regularise (or at least recognise and encourage) cooperation among diplomats and scientific experts. The Agreement, which reiterates the norm of cooperation in the region in the form of scientific research, could have been designed to be more substantive and achieve more specific outcomes, for instance, by making the provision of access for foreign scientists to territories and maritime zones mandatory rather than discretionary. A more functional agreement might also have required the inclusion of scientific knowledge in decision making, given that the science-policy interface is central to most of the issues in Arctic international cooperation. However, it is questionable whether this would have been acceptable to all the Arctic states. The point being, that, even if a soft treaty was the most that could be agreed, it can still have discernible and even important effects.

Initially planned to be a non-binding instrument in the form of a Memorandum of Understanding, the Scientific Cooperation Task Force decided issues such as facilitating research collaboration across borders that would require governments to 'conform to the policy' would be better addressed with a binding instrument instead.[57] This demonstrates at least one of the reasons why Arctic states wanted a treaty even if its provisions are all soft. This Agreement was concluded in its binding form in order to meet both the United States and Russia's demands.

---

55 Ibid., Art. 1.
56 Paul Arthur Berkman, Lars Kullerud, Allen Pope, Alexander N Vylegzhanin, and Oran R Young. "The Arctic Science Agreement Propels Science Diplomacy," *Science* 358, no. 6363 (2017): 596–598.
57 See Smieszek, note 57.

When negotiating an international instrument, the option of a soft treaty may have also been attractive for constitutional considerations; considerations that will differ from state to state, depending on their domestic systems. This Agreement was concluded in its binding form in order to meet both the United States and Russia's demands. For example, calling an instrument an 'agreement' instead of a 'treaty' can help to free the executive branch of the US government from having to secure the 'advice and consent' of two-thirds of the Senate for ratification.[58] The three treaties negotiated under the umbrella of the Arctic Council were all treated as 'executive agreements' and not referred to the Senate. This approach did not undermine their status as treaties in international law, where the term 'treaty' is not determinative of legal status,[59] but it did ensure that the United States could quickly become party to them. The content of the treaties would also have mattered here, with the absence of any new, clear, mandatory provisions making it easier to treat them as executive agreements.

In contrast to the US, Russian diplomats admit to preferring treaties to non-binding instruments because funding from the Russian Duma for the implementation of a treaty is assured under Russian constitutional law, while funding for the implementation of a non-binding instrument is not. The Russian representatives argued for a binding instrument that would better facilitate 'coordination among the relevant Russian ministries'.[60] Therefore, it is likely that in order to find a particular balance that would have been acceptable to the US and Russian, Arctic Council members negotiated a treaty with only soft provisions.

The softness in the Agreement on Arctic Scientific Cooperation is of a different character than the preceding two Agreements: instead of involving redundancy, it involves a lack of mandatory language. This could be explained on the basis that no previous treaties on scientific cooperation existed, which meant that the Arctic states were breaking new ground – and doing so cautiously.

Another possible reason for negotiating a soft treaty is that the member states saw the Agreement on Arctic Scientific Cooperation as an opportunity to match the accomplishments of the previous two Arctic treaties and further demonstrate that regional cooperation had survived the 2014 Russian annexation of Crimea.[61] In order words, a soft treaty can signal a higher level of coop-

---

58   See United States Constitution Art. II sec. 2.
59   Vienna Convention on the Law of Treaties 1969, Art. 2(1).
60   Smieszek, note 57, 3.
61   Michael Byers, "Crises and International Cooperation: An Arctic Case Study," *International Relations*, no. 31(4) (2017): 375–402.

eration than traditional soft law even if it contains no new mandatory content. Indeed, the soft character of the Agreement on Arctic Scientific Cooperation has not stopped the promoters of scientific cooperation from championing its significance.[62] This championing could have political and ultimately legal effects, by helping a soft treaty gain legitimacy and therefore effectiveness. In other words, the fact that any kind of treaty exists may create a point of leverage for those who wish to see its provisions implemented through action. And so, the 'reason' for negotiating a soft treaty rather a non-binding instrument may have been to achieve the goals of the treaty through its non-obligatory implementation, in circumstances where it was impossible to conclude a hard treaty because of a broader situation of mutual suspicion between Russia and the other Arctic states.

6.4 *2019 Arctic Council Chair's Statement*

For the first time in the Arctic Council's history, member states were unable to agree on a declaration at the 2019 Ministerial Meeting in Rovaniemi, Finland. Instead the Chair, Finland, released a unilaterally worded statement which did not require the consensus of the member states but would have nonetheless reflected discussions and widespread agreement, even if behind closed doors. The USA was against the use of any language recognising the risk that climate change poses in the Arctic. However, since the remaining seven members were insistent on the inclusion of such language, a Ministerial Declaration – which would have to be agreed on the basis of consensus – was not achieved.

The soft character of the 1996 Ottawa Declaration (i.e. the founding document of the Arctic Council) may provide the flexibility to adopt or release documents that reflect outcomes of different configurations of Arctic states, including on different issues (some of which had the support of all eight members; others only of seven) and that the Statement of the Chair is thus, in reality, just about as significant as a full Ministerial Declaration, because it shows that the US is not a hegemonic or perhaps even necessary actor in international affairs, at least within these circumstances. In short, it is not the soft or hard character of the instrument that matters, or even if it conforms to previous practice, but rather the fact that majority of the states are continuing to express a substantial amount of political will even/especially in difficult circumstances.

While the Arctic Council members may have been unable to agree on a ministerial declaration, the Chair's statement as well as the unwillingness for the rest of the member states to yield to demands made by a powerful state

---

62   See Berkman et al., note 62.

result in two key takeaways. First, the responsibility as well as the stalwartness of the Chair resulted in a unilaterally produced statement that includes language that majority of the member states would clearly have agreed upon – and probably did agree upon in advance behind closed doors. Second, is the strength in the alliance of smaller and, by most counts, less powerful states, to stand their ground against a more powerful outlier. This flexibility of soft law instruments reflected in instruments such as the Ottawa declaration, ministerial declarations and chair's statements may be a key enabler of Arctic cooperation moving forward despite some current opposition from the world's most powerful state.

The 2019 Ministerial Meeting was the first high level meeting among Arctic Council states since the US withdrew from the Paris Climate Agreement. This raises two additional interesting questions. First, why did Russia not joint the USA in its opposition to including language on climate change? Was it simply sitting back and watching NATO allies disagree, or did it see value in having Arctic cooperation continue? Second, will similar events might unfold at the next Ministerial Meeting in 2021, should Donald Trump be re-elected, and what this might mean for the Arctic Council?

7 Implications

Non-security aspects of the Arctic have generally been managed among the Arctic states on a cooperative basis since the end of the Cold War, even during and after Russia's annexation of Crimea, along with some more recent cooperation involving non-Arctic states such as China. The legal regime, as described earlier in this chapter, is largely made up of soft law instruments both in their binding and non-binding variations. A regime complex of hard law supplemented extensively by soft law instrument can be credited for cooperation in a region with several mutually suspicious states, such as the US, Russia, and China, which may not trust each other enough to make purely hard law commitments. At the same time, a shared commitment to cooperation in the Arctic may explain the ability of these states to enter into binding legal agreements – even if some of them are soft treaties.

While binding instruments may be more difficult to negotiate because of the sovereignty and transaction costs involved, the literature often explains the choice of non-binding soft law on the basis that it is a simpler alternative.[63] This, however, can be observed to be contrary in the Arctic as exemplified by

---

63   See Abbott and Snidal, note 12, 422.

the deadlocks that arose during the 2019 Ministerial Meeting. It is also useful to note here that the failure to adopt a declaration at this Meeting is not the first time that plans for a soft law instrument were shelved due to deadlock over negotiations. In 2012, for example, for the first time in Association of Southeast Asian Nations' (ASEAN) 45-year history, member states were unable to agree on a joint statement due to disagreements over the South China Sea disputes.[64] The 2019 US-Democratic People's Republic of Korea (DPRK) Summit held in Hanoi, Vietnam is yet another example whereby the negotiations reached a deadlock. This is unlike the preceding meeting between the two states in Singapore which saw the vague, but nonetheless mutually agreed declaration which was not adopted in Hanoi. Such instances, where even a non-binding instrument is unable to be agreed upon are perhaps indications that non-binding soft law instruments are not benign and egalitarian as the literature may make them out to be. Sometimes the soft character of these agreements allows for imaginative ways around the deadlock – such as the 2019 Statement of the Chair which is essentially a ministerial declaration of 8 plus a side agreement of 7 that will enable Arctic cooperation to continue apace.

Several of the binding instruments, whether hard or soft, examined in this chapter evolved from a non-binding instrument. This lends support to existing theories of soft law's evolution towards the hard law end of the spectrum. However, it should be noted that most of these instruments are soft treaties rather than hard treaties. The reasons for the evolution in each of these cases often differs as well. Soft treaties may become hard over time, for instance, through the practices of their parties, or more specific sub-agreements. Some environmental treaties, such as the UN Framework Convention on Climate Change, provide examples of this process. The point is that the legal/cooperative landscape is constantly evolving, and that both soft and hard instruments are therefore part of a political and normative process.

Whatever the outcome, when Arctic states come together to negotiate, communication is taking place among them, and in some instances, among them and non-Arctic States. Cementing that conversation in some form of a legal document legitimises the effort to cooperate. Diplomacy is always taking place in the sidelines and epistemic communities are continually being strengthened, thus adding to the resilience of cooperation. Additionally, soft law instruments may provide some resilience in favour of continued regional cooperation among distrusting states, in circumstances where hard treaties

---

64   BBC. "Asean nations fail to reach agreement on South China Sea", July 13, 2012, https://www.bbc.com/news/world-asia-18825148 (accessed 10 November 2019).

and formal international organisations are not possible, or might suffer full breakdowns if they were. The production of a soft law instrument can be as much a reason for diplomacy as it is a conclusion of diplomacy. And by reducing or eliminating the costs associated with the instrument, by making it soft, the initiation of diplomacy becomes much easier.

Negotiations on soft law instruments can thus amplify the path dependency to cooperation. Despite exogenous factors such as the annexation of Crimea, the Arctic has continued to be a region with considerable cooperation, including between Russia, China, the US and a number of other NATO states. Therefore, the negotiation of soft treaties and non-binding soft law instruments is perhaps not just about flexibility and sub-optimal outcomes, but rather about creating interdependence, building trust, and cushioning cooperation against exogenous shocks.

8 Conclusion

Each of the binding instruments, whether hard or soft, examined here evolved from a non-binding instrument lending support to existing theories of soft law's evolution towards the hard law end of the spectrum. However, it should be noted, that most of these instruments have ended up being designed as soft treaties, and not hard law, at least not yet. The reasons in each of these instruments often differ as well. Soft treaties may be made hard in other ways, such as through the practices of their parties, or more specific sub-agreements. The environmental legal regime is characteristic of the latter in particular. The point is that the legal cooperative landscape is constantly evolving and that both soft and hard instruments are therefore part of a political and normative process.

To strengthen or even verify the argument this article makes, subsequent research could expand the analysis to other case studies or include more instruments within the cases already examined here. Much like the Antarctic Treaty System and the Outer Space Treaty, other frontier regions and issue-areas have much to extrapolate from existing legal regimes built around extensive networks of soft law instruments such as the deep seabed and cyberspace. Aside from such cases, governance within the field of international finance has been a growing field of research within the soft law sphere making it an ideal case study.[65] In questioning, if soft law is increasing, future research could also

---

65 Abraham L Newman and Elliot Posner, *Voluntary Disruptions: International Soft Law, Finance, and Power*, (Oxford University Press, 2018).

question the reverse: Is there a decline in hard treaties? If so, why? And, has the decline in hard treaties caused a rise in soft law instruments? Or has the ease with which soft law instruments are being negotiated resulted in a decline in hard treaties? Additionally, while a highly simplified empirical method was used to verify soft law's prevalence within the Arctic, future research could build upon this methodologically by supplementing the process-tracing method utilised in here by using regression analysis to quantify the degree to which each independent variable can be held accountable for the conclusion of soft law instruments relative to harder alternatives.

Soft law's increasing use in the international system and the gaps in the current literature examining its prevalence and implications, calls for a re-examination and further theorising of this now ubiquitous feature of the international system. The methodological approach employed in this research contributes to the literature by: (1) empirically accounting for the increased recourse to soft law within the Arctic; (2) identifying a particular strand of soft law (i.e. 'soft treaties') that has not been sufficiently analysed within the Arctic and; (3) identifying the existence of soft treaties and analysing the role and consequences of soft law more broadly enables us to better understand the complex relationship between international law and international relations.

States choose forms of instruments based upon careful considerations of objectives, obstacles, opportunities, and the relative benefits and drawbacks of the options available to them. Such an analysis will not only help us gain a better understanding of the international system, as it exists today, and how it has changed, the role of negotiation, the deliberate use of legal language, and the importance of the context within which each agreement was negotiated. More broadly, it could also inform decision-makers and relevant stakeholders of the relative costs and benefits of the various forms of international instruments.

From the Indian Ocean to the Arctic: What the Chagos Archipelago Advisory Opinion Tells Us about Greenland

*Rachael Lorna Johnstone**

Abstract

On February 25, 2019, the International Court of Justice issued its advisory opinion on *Legal Consequences of the Separation of the Chagos Archipelago from Mauritius in 1965*. The judges held by a majority of 13:1 that the process of decolonisation of Mauritius is incomplete, owing to the separation of the Chagos Archipelago shortly before Mauritian independence, that the United Kingdom should end its administration of the Chagos Archipelago as rapidly as possible, and that all Member States of the United Nations should cooperate to complete the decolonisation of Mauritius.

The (partial) decolonisation of Mauritius in 1968 and the treatment of the Chagos islanders (Chagossians) have important parallels with the purported decolonisation of Greenland in 1952–54. In both cases, the consultative body of the colonised people was neither fully independent nor representative of all the people concerned. No real choice was given to either body; rather the colonial power offered only the continuation of the status quo or professed self-determination on terms defined by the colonial power itself. Furthermore, the process of decolonisation was inherently linked to the forcible transfer of people in order to make way for a United States military facility.

Nevertheless, there are some relevant differences. First of all, Greenland was purportedly decolonised in 1953, some seven years before the UN General Assembly Declaration on the Granting of Independence to Colonial Countries and Peoples (UNGA Res. 1514(XV) 1960). Second, the UN General Assembly accepted the Danish government's representations regarding the full decolonisation of Greenland (UNGA Res. 849 (1954)), in contrast to their position regarding Mauritius that decolonisation was and remains incomplete, owing to the separation of the Chagos Archipelago (UNGA Res(XX) 1965). Third, though the Chagossians have been recognised as indigenous at the UN, the British government has continually denied this status and

---

* Professor, University of Akureyri, Iceland. rlj@unak.is.

(mis)characterises them as a transient people, while Denmark has accepted the status of the Greenlanders as both an indigenous people and a colonial people, entitled to self-determination.

This article examines the implications for the judgment for the Greenland case as well as broader questions of self-determination of peoples. It concludes that the colonial boundaries continue to govern in decolonisation cases, with the consequence that the Greenlanders are likely to be held to be a single people; that the *erga omnes* character of the right to self-determination means that all States must cooperate to facilitate Greenlanders' choices for their future; and that there remain significant procedural hurdles that prevent colonial and indigenous peoples having their voices heard, even in the matters that concern them most of all.

Keywords

decolonisation – Greenland – Chagos Archipelago – indigenous peoples

1 Introduction

The Chagos Archipelago, located in the Indian Ocean, could barely be further away from the Poles. Nevertheless, the International Court of Justice's advisory opinion on *Legal Consequences of the Separation of the Chagos Archipelago from Mauritius in 1965*[1] (Chagos Advisory Opinion) tells us important things about contemporary international law of relevance to Polar law and to Greenland in particular. The Chagossians and the Greenlanders have a shared experience of colonisation and an unsatisfactory and incomplete process of decolonisation. In both cases, the consultative body of the colonised people was neither fully independent nor representative of all the people concerned. No real choice was given to either body: rather the colonial power offered only the continuation of the status quo or professed self-determination on terms defined by the colonial power itself. In both territories, the process of decolonisation was inherently linked to the forcible transfer of people in order to make way for a United States military facility.

This article will present the history of the Chagossians, highlighting the features of most relevant to the questions of decolonisation, self-determination,

---

1 *Legal Consequences of the Separation of the Chagos Archipelago from Mauritius in 1965*, Advisory Opinion, ICJ GL No 169, ICGJ 534 (ICJ 2019), February 25, 2019 (Chagos Advisory Opinion).

territorial integrity, and forced relocation. The findings of the Court are then explained. Readers of the *Yearbook* are likely familiar with the history of Greenland, so a more succinct outline of the colonisation and purported decolonisation of Greenland is presented, drawing relevant comparisons with the Chagossians' case. Fuller accounts of Greenland's legal history are available elsewhere.[2] The article then considers how the process before the International Court of Justice, even in advisory opinions, prioritises States and excludes the people at the heart of the matter. It concludes that the colonial boundaries continue to govern in decolonisation cases, with the consequence that the Greenlanders are likely to be held to be a single people; that the *erga omnes* character of the right to self-determination means that all States must cooperate to facilitate Greenlanders' choices for their future; and that there remain significant procedural hurdles that prevent colonial and indigenous peoples having their voices heard, even in the matters that concern them most of all.

2   The History of the Chagossians

The Chagos archipelago was uninhabited when discovered by Portuguese and Dutch sailors in 16th C.[3] The Maldivians probably knew of the islands but did not use them and made no efforts at *occupation*. France administered the archipelago from 1715 but the British claimed it as a prize of the Napoleonic Wars in 1814.[4] The first people were sent to work as slaves in 1776, from Mozambique and Madagascar. After the transfer of the islands, the United Kingdom (UK)

---

2   See, e.g., Gudmundur Alfredsson, "Greenland and the Law of Political Decolonization," *German Y.B. Int'l L.* 25 (1982): 290; Gudmundur Alfredsson, "Greenland and the Right to Self-Determination," *Nordisk Tidsskrift Int'l Ret* 51 (1982): 39; Rachael Lorna Johnstone, "The Impact of International Law on Natural Resource Governance in Greenland," *Polar Record, Special Issue: International Law for Sustainability in Arctic Resource Development*, 2019; Søren Rud, *Colonialism in Greenland: Tradition, Governance and Legacy* (Cham: Palgrave Macmillan, 2017).

3   See, David Vine, "From the Birth of the Ilois to the 'Footprint of Freedom': A History of Chagos and the Chagossians", in *Eviction from the Chagos Islands: Displacement and Struggle for Identity Against Two World Powers*, eds. Sandra JTM Evers and Marry Kooy (Leiden: Brill, 2011), 11–39 (for the early history of the Chagossians). See also Peter H Sand, *United States and Britain in Diego Garcia: The Future of a Controversial Base* (New York: Palgrave Macmillan, 2009) (for history and analysis of the creation of BIOT and the forced relocation of the Chagossians, including reproduction of official UK documents).

4   See Vine, note 3, 17.

continued to send slaves to live and work there.[5] Slavery was abolished in 1835, but the Chagossians continued to work as contract labourers and their conditions barely improved.[6] Some other workers came voluntarily and settled, including from Malaysia and India. Today's Chagossians are descendants of those people.

The UK administered the Chagos Archipelago as a dependency of Mauritius, also a British colony over 2000km away. Prior to colonisation, the Mauritians had no links to the islands nor to the people that would be brought there from the 18th century onwards. The Chagossians are ethnically and culturally distinct from the people of Mauritius.[7] The British government presents the Chagossians as a transient population even if their own records, released many years later, prove otherwise.[8] The Chagossians self-identify as a distinct people, were recognised by the UN Working Group on Indigenous Populations in 1997, and have also been recognised as an indigenous people by the English courts.[9]

From 1946 to 1968, the UK submitted reports regarding Mauritius as a colony under article 73(e) of the UN Charter in which it referred to the Chagos Archipelago as a 'dependency' of Mauritius.[10] The new 1947 constitution established a Legislative Council (from 1964 'Legislative Assembly') in Mauritius which consisted of the governor presiding, 12 members nominated by the governor, 3 members *ex officio* and 19 members elected by (some of) the Mauritians (though not at that time the Chagossians).[11] The party system meant that the Mauritian vote was inevitably split making it almost impossible

---

[5] See Chagos Advisory Opinion, note 1, para 113; See also Julian Durup, "The Chagos. A Short History and its Legal Identity" *Études ocean Indien* 49–50 (2013), DOI: 10.4000/oceanindien.2003.

[6] Stephen Allen, "Looking Beyond the Bancoult Cases: International Law and the Prospect of Resettling the Chagos Islands," *Human Rights Law Review* 7, no. 3 (2007): 441–482, 445.

[7] Ibid, 471.

[8] See Sand, note 3, 16–18; Vine, note 3, 33–34. See also UK Foreign and Commonwealth Office, Resettlement Memorandum, 1971, reproduced in Sand, *United States and Britain*, 18–23.

[9] See Allen, note 6, 473; Vine, note 3, 34; *R v Secretary of State ex parte Bancoult* 2000, [2000] EWHC Admin 413, [2001] QB 1067; *Eviction from the Chagos Islands*, xii. See also Maureen Tong, "Self-Determination in the Post-Colonial Era" in Evans and Kooy, note 3, 173–74.

[10] Charter of the United Nations. (1945). Adopted 26 June 1945, entered into force 24 October 1945. United Nations Treaty Series 1 (1945): XVI, article 73(e); Chagos Advisory Opinion, note 1, para 29.

[11] See Chagos Advisory Opinion, note 1, para 63. Chagos Advisory Opinion, Written Statement of the Republic of Mauritius, March 1, 2018, para 3.4. The members *ex officio* were the Colonial Secretary, the Procureur and Advocate General, and the Financial Secretary.

for any Mauritian party to hold a majority on the Legislative Council.[12] Four of the elected members served on the Executive Council (from 1964 'Council of Ministers'). In 1958, the Legislative Council was expanded to include 40 elected members, 12 appointees of the governor, and 3 *ex officio*.[13]

In any case, the Legislative Council could not, in fact, legislate, absent the assent of the British governor.[14]

The UN Committee of Twenty-Four characterised the system in the following manner:

> The Special Committee is of the opinion that the present Constitution of Mauritius ... do[es] not allow the representatives of the people to exercise real legislative or executive power, and that authority is nearly all concentrated in the hands of the United Kingdom Government and its representatives ... All laws passed by the Legislative Assembly are subject to the assent of the Governor, who is empowered, moreover, to give legal effect to any bill before the Assembly even if it has not been voted upon.[15]

Having created a body that existed only at the pleasure of the British governor and over which the governor had the ultimate authority, the United Kingdom then entered into independence negotiations with it.[16] The British made it clear that they had no intention of including the Chagos Archipelago in the Mauritian independence package: it was the British deal or no deal.[17]

On November 8, 1966, the UK separated the Chagos Archipelago administratively from Mauritius and joined it with three islands annexed from the Seychelles to create British Indian Ocean Territory (BIOT).[18] (The three islands of the Seychelles were returned in 1976.) BIOT was never registered as a colony within the UN system, a position that also suits Mauritius as should the archipelago be registered as a distinct territory, the Chagossians would have a much firmer recognition of their right to self-determination.[19] The UN General

---

12 See Chagos Advisory Opinion, note 1, para 64; Written Statement of the Republic of Mauritius, note 11, para 3.5.
13 See Written Statement of the Republic of Mauritius, note 11, para 3.8.
14 Ibid.
15 UN General Assembly, Implementation of the Declaration on the Granting of Independence of Colonial Countries and Peoples: Report of the Special Committee, 1964–65, UN Doc. A/5800/Rev.1 (1964–65), para 154.
16 See Chagos Advisory Opinion, note 1, para 98.
17 Ibid, paras 98–112.
18 Ibid, para 33; BIOT Order 1965, No. 1, *The British Indian Ocean Territory Official Gazette*, 1, vol. 1 (December 1965): 1.
19 See Tong, note 9, 168.

Assembly responded with Resolution 2232 (XXI) in which it reiterated that breaches of the territorial integrity of colonies and the establishment of military bases thereon violate the UN Charter and Resolution 1514.[20] Nevertheless, on December 30, 1966, following years of secret negotiations, the UK entered a defence agreement with the United States that would allow the Americans to build a military base at the largest of the Chagos islands, Diego Garcia and required, *inter alia*, relocation of the population of the islands.[21]

Mauritius became independent on March 12, 1968 – without the Chagos Archipelago.[22]

Between 1967–1973, Chagossians who left their islands to obtain healthcare, visit relatives, or take a vacation, were prevented from returning. The rest were forcibly removed.[23] Before the last shipment of the human cargo sailed, the Chagossians' pet dogs were rounded up, gassed, and their corpses burned in from of the families.[24] The implicit message of this demonstration of British force was not lost on those who might have wavered before boarding the overcrowded cargo ships. From 1971 onwards, one could only enter the Chagos islands with a permit – which was almost impossible to acquire if you were not British government, US Military or a contractor to the base, a compliant scientist, or an affluent private yacht owner seeking to moor at one of the smaller islands.[25]

---

20 UN General Assembly, Resolution No. 2232 (XXI), Question of American Samoa, Antigua, Bahamas, Bermuda, British Virgin Islands, Cayman Islands, Cocos (Keeling) Islands, Dominica, Gilbert and Ellice Islands, Grenada, Guam, Mauritius, Montserrat, New Hebrides, Niue, Pitcairn, St Helena, St Kitts-Nevis-Anguilla, St Lucia, St Vincent, Seychelles, Solomon Islands, Tokelau Islands, Turks and Caicos Islands and the United States Virgin Islands, 1966, UN Doc. A Res 2232 (XXI), December 20, 1966, para 4; Chagos Advisory Opinion, note 1, para 35.

21 Agreement concerning the Availability for Defence Purposes of the British Indian Ocean Territory. Adopted December 30, 1966, *United Nations Treaty Series* 8737 (1967): 273; Chagos Advisory Opinion, note 1, para 36–37. See also Vine, note 3, 32–33.

22 See Chagos Advisory Opinion, note 1, para 42.

23 Ibid, para 433.

24 David Vine, *Island of Shame: The Secret History of the U.S. Military Base on Diego Garcia* (Princeton, NJ: Princeton University Press, 2011), 114.

25 See Chagos Advisory Opinion, note 1, para 115. See also Sand, note 3, 31. The Agreement requires the US to hire Mauritian and Seychellian workers at the base 'to the maximum extent practicable, consistent with United States policies, requirements and schedules'. See, Agreement concerning the Availability for Defence Purposes, note 21, article 7(a). See Steffen F Johannessen, "Cleaning for the Dead: The Chagossian Pilgrimage to their Homeland," in Evans and Kooy, note 3, 204 (explaining that it was not until 2006, after decades of explicit discrimination, that the US base hired the first Chagossians and then only three).

Only in 2006 would the first group of Chagossians be permitted to join a carefully choreographed 'heritage visit' to their homeland to, amongst other things, care for the graves of their relatives.[26]

The UK paid 650,000 GBP *to Mauritius* in 1972 for the costs of resettling the Chagossians who had been left utterly destitute on the jetties of Mauritius and the Seychelles.[27] Ten years later, the UK paid a further 4,000,000 GBP, again to Mauritius, in 'full and final settlement' but with no admission of liability.[28] This sum was to be disbursed to surviving Chagossians in Mauritius (though not those in the Seychelles or in the UK) on condition they signed a one-page form, in English, renouncing any right to return, as required by the British authorities.[29] One Chagossian estimated the total compensation package as less than one month's average British wage for each survivor.[30] The Chagossians in the Seychelles have been largely overlooked but the British government funded a new airport for the Seychelles, which helped it develop its extensive tourism industry.[31]

In 1992, Mauritius amended its constitution to incorporate explicitly the Chagos Archipelago as part of its territory.[32]

The General Assembly and the African Union (erstwhile Organisation of African Unity) have repeatedly held the decolonisation of Mauritius to be incomplete, because of the separation of the Chagos islands.[33] Exiled Chagossians have brought litigation in the British courts and before the European Court of Human Rights with limited impact. Following a Chagossian win in the English courts in 1998, the UK government accepted the formal legal right of return to some of the islands, excluding *Diego Garcia*, but ensured this was practically impossible and reversed their position before anyone could return.[34]

---

26 Johannessen, Ibid.
27 Chagos Advisory Opinion, note 1, para 117; Vine, note 3, 160–161.
28 Chagos Advisory Opinion, note 1, para 119.
29 Ibid, para 120; Laura Jeffrey and David Vine, "Sorrow, Sadness, and Impoverishment: the Lives of the Chagossians in Mauritius," in Evans and Kooy, note 3, 99.
30 Laura Jeffrey, "Charlesia Alexis: The Struggle of the Chagossian Women" in Evans and Kooy, note 3, 82. The amount was around 4000 GBP; see Jeffrey and Vine, note 29, 100.
31 See, "Bernadette Dugasse: Born in Diego Garcia December 1956" in Evans and Kooy, note 3, 103–4; and David Vine, "Chagossians Twice Forgotten: Exile in the Seychelles" in Evans and Kooy, note 3, 105–124 (on the experience of the Chagossians in the Seychelles).
32 Constitution of Mauritius, Part XI; see also, *In the Matter of the Chagos Marine Protected Area Arbitration (Mauritius v United Kingdom)* Permanent Court of Arbitration, March 18, 2015, *Reports of International Arbitral Awards* XXXI (2018): 359–606, para 104.
33 See Chagos Advisory Opinion, note 1, paras 47, 49, 52, and 173.
34 Ibid, paras 121–130.

On April 1st 2010, the UK declared an enormous marine protected area (MPA) around the entire Chagos Archipelago, creating the largest 'no-take' zone in the World. This was celebrated by, *inter alia*, Greenpeace and the Royal Society for the Protection of Birds (RSPB).[35] As a British diplomat candidly explained, the British "environmental lobby is far more powerful than the Chagossians' advocates."[36] However, the MPA is not entirely 'no-take': 3000–5000 US military personnel and contractors are permitted to fish for food and recreation.[37] The base population is almost as high as the surviving Chagossian community and probably higher than the number who would return if given the opportunity;[38] yet the MPA would prohibit them from fishing in their own waters. Later the same year, *wikileaks* released a cable from 2009 in which a US diplomat explains unambiguously the intentions behind the MPA: "Establishing a marine reserve might, indeed, as the FCO's Roberts stated, be the most effective long-term way to prevent any of the Chagos Islands' former inhabitants or their descendants from resettling in the British Indian Ocean Territory".[39]

Mauritius challenged the MPA under the UN Convention on the Law of the Sea (UNCLOS) and the Permanent Court of Arbitration held in 2015 that it was unlawful owing to the failure to consult with Mauritius (that is, on relatively narrow, procedural grounds).[40] The majority declined to rule on the

---

35 Willie, "Why Greenpeace supports a Marine Reserve in the Chagos," Greenpeace, March 2, 2010, accessed December 18, 2019 from archive, https://storage.googleapis.com/gpuk-archive/blog/oceans/why-greenpeace-supports-marine-reserve-chagos-20100224.html (accessed 1 July 2020); Mark Avery, "Chagos – a Great Result for Wildlife," Royal Society for the Protection of Birds, April 2, 2010, https://community.rspb.org.uk/ourwork/b/markavery/posts/chagos-a-great-result-for-wildlife?CommentId=269284cd-12f3-4ac2-961d-0e2af689a716 (accessed 1 July 2020). The RSPB is a well-respected British conservation charity with over one million members. Gross income in the 2018–19 was 144.6 million GBP, see, RSPB, *Annual Review 2018–19*, 2019, 49, https://www.rspb.org.uk/about-the-rspb/about-us/how-the-rspb-is-run/annual-review/ (accessed 1 July 2020).
36 "HMG Floats Proposal For Marine Reserve Covering The Chagos Archipelago (British Indian Ocean Territory)," May 15, 2009, https://wikileaks.org/plusd/cables/09LONDON1156_a.html, para 7.
37 See Vine, note 3 (for estimates of base numbers). See also, Sand, note 3 (on the US military's poor environmental record on Diego Garcia).
38 See, Sandra JTM Evers and Marry Kooy, "Redundancy on the Installment Plan: Chagossians and the Right to be Called a People" in Evans and Kooy, note 3, 2 (estimating the surviving population of the evicted at approximately 750 in 2011; with around 5,500 survivors and descendants in total estimated in 2008).
39 See HMG Floats Proposal For Marine Reserve, note 36, para 15.
40 See *In the Matter of the Chagos Marine Protected Area Arbitration*, note 32.

substantive questions of sovereignty over the islands.[41] The UK and Mauritius continue to negotiate but at the time of writing, the MPA remained in effect.

3   The 2019 Chagos Advisory Opinion

The General Assembly sought an advisory opinion from the Court in 2017 on two questions:

(a) Was the process of decolonization of Mauritius lawfully completed when Mauritius was granted independence in 1968, following the separation of the Chagos Archipelago from Mauritius and having regard to international law, including obligations reflected in General Assembly resolutions 1514 (XV) of 14 December 1960, 2066 (XX) of 16 December 1965, 2232 (XXI) of 20 December 1966 and 2357 (XXII) of 19 December 1967?;

(b) What are the consequences under international law, including obligations reflected in the above-mentioned resolutions, arising from the continued administration by the United Kingdom of Great Britain and Northern Ireland of the Chagos Archipelago, including with respect to the inability of Mauritius to implement a programme for the resettlement on the Chagos Archipelago of its nationals, in particular those of Chagossian origin?[42]

It was not a foregone conclusion that the Court would agree to consider the case. The UK (and others) objected, insisting that this was in reality a contentious, bilateral dispute between Mauritius and the UK to which the UK had not accepted the Court's jurisdiction.[43] However, the majority concluded that the advisory opinion was rather directed to the organ that sought it, namely the General Assembly, for whom it would contribute importantly to its ability to conduct its task of overseeing decolonisation. The inclusion of matters on which two States happened to disagree did not render the issue a bilateral dispute and therefore their consent to the Court's jurisdiction was not necessary.[44] While the Court's position on this matter follows *Western Sahara*,[45] it does indicate a departure from *East Timor*[46] in which a bilateral dispute os-

---

41   Ibid, para 213 *et seq*.
42   UN General Assembly, Resolution 71/292, Request for an advisory opinion of the International Court of Justice on the legal consequences of the separation of the Chagos Archipelago from Mauritius in 1965, UN Doc. A/Res/71/292, June 22, 2017.
43   See Chagos Advisory Opinion, note 1, paras 83–91.
44   Ibid, paras 89–90.
45   *Western Sahara*, Advisory Opinion, ICJ Reports (1975): 12.
46   *East Timor (Portugal v Australia)*, ICJ Reports (1995): 90.

tensibly between Portugal and Australia was not admissible in contentious proceedings because it in reality concerned a dispute between Indonesia (that had not consented to jurisdiction) and the colonised East Timorese people. It is not self-evident that the Court would hear a contentious dispute between two States that regarded inherently the failure to decolonise of a third State. Nevertheless, the Court emphasised in the Chagos Advisory Opinion the *erga omnes* nature of the norm of self-determination (as it did in *East Timor*) and specified the 'legal interest' of all States 'in protecting that right'.[47] If the Court continues to follow *East Timor*, this would still not open the door to contentious proceedings brought by third States but it could potentially justify counter-measures by third States in order to pressure colonial powers to facilitate self-determination.

The Court held on the facts that the decolonisation of Mauritius in 1968 was incomplete, owing to the separation of the Chagos Archipelago.[48] Although this is an advisory opinion, directed at the General Assembly that requested it, the Court concludes strongly that:

> The United Kingdom is under an obligation to bring an end to its administration of the Chagos Archipelago as rapidly as possible, thereby enabling Mauritius to complete the decolonization of its territory in a manner consistent with the rights of peoples to self-determination.[49]

It then turns the matter back to the General Assembly, refraining from identifying any particular steps the General Assembly should take.[50] In light of the *erga omnes* character of the norm of self-determination, the Court reminds all Member States of their duties to cooperate to promote the end of decolonisation *of Mauritius*.[51]

What is implicit in the opinion is that the Court views the Chagos Archipelago *as part of Mauritius*, notwithstanding the lack of any historic connection before the *British* decision to administer the territories together for its own convenience. It seems the Chagossians, who consider themselves a distinct people, are pawns to be transferred once more from one foreign regime to another. It is the colonial boundaries drawn up by States thousands of miles away that continue to govern and not the identities of the peoples concerned. The principle of self-determination is thus radically constrained for minorities

---

47 See Chagos Advisory Opinion, note 1, 180.
48 Ibid, para 174.
49 Ibid, para 178.
50 Ibid, para 179.
51 Ibid, para 180.

within colonised regimes. As will be explained later, the *process* before the Court further marginalises such peoples.

4 A Brief Legal History of Greenland

Polar lawyers are mostly familiar with the legal history and status of Greenland so a briefer account of that country follows, focusing on relevant similarities and differences to the Chagossians' case. The following account summarises an account presented elsewhere.[52]

Greenland's west and south coasts were colonised by Norway from 1721 onwards. The Scandinavian colonisation of the East Greenlanders began in 1883. The Greenlanders in the south seem to have been aware that there were settlements to the east but there was no regular contact between them. (Similarly, Mauritius had no relations with the Chagos Archipelago prior to European colonisation.) The Danes reached North Greenland around the same time but Danish sovereignty over North Greenland was not conclusively settled until 1916 when the US renounced any claim (as part of a package deal to purchase the Danish West Indies, now the US Virgin Islands). The native Greenlanders are all Inuit but the North and East Greenlanders are culturally and linguistically distinct from the majority of the Greenland population.

In the 1933 *Eastern Greenland* case, the Permanent Court of International Justice evaluated the competing claims of Denmark and Norway – based on their respective efforts at occupation. The Court held that the entire island was under Danish sovereignty, notwithstanding relatively little effective occupation by the Danish of the East coast. The Inuit are considered only wards of the colonial power.

During World War II, Denmark was occupied by Germany and the US established defence facilities in (unoccupied) Greenland. Following the war, Denmark reported on Greenland as a non-self-governing territory under article 73(e) of the Charter.

In 1952, an entirely Danish Constitutional Commission presented proposals for integration of Greenland to the *Grønlands Landsråd* (the Greenland Provincial Council). The Council was a partly elected body but did not include any representatives from North or East Greenland and it was chaired by the Danish Governor. It was not an independent body and had, up until this point, been granted only minor powers. It had been elected in 1951, before anyone had mentioned potential constitutional upheaval to the Greenlanders.

---

52 See Johnstone, note 2.

The Council had only two days to discuss the Danish offer of integration before agreeing. No alternatives were proposed, despite the fact that the Faroe Islands had enjoyed Home Rule since 1948. It was the Danish offer of integration or the *status quo*. The members of the Provincial Council were shown only the draft articles concerning the status of Greenland but not the rest of the Danish Constitution to which they were to sign up. There was no discussion amongst the wider community and certainly no popular vote before the Provincial Council agreed to the integration.

Just days before the new Constitution would take effect, bringing Greenland into the realm as a formally equal county of Denmark and making the Greenlanders Danish citizens, the Inughuit people were forcibly relocated from Uummannaq – to make way for expansion of the US base. (David Vine finds similar examples in Alaska, the Bikini Atoll, Culebra, Guam, Hawaii, the Marshall Islands, Okinawa, Panama, the Philippines and Puerto Rico.[53]) Denmark paid compensation much later to the Greenland Home Rule government in 1997 and to the Inughuit families in 2003.[54] Differing from the Chagossians' case, the UN General Assembly accepted the Danish presentation of the decolonisation of Greenland as having been completed in 1954.[55]

Table 1 summarises the most important similarities and differences in the colonisation and decolonisation processes regarding the Greenlanders and the Chagossians.

The dates are important. Resolution 1514 was not agreed until 1960. Judge Robinson, in his separate opinion in the Chagos Advisory Opinion, holds that 1960 is the most convincing date to hold the principles of Resolution 1514 as customary law. At best, they might have crystallised in 1957.[56] Therefore, the *contemporary* law on decolonisation at the time of Greenland's integration into Denmark is not as well developed and does not emphasise to the same degree the need to follow the wishes of the people of the territory. The less developed state of international law may explain in part why the General Assembly accepted the Danish report of the decolonisation at face value whereas they have never accepted the decolonisation of Mauritius as complete. Another factor is simply the international relations of the time: the Greenlanders had no

---

53 See Vine, note 24, 65–68.
54 *Hingitaq 53 v Denmark*, Application no. 18584/04, European Court of Human Rights, Decision on Admissibility, January 12, 2006.
55 UN General Assembly, Resolution 849 (IX), Cessation of the transmission of information under Article 73 e of the Charter in Respect of Greenland, UN Doc. A/RES/849(IX), November 22,1954.
56 See Chagos Advisory Opinion, note 1, Separate Opinion of Robinson, para 42.

TABLE 1 Comparison of Greenland and Chagossian legal history

Greenland	Chagos Archipelago
KEY SIMILARITIES	
Bilateral dispute between two colonial powers (DK and NO).	Bilateral dispute between colonial power (UK) and one post-colonial power (MU); and advisory opinion.
People ethnically and culturally distinct from colonial power (DK) and contesting power (NO); minorities in East and North Greenland also culturally distinct from post-colonial power (Nuuk).	People ethnically and culturally distinct from colonial powers (UK and France) and contesting post-colonial power (MU).
Reported as a colony under article 73(e) UN Charter.	Reported as a part of a colony under article 73(e) UN Charter.
Negotiations on decolonisation with a non-representative body; "take it or leave it".	Negotiations on decolonisation with a non-representative body; "take it or leave it".
Indigenous population prior to European colonisation; widely recognised as indigenous people.	Descendants of slaves and immigrant workers brought by colonial powers as well as later arrivals; recognised as indigenous people by UNWGIP, English courts.
Forced relocation of part of population and prevention of return (1953).	Forced relocation of whole population and prevention of return (1967–1973).
US military defence agreement.	US military defence agreement.
Compensation paid later to those relocated and to the post-colonial power (Gl Home Rule).	Compensation paid later to those relocated and to the post-colonial power (MU).
Territorial integrity paramount, based on colonial boundaries.	Territorial integrity paramount, based on colonial boundaries.
Voice of colonial people excluded in legal process.	Voice of colonial people excluded in legal process.
KEY DIFFERENCES	
Purported decolonisation prior to UNGA Res. 1514.	*Partial decolonisation (of MU) post UNGA Res. 1514.*
UNGA accepted decolonisation complete.	*UNGA never accepted decolonisation complete.*

kin to speak up for them in the General Assembly in the 1950s in contrast to the burgeoning African movement for decolonisation of the 1960s and 1970s.

In neither case was the population consulted. In the Chagos Advisory Opinion, the majority notes that it is not necessary *in every case* to have a vote of the whole people concerned, citing the *Western Sahara* opinion. The General Assembly has a 'measure of discretion' in accepting the procedures used to identify the 'freely-expressed will of people'.[57] A consultation may be 'totally unnecessary, in view of special circumstances'.[58] One might imagine that in 1953, the General Assembly considered such 'special circumstances' to apply to Greenland. However, the Court on this point quotes directly from the *Western Sahara* opinion, which concerns the (very) special circumstances of a colonial power deliberately transferring population to upset the natural demographics to give the colonial power a majority in any popular vote. There was nothing particularly 'special' about the purported decolonisation of Greenland. It is a better view that it is the date of decolonisation that is the important factor: in 1953 there was not yet an expectation that a popular vote of the colonised population was required.

As described earlier in this article, the Chagossians arrived relatively recently on the archipelago – from the 18th century onwards. Nevertheless, they are the 'first settlers,' even if they settled against their will in the first place. They have been recognised as an indigenous population in the UN. Judge Cançado Trindade refers in his separate opinion to a series of indigenous cases from the Inter-American Court, implying that he considers indigenous rights to be relevant to the Chagossians' case. In any case, like the Greenlanders, whether indigenous or not, the Chagossians have the *stronger* status of a colonial people and the right of external self-determination that comes with it.[59]

5   The Significance of the Chagos Advisory Opinion for Greenland

The Chagos Advisory Opinion confirms once more that it is the *colonial* boundaries that continue to govern: the boundaries *drawn by the colonial power at the moment of decolonisation*.[60] These boundaries need make no historic, ethnographic, or geographic sense but simply be an administrative convenience of the colonial power. The Chagos Islands are part of Mauritius *because the British*

---

57   Chagos Advisory Opinion, note 1, para 157.
58   Ibid, para 158.
59   See also, Tong, note 9, 171–72.
60   Chagos Advisory Opinion, para 170.

made them so.[61] Judge Dillard famously opined in the *Western Sahara* case that, "It is for the people to determine the destiny of the territory and not the territory the destiny of the people."[62] However, there is no provision for the people to identify themselves *qua people* in the first place; rather the people is identified by the colonial boundaries. The people entitled to self-determination is thus a construction of the colonial power, created by the drawing of colonial boundaries, even if these were drawn on a completely arbitrary basis. Thus in a very real sense, the territory does continue to determine the destiny of the people.

The consequence for Greenland is that this reinforces the historic Danish position, now endorsed by the government of Greenland, that the Greenlanders are one single people. The Danish position that Greenland is a single integral territory was first presented to stave off the ambitious Norwegians in the *Eastern Greenland* case. It was then adapted to the position that the Inuit inhabitants of Greenland are a single integral people in order to defeat the claims regarding the forced relocation of the Inughuit.[63] Today, this position suits the government of Greenland as to recognise the cultural and linguistic minorities within Greenland as indigenous would bring obligations to protect their rights against the Greenland and Copenhagen administrations *qua* indigenous peoples.

The Danes drew the line around Greenland that encircled all the Inuit therein, ignoring the historic isolation of the East and North Greenlanders and their cultures and languages that remain distinct to this day.[64] The territory – according to the boundaries drawn up by the Danes – determines the destiny of the minority Greenlanders. The East and North Greenlanders are unlikely to be recognised as distinct peoples, notwithstanding their significantly different

---

61   See, ibid, para 160. See also UN General Assembly, Resolution 73/295, Advisory opinion of the International Court of Justice on the legal consequences of the separation of the Chagos Archipelago from Mauritius in 1965, UN Doc. A/RES/73/295, May 24, 2019, paras 2(a) and (b), 4, 6 and 7. See also, Conference on Yugoslavia Arbitration Commission: Opinions on Questions Arising from the Dissolution of Yugoslavia, January 11 and July 4, 1992, *International Legal Materials* 31 (1992): 1488, 1498–1500 (Opinion no. 2).

62   See *Western Sahara*, note 45, Separate Opinion of Judge Dillard, 114.

63   Report of the Committee set up to examine the representation alleging non-observance by Denmark of the Indigenous and Tribal Peoples Convention, 1989 (No. 169), made under article 24 of the ILO Constitution by the National Confederation of Trade Unions of Greenland (Sulinermik Inuussutissarsiuteqartut Kattuffiat – SIK) (*SIK v Denmark*), GB.277/18/3; GB.280/18/5, para 20.

64   See Terto Ngiviu, "The Inughuit of Northwest Greenland: An Unacknowledged Indigenous People," *The Yearbook of Polar Law* 6 (2016): 142–161 (on the North Greenlanders); and see Gustav Holm, et al, The Ammassalik Eskimo: Contributions to the Ethnology of the East Greenland Natives, William Thalbitzer, ed., Parts I and II (English translation) (Copenhagen: Bianco Luno, 1914) (on the East Greenlanders).

experiences of colonisation, cultures, languages, and – most important of all – self-identification as distinct.[65] In an independent Greenland, they *might* have some protections as minorities or even as indigenous peoples but they are not considered distinct colonial peoples – *because this is what Denmark decided* in the 20th century in response to the Norwegian challenge. The East and North Greenlanders can be transferred from Copenhagen to Nuuk, just as the majority of the Court calls, effectively, for the Chagossians to be transferred from British to Mauritian rule in due course.

Another side of this principle of integrity of colonial boundaries is that it indicates that for Greenland to become fully independent, the Pituffik (Thule) area on which the US military base sits must be included. Neither Denmark nor the US can annex the base area prior to independence.[66] An independent Greenland is free to negotiate with the US (or not) for the continuation of the base as it sees fit.

The recognition of the right to self-determination as a norm *erga omnes* presents the Court with an opportunity to emphasise the duty to comply and to promote this norm. It pronounces, fairly meekly, that:

> while it is for the General Assembly to pronounce on the modalities required to ensure the completion of the decolonization of Mauritius, all Member States must co-operate with the United Nations to put those modalities into effect.[67]

Thus the Court emphasises the primary role of the General Assembly and indicates that individual States have a subsidiary role, only in support of the United Nations, rather than taking measures to promote the norm themselves. The Court falls short of an express recognition of the *ius cogens* character of the norm – and is rebuked on this count in three separate opinions.[68] Nevertheless, the *erga omnes* status of the norm implies that any State has standing to bring a *contentious* case where self-determination is denied.[69] All States have a legal interest[70] indicating that all and any states can invoke responsibility in cases

---

65   See *Hingitaq*, note 54, 53.
66   See Chagos Advisory Opinion, note 1, para 160.
67   Ibid, para 180.
68   Ibid, Separate Opinions of Judge Cançado Trindade, Judge Sebutinde and Judge Robinson.
69   See also, *Questions Relating to the Obligation to Prosecute or Extradite (Belgium v Senegal)* Judgment, ICJ Reports (2012): 422; and Rachael Lorna Johnstone, "Invoking Responsibility for Environmental Injury in the Arctic Ocean" *Yearbook of Polar Law* 6 (2015): 3–35 (on the right to invoke responsibility for violation of norms *erga omnes*).
70   See Chagos Advisory Opinion, note 1, para 180.

where self-determination is denied. While a contentious judicial settlement would still likely require consent to jurisdiction by the colonial State (following *East Timor*), the advisory opinion implicitly indicates a potential for countermeasures against recalcitrant colonial powers.

That all States must cooperate to uphold and ensure norms of *ius cogens* should go without saying in the 21st century. When it comes to the right to self-determination, States might not go out of their way to put pressure on their allies to decolonise or cease unlawful occupations but they tend not openly to promote policies of colonialism or occupation. As regards Greenland, all States should respect the rights of the Greenlanders to determine their own future, including in the fairly unlikely event that the Danish government reverses its policy and stands in their way. Until recently, this would simply be stating the obvious. However, the inquiries of the United States regarding the potential to simply purchase the territory – and furthermore considering the Danish government the relevant negotiating partner for such an objective – indicate that the obvious bears restating.[71]

More likely to be of relevance in real world diplomatic relations are questions regarding the maintenance and future of the US base at Pituffik. The Greenland government must have a leading role in any negotiations and must approve of any bilateral treaty agreed between Denmark and the US regarding the territory.

6   Procedure and Its Limitations

The Chagos Advisory Opinion also constrains the right to self-determination for procedural reasons. The rules of the Court remain based fundamentally on the 1922 rules of the Permanent Court of International Justice, when international law was very much about State to State relations and there was precious little in the way of rights or responsibilities of non-State actors.[72] The current rules are substantially from 1972, with minor amendments in 2005 and 2019.[73] Only States can be party to contentious proceedings though interna-

---

[71]   Paul LeBlanc, "Danish Prime Minister Calls Trump's Interest in Buying Greenland 'Absurd'," CNN, August 19, 2019), https://www.cnn.com/2019/08/18/politics/us-buy-greenland-danish-prime-minister/index.html (accessed 1 July 2020).

[72]   Permanent Court of International Justice, Rules of the Court, Adopted March 24, 1922, https://www.icj-cij.org/files/permanent-court-of-international-justice/serie_D/D_01.pdf (accessed 1 July 2020).

[73]   International Court of Justice, Rules of the Court, Adopted April 14, 1978, as amended, https://www.icj-cij.org/en/rules (accessed 1 July 2020).

tional organisations (or organs thereof) can request advisory opinions and they may submit information to the Court, on invitation by the Court or on their own initiative.[74] The Court is also obligated to advise international organisations of any case in which its treaty or treaties is under review.[75] Conversely, notwithstanding the supposed gains in the right to self-determination of colonial and indigenous peoples, there is still no procedural mechanism that enables them to be heard.

In the 1933 *Eastern Greenland* case, the Permanent Court made no reference to the views of the Greenlanders. The Danish agents argued that they would better protect the Inuit of Greenland, and this paternalistic view was implicitly accepted by the Permanent Court. There was no expectation in the 1930s that the views of the colonised might be relevant in proceedings regarding their future.

In the following decades, however, the UN Charter, General Assembly Resolutions 1514, 1541 and the Friendly Relations Declaration, the International Covenant on Economic, Social and Cultural Rights, the International Covenant on Civil and Political Rights, and the UN Declaration on the Rights of Indigenous Peoples all promise the right to self-determination of colonised peoples. Yet the procedure has not evolved. The process still privileges States and eliminates colonial voices.

During the Chagos hearings, 31 States plus the African Union submitted written evidence to the Court.[76] Niger even submitted its statement late but the Court admitted it in any case, 'on an exceptional basis,' indicating that flexibility is possible as long as it does not upset any of the basic presumptions about who may speak.[77] 10 States plus the African Union made follow-up statements.[78] 22 States participated in the oral hearings.[79] The Court also relied extensively on resolutions of the General Assembly (who had of course sought the advisory opinion in the first place) – a forum in which only States participate.

The Chagossians had no way to present their own perspective. Reflecting even a step back from the *Eastern Greenland* case, the Court does not even inquire into the *welfare*, let alone the *wishes* of the Chagossians. The Chagossians have experienced decades of social exclusion and discrimination in Mauritius

---

74 Ibid, Rules 67 and 105; see also Statute of the International Court of Justice, adopted June 26, 1945, entered into force October 10, 1945, *Bevans* 3 (1945): 1179, article 34.
75 Statute of the Court, article 34(3).
76 Chagos Advisory Opinion, note 1, para 9.
77 Ibid, para 11.
78 Ibid, para 15.
79 Ibid, para 23.

and have little cause to trust the Mauritian government to protect them.[80] Three Chagossians attended the Court proceedings as fig leaves of the Mauritian delegation. They did not speak before the Court. One Chagossian, Marie Liseby Elysé, had made a pre-recorded video – edited and approved by the Mauritian legal team before being submitted as part of the Mauritian case.[81]

Thus, for all the substantive law – both custom and treaty – on the importance of self-determination of peoples, a process that privileges states undermines the principle in practice. In international legal proceedings that are ostensibly about self-determination, there is no way for the self to present whatever it determines.

7 Conclusions

Although over 12,000km separate Diego Garcia and Nuuk, the colonial experience and inadequacy of the decolonisation processes unite them. The Greenlanders and Chagossians are both indigenous and colonial peoples and the rights which attach to that status are non-derogable. The Chagos Advisory Opinion restates the *erga omnes* character of the norm of self-determination, and three judges separately emphasise its *ius cogens* nature. There are, however, some limitations to self-determination in practice, mainly due to the priority given to colonial boundaries and to the procedural restrictions on non-State actors before international institutions, in particular, the Court.

As a result of the single boundary around Greenland drawn by the Danish administration, under international law, the Greenlanders are a single people in a single territorial unit, irrespective of the unique histories, languages, cultures and practices of the minorities in the north and the east. Greenland also includes the Pituffik area with the US base. The duty of all States to uphold the right to self-determination means that the Greenland government must be at the heart of any negotiations regarding the base and that the area may not be annexed prior to independence without the genuine consent of the Greenlanders (something that seems at the time of writing politically improbable). Meanwhile, the Greenlanders remain in the catch-22 of colonial peoples the World over when it comes to claiming their right to self-determination.

---

80 Atman Ramchalaon, "Seeking the Facts" in Evers and Kooy, note 3, 59–60; Laura Jeffrey and David Vine, note 29, 83–103.

81 Chagos Advisory Opinion, Public sitting, verbatim record, September 3, 2018, para 4, https://www.icj-cij.org/files/case-related/169/169-20180903-ORA-01-00-BI.pdf para 4. (Chagossians Louis Olivier Bancoult and M. Louis Rosemond Saminaden were also in the courtroom.)

As they are not a State, they cannot speak before the International Court of Justice and do not participate in the UN General Assembly which is tasked with overseeing the decolonisation process. They must rely on the one hand on the goodwill of the colonial power (Denmark, which to its credit has, since 2009, shown goodwill in this regard) and the attention of other States (which is extremely low). Relying on the goodwill of another country is the very definition of colonialism.

Assessing Japan's Arctic Engagement during the ArCS Project (2015–2020)

Romain Chuffart,* Sakiko Hataya,** Osamu Inagaki,*** and Lindsay Arthur****

Abstract

As Japan is considered a non-regional actor in Arctic governance, this paper begins with analysing how Japan navigates the web of Arctic governance and how it manages to create a coherent Arctic narrative and engages with the Arctic both inside and outside the region. The present research argues that the construction of an Arctic identity is a praxis performed through time that needs to be constantly reaffirmed. To illustrate this point, the paper then uses a lateral rather than linear approach to assess the influence of the Arctic on Japan at present. This paper assesses Japan's engagement on the main stage where Arctic governance is performed (i.e. The Arctic Council) since the release of Japan's Arctic Policy and under the Arctic Challenge for Sustainability project, Japan's flagship program for Arctic research. Looking to the future, countries such as Japan who are willing to be involved in all parts of Arctic governance will have to make a choice about what kind of Arctic relationships they want to create and in which of these relationships Japan could invest more.

Keywords

Arctic governance – rule of law – Japan's Arctic policy – ArCS

---

* DurhamARCTIC PhD candidate in law, Durham Law School, Durham University (UK). romain.f.chuffart@durham.ac.uk.
** PhD student in law, Kobe University (Japan), and a research fellow of the Japan Society for the Promotion of Science.
*** Researcher at Polar Cooperation Research Centre (PCRC), Graduate School of International Cooperation Studies (GSICS), Kobe University (Japan).
**** Arctic Specialist at the Icelandic Ministry of Education, Science and Culture and MA candidate in Polar Law, University of Akureyri (Iceland); Disclaimer: all views expressed in the present article are the authors' own and does not reflect the views of the authors' current employers.

1   Introduction

The Arctic is a web of multi-level, multi-purpose relationships, but there is a lack of cohesion between achieving sustainable development and working toward a more developed framework for Arctic governance. Looking to the future, countries such as Japan which are willing to be involved in all parts of Arctic governance will have to make a choice about what kind of future Arctic relationships they want to create and in which of these relationships Japan could invest more. At present, it is intellectually challenging to both fulfil resource development goals while protecting the global environment. A creative path to rethinking and investing in real sustainability is one of the potential avenues through which Japan can make a difference in Arctic governance.

According to Japan's Arctic Policy released in 2015, Japan needs to be involved appropriately in formulating international agreements and rules regarding the Arctic. From 2015 to 2020, the Japanese government funded the Arctic Challenge for Sustainability (ArCS) project to play a role in shaping Arctic governance and rethink sustainability from both a scientific and an academic perspective. As the first phase of the ArCS project is coming to an end in 2020, there is a need to reassess Japan's involvement in order to fully realise its policy and strengthen Japan's engagement at the Arctic Council (AC) in the post-ArCS (2020–2025) phase. A central theme of this paper is to specifically highlight further opportunities for Japan to engage as an AC Observer State from 2020–2025. A post-ArCS interdisciplinary (natural sciences, social sciences, as well as legal and political studies) approach is necessary to foster increased and better cohesion between the different stakeholders within Japan.

Section 2 of this article gives an overview of Japan's Arctic engagement through time. This section traces the history of Japan's Arctic engagement and how such engagement has been used over time to legitimise Japan's current status as a credible and relevant Arctic actor. As the next section will illustrate, a lateral rather than linear approach will be used to assess the influence of the Arctic on Japan at present. The construction of an Arctic identity is a praxis performed through time and one that needs to be reaffirmed in the present. A lateral outlook of Japan's Arctic engagement might help to map out the scope of Japan's Arctic identity and its impact on Arctic governance. Section 3 (Japan as an Arctic Council Observer State) analyses Japan's involvement and contribution to the Arctic Council since 2015. Section 4 (Implementation of the Japanese Arctic Policy) focuses on the domestic implementation of the Arctic-specific legal framework and its impact on Japan. This section also illustrates Japan's role in Arctic law-making at the international level and the domestic implementation of this new legal framework. This paper concludes by laying out a roadmap for improving Japan's involvement in the Arctic and how this can help inform Japan's opportunities for future Arctic engagement.

2 Japan's Arctic Engagement

In the Arctic, as elsewhere, regional governance is an intricate web of relationships. From local cross-border people-to-people cooperation to multilateral State-led governance, all stakeholders carefully weave relationships together to affirm, for some, or confirm, for others, their place in this complex multilevel framework that the Arctic, as an integrated region, has become. This section aims to focus on how Japan navigates the web of Arctic governance and concentrates on how Japan creates a coherent Arctic narrative and engages with the Arctic both inside and outside the region. To do so, this section offers a brief history of Japan's polar engagement which begins with building Antarctic expertise through scientific research.

2.1 *Performing Japan's Polar-ness*

Much of the literature on traditional non-Arctic states (i.e. states that are not part of the Arctic 8[1]) begins with demonstrating that their Arctic identity is not determined by their topographical geography, but rather by their willingness to engage in Arctic affairs. As Depledge argues, proximity to one region is not only about topography.[2] National projection to regional areas outside of a country's geographical boundary or traditional sphere of governance is used as a tool to extend linkages beyond the region and create a coherent narrative that legitimises a country's presence in specific regional arenas. A coherent national narrative built on performing a polar identity is essential for non-Arctic states. Japan's turn to the North is no different. The northern Japanese waters of the Sea of Okhotsk border the southern edge of the Russian South-East, but they do not stretch as far as what is typically viewed as the narrow definitions

---

1 Commonly referred to as the Arctic 8 (A8), the eight member states of the Arctic Council are Canada, the Kingdom of Denmark, Finland, Iceland, Norway, Russia, Sweden, and the United States. Other State actors are labelled "non-Arctic states", although in recent years countries such as China and the United Kingdom have respectively described themselves as being "near-Arctic" or "the Arctic's nearest neighbour"; see The State Council of the People's Republic of China, *China's Arctic Policy* (2018) <http://english.www.gov.cn/archive/white_paper/2018/01/26/content_281476026660336.htm>, see also Polar Regions Department, *Adapting To Change UK policy towards the Arctic* (London: Foreign and Commonwealth Office, 2013), ii.
2 Duncan Depledge, *Britain and the Arctic* (London: Palgrave Macmillan 2017) 13–14.

of the Arctic that prevail nowadays.[3] Japan's Arctic engagement thus needs to be thought less in terms of traditional topography and more as creating a polar identity that makes sense in both a domestic and an international context.

As many scholars have pointed out, Japan projects itself as a maritime state with a robust polar tradition and with an extended polar identity via both scientific engagement and concerns about global climate change.[4] Japan's Arctic identity-building is therefore reliant on its scientific engagement. It is the main driver of Japan's involvement in the Arctic, but it is not Japan's sole area of interest in the region. Changes in the Arctic environment have political, economic, and social effects, not only in the Arctic but also globally. Based on some of the measures to respond to changes in the Arctic Ocean outlined in the Second Basic Plan on Ocean Policy adopted by the Japanese Cabinet in 2013,[5] Japan's Arctic interests can be grouped in three categories: (1) Arctic observation, including scientific research, (2) the development of Arctic sea routes, and (3) participation to the international meetings related to the Arctic.

2.2   *Constructing Japan's Polar Identity*

To better understand the development of Japan's present stance in Arctic governance, it is necessary to put together a timeline of Japan's interaction with the poles. Framing Japan as a country with a robust polar tradition is, as Julie Babin points out, a means for the Japanese government to legitimise its interests in Arctic affairs.[6] However, an important caveat highlighted by Babin, is

---

3   There are many ways to define the Arctic with the Arctic circle being the most commonly used, but other definitions such as the southern boundaries of the High Arctic and the subarctic delineated on the basis on vegetation (treeline), the 10°C July isotherm, and the marine Arctic that focuses more narrowly on the Central Arctic Ocean and its coastal states.

4   See e.g. Aki Tonami and Steward Watters, "Japan's Arctic Policy: The sum of many parts" in L. Heininen (ed.) *Arctic Yearbook* 2012 (Akureyri: Northern Forum, 2012); Elana Wilson Rowe, Arctic Governance: Power in cross-border cooperation (Manchester: Manchester University Press, 2018), 47 (table 3); Fujio Ohnishi, 'Japan's Arctic Policy Development: from engagement to a strategy' in Leiv Lunde, Jian Yang and Iselin Stensdal (eds.) *Asian Countries and the Arctic Future* (World Scientific 2016): 171–182.

5   The Basic Plan on Ocean Policy is an implementation of Article 16 of the Basic Act on Ocean Policy (Act No. 33 of April 27, 2007). The Basic Plan prescribes the basic policy of measures with regard to the oceans (art. 16.2.i), the measures that the Government shall implement with regard to the oceans comprehensively and systematically (art. 16.2.ii), and any items necessary for promoting measures with regard to the oceans comprehensively and systematically (art. 16.2.iii). The most recent revision of the Basic Plan on Ocean Policy was released in May 2018 <https://www8.cao.go.jp/ocean/english/plan/pdf/plan03_e.pdf> (accessed 9 January 2020).

6   Julie Babin, "Diplomatie Scientifique et Engagement du Japon dans l'Arctique: L'exemple du Conseil de l'Arctique," *Relations internationales* 2, no. 178 (2019): 119–133.

that overall the Arctic is far from being a high priority area in Japanese domestic politics.[7] Japan has constructed its polar identity via scientific engagement since the expedition of Nobu Shirase to Antarctica (1911–1912) and by being one of the first twelve signatories of the Antarctic Treaty in 1959 despite Japan not being a claimant state in the Antarctic. Since then, Japan has been a prominent actor in Antarctic governance mainly through scientific output. Japan's turn to the Arctic also began out of scientific research interest with observations of and research on Arctic environmental changes in the 1950s.

Two key events for Japan in the evolution of its turn to the Arctic are the research expedition of Professor Nakaya, a glaciologist from Hokkaido University, to Greenland in 1957 as a member of the United States expedition for the International Geophysical Year and the founding of the National Institute for Polar Research in 1973. At the local level, the government of Hokkaido also projected itself to the North as they raised the idea of creating a cross-border organisation for northern regional governments during the First International Conference on Human Environment in Northern Regions held in Sapporo in 1974 which led to the establishment of the Northern Forum in 1991.[8] Japan furthered its Arctic research capacity throughout the 1990s with the creation of the Arctic Environment Research Center at NIPR. In 1991, Japan became the first non-Arctic state to establish an observation station (Ny-Ålesund Research Station) in the Arctic. The following year, Japan was also the first non-Arctic State to join the International Arctic Science Committee (IASC). Continuing its Arctic journey, Japan joined the Barents Euro-Arctic Council in 1993 and was present at the signing ceremony of the Arctic Council's Ottawa Declaration in 1996. Furthermore, between 1993 and 1999, the Ship and Ocean Foundation, which later became the SPF Ocean Policy Research Institute, partnered with Norway's Fridtjof Nansen Institute and the Russian Central Marine Research and Design Institute to create the International Northern Sea Route Programme (INSROP), a multidisciplinary research program to help map out the potential shipping opportunities of Russia's Northern Sea Route (NSR).[9] INSROP concluded that NSR shipping was economically, technologically and environmentally viable, but that there were many issues that would need to be dealt with before commercial shipping could take place.[10] As Tonami explains,

---

[7] Ibid.
[8] Northern Forum, History of the Northern Forum, <https://www.northernforum.org/en/the-northern-forum/history> (accessed 8 January 2020).
[9] Kentaro Nishimoto, "The Rights and Interests of Japan in Regard to Arctic Shipping," in Robert C. Beckman et al. (eds.) Governance of Arctic Shipping: Balancing Rights and Interests of Arctic States and User States (Leiden: Brill, 2017), 358.
[10] Ibid.

these developments in Arctic research in the 1990s coincide with the enactment of the Science and Technology Basic Law[11] that provided the basis of Japan's science and technology policy and formally recognised the role of science and technology in the country's economic development and diplomacy.[12]

Having submitted its application to be an AC Observer in 2009, Japan's engagement in Arctic affairs culminated in 2013 as Japan was granted the observer status at the Kiruna Ministerial Meeting alongside other Asian states (China, India, South Korea and Singapore) and Italy. The AC is often regarded as the center of the Arctic governance web and the main venue for governance to be performed. Japan's observer status at the AC thus helps to further legitimise Japan as a genuine Arctic stakeholder with the potential to contribute and strengthen Arctic legal order.[13] However, the AC is not an international organisation and does not have a law-making mandate. This unique set up, as Tonami remarks, limits Asian states or actors' participation but also allows them "to play a different but not insignificant role in developing norms in/about the Arctic".[14] Tonami highlights, for example, the requirement for observer states to submit projects via one of the A8 states or a Permanent Participant[15] which helps deepen cooperation between AC stakeholders.

In recent years, the cornerstone of Japan's Arctic involvement has been Japan's Arctic Policy.[16] Produced by the Headquarters for Ocean Policy[17] and announced publicly in October 2015 at the third Arctic Circle Assembly in

---

11   Law No 130 of 1995 (effective on 15 November 1995).
12   Aki Tonami, *Asian Foreign Policy in a Changing Arctic: The diplomacy of economy and science at new frontiers* (Palgrave Macmillan 2016): 49.
13   For an overview of Japan's role in shaping Arctic governance, see Keiji Ide, "Japan's Role in Formation and Strengthening of Arctic Legal Orders" in A Shibata et al. (eds.) *Emerging Legal Orders in the Arctic: The role of non-Arctic actors*, (Oxon and New York: Routledge, 2019): 42–48.
14   Aki Tonami, "The Rise of Asia and Arctic Legal Order Making: Political-economic settings" in Shibata et al. (eds.) note 13, 27.
15   The Permanent Participants are the six international organisations representing Arctic Indigenous Peoples at the Arctic Council (Aleut International Association, Arctic Athabaskan Council, Gwich'in Council International, Inuit Circumpolar Council, Russian Association of Indigenous Peoples of the North, and the Saami Council).
16   Headquarters for Ocean Policy, Japan's Arctic Policy, provisional translation (16 October 2015) <https://www8.cao.go.jp/ocean/english/arctic/pdf/japans_ap_e.pdf> (accessed 9 January 2020).
17   Headed by the Prime Minister's office, the Headquarters for Ocean Policy's aim is to comprehensively and systematically address ocean policy across all government ministries and agencies.

Reykjavik by then-Ambassador for Arctic Affairs Kazuko Shiraishi,[18] Japan's Arctic Policy is a comprehensive statement of Japan's fundamental policy outlook towards the Arctic with a strong emphasis on international cooperation. Covering scientific research, environmental protection, fishing and natural resource exploitation, Japan's Arctic Policy provides specific initiatives to carry Japan's engagement forward and to play a normative role in the Arctic region. Modelling the approach of the Basic Plan for Ocean Policy, Japan's Arctic Policy outlines the following three specific initiatives of Japanese interests in the Arctic: (1) Research and Development, (2) International Cooperation, and (3) Sustainable Use. Japan's Arctic Policy also highlights the leading role of Japan in formulating several international environmental agreements such as the Kyoto Protocol, Aichi biodiversity targets and other agreements through which the international community has responded to global environmental problems such as global warming and the loss of biodiversity. The policy document also points to the needs for Japan to contribute to sustainable development which benefits Arctic Indigenous peoples.

Japan was involved in shaping the Arctic legal order by participating to the Five-plus-Five process that resulted in the Central Arctic Ocean Fisheries (CAOF) Agreement.[19] Given the central place given to science in Japan's approach to Arctic governance, Joji Morishita argues that the CAOF Agreement and, specifically, Article 4 on scientific cooperation provide a useful platform for Japan to promote its Arctic scientific activities.[20] Science and science diplomacy[21] have always been a key priority for Japan. During the negotiations of the 2017 Agreement on Scientific Cooperation[22] under the auspices of the AC, Japan was among a few key numbers of observer states to make a positive contribution to the negotiations given the limitations inherent to an AC

---

18   Arctic Portal, "Japan's Arctic Policy Released at the Arctic Circle" (21 October 2015) <https://arcticportal.org/ap-library/news/1589-japan-s-arctic-policy-released-at-the-arctic-circle> (accessed 9 January 2020).

19   Agreement to Prevent Unregulated High Seas Fisheries in the Central Arctic Ocean, signed on 3 October 2018 (not in force), European Commission, Doc. COM (2018) 453, Annex (12 June 2018).

20   Joji Morishita, "The Arctic Five-plus-Five Process on Central Arctic Ocean Fisheries Negotiations" in Shibata et al. (eds.), note 13, 125.

21   For an in-depth study of Japan's science diplomacy, see Babin, note 6; see also Atushi Sunami, Tomoko Hamachi, and Shigeru Kitaba, "The Rise of Science and Technology Diplomacy in Japan," *Science and Diplomacy* 2, no. 1. (2013) <http://www.sciencediplomacy.org/article/2013/rise-science-and-technology-diplomacy-in-japan> (accessed 9 January 2020).

22   Agreement on Enhancing International Arctic Scientific Cooperation, signed on 11 May 2017 (entered into force 23 May 2018) <https://oaarchive.arctic-council.org/handle/11374/1916>.

Observer. Japan attended and gave a presentation at the Scientific Cooperation Task Force (SCTF) meeting in Copenhagen in August 2015 and submitted a written statement at the SCTF meeting in Arlington the following year. At the final SCTF meeting in Ottawa, Japan, alongside other AC Observers, was allowed to express its views on the draft agreement, especially on the provision regarding non-Parties.[23] As Shibata points out, the active participation and involvement of non-Arctic states during the negotiation process helped extend benefits under the 2017 Agreement to non-Parties including AC Observers.[24] Japan hosted the Arctic Science Summit Week in Toyama in 2015 and it is set to co-host the third Arctic Science Ministerial Meeting in Tokyo in November 2020 with Iceland. This will also be the first Ministerial-level Arctic meeting in Asia.

Universities and research centers have also played an important role in putting Japan at the forefront of Arctic scientific and academic research. Under Japan's Arctic Policy's specific initiative of Research and Development, one of the highlighted priorities was to establish research network and promote better cohesion between all these stakeholders. In the fiscal year 2015, the Japanese government started to finance the Arctic Challenge for Sustainability Project (ArCS) as a means to promote Arctic scientific research and to contribute to policy decision making and problem solving. Often described as Japan's flagship program for Arctic research, ArCS is funded by Ministry of Education, Culture, Sports, Science and Technology (MEXT) with the National Institute of Polar Research (NIPR), Japan Agency for Marine-Earth Science and Technology (JAMSTEC) and Hokkaido University all playing key roles in further developing the project and cooperating with other related Japanese institutions.[25] Thus far, although ArCS aims at developing a comprehensive, multidisciplinary approach to Arctic research, the vast majority of projects under ArCS have mainly been in climate and environmental sciences. The first phase of ArCS has been running from September 2015 to March 2020 while the second phase is meant to begin from the start of the Japanese fiscal year in April 2020 and run for another five years until 2025.

To this day, there is still no cross-ministerial, unified domestic Japanese organisation dealing with Arctic issues.[26] The Ambassador for Arctic Affairs does not seem to have an overarching role in coordinating Japan's national Arctic

---

23 Akiho Shibata, "The Arctic Science Cooperation Agreement: A perspective from non-Arctic actors" in Shibata et al. (eds.), note 13, 216.
24 Ibid, 217.
25 Arctic Challenge for Sustainability (ArCS) website, <https://www.arcs-pro.jp/en/about/> (accessed 9 January 2020).
26 Aki Tonami, "The Arctic Policy of China and Japan: multilayered economic and strategic motivations," *The Polar Journal* 4, no. 1 (2014): 115.

involvement, and many stakeholders work with different agendas and goals within Japan's domestic political landscape. Between MEXT, MoFA, MLIT, JAMSTEC, JOGMEC, NIPR, OPRF,[27] there are several ministries, government agencies, and research institutes whose focus on the region covers the complex reality of engaging in a multi-layered environment.

3   Japan as an Arctic Council Observer State

Japan's Arctic policy in 2015 proclaims further contribution to activities of the Arctic Council.[28] This section reflects on Japan's involvement in the Arctic Council from 2009 (when Japan obtained ad-hoc observer status) to 2019, and draws lessons and improvements for Japan's involvement in the post-ArCS period from this reflection.

3.1   *Japan's Involvement in the Arctic Council 2009–2019*
3.1.1   Attendance of the Meetings[29]

One useful indicator to evaluate Japan's involvement in the Arctic Council is its attendance of meetings. Since Japan obtained an ad-hoc observer status in 2009, Japan has attended almost all Senior Arctic Officials (SAO) meetings, deputy minister's meetings and Ministerial meetings. Until the appointment of Arctic Ambassador on 19 March 2013, the members of Japanese delegation

---

27   MLIT: Ministry of Land, Infrastructure and Transport; MoFA: Ministry of Foreign Affairs; JOGMEC: Japan Oil, Gas and Metals National Corporation, OPRF: Ocean Policy Research Foundation. For an in-depth analysis of Japan's different ministries and government agencies and their respective stakes in Arctic affairs, see Fujio Ohnishi, 'Japan's Arctic Policy Development: from engagement to a strategy' in Leiv Lunde, Jian Yang and Iselin Stensdal (eds) *Asian Countries and the Arctic Future* (World Scientific 2016) 171–182.

28   See Japan's Arctic Policy, note 16, 8.

29   The description on Japan's attendance of AC meetings below is based on following six sources: (1) Japan's Observer Reports in 2016 and 2018 <https://oaarchive.arctic-council.org/handle/11374/1868> and <https://oaarchive.arctic-council.org/handle/11374/2259>; (2) ArCS Project Outcome Report from AY2015 to AY2018 (in Japanese) <https://www.nipr.ac.jp/arcs/achievement/index.html#report>; (3) Sebastian Knecht, "Stakeholder Participation in Arctic Council meetings 1998–2015 (STAPAC) Dataset" Harvard Dataverse 2016 <https://dataverse.harvard.edu/dataset.xhtml?persistentId=doi:10.7910/DVN/OMQAEW>; (4) MoFA, "MoFA's Efforts for the Arctic" (in Japanese) <https://www.mlit.go.jp/common/001067920.pdf>; (5) ArCS Blog, "Dispatching Experts Archive," <https://www.nipr.ac.jp/arcs/blog/en/cat270/index.html>; and (6) other relevant AC documents, in particular, participants lists of meetings available at <https://oaarchive.arctic-council.org/> (all accessed 24 October 2020).

were MoFA officials or diplomats of Japanese embassies in the countries where the meetings were held. After the appointment, the Japanese Arctic Ambassador has attended almost all SAO and Ministerial meetings.

As to the working group level meetings, Japan has attended plenary meetings of AMAP, EPPR, CAFF, PAME and SDWG thus far. When Japan was an ad-hoc observer, Japan attended AMAP and SDWG meetings only a limited number of times. After Japan became an official observer in May 2013, Japan's attendance expanded to PAME and CAFF working groups and the total number of attendances also increased. When the ArCS project launched with the "dispatch of experts to the AC or related [working groups]"[30] as one of its principal components in September 2015, the number of Japan's attendance further increased. During the ArCS period, Japan has regularly attended the meetings of AMAP, CAFF, PAME and SDWG. However, as far as available information verifies, Japan has attended an EPPR meeting only once in June 2014 and Japan has never attended an ACAP working group meeting.

Before the commencement of the ArCS project, Japanese participants to the working group meetings are government officials from MoFA, MEXT or Ministry of Environment (MoE) accompanying some scientists from JAMSTEC or NIPR. Thanks to the "dispatch of experts to the AC or related [working groups]" initiative launched by the ArCS project, scientific experts affiliated with ArCS became main participants in the working group meeting during the ArCS period. At the same time, Japanese government officials ceased to attend working groups except for CAFF meetings which MoE officials continue to attend.

Japan also has attended several expert groups or specific projects meetings under the working groups. These meetings include AMAP Short-lived Climate Pollutants (SLCP) Expert Group expert group; CAFF CBird; and other ad-hoc conferences, workshops and symposia held by CAFF, AMAP and PAME. The most of Japanese participants in these meeting are experts dispatched by ArCS.

Japan has been a diligent participant of the meetings of the several Task Forces and an Expert Group established by the Ministerial meeting. So far, Japan has attended Task Force on Arctic Marine Oil Pollution Prevention (TFOPP) (2013–15); Task Force on Black Carbon and Methane (TFBCM) (2013–15); SCTF (2013–17) and Expert Group on Black Carbon and Methane (EGBCM) (2015–). More specifically, Japan attended 6 out of 9 SCTF meetings, the only treaty negotiation in the Arctic Council where observer states were allowed to

---

30 See ArCS website <https://www.nipr.ac.jp/arcs/e/achievement/project/dispatch.html> (accessed 24 October 2020).

attend.[31] Moreover, Japan has attended all the meeting of EGBCM so far. The Japanese participants in SCTF and EGBCM were scientific experts dispatched by the ArCS project. However, there are also Task Force meetings which Japan seems not to have attended. Regrettably, Japan seemed not to have attended the Task Force of Arctic Marine Cooperation (TFAMC) (2015–19). The task force was initially established to "to assess future needs for a regional seas program or other mechanism, as appropriate, for increased cooperation in Arctic marine areas."[32] Given this ambitious mandate, Japan should have attended the meetings of the task force.

3.1.2 Contribution to Specific Projects

Contribution to specific projects is also an important indicator to evaluate Japan's involvement, since attendance of meetings itself does not necessarily mean Japan's positive influence on the work of the Arctic Council. According to the reports developed by the AC secretariat in 2018 and 2019, Japan has been substantially involved in 6 AC projects: AMAP Adaptation Action for Changing Arctic (AACA); AMAP Air Pollution including SLCF; AMAP Sustaining Arctic Observing Network (SAON); CAFF Arctic Migratory Bird Initiative (AMBI); CAFF Actions for Arctic Biodiversity 2013–2021; and EGBCM.[33]

Regarding AMAP AACA, a Japanese expert contributed as an author of the report, *Adaptation Actions for a Changing Arctic: Perspectives from the Bering-Chukchi-Beaufort Region* (2017). Along with this AACA report, Japanese researchers have worked as authors or reviewers of several of AMAP's scientific reports such as *AMAP Assessment 2013: Arctic Ocean Acidification* and *Snow, Water, Ice and Permafrost in the Arctic (SWIPA) 2017*.

---

31   Erik J Molenaar, "The Arctic, the Arctic Council and the Law of the Sea" in Robert C. Beckman et al. (eds.) note 9, 52–3.
32   Iqaluit Declaration 2015 on the Occasion of the Ninth Ministerial Meeting of the Arctic Council, 24 April 2015, Iqaluit, Canada, para 43 <https://oaarchive.arctic-council.org/handle/11374/662> (accessed 13 January 2020).
33   These reports named "Amarok: The Arctic Council tracking tool; Maxi-report" are a compilation of the questionnaires made by Secretariat to all the projects under the Arctic Council. One of the questions in this questionnaire is particularly relevant: "Have any Observers contributed in a particularly meaningful way to this initiative?"; see AC Secretariat, *Amarok: The Arctic Council tracking tool; Maxi-report* (2018) available at <https://oaarchive.arctic-council.org/handle/11374/2131>; see also AC Secretariat, *Amarok: The Arctic Council tracking tool; Maxi-report* (2019) available at <https://oaarchive.arctic-council.org/handle/11374/2416>; see also Sebastian Knecht and Jennifer Spence, "State Observers and Science Cooperation in the Arctic Council" in Shibata et al. (eds.), note 13, 226–43.

Mitigation of SLCP is an issue that Japan has been actively involved in. Since emissions of SLCP not only from Arctic states but also from non-Arctic states affect the Arctic environment, the Arctic states particularly need the cooperation with non-Arctic observer states. Thus, the Arctic states encourage observer states to submit a national report on the emission of black Carbon and methane in the Framework for Enhanced Black Carbon and Methane Emission Reduction.[34] Responding to this request, Japan submitted national reports in 2015 and 2017. Japan has also been engaged in the AMAP SLCP expert group. Japan contributed to developing updated assessment of SLCP by Japan's advanced measurement technologies for airborne BC particles.[35]

Japan has also been working on the issue of conservation of migratory birds. This issue has a similar character with the SLCP issue in that the cooperation of non-Arctic states is particularly necessary as migratory birds migrate to the Arctic from or through non-Arctic states. In CAFF Seabirds (CBird) expert group, for example, scientists from NIPR provided the preliminary results on the winter migration of 5 Arctic breeding seabirds obtained in the Pacific Arctic as part of the ArCS.[36] Also, Japan contributed to Arctic Migratory Bird Initiative (AMBI) through participating in the AMBI workshops. Specifically, an official of the Ministry of Environment presented Japan's domestic legal framework on conservation and hunting issues in AMBI East Asian-Australasian Flyway Workshop held in January 2017 in Singapore.

In addition, though not mentioned in the secretariat's report above, Japan's contribution to the work of SCTF is noteworthy. During the meetings of the SCTF, observers were allowed not only to attend the meetings but also participate substantially in the discussion. At the 8th meeting of the SCTF, Japan submitted a written statement on the draft Agreement on Enhancing International Arctic Scientific Cooperation.[37] Furthermore, the opinions of observer states were reflected in the final text of the Scientific Cooperation Agreement, especially the provisions relating to benefits of non-Arctic states.[38] This case is particularly notable in that the observer states contributed to the policy level

---

34 Senior Arctic Officials (SAO) Report to Ministers, 24 April 2015, Iqaluit, Canada, 118–30 <https://oaarchive.arctic-council.org/handle/11374/494> (accessed 14 January 2020).
35 MoFA, *Japan's 2018 Observer Review report* (2018): 5 <https://oaarchive.arctic-council.org/handle/11374/2259> (accessed 14 January 2020).
36 Ibid.
37 MoFA, *Japan's 2016 Observer Review report* (2016): 3 <https://oaarchive.arctic-council.org/handle/11374/1868> (accessed 14 January 2020).
38 See Shibata, note 23, 217.

discussion within the Arctic Council, given that most of observer's contribution to the Arctic Council were scientific in nature.[39]

3.2 Lessons and Improvements for Post-ArCS Period

Based on the description of Japan's involvement in the Arctic Council above, let us draw lessons and improvements for the post-ArCS period. First, it is desirable for Japan to be more substantially engaged in SDWG, PAME, EPPR and ACAP working groups. While Japan attends SDWG and PAME working groups meetings consistently, it appears that it has not made concrete contributions to those two working groups. Furthermore, as mentioned above, Japan has seldom attended the meetings of EPPR and ACAP working groups. As former Japanese Arctic Ambassador Keiji Ide pointed out in his statement, Japan should seek to build up cooperation with these working groups.[40] On the other hand, Japan has made substantial contribution to AMAP and CAFF so far. In the post-ArCS period, Japan needs to continue the efforts for those two working groups.

Second, in the post-ArCS period, Japan should pursue more strategic involvement in the Arctic Council. Certainly "dispatch of experts to the AC" launched by the ArCS project contributed to an increase in attendance of the Arctic Council meetings. However, it also seems to have weakened the engagement of the Japanese government, especially with working groups or subsidiary bodies meetings, and to have made Japan's involvement based on individual scientists' interests or expertise rather than on a strategy. One of the reasons why Japan missed TFAMC meetings could be this lack of a strategy. In order not to miss important developments or opportunities within the Arctic Council, it is necessary for Japan to develop a strategy towards the Arctic Council through discussion between Japanese government and scientific experts including social scientists. In this context, it should be noted that so far two round tables have been held between government and ArCS scientists in 2018 and 2019 to facilitate their cooperation.[41] These are a good step towards pursuing more strategic involvement in the Arctic Council.

---

39 Sebastian Knecht and Jennifer Spence evaluate the amendment of rules of procedure and the introduction of an observer manual to subsidiary bodies in 2013 as 'scientification' of observer status; see Knecht and Spence, note 33, 241.

40 Japan, *Statement of Mr. Keiji Ide, Ambassador in charge of Arctic affairs of Japan at the Arctic Council* SAO Meeting at Oulu, 26 October 2017, available at <https://oaarchive.arctic-council.org/handle/11374/2102> (accessed 14 January 2020).

41 See Arctic Challenge for Sustainability (ArCS), "First round-table conference on Arctic between government officials and researchers" (7 March 2018) <https://www.nipr.ac.jp/arcs/blog/en/2018/03/first-round-table-conference-on-arctic.html>; see also ArCS,

4   Implementation of the Japanese Arctic Policy

Recently, the AC has provided a forum for the negotiation of three important legally binding agreements among the eight Arctic states: Agreement on Enhancing International Arctic Scientific Cooperation, Agreement on Cooperation on Marine Oil Pollution Preparedness and Response in the Arctic, and Agreement on Cooperation on Aeronautical and Maritime Search and Rescue in the Arctic.[42] According to the Japan's Arctic Policy, Japan will ensure the rule of law, and promote international cooperation in a peaceful and orderly manner.[43] It could be assumed that Japan would implement both hard and soft law mechanisms which can be adapted to the Arctic region, as in the case of the 1982 United Nations Convention on the Law of the Sea (UNCLOS). Additionally, The Third Basic Plan on Ocean Policy, approved by the Meeting of the Headquarters for Ocean Policy followed by Cabinet a decision in 2018, affirms that engaging in scientific-based evidence discussion is necessary. And what more, ensures that the rule of law is vital to the oceans, which includes the Arctic Ocean.[44] The Basic Ocean Plan also mentioned the formulation of international rules regarding the conservation and management of fishery resources in the high seas,[45] of which there is no mention in Japan's Arctic policy in 2015. From this context, we can observe Japan's positive attitude to participate the law-making process which is relevant to Japan.

Mr. Keiji Ide mentioned "the ocean is very important for Japan in the context of trade routes, sources of various resources (including fish and minerals) and security as a whole."[46] It was in this context that the Nippon Foundation, National Graduate Institute for Policy Studies, and the Sasakawa Peace Foundation, established the "Study Group for the Future of the Arctic."[47] The study group discussed marine oil pollution preparedness and response, as well

---

"Second round-table conference on Arctic between government officials and researchers" (19 June 2019) <https://www.nipr.ac.jp/arcs/blog/en/2019/06/second-round-table-conference-on-arctic.html> (accessed 24 October 2020).

42   Arctic Council," Engagements" (6 December 2018) <https://arctic-council.org/index.php/en/our-work/agreements> (accessed 28 January 2020).

43   See Headquarters for Ocean Policy, note 16, 2.

44   The Third Basic Plan on Ocean Policy, 38 <https://www8.cao.go.jp/ocean/english/plan/pdf/plan03_e.pdf> (accessed 26 January 2020).

45   Ibid.

46   See Ide, note 13, 43.

47   The Nippon Foundation, National Graduate Institute for Policy Studies and The Sasakawa Peace Foundation, "the Arctic challenge and policy which Japan strongly need to deal with," <https://www.spf.org/_opri_media/docs/Policy_Recommendation_Arctic_Governance_Japan.pdf> (accessed 8 January 2020).

as aeronautical and maritime search and rescue. In the meeting report there is no direct mention about the agreement (Agreement on Cooperation on Marine Oil Pollution Preparedness and Response in the Arctic, and Agreement on Cooperation on Aeronautical and Maritime Search and Rescue in the Arctic); however, regarding marine oil pollution preparedness and response, the report mentioned that there are concerns about marine environmental problems and pollution caused by vessels which use the Arctic sea route through the Sea of Japan, Tsushima, Tsugaru, Soya canals, due to the marine accidents and encounters with marine mammals. Therefore, they concluded that is necessary to take measures domestically, such as designating the channel and examining the pre- and post-action measures to prevent marine environmental damage such as oil pollution.[48] The study group also identified that if economic activity in the Arctic Ocean expands in the future, traffic congestion is expected to increase along the Arctic Sea Route, necessitating attention for response and preparedness in the case of a marine disaster. The group also identified the opportunity to enhance safety at sea in the Arctic Ocean by making use of Japan's strengths, such as creating ice bulletin maps.[49]

However, these recommendations related to the marine oil pollution preparedness and response, and aeronautical and maritime search and rescue were not reflected in the final versions of the Third Basic Plan on Ocean Policy. Thus, implementation of the Agreement on Enhancing International Arctic Scientific Cooperation is the most viable option for making progress in the future implementation of the hard laws and soft laws adopted under the auspices of the Arctic Council.

4.1 Scientific Cooperation Agreement

The Agreement on Enhancing International Arctic Scientific Cooperation serves as a good opportunity for the future implementation of Japan's Arctic policy. The purpose of the Agreement is to enhance cooperation in scientific activities in order to increase effectiveness and efficiency in the development of scientific knowledge about the Arctic.[50] Recognising their importance and input to Arctic research as well as already existing partnerships between Arctic and non-Arctic states and research organisations, the AC Observers were invited to present comments on proposed drafts and were actively involved throughout the negotiation process.

---

48   Ibid, 7.
49   Ibid, 11.
50   See Agreement on Enhancing International Arctic Scientific Cooperation, note 22.

Japan's Arctic Policy mandates that Japan, – "Promote scientific and technical cooperation on the basis of bilateral scientific and technical cooperation agreements with interested states, including the Arctic states, in polar research and related fields."[51] The Third Basic Ocean Plan mandates that Japan "will promote scientific and technology cooperation in polar research and related areas with the Arctic states and other relevant countries on the basis of bilateral agreements on cooperation in science and technology.[52]

Japan engaged as an Observer during the negotiation of the new instrument for Scientific Cooperation by the Arctic Council. In 2015 at the Scientific Cooperation Task Force Meeting, a joint statement was submitted from other Arctic Observers: France, the UK and Germany, with strong support by Japan. The Joint statement influenced the definition of "participants" and "joint activities" related to article 1, and article 18 regarding "cooperation with non-member states" in the Copenhagen Draft. One of the goals of Japan's policy is to "participate actively in discussions of expanding the role of observers,"[53] so the negotiation process of the agreement reveals a burgeoning interest from Japan towards this goal.

Scientific data collection and observation is a strong point for Japanese scientific research and a deeply important component of the future of Arctic research. Japan has an opportunity to continue to engage on this front and actively participate in the development of cooperation in international Arctic science research. Through the Agreement on Enhancing International Arctic Scientific Cooperation, observer states are recognised in paragraph 11 of the preamble which acknowledges the significant scientific expertise and invaluable contribution to scientific activities by observer states. Japan can also expect through Article 17, where cooperation with non-parties will be actively utilised by cooperating with scientists in Arctic states, that they may have opportunity to engage through bilateral agreements. For example, through the Agreement between Russia and Japan on Scientific and Technical Cooperation signed on 02 September 2000, Japanese scientists may engage in future scientific cooperation in the Arctic.[54] In order to fully realise the opportunities possible through the Agreement on Enhancing International Arctic Scientific Cooperation, Japan must participate actively in the MOP of the agreement, which affords the unique opportunity for non-Arctic states to engage.

---

51 See Headquarters for Ocean Policy, note 16, 8.
52 See The Third Basic Plan on Ocean Policy, note 44, 106.
53 See Headquarters for Ocean Policy, note 16, 8.
54 Akiho Shibata, "Arctic Scientific Cooperation Agreements Being Attracted-Implications for Japan to Russian Marine Sciences Survey", the Sasakawa Peace Foundation: Ocean Newsletter, <https://www.spf.org/opri/newsletter/421_3.html> (accessed 26 January 2020).

Mr. Ide refers to the 'importance of cooperation with holders of traditional and local knowledge' which is described in Article 9. He raises the concrete example of Japanese scientists and researchers who have been cooperating with Indigenous peoples, especially in Greenland.[55] In terms of Indigenous peoples, Japan's Arctic Policy mentioned that "Japan needs to examine how we can contribute to achieve sustainable development of which the [I]ndigenous peoples can see benefits while protecting the foundations of traditional cultures and lifestyles."[56] There are examples from Japanese scientists who individually cooperate with Indigenous peoples, however there is no concrete policy from the Japanese government framing ways for how Japan "can contribute to achieve sustainable development" for Indigenous peoples, nor has there been evidence of Japan supporting the self-determined research goals of Arctic Indigenous peoples through the AC working groups or otherwise.

4.2 Shipping and the Arctic Sea Route

The Polar Code covers the full range of design, construction, equipment, operational, training, search and rescue and environmental protection matters relevant to ships operating in the inhospitable waters surrounding the two poles.[57] Japan's Arctic Policy reveals that as shipping opportunities expand, increasingly active discussions are underway regarding the effect of shipping on the marine environment and on securing the safety of navigation. The policy advises that Japan participate actively in the international debates regarding the drafting of new rules. Since the 1990s, Japan has demonstrated leadership in the IMO, and when Japan joins the process of law-making in the Arctic region with the Polar Code, it's mainly through IMO. Japan's engagement with the Polar Code began in 2009, by participating in the drafting of the "Guidelines for Ships Operating in Polar Waters", when the Ministry of Land, Infrastructure, Transport and Tourism (MLIT) started sending delegates to the IMO committee about the Polar Code. In 2010, Japan started joining the Correspondence Group, which modified the plan from the Working Group. MLIT is now preparing to implement the Polar Code domestically. Japan's plans for domestic implementation for the Polar Code includes: the development of the vessels that correspond to Polar Code, training for sailors, and security measures after

---

55   Ide, note 13, 47.
56   Headquarters for Ocean Policy, note 16, 3.
57   International Maritime Organization, "Shipping in polar waters: International Code for Ships Operating in Polar Waters (Polar Code)" <http://www.imo.org/en/MediaCentre/HotTopics/polar/Pages/default.aspx> (accessed 28 January 2020).

the vessels enter Japanese ports. This demonstrates that Japan is proactive in implementing the Polar code.

4.3 Strengthening Collaboration between Asia Pacific States

While strengthening international cooperation, including collaboration with Asian Pacific states, Japan has proposed advanced efforts in both mitigation and adaptation.[58] By proposal from Korea in 2016, the First Trilateral High-Level Dialogue on the Arctic was joined by the Republic of Korea, Japan, and the People's Republic of China. The three countries "discussed the guiding principles of the trilateral Arctic cooperation and shared the view that they should continue their commitments of contribution to the Arctic Council and enhance their cooperation within various international fora, and also explored the possibilities to cooperate in areas such as scientific research, which is the most promising area for their joint activities and trilateral cooperative activities.[59] The most recent Fourth Trilateral High-Level Dialogue on the Arctic was held in Korea in June 2019, and the three Heads of Delegation reconfirmed they contribute to the work of the Arctic Council and encouraged continued engagement with Arctic related international events.[60] Japan seems to be seeking to strengthen international cooperation through these Trilateral High-Level Dialogues under the Policy. However, tangible cooperation between these three countries has not yet occurred.

5 Conclusion

Geographically, Japan will never be an Arctic State, but as section 2 highlights, the creation of an Arctic identity is not solely determined by geography or topography. Although the Arctic does not yet seem to be a high priority in Japanese domestic politics, Japan has created a coherent narrative that legitimises the country's presence and involvement in Arctic governance. This

---

58   See Headquarters for Ocean Policy, note 16, 3.
59   Arctic Portal, "Joint Press Release of the First Trilateral High-Level Dialogue on the Arctic among the Republic of Korea, Japan, and the People's Republic of China" <https://arcticportal.org/ap-library/news/1742-joint-press-release-of-the-first-trilateral-high-level-dialogue-on-the-arctic-among-the-republic-of-korea-japan-and-the-people-s-republic-of-china> (5 January 2020).
60   Ministry of foreign affairs Republic of Korea, "The Fourth Trilateral High-Level Dialogue on the Arctic, Busan, June 25–26, 2019" <http://www.mofa.go.kr/eng/brd/m_5676/view.do?seq=320574> (5 January 2020).

narrative is built on performing a polar identity and heavily relies on science as its main driver. Building an Arctic identity is a praxis that needs to be performed through time and must be reaffirmed. A linear historical outlook does not suffice to map out the breadth of Japan's Arctic identity and the scope of its current impact on Arctic governance. To evaluate Japan's Arctic engagement and relation to the region during the ArCS period (2015–2020), this paper chose to focus on two indicators (i.e. Arctic Council involvement as an Observer and domestic implementation of Arctic-related policies). To conclude, this paper provides several recommendations for Japan to further develop its Arctic engagement and more fully realise the objectives set forth in the 2015 Arctic Policy.

Both attendance and contribution are two excellent indicators to assess Japan's involvement at the Arctic Council. This paper showed that at the working group level, Japan has regularly attended AMAP, CAFF, PAME and SWDG meetings since the start of ArCS (2015). However, Japanese experts only attended an EPPR meeting once and never attended ACAP meetings. Furthermore, Japan still lacks a strategy to map and enhance its interaction at the Arctic Council. ArCS's objective of funding Japanese experts to working groups meetings has contributed to an increased attendance, but it also seemed to have weakened the involvement of the Japanese government, which often results in experts attending meetings based on individual interests rather than on a coherent strategy. Thus the first recommendation is Japan should seek to develop a strategy to better streamline the engagement of all the domestic stakeholders with an Arctic interest (e.g. government officials, ministries researchers, and scientific experts including social scientists) at the Arctic Council.

In terms of domestic implementation, the analysis of Japan's Arctic Policy highlights that Japan is willing to follow the rule of law in the Arctic and implement both hard and soft law mechanisms (e.g. UNCLOS and Basic Plan on Ocean Policy). Japan's focus seems to relate to the maritime Arctic. Consequently, the Arctic Ocean becomes important to ensure the rule of law related to the oceans. The importance given to the Arctic Ocean is also demonstrated by Japan's involvement in the development of shipping routes and in the IMO Polar Code and guidelines, and their subsequent domestic implementation. Additionally, scientific research cooperation is an area where Japan excels. International Arctic scientific research and the promotion of science are two gateways through which Japan approaches Arctic governance. This was highlighted by Japan's role, as an Observer State, during the negotiations of the 2017 Agreement on Enhancing International Arctic Scientific Cooperation. The second recommendation is that Japan should seek to better integrate Arctic science into policy and build synergy between international and domestic Arctic policies to promote scientific international cooperation in the Arctic.

Arctic governance is best viewed as a web of multilevel, multi-purpose relationships with the Arctic Council at the center. While scientific collaboration and Arctic Council engagement have played a large part in Japan's Arctic activities, it is also crucial to enhance cooperation with different kinds of Arctic actors within various international fora, and explore the possibilities to cooperate in areas beyond scientific research. For instance, Japan often privileges state-to-state relationships and it could invest more in strengthening Arctic-specific international collaboration with other non-Arctic actors, especially in the Asia Pacific region. Thus, the third recommendation is that Japan should invest in more integrated relationships with all Arctic stakeholders in order to be a fully realised Arctic actor with a cohesive strategy between science, policy and Arctic networking. Building on the third recommendation, one specific area where Japan is currently lacking is engaging with non-State actors, especially indigenous representatives. Japanese researchers already engage with Indigenous communities on an ad-hoc, individual basis. For instance, Japan should seek to better engage with the Permanent Participants at the Arctic Council. While Japan attends SDWG working group meetings regularly, Japan has not made concrete contributions. Better involvement in working groups such as SDWG could provide an avenue for supporting and fostering relationships with Indigenous representatives and other non-state actors at the Arctic Council. The fourth recommendation is that Japan should develop its Arctic policy to outline concrete contributions to achieve sustainable development in support of Indigenous peoples as one way to enhance its engagement with non-State actors.

This creative path to rethinking and investing in more meaningful relationships with Indigenous communities and organisations in support of sustainable development could be one of the potential avenues through which Japan could make a difference in Arctic governance. The second phase of the ArCS project (2020–2025) could help coordinate all Japanese stakeholders (e.g. the Japanese government) as well as scientific experts including social scientists for them to engage even more with the Permanent Participants and the working groups. Many observer states wish for more influence "at the top" of the Arctic Council, failing to recognise that all of the influence and relationship-building happen at the working group level, where they are free to participate equally. The final recommendation is that Japan should develop a strategic plan for engaging more broadly and deeply in the AC working groups. After all, the real work of the Arctic Council happens in the working groups with Indigenous peoples as key partners.

Recommendations for Japan to further develop its Arctic engagement and more fully realise the objectives set forth in the 2015 Arctic Policy:

1. Japan should seek to develop a strategy to better streamline the engagement of all the domestic stakeholders with an Arctic interest (e.g. government officials, ministries, researchers, and scientific experts including social scientists) at the Arctic Council.
2. Japan should seek to better integrate Arctic science into policy and build synergy between international and domestic Arctic policies to promote scientific international cooperation in the Arctic.
3. Japan should invest in more integrated relationships with all Arctic stakeholders in order to be a fully realised Arctic actor with a cohesive strategy between science, policy and Arctic networking.
4. Japan should develop its Arctic policy to outline concrete contributions to achieve sustainable development in support of Indigenous peoples as one way to enhance its engagement with non-State actors.
5. Japan should develop a strategic plan for engaging more broadly and deeply in the AC working groups.

Acknowledgements

The authors would like to thank Kobe University's Polar Cooperation Research Centre and the Japanese Society for the Promotion of Science (JSPS) for their support. The present research was made possible by the partial financial support of the KAKENHI Project Number 16H03551 (PI: Akiho Shibata, Kobe University) which allowed most of the authors to attend and present their research at the 12th Polar Law Symposium in December 2019 in Hobart, Australia.

The Polar Code and Telemedicine

*Johnny Grøneng Aase, Henrik Hyndøy, Agnar Tveten,
Ingrid Hjulstad Johansen, Hege Imsen, Eirik Veum Wilhelmsen,
Trude Duelien Skorge, Alfred Ingvar Halstensen, Arne Johan Ulven,
Jon Magnus Haga**

Abstract

One result of a warmer global climate is increased maritime activity in the Arctic. Areas that used to be covered by ice and snow are now accessible for the scientific community and commercial users. The Norwegian government has chosen tourism as a pillar of the economy of Svalbard and facilitates the development of the tourism industry. Aase and Jabour have shown that tourist vessels sail as far north as 82° N, beyond the range of geostationary satellites.

The Polar Code states that appropriate communication equipment to enable telemedical assistance in polar areas shall be provided. This paper describes a series of functional telemedicine tests carried out on board the Norwegian Coast Guard vessel

---

* Johnny Grøneng Aase, Institute for Marine and Antarctic Studies, University of Tasmania, Hobart, Australia / Norwegian Cyber Defence Forces, Lillehammer, Norway. Email johnny.aase@utas.edu.au. Orcid ID 0000-0003-4793-6749; Henrik Hyndøy, Norwegian Army Medical Battalion, hhyndoy@gmail.com. Orcid ID 0000-0002-3910-2675; Agnar Tveten, The Norwegian Centre for Maritime and Diving Medicine, Haukeland University Hospital, Bergen, Norway. E-mail agnar.strom.tveten@helse-bergen.no; Ingrid Hjulstad Johansen, The Norwegian Centre for Maritime and Diving Medicine, Haukeland University Hospital, Bergen, Norway. E-mail ingrid.hjulstad.johansen@helse-bergen.no. Orcid ID 0000-0003-4143-2785; Hege Imsen, The Norwegian Centre for Maritime and Diving Medicine, Haukeland University Hospital, Bergen, Norway. E-mail hegesofie@hotmail.com; Eirik Veum Wilhelmsen, The Norwegian Centre for Maritime and Diving Medicine, Haukeland University Hospital, Bergen, Norway. E-mail eirik.veum.wilhelmsen@helse-bergen.no; Trude Duelien Skorge, The Norwegian Centre for Maritime and Diving Medicine, Haukeland University Hospital, Bergen, Norway. E-mail trude.duelien.skorge@helse-bergen.no; Alfred Ingvar Halstensen, The Norwegian Centre for Maritime and Diving Medicine, Haukeland University Hospital, Bergen, Norway. E-mail alfred.ingvar.halstensen@helse-bergen.no; Arne Johan Ulven, The Norwegian Centre for Maritime and Diving Medicine, Haukeland University Hospital, Bergen, Norway. E-mail arne.johan.ulven@helse-bergen.no; Jon Magnus Haga, The Norwegian Centre for Maritime and Diving Medicine, Haukeland University Hospital, Bergen, Norway. E-mail jon.magnus.haga@helse-bergen.no.

NoCGV Svalbard during her transit between Svalbard and the Norwegian mainland in September 2019. Communication was established between the vessel and Haukeland University Hospital in Bergen, Norway, using the new Iridium NEXT constellation of communication satellites. Our tests show that medical services that require low bandwidths work.

Keywords

Arctic – Polar Code – telemedicine – satellite communications – patient data protection

1   Introduction[1]

One result of a warmer global climate is increased maritime activity in the Arctic. Areas that used to be covered by ice and snow are now accessible for the scientific community and commercial users. The Norwegian government has chosen tourism as a pillar of the economy of Svalbard and facilitates the development of the tourism industry. Aase and Jabour have shown that tourist vessels sail as far north as 82° N, beyond the range of geostationary satellites.[2]

The Polar Code states that appropriate communication equipment to enable telemedical assistance in polar areas shall be provided. This paper describes a series of functional telemedicine tests carried out on board the Norwegian Coast Guard vessel *NoCGV Svalbard* during her transit between Svalbard and the Norwegian mainland in September 2019. It begins by describing the location, the western Arctic.

2   The Western Arctic

The western Arctic (Figure 1) is a region that has seen climate change over the last decades. Regions that used to be inaccessible due to ice and snow are now high-end tourist destinations. Historically, activity was mainly fishery based,

---

1   Johnny Grøneng Aase and Julia Jabour, 'Can monitoring maritime activities in the European High Arctic by satellite-based Automatic Identification System enhance polar search and rescue?' *The Polar Journal*, 2015: DOI: 10.1080/2154896X.2015.1068534.
2   Ibid.

and saw some minor transport and cruise activity.[3] Sea traffic at Svalbard is limited during winter season because of ice. Ship traffic can be divided into nine categories:
- The major overseas cruise ships that call at fjords on the west coast of Spitsbergen
- Expedition cruise ships that go all around Svalbard
- Day cruise ships that operate from Longyearbyen
- Bulk carriers shipping coal from Svalbard
- Cargo ships with supplies to Longyearbyen, Barentsburg, Ny-Ålesund and Hornsund which sail most of the year when ice in the fjords are limited
- Fishing vessels are active in the Svalbard waters throughout the whole year
- Research vessels
- Smaller leisure crafts, such as sail boats, cabin cruisers and kayaks are used by the locals of Svalbard. From time to time people sail between the Norwegian mainland and Svalbard
- Military vessels, like Norwegian Coast Guard vessels

The Joint Rescue Coordination Centre of the Norwegian High North is in Bodø. Several Rescue Sub Centres (RSC) are manned by the Norwegian police. The RSC at Svalbard is organised directly under the Governor of Svalbard.

Hospitals are located along the coast of the Norwegian mainland and in Longyearbyen. A patient can be evacuated by helicopter or air jet ambulance. The Governor of Svalbard has at her disposal the *MS Polarsyssel*, a modern vessel with helicopter landing facilities. The Norwegian Polar Institute operates the new research vessel *FF Kronprins Haakon*, which also has helicopter landing facilities.

3   Effects of Climate Change

Aase and Jabour use data from Norwegian satellites equipped with Automatic Identification System (AIS) receivers to quantify maritime activities in three regions of the Arctic.[4] The three areas are located north of Svalbard, along the eastern and northern coast of Greenland and in the waters surrounding Russia's Franz Joseph Land. The vessels are organised in relevant groups. As an example, in the waters north of Svalbard the groups were passenger (tourist)

---

3 Fjørtoft, et al., Analysis of Maritime Safety Management in the High North, 10 September 2010.
4 Aase and Jabour, note 1.

vessels, trawlers/fishing vessels, research/survey vessels, Norwegian coast guard vessels, sailing vessels/yachts, cargo vessels, non-military Norwegian government vessels, ice breakers, sealers and other vessels. Similar natural groups were identified in the waters of Greenland and Russia. The study focused upon tourist vessels. It covers the period 2010–2014. The authors found that tourist vessels in the Svalbard area sail as far north as 82° N, beyond the range of geostationary satellites. The study also found that a significant number of tourist vessels are north of 80° N only one to three times during the tourist season. This means that the crew has a limited experience with handling Arctic conditions.

ClimeFish[5] is a European Union-supported program to investigate the effects of climate change on fisheries and aquaculture at European and regional scale, and to collect and harmonise relevant data. It consists of a total of 16 case studies. Two are relevant here: case study #1 (North East Atlantic) and case study #5 (Barents Sea). The first ClimeFish case study covers species like herring, mackerel, capelin, blue whiting, sprat, anchovy and sardine in the North East Atlantic which includes the Barents Sea, the Norwegian Sea, West of Scotland, Faroese waters, Icelandic waters and the Deep basin area located between the North Sea, Norway, Iceland and Svalbard. The main effects of climate change are an increase in ocean temperature, extreme water events, waves and rainfall. Increased storminess and waves reduce safety at sea for the crew.

The Barents Sea Fisheries case study considers the shelf area bordering the Arctic Ocean, Russia, Norway and the Norwegian Sea. This area supports three main fisheries: demersal trawl fisheries targeting North East Arctic cod and haddock and a pelagic trawl fishery for capelin. In 2014 the cod fishery yielded more than €600 million. The Barents Sea includes species like saithe, redfish, Greenland halibut and crustaceans like deep-water prawns, king crab and snow crab. Sea surface temperatures are expected to increase in the next decades. Cod and haddock, which prefer cold waters, are migrating northward. The snow crab population has spread westward into the Norwegian part of the Barents Sea. The northward fish migration and shrinking sea ice will probably lead to trawlers moving further north.

---

5   ClimeFish, Project Description, https://climefish.eu/aims-and-goals/ (accessed 6 March 2020).

4 The Polar Code

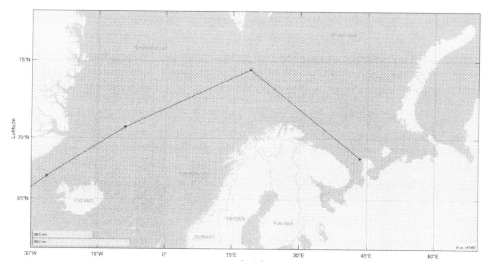

FIGURE 1   Polar Code area of application in the western Arctic

The International Maritime Organization (IMO) has adopted the *International Code for Ships operating in Polar Waters* – the Polar Code[6] which entered into force on 01 January 2017. The goal of the Code is to provide for safe ship operation and the protection of the polar environment. Article 10.2.1.4 of the Polar Code states that "Appropriate communication equipment to enable telemedical assistance in polar areas shall be provided."

In the North Atlantic and Barents Sea, the Polar Code applies in the area north of a series of straight lines drawn between Cape Kanin Nos in Russia, Bear Island (Norwegian: Bjørnøya) and Jan Mayen Island that continues further west through waypoints located in the ocean between Iceland and Greenland (Figure 1). The search and rescue responsibilities in the waters north of the European landmass are shared by Norway and Russia.[7] The national areas of responsibility (AoR) for maritime and aeronautical search and rescue (SAR) in the Arctic were defined by the Arctic Council in 2011. As a first approximation, the Norwegian SAR AoR is located between the North Pole and the coast of the

---

6   International Maritime Organization, International Code for Ships Operating in Polar Waters (Polar Code). Two IMO Resolutions establish and adopt the Polar Code: MSC.385 (94) (London, November 21, 2014) and MEPC.264 (68) (London, 15. May 2015).
7   The Arctic Council, 'Agreement on Cooperation on Aeronautical and Maritime Search and Rescue in the Arctic', https://oaarchive.arctic-council.org/handle/11374/531 (accessed 30 January 2020).

Norwegian mainland, and in the east–west direction between the zero meridian and 35 degrees east. The line separating the Norwegian and Russian SAR AoRs deviates somewhat from this simple description as one approaches the Norwegian and Russian coasts. However, it is also possible that a ship (or aircraft) may be required to assist in rescue operations outside its national AoR.

5 Telemedicine Requirements in the Polar Code

The term 'telemedical assistance', or derivations of the term, like 'telemedicine', are not defined in the Polar Code. The safety aspects of the Polar Code are made mandatory by the International Convention for the Safety of Life at Sea (SOLAS). Under the SOLAS Convention we also find *The International Aeronautical and Maritime Search and Rescue (IAMSAR) Manual*.[8] The IAMSAR Manual states that 'SAR services includes providing medical advice'. IAMSAR defines medical advice as 'exchange of medical information and recommended treatment for sick or injured persons where treatment cannot be administered directly by prescribing medical personnel'.[9]

Several legal documents demand the availability of services providing advice and onboard healthcare. The most senior publication is the Maritime Labour Convention, 2006 (MLC-2006), by the International Labour Organization (ILO). The MLC-2006 states that medical care on board should be 'as comparable as possible to that which is generally available to workers ashore'.[10] One can therefore easily argue that telemedical equipment should be used if this contributes to narrowing the gap between the healthcare that can be provided ashore and on board.

The Norwegian Centre for Maritime and Diving Medicine (NCMDM) is the national centre with competence for maritime medicine in Norway,[11] and provides the maritime telemedical assistance service called Radio Medico Norway. The centre was established by decision of the Norwegian Parliament in 2004 and has had regular activity since 2006. NCMDM is a section of the

---

[8] International Maritime Organization (IMO) and International Civil Aviation Organization (ICAO), *IAMSAR manual* Vol II – Mission Co-ordination. 2016.

[9] International Maritime Organization (IMO) and International Civil Aviation Organization (ICAO), *IAMSAR manual* Vol III – Mobile facilities. 2016.

[10] International Labour Organization (ILO), Maritime Labour Convention, 2006 (MLC-2006), Regulation 4.1.4.

[11] Norwegian Centre for Maritime Medicine, 'About the Norwegian Centre for Maritime Medicine', http://www.ncmm.no/about-ncmm (accessed 30 January 2020).

Department of Occupational Medicine at Haukeland University Hospital in Bergen and is also affiliated to the University of Bergen.

Radio Medico Norway can be contacted by all possible means of communication from vessels. This includes VHF Channel 16 calls, HF telephony, INMARSAT telex or telephone, direct telephone or e-mail. The Radio Medico doctor evaluates available information and gives advice on treatment. When necessary, the doctor will order evacuation of the patient. The responsible officer on board gives the treatment ordered and informs the Radio Medico doctor of further developments at agreed intervals. The doctor decides when the treatment can be terminated.

The Coast Guard is one of Norway's main tools to monitor activities in the Arctic. Coast Guard vessels provide a point of presence for exercising jurisdiction, monitoring the environment and supporting scientific research. All Coast Guard vessels have enhanced medical facilities compared to ordinary ship sickbays.

The Coast Guard provides free medical services to mariners in distress. A medical doctor can be transported to a vessel, e.g. a trawler, to provide medical care to a mariner on board his own vessel, or the patient can be transferred to the medical facilities on board the Coast Guard vessel. A patient can also be evacuated by helicopter to a hospital on the Norwegian mainland or in Longyearbyen.

The purpose of this test was to investigate if current communication systems and off-the-shelf equipment can assist a doctor at sea. It should be stressed that the authors do not question the skills, dedication and professionalism of medical personnel serving at sea. However, from time to time all professionals need to discuss cases with colleagues to verify the conclusions or to get a second opinion. Telemedicine is an excellent tool for this.

6   Communications

The field of telemedicine is developing rapidly. New commercial, off-the-shelf equipment can perform numerous health and vital signs checks, just like in a doctor's surgery. Some even provide live voice and video at relatively low bandwidth. However, this is a niche and the technology mainly relies on broadband services. In most of the world, this is not a problem.[12]

---

12   Johnny Grøneng Aase and Julia Jabour, 'How Satellites Can Support the Information Requirements of the Polar Code' *The Yearbook of Polar Law* Volume 8, 2018.

Geostationary communications satellites have a theoretical coverage to 81.3° North and South latitude. Vessels sailing in Antarctic waters and in the southern regions of the Arctic will always be in the coverage area of broadband services from geostationary communication satellites. In the Norwegian SAR Area of Responsibility, the north coasts of the islands Spitsbergen and Nordaustlandet are located at approximately 80° N. At such latitudes a geostationary satellite is barely above the local horizon and a vessel could very easily experience satellite outage when it is in the shadow of a mountain or an island to the south.

Mariners have not agreed upon the line for robust geostationary satellite communications in the Arctic. Some professionals state that it is at 78° N, approximately the latitude of the two settlements of Longyearbyen and Barentsburg. Others put the line at 75° N, near Bear Island (Norwegian: Bjørnøya). An exact line might not even be relevant as the coverage and robustness are greatly affected by the sea state, terrain southwards and the azimuth of the geostationary satellite.

Broadband satellite coverage is still available in the High Arctic through other forms of satellite communications. The Soviet Union/Russia has used communication satellites in highly elliptical orbits that overlook the Arctic since the mid-1960s. To the best knowledge of the authors, this service is not available for Western users. Norway is currently planning the Arctic Satellite Broadband Mission (ASBM), which is scheduled for launch in December 2022. The two satellites will, among other payloads, carry an Inmarsat transponder which will provide seamless global services for commercial users, alternating between geostationary and polar broadband satellites. Two satellites in a 16-hour three apogee (TAP) orbit will provide 24/7 broadband services north of 65° N. The satellites orbit the Earth three times every two days. The apogeum, or the point in the orbit where the satellite is furthest from the Earth and provides communication services, will alternate between the southern tip of Greenland, the Ural Mountains and the Bering strait.

As of today, Iridium NEXT is the only satellite broadband service with coverage in the High Arctic that is commercially available in the West. This is a new constellation, entering service in 2019. The Iridium NEXT constellation consists of 66 communication satellites flying in low polar Earth orbit. These satellites pass over vessels in the Arctic Ocean and provide low latency, decent bandwidth and high reliability.

For the tests described in this paper, we used the Certus 350 plan that permitted speeds up to 352 kbps, significantly faster than what was available through the old Iridium constellation. During a series of communications tests in 2015, the lead author experienced that services that worked fine in

Bergen, a city on the Norwegian mainland located at 60° N, failed when repeated in the waters surrounding Svalbard. The technical literature available that describes the Iridium NEXT constellation does not address the engineering choices that lead to a significant reduction in available bandwidth in the Arctic. This was therefore an unanswered question when we deployed for the tests in September 2019.

7 Maritime Activities in the Svalbard Area

The Automatic Identification System (AIS) automatically provides information about a ship's identity and location to other ships and to coastal authorities.[13] The purpose of AIS is to increase safety at sea. These transmissions can also be received by satellites in low Earth orbit. Norway launched its first satellite with an AIS receiver payload in 2010 to monitor maritime activities in the North Atlantic and Barents Sea.

Regulation 19 of SOLAS Chapter V – *Carriage requirements for shipborne navigational systems and equipment* – sets out navigational equipment to be carried on board ships, according to type. In 2000, IMO adopted a new requirement (as part of a revised new Chapter V) for all ships to carry AIS capable of automatically providing information about the ship to other ships and to coastal authorities. The regulation requires AIS to be fitted aboard all ships of 300 gross tonnage and upwards engaged on international voyages, cargo ships of 500 gross tonnage and upwards not engaged on international voyage and all passenger ships irrespective of size. The requirement became effective for all ships by 31 December 2004. Ships fitted with AIS are always required to maintain AIS in operation except where international agreements, rules or standards provide for protection of navigational information. For example, military vessels are not required to shine their AIS transponder.

To quantify the increase in marine activities in the Svalbard area, AIS data from 2015 and 2019 have been analysed. Figure 2 shows the area of interest, as a box between 6° W and 31° E longitude, and 75° to 82° latitude. The box surrounds most of the Svalbard archipelago, including the banks north of the archipelago and in the waters between Spitsbergen and Hopen Island.

Figures 3 and 4 illustrate the increase of maritime activities in the Svalbard area from 2015 to 2019. The x-axis shows the day of year (DOY), and the y-axis the number of unique vessels seen by Norwegian AIS satellites in the waters in

---

13   International Maritime Organization, 'AIS transponders', http://www.imo.org/en/Our Work/Safety/Navigation/Pages/AIS.aspx (accessed 30 January 2020).

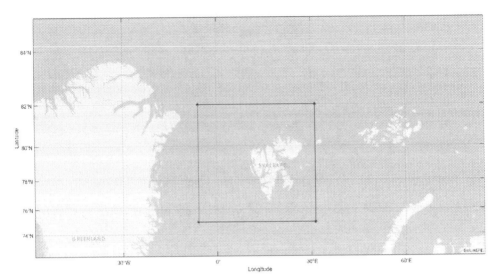

FIGURE 2   Area of analysis

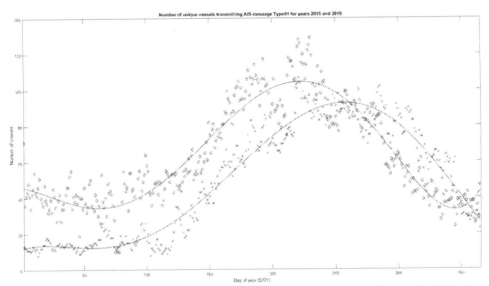

FIGURE 3   Number of unique vessels transmitting AIS-message Type01 in 2015 and 2019 in the Svalbard area

the area of interest for each day of the years 2015 and 2019. It should be noted that each vessel is counted only once per day, even if it is seen during several satellite passes on a day.

Figures 3 shows the number of unique vessels transmitting AIS-messages Type01 for each day of the years 2015 (x) and 2019 (diamonds). In layman's

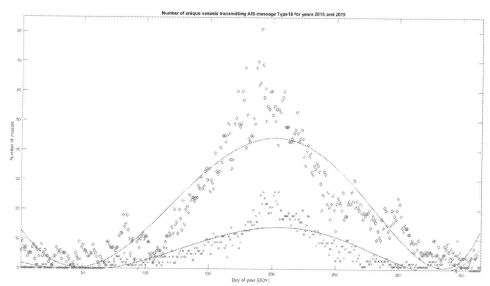

FIGURE 4 Number of unique vessels transmitting AIS-message Type18 in 2015 and 2019 in the Svalbard area

terms, "large vessels" (e.g., cruise vessels, trawlers or cargo vessels) transmit this type of AIS message. The lines in Figures 3 and 4 are 5th order polynomials fitting the data sets. When comparing the data sets for 2015 and 2019 we see that the number of vessels in the area double for the first four months of the year. The number of vessels during summer season is slightly higher in 2019 than in 2015. During autumn and early winter 2019 the number of vessels is lower than in 2015.

The increase is more dramatic for vessels transmitting AIS messages Type18, or "small vessels" (Figure 4). In 2015, hardly any small vessels like yachts and leisure craft were seen during January, February or December. In 2019 small vessels were seen during the entire year. The number of vessels more than doubles from 2015 to 2019 during Spring, Summer and early Autumn.

The numbers of vessels detected by tracking these AIS signals should be regarded as minimum values. Military vessels are not required to transmit AIS messages all the time. Illegal fishing vessels may turn off their AIS transponders to avoid detection by Russian and Norwegian Coast Guard and maritime patrol airplanes. It is hence likely that the real number of vessels in this area is higher than depicted.

Overall, the figures show that the maritime activities in the waters surrounding Svalbard have increased significantly over the last five years. The increased maritime activity highlights the need for reliable medical services for mariners in the Arctic. The need is expected to increase as these remote waters become more accessible.

8   Test Set-Up

The tests described in this paper were carried out on board the Norwegian Coast Guard vessel *NoCGV Svalbard* from 11–13 September 2019 during her transit between Svalbard and the Norwegian mainland.

The vessel was equipped with a Tempus Pro version v04.16. It is a lightweight, rugged vital signs monitor that enables patient data collection and sharing, real-time data streaming and storage.[14] Tempus Pro monitors are used by first responders and the medical services of several NATO nations. Video communication was achieved via Web RTC protocol and Cisco meeting app Version 1.11.15.0. No attempts were made to optimise either the Tempus Pro or the communication equipment. They were used as is.

Besides the Tempus Pro's built-in FIPS 140–2 encryption,[15] no additional attempts were made to encrypt the transmitted data. Encryption adds a data overhead that must be transmitted in addition to the medical data.

The test scenario was based on a doctor needing collegial assistance for decision-making and treatment of a patient, and we intended to test if telemedicine over Iridium NEXT could support the doctor through information exchange with a more experienced doctor at a hospital. This is translatable to similar situations in which the person providing assistance on the scene has minimal medical qualifications, e.g. a trawler captain with a sick crew member, a tourist expedition leader with a sick patient, or expedition participants who have fallen ill.

The standard Radio Medico Norway procedure for evaluating telemedical video consultations was used. This procedure asks the receiving doctor to assess the quality of the transmitted telemedical information, and whether the information is of sufficient quality to add clinical value. Table 1 presents the different telemedical channels of communication that were tested. Each channel was tested by transferring data from the ship to a doctor on call at Radio Medico Norway.

---

14   Remote Diagnostic Technologies, https://www.rdtltd.com (accessed 6 March 2020).
15   Remote Diagnostic Technologies, Tempus ProTM Monitoring Platform https://promedtech.co.nz/wp-content/uploads/2015/08/Tempus-Pro-Capability-Sets-Sept-2013-.pdf (accessed 6 March 2020).

Upon reception the doctor would score each channel according to four evaluation criteria. Each criterion strictly evaluates if the information transferred has the necessary quality to be used in the clinical assessment of the patient. The content of the information or the type of diagnostic information is not part of the evaluation.

The four criteria were:

N/A: Not available/tested

–: Unsatisfactory, connected but with quality not suitable for diagnostics or treatment purposes

+: Satisfactory, quality good enough to give added diagnostic value to the consultation, but better quality or real time/more rapid transfer would provide even more/better information

++: Good quality, suitable for diagnostic purposes and treatment without any expected value of further increased quality

The tests were repeated at intervals of one degree of latitude. Due to practical considerations, the tests started in Longyearbyen at 78° N.

Table 1 shows the results of the tests. The satellite phone was used for both calling and data transfer. Contact between the ship and Radio Medico Norway was attained at all locations, generally without problems. At 73° N the connection was lost. After reconnection the transfer was without problems.

When used for telephony, sound quality was good at all locations. E-mail was sent from all latitudes and was received without delay. For video, connection was established, but in all tests picture and sound was either not present or unstable and of low quality. The information transferred by video was therefore not suitable for diagnostics or treatment purposes. Connection of

TABLE 1   Clinical value of transferred information scored by quality

Latitude (°N)	78	77	76	75	74	73	72	71
Satellite phone – connection	++	++	++	++	++	+	++	++
Satellite phone – sound quality	++	++	++	++	++	++	++	++
Satellite phone – availability	++	++	++	++	++	++	++	++
E-mail	++	++	++	++	++	++	++	++
Video connection	–	–	–	–	–	–	–	–
Video/sound/shared desktop	–	–	–	–	–	–	–	–
Tempus monitor connection	++	++	++	++	++	+	++	++
Tempus image transfer	++	++	++	++	++	++	++	++

the Tempus monitor with transfer of data through Tempus's own third-party server and picture had good quality at all locations.

9 Patient Data Protection

Patient privacy has always been an important aspect in medicine. The Hippocratic oath is one of the oldest binding doctrines in history.[16] A medical doctor swears to treat the ill to the best of one's ability, and to preserve a patient's privacy.

Telemedicine has inherent challenges to preserving a patient's privacy. In this functional test medical data were transmitted over large distances, using both satellite and terrestrial communication links. Such communication links may be compromised and allow unauthorised users to access patient information.

In Europe, a person is protected by the General Data Protection Regulation (GPDR).[17] Norway is not a member of the European Union but has as an EEZ country adopted the GPDR to the benefit of its citizens. Article 1 says that the

> Regulation lays down rules relating to the protection of natural persons with regard to the processing of personal data and rules relating to the free movement of personal data. [It] protects fundamental rights and freedoms of natural persons and in particular their right to the protection of personal data.

Article 4 defines 'personal data' as

> any information relating to an identified or identifiable natural person ('data subject'); an identifiable natural person is one who can be identified, directly or indirectly, in particular by reference to an identifier such as a name, and identification number, location data, and online identifier or to one or more factors specific to the physical, physiological, genetic, mental, economic, cultural or social identity of that natural person.

---

16   William C. Shield Jr, 'Medical Definition of Hippocratic Oath', https://www.medicinenet.com/script/main/art.asp?articlekey=20909 (accessed 30 January 2020).

17   REGULATION (EU) 2016/679 OF THE EUROPEAN PARLIAMENT NAD OF THE COUNCIL of 27 April 2016 on the protection of natural persons with regard to the processing of personal data and on the free movement of such data, and repealing Directive 95/46/EC (General Data Protection Regulation) (Text with EEA relevance).

Data concerning health means

> personal data related to the physical or mental health of a natural person, including the provision of health care services, which reveal information about his or her health status.

As the search and rescue area for this project is under Norwegian jurisdiction, and the *NoCGV Svalbard* is a Norwegian government vessel, there are several laws and regulations regarding the data protection aspect. The most significant is the Norm of Information Security of Norway, issued by the Norwegian National Security Authority (Norwegian: Nasjonal sikkerhetsmyndighet). It states that all communication, regardless of whether it is wireless or not, is to be encrypted to the standards described in NSM Cryptographic Requirements Version 3.1.[18] If there are lives at risk, the right to break these regulations in order to save lives takes priority.

10 Discussion

These tests show that telemedicine using Iridium NEXT and equipment like Tempus Pro can play a role in improving medical services in remote areas in the future. Used as is, it facilitated exchange of information between a vessel in the Arctic and a hospital. In addition to telephony and e-mail that is currently in use in these areas, picture transfer via the Tempus unit and real time transfer of monitoring data also functioned well. However, the video system proved not to function over this bandwidth with the Iridium NEXT.

While the tests did confirm that telemedicine could be performed via Iridium NEXT at these high Arctic latitudes, the connection was not without challenges. In next steps the authors will report these problems to Iridium and seek to repeat the test at higher latitudes. In addition, other kinds of commercial medical equipment should be tested over Iridium NEXT, as well as by other means of communications (e.g., 4G and 5G mobile telephone services) and encryption of data.

It should be noted that Iridium NEXT is a new constellation of satellites. From an engineer's perspective, it is expected that a new service experiences technical issues. Iridium NEXT should be recognised for, even at this early stage

---

18   Norwegian National Security Authority: NSM Cryptographic Recommendations, https://www.nsm.stat.no/globalassets/dokumenter/veiledninger/systemteknisk-sikkerhet/nsm-cryptographic-recommendations-juli19.pdf (accessed 9 March 2020).

in the life of constellation, supporting most of the services tested during this campaign. Further testing and sharing of results are encouraged to improve the quality of the service further.

Due to practical considerations the tests started in Longyearbyen at 78° N. As tourist vessels have been observed sailing beyond 82° N, tests should also have been carried out even further north. This is deferred to future campaigns.

The arrangement as tested does not meet requirements for patient data protection. Cruise vessels sail in both Arctic and Antarctic waters. A standard for encrypting medical data for the cruise industry and hospitals in Polar regions should be developed. A tourist vessel may use Ushuaia as a port in November to March, and Tromsø or Longyearbyen from June to September. As many cruise vessels sailing in the Polar areas are EU or EEA flag states, it is recommended to develop a standard for exchange and encryption of medical data that meets the requirements of the GDPR as a minimum standard. As it turns out that Iridium NEXT can support basic telemedicine, future work should include establishing a regime for encryption of medical data. Data encryption is vulnerable for data package loss. The Iridium NEXT is a new constellation, and little is known of its package loss properties. This was not measured during this campaign.

11   Conclusions

These tests show that telemedicine using Iridium NEXT and off-the-shelf equipment can play a role in improving medical services in remote areas in the future. However, current bandwidth limits the use of video systems. Future work should include a) similar tests at latitudes beyond 78°, b) establishing a standard for encryption of patient data to be used by e.g. the tourist industry and c) exploration of package loss properties of Iridium NEXT and future Arctic SATCOM systems.

Acknowledgements

The authors would like to thank the Norwegian Coast Guard vessel *NoCGV Svalbard* and her fine crew for assistance and hospitality during the tests in the Arctic. We would also like to thank the Medical Services of the Royal Norwegian Navy and the crew of the Norwegian Navy's new hospital ship, the *HNoMS Maud*, for lending us equipment and test facilities.

We thank the Norwegian Coastal Administration for providing data from the Norwegian AIS satellites, and Prof Kjellmar Oksavik at Bergen University for assistance with improving our data analysis tools.

We would also like to thank Mr Jostein Olsen at Airbus for negotiating time on the Iridium NEXT constellation.

The tests have received funding from the *EP1901 SATCOM in the Arctic – Iridium NEXT* project.

Indigenous Peoples' Rights

Corporate Behaviour towards the Upholding of Human Rights – Exploring the Possibilities of Human Rights Impact Assessment in the Sápmi Region

Anna Petrétei*

Abstract

One of the most current challenges the Sámi are facing is the rapid expansion of extractive industries throughout the Arctic region, creating obvious conflicts between states and Sámi people. European High North has already proven to be rich in mineral deposits. Furthermore, it is suggested that the world's largest remaining untapped gas reserves and undeveloped oil reserves are located in the Arctic. Therefore, there is a growing pressure to conduct extractive industrial activities on the territories important for the Sámi, for instance on reindeer herding areas and reindeer migration routes. The expansion of extractive industrial developments causes significant challenges to the enjoyment of their human rights, unless effective procedural measures are in place to mitigate adverse impacts. The aim of this paper is to explore the possibility of integrating human rights impact assessment (HRIA) in existing license granting mechanisms, to examine how particular companies comply with human rights norms applicable to local and indigenous, and to scrutinise the possibility of these and other Northern mining companies to carry out HRIA in the future. The integration of HRIA would ensure that the special status and interests of Sámi people is properly taken into consideration when planning and implementing extractive industrial projects.

Keywords

Arctic – indigenous peoples – human rights – mining – Sámi

---

* Northern Institute for Environmental and Minority Law, Arctic Centre, University of Lapland. anna.petretei@gmail.com.

1   Introduction

The term *corporate behaviour* typically relates to the general conduct of companies, including different aspects of their operations. The corporate behaviour of companies may affect their reputations, as well as their relationship with other organizations and individuals. An important factor of corporate behaviour is corporate social responsibility, which generally refers to actions taken by firms with respect to their employees, communities, and the environment that go beyond legal requirements.[1] Especially in the extractive industrial sector, another important factor of corporate behaviour is the extent to which companies consider the human rights of people affected by the company's operations, starting in the early phase of licensing processes. The means by which human rights impacts are assessed within the conduct of companies is the focus of this article.

The Arctic is a unique region in many ways, characterised by a cold and harsh environment and challenged by global warming, which is twice as fast in this region as the global average. This rapid warming has contributed to the dramatic melting of Arctic sea ice and spring snow cover.[2] The Artic is generally rich in natural resources; however, as a result of environmental changes, its natural resources are becoming more and more accessible. The presence of indigenous peoples, the changing environment, and the more accessible natural resources are the roots of specific human security threats. The rapid expansion of extractive industries throughout the Arctic region is one of the most serious challenges the indigenous people and local communities are currently facing. *Sápmi*, the region traditionally inhabited by the *Sámi* people, stretches through the northern parts of Norway, Sweden, Finland, and the Kola Peninsula in Russia. Hence, the extractive development creates obvious conflicts between states and the interests of the Sámi people.[3] European High North, including the Sápmi region, is rich in mineral deposits: Finland and

---

1   Amir Rubin and Amir Barnea, "Corporate Social Responsibility as a Conflict Between Shareholders" (March 10, 2006) EFA 2006 Zurich Meetings, 2.
2   Judah Cohen, et al., "Recent Arctic amplification and extreme mid-latitude weather" *Nature Geoscience* 7, (2014): 627–637.
3   It must be noted that in terms of extractive industrial activities, there is no clear common interest of Sámi people that reflects the views of all Sámi. The interest of a given Sámi community may depend on many factors, such as which region they live in, how they suffer from commercial activities, or what benefits they get from those. Naturally, the views of different Sámi communities on extractive industries may vary. By referring to the interest of Sámi, I mean the actual interests of the given communities, which may be related to any issue that is important for the community in question.

Sweden has long been amongst the most attractive countries for mineral investments worldwide.[4]

There is growing pressure to conduct extractive industrial activities on the territories that have traditionally been important for indigenous peoples. Natural resource extraction and other major development projects in or near indigenous territories are amongst the most significant sources of abuse of the rights of indigenous peoples worldwide.[5] Indigenous peoples generally live in close connection to nature, and their traditional ways of living often relate to land, water, and other natural resources, which makes them especially sensitive to environmental changes. Adverse impacts on the environment may even endanger traditional indigenous livelihoods. These livelihoods are not only a source of food for indigenous peoples but are also a part of their heritage and culture, some of them even indicators of 'indigenousness'.[6] Therefore, major impacts on the environment not only threaten their traditional livelihoods but may also jeopardise the unity and established structure of Sámi society.[7] The establishment of a mine has a significant socio-economic impact on the affected local and indigenous communities. Environmental security (the protection of the environment while allowing for the sustainable use of natural resources now and by future generations) and community security (including the protection of community values and identities) are both significant aspects of human security.[8] Therefore, it is apparent that environmental and social challenges are amongst the most significant and relevant aspects of human security threats against indigenous peoples.

---

[4] Survey of the Fraser Institute published in March 2014, available online at: http://www.fraserinstitute.org/research-news/news/display.aspx?id_20902; and Fraser Institute Annual Survey of Mining Companies: 2014, https://www.fraserinstitute.org/sites/default/files/survey-of-mining-companies-2014.pdf (accessed 1 July 2020). See also: Kamrul Hossain and Anna Petrétei, "Resource Development and Sámi Rights in the Sápmi Region: Integrating Human Rights Impact Assessment in Licensing Processes", *Nordic Journal Of International Law* 86, no 2, (2017):302–340.

[5] S James Anaya, former UN Special Rapporteur on the rights of indigenous peoples, "Report on extractive industries operating within or near indigenous territories" (2011). A/HRC/18/35, para 82.

[6] For instance, reindeer herding can only be practiced by Sámi people in Sweden and Norway. (Although reindeer herding is practiced by Sámi also in Finland and Russia, it is not the exclusive right of the Sámi indigenous peoples of those countries.)

[7] Anna Petrétei, "Securing Sámi Livelihoods – Does Mining Undermine Traditional Ways of Living", in Kamrul Hossain and Anna Petrétei (eds), *Understanding the Many Faces of Human Security – Perspectives of Northern Indigenous Peoples*, (Brill Academic Publishers, 2016), 158.

[8] Kamrul Hossain, et al., "Constructing Arctic security: an inter-disciplinary approach to understanding security in the Barents region" *Polar Record* 53, (2017):54.

The problem is clearly visible within the Sámi territories, where mines and other development projects have recently been established, endangering traditional Sámi livelihoods and culture. Both national and international mining companies operate in the region, and the global interest towards mining in Sápmi is constantly growing. In order to evaluate the impacts of development projects and to mitigate the conflicts, several procedures are in place in most countries, such as the environmental impact assessment (EIA) and the social impact assessment (SIA). It is suggested that in the case of activities related to resource development, the process of human rights impact assessment (HRIA) should be integrated with existing license-granting mechanisms.[9] The integration of HRIA would ensure that the special status and interests of the Sámi people are properly taken into consideration when planning and implementing mining and other extractive industrial projects. By the integration of tools to assess the impacts on human rights before project operations begin, such conflicts between communities and companies may even be mitigated.[10]

The aim of this article is to examine how particular companies in the region comply with the human rights norms applicable to local and indigenous peoples in the region. It is argued here that the effective consideration of human rights (possibly via implementing HRIA) in the course of extractive activities enhances human well-being, which promotes human security and therefore provides societal security for local and indigenous peoples. The article sheds light on the increasing importance of the assessment of human rights impacts within the Sápmi region. Specific human rights instruments are applicable to indigenous peoples, and companies are therefore required to pay special attention to protect the rights of the indigenous Sámi people inhabiting the region. This issue is examined through an analysis of the existing literature on HRIA and indigenous peoples' rights in the human rights context. Corporate behaviour of extractive industrial companies is investigated through selective case studies, by examining the relevant policies of companies and by conducting interviews with company representatives. The performance of the selected companies is not scrutinised, as the main focus of the article is to explore the possibility of these and other northern mining companies that currently do not conduct HRIA carrying out such assessments in the future.

---

9   See Hossain and Petrétei, note 4.
10 Ibid, 333.

2 Human Rights Impact Assessment (HRIA)

2.1 *The Importance and Development of HRIA*

HRIA has developed from other types of impact assessments, such as environmental and social assessments.[11] HRIA is carried out to evaluate proposed policies, programs, and projects, with special regard to their human rights implications. The primary aim of HRIA is to minimise human rights risks, lessen adverse impacts, and strengthen positive outcomes of business investments on affected populations. The most important and specific features of HRIA are the normative framework of binding international human rights law, the assessment of compliance with human rights, and comprehensiveness. Unlike other assessments, HRIA considers economic, socio-cultural, civil, and political aspects, thus enabling parties to focus on more vulnerable groups such as local and indigenous peoples.[12] Due to globalization, the impact of multinational enterprises on communities has significantly increased. Unfortunately, human rights violations related to the activities of such enterprises have also become more common. As HRIA assesses actions that have or may have an impact on human rights, the actual use of such assessments in the extractive sector would greatly enhance the protection of local and indigenous communities, and therefore would help to avoid conflicts between the companies and communities.[13]

By the adoption of the UN Guiding Principles on Business and Human Rights[14] (hereinafter referred to as Principles) in 2011, businesses for the first time were placed under an obligation to ensure that human rights are protected in the course of their operations. According to the Principles, states are obliged to protect against human rights abuses within their territories, and therefore business entities and corporations are responsible for respecting human rights in their operations by performing due diligence in accordance with national and international regulations.[15] Thus, states have the duty to protect human rights, while companies are responsible for respecting human

---

11   "Human Rights Impact Assessments: A Review of the Literature, Differences with other forms of Assessments and Relevance for Development" (February 2013) Nordic Trust Fund, The World Bank, x.
12   Ibid.
13   See Hossain and Petrétei, note 4, 302–340.
14   Special Representative of the Secretary-General, "UN Guiding Principles on Business and Human Rights: Implementing the United Nations 'Protect, Respect and Remedy' Framework" (2011).
15   Ibid, Principle 18.

rights within their sphere of influence.[16] Importantly from a business perspective, the UN High Commissioner for Human Rights later endorsed the "Corporate Responsibility to Protect Human Rights – An Interpretive Guide",[17] in order to support the effective implementation of the Principles focusing on corporate responsibility to respect human rights in business.

Although the number of HRIA case studies and tools is relatively low, their growing number undoubtedly indicates that a body of knowledge on HRIA is developing.[18] Three motivations seem to underline HRIAs: the concern over the enjoyment of particular (mostly economic, social, and cultural) rights,[19] the concern over the impacts of certain policies and projects, and the assessment of the impact of the work by human rights organizations. The importance of the latter has emerged due to the increased pressure on human rights organizations to demonstrate a positive correlation between donor contributions and human rights outcomes, especially since investors (donors) started to be concerned about whether their investments in human rights were paying off. For instance, the Office of the United Nations High Commissioner for Human Rights (OHCHR) applied results-based budgeting techniques to develop and report on its Strategic Management Plan with impacts demonstrated in its annual reports.[20]

Even though HRIA aims to bring beneficial changes in policies and to have a positive effect on practices, it is important to be aware of the possibility of HRIAs to undermine their own ability to have such impacts. First and foremost, clear conclusions and concrete recommendations would be essential for an effective HRIA. However, in many cases HRIAs do not formulate such recommendations, or the conclusions are weak and unrelated to the identified problems. Another problem with HRIA processes concerns the end of the process. Although HRIA is supposed to be a dynamic process where the implementation of recommendations and future human rights impacts are

---

16 The guiding principles endorse three pillars in human rights and business: 'protect,' 'respect' and 'remedy' – a framework proposed by UN Special Representative John Ruggie.
17 The Guide, http://www.ohchr.org/Documents/Publications/HR.PUB.12.2_En.pdf (accessed 1 July 2020).
18 Simon Walker, "Human Rights Impact Assessments – Emerging Practice and Challenges" in Eibe Riedel, Gilles Giacca and Christophe Golay (eds), *Economic, Social and Cultural Rights in International Law* (Oxford University Press, 2014), 391–392.
19 For instance, food impact assessment checklist by the Food and Agriculture Organization (FAO), equality impact assessment by public authorities in the UK.
20 See Walker, note 18, 393–394.

monitored, in reality such reviews are seldom conducted.[21] Therefore, appropriate methodologies and long-term goals should be carefully balanced when carrying out HRIAs.

2.2 The Relevance of HRIA in the Extractive Industrial Sector

Due to the special features of the Sápmi region and the distinct threat by the extractive sector towards local and indigenous peoples, the consideration of human rights impacts is especially important in the extractive industrial context.[22] The increased accessibility of rich natural resources in the region has led to rapidly expanding extractive industrial development, resulting in multiple challenges for local and indigenous communities. Therefore, there is an ever growing need for effective means to reduce adverse impacts of development projects and to avoid conflicts arising from such projects.

The guiding Principles include provisions for victims to access effective remedy. In other words, when companies violate human rights, governments must provide appropriate recourse for those affected. This is especially important in the extractive sector, where projects have negative impacts on the environment and therefore on the rights and livelihoods of affected communities. Assessing the human rights impacts of extractive activities is facilitated by the sector's strong background in data collection, giving assessors the access to review robust sets of environmental, health, engineering, and workforce data. However, for a HRIA to fulfil this purpose, it must consider the perspectives of everyone affected by a company's operations.[23]

Companies often fail to recognise the immediate costs of poor human rights performance, and tend to overlook the prevention of conflicts due to the time-consuming nature of building sustainable relationships with local communities. Nevertheless, the ignorance towards community concerns is usually a detrimental mistake, and a project that goes through the planning phase without consultation with affected communities carries a serious risk of local conflict.[24] These conflicts not only delay the project operation but also imply

---

21 James Harrison, 'Measuring Human Rights: Reflections on the Practice of Human Rights Impact Assessment and Lessons for the Future' (November 10, 2010) 26 *Warwick School of Law Research Paper*, 23.
22 For a thorough description of international law background of indigenous peoples' and human rights, see: Hossain and Petrétei, note 4.
23 Community Voice in Human Rights Impact Assessments – Oxfam America, 1.
24 Rachel Davis and Daniel Franks, "Costs of Company–Community Conflict in the Extractive Sector" *Corporate Social Responsibility Report* 66 (Shift/Kennedy CSRI Initiative/University of Queensland), (2014):8–9.

high costs, such as operational, personnel, legal, and reputational costs.[25] By conducting meaningful HRIA, conflicts with local communities may be mitigated, and therefore costs may be reduced.[26]

The importance of human rights protection in the extractive sector is also shown by the US–UK Voluntary Principles on Security and Human Rights,[27] established in 2000. This initiative aims to ensure security and human rights in mining and other extractive industries. It is a multi-stakeholder[28] initiative seeking to improve security by ensuring human rights in the oil, gas, and mining industries through regular consultation with host governments, local communities, civil society, and companies. The Principles provide guidance for companies in conducting a comprehensive human rights risk assessment to ensure that human rights are respected.[29]

3   HRIA – the Sámi Perspective

3.1   *HRIA in the Sápmi Region – Prospects and Challenges*

Generally, human rights are fairly well protected in Nordic states constituting the Sápmi region.[30] However, due to the above-described specific challenges in the region, special measures need to be considered in order to ensure efficient protection for local and indigenous peoples. Although different measures[31] are available to reduce the negative impacts of development projects, these procedures often fail to provide effective protection, as the outcome of such assessments is in many cases not considered during the practical implementation of

---

25   Ibid, 15–16.
26   Luckily, there are examples of successful HRIAs in the mining sector, such as the one carried out by the human rights organisation Ecuadorian Ecumenical Commission for Human Rights in 2009, focusing on FPIC (see also: Community Voice, note 23, 38.); and the work of Business for Social Responsibility (BSR) with a Canadian mining company Teck Resources to develop a global human rights due diligence system (see also: Conducting an Effective Human Rights Impact Assessment – Guidelines, Steps, and Examples, (2013):8–9).
27   For the text of the Principles, see http://www.voluntaryprinciples.org/wp-content/uploads/2019/12/TheVoluntaryPrinciples.pdf (accessed 1 July 2020).
28   Including governments, major multinational extractive companies and NGOs. More information on the Principles and their implementation, https://www.voluntaryprinciples.org/ (accessed 1 July 2020).
29   Amongst the countries with Sámi populations, Norway is the only country to participate in this initiative.
30   For more information about human rights and international law instruments in the region, please see Hossain and Petrétei, note 4.
31   Such as environmental impact assessment (EIA) and social impact assessment (SIA).

the projects.[32] As the extractive sector is the industrial sector giving rise to the highest number of human rights reports, it is of crucial importance to reduce human rights abuses caused by extractive industrial companies,[33,34] and HRIA is suggested as an effective tool for doing so.[35] Such form of impact assessment has not been used in mining developments in the Nordic countries; hence, examples and guidance may only be drawn from assessments conducted in other parts of the world.[36]

When suggesting the implementation of HRIA, it is important to be aware of the possible difficulties of such procedures. The most significant difficulty with impact assessments in general is that they require considerable human capital, time, and financial resources. Additionally, HRIA poses some specific challenges, as it requires a high level of understanding of the human rights framework itself. Furthermore, the framework applied by HRIA is essentially highly political and partisan,[37] which is especially problematic in the case of extractive industries where the interest of states and local communities are in clear contradiction – and therefore even more challenging in the Sápmi region, where the rights of indigenous peoples are to be considered. A clear-cut example of such tension is the Finnish Sámi parliament expressing its explicit opposition against mining and extractive activities.[38]

To carry out effective HRIA, several criteria can be identified.[39] HRIA should reflect the company's unique operating context and availability of human and financial resources. This is crucial in the mining sector, where activities are expensive to conduct and economic circumstances are far from favourable

---

32 See Hossain and Petrétei, note 4, 335.

33 Menno T. Kamminga, "Company Responses to Human Rights Reports: An Empirical Analysis" *Business and Human Rights Journal* 1, no. 1 (Cambridge University Press, 2016), 108.

34 The protection of Sámi cultural rights related to land use activities has been dealt by the Human Rights Committee (HRC). In the case of *Länsman et al. vs. Finland*, the Committee clearly indicated that any future large-scale mining activities would constitute a violation of the rights of the Sámi under article 27 of the ICCPR. For more information, see also Hossain and Petrétei, note 4, 338–340.

35 For structured information on the theory and benefits of HRIAs, see Hossain and Petrétei, note 4.

36 HRIA are apparently more widely used in South America, related to different development projects. Examples may also be found from other parts of the world, such as the Philippines, Ivory Coast and Kenya.

37 See Walker, note 18, 406–413.

38 Timo Koivurova and Anna Petrétei, "Enacting a New Mining Act in Finland – How were Sami Rights and Interests Taken into Account?" *Nordisk Miljörättslig Tidskrift/Nordic Environmental Law Journal* 1, (2014), ed Gabriel Michanek. ISSN: 2000-4273.

39 Conducting an Effective Human Rights Impact Assessment – Guidelines, Steps, and Examples. Business for Social Responsibility, March (2013):8.

amidst the global financial crisis. Although state economies are fairly stable within the Sápmi region, there have been recent examples of mines closing down their operations due to the bankruptcy of mining companies.[40] Even though different legislative instruments aim to provide more security against such scenarios,[41] this factor must specifically be considered within the current economic setting.

For an effective HRIA, a company's due diligence pertaining to human rights should be continuous, recognizing that the human rights risks may change over time as the business enterprise's operations and operating context evolve.[42] Mining companies face very different human rights risks during the construction, operation, and closure of a mine. Additionally, companies operating in the Sápmi region should pay special attention to enhance and protect the specific rights of the Sámi people. Engagement with potentially affected rights holders is often worrisome for companies, due to the cost and time pressure associated with engagement, and companies' fear of discussing sensitive issues with stakeholders who are critical towards their operations.[43] Although stakeholder engagement is prescribed by national legislations and recognised in most existing regulatory licensing processes within the Sápmi region, the outcome of those engagements is often not properly considered during the implementation of projects. Therefore, despite the fact that stakeholder engagement is an existing concept in the region, its use fails to fulfil the criteria for effectiveness.[44]

Transparency of a company's human rights performance is amongst the most significant aspects of trust-building and an essential component of human rights due diligence.[45] However, transparency is often a major challenge for companies that are cautious of disclosing sensitive information and worried about drawing attention to problems. Nevertheless, there have been examples in the Sápmi region where companies were able to establish fruitful cooperation with the affected Sámi community. For instance, a Swedish

---

40 For instance, the Kaunisvaara iron-ore mine in Pajala (Swedish Lapland) closed down as mining company Northland Resources bankrupted in December 2014.

41 For instance, companies in Sweden have to provide information on their economic security and ensure that they have enough money to cover damages caused by their operation. The reason for introducing this rule was an unfortunate case where a company went bankrupt and was unable to pay the adjudicated compensation to the affected Sámi village.

42 See UN Guiding Principles, note 14, Principle 17.

43 "Conducting an Effective Human Rights Impact Assessment – Guidelines, Steps, and Examples. Business for Social Responsibility" (March 2013):14.

44 See Hossain and Petrétei, note 4, 302–340.

45 See UN Guiding Principles, note 14, Principle 21.

mining company managed to establish a special agreement with the Sámi villages affected by its activities.[46] The agreement regulates the ways in which they provide each other with relevant information. For example, the Sámi people inform the company of their activities in different parts of the affected area, which helps the company to measure the cumulative effects of its operation. Gaining the trust of the affected Sámi villages and establishing fruitful discussion with them is crucial for the company, especially if it plans to expand its operations in the future.[47]

In order to conduct an effective and meaningful HRIA, companies should ensure that the HRIA process is thorough, that community participation is meaningful, that the company's human rights conclusions are clearly communicated, and that vulnerable groups are heard. Furthermore, companies should be willing to implement the findings of HRIA, internalise lessons learned from HRIAs, and apply this knowledge to future projects. This is especially significant within the Sápmi region, where Sámi communities tend to be more accommodative with companies with whom they already have a history of cooperation.[48]

Besides HRIA, an important concept for company-community relations is that of the social license to operate (SLO), which is increasingly being used nowadays worldwide. The SLO describes a specific aspect of company-community relations in extractive projects, with special regard to the interaction of different actors to resolve the social and economic impacts on local communities and other stakeholders.[49] The SLO is not a legal tool, but an intangible process whereby the company obtains social acceptance in the community affected by its operations. Also, it is suggested that the thorough consideration of human rights impacts by a company (for instance, within the framework of HRIA) helps companies to gain the SLO.[50]

3.2   *Case Studies from the Sápmi Region*

As stated above, the Sápmi region offers rich mineral deposits to extractive companies. As opposed to the often unfavourable socio-political settings in

---

46   Timo Koivurova, et al., "Legal Protection of Sami Traditional Livelihoods from the Adverse Impacts of Mining: A Comparison of the Level of Protection Enjoyed by Sami in Their Four Home States" (2015)6, 1 *Arctic Review on Law and Politics*, 11–51, 29.
47   Ibid 29.
48   Pamela Lesser, Thomas Ejdemo, Leena Suopajärvi and A Petrétei, *Sustainable mining – Nordic knowledge synthesis guidebook. Good practices and knowledge gaps* (Lapin yliopisto, 2016), 29–30.
49   Timo Koivurova, et al., "Social license to operate': a relevant term in Northern European mining?" *Polar Geography* 38, no. 3 (2015):194–227.
50   See Hossain and Petrétei, note 4, 302–340.

the developing states, the importance of the rule of law in Nordic countries is a clear asset for mining companies.[51] Finland and Sweden are especially attractive for mining investors, not only because of their valuable deposits, but also because of the high technical standards required during mining operations, as well as the favourable political environment for mining and mining legislation. Currently, several companies are conducting mining operations in these countries. For the sake of this article, two cases have been chosen: the Kittilä gold mine operated by Agnico Eagle Mines Limited in Finland and the operations of LKAB mining company in Sweden. The main purpose of the case studies is to explore how companies see their actions complying with human rights standards and perspectives. In the first case, the mine is located close to the Finnish Sámi homeland, and the company has had strong cooperation with affected communities, including reindeer herders. Although the mine is not located within the Sámi homeland, and therefore the operations have not yet directly impacted Sámi communities, Agnico Eagle's community engagement policy serves as an outstanding example. Furthermore, the company is about to start operating in Sámi areas in Sweden. In the second case, LKAB mining company has had a long history of cooperation with affected Sámi villages, resulting in agreements with those communities, active community engagement, and several indigenous-specific policies.

3.3 Agnico Eagle Mines Ltd. – Kittilä Gold Mine

The Kittilä mine in northern Finland is the largest gold producer in Europe, operated by the Canadian company Agnico Eagle Mines Ltd. The mine is the company's first mine outside of Canada. Since the opening of the Kittilä mine, Agnico Eagle Mines Ltd. has expanded its operations to Mexico. Ore production in the Kittilä mine started with two open pits in 2008 and continued as an underground operation two years later. Open pit mining was completed in 2012, and Kittilä has been an underground-only operation since then. The annual extraction of the mine is about 1.6 million tons of ore, yielding about 6,200 kg of gold. Approximately 14 km of new tunnel is excavated yearly. The current ore reserves are expected to be productive until about 2035, but further exploration works are in progress with the aim of expanding the

---

51 Naturally, the rule of law entails respect towards human rights and the rights of indigenous peoples. These aspects are to be specifically considered in the case of extractive industry. This could be enhanced by the use of HRIA.

lifespan of the mine.[52] The mining site is located approximately 50 km from the Finnish Sámi homeland.

The Kittilä mine aims to contribute to the social and economic development of the region in several ways. Being amongst the largest employers in Lapland, the mining company employs about 480 people year-round and provides jobs for over 450 employees of subcontractors working in the mine or in exploration operations. The company emphasises the maximisation of local employment, and the vast majority of its employees are from the region surrounding the mine. The mine is one of the reasons for the increasing population in the region. Regional development is promoted by purchasing all the necessary products and services locally, thus boosting other industrial sectors, such as hotel and restaurant services, and health care. The company enhances the municipal and state economy by paying different kinds of taxes and royalties.[53] Agnico Eagle Mines Ltd. also strives to support community well-being in the area nearby its operation.[54]

The company aims to present the image of greatly emphasising environmental and social sustainability. According to Agnico Eagle, special measures are taken in order to minimise the impacts on the environment, to reduce the ecological footprint of its mining operations, and to sufficiently restore mining areas after the closure of operations.[55] The company also promotes societal, economic, and sustainable development in the communities affected by its operations. In order to do so, Agnico Eagle offers communities a confidential reporting system to inform them about any unethical, illegal or irresponsible activities; acknowledges and respects affected people's basic human rights, cultures, and customs; promotes open, transparent, and respectful dialogue with all stakeholders; and follows nationally and internationally accepted principles of operation.[56]

Agnico Eagle strives to demonstrate its endeavours to engage its stakeholders as actively as possible. In order to do so, a Community Liaison Committee was established, including the most important interest groups such as the Kuivasalmi reindeer herding cooperative, local villages, the Levi Tourist Office,

---

52   "The Kittilä Mine – an Important Player in the Development of Finnish Lapland" (Euromines Newsletters 1/2013).
53   General brochure of Agnico Eagle Finland Ltd.
54   This is done for instance by participating in the renovation of the Kittilä football pitch and ice-hockey arena, and by sponsoring several local societies and hobby groups.
55   Environmental sustainability measures of the company.
56   Community sustainability measures of the company.

the Kittilän Luonto association for environmental protection, the local parish, the local government of Kittilä, and Lapland Vocational College.[57]

3.4 LKAB Mining Company

Luossavaara Kiirunavaara Aktiebolag (LKAB) is a mining company owned by the Swedish government. It is a high-tech international minerals group, a world-leading producer of processed iron ore products for steelmaking, and a growing supplier of mineral products for other industrial sectors, providing minerals and iron ore products in Europe, North Africa, the Middle East, South East Asia, and the USA. In 2016, LKAB produced 26,9 million tons of iron ore products. This amounts to 76% of the iron ore in Europe, making the company the largest iron ore producer in that continent.[58]

The operations of LKAB take place in the underground mines in Kiruna and Malmberget, and at the Gruvberget and Leveäniemi open pit mines in Svappavaara in Northern Sweden. Corporate governance at LKAB is based on Swedish legislation, the Swedish Code of Corporate Governance,[59] the state's ownership policy, and internal control documents.[60]

The company promotes itself as aiming to be one of the most innovative, resource-efficient, and responsible companies in the mining industry, indicating that sustainability is amongst their core strategies. The sustainability goals of the company include economic, social, and environmental dimensions. LKAB is devoted to continuously improving its energy performance and to preventing and minimising its environmental impact. According to the company's communication, its aim is to achieve a long-term, sustainable business by ensuring that resources are available for achieving its environmental and energy targets; complying with the applicable laws, regulations, and other environmental and energy requirements of the countries in which it operates; actively working to ensure that its employees and suppliers are trained, committed, and motivated to participate in its environment and energy efforts; using and helping develop new technology in the extraction and processing of minerals; striving to find alternatives that are energy efficient and environmentally

---

57 Stakeholder information of the company.
58 "LKAB develops Europe's biggest iron ore project" (Euromies Newsletters 3/2014); Malmberget Iron Ore Mine, Sweden.
59 The Swedish Corporate Governance Code, Applicable from 1 December 2016.
60 See "LKAB develops Europe's biggest iron ore project", note 58.

friendly when purchasing goods and services; and being open in its communication and collaboration with stakeholders.[61]

The environment and energy policy of LKAB applies equally to the LKAB Group and its suppliers. The company gives the impression of putting a great emphasis on environmental cautiousness, and thus has a goal to reduce its emissions of greenhouse gases per ton of finished product by 12% by 2021, compared to the 2015 level.[62]

4 Human Rights Performance of Companies in the Sápmi Region – How Well Is Theory Implemented in Practice?

In order to find out how the general human rights policies are implemented in practice, and in what ways human rights are considered during the implementation of development projects, semi-structured interviews were conducted with the representatives of the above companies, as well as with experts on social license to operate and corporate social responsibility. The aim was to draw a realistic picture about the implementation of human rights policies and to explore the possibilities of carrying out actual human rights impact assessments. In doing this, it might be possible to find gaps between regulations and practice, as well as identify issues that need to be further researched.

4.1 Agnico Eagle Mines Ltd – General Human Rights Policy

In 2016, Agnico Eagle formally adopted the Voluntary Principles on Security and Human Rights.[63] The Voluntary Principles are standards to help companies in the extractive sector balance the obligation to respect human rights while protecting the assets and people at their operations. Agnico Eagle is committed to implementing a human rights and security approach consistent with the Voluntary Principles, and to reporting on the implementation in its annual progress report. The Principles contain provisions on risk assessment including the identification of security risks, awareness of past human rights abuses, and consideration of the capacity of the local prosecuting authority and the judiciary to hold accountable those responsible for human rights abuses. The

---

61   LKAB's sustainability goals, https://www.lkab.com/en/sustainability/our-sustainability-work/sustainability-goals/ (accessed 1 July 2020).
62   LKAB's measures to reduce climate impacts, https://www.lkab.com/en/sustainability/environment/energy-and-climate/lkab-actively-minimises-its-climate-impact/ (accessed 1 July 2020).
63   The Voluntary Principles, http://www.voluntaryprinciples.org/what-are-the-voluntary-principles/ (accessed 1 July 2020).

Principles also encompass the interactions between companies and public security, as well as private security. These include regular consultations between companies and communities, transparent communication, safeguarding of human rights, promotion of international law enforcement principles, lawfulness, and the recording of human rights abuses.

Agnico Eagle has also incorporated respect for human rights into its management and governance practices and programs. The clear intention of the company's Board of Directors is to conduct business only in regions where human rights laws are respected and promoted. As a Canadian company, Agnico Eagle is committed to the Canadian Charter of Rights and Freedoms while operating internationally, ensuring that all employees and communities are treated with respect and dignity. Furthermore, the Government of Canada has identified the Voluntary Principles as one of six leading standards in Canada's Corporate Social Responsibility (CSR) Strategy for the Extractive Sector, which makes the company's commitment to the Principles even stronger.

Agnico Eagle specifically emphasises that it does not support or facilitate child labour or forced labour practices in any of their operations, including outsourced or subcontracted activities across the entire supply chain. When working on private lands or lands important for indigenous peoples, the company applies the principle of informed consent by seeking the consent of the land owner, usually by a formal agreement acknowledging that Agnico Eagle will conduct work in a certain area and under certain conditions. Stakeholder engagement is also a key standard of Agnico Eagle. The company has established a Stakeholder Advisory Committee (SAC) in order to get feedback on their corporate social responsibility efforts, and to help them engage local stakeholders. The endeavour of the company is to conduct a regular and meaningful stakeholder dialogue.[64]

The respect for human rights is an important criterion in Agnico Eagle's Supplier Code of Conduct.[65] The company requires all its business partners to uphold the highest standards of human rights, especially in terms of treating workers and contractors with dignity and respect, and by prohibiting child employment and forced labour.[66]

In order to further assess the human rights impacts of its operations, Agnico Eagle produces a sustainable development report. This report is published annually, is available to the public, and keeps record of the activities of the

---

64   Sustainability standards of Agnico Eagle.
65   Supplier Code of Conduct of Agnico Eagle.
66   Supplier Code of Conduct, page 1.

company in respect of sustainable development. The report addresses specific indicators on human rights performance that correspond to the indicators of the Global Reporting Initiative (GRI). This report is also part of the company's Responsible Mining Management System (RMMS), that is, their in-house health, safety, environment, and social acceptability management system, aimed at improving the performance of the company and ensuring that compliance requirements and industry standards are met.[67]

In 2015, Agnico Eagle adopted an Aboriginal Engagement Policy for its operations in Canada, followed by an international Indigenous Peoples Engagement Policy in 2016.[68] According to the policy, the company aims to work in partnership with indigenous peoples in order to establish a mutually beneficial, cooperative, and productive relationship. The approach is characterised by effective two-way communication, consultation, and partnership. Therefore, the company is committed to improving the understanding of the concerns and aspirations on both sides through meaningful consultation and cooperation with the indigenous communities. To achieve this goal, Agnico Eagle strives to fully inform indigenous communities and consult with them on the likely impacts and opportunities arising from its activities; to share information on business imperatives and constraints to help indigenous communities and business partners understand the reasoning behind business decisions; and to provide indigenous people with the opportunity to reach mutually beneficial agreements with the company on new projects.

According to the Engagement Policy, capacity-building strategies are to be identified with and for indigenous peoples, especially by increasing the number of indigenous employees within the company and service providers; by developing partnerships with the indigenous people and government and community organizations in the delivery of indigenous employment and training; and by promoting the development of indigenous business opportunities to service the company's projects and operations. Agnico Eagle recognises the importance of indigenous culture by its commitment to consider the sustainability of indigenous culture when managing the impacts of its operations; to consider the use of land by indigenous peoples and their information

---

[67] These requirements and standards include: Carbon Disclosure Project (CDP), Global Reporting Initiative (GRI), International Cyanide Management Code, Towards Sustainable Mining (TSM) Initiative, Disclosure of payments to governments, Conflict-Free Gold Standard. For more information on the Responsible Mining Management System, see also https://www.agnicoeagle.com/English/sustainability/standards/default.aspx (accessed 1 July 2020).

[68] Indigenous People Engagement Policy of Agnico Eagle.

concerning the land in the project planning phase; to implement indigenous culture awareness courses for its employees; and to provide a working environment that is culturally sensitive and supportive for all employees.[69]

Agnico Eagle also implements the Towards Sustainable Mining (TSM) initiative, which is a commitment of the Mining Association of Canada to responsible mining. The initiative includes a set of tools and indicators to drive performance and ensure that key mining risks are managed responsibly. Companies committing to the TSM initiative are to comply with several principles, including engagement with communities, world-leading environmental practices, and commitment to the safety and health of employees and surrounding communities. The main objective of the program is to enable mining companies to operate in the most socially, economically, and environmentally responsible way. The core strengths of TSM are transparency, credibility, and accountability. This is the only program worldwide where assessments are conducted at the facility level where the mining activity takes place – thus providing affected local communities with meaningful information on the development of the mine.[70] Building strong relationships with communities of interest, including Aboriginal communities, is a fundamental component of TSM, and therefore a specific protocol for Aboriginal and community outreach is implemented.[71]

4.2 *Agnico Eagle Mines Ltd – Practice from the Company Perspective*

Interviews were conducted with the representatives of the Finnish branch of Agnico Eagle Mines Ltd., in order to explore the human rights impacts of mining in Lapland and the implementation of the company's human rights policy. Company representatives from the Canadian headquarters also contributed to the interviews.[72]

As the company's above-described policies show, Agnico Eagle pays particular attention to its relationship with affected communities and to gaining their acceptance of their development projects. In order to earn and maintain the social license to operate, the company fosters a level of trust with its

---

69 Indigenous People Engagement Policy.
70 For more information about TSM see also the Canadian Mining Association, http://mining.ca/towards-sustainable-mining (accessed 1 July 2020).
71 TSM Aboriginal and Community Outreach Protocol; TSM Aboriginal and Community Outreach Framework.
72 The chapter builds on interviews conducted with company representatives. Naturally, the views of affected Sámi and local communities may differ from the perspectives of the company.

partners through its engagement policies (for instance, through the Aboriginal Engagement Policy described above) and sustainable development policies.[73]

Furthermore, a 'due diligence' template was recently developed by the company in order to assess the risks and opportunities of a project. The template is in line with the policies of the company and considers issues of concern of the company's partnering communities. In order to ensure the protection of human rights and compliance with the company's policies, the social acceptance of local and indigenous peoples is considered during the EIA and SIA conducted by the company. For instance, Agnico Eagle is engaged in conducting a consultative and information process with local and indigenous peoples. This is done in order to obtain the traditional knowledge of affected peoples, to hear their concerns and other possible input towards improving the mine design, and to reduce the anticipated social and environmental impacts as much as possible.[74]

Agnico Eagle does not currently have any operations within the Sámi homeland in Finland. However, the company is currently conducting exploration activities in the Barsele area in northern Sweden, which is an important territory for the Sámi people. The company has conducted extensive dialogues with the potentially affected Sámi villages and local people, with promising results.[75] During all its operations, the company strives to develop and maintain trustful partnerships with the indigenous peoples affected by its operations. In order to enhance a cooperative and productive relationship, the company aims to ensure the social acceptance of its presence in a particular region. This is done by continuous consultation with and engagement of local and indigenous communities, as well as specific interest groups during different phases of the project. In Finland, for instance, the operations of Agnico Eagle affect the reindeer herding area nearby the mine site. The company arranges regular meetings with reindeer herders, and the open dialogue has led to good results.[76]

Although Agnico Eagle does not conduct specific HRIA in order to assess human rights impacts of its operations, its template of risk and opportunity assessment has been inspired by different recognised models of social acceptance recommended by the industry and the stakeholders of the company. As for conducting a HRIA *per se*, Agnico Eagle has not yet carried out any specific HRIA procedure. However, when more familiar with the HRIA process, the company may consider using HRIA or parts of it in order to continuously

---

73   Interview with company representative, February 2017.
74   Ibid.
75   Ibid.
76   Ibid.

improve the risk and opportunity assessment processes, to better consider the human rights of affected people, and to minimise the human rights risks caused by its operations.[77]

4.3   LKAB – General Human Rights Policy

In order to minimise the impact on human rights by company operations, LKAB has adopted a human rights policy.[78] The policy focuses on the social impact of mining, operations, and production in high-risk countries, working conditions and safety, indigenous populations, and diversity and discrimination. Issues relating to human rights are also part of the Code of Conduct of the company.[79] Specific international guidelines are considered in its Code of Conduct, such as the UN Global Compact, including its ten principles on human rights;[80] UN Guiding Principles on Business and Human Rights;[81] OECD Guidelines for Multinational Enterprises;[82] and Children's Rights and Business Principles.[83]

In its human rights policy, LKAB acknowledges that its operations affect the environment, both positively and negatively, and may also directly or indirectly impact the human rights of affected people. Therefore, the company strives to maximise positive impacts and minimise negative ones by clear and transparent dialogue with stakeholders and by continuous risk assessment.[84] The policy is not only applicable to LKAB but also to its subsidiaries and business partners.[85]

The company is committed to conducting a continuous dialogue with stakeholders, especially with those who may be affected negatively by its operations. Therefore, indigenous peoples and those who will be affected by land claims are specifically considered in the course of such dialogues. As these stakeholders might not be aware of their rights in relation to the operations

---

77   Ibid.
78   LKAB's human rights policy.
79   Code of Conduct of LKAB.
80   The Principles, https://www.unglobalcompact.org/what-is-gc/mission/principles (accessed 01 July 2020).
81   The Guiding Principles, http://www.ohchr.org/Documents/Publications/GuidingPrinciplesBusinessHR_EN.pdf (accessed 01 July 2020).
82   The OECD Guidelines, http://www.oecd.org/daf/inv/mne/48004323.pdf (accessed 01 July 2020).
83   The Principles, http://childrenandbusiness.org/the-principles/introduction/ (accessed 01 July 2020).
84   Section 1 of the Human rights policy.
85   Section 2 of the Human rights policy.

of the company, LKAB aims to conduct the dialogues in a manner understandable for all parties.[86]

The company regularly conducts due diligence processes to identify, prevent, limit, and report on the human rights impacts of company operations. Also, each part of the business is responsible for identifying its impact on human rights annually and for taking measures to reduce impacts.[87] In cases where negative impacts on human rights are identified, or when obvious risk exists, necessary measures are to be taken in collaboration and consensus with the affected group or individual. Relevant incidents, actions, and monitoring of the work on human rights are reported in the annual and sustainability report, and external experts are consulted if necessary in order to ensure accurate and objective assessments.[88]

4.4   LKAB – *Practice from the Company Perspective*
Interviews were conducted with the representatives of LKAB to scrutinise the practical application of the measures the company takes to mitigate adverse human rights impacts.

LKAB considers dialogue and transparent information as the first step towards creating mutual understanding and cooperation. In order to monitor and handle the human rights impacts of its operations, the company conducts due diligence processes. In order to maintain the social license to operate, LKAB strives to comply with all rules, regulations, and policies applicable to them. The company conducts its business in a professional manner, with the aim to increase and enhance positive impacts and decrease negative impacts throughout its value chain. LKAB also produces a sustainability report, which is published annually.

The value chain of the company is large as it imports goods from all over the world for production. In order to mitigate risks in the value chain, including negative impacts on human rights, LKAB implements a supplier Code of Conduct[89] and performs audits on selected high-risk suppliers based on location and line of business.

Since a significant part of LKAB's operation is conducted on lands that are important for indigenous peoples, the company has found ways to cooperate with the indigenous population. For instance, LKAB has made agreements with Sámi villages affected by its operations. These agreements specify the means

---

86   Section 3 of the Human rights policy.
87   Section 4 of the Human rights policy.
88   Section 5 of the Human rights policy.
89   Code of conduct of LKAB.

of communication between the parties, as well as contain provisions on how often their meetings are organised. As a company representative points out, having an agreement does not mean that LKAB and the Sámi villages always agree – rather, it means that they have agreed on a way for communication to take place, and also that if their dialogue fails, there is a third-party mediator on hold.[90] An important by-product of the meetings is the methodology for evaluation of the impacts on reindeer herding, worked out together by the company and the Sámi villages. So far, the company has been able to reach agreements concerning the terms of its operations, mitigation mechanisms, and compensation measures with the Sámi villages. Since reindeer herding is valued as a national interest in Sweden, companies are obliged by law to describe in their EIAs how their operations may affect such activities. The possible impacts on reindeer herding are evaluated by representatives from the Sámi villages according to the methodology mentioned above. Although LKAB does not carry out separate SIAs, the social context is considered within the EIA.[91] Furthermore, LKAB follows several policies and guidelines in order to engage communities and to gain the trust of affected indigenous peoples. These guidelines include, for instance, land-use guidelines and compensation agreements regarding urban transformation.

LKAB has clearly adopted a fruitful way of working with indigenous peoples, mostly by complying with legislative demands, as well as by conducting additional dialogue. Moreover, the company provides education on human rights, which is compulsory for all of its co-workers. Although there is no available training specifically on Sámi culture and rights, the company's legal experts are involved in most of the cooperation with the Sámi villages, giving information on various occasions concerning the legal grounds for the work with the Sámi villages. LKAB considers its way of cooperation with the Sámi as encouragement to learn more about one another, both in terms of business and culture.[92]

LKAB strives to develop its routines in accordance with its human rights policy.[93] This policy is based on worldwide principles that essentially correspond to the concept of HRIA. Due diligence processes have been conducted in two primary risk areas of the company: urban transformation[94] and the im-

---

90 Interview with company representative, March 2017.
91 Ibid.
92 Ibid.
93 Human rights policy of LKAB.
94 In order to carry on mining iron ore, LKAB must ensure the availability of the land that the mining affects. For this reason, the company has to relocate parts of their operating locations, Kiruna and Malmberget. For more information on urban transformation, see also https://samhallsomvandling.lkab.com/ (accessed 01 July 2020).

pact on indigenous peoples. In the latter case, the notion of FPIC was used as an inspiration for further development of the company's working methods. Therefore, it can clearly be stated that LKAB emphasises and strives to consider the impacts of its operations on indigenous peoples.

Although LKAB does not carry out separate HRIAs, its policies and conduct comply with human rights legislation and instruments. The company has chosen to separate due diligence processes from human rights impacts, as well as from EIA and SIA, and is working on a tool for higher executives to help simplify the risk-defining process. The company also emphasises that these processes must be conducted continuously, not only during the ongoing EIA process. Therefore, parts of HRIA are applied as tools for risk assessment. Furthermore, some aspects of HRIA are considered during the due diligence and impact assessment processes. According to the company representative, it is in the company's utmost interest to approach human rights issues proactively. It is not a matter of any separate tool determining what conflicts arise and how those can be mitigated or solved.[95]

5   Assessment of Possibilities

Based on the human rights policies of Agnico Eagle and LKAB and the interviews conducted with company representatives and experts, we can conclude that both companies strive to comply with national and international norms in order to protect the human rights of local and indigenous peoples affected by their operations. In addition to emphasising conformity with the above-described international human rights norms, both companies acknowledge the distinctiveness of Sámi rights as collective human rights requiring special protection, and both companies have embodied such protection in their policies. Sustainability, community engagement, and respect for human rights are at the top of the agenda of both mining companies. The actual implementation of the above concepts is manifested through different tools. Agnico Eagle emphasises the importance of community relations, addresses the indicators of its human rights performance in the annual sustainable development report, follows the Towards Sustainable Mining initiative that ensures the provision of meaningful information to local communities, and implements a specific protocol for indigenous and community outreach. Furthermore, the social acceptance of its operations by local and indigenous communities is assessed in the company's EIA and SIA processes. The human rights policy of LKAB also

---

95   Interview with company representative, March 2017.

addresses affected indigenous peoples, and human rights issues are considered both in the Code of Conduct and in the due diligence process of the company. Moreover, LKAB provides compulsory education on human rights to its employees, and conducts audits of its high-risk suppliers to reduce possible negative human rights impacts. The company pays special attention to dialogue with affected local and indigenous communities and has a long history of cooperating with indigenous peoples. Although neither of the companies conducts separate assessments of the human rights impacts of their operations, it is clear that human rights issues are taken into account during the companies' conduct. Their human rights policies are in line with different human rights instruments – the same instruments that should serve as the basis of HRIA as well. During the interviews, company representatives indicated that their company would consider conducting HRIAS when it was more familiar with the concept of such assessments. This was also confirmed by experts on social license to operate and corporate social responsibility, who pointed out the absence of awareness about HRIA.

According to SLO experts, the chances of the companies conducting separate HRIAS in the near future in the Sápmi region are rather low, mostly because of the lack of general knowledge about HRIA. It is suggested that if both the companies and communities were made aware of the advantages of such assessments, the companies would probably opt for conducting HRIAS on their own initiative.[96]

As it stands now, carrying out such assessments would create an extra burden from the company viewpoint. Companies would have to invest a great amount of human and financial resources, and additional impact assessments would be somewhat time-consuming and may even cause significant delay to company operations. Therefore, experts assume that unless HRIA is prescribed by law, companies will show less willingness to undertake this form of impact assessment. Ideally, there should be international legal requirements for conducting HRIA, as HRIA does not necessarily offer any greater protection unless it is backed by the enforcement of the courts or other higher entities.[97]

The picture is complex from the community perspective as well. Although communities generally wish to be part of the dialogue with mining companies, they are not experts on impact assessments, nor are they used to dealing with such processes. On the practical level, the most important thing for communities is that their interests are being considered during the mining

---

96   Interview with SLO expert, June 2017.
97   Ibid.

process.[98] They are almost indifferent as to what processes companies use in order to achieve this and what forms of impact assessments they carry out. For instance, if a community wishes their traditional knowledge to be considered in the mining process and used throughout the mining operation, it is not relevant for them whether this knowledge is contemplated during the SIA, HRIA, or possibly within the EIA – as long as it is considered. In fact, communities may not even be able to tell apart the different impact assessment processes, and they certainly cannot be expected to do so.

If companies see that HRIA can enhance their cooperation with communities and recognise the other benefits it can bring them, and communities understand how they can profit from such assessments, it may be possible to actually implement HRIA. However, both parties would need to be made aware of the added benefits of HRIA and see the value of HRIA for themselves. The most realistic idea would be to incorporate HRIA in other impact assessments, for instance to include a section on human rights impacts in the EIA report. For a start, it would be ideal to conduct a social and human rights impacts assessment in addition to the EIA. This way, social issues would be better highlighted, and human rights would also be emphasised – both of which are significantly important in the Arctic but often get lost during the impact assessment.[99]

Experts suggest that if the concept of HRIA were more widely known, it could have the potential to grow over time, similarly to SIA. This process is difficult to start as long as there is no test case in the Sápmi region. However, if HRIA were more generally used around the world, companies would most probably follow the example.[100]

6   Conclusion

The impact of expanding the mining industry in indigenous communities in the Sápmi region is apparent. Evidently, special attention is to be paid to the protection of the human rights of the Sámi people. The tension between indigenous communities, mining companies, and governments is also obvious. It is therefore of great importance to find solutions for the human rights violations emerging as a consequence of mining and to mitigate conflicts between these parties. It is suggested that an effective way for that would be the implementation of HRIA. Although research has shown that companies are

---

98   Ibid.
99   Ibid.
100 Interview with SLO expert, June 2017.

becoming more aware of the possible costs of poor human rights performance, and hence a body of knowledge on HRIA is developing, the relevance of HRIA is not yet reflected in practice.

The aim of this article was to investigate the possibilities of conducting HRIAS in Sápmi in order to ensure greater protection for indigenous peoples' rights and to analyse companies' corporate behaviour regarding human rights. These questions were investigated from the viewpoint of companies and SLO experts, to see how companies view their own operations as complying with international human rights norms and with the possible requirements of HRIA. It is suggested that HRIA could be an effective way to develop the corporate behaviour of companies, which would also positively affect their reputations. This is especially important in the Sápmi region amidst the growing tension between companies and communities, where communities tend to be more accommodative towards companies with a history and longer experience of cooperation with indigenous communities. It is apparent that the conduct of the selected companies follows the respective human rights regulations, and that human rights issues are considered both within the policies and during the operation of the companies. Therefore, especially considering the generally high level of protection of human rights in the Nordic countries, we can conclude that companies in the region normally comply with the applicable human rights instruments. Some of the human rights impacts are assessed throughout the different impact assessment procedures, and human rights aspects are considered during the companies' due diligence processes. Hence, a significant body of knowledge is produced on the human rights impacts of company operations during different assessment and due diligence processes. The next step should be to actually perform the process of HRIA – part of which is already done through the above-mentioned mechanisms. By doing so, it would be possible to further emphasise the legal protection of local and indigenous communities.

Company representatives have implied that companies would probably undertake HRIA if they were more familiar with the process. In order to conduct HRIA, experts suggest that awareness about its benefits should be raised both from the company and from the community perspective, and that the implementation process should be done step by step. The integration of HRIA with other forms of impact assessment would be a good way to start the process. Although there are no test cases in the Sápmi region, examples of effective HRIA from other parts of the world may encourage companies in Sápmi as well.

Finally, as the experts have pointed out, conflict resolution cannot be expected from a single tool, no matter if the use of such tool is an obligation prescribed by law or a voluntary measure of companies. Communication, respect, and time are the keys to resolving problems, both from the company and the community sides. Considering that many tools have defined good practices, a first step is to be inspired and learn from these in order to create a routine that works for both parties – and the next step should be the actual implementation of HRIA and thus the enhancement of the protection of local and indigenous communities.

Communities' Reflections on Oil Companies' Corporate Social Responsibility Activities in Utqiaġvik, Alaska

*Yu Cao**

Abstract

This paper explores the reflections of Utqiaġvik community members on oil companies' Corporate Social Responsibility (CSR) activities within the region of North Slope, Alaska. The research question is: how have the people of Utqiaġvik responded to the CSR activities of oil companies whose oil extractive industry operations impact the region's social, economic, and environmental welfare? In particular, this paper seeks to understand why CSR activities sometimes fail to achieve their purported goals. By interviewing residents from the community of Utqiaġvik, this paper obtained perspectives on the impacts of oil development on the local environment and community, bringing to light the limits of current CSR activities, such that this research might provide recommendations for rectifying CSR shortfalls. The argument is: while oil companies' profit motives tend to restrict the potential of CSR activities, local people should be able to influence the types of CSR activities corporations pursue, given that they experience the local impacts of the industry. The paper concludes by offering recommendations to the oil companies regarding the nature and desired impacts of their CSR activities.

Keywords

Corporate Social Responsibility – extractive industry – oil companies – Utqiaġvik, Alaska – community perspectives – indigenous people

---

* PhD Student, Northern Arizona University. yucao.kim@gmail.com.

1 Introduction

Northern Alaska has an abundance of oil and gas reserves with the geology above the Arctic Circle holding an estimated 90 billion barrels of oil and 1669 trillion cubic feet of natural gas. With its abundant natural resources, communities within the North Slope region have been greatly affected by oil activities since commercial oil production began in the Prudhoe Bay area in the 1960s. The effects of oil production included economic development, interference with subsistence activities, changes in social norms and environmental contamination. For example, Arctic conditions such as moving sea ice and a poorly developed emergency response infrastructure present enormous challenges to clean-up and recovery in the event of oil spills and pollutants.[1]

Climate change has diminished Arctic sea ice coverage, thus increasing the accessibility of Arctic oil and gas reserves and rendering exploration, development and extraction in the region more economically feasible than ever before. Concerns regarding the well-being of northern Alaska's people are increasing along with calls for more sustainable development.[2]

International organisations are paying more attention to the issue of transnational extractive industries' social responsibilities in the countries they operate, especially human rights abuses. The United Nations (UN) Framework on "Protect, Respect and Remedy" and the United Nations Guiding Principles on Business and Human Rights (UNGP) are the two foundational principles which address the issue of human rights and natural resource governance. According to these two frameworks, corporations need to identify and prevent risks related to their businesses and perform due diligence to protect human rights. Extractive industries should also consider indigenous rights. According to International Law terms on indigenous peoples' participation rights, indigenous peoples have the right to Free, Prior, and Informed Consent (FPIC) regarding any business operations on their land.[3] Indigenous knowledge also

---

1   John Kruse, "Subsistence and the North Slope Inupiat: the Effects of Energy Development," *Contemporary Alaskan Native Economies, Maryland: University Press of America* (1986): 121–152; Terrence M. Cole, "Blinded by Riches: the Permanent Funding Problem and the Prudhoe Bay Effect," *Institute of Social and Economic Research, University of Alaska Anchorage* (2004): 1–114.

2   W. Rickerson et al., "Renewable Energies for Remote Areas and Islands (REMOTE)," *International Energy Agency-Renewable Energy Technology Deployment (IEA-RETD)*, Paris, France (2012).

3   Mark Nuttall, "The Isukasia Iron Ore Mine Controversy: Extractive Industries and Public Consultation in Greenland," *Nordia Geographical Publications* 41, no. 5 (2012): 23–34.

plays a significant role in fulfilling indigenous rights. Indigenous people are both rights holders and stakeholders.[4]

Meanwhile, non-governmental organisations (NGOs) focused on environmental protection are watching oil companies' operational procedures more closely. NGOs are demanding more of oil and gas operations in terms of environmental responsibility. These influences have heightened oil company's awareness of how the public perceives the environmental impacts of their activities.[5] Such scrutiny pressures oil companies to take more active measures to mitigate environmental impacts and to expand sustained social and economic benefits of oil developmental activities.[6]

International instruments constraining oil companies' activities include the binding treaties and the 'soft laws'. International Labor Organization (ILO) conventions, Bilateral Investment Treaties (BITs), industrial pollution-related treaties are examples of the binding treaties. 'Soft laws' comprise the Organization for Economic Co-operation and Development (OECD) guidelines, the UN norms, the Preamble to the 1948 Universal Declaration on Human Rights (UDHR), the Rio Declaration on Environment and Development and others.[7] State directly addresses these obligations to corporations through domestic legislation.[8] For instance, in the United States, both federal and state environmental regulations of oil and gas exploration and production (E&P) legally bind companies' activities. Federal environmental regulations include the Resource Conservation and Recovery Act (RCRA), which regulates waste disposals; the Clean Water Act (CWA), which is the primary federal law governing water pollution; Comprehensive Environmental Response, Compensation, and Liability Act (CERCLA) which regulates companies' actions in cleaning

---

4   Arun Agrawal, "Dismantling the Divide between Indigenous and Scientific Knowledge," *Development and change* 26, no. 3 (1995): 413–439; Marjo Lindroth, and Heidi Sinevaara-Niskanen, "Adapt or Die? The Biopolitics of Indigeneity – From the Civilising Mission to the Need for Adaptation," *Global Society* 28, no. 2 (2014): 180–194; John Ruggie, "Protect, Respect and Remedy: A Framework for Business and Human Rights," *Innovations: Technology, Governance, Globalization* 3, no. 2 (2008): 189–212; John Ruggie, "Report of the Special Representative of the Secretary-general on the Issue of Human Rights and Transnational Corporations and Other Business Enterprises: Guiding Principles on Business and Human Rights: Implementing the United Nations 'Protect, Respect and Remedy' Framework," *Netherlands Quarterly of Human Rights* 29, no. 2 (2011): 224–253.
5   Abagail McWilliams and Donald Siegel, "Corporate Social Responsibility: A Theory of the Corporation Perspective," *Academy of Management Review* 26, no. 1 (2001): 118.
6   Stefan Ambec and Paul Lanoie, "Does It Pay to Be Green? A Systematic Overview," *The Academy of Management Perspectives* 22, no. 4 (2008): 45–62.
7   Ilias Bantekas, "Corporate Social Responsibility in International Law," *BU Int'l LJ* 22 (2004): 309–347.
8   Ibid, 334.

up sites contaminated with toxic chemicals; the Clean Air Act (CAA); the Oil Pollution Act (OPA); the Endangered Species Act (ESA), which addresses the conservation of endangered species and others.[9] In the state of Alaska, the Alaska Department of Natural Resources "manages all state-owned land, water, and natural resources,"[10] and the Division of Oil and Gas manages oil and gas leasing programs such as exploration licenses and production tax, and performs other resource management related activities.[11] The Alaska Oil and Gas Conservation Act manages leasing programs while also regulates waste disposals.[12] The U.S. Environmental Protection Agency (EPA) monitors existing laws (such as Alaska Human Rights Law and other acts ensuring indigenous rights) and statutes regarding environmental and human health within native Alaska communities.[13]

These laws and regulations constrain oil companies' activities in the areas of environmental protection and human rights. In this context, state plays a leading role in overseeing companies' activities.[14] But considering the implementation of these laws and regulations, state has limited capacity in controlling the on-the-ground behaviors of oil companies within each community. Because each community has its unique demographic and economic features, oil companies apply different communication and managerial strategies to each community. Moreover, corporation also has the innovative capacity to develop new technologies regarding oil exploration and pollutant management. State does not have this kind of capacity.[15] In this instance, CSR serves to close weaknesses in the existing regulatory framework.

---

9 "Federal Environmental Regulations Affecting Oil and Gas Operations," *the Lexis Practice Advisor Journal*, Energy & Utilities Special Edition (2019).
10 "Alaska Natural Gas Flaring and Venting Regulations," Office of Oil and Natural Gas, U.S. Department of Energy, https://www.energy.gov/sites/prod/files/2019/08/f66/Alaska.pdf (accessed 29 March 2020).
11 "Regulations," Division of Oil &Gas, Alaska Department of Natural Resources, http://dog.dnr.alaska.gov/About/Regulations (accessed 29 March 2020).
12 "S.49-Alaska Oil and Gas Production Act," Congress.Gov, January 5, 2017, https://www.congress.gov/bill/115th-congress/senate-bill/49/text#toc-idb27c755caad84bc28246933be95b73a6 (accessed 29 March 2020).
13 "Laws, Regulations and Policies that Affect Tribes and Native Alaska Villages," United Sates Environmental Protection Agency, https://www.epa.gov/tribal/laws-regulations-and-policies-affect-tribes-and-native-alaska-villages, (accessed 29 March 2020); "Alaska State Commission for Human Rights," Alaska State Commission for Human Rights, https://humanrights.alaska.gov/ (accessed 29 March 2020).
14 See Bantekas, note 7, 335.
15 Ibid, 335.

Companies themselves introduced the concept of CSR into their operational strategies. CSR rests on voluntary bases.[16] CSR in the extractive industry refers to actions taken by corporations to improve the quality of life for its employees, local community members, and the environment, while also contributing to its own economic development.[17] For oil companies, CSR activities include improving risk management strategies such as oil spill prevention measures; working on energy efficiency and renewable energy; building relations with the local communities where they operate; improving employees' life quality and contributing to society at large.[18]

However, since its implementation, oil companies have shown mixed reception to CSR. Some companies have integrated CSR as a core value that guides each development plan, while others use CSR merely as a "window-dressing" to placate the public.[19]

This paper solicited Utqiaġvik community members' opinions through interview process to explore the role of CSR in oil companies' strategic plans. The research question is: how have the people of Utqiaġvik responded to the CSR activities of oil companies whose oil extractive industry operations impact the region's social, economic, and environmental welfare? This paper seeks to understand why CSR activities sometimes fail to achieve their purported goals. The argument is: while oil companies' profit motives tend to restrict the potential of CSR activities, local people should be able to influence the types of CSR activities corporations pursue, given that they experience the local impacts of the industry.

This paper finds that local people of Utqiaġvik desire 1) improved environmental responsibility, 2) more efficient sharing of information with the community, 3) long-term commitment to the community, and 4) more utilisation of local knowledge from the oil companies. These four themes strengthen the argument for local people being able to define the nature of CSR activities undertaken by oil companies. The themes also support the argument that the profit

---

16   Ibid, 317.
17   See McWilliams and Siegel, note 5, 117–127.
18   Jedrzej George Frynas, "The False Developmental Promise of Corporate Social Responsibility: Evidence from Multinational Oil Companies," *International Affairs* 81, no. 3 (2005): 581–598; Williams and Siegel, note 5, 117–120; Manuel Castelo Branco and Lúcia Lima Rodrigues, "Corporate Social Responsibility and Resource-based Perspectives," *Journal of Business Ethics* 69, no. 2 (2006): 111–132.
19   Ruth V. Aguilera et al., "Putting the S Back in Corporate Social Responsibility: A Multilevel Theory of Social Change in Organizations," *Academy of Management Review* 32, no. 3 (2007): 836–863.

motive of oil companies restricts the reach and potential of CSR activities. The profit motive can compete with environmental protection imperatives.

Using the community of Utqiaġvik for the case study on CSR offers insight into relationships between communities and oil companies, in a region as they make choices. Oil companies can improve their strategies, before practices become entrenched and before damages resulting from oil and gas production are irreparable.[20] Local people's reflections on CSR activities in Utqiaġvik thus provide a viable case study to test the limitations and potential of CSR. Identifying the limitations of CSR is vital to communities' ability to make informed decisions about future community developmental plans.

The next section of this paper examines oil companies' CSR activities in the existing literature. It then follows with the case study of oil companies' CSR activities in the community of Utqiaġvik, Alaska, including the analysis of the interview data. This paper concludes with providing recommendations to oil companies' CSR initiatives in general.

2   Why Does CSR Sometimes Fail to Achieve Its Goals?

A review of the existing literature finds that research on oil companies' CSR activities outside of Alaska under-represents non-business actors' perspectives, such as those of local community members.[21] Kelman and Loe conducted 18 interviews of Hammerfest's residents; they claim that their research was the first to examine local perceptions of the petroleum industry's CSR activities in the Hammerfest area of the Norwegian Arctic.[22] Kelman and Loe discuss the responsibilities that they believe petroleum companies should shoulder on behalf of society and the environment. Their interviews demonstrate that the local population is focused on job creation and economic ripple effects, both decisive in making the community an attractive place to live and work. Thus, petroleum companies' responsibilities are to contribute actively to employment.[23] Kelman and Loe's research is part of a broader, comparative case study, in which they conduct interviews with a view to comparing local perceptions of CSR in Hammerfest, Murmansk, the Nenets Autonomous Okrug (NAO) and the Komi Republic. Their study has explored local, especially non-business,

---

20   See McWilliams and Siegel, note 5, 117–120.
21   Ilan Kelman et al., "Local Perceptions of Corporate Social Responsibility for Arctic Petroleum in the Barents Region," *Arctic Review* 7, no. 2 (2016): 154.
22   Julia SP Loe and Ilan Kelman, "Arctic Petroleum's Community Impacts: Local Perceptions from Hammerfest, Norway," *Energy Research & Social Science*, no. 16 (2016): 25–34.
23   Ibid, 25–34.

perspectives on petroleum development in the Arctic. Interviews show that opinions of CSR varied substantially across and within the case studies and suggest that "those who gain directly from the petroleum industry and do not directly experience negative impacts were more inclined to be positive about the industry," which illustrates what the authors define in this article as the "insider-outsider lens."[24] The term *insiders* refers to those who are close to both the petroleum industry and the accompanying CSR benefits, while *outsiders* refers to those who are far removed from the industry and the benefits. Some cases show that positive economic benefits resulted in greater tolerance of environmental risks. Differential access to information among communities and different levels of trust between people and oil companies cause the "insider-outsider" tension. Their research reveals the importance of understanding local perspectives and shows that successful CSR practices require open-mindedness and willingness to engage in open dialogue with people who are directly affected, as well as those who are indirectly affected by oil activities.[25]

Why do oil and gas corporations increasingly engage in CSR activities? Corporations increasingly engaging in CSR activities in response to social pressure to operate responsibly. Such social pressure has been animated by globalisation, which has placed problems caused by corporations' operational-failures (such as human rights abuses and pollutions) into a broader context.[26] Corporations also engage in CSR activities to address six issue areas: societal legitimacy, which illustrates corporations' willingness to obtain social licenses to operate; public support, which indicates corporations' desire to control public opinions; moral responsibility to local communities; transparency of reporting disclosures as indicated by the Extractive Industries Transparency Initiative (EITI); protection of the environment; and assessment of risk-management concerns.[27]

Corporations have freedoms to pursue CSR in ways that benefit themselves. There is no defined standard for measuring CSR commitment-level. Corporations' actual practices of CSR often deviate from their proposed CSR

---

24   See Kelman et al., note 21, 152.
25   Ibid.
26   Adam Lindgreen and Valérie Swaen, "Corporate Social Responsibility," *International Journal of Management Reviews* 12, no. 1 (2010): 1–7; Aguilera et al., note 19, 836–863; Branco and Rodrigues, note 18, 111–132.
27   Willice O. Abuya, "Mining Conflicts and Corporate Social Responsibility: Titanium Mining in Kwale, Kenya," *The Extractive Industries and Society* 3, no. 2 (2016): 485–493; Benedict Y. Imbun, "The Chinese, Political CSR, and A Nickel Mine in Papua New Guinea," *Routledge* (2017): 57–70.

initiatives. Thus, evaluating CSR performances' impacts on the ground is very important. How well a corporation performs depends a lot on how a local community or society views it.[28] Communities' expectations are contingent and are subject to change at different times and places.[29] In this way, the tensions between corporations and local communities can be accelerated by inadequate CSR activities.

So, why do CSR activities sometimes fail to achieve their purported goals? Researchers have argued that CSR can fail when 1) it is used as mere "window-dressing;" and 2) the micro-level CSR activities fail to adequately address macro-level problems.

Operating within a capitalist market, corporations always tend to prioritise maximising their profits. Thus, they characterise CSR as a form of investment. CSR could thus fail when corporations do not take it seriously and use it as a "window-dressing" tool to placate consumers and their stakeholders.[30] Garipova argues that rather than integrate it as core value, corporations can misuse CSR as a "marketing" tool to greenwash their reputation or images. Greenwashing is defined as companies using CSR deceptively to give the impression that damaging activities in the communities in which they operate are environmentally friendly. Garipova points out that, corporations view CSR as optional, as it does not have the force of law behind it.[31] Mishin also expresses concern about CSR being used as a tool for regulation-dodging purposes. He argues that corporations are now playing key roles in defining CSR policies; therefore, they tend not to consider local people's interests. He suggests that corporations need to participate more actively in CSR and contribute to social wellbeing.[32] Aluchna and Idowu argue that, "practical adoption of CSR cannot be isolated from the company's core strategy," and companies need to reconcile the conflict between social and business goals.[33]

CSR comprises at least two levels, the micro- and macro-levels. Micro-level CSR relates to small-scale projects such as local community education and

---

28 Gabriel Eweje, "Multinational Oil Companies' CSR Initiatives in Nigeria," *Managerial Law* (2007): 218–235.
29 Ibid. See also Marydee Ojala, "Finding Socially Responsible Companies," *Database* 17, no. 5 (1994): 86–89.
30 See McWilliams and Siegel, note 5, 117–127; Keith Slack, "Mission Impossible? Adopting A CSR-Based Business Model for Extractive Industries in Developing Countries." *Resources Policy* 37, no. 2 (2012): 179–184.
31 Leana Garipova, "Corporate Social Responsibility in the Arctic," *Geo. LJ* 104 (2015): 992.
32 Matvey Mishin, "Corporate Social Responsibility of British Petroleum in Azerbaijan," *Lund University* (2013): 7–8.
33 Maria Aluchna, and Samuel O. Idowu, "The Dynamics of Corporate Social Responsibility," *Springer International Publishing* (2017):85.

health projects, and small business developmental projects. Macro-level CSR is more concerned with social development, human rights and good governance.[34] Oil companies' micro-level interventions can produce problems, for instance, because they do not address the macro-level effects of oil production, especially over-dependence on one non-renewable resource. Karl defines this 'resource curse' as 'the inverse relationship between high natural resource dependence and economic growth rates',[35] a phenomenon that often results in public sector corruption, and negative effects on other sectors of the economy. Frynas argues that oil corporations' failure to integrate local initiatives into larger developmental plans limits the potential of CSR.[36] In a similar vein, Odogwu provides suggestions to oil companies that have their operational sites in Nigeria, for improving community relations, including raising mitigation payments to cover the cost of damages from oil drilling activities. He urges oil companies to develop their environmental management capacities and to integrate their community assistance programs in ways that respond to communities' expressed priorities.[37]

Gulbrandsen and Moe identify an additional CSR-related challenge. Oil companies often only perceive a social responsibility towards one community, the "host community," which is located closest to their oil facilities. This ideology causes dissatisfaction and jealousy amongst other communities in the vicinity, which can give rise to intercommunal conflict.[38] Gulbrandsen and Moe provide an example of successful combination of micro-level CSR and macro-level CSR. British Petroleum (BP) has engaged in CSR activities in Azerbaijan since 1997.[39] Azerbaijan has an abundance of oil reserves but suffers from serious governmental corruption. At the micro-level, BP sponsored several community developmental programs during construction of the BTC (Baku-Tbilisi-Ceyhan) pipeline, which carries crude oil through Azerbaijan. The Community Investment Program included providing job opportunities for unemployed people from local communities. This program also provided funding for local communities to build infrastructure such as houses and

---

34 Lars H. Gulbrandsen and Arild Moe, "BP in Azerbaijan: A Test Case of the Potential and Limits of the CSR Agenda?" *Third World Quarterly* 28, no. 4 (2007): 813–830.

35 Terry Lynn Karl, "Understanding the Resource Curse," *Covering Oil: A Guide to Energy and Development* (2005): 23.

36 See Frynas, note 18, 581–598.

37 Emmanuel C. Odogwu, "The Environment and Community Relations: The Shell Petroleum Development Co. of Nigeria Experience," In *SPE Health, Safety and Environment in Oil and Gas Exploration and Production Conference*. Society of Petroleum Engineers (1991).

38 See Gulbrandsen and Moe, note 34, 813–830.

39 Ibid.

clinics. Consequently, local people's quality of life improved. BP also initiated the Future Communities Program, aimed at teaching local community members' skills and means to manage their future developmental plans and projects. BP sent education specialists to Azerbaijan. Explaining this initiative, Gulbrandsen and Moe write, "the community is trained to work out a budget, write a proposal, a procedure plan, project implementation plan, and long-term management plan."[40] This training process has changed community-building fundamentally, because local people had opportunities to learn and use what they have learnt to work independently. This program helps local people build their communities in durable ways. The researchers note with approval that the program represents a "bottom-up" approach to community-level governance of Azerbaijan.[41] BP's macro-level CSR activities were also effective in achieving their goals. BP contributed to local governmental development in the country by providing financial supports and by helping elites.

The reviewed CSR literature suggests that, first, corporations could utilise CSR as a tool to satisfy social needs while making profits. Corporations can gain more profit when they act socially responsibly. In this way, the primary driver of CSR is the business case. Second, CSR can fail when it is used merely as "window-dressing" in marketing campaigns and when its micro-level activities do not address macro-level concerns. The review has also indicated that, too often, oil and gas companies fail to gauge local interests and perspectives, whereas this effort should be perceived as CSR's *sine qua non*.

3 Case Study of Utqiaġvik, Alaska

Utqiaġvik lies on the Chukchi Sea coast at the northern most point of Alaska. It is approximately 350 miles north of the Arctic Circle.[42] It is the largest city of the North Slope Borough and the northernmost city in the United States. The population of Utqiaġvik is approximately 4,900 residents, and the major ethnic group, at 63 percent, is the Inupiaq people.[43] Utqiaġvik has a polar climate with the weather posing challenges to human comfort and safety much

---

40 Ibid.
41 Ibid.
42 Lisa Demer, "Barrow's New Name is Its Old One, Utqiaġvik. Local Iñupiaq Leaders Hope Its Use Heals as It Teaches," *Alaska Dispatch News*, https://www.adn.com/alaska-news/rural-alaska/2016/10/29/barrows-new-name-is-its-old-one-utqiagvik-local-inupiaq-leaders-hope-its-use-heals-as-it-teaches/ (accessed 29 March 2020).
43 "Utqiagvik," *Official Website of the North Slope Borough*, http://www.north-slope.org/our-communities/utqiagvik (accessed 24 July 2020).

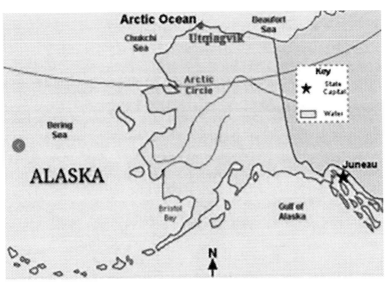

FIGURE 1   Utqiaġvik, Alaska. Derived from: https://www.enchantedlearning.com/usa/states/alaska/map.GIF and has been modified

of the year.[44] While Utqiaġvik is a modern community, many still engage in subsistence activities to feed themselves, their families and the wider Utqiaġvik community, as is their tradition. Their food sources include whale, walrus, seal, fish and caribou, which they harvest along the coast or from coastal waters. The bowhead whale has played and continues to play a central role in Inupiaq life and culture.[45] The National Petroleum Reserve–Alaska surrounds Utqiaġvik with the community lying on the doorstep of offshore oil development. Oil production has affected the local environment, including its flora and fauna. It has altered caribou migration routes, and seismic testing has also affected the lives of the sea mammals such as the bowhead whales.[46] This economic enterprise, therefore, has impacted the subsistence activities of local inhabitants.

3.1   Interview Evidence and Analysis

Interview data for this research was collected during a fieldtrip in the community of Utqiaġvik, Alaska in April 2017 and at the World Eskimo-Indian

[44]   "Summary about Barrow NWS Station," *climate.gi.alaska.edu*, (accessed 1 April 2018).
[45]   "State of Alaska Community Database," https://dcra-cdo-dcced.opendata.arcgis.com/ (accessed 23 July 2020).
[46]   "Cumulative Environmental Effects of Oil and Gas Activities on Alaska's North Slope," *Washington, DC: The National Academies Press* (2003).

Olympic Games (WEIO), which took place at Carlson Center in Fairbanks, Alaska in July 2017. Interview was conducted using the "snowball sampling" method. The 12 respondents, all adults and all participating in the research voluntarily, represented a cross section of ages, genders, and occupations and were either residents of Utqiaġvik or individuals with ties to the community. Most of the interviewees were born and raised in Utqiaġvik even if they now reside elsewhere, and all of them have some knowledge of the oil activities and economic conditions of the area. This sample does not represent all professions, nor does it account for all community perspectives.

The interview protocol comprised both semi-structured and open-ended questions that sought to uncover and explore their thoughts on oil companies' CSR activities. Many respondents were not familiar with the term "CSR". The contents of CSR were explained to the respondents at the beginning of every interview session. This research does not point to a specific oil company's CSR strategy. As according to the respondents, oil companies always tend to work together in the community of Utqiaġvik.

Four central themes emerge from the interview data: interviewees desire 1) improved environmental responsibility, 2) more efficient sharing of information with the community, 3) long-term commitment to the community, and 4) more utilisation of local knowledge, from the oil companies. These four themes strengthen the argument for local people being able to define the nature of CSR activities undertaken by oil companies.

3.2   *Improved Environmental Responsibility*

According to the respondents, the changing flora and fauna of the Arctic makes depending on environment even more tenuous for the locals. Interviewee A, 72-year-old and a long-term resident of Utqiaġvik, said that, "you could not have lived on the slope and not be impacted by the oil." Respondents expressed concerns of oil industry regarding contamination of local environment and food sources, disturbance of subsistence activities, and health issues. They all questioned CSR's ability and effectiveness in protecting local environment and preventing harms.

Interviewee E, who was born and raised in Utqiaġvik, has been working as a whaling captain for more than 30 years. He experiences marine environment's changing patterns and worries about oil activities' disturbance of the marine mammals' lives. Whaling is central to Inupiat lifeways. As a whaling captain, he speaks of his own experience:

> So last year, we went 50 miles from my home, from Utqiaġvik to the Arctic ocean and we didn't see anything, so that was odd, because a few years

before that, I just put my boat in the water, we just start (teasing) hunting whales right there. So last year, we had to go a great distance to see any whales.

He'd like oil companies to eliminate negative effects to the marine mammals and ensure locals' ability to harvest whales. Interviewee D, born in Juneau, Alaska, has lived in Utqiaġvik for 8 years. He expressed his concern that the current CSR agenda on research of whaling and other subsistence activities is insufficient. He believes that oil companies' research teams should encompass the community's subsistence way of living, not only whaling, but other hunting activities too.

Interviewee F, who was born and raised in Anchorage and has family in Utqiaġvik, was an employee for Petro Star Inc.[47] She argues that CSR plays a significant role in preventing harms from oil activities. She also demonstrated her concern over the health issues that Alaskans are experiencing now, such as heart problems and diabetes. According to her argument, oil development has affected the accessibility of traditional food sources. People are having health problems because they are not eating their traditional food. She said, "people may think that it (oil) is just a business, but it is not. It (the Arctic) used to be pristine."

Interviewee E said that he worried about potential oil spills. He also expressed concerns about the well-being of the Arctic ocean. "There's ice in the ocean, sea ice. There (is) no documentary for (cleaning up oil spills), there's nothing that can clean oil out of ice. Especially with the currents out there, an oil spill in Arctic water would be catastrophic. And it could affect the whales, the seals and the fish." For him, the oil companies' first responsibility towards the community of Utqiaġvik is ensuring the protection of the Arctic environment. He said,

> People all come after the profit. Environment is the number one thing that we must guard. Because my father and his father, and his father, they all subsist out of the ocean, we got to keep it at the same level they were able to subsistent. So, (when) an oil spill changed the history of that, we got to stop the oil spill. For the oil companies I would say, you leave how you found ocean, pristine.

Interviewee C, who was born and raised in Utqiaġvik in the 1970s, now works for the village and the regional Alaska Native Claims Settlement Act (ANCSA)

---

47 Petro Star Inc. is the only Alaska owned refining and fuel marketing operation in the state.

corporations for the North Slope in their Anchorage offices. She also questioned about oil companies' capacity to clean up oil spills. She mentioned her concern over cumulative effects. She said:

> I've heard talks about cumulative impacts, and I think when one or two oil companies were coming on, nobody was really thinking about cumulative, and then they didn't really start to think about the series of impacts until oil spill happened.

The cumulative effects, which refer to changes in local environment caused by actions in combination with other past, present and future actions, reinforce the urgency for the oil companies to develop their spill and pollution prevention strategies.[48]

Several respondents expressed concerns and uncertainties regarding offshore oil exploration. Interviewee C, who has worked for the oil companies and the Alaska's Whaling Commission, has seen all the sides of oil development and commented from her unique perspective that oil companies should stay onshore.

3.3 *More Efficient Sharing of Information within the Community*

The sharing of information within the community involves the participation of both oil companies and local community members. According to Interviewee C, oil companies' information-sharing practices are sufficient now. Based on her own experience, she described that within community meetings, BP would outline a project or a schedule and inform any potential impacts generated by oil exploration and extraction activities. Anybody in the community would be welcomed to attend the meetings and review the projects. Community members would be informed of whom to contact when an emergency occurs. Interviewee D, however, emphasised that oil companies did not advertise these meetings well. He said that,

> There needs to be a record of something that says there are all these opportunities to learn about what's going on have been available, so it's really knowing whether they have them available to the communities. And, also marketing it, people don't always know what is going on.

---

48 "Cumulative Effects Assessment Practitioners' Guide," *Canadian Environmental Assessment Agency*, https://www.canada.ca/en/impact-assessment-agency/services/policy-guidance/cumulative-effects-assessment-practitioners-guide.html (accessed 23 July 2020).

According to Interviewee D, oil companies hold community meetings only occasionally. People do not always know the timing of these meetings, as they do not always make efforts to find out. Also, there does not appear to be a clear record or schedule of the meetings or other opportunities for people to learn about oil activities. Interviewee D suggested that oil companies create more thorough and transparent systems of community engagement techniques, for instance, publicising the learning sessions or the time and place of community meetings. When being asked about suggestions for oil companies' CSR, Interviewee D replied:

> We are talking about promotions, just really going out showing or marketing what it is, being able to tell everybody, what's the good, what's the bad, and letting the community really have a survey or something like that, again, that's only to the people who show up, so that's only the people that find that important.

Interviewee D argues that, community members perceive the purpose of CSR to be 'window-dressing' because it involves promotions like gifts. He also argues that community perspectives have little influence because the person in power ultimately makes the decisions. He recommended that oil companies establish a responsible leadership and have a sit-down meeting with other corporations and members of the borough assembly. During the meeting, the participants could discuss a pre-prepared list of questions, so the meeting would be efficient. Interviewee D also recommended the oil companies to establish a radio channel which is responsible for informing the whole community of the oil developmental activities. He said:

> Maybe just having something where people can tune in over the radio, where they are able to submit questions ahead of time and then listen to the responses on the radio. It's a little harder to take all the questions when you haven't seen them right? So, they (the local people) are just trying to make something up on the spot, they are very bland, but if you (the oil companies) give them time to think about what they are wanting to know, then you will expect real answers and full answers. Just giving them something so they can sit down, like we said, or the radio or TV show.

Respondents worry about the unknown future of oil development. Interviewee B emphasised that local people would like to know where oil companies will drill, how deep they are going to drill and how they will clean up oil spills in a timely manner. Interviewee E also mentioned that he would like to learn more about oil companies' long-term developmental plans such as how far they are going to expand their industries on Alaska's North Slope.

3.4 Long-Term Commitment to the Community

According to the respondents, oil companies support the local community by providing employment opportunities, funding higher education and supporting local businesses. According to Interviewee C's experience, oil companies such as BP funds higher education because it is so expensive for students from the North Slope to go to college. BP provides financial assistance for students to go to college. Oil revenue allows the Arctic North Slope Borough to support K-12 education in the region. Interviewee B noted that many community-based businesses are supported by oil companies.

However, oil development has changed residents' traditional values and subsistence lifestyles. Thus, respondents desire oil companies' long-term commitment to the community.

Interviewee A said that, oil industry opened up many employment opportunities. Before the oil companies came, residents lived a mostly subsistence lifestyle. Eventually, Utqiaġvik developed more of a cash economy. Interviewee D expressed concern about the broader and longer-term impacts of oil development to the landscape and to the way of life:

> On the negative side, you question, what are they (the oil companies) actually doing to our land? What are they doing to our animals? So, this problem can never be settled until they either stop doing it (oil development), or they do it so much that cause a huge crisis.

According to Interviewee A, earlier in the 70s, oil companies did very little in terms of meaningful or effective CSR:

> Oil company's money was cheap. They were quick to pour money into stuff, but as far as being associated with Inupiat people, they were not that active. Oil companies would throw money at the community. People would get a case of oranges, a case of apples from them (the oil companies). But they (the oil companies) were not really accepted as part of the community.

Community engagement does not only mean giving residents pay checks and cases of oranges. It includes understanding resident's real, long-term needs. The lack of engagement with local community affects oil companies' reputation and has resulted in a lack of support from the locals.

3.5 Utilisation of Local Knowledge

According to BP's report, recruiting, training and hiring Alaskans remain its top priorities. BP also encourages its contractors to hire Alaskans.[49] But, according to this research, respondents still want the oil companies to utilise more local knowledge. Interviewee A said that, according to his experience, most oil companies' employees have no knowledge of local conditions. Oil companies would thus benefit from hiring more locals who have enough knowledge of local conditions.

> They will come here by helicopters, with their questions and most questions are stupid. These people know nothing, so you try to explain our lifestyle and try to explain the country to them. Little simple things like, I can tell the difference between freshwater ice and saltwater ice. But you just flew a guy from Texas on a helicopter, he had no idea if he's looking at freshwater ice or from the ocean. So, you just teach them things, simple facts that made life easy to survive.

Interviewee F also expressed her concern over corruption. She indicates that oil companies need to run transparent operation to avoid corruption. According to Swaen and Lindgreen, to improve company morale and fulfill their CSR, companies should provide equal opportunities for all their employees.[50] When asked for suggestions regarding oil companies' CSR activities, Interviewee F suggested that oil companies, indigenous people, and environmental scientists should all work together to protect the long-term sustainability and quality of life in the North Slope region. She argues that CSR activities could contribute to the future development of the oil companies themselves, their shareholders, their business partners such as Native corporations, and local people from the communities where they operate.

Overall, the interview data demonstrates the main concerns from the community members of Utqiaġvik over oil companies' CSR activities in the aspects of environmental protection, information-sharing techniques, long-term community developmental plans, and utilisation of local knowledge. The interview evidence speaks to the existing CSR literature in that it demonstrates that current CSR strategies are falling short in addressing local needs. The interview

---

49 "BP Alaska Hire, 2016," *BP Exploration (Alaska), Alaska Press Office*, https://www.bp.com/content/dam/bp/country-sites/en_us/united-states/home/documents/careers/alaska-hire-report-2017.pdf (accessed 23 July 2020).
50 See Lindgreen and Swaen, note 26, 1–7.

data also suggests that other than defining and operating CSR initiatives from oil companies' perspectives, local people should realise that they need to express their concerns if they are worrying about their communities' future, and that they should be able to influence the types of CSR activities corporations pursue, given that they experience the local impacts of the industry.

4 Conclusions

Relying upon data collected from interviews with local members of Utqiaġvik, this paper has argued that CSR measures related to oil industry extractive activities on the North Slope of Alaska ought to be dictated by residents whose lives are impacted by that industry. This paper has sought to address 1) how the people of Utqiaġvik have responded to the CSR activities, presently defined, of nearby oil companies; and 2) how and why CSR has sometimes failed to achieve its purported goals.

Regarding the first question, respondents' reflections indicated that they were pleased with the job opportunities and their dividends and the financial support the oil companies have provided for education. But they also demonstrated concerns regarding oil company's CSR activities in Utqiaġvik. Some broad concerns among the residents over oil companies' CSR strategies include: 1) limited risk management capacities of potential environmental problems such as oil spills, 2) insufficient sharing of information at community meetings regarding oil activities and oil impacts, 3) insufficient long-term commitment to the community and 4) insufficient utilisation of local knowledge.

Regarding the second question, the analysis reflects that the current CSR activities have been insufficient in meeting local people's needs, in particular with regard to safeguarding the environment upon which the traditional culture and indigenous lifeways depend. This may be partly because of local people's voices have not been sufficiently sought out. The paper's analysis has reinforced its argument: oil company's CSR activities, when overly determined by its profit motive, tend to restrict the potential of its CSR obligations. Further, the paper has suggested that residents should be able to define for themselves relevant and appropriate CSR activities given that they experience the local impacts of the resource extraction industry.

Drawing upon Utqiaġvik's circumstances and respondents' perspectives, this paper makes the following general policy recommendations to all oil companies to examine and address the limitations of their presently defined CSR obligations among the communities of Alaska's North Slope region.

First, oil companies need to improve their safety standards and develop their risk-management approaches. Oil companies need to conduct more research on the local ecological conditions of the region where they operate, including land conditions, marine environment, flora and fauna, and on the impacts of oil exploration and extraction activities. The Arctic environment is vulnerable, especially considering the changing climate. Moreover, according to the respondents, offshore oil drilling could harm the well-being of marine mammals. For instance, whale migration patterns have been affected by oil industries. Whaling plays a key role among all the subsistence activities in Utqiaġvik. Therefore, it is essential for oil companies to conduct more research on the local environment.

Second, oil companies need to inform local people of their oil developmental plans and the potential impacts through improved communication techniques such as broadcasting information through the local radio stations and holding more organised community meetings. As Interviewee D mentioned, a radio program can serve as a tool for oil company to broadcast information. Moreover, as Interviewee C suggested, oil companies' leadership ought to present in community meetings to promote greater transparency, and to encourage greater public participation.

Third, oil companies need to demonstrate long-term commitment to local communities and utilise local knowledge. As Interviewee A indicated, oil workers who came from other states other than Alaska have limited knowledge of the local environmental and local ecological conditions. Hiring local employees helps oil companies better understand local environment and ease their operations. Treating them equitably improves employee morale. Oil companies ought to listen to local people's voices and formally incorporate their perspectives into the companies' decision-making processes regarding CSR initiatives.

These recommendations rest on the remarks of respondents. Oil companies should realise the importance to improve their CSR practices, and continue to contribute to local communities' environmental, economic and social well-beings. This paper suggests that CSR can fail if oil companies only focus on generating profits and ignore local people's needs. Oil companies cannot determine the success and failure of CSR only by themselves, as CSR ties closely to the local communities where oil companies operate.

Future studies should focus on exploring relations between oil companies and local communities, in regard to oil companies' CSR activities. More broad-based, comparative case studies would shed further light on the potential and limitations of CSR activities. Comparative case studies of the effectiveness of oil industries' CSR activities in other regions of the world would be especially enlightening.

Polar Comparisons

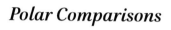

Ethics of Observation in the Polar Regions

*Alexandra L. Carleton**

Abstract

Whilst satellite observations over the Polar Regions yield vastly beneficial scientific knowledge, ethical questions complicate their use in the context of the Polar Regions, in particular, questions about military or strategic advantage vis-à-vis human security concerns. The Antarctic Treaty System is committed to use of its space for peaceful purposes which, in the fulfilment of high-level science, seems plausible. Yet where military endeavour is coupled with such scientific endeavour, or where global security concerns seek an entrée to the knowledge acquired by such observation, the question of whether either Pole can remain free from human non-peaceful purpose is bedevilling.

Keywords

satellite surveillance – polar – ethics – peaceful use – military

1   Introduction

The positioning of satellites over the Arctic and Antarctic gives rise to extended national surveillance capability. Ethical considerations in the use of data gained from observation using platforms in the Arctic and Antarctic include questions around privacy and military purpose. Data received from satellites retain possible uses extending to predictive capabilities in relation to disease outbreak, monitoring conflict zones, tracking illegal conduct, as well as the use of espionage for national security interests. All this regardless of the territorial jurisdictional complications which may hinder collaborative effort as regards terrestrially-bound resources.

---

*   Independent researcher. alexandracarleton@gmail.com.

This paper examines the ethical issues surrounding surveillance and the collection of data at the Poles. The first part of this paper examines the use of the polar skies and spaces for observation, followed by consequent ethical issues surrounding such use. Once infrastructure and data is located then come the questions of access and ownership rights, complicated in spaces where jurisdiction is compromised. Finally, the paper mentions briefly those factors needing to be considered in governance.

2 Earth Observation Stations in the Polar Wilderness

2.1 *Where Are They? Who Are They?*

Earth stations in the Arctic include Svalbard satelittstasjon (Svalsat) in Spitsbergen, Svalbard. In Antarctica there is Troll satelittstasjon (TrollSat) in Queen Maud Land, owned and operated jointly by the Norwegian Space Centre and Kongsberg Defence Systems (KDS), the latter one of four wholly owned subsidiaries of Kongsberg Gruppen, an Oslo Stock Exchange (OSE) listed company. The Government of Norway controls half the company, the next major shareholder being Arendals Fossekompani ASA who controls 7.96%.[1] Four satellites use Trollsat: RADAR (Canadian), GeoEye and Worldview (both American and listed on the NYE[2]), and Galileo (EU). China also has a new satellite over Antarctica.[3] Additionally, there are numerous non-Polar land-based relay sites and non-territorially based satellite observation systems that do not use the Polar-located earth stations but still pass through the space above Polar territory, such as the American DSCS-3 B7 satellite which maintains a geosynchronous orbit.

---

1 According to website 4-traders, http://www.4-traders.com/KONGSBERG-GRUPPEN-AS-1413189/company/ (accessed 1 September 2017).

2 At end June 2017, the companies have 223 institutional equity holders and 310 fund owners, thus fracturing ownership. The largest investor is institutional player T. Rowe Price Associates Inc with 14.14% ownership. Together with their affiliate fund T. Rowe Price Mid-Cap Growth which has 7.22%, the group control 21.36%. The second player is Dimensional Fund Advisers Inc whose institutional arm has 8.45% and fund, DFA US Small Cap Value II has 3.76% thus making a total of 12.21%. Third on the list is institution Vanguard Group Inc with 7.90% and fund Vanguard Small Cap Index with 2.3%, total 10.1%. Institution Shapiro Capital Management Co Inc has 6.46%. These companies combined control 50.13% of the company, giving American enterprise majority ownership. Data was obtained from Morningstar, found at http://morningstar.com.au (accessed 1 September 2017).

3 Andrew Darby, 'China's Antarctica satellite base plans spark concerns', November 12 2014, *The Sydney Morning Herald*, https://www.smh.com.au/world/chinas-antarctica-satellite-base-plans-spark-concerns-20141112-11l3wx.html (accessed 17 December 2019).

2.2 Observation in Antarctica and the Arctic

The 1959 Antarctic Treaty[4] allows for aerial observation which may include that conducted from within the biosphere and also, arguably, within the stratosphere. It states: 'Aerial observation may be carried out at any time over any or all areas of Antarctica by any of the Contracting Parties having the right to designate observers' (Article VII (4)). Within the context of Antarctica there is a direct clash of interests or concerns where the use of satellites can infringe international or national restrictions on data collection for military use and whether and to what extent this would compromise Article 1(1) of the Antarctic Treaty whereby 'Antarctica shall be used for peaceful purposes only. There shall be prohibited, inter alia, any measures of a military nature, such as the establishment of military bases and fortifications, the carrying out of military maneuvers [sic], as well as the testing of any type of weapons' (Article 1 (1)). As a treaty-based governance region, Antarctica is under the stewardship of the Parties to the treaty. Under the Antarctic Treaty, prior claims to territorial sovereignty in Antarctica are not affected by the treaty (Article IV (1) (a)), and sovereign claims have been effectively frozen.[5]

The mandate of the Arctic Council is founded on international consensus pertaining to the environmental stewardship and sustainable development of the Arctic Region. It makes mandatory certain involvements for observer-states and indigenous peoples. As a broad framework for inclusion in Arctic affairs it has so far served its purpose well, given the high-level diplomatic eye that has fallen on the Arctic Circle Assembly.[6] The Agreement[7] itself excludes the general area of observation: firstly specifically excluding the Arctic Council from dealing with matters related to military security (in footnote 1 of the Agreement); and secondly in making no *specific* provision for meteorological or other forms of observation and data collection, however much it may fall under the general environmental direction of the Agreement.

Polar observation for scientific benefit, whether to understand climate change[8] or ice-shelf alterations,[9] is known. What of the considerations for

---

4 Antarctic Treaty, 402 *United Nations Treaty Series* 71, entered into force 23 June 1961.
5 Christy Collis, "Territories beyond possession? Antarctica and Outer Space" *The Polar Journal* 7 (2017): 287–302, DOI: 10.1080/2154896X.2017.1373912.
6 In 2016 both Nicola Sturgeon, First Minister of Scotland, and Ban Ki Moon, Secretary-General of the United Nations, were present.
7 *Declaration on the Establishment of the Arctic Council* (Ottawa, Canada, 1996).
8 Jan Lenaerts et al, "Polar clouds and radiation in satellite observations, reanalyses, and climate models" *Geophysical Research Letters* 44 (2016): 3355–3364, DOI: 10.1002/2016GL072242.
9 JA Griggs and JL Bamber, "Antarctic ice-shelf thickness from satellite radar altimetry" *Journal of Glaciology* 57 (2011): 485–498.

unethical use of observation? The 2017 Arctic Circle Assembly gave a clear direction in favour of 'observation' becoming a pivotal role for the Arctic Council of the future.[10] This role is not unexpected. Since the 1980s many of the United Nations (UN) agencies have advertised their use of satellite data to aide in their work. In particular, the World Meteorological Organisation (WMO) are playing an ever-increasing role in the collection of satellite data or observation data and policy development. The ease with which observation is included as part of the geopolitical framework in the Arctic serves as a stark contrast to that in Antarctica, although the latter has its own observation allowances.[11] The Poles' capabilities and usage are similar in many respects, but the geopolitical framework and the movement of the players in the Arctic appear much more transparent.

3 Pros and Cons of Observing

3.1 *Privacy*

Far-reaching capability of surveillance at the Poles has implications for privacy and breaches of privacy, not simply of the individual but also of the nation. Espionage, as an act of collecting information through deception or disguise, is historically attributable to an individual.[12] Insofar as this is the definition, espionage then is the theft of information about a nation by a disguised individual. It is the severest form of invasion of national privacy short of physical infiltration. Deeks[13] posited the idea that an infringement on privacy occurs at the point of observation by a human[14] rather than at the time of any computer processing or collating. In the sense of simple data about an individual perhaps this definition is easier to apply. In the case of national privacy (or

---

10   In particular the session entitled, "Observing and Responding to a Changing Arctic" found at http://www.arcticcircle.org/assemblies/2017/program-news (accessed 1 September 2017).

11   As stated by Tony Press, former head of the Australian Antarctic Division, 'any party has complete freedom to access all parts of Antarctica at any time to inspect ships, aircraft, equipment, or any other facility, and even use "aerial observations" for inspection.' In Tony Press, "Australia wants to install military technology in Antarctica – here's why that's allowed", 23 August 2019, *The Conversation* http://theconversation.com/australia-wants-to-install-military-technology-in-antarctica-heres-why-thats-allowed-122122 (accessed 17 December 2019).

12   Ashley Deeks, "An International Legal Framework for Surveillance" *Virginia Journal of International Law* 55 (2015): 291–368, 298–300.

13   Ibid, 357.

14   Ibid.

security), applying the same standard so cleanly is difficult. There is a tentative alignment insofar as the infringement occurs by an individual observing or collecting information 'undercover'. Crafting the idea broadly in this way, the new infiltration of information in the technology age is still capable of falling within a definition of espionage.

The laws around espionage are the founding basis upon which the more politically digestible idea of allowable invasion of privacy for the purposes of ensuring the greater security of the nation and globe are premised. A quick perusal of the international accords in relation to setting some standard or ethical framework around observation of humans by states reveals the pre-eminence of the human rights concerns around privacy, embedded in Article 17 of the International Covenant on Civil and Political Rights (ICCPR).[15] Interestingly, the codification of non-military means of use in the Antarctic Treaty would also lend a hand to the preference for privacy, albeit via the back door. Conversely, Article 17 of the ICCPR may inherently lend support to the non-invasive use of data collection, that is, by limiting it to scientific use. But this is unlikely.

More likely, is the unravelling of protections to privacy,[16] particularly in Antarctica, where the territorial claims are yet to be confirmed. Access to and control over land and the natural resources embedded in or existing within the land, significantly alters notions of 'sovereignty', though the notion of the sovereign is mostly tied to the mechanism which controls the geographical boundedness of territory.[17] (This leaves aside altered forms of sovereignty that come about when self-determination is sought absent of a current territorial nexus, as it may in a migrated or displaced diaspora.) How much such national observation impedes the privacy of other nations and their nationals and how much such actions to collect information can be construed as invasion of a new variety, remains open for discussion.

In the context of data collected from Polar stations, ownership can be at once the domain of the satellite owner, the image owner, the image subject, the earth station, or the owner of the air spaces through which the data travels.

---

15   UN General Assembly, International Covenant on Civil and Political Rights, 16 December 1966, 999 *United Nations Treaty Series* 171, available at: https://www.refworld.org/docid/3ae6b3aa0.html (accessed 20 March 2020).

16   Courtney Walsh, "Surveillance Technology and the Loss of Something A Lot Like Privacy: An Examination of the 'Mosaic Theory' and the Limits of the Fourth Amendment", 24 *St. Thomas L. Rev* (2012): 169.

17   Montevideo Convention on Rights and Duties of States, opened for signature 26 December 1933, entered into force 26 December 1934, 165 *League of Nations Treaty Series* 19.

An invasion/infringement of privacy then, could here be distinct – infringements on privacy occurring in human interaction with the data – from theft, depending on who is deemed the effective owner of the data. Privacy, both of a personal variety and national, can now take place extra-territorially, so that data collected by the voyeur do not penetrate physically the boundaries of another state.[18] Systems of sharing communications networks has meant a more extensive ability to monitor larger numbers of people, yet despite the new political pressure to find balance between privacy and national security,[19] there is not likely to be a willingness to even discuss this since there is no actual violation or physical infringement that occurs.

Moreover, where the territorially unrestricted area of Antarctica is used for such purposes, there is no jurisdictional mandate to resolve any disagreement. This is new ground perhaps. Grounds for basing complaints of unlawful interference are weak where physical actions within foreign borders are no longer a necessary requirement for collecting information. An examination of sovereignty over space may be useful, in that space, as a whole, is not inhabited physically by any nation. Whereas the property that enters the territory of space (for example, a satellite) may be owned. But the jurisdiction of space itself is part of the common domain. There is an argument for an extraterritorial right to privacy.[20] It remains undecided whether territorial integrity is violated if interception of data packets occurs without entering foreign jurisdiction.[21]

To use the example of an image of a corn field: The image is taken by a satellite owned by GeoEye and relayed to Troll in Queen Maud Land, Antarctica. The satellite is owned by majority US equity stakeholders, the earth station by Norway, and the land of the earth station contentiously by Norway. The image at once could be owned by several players depending on the specific purpose and use of the data perhaps. If we take Deeks' definition that an infringement of privacy (privacy violation) is considered the point at which information is exposed to human observation rather than collated, copied or processed by a computer,[22] then the likelihood for several infringements in several locations is high depending of the distribution of the data packet. What if the image is accompanied by data whose collection was made possible by remotely positioned cameras? Or where national privacy laws of the nation where the corn field lies dictates all images belong to the government?

---

18 See Deeks, note 11.
19 Ibid, 316–318.
20 Ibid, 306.
21 Ibid, 305.
22 Ibid, 357.

Ethical dilemmas resulting from unknown intrusions sit with those who do the observing.[23] The lack of knowledge by a subject or owner of, for example, a field brings to the fore the question of whether an infringement actually took place. Is privacy violated when the human factor partakes in observation? Or can it involve the collection and storage of data by computers only with the stored potential of being humanly observed? Perhaps it could be said that an invasion of privacy (ethically speaking) is only one where it is known (otherwise there are potential invasions of privacy all the time).[24] Which brings the world of espionage closer to that of privacy infringements and, in so doing, somewhat lessens the gravity of the offence of espionage. Given that technology can breach jurisdictional boundaries without physical breach, that technology is widespread, and that the individual is taken out of the equation more and more (through computer systems and teams of people utilising the information), the world of espionage is almost a thing of the past. Or, it has entered a new age, where national agricultural and mineral production, technological development and energy advances are more easily discoverable. In a world increasingly homogenised, with lowered resilience and less territory to buffer our ever-expanding population, perhaps this is a good thing. Perhaps the accurate question or standard is to ask to what extent an invasion of privacy threatens *global* security? That is, can we apply a public purpose test? Standards for espionage, if developed, could indicate a preference for finding jurisdiction over a violation of privacy where a) use of data transits locally, irrespective of source of data package; b) the violation is necessary and proportionate to the end, as under the ICCPR and incorporated into European Court of Human Rights (ECtHR) standards;[25] or c) there is a spatial model of jurisdiction which relies on an effective control test.

---

[23] Bender, The Fourth Amendment in the Age of Aerial Surveillance: Curtains for the Curtilage?, 60 *N.Y.U. L. Rev.* (1985): 725.

[24] In arguing for a tort of invasion of privacy, four different models are mentioned, all which involve the action of the invader: "unreasonable intrusion upon the seclusion of another, public disclosure of private facts, displaying another in a false light before the public, and appropriation of another's name or likeness". See Des Butler, "A Tort of Invasion of Privacy in Australia" *Melbourne University Law Review* 11 (2005): 339.

[25] Juliane Kokott and Christoph Sobotta, "The distinction between privacy and data protection in the jurisprudence of the CJEU and the ECtHR" *International Data Privacy Law*, 3 (2013): 222–228. The principles of necessary and proportionate formed the basis of 13 principles agreed by the International Principles on the Application of Human Rights to Communications Surveillance; discussed in Electronic Frontier Foundation, "Necessary and Proportionate International Principles on the Application of Human Rights to Communications Surveillance", *Electronic Frontier Foundation*, May 2014.

Our approach to data security and/or privacy needs a new level of nuance. In particular in relation to the subject of surveillance versus the point of observation versus the point of collection/storage. The real issue is whether invasion of national privacy is a concern in disrupting collaborative efforts which are important, for example with the emerging trans-border health surveillance.

With the use of the Polar Regions, collaborative endeavours and space and the unfinished debate around jurisdiction, it appears trite to begin examination of data surveillance and question standards of privacy as a human right. Particularly, when it involves military surveillance for national security or global security. Furthermore, whether surveillance threatens privacy but has no direct effect on a subject's life until the point of actual physical act or cyber-restraint or even perhaps knowledge by the subject, (emotional impact as well) adds another dimension to infringement. The threat would be either established upon knowledge or as a matter of fact, particularly where individual action, aggregated or otherwise to collective action, may in even 'lesser' situations pose direct threats to security.

Ethical decision-making in the collection and dissemination of data ought not to be exclusively either normative or utilitarian, but rather needs to balance the competing demands of the individual, the nation and the greater good, and even then each of these is defined differently in different contexts. In the case where a choice of ethical matrix must be preferred, ethics must take more than a normative stance and rather begin to look at the greater good.[26] With the emergence of new pathogens and the growing body of evidence that pathogeneses may be affected by increased activity in previously frozen parts of the planet, collaboration is not an option for consensus-building, nor is it a choice. It is essential. The underlying question addressed here is what balance between national security/ownership over components of the satellite network and the need for global consensus will be tolerated politically? More specifically, how do we build global consensus while respecting changing issues of sovereignty?

3.2   Global Goods

There is an emerging group of concerns which demand international collaboration and demonstrate the importance of consensus. Local to global monitoring

---

https://www.ohchr.org/Documents/Issues/Privacy/ElectronicFrontierFoundation.pdf [accessed 18 December 2019].

26   Greater goods may include those described as legitimate aims by Kokott and Sobotta, "interests of national security, public safety, the economic well-being of the country, the prevention of disorder or crime, the protection of health or morals, and the protection of the rights and freedoms of others"; Kokott & Sobotta, note 23, 224.

that is being built upon is important for this mapping. The sweeping scale of preventive measures that can be installed through accurate satellite observation/interpretation and associated radar telemetry, in relation to disease and conflict, biosecurity and natural disasters, is massive.

Increased role of cyber-tools in the functioning of society[27] may meet the burden of a concurrent rise in genetic drift and pathogenic virulence and resilience.[28] Real-time data on clustering and prevalence of epidemics is a fair reason to approve of potentially invasive observation efforts at the Poles of the world. Within the context of abstract theories on ethics, it not only satisfies utilitarian thought but also satisfies virtue ethics where the action taken is both out of and with respect for human dignity or for the moral good, despite temptations to act otherwise.[29] The same could be said for other scenarios including conflict, mapping efforts of the exploration and exploitation of mineral and other natural resource tenements, tracking shipping movements, identifying breaches of the international laws of the sea, and meteorological and climate change phenomena including melting ice caps.

The relevance of satellite geodesy, the collection and storage of cartographic data, mapping of natural resources and terrain modelling has been an active part of many United Nations organs for a number of decades.[30] In 1992, the same time as the Convention of Biological Diversity was gaining its greatest momentum, it was noted that long-term satellite surveillance was essential for both understanding the complexity of climate variation and the loss of ecosystem space due to human activity and pressure of population growth.[31]

3.3 Search and Rescue

Drones are used in the Arctic and the Antarctic, and their usage will likely increase, particularly as a non-invasive method of observation in response to shipping disasters and search and rescue, areas which are of increasing interest.[32] The question of ethics regarding an invasion of national and individual

---

27 Myriam Dunn Cavelty and Andreas Wenger, "Cyber security meets security politics: Complex technology, fragmented politics, and networked science" *Contemporary Security Policy* 41 (2020): 5–32, 15.
28 DA Kennedy and G Dwyer, "Effects of multiple sources of genetic drift on pathogen variation within hosts" *PLOS Biology* 16 (2018): DOI: 10.1371/journal.pbio.2004444.
29 RB Louden, "Kant's Virtue Ethics" *Philosophy* 61 (1986): 473–489.
30 These uses were noted in the 5th UN Regional Cartographic Conference 11–15 January 1993, New York. Noted in *Update: Science and Technology for Development*, 51, Spring 1993.
31 "Tracking the Ebb and Flow of Life on Earth", *Update: Science and Technology for Development*, 50, Summer 1992.
32 Draft proposal for a Ministerial Declaration on Oil and Gas Exploitation in the Arctic. 2008 Arctic Monitoring and Assessment Programme (AMAP) submitted to Senior Arctic

security is by far a narrower ethical issue in the field of polar observation than the broader functional ethical concern around the spread of disease, the need for trade monitoring and biosecurity.[33] Going forward, governance on these more expansive questions are at the very least equally as important to global security as the international/national sovereign divide. This is because the threat to our functional ecosystems, the role that biodiversity plays and the existence of dynamic equilibrium is crucial to a healthy living relationship of human, animal and environment; it is a planetary concern.[34] This is the crucial aspect that needs to be recognised in management and collaboration in resolving disputes at the Poles into the twenty-first century.

Officials (SAOs) at the Arctic Council's SAO Meeting, 19–20 November 2008, Kautokeino, Norway, AC-SAO-NOV08-3.3b; Agreement on Cooperation on Aeronautical and Maritime Search and Rescue in the Arctic. Nuuk, 2011. The Government of Canada, the Government of the Kingdom of Denmark, the Government of the Republic of Finland, the Government of Iceland, the Government of the Kingdom of Norway, the Government of the Russian Federation, the Government of the Kingdom of Sweden, and the Government of the United States of America, hereinafter referred to as "the Parties" https://oaarchive.arctic-council.org/handle/11374/531. The Fairbanks Declaration welcomed "the operational exercises that have advanced the implementation of the Agreement on Cooperation on Aeronautical and Maritime Search and Rescue in the Arctic, as well as cooperation through the Arctic Coast Guard Forum, and request continued actions within the framework of that Agreement to promote regional capability and readiness. In relation to Antarctica see general considerations in D Leary, "Drones on ice: an assessment of the legal implications of the use of unmanned aerial vehicles in scientific research and by the tourist industry in Antarctica", *Polar Record*, 53 (2017): 343–357; C Watson, "This week at Davis: 7 September 2018", Australian Antarctic Division, at https://www.antarctica.gov.au/news/stations/davis/2018/this-week-at-davis-7-september-2018/ (accessed 4 June 2020).

33 Surveillance also gives ability to tracking geomorphological changes and land alterations as well as climatic data, which can aid in the forecast of Polar Regions to disease and ecotoxicological events. Similarly, the prevalence of disease epizootics threatening food sources and environment, may give impetus to the use of agrometeorological and hydrological tele-medicine, already used in remote places for vulnerable populations. See World Health Organization, "Emerging Zoonoses" https://www.who.int/zoonoses/emerging_zoonoses/en/ [accessed 18 December 2019]; RS Ostfeld, "Biodiversity loss and the rise of zoonotic pathogens" *Clinical Microbiology and Infection* (2009): 15 Suppl 1:40–3. DOI: 10.1111/j.1469-0691.2008.02691.x. CO Bagayoko, H Müller and A Geissbuhler, "Assessment of Internet-based tele-medicine in Africa (the RAFT project)" *Computerized Medical Imaging and Graphics* 30 (2006):407–416.

34 PA Sandifer, AE Sutton-Grier and BP Ward, "Exploring connections among nature, biodiversity, ecosystem services, and human health and well-being: Opportunities to enhance health and biodiversity conservation", *Ecosystem Services* 12 (2015): 1–15, https://doi.org/10.1016/j.ecoser.2014.12.007; Cf RS DeFries, JA Foley and GP Asner, "Land-use choices: balancing human needs and ecosystem function" *Frontiers in Ecology and the Environment* 2 (2004): 249–257.

3.4 Bones of Contention

Ethical observation conflates national security concerns, international collaboration and individual privacy rights. Which aspect takes precedence in a situation is a question of functional or utilitarian ethics. The jurisprudential query meandering in the shallows of this ethics question is whether and how equity entitlements or ownership over both the infrastructure of cyberspace and the abstract information floating through such infrastructure, alters the sovereign landscape. Access and control over the resource and the associated interplay of political sovereignty are the hallmarks of international relations. Collaboration has been pragmatically ensured through the evolution of international organisations, though where collaboration requires a softening of sovereignty, the process of consensus is only achieved through the sovereign retaining individual power. How fractured ownership over the same infrastructure will affect sovereignty appears to have been conveniently forgotten, in particular ownership over *data* given the international collaborative effort utilised to receive, store and retrieve it. Ownership over data either alters terrestrial sovereign entitlement or creates multiple overlapping interests where data 'occupies' the same space as land. Non-Polar land-based relay sites add a further layer of contention according to whether ownership of the data arises at the point of collection, aggregation, dissemination or human observation. Scholarship has suggested it is the latter[35] which means that control of information flow remains in the hands of the receiving station.

One aspect of sovereignty is the use of the military to secure national interest.[36] Involvement of the military in situations of epidemiological concern, for example, may be expected given the technological advantage offered by military capability and the fact that the Antarctic Treaty System (ATS) and the Arctic accords do not strictly restrict the presence of the military or military personnel. Military involvement may not necessarily breach the requirement for peaceful purpose under the Antarctic Treaty, particularly when paired with scientific research. It is possible that military involvement in the Polar Regions will not be synonymous with the protection of national security interests. Where military security may be understood more broadly as that which relates

---

35 Deeks, note 11. Deeks suggests it is the point of human observation which becomes the point of an infringement of privacy which could indicate the point of ownership, though this is contentious.

36 "As national security becomes defined as much by law as politics, the military will assume an increasing role in law enforcement, particularly overseas": Christopher Donesa, "Protecting National Interests: The Legal Status of Extraterritorial Law Enforcement by The Military." *Duke Law Journal*, 41 (1992): 867–906.

to a protection mandate (Mazzone[37] refers to it in the USA constitution as the Protection Clause) then the idea of military involvement at the Poles serves a general protection ideal. Alternatively, military security can be considered as a constitutional prerogative. However neither treaty – the Antarctic Treaty or the Ottawa Declaration establishing the Arctic Council – have the mandate to deal with issues of military security and it may prove difficult to enforce a mandate to govern Polar territory when there is no effective mandate to either adjudge military involvement or independently defend that territory. Both the Arctic and Antarctic governance bodies suffer from Member governments' reluctance "to contribute to the costs of defending other states although the cost of an attack is not geographically confined."[38] Additionally, without the ability to develop a greater security role, these international bodies may never be considered with sufficient weight. Without taking the national domain of security away from nations, the international Polar bodies run less risk of being sidelined. The Arctic Council for example, in focusing on the scientific and traditional access rights issues, runs the risk of becoming politically irrelevant at such time as exploration and private commercial interests take the ear of government. Restrictions on military access would be difficult to uphold where disguised by scientific purpose. It may mean the Antarctic Treaty System (ATS)[39] Consultative Meeting and the Arctic Council develop profiles as environmental inter-government stewards and in this more neutral position develop into a pseudo judicial body able to start developing a set of constitutional principles.

---

[37] Jason Mazzone, "The Security Constitution", *UCLA Law Review* 53 (2005), Brooklyn Law School, Legal Studies Paper No. 32.

[38] Ibid, 36.

[39] The Antarctic Treaty System includes: Conference on Antarctica Final Act, 1 December 1959; The Antarctic Treaty, 402 U.N.T.S. 71, entered into force June 23, 1961; Final Act of the Eleventh Antarctic Treaty Special Consultative Meeting, November 1991; Protocol on Environmental Protection to the Antarctic Treaty, signed October 4, 1991 and entered into force in 1998, including Annexes I: Environmental Impact Assessment, II: Conservation of Antarctic Fauna and Flora, III: Waste Disposal and Waste Management, IV: Prevention of Marine Pollution, V: Area Protection and Management and VI: Liability Arising from Environmental Emergencies (not in force); Final Act of the Conference on the Conservation of Antarctic Marine Living Resources; Convention on the Conservation of Antarctic Marine Living Resources (1980) (CCAMLR); Convention for the Conservation of Antarctic Seals (1972); Special Permits for the Killing or Capturing of Seals; Headquarters Agreement for the Secretariat of the Antarctic Treaty; Staff Regulations for the Secretariat of the Antarctic Treaty; Financial Regulations for the Secretariat of the Antarctic Treaty; and Measure 1 (2003): Secretariat of the Antarctic Treaty. There are also special rules of procedure. See "Key Documents of the Antarctic Treaty System", Secretariat of the Antarctic Treaty, https://www.ats.aq/e/key-documents.html.

The omission from both mandates may in time question the role of governor or government and add another divergence in the broader question of what the sovereign is and what the fundamental entitlements of the sovereign are which continue to pervade the discourse and judicial decisions on international law.[40] Yet, leaving the military question to one side has strategic advantage for all players. Given the dearth of case law delineating 'military purpose', perhaps the Polar Regions will escape the arms race which has taken most of the world in its arms in various guises.[41] Excluding military security from the purview of both the Antarctic and Arctic Governance regimes may work to strengthen the relevance of the international collaborative and diplomatic bodies in existence. Although, military presence at either Pole may become a great distraction from more important concerns such as monitoring disease prevalence or trans-border pollution.

4   Governance of the Observation Paradigm: the Way Through

4.1   *International Organisations and Collective Responsibility*

Beyond the normative question about the use of any observations collected in those regions of the world where clearer skies predominate, and leaving aside the abuse of those collections for mutual espionage, there is a greater ethical question supplanting these other more obvious ones: the framework for consensus and the reality of sovereign respect.

Consensus building is a method used to facilitate agreement.[42] International consensus-building on the role of satellite remote observation has been underway for a number of decades.[43] Indeed the presence of satellites could be considered a driver behind both the implementation and due regard given to consensus-building as a major tool of international treaty negotiation, the very nature of its geosynchronous orbit a strong motivation to ensuring space exploration and international space treaties emphasise the peaceful purposes of

---

40   *Obligations concerning Negotiations relating to Cessation of the Nuclear Arms Race and to Nuclear Disarmament, Marshall Islands v United Kingdom*, Preliminary Objections, ICGJ 500 (ICJ 2016), 5th October 2016, International Court of Justice [ICJ].
41   From SALW (small arms and light weapons) to NNP (nuclear non-proliferation) treaties.
42   Eilen Gallway, "Consensus as a Basis for International Space Cooperation" 20 *Proc. on L. Outer Space* 20 (1977): 105, 111.
43   "Moscow Conversion Conference Explores New Directions for Aerospace Industry", 12–17 October, recorded in Update: Science and Technology for Development, No. 51, Spring 1993. This conference discussed the possibilities of converting military aerospace technology to civilian use.

space.[44] In a sense satellites and consensus-building go hand-in-hand. It is in the practical implementation of local-to-global that observation ethics come into their own. International bodies, set up as a demonstrable attempt at international collaboration and responsible for data collection, work in sync with local groups organised for monitoring and practical implementation of the global order.

The World Meteorological Organisation (WMO) is the international organ with responsibility for the oversight of data collection and aggregation.[45] The types of data likely to be collected under the auspices of the WMO would be many and varied and perhaps the existence of such a body may mean a better regulation of surveillance systems. Their function in the future would likely intersect with that of the International Telecommunications Union (ITU) and, possibly the International Atomic Energy Agency (IAEA). The Space Services Department (SSD) of the ITU is responsible for: the coordination and recording procedures of space systems and earth stations; examination for inclusion in MIFR (Master International Frequency Register); capture, processing and publication of data; and the registration of satellite networks. The depository of satellite competitive advantage a nation is thus kept by an international organisation. These international monitoring bodies are responsible for administration and playing a significant role both in protecting sovereignty and in facilitating consensus. This is the hallmark of international organisations; that their very existence is the means through which consensus is achieved.

Granting oversight to an international body is acceptable for mutually respectful sovereign relations. It also carries the flavour of consensus and leaves the marks of sovereignty intact. In the case of the Arctic for example, the WMO[46] can perform its data collection function and utilise it for the benefit of consensus-building among nations that operate in the region. Its function

---

44　Gallway, note 42, 110.

45　The World Meteorological Organisation (WMO) has increased their attention and energies in relation to Polar observation. "WMO polar initiatives showcased at Arctic Circle Assembly: Observing and responding to a changing Arctic", 11 October 2017, Press Release, World Meteorological Organization https://public.wmo.int/en/media/press-release/wmo-polar-initiatives-showcased-arctic-circle-assembly. The WMO appears to be becoming the global facilitator of climate predictive capability, see "Innovation and cooperation for a safer Arctic", Meeting announcement, World Meteorological Organisation https://public.wmo.int/en/events/meetings/innovation-and-cooperation-safer-arctic [accessed 2 December 2017].

46　The WMO calls for greater international collaboration at the 2017 Arctic Assembly. "Innovation and cooperation for a safer Arctic", Meeting announcement, World Meteorological Organisation https://public.wmo.int/en/events/meetings/innovation-and-cooperation-safer-arctic [accessed 2 December 2017].

may be replicated either by itself at the southern pole, or by another already existent organisation. Here then, in the ethics of observation and data collection at the polar ends of the world is a case of consensus achieved through sovereignty. The truth is that one is not achieved without the other.[47] Where such an organisation is simply the *de facto* collector and not actually controller of what is collected, remains undetermined.

In the Arctic, the need to "increase cooperation in meteorological, oceanographic and terrestrial observations, research and services ... [and] the importance of scientific assessments and projections to informed decision-making in the Arctic ... [and] the need for an ecosystem approach to management in the Arctic" was announced at the Fairbanks Declaration[48] made at the changing chairmanship of the Arctic Council from the United States to Finland in 2017.

4.2 Involving the Local

Despite the foremost role played by the international bodies governing the collecting and aggregation of data and the various national interests which play a role in the scope of authority these bodies have, it is the under-explored role of locally-based peoples which may prove an increasingly important factor in the future. Telemetry requires local-level maintenance. Earth observation stations require local management. Whether implanted or built from an indigenous base, peoples who live in the remote deserts of observation units tend to form highly specialised units which develop both a keen awareness of their responsibilities and a fondness for the often endemic issues which pervade the landscape in which they live.[49] The Fairbanks Declaration, along with recognising the importance of meteorological observation and monitoring by the WMO, also recognised 'the need for well-maintained and sustained observation networks' [para 30] which may include locally based peoples. Together with recognizing the important of scientific assessment, also affirmed the importance

---

[47] It may be an interesting study to determine whether the number of international agreements, in particular those creating international organisations, proliferates during periods of heightened tension, almost as a diplomatic reassurance that sovereignty will be respected, thus quelling fears of usurpation.

[48] "Fairbanks Declaration 2017: On the Occasion of the Tenth Ministerial Meeting of the Arctic Council", Signed by Representatives of the Arctic Council 11th Day of May, 2017, Fairbanks, Alaska, https://oaarchive.arctic-council.org/bitstream/handle/11374/1910/EDOCS-4072-v5-ACMMUS10_FAIRBANKS_2017_Fairbanks_Declaration-2017.pdf?sequence=9&isAllowed=y (accessed 1 September 2017) paras 30–32.

[49] Informed by the author's twelve months living in Longyearbyen, Spitsbergen, Svalbard in 2013.

of 'traditional and local knowledge, and the reliance of Arctic biodiversity and inhabitants on the availability of freshwater'.[50]

Both the Arctic and Antarctic are home to a collection of people who have, at their core, a very different way of living.[51] Theirs is formed from a unique attachment to land and one that in Kolerian theory[52] is mutually formed between themselves and the landscape. The land of their choosing is the Arctic and Antarctic respectively. In these places alone are the land and people subject to conditions of living not experienced elsewhere. The experience of those conditions does not go without affect.

Out of the unique set of circumstances faced by such peoples, a new knowledge about the global to local interface develops and as these people become both highly specialised and highly adapted, their role in global observation structures will become ever increasingly important. Questions proliferate here: what is the local? What is national? What is local ownership? Who are the indigenous? Not only are these local-to-global groups altering the conception of sovereignty, but as autonomous communities – Svalbard and Antarctica are ontologically their own places – issues of ownership and power in the collection, dissemination and control of data will undoubtedly be future political roles. Satellite bases and their personnel, local or visitor, lie within a community that has its own ontology and one that often has an intimate connection with the land. The perpetuation of nationalist concern and the overarching framework (kept in place tenuously) driven by international collaborative bodies cannot replace the operationality on the ground, which is formed by the interactions with highly ontological societies.

In these types of situations, systems of Polar Surveillance are a unique example of the local to global geopolitical interface so necessary for increasing the resilience of the Polar Regions. International collaborative efforts to measure and monitor meteorological data[53] take place within a local network, by people who form part of an ontological network. In this, the perpetuation of nationalistic concern and the overarching framework (kept in place tenuously)

---

[50] Fairbanks Declaration, note 61, para 31.

[51] Informed by the author's twelve months living in Longyearbyen, Spitsbergen, Svalbard in 2013.

[52] Avery Kolers, *Land, Conflict, and Justice: A Political Theory of Territory* (Cambridge: Cambridge University Press, 2009).

[53] The WMO calls for greater international collaboration at the 2017 Arctic Assembly. "Innovation and cooperation for a safer Arctic", Meeting announcement, World Meteorological Organisation https://public.wmo.int/en/events/meetings/innovation-and-cooperation-safer-arctic (accessed 2 December 2017).

driven by international collaborative bodies somewhat irrelevant to the cultural distinctness of the place.

5 Conclusion

Surveillance and cyber-systems at the Poles are fraught with difficulties. Although there is a clear greater good argument for their use and maintenance, and one that easily trumps concerns about the individual in the short-term, whether they are capable of contributing to a peaceful purpose for the Poles is another question entirely.

Ethical decision-making ought not to be exclusively either normative or utilitarian, but rather needs to balance the competing demands of the individual, the nation and the greater good, and even then each of these is defined differently in different contexts. In the case where a choice of ethical matrix must be preferred, it is the opinion of this paper that ethics must begin to look normatively at the greater good. The underlying question addressed is what balance between national security over components of the satellite network and the need for global consensus will be tolerable politically. More specifically, how can global consensus be built while respecting changing issues of sovereignty.

Satellites satisfy both national requirements and also the international collaborative efforts to measure and maintain a team of scientific personnel who are responsible for data collection on meteorological phenomena. However much the satellite stations represent international surveillance efforts and nationalistic requirements, the stations are run from a local base, by people who form part of an ontological community who may be part of an entirely different formulation of geopolitics. In this, the understanding of the local to global is distinct: highly ontological society, the perpetuation of nationalistic concern and the overarching framework (kept in place tenuously) driven by international collaborative bodies. As such, the ethics of observation at the Poles is part national power, part international collaborative effort and part local monitoring: it is at once governed by an overarching international framework, subject to nationalist concern, and based in a highly ontological society.

Lessons from International Space Law: The Role of International Relations in Governing Global Commons Regions

Edythe E. Weeks*

Abstract

Drawing from an analysis of experiences in outer space law, this paper provides insights into challenges involved with managing the global common spaces of the polar regions. The literature concerning governance of the international commons regions focuses on justice and equity concerning natural resources, climate change, the speed, uncertainty and consequences stemming from key actor activity in the Polar Regions. This usually boils down to successes and failures of treaty noncompliance and enforcement mechanisms, or the lack thereof. This paper highlights a current political process aimed at dismantling agreed upon terms outer space international agreements. This offers a snapshot of a political process, likely to influence evolving polar legal norms for the rapidly melting Arctic and Antarctic regions. This is a conceptual paper borrowing theoretical and methodological approaches from political science and international relations such as a Gramscian analysis, constructivism theory and critical discourse analysis, to present several interesting ideas. The purpose is to enable people to understand and explain that future colonisation patterns are unfolding today. It calls attention to issues likely to challenge and define our world in the twenty-first century.

Keywords

international treaty compliance – global commons governance – polar law development – space law – asteroid mining

---

* Northern Arizona University, Flagstaff, Arizona, USA. Edythe.Weeks@nau.edu.

1 Introduction

Five hundred years from now, it is possible that outer space and polar regions territories may be populated into nation states. If this happens in a manner involving environment devastation, poverty and wider inequality and conflict, it will be because of what is happening today, in our lifetime. Our lofty endeavours to preserve Earth and to uplift humanity are failing because we allow international treaties to fail. Will this pattern continue with treaties governing the global commons regions? Before treaty noncompliance, something else happens – strategic discourses, in various forms. Illustrating current dynamics related to outer space strategic discourses, intended to undo international space law provisions, this paper adds to the current literature on international law. When this process plays out, the *res communis* provisions in the Outer Space Treaty and Moon Treaty and restrictions against owning territories, could become disavowed. Political efforts to counter the international space law *res communis* provisions can be found in various strategic discourses, aimed at producing new norms. These new norms are being positioned to match the dominant ideology of current times. This strategy's success could make the granting of private property rights to outer space acceptable. This could then proceed to become custom in international law, and a forerunner for the polar regions. The international community's reaction to new national legislation promoting asteroid mining and private property rights serves as a precursor to this emerging pattern.

2 International Treaty Compliance Issues

Ozone depletion, global climate change, rising sea levels, exploitation of the environment and natural resources, war, conflict, human rights violations and refugee crises, can only be resolved through cooperation of humanity. All these phenomena are occurring despite a myriad of international treaties designed with the best intentions to prevent these catastrophes. In *Making Treaties Work: Human Rights, Environment and Arms Control* experts on international treaty compliance warn that there is a need for ensuring compliance mechanisms since traditionally, enforcement tends to be left up to the individual parties. The edited book contains insights from scholars who examine three forms of mechanisms: dispute settlement procedures in the form of international courts, non-compliance procedures of an administrative character, and enforcement of obligation by coercive means. The fields examined include human rights, international environmental law, and arms control and disarmament.[1]

2.1   *Potential Conflict and Using Commons Resources*

Scholars have voiced concern over potential conflict in the rapidly melting polar regions territories.[2] For example, Leary argues that 'states should also consider the introduction of review processes to soft law and other processes to bolster compliance and effectiveness' and should 'consider closely the need to strengthen Arctic environmental governance both within and beyond areas of national jurisdiction'.[3] The tendency to take action to 'appropriate emerging resources to the exclusion of other states and to the detriment of a global common use doctrine', despite prior agreements, 'securing global interests and common values to secure resources for common use and humanity's benefit', has been noted. Specifically, regarding the Arctic region, 'The world is not witnessing a paradigm shift in the High Arctic; it is witnessing iterations of a state-sponsored possessory interest to territorialise geo-spatial resources, iterations amply demonstrated throughout history and especially in the ambit of the law of the sea'.[4] In addition, Timo Koivurova has pointed out the problem of grey areas or apertures between various norms and beliefs about favoured styles of governance, in the Arctic context.[5]

Regarding international law affecting the Antarctic continent, Joyner asserted that although enforcing compliance with recommendations is difficult, 'it is inaccurate to infer that these measures are not enforceable'.[6] He further stated

---

1 Geir Ulfstein (ed), *Making Treaties Work: Human Rights, Environment and Arms Control* (Cambridge: Cambridge University Press, 2010).
2 See Peter Beck, 'Keeping Conflict on Ice', *History Today* 59 (December, 2009): 16–18; Doaa Abdel-Motaal, *Antarctica: The Battle for the Seventh Continent* (Westport Connecticut: Praeger, 2016); and Michael Byers, *Who Owns the Arctic?: Understanding Sovereignty Disputes in the North* (Vancouver: Douglas & McIntyre, 2010).
3 David Leary, 'Looking beyond the International Polar Year: What are the Emerging and Re-Emerging Issues in International Law and Policy in the Polar Regions' *Yearbook of Polar Law* 1 (2009): 1–20.
4 Christopher R Rossi, 'A Particular Kind of Dominium: The Grotian Tendency and the Global Commons in a Time of High Arctic Change,' *Journal of International Law and International Relations* 11 (Spring 2015): 1–60.
5 Timo Koivurova, 'Gaps in International Regulatory Frameworks for the Arctic Ocean' in *Environmental Security in the Arctic Ocean*, eds. PA Berkman & AN Vylegzhanin (Dordrecht: Springer, 2013), 139.
6 Christopher C Joyner, 'Recommended Measures under the Antarctic Treaty: Hardening Compliance with Soft International Law' *Michigan Journal of International Law* 19 (Winter 1998): 401–444.

that the 1959 Antarctic Treaty[7] provides for certain recommended measures to be adopted and approved as policies by the Antarctic Treaty Consultative Party (ATCP) states and that by 1998, meetings had brought forth at least 228 adopted recommendations. However, he pointed out that these measures adopted at Antarctic Treaty Consultative Party Meetings are 'soft law', or nonbinding instruments. He states that the 'legal value attached to recommendations remains vague and subject to varying interpretations by Member States'. On balance, this process of adopting recommended measures as soft law has worked sufficiently well, as nearly all Antarctic activities have been directed and supported by governments and that they have been accepted and implemented as agreed-upon measures, which contributes to their evolution from nonbinding, so-called 'soft' law into customary law or hard legal principles.[8]

Relatedly, here is what is happening regarding private property rights in outer space.

3   Exercising Power over the Global Commons: the US Asteroid Mining Act of 2015

On 23 November 2015, the 'Asteroid Mining Act' – the US *Commercial Space Launch Competitiveness Act* – was enacted as Public Law No. 114-90.[9] More recently, on 6 April 2020 US President, Donald Trump issued an Executive Order supporting this initiative. This political-legal strategy seems to assert the legality of asteroid mining rights for US citizens. Since outer space is a global commons territory, tensions, at least on paper, are heating up because of this national asteroid mining legislation. This law is potentially at odds with international legal authority over the issue of sharing and private property rights of natural space resources.[10]

3.1   *International Space Law Authorities Reaction*

Space law experts have indicated that how the US decides to interpret the new US commercial law in conjunction with the Outer Space Treaty of 1967 and

---

7   The Antarctic Treaty, 1 December 1959, 12 UST. 794, 402 U.N.T.S. 71.
8   See Joyner, note 6.
9   H.R.2262 – US Commercial Space Launch Competitiveness Act Public Law No: 114-90 (11/25/2015), file:///E:/IAC%202019/ABSTRACT/2015%20US%20Law%20Asteroid%20 Mining.pdf [Accessed 4 January 2020].
10 See the IISL website at: https://iislweb.org/spacewatchgl-perspective-on-us-space-re sources-executive-order-iisl-president-kai-uwe-schrogl-on-the-clarity-of-existing-space -law/ [Accessed 17 January 2020].

the Moon Agreement, may be at odds with the international community in the near future. Advocates for the new US law suggest that the law is perfectly in-line with international space law.[11] However, the International Institute of Space Law (IISL) issued a Statement in December of 2015 indicating some skepticism about how the US will decide to interpret the new law in an actual legal situation.[12]

Asteroid mining operations are scheduled and are anticipated to accrue trillions, or quadrillions of dollars in natural resources including gold, iridium, osmium and other platinum group metals, which have been discovered on Near Earth asteroids. For example, news reports estimate asteroids worth in quadrillions of dollars.[13] Companies such as Deep Space Industries and Planetary Resources have formed. Therefore, this is a critically pivotal matter of international law. Additionally, the *Zeitschrift für Luftrecht und Weltraum-Rechtsfragen* journal subsequently published the article entitled 'The International Institute of Space Law adopts Position Paper on Space Resource Mining'.[14] In addition, on 18 December 2015, Ridderhof posted an article entitled 'Space Mining and (US) Space Law' on the Hague's Peace Palace Library blog. The article outlines concerns and foreseeable issues regarding the passage of this legislation.[15]

Blount and Robison explain that the United States Congress passed the US *Commercial Space Launch Competitiveness Act* (CSLCA) and in Title IV of the Act, Space Resource Exploration and Utilisation, ultimately 'recognized

---

11   Sagi Kfir, 'Is Asteroid Mining Legal? The Truth Behind Title IV of the Commercial Space Launch Competitiveness Act of 2015' General Counsel, http://deepspaceindustries.com/is-asteroid-mining-legal [Accessed 17 January 2020].

12   The International Institute of Space Law, *Position Paper on Space Resource Mining*, Adopted by consensus by the Board of Directors on December 20, 2015, http://www.iislweb.org/docs/SpaceResourceMining.pdf [Accessed 17 January 2020].

13   An example of these types of reports is entitled 'NASA plans mission to asteroid that may hold treasure trove of minerals' CBS News This Morning (January 19, 2017), https://www.cbsnews.com/news/nasa-mission-16-psyche-asteroid-metals-worth-ten-thousand-quadrillion-dollars/ indicates that some scientists estimate, for example, an asteroid named 16 psyche, to be worth '$10,000,000,000,000,000,000 ten thousand quadrillion dollars'. There are tens of thousands of asteroids in Near Earth orbit. Several companies such as Deep Space Industries and Planetary Resources, Inc. are articulating plans to lead the way in this new industry, https://www.youtube.com/watch?v=50g3yxVZRKk&t=35s [Accessed 11 April 2020].

14   Stephan Hobe, *Zeitschrift für Luftrecht und Weltraum-Rechtsfragen* 65 (2016): 204–209.

15   See https://www.peacepalacelibrary.nl/2015/12/space-mining-and-u-s-space-law/ [Accessed 4 January 2020]; and Debra Werner, 'Space Law Workshop exposes rift in legal community over national authority to sanction space mining' *Space News* (April 17, 2018), https://spacenews.com/space-law-workshop-exposes-rift-in-legal-community-over-national-authority-to-sanction-space-mining/ [Accessed 10 April 2020].

commercial property rights in resources extracted from celestial bodies' and that 'the CSLCA was met with exuberance by the commercial space sector, but many scholars declared that the legislation was a violation of international space law'.[16] Lee further states that pursuant to this new US law, former US President, Barack Obama authorised commercial exploitation of asteroid and space resources, and also recognised property rights in those resources.[17]

3.2 Contributing to the Literature and What Needs to Be Stated

Notwithstanding international space law's track record for promoting commercial opportunities throughout the world, criticisms assert international space law is a hindrance to space enterprise and space industry.[18] Strategic discourse and political strategies aimed at dismantling international space law, predate the passage of the 2015 US Asteroid Mining Act legislation. Jakhu and Buzdugan explain that the path of gradual commercialisation of current space applications, such as launch services, satellite communication services, direct broadcasting services, satellite remote sensing and navigation services, and satellite weather monitoring services, will most likely be followed by future activities of use of space resources – space mining ventures.[19] They argue that 'the perceived regulatory barriers, i.e., the licensing requirement, the "common heritage of mankind" principle of international space law, and protection of intellectual property rights, are not obstacles to economic development'. Rather than property rights, there are other ways to encourage space mining

---

16 PJ Blount and Christian Robison, 'One Small Step: The Impact of the US Commercial Space Launch Competitiveness Act of 2015 on the Exploitation of Resources in Outer Space' *North Carolina Journal of Law & Technology* 8 (December 2016): 160–186.

17 Katie E Lee, 'Colonizing the Final Frontier: Why Space Exploration beyond Low-Earth Orbit Is Central to US Foreign Policy, and the Legal Challenges It May Pose' *Southern California Interdisciplinary Law Journal*, 27 (Fall 2017): 231–253, 242; and US Commercial Space Launch Competitiveness Act, Pub. L. No. 114-90, 129 Stat. 704 (2015).

18 See Timothy G Nelson, 'The Moon Agreement And Private Enterprise: Lessons From Investment Law' *ILSA Journal of International & Comparative Law* 17 (Spring, 2011): 393–416; LM Fountain, 'Creating Momentum in Space: Ending the Paralysis Produced by the "Common Heritage of Mankind" Doctrine', *Connecticut Law Review* 35 (2003): 1753–1787; Carol R Buxton, 'Property in Outer Space: The Common Heritage of Mankind Principle vs. the "First in Time, First in Right" Rule of Property Law', *Journal of Air Law & Commerce* 69 (2004): 689; M Schwind, 'Open Stars: An Examination of the United States Push to Privatize International Telecommunications Satellites', *Suffolk Transnational Law Review* 10 (1986): 93.

19 Ram Jakhu and Maria Buzdugan, 'Development of the Natural Resources of the Moon and Other Celestial Bodies: Economic and Legal Aspects,' *Astropolitics* 6, (4 November 2008): 201–250, 201 https://doi.org/10.1080/14777620802391778 [Accessed 27 January 2020].

industry development. For example – enterprise rights could prove to settle these burgeoning tensions between perspectives.[20]

Thus, the US Asteroid Mining Act of 2015 represents a furtherance of consistent attempts to dismantle the commons provisions and restrictions against private property ownership and exclusive territorial rights, which are contained in the body of international space law.[21]

3.3 *Space Law's Track Record for Promoting Commercial Industries*

The record of space lawmaking disproves these assumptions that international space law will hinder the asteroid mining plans. A myriad of resulting space industries including private space transportation, International Space Station commerce, satellite telecommunications, remote sensing and various related enterprises, serve as proof. International Telecommunications Union (ITU) orbital slot allocation in 1988, there are other examples of how the equitable sharing principle has worked well between private and public key plays. The Communications Satellite Act of 1962 (The COMSAT Act) was passed by the US Congress for the purpose of commercialising space satellite technologies. President Kennedy had 'charged his administration with the need to develop a coherent and cohesive policy with respect to communications satellites' and by July 1961 he called for joint ownership with other nations of a communications satellite system, non-discriminatory access for all countries of the world, and a constructive role for the United Nations in international space communications. Shares were offered to the international community when the COMSAT corporation developed into International Telecommunications Satellite Organization (INTELSAT) via a US-led international agreement. Many nations participated in space commerce associated with this bourgeoning technology. During the 1980s, the International Telecommunications Union granted orbital slots, regions in outer space, to member nations. Commercialisation trends established by the COMSAT and INTELSAT corporations were followed by the establishment of similar industries who launched their own regional satellite systems – for example, EUTELSAT in Europe and ARABSAT in the Middle East.

---

20 Leslie I Tennen, 'Enterprise Rights and the Legal Regime for Exploitation of Outer Space Resources,' *The University of the Pacific Law Review 47* (2017): 281, https://scholarlycommons.pacific.edu/uoplawreview/vol47/iss2/14 [Accessed 1 June 2020].

21 Edythe E Weeks, *Outer Space Development, International Relations and Space Law: A Method for Elucidating Seeds* (Newcastle upon Tyne, United Kingdom: Cambridge Scholars Publishing, 2012); and Edythe E Weeks, 'Continuing Patterns of Inequality Between North and South in Outer Space', *Revue de Droit International de Sciences Diplomatiques et Politiques* 79 (May–August, 2001): 167–195.

These examples should serve as evidence that international space law works to promote and foster commercial space enterprises.

4 Honouring the Space Law Negotiators: the Framers Who Wanted to Prohibit World War III in Outer Space

Claims over outer space territory, for example, Lunar Embassy and Orbital Development have been deemed illegal by the International Institute of Space Law Board of Directors Statements of 2004 and 2009.[22] Still, efforts are being made to create private property rights to territories in outer space. It is clear from the *travaux préparatoires* and related documents that the nations of the world, as they worked towards negotiating and creating laws to govern outer space, were concerned with preventing World War III from occurring over the new territory in outer space. This prompted the stance against ownership of outer space territory, whether by individuals, or private, corporate, international, or governmental bodies.

4.1 *Extracting Natural Resources*

It is generally understood within the space law authorities that extracting space resources is allowable, even by private companies for profit. However, international space law prohibits property rights over territories and outer space land.[23] Hobe explains that the Outer Space Treaty 'explicitly and implicitly prohibits only the acquisition of territorial property rights' – public or private. Hobe further explains that there is no mention of 'the question of the extraction of natural resources which means that such use is allowed under the Outer Space Treaty' (2006: 211).[24] He also points out that there is an unsettled

---

[22] Both the 2004 and 2009 International Institute of Space Law Board of Director's Statements are available online at: http://www.iislweb.org/docs/IISL_Outer_Space_Treaty_Statement.pdf; http://www.iislweb.org/docs/Statement%20BoD.pdf [Accessed 4 January 2020].

[23] The International Institute on Space Law, an academic body granted the advisory capacity for the United Nations Office for Outer Space Affairs and Legal Subcommittee, takes the position that it is uncontested that claims over outer space territory, are unlawful because their violate the Outer Space Treaty, and that it is less clear whether the treaty also prohibits the extracting and taking of resources. The International Institute of Space Law, Position Paper on Space Resource Mining, adopted by consensus by the Board of Directors on December 20, 2015, http://www.iislweb.org/docs/SpaceResourceMining.pdf [Accessed 23 October 2020].

[24] Stephan Hobe, 'Adequacy of the Current Legal and Regulatory Framework Relating to the Extraction and Appropriation of Natural Resources', Session 4, Conference and Workshop

question regarding the division of benefits from outer space resources in accordance with Article, paragraph 1 of the Outer Space Treaty.[25]

It is important to note that even the Moon Agreement with its common heritage of mankind clause, arguably, allows space mining, extraction, private property rights and exclusive ownership rights over natural outer space resources, if removed from their natural place. Taking natural resources out of their location, from the surface or subsurface, interpreted by space law authorities as meaning that those resources are no longer tied to the 'in place' restrictions against ownership, and thus legally permissible to take.[26]

4.2 The Bargained for Exchange

It is also clear from the record that the less powerful nations participating in the outer space treaty negotiations made a bargained for exchange. In negotiating the space law treaties, nations agreed to define outer space as a *res communis* territory.[27] Prior to this, outer space could have been defined as belonging to each nation in accordance with its sovereign territory, similar to air space. This is why one of the key principles of space law is that space activities are to be for the benefit of all nations, 'irrespective of their stage of economic

---

Proceedings of the Policy and Law Relating to Outer Space Resources: Examples of the Moon, Mars, and Other Celestial Bodies Workshop, McGill Institute of Air & Space Law, Montreal, June 28–30, 2006 (2006): 203–214: https://www.mcgill.ca/iasl/files/iasl/Moon-Proceedings-Part_4_2006.pdf [Accessed 21 October 2020].

25   Ibid, 211. Hobe explains that the Declaration on International Cooperation in the Exploration and Use of Outer Space for the Benefit and the Interest of all States, Taking into Particular Account the Needs of Developing Countries, UNGA res. 51/122 13 December 1996 grants states the right to make this determination on how to cooperate with the international community to comply with the international space law provision which requires equitable sharing of outer space resources. In addition to the five outer space treaties, international space law also includes five declarations and legal principles. These include: The Declaration of Legal Principles Governing the Activities of States in the Exploration and Uses of Outer Space (General Assembly resolution 1962 (XVIII) of 13 December 1963); The Principles Governing the Use by States of Artificial Earth Satellites for International Direct Television Broadcasting (resolution 37/92 of 10 December 1982); The Principles Relating to Remote Sensing of the Earth from Outer Space (resolution 41/65 of 3 December 1986); The Principles Relevant to the Use of Nuclear Power Sources in Outer Space (resolution 47/68 of 14 December 1992); The Declaration on International Cooperation in the Exploration and Use of Outer Space for the Benefit and in the Interest of All States, Taking into Particular Account the Needs of Developing Countries (resolution 51/122 of 13 December 1996).

26   Carl Q Christol, 'The Moon Treaty: Fact and Faction', *The Christian Science Monitor*, (2 April 1980): https://www.csmonitor.com/1980/0402/040234.html (accessed 11 April 2020).

27   Nandasiri Jasentuliyana and Roy SK Lee, *Manual on Space Law*, Volumes I, II, III and IV (Dobbs Ferry, New York: Oceana Publication, 1979–1981): 304.

or scientific development'.[28] However, today, this provision of international space law is being challenged. Around the world today many people use cell phones, the Internet, money transfer systems and enjoy increased GNP due to these space industries.

It is widely known within the space community that in 1988 the ITU equitably allocated slots in the geostationary orbit to member states in accordance with the *res communis* principles of existing international space law.[29] This has worked well to promote global cooperation and peaceful uses of outer space for people across the globe. It has helped many nations increase their GNP, GDP, telecommunications capability – and access of information via the Internet. For many, this satisfied the requirement of international space law that space activities benefit all mankind.

5 Thwarting Utopian Ambitions

International space law can help explain why utopian statements and grandly stated goals, written into international treaties, are seldom actually realised. Often invisible and hard to trace, nevertheless, influence occurs and predictable outcomes happen. This seems to be why, perhaps, Kai-Uwe Schrogl felt the need to ask the question regarding the global commons in Antarctica, outer space and the high seas-deep seabed regions: What is the future for the global commons?[30] An analysis of space law reveals that legal provisions intended to promote equality, peace and environmental stewardship and sustainability are in the process of being undermined, due to the high profitability reports for the emerging asteroid mining industry. This represents a political calculus related to change in international law. By being able to snapshot strategic hegemonic discursive practices mid-flight, a scholar can highlight these strategies to initiate counter hegemonic legal activities. This can enable new key actors to ensure humanity's awe inspiring treaty terms are not repeatedly

---

28 MJ Von Bencke, *The Politics of Space: A History of US–Soviet/Russian Competition and Cooperation in Space* (Boulder, Colorado: Westview Press, 1997), 43.

29 The ITU is a specialised agency of the United Nations with a Convention, a Constitution, and two sets of operating regulations, and all these have Treaty status. The international community granted this intergovernmental organisation the authority of being the regulatory regime for assigning rights to use various orbital slots (in the orbit spectrum – thus, a limited natural resource) for various goods and services deriving from satellite communications. See Lawrence D. Roberts, 'A Lost Connection: Geostationary Satellite Networks and the International Telecommunication Union,' *Berkeley Technology Law Journal* 15 (Fall 2000): 1095–1114.

30 Kai-Uwe Schrogl, 'Which Future for the Global Commons' *Proceedings of the International Institute of Space Law* 61 (2018): 935.

undermined by a clever few. Humanity deserves to experience the full spectrum of legal rights and treaty entitlements, which are written into our international laws. Towards, this end, we much encourage and promote the critical analytical study of the process of change in international law, as a function of international politics.

6   Space Law

Despite the fact that outer space is further away that Earth's polar regions, international space law is more extensively developed than polar law. The global satellite telecommunications infrastructure, located in Earth's now fully colonised geostationary orbit, serves as evidence that a phase of outer space development has already happened. The outer space global satellite and telecommunications infrastructure provides the world with essential tools such as cell phones, email, the Internet, social networks, geospatial maps, credit/debit cards, and wireless financial transactions. Space law was instrumental to the growth and development of these industries. Thus, space law is voluminous.

6.1   *The Outer Space Treaty of 1967*

After ten years (1957–1967) of negotiations, between approximately one hundred nations, the Outer Space Treaty terms were solidified; it opened for signature on 24 January 1966. It entered into force as the constitution for outer space on 10 October 1967. The outcome has been that the basic foundation of international space law consists of five (arguably four)[31] international space treaties,

---

31   The five international treaties are as follows: The Treaty on Principles Governing the Activities of States in the Exploration and Use of Outer Space, including the Moon and other Celestial Bodies (the 'Outer Space Treaty') – adopted on 19 December 1966 in General Assembly resolution 2222 (XXI), opened for signature on 27 January 1967, entered into force on 10 October 1967; The Agreement on the Rescue of Astronauts, the Return of Astronauts and the Return of Objects Launched into Outer Space (the 'Rescue Agreement') – adopted on 19 December 1967 in General Assembly resolution 2345 (XXII), opened for signature on 22 April 1968, entered into force on 2 December 1968; The Convention on International Liability for Damage Caused by Space Objects (the 'Liability Convention') – adopted on 29 November 1971 in General Assembly resolution 2777 (XXVI), opened for signature on 29 March 1972, entered into force on 1 September 1972; The Convention on Registration of Objects Launched into Outer Space (the 'Registration Convention') – adopted on 12 November 1974 in General Assembly resolution 3235 (XXIX), opened for signature on 14 January 1975, entered into force on 15 September 1976; The Agreement Governing the Activities of States on the Moon and Other Celestial Bodies (the 'Moon Agreement') – adopted on 5 December 1979 in General Assembly resolution 38/68, opened for signature on 18 December 1979, entered into force on 11 July 1984. Each treaty is available on line at: http://www.unoosa.org/pdf/publications/STSPACE11E.pdf [Accessed 4 January 2020].

along with various written resolutions and declarations. The main international treaty is the Outer Space Treaty of 1967. It was well received; it was ratified by ninety-six nations and has been signed additional nations. As the first effort to regulate activities occurring in outer space, it established several principles of international law, making it the most important treaty in the field of space law. Moreover, it incorporated the principles of peaceful use of outer space, cooperation between space-faring nations, and the extension of the rule of law into outer space; thus it is considered the cornerstone of international space law. The principles which make up the Outer Space Treaty are considered the source and substance upon which all of the subsequent four agreements were derived.

The framers of Outer Space Treaty initially focused on solidifying broad terms first, with the intent to create more specific legal provisions later.[32] The members of the United Nations Committee on Peaceful Uses of Outer Space later expanded the Outer Space Treaty norms by articulating more specific understandings which are found in the 'three supplemental agreements' – The Rescue and Return Agreement of 1968, the Liability Convention of 1973, and the Registration Convention of 1976. After these three additional treaties were produced and enacted, key actors involved in space law negotiations, set out to establish and confirm a few more of the still unsolidified legal norms.[33]

6.2 The Moon Treaty/Agreement

The rules, terms and agreements considered by space law authorities to be part of the active body of international space law are the five international space treaties and five UN declarations. In 1979, the fifth outer space treaty, the Moon Treaty Agreement opened for signature.[34] The Moon Treaty, embodied issues such as the environment, public health and sharing to benefit all mankind, which were left open after the first fourth treaties were established. Many of

---

32　Nancy Griffin, 'The Americans and the Moon Treaty,' *Journal of Air Law and Commerce* 46, (1981): 729, 733–734.

33　Antonella Bini, 'The Moon Agreement in the 21st century' *Acta Astronautica* 67 (August–September 2010): 496–501.

34　The United Nations Office for Outer Space Affairs (UNOOSA) provides information and advice to governmental bodies, nongovernmental organisations as well as the general public. This office also provides copies of the treaties, declarations, working papers, minutes and other documents related to the creation and development of space and it prepares legal studies and informative documents on space law and acts as the secretariat for the Legal Subcommittee of the United Nations committee on the Peaceful Uses of Outer Space – the primary international forum for the development of laws and principles governing outer space and its resources. For updates of the status of the Moon Treaty see https://www.unoosa.org/oosa/en/ourwork/spacelaw/treaties/status/index.html [Accessed 10 April 2020]. Member states use this forum to come together, discuss, deliberate and make decisions concerning space law. The International Institute of Space Law (IISL) cooperates with international organisations and national institutions in the field of space law and helps to foster space law development.

the terms written into the Moon Treaty were sticking points during early negotiations. In addition, The Common Heritage of Mankind principle, the equity clause, the requirement to form an international regime have caused the Moon Treaty to be disliked. Generally, many opponents who lobbied against the Moon Treaty within the US, have articulated the belief 'such provisions are highly detrimental to a free enterprise system and would therefore have an adverse effect on America's future in space exploration'.[35] Thus, some critics on international space law accept the Outer Space Treaty, but reject the Moon Agreement. Currently, twenty nations have ratified the Moon Treaty.

6.3 Is the Moon Agreement Considered Real Law?

In comparison to the Outer Space Treaty, in accordance with the terms of the Moon Treaty, five nations ratification was required to enter it into force, however it opened for signature on 18 December 1979 and took five years to get the five requisite signatures. This is why many people suggest and seem to believe that the Moon Agreement is a failed treaty and due to its inability to gather widespread international acceptance.[36] Despite this common misinterpretation of space law, the Moon Treaty is a valid part of international space law.[37]

Many have also asserted that since the Moon Agreement was not signed by the major spacefaring nations, it is was never actually enacted. Wiles[38] explains

---

35 See Griffin, note 32, 749–750.
36 See Report of the Legal Subcommittee on Its Fortieth Session, UN Committee on the Peaceful Uses of Outer Space, 40th Session, 22(a), United Nations' Document A/AC.105763 (2001). Since the Moon Treaty has garnered such a low level of international support, some space law experts have reasoned it is 'obviously unacceptable'. See Kelly M Zullo, 'The Need to Clarify the Status of Property Rights in International Space Law,' *The Georgetown Law Journal* 90 (2002): 2414–2444, note 12, citing Eilene Galloway, 'Guidelines for the Review and Formulation of Outer Space Treaties', Presentation at the International Astronautical Federation 41st International Colloquium on the Law of Outer Space, Melbourne, Australia, at 2, 2 October 1998.
37 See F Von der Dunk, 'The Acceptability of the Moon Agreement and the Road Ahead, International and Interdisciplinary Workshop on Policy and Law Relating to Outer Space Resources: Examples of the Moon, Mars, and Other Celestial Bodies' (June 28–30, 2006) Montreal, *Proceedings of the Policy and Law Relating to Outer Space Resources: Examples of the Moon, Mars, and Other Celestial Bodies Workshop*, McGill Institute of Air and Space Law, http://www.mcgill.ca/files/iasl/Moon-Proceedings-Part_5_2006.pdf [Accessed 15 January 2020]. Also see H Tuerk, 'The Negotiation of the "Moon Agreement"', *Space Law Symposium on '30th Anniversary of the "Moon Agreement": Retrospect and Prospects'*, sponsored by the International Institute of Space Law and the European Centre for Space Law (23 March 2009) http://www.unoosa.org/oosa/en/COPUOS/Legal/2009/symposium.html [Accessed 15 January 2020].
38 Gladys E Wiles, 'The Man on the Moon Makes Room for Neighbors: An Analysis of the Existence of Property Rights on the Moon Under a Condominium-Type Ownership Theory' *International Review of Law Computers & Technology* 12 (1998): 513–534, 531.

why and how the Moon Agreement went into force and effect upon the fifth signature and ratification, irrespective of their classification. The Outer Space Treaty explicitly required the involvement of the USSR, the UK and the US, whereas, the Moon Agreement did not. Technically, consensus was achieved and the Moon Agreement entered into force on 30 July 1984, which would be the 'thirtieth day following the date of deposit of the fifth instrument of ratification', since 11 July 1984 marked the date of the fifth instrument of ratification which was deposited with the Secretary-General of the United Nations. As with the initial four international space treaties, the international community agreed that this one would be enacted upon the achievement of a consensus of five nations.[39] In recent, years more nations have ratified this treaty.

6.4 *The Common Heritage of Mankind Principle and Space Law*

The Common Heritage of Mankind (CHM) principle is generally defined as requiring a global sharing of resources mined in outer space. The Moon Agreement's lack of widespread international acceptance is often blamed on that the fact that it contains the CHM principle and that this is what turned off many nations. The working papers indicate that this was why the Outer Space Treaty does not contain the CHM principle. Rather, it contains something created called the *province of mankind*. The province of mankind principle was never specifically defined, thus allowing the superpowers to pursue their interests. The space treaties cover many major issues such as arms control, non-appropriation of space, freedom of exploration, liability for damages, safety and rescue of astronauts and spacecraft, prevention of harmful interference with space activities and the environment, notification and registration of space activities, and the settlement of disputes.[40]

Other criticisms include that the Moon Agreement include that it is contrary to business interests, especially to property rights; it allows too much political control to developing nations and/or the soviet union; the equity and benefitting all humankind provisions; and suspicions about the international

---

[39] The Moon Treaty has been ratified by Australia, Austria, the Netherlands, Uruguay, Peru, Philippines, Kazakhstan, Lebanon, Mexico, Morocco, Belgium, Chile, Turkey and Saudi Arabia. For updates see the United Nations Office for Outer Space Affairs, Status of International Agreements relating to activities in Outer Space, http://www.oosa.unvienna.org/pdf/publications/ST_SPACE_11_Rev2_Add3E.pdf, [Accessed 15 January 2020]. See also Nandasiri Jasentuliyana, *Space Law: Development and Scope* (Westport, CT: Praeger, 1992), 36.

[40] Jasentuliyana, note 38.

regime in that this could provoke fears of a moratorium, or 'chilling' business investors.[41]

7   International Relations Theories and Concepts

The discipline of political science/international relations and the theories and concepts can enable a wide range of scholars and practitioners to deepen and broaden their understanding of wild card dynamics. Often these types of overlooked dynamics and factors include invisible political exercises of power. This section will illustrate how a Gramscian analysis, constructivism theory and a critical discourse analysis contributes to international law.

7.1   *Gramsci:*[42] *Historicism, Hegemony & the Dominance of Free Market Ideology and Matching Strategic Discourses*

Historical analyses, or what Gramscians call historicism, involves understanding ideas and social forces within their historical context. This includes interrogating the mechanisms of hegemony including the relationship between the ideological and political environment at various historical moments, mechanisms of influence such as laws, policies, and institutions, and how these social forces and mechanisms shape change.

7.2   *Political Mood Swings*

In the case of space law, noticeable shifts occurred in international space law activities into three distinct periods: the first epoch (1957–1979), the second epoch (1980–1991) and the third epoch (1992–2005). During the first epoch space activities were perceived through the lens of the Cold War balance of power. The dominant ideology shaped our view of outer space as a matter of national competition, and space activities were purely a governmental enterprise. Around 1980, the Reagan era ushered in profound changes and a new marked and noticeable shift occurred. In the second epoch, space lawmaking shifted from the international arena into the domestic arena and was marked by the drastic increase in US domestic space laws and policies triggering an increase in space commercialisation and participation by private corporations.

---

41   See Thomas Gangale, *The Development of Outer Space: Sovereignty and Property Rights in International Space Law* (Westport, CT: Praeger, 2009) and Griffin, note 32, 730.

42   Antonio Francesco Gramsci (1891–1937), an author and Italian neo-Marxist philosopher, imprisoned by Benito Mussolini's Fascist regime, is best known for his explanations of seeing the connections between invisible factors and dynamics of exercises of power.

Space law had been shaped through the United Nations from 1957 until 1979. In addition to causing the space lawmaking forum to shift to the domestic sphere, the Reagan Administration took a series of actions triggering a global pattern of space privatisation and commercialisation. Many domestic laws were created following the logic of cutting cost and maximising profit. Within the domestic arena, laws were created to facilitate the commercial success of certain space industries – telecommunications, direct television broadcasting, remote sensing, and space transportation and launch services. These actions paved the way for the acceptance of further commercialisation and privatisation during the third epoch. The third epoch is marked by activities that promote the hyper-privatisation of outer space.

7.3   Explaining Marked Periods of Change

Theories of International Relations can explain changes in space law for each period. The first epoch of outer space development was seen in terms of the Cold War bipolar superpower balance of power. Lawmaking was motivated by the shape of period politics. The first epoch was influenced by the predominant political mood best described by realism theory. In 1957, the initial phase of international space lawmaking, discourse strategies constructed the need for law as a matter of national competition between the two superpowers. Space activities were purely a governmental enterprise during this period. Space law focused on fears raised due to the launching of Sputnik by the Soviet Union in 1957. Key actors included the United States and the Soviet Union and about 100 other states, who were willing to forego self-interest and perform extensive trade-offs during the space law negotiations as they worked through the United Nations. This includes non-spacefaring and non-superpower nations who were also involved in negotiating processes (1957–1967) to produce clauses ensuring the prevention of militarisation and colonisation of outer space by the US or the USSR. Of primary concern to the other nations was getting the US and USSR. to sign a treaty preventing either from placing nuclear weapons in outer space. World War II had recently ended at this time. Therefore, the preeminent concern of people's mind was to prevent World War III from happening in outer space or over outer space territories. In exchange for these types of assurances, these other nations acquiesced to US and Soviet proposals to treat outer space as a commons territory which belonged to no one state.

7.4   Critical Discourse Analysis

In the case of current strategic discourses permitting private property rights, they seem aimed to shift ideology and norms to suit key actor interests and this can happen even in regions designated to belong to the global commons.

The Gramscian concept of hegemony is useful in understanding relations of domination and subordination in global politics within the context of historic blocs, or epochs, and the world order. According to Cox, a historic bloc is 'a dialectical concept in the sense that its interacting elements create a larger unity' in which the interacting elements of superstructure (political, ideological, spiritual spheres) interact with the substructure (the economic sphere) to form an 'ensemble of social relations of production' (Cox, 1993: 56). In addition, 'organic intellectuals' played and continue to play a key role in the formation of new types of actions and activities within specific historic blocs, as they build hegemonic discourses of legitimisation regarding outer space. Current political activities suggest that we may entering a new epoch, wherein private property rights will be normalised in outer space. Other scholars have voiced similar concerns about emerging patterns towards economic exploitation of the global commons, as preparations for large scale mining operations steps up[43] and as new types of property regimes begin to form,[44] and that this is especially likely given that the time is ripe in free market ideology's dominance.[45]

As Gramscians argue, ideas build broader systems of thought, and thus can shape the way individuals and groups are able to understand their social situation, This provides the hope that possibilities exist for social change.[46] Future change makers do not have to settle for past patterns of inequality, conflict, injustice, etc. The role of organic intellectuals is important in counter-hegemonic movements as well. Key thinkers on space law matters recognise that the current international legal and political order governing space activities is inadequate to meet humanity's needs, challenges and developments in the 21st Century. One example of a team effort towards this goal is a McGill University Air & Law Institute project, which resulted in a book entitled *Global Space Governance: An International Study*.[47]

---

[43] Isabel Feichtner and Surabhi Ranganathan, 'International Law and Economic Exploitation in the Global Commons: Introduction', *European Journal of International Law* 30 (2019): 541–546.

[44] Hope M Babcock, 'The Public Trust Doctrine, Outer Space, and the Global Commons: Time to Call Home ET,' *Syracuse Law Review* 69 (2019): 191.

[45] Cameron Hepburn and Chester Brown, 'Privatising the Commons – A Global Greenhouse Emissions Trading Regime', *Australian Mining & Petroleum Law Journal* 19 (June 2000): 157–179.

[46] Stephen Gill and David Law, 'Global Hegemony and the Structural Power of Capital' in Stephen Gill (eds.) *Gramsci, Historical Materialism, and International Relations* (Cambridge: Cambridge University Press, 1993), 93–124.

[47] Ram Jakhu and Joseph Pelton (eds.) *Global Space Governance: An International Study* (Manhattan, New York City: Springer, 2017).

7.5 Constructivism

Constructivism in a theory of international relations, which suggests that significant aspects of international relations are caused to happen by human factors, which are constructed historically and socially. Applying this methodological approach give permission to researchers to investigate key actor activities behind key periods of change in international space law. Legal norms, arguably are in the process of being changed. Key actors and thus effectuate new norms and can also work to establish widespread acceptance of practices and behaviours. Once this happens an international custom can form and a new legal regime. Hence, a Gramscian analysis and constructivism, along with a critical discourse analysis enables us to understand the discursive practices and micro-level processes and activities, which are usually written out in the form of policies, laws and various documents created during the lawmaking processes. Articulated strategies and their stated intention are usually locatable. Treaties, declarations, working papers, laws, policies, legislative intent statements, working papers, speeches, Executive Orders, policy memos, published articles, books, discussions and debates in public forums can be located and analysed.[48] This allows us to determine key actors, power and influence involved in the politics of change in international space law. The constellation of forces involved are often obscurely connected. A process exists which involves strategic influence of thinking patterns to reshape old norms, into new norms, and thus reshape what is to be considered acceptable behaviours.[49] As such, this process and associated processes involve an exercise of power.

7.6 Colonisation: Money Changes Things

Strategic discursive challenges to international space law represent something other than the often-stated request for private sector participation, since existing international space law mechanisms have served both public and private commercial space enterprises for over sixty years. This pattern contradicts the purpose of having international law. The purpose of international space law, as Manfred Lachs informs, was to be classified as international law, 'known to all of us as the system of law that has for centuries been regulating relations among States'.[50] International space law, as a form of international law, is in-

---

48 See Weeks (2012), note 21.
49 Jack M Beard, 'Soft Law's Failure on the Horizon: The International Code of Conduct for Outer Space Activities,' *University of Pennsylvania Journal of International Law* 38 (Spring 2017): 335–424.
50 Manfred Lachs, Warsaw & The Hague, 'The Law-Making Process of Outer Space' in Edward McWhinney and Martin A. Bradley (eds.) *New Frontiers in Space Law* (AW Sijthoffs, Leynden & Oceana Publications, New York, 1969), 13.

tended to create norms and rules so that international actors understand and comply with expectations and agreements.[51] Despite this, international space law may wind up being changed, as profitable industries exponentially expand. Asteroid mining proposals, laws and companies aimed at making space mining a new industry exist. As stated earlier, asteroid mining is projected to create a multi-quadrillion dollar industry. Analogously, in the Arctic, the melting ice means that natural resources such as nickel, copper, coal, gold, uranium, tungsten, diamonds, natural gas, and oil are becoming more accessible. As one scholar on the subject has stated 'the international legal system has been marked by continuous development and redefinition to reach objectives which have been formulated for it'. The process involves the intentional acts of individuals – or groups of individuals. This implies that someone, perhaps anyone, has the power and authority to make the decision to change international law, and to decide how it should be changed. Someone has the power to define what the new objectives should be. Hager also asserts that international law is more accurately characterised *as de lege ferenda* (that which is developing to attain the objectives contemplated for it), rather that *de lege lata* (that which is established); and he relies on Hoffman's[52] argument that international law must be studied as a product of international systems and as a repertory of normative theory about each one of them'. Hager explains this to mean that international law is shaped by all the elements that compose the international system and is 'reflective of the structure of the world, transnational forces, the pattern of power and the political cultures of the main actors, and the relations among the units'.[53]

7.7 *When a Widespread Acceptable Practice Becomes 'Custom'*

Goldsmith and Posner explain that a *custom* arises, having the effect of law when there is a is a 'widespread and uniform practices of states and states must engage in the practice out of a sense of legal obligation'.[54] Widespread acceptance of practices can be treated as law and failure to contest practices can result in losing the right to contest once the practice has been established

---

51 Nandasiri Jasentuliyana, *Perspectives on International Law* (London: Kluwer Law International, 1995).
52 Stanley Hoffman, *The State of War: Essays on the Theory and Practice of International Politics* (Westport, CT: Praeger, 1965), 96.
53 David Russell Hager, 'Space Law: The United Nations, and the Superpowers: A Study of International Legal Development and Codification, 1957–1969,' (PhD diss., University of Virginia, 1970): 8.
54 Jack L Goldsmith and Eric A Posner, *The Limits of International Law: The Limits of International Law* 1st Edition (Oxford: Oxford University Press, 2006), 23.

as custom. Hence activities are heating up in both polar regions. With the continued melting of polar ice, we can expect northern international waters to expand. Inaccessible lands, once frozen, present new resources, territories and opportunities for key actors including nation states, private sector interests, community groups and organisations.

8 Conclusion

Imagine what our world might be like, if past colonisation and development scenarios had involved a broader range of people. Humankind has this type of opportunity today. Polar law academics, students and legal practitioners from all nations, have a chance to play key roles in the development polar regions. Micro-level discursive practices eventually create global futures. Understanding that inequality, poverty and lack of opportunity tend to produce conflict, we can examine the processes, dynamics and factors earlier on and while they are mid-flight. Otherwise, allowing activities outlines in this paper to effectuate patterns of winner take all, will continue to rob everyone of precious once in a life time opportunities. Once such a pattern takes hold it could become an international custom, thus able influence other international laws governing global commons territories.

Book Reviews

∴

Monica Tennberg, Hanna Lempinen and Susanna Pirnes (eds), *Resources, Social and Cultural Sustainabilities in the Arctic* (Routledge 2019) 192 pp.

The book *Resources, Social and Cultural Sustainabilities in the Arctic* is a timely and needed piece on Arctic sustainabilities and resources. The driving force throughout the book is the concept of resources and their entanglements with sustainabilit(ies). The question of resources is approached from a wide, innovative viewpoint. In the midst of the global rush towards the energy resources of the Arctic, this volume offers an inspiring reminder of what can be approached as a resource. For the editors of the work resources are understood as socially and culturally constructed components, and their connection with Arctic sustainabilities is discussed from various viewpoints. The geographical context of the book is the European Arctic, however, several of the themes are also relevant for the broader circumpolar world. The volume is part of the Routledge Research in Polar Regions series, which offers a rather extensive outlook to the Arctic and Antarctic research.

The work lays out a broad overview of the current issues in the European Arctic, combining different approaches and methodologies, shifting from local to global. The book avoids the rather common mystification of the Arctic within research, which is prone to present the Arctic as an empty and harsh 'oneness'. The volume focuses both on indigenous and non-indigenous peoples, as well as tangible and intangible entities. Navigating from a small Finnish town, Salla, to a statue in Murmansk, visiting a demonstration in Nuuk on the way, the book tackles multiple levels of everyday life in the Arctic. The authors approach the topics from different disciplinary backgrounds, such as political science, history, arts and sociology, which brings a fascinating combination of case studies and their examination.

The book is an edited volume, which consists of two parts and 13 chapters, with each chapter focusing on northern resources, in one way or another. After an introduction by the editors, Marjo Lindroth opens the first part of the volume. In her chapter she takes the reader to Greenland and sheds light on Greenland's hopes of possible future independence, which are strongly entangled with its natural resources. Aspiring for independence, natural resources (especially uranium) are crucial in achieving economic security. The imaginaries of the future and the elusive hopes of independence are strongly connected to the utilisation of natural resources. Lindroth's own fieldwork and discussion brings a personal touch to the piece, and the chapter works well as the opening chapter of the book.

Hannah Strauss-Mazzullo continues this train of thought by considering the implications of uranium as a resource in Finland. In doing so, she highlights divergences between local, national, and international perceptions of nuclear power and sustainability. In her chapter she focuses especially on the planned power plant in Pyhäjoki, which is a small municipality located on the Gulf of Bothnia. The proposed project is located on the peninsula of Hanhikivi, of which a part belongs to a NATURA natural reserve. The environmental heritage aspect of the proposed nuclear project is mentioned in the chapter but not discussed in detail. She focuses on the local dimensions of the planned nuclear plant, leaving the much debated power politics related to Russia's role in the project aside. She captures the historical development of nuclear power in Finland, tying it to recent developments within the case of Pyhäjoki. An interesting notion that Strauss-Mazzullo makes is that the local community is willing to live with the risk of nuclear accident, as the project brings jobs and wealth to the area. This shows the complexity of nuclear power, or any other large-scale extractivist project, in relation to the local community and its economic needs. The chapter captures and questions sharply the direction of Finnish nuclear politics – while the rest of Europe is aiming to shift away from nuclear power, Finland is planning and building new nuclear power plants.

The next chapter, written by Joonas Vola, offers a curious viewpoint on the governance of natural resources, in this case the resource being the river Kemijoki, Finland's longest river. The chapter presents an innovative way of combining different elements, such as the history of language and cultural metaphors in examining the northern river as a resource. The chapter differs slightly from the other chapters in its style, however it tells the reader a comprehensive story about the genealogy and etymology of the language of a river. Kemijoki flows across Northern Finland and flood management is a central question for people living on its shores. Vola shows how the framing of the river as a resource by the state also enables the management of it.

Moving forward, Hanna Lempinen examines Arctic energy and the concept of social sustainability. She captures the change that has occurred within the framing of Arctic energy, perhaps the most discussed form of Arctic resources.

From discussing merely the Arctic oil and gas industry, the discussion has evolved to include climate change and its implications in the past few decades, while pondering possibilities of alternative energy sources. However, as Lempinen notes, the future is still imagined in the frame of fossil fuels. Arctic energy in this paradigm is seen as vital both locally, to the communities, as well as globally. While the Arctic oil and gas reserves are seen as crucial for global energy demands, the social dimensions of energy production are given less attention within the discussions. Lempinen points out the paradox of producing fossil fuels with 'zero emissions' while paying little attention to their consumption elsewhere in the world. The chapter critically addresses the concepts of 'sustainability' and 'development', two commonly used terms within Arctic discussions.

A chapter by Adrian Braun addresses the topic of resources in the Arctic, again using another approach, focusing on the financial investments and especially climate bonds in relation to municipalities in the European Arctic. The chapter differs from the other chapters slightly in that it is more of an economic review of the current situation of socially responsible investments (SRI) in each European Arctic country and not so much a case study. The chapter brings valuable contributions to the reader (especially a reader from social sciences) by introducing the functioning mechanisms and effects of these investments. His chapter notes that the European Arctic actors do have many possibilities to achieve social and ecological sustainability through these different mechanisms.

Paula Tulppo finishes the first part of the book with a chapter looking at Arctic borders and resources. Tulppo examines the EU cross-border program as well as municipal strategies of northern border regions of Finland. A specifically insightful notion is that in addition to the people, culture and natural resources of a municipality, the geographical location of the municipality and its proximity to a border can also be seen as a resource. Border towns often have rich culture, emerging from the shared history and cooperation between neighboring countries. Tulppo notes that while EU programs emphasise economic resources, local strategies and people value cultural and social resources.

Opening the second part of the book, Gemma Holt takes a critical look at the production of knowledge. After introducing the Arctic Council (AC) she focuses on the formation of a report of AC and the concept of adaptation. She notes that the role of indigenous knowledge is highlighted and seemingly appreciated within the scientific discussions of the Arctic. However, the knowledge production process is still very much incorporated within 'Western science', whereas indigenous knowledge is only given the possibility to serve as an add-on. Her chapter is indeed thought-provoking and a needed contribution to this volume, bringing attention to knowledge as a resource and raising the question, whose knowledge matters?

Monica Tennberg continues by examining the discourse of Arctic expertise in the light of social sustainability. 'Arctic expertise' has become a common phrase within national discussions and in her chapter Tennberg takes a closer look at the meaning and possession of this expertise. She focuses on Finnish Lapland, examining both regional and national discourses of Arctic expertise. In doing so, Tennberg questions the role of social sustainability within the discourse of skilled people (as a resource) in the North – if there are no sufficient measures to gain expertise, can there be experts? In addition, her chapter compares the situation with that of the neighboring areas of Northern Finland and finds Finland lagging behind in many ways.

Heidi Sinevaara-Niskanen continues with a chapter on the meaning of gender within Arctic sustainability. She draws attention to the social resources of the Arctic, which have been neglected in Arctic research, and focuses on the gendered currents of Arctic development as well as academic discussions. She brings the waves of feminist thinking brilliantly together to Arctic 'waves of equity', showing an overview of the historical development and the different steps that Arctic research has taken. From questions of equal participation and understanding of gendered vulnerabilities, the discussion has evolved to emphasise the importance of intersectional approaches in the Arctic. Her chapter encourages actors to examine gendered knowledge and intersectionality as supporting tools to sustainability within the Arctic.

The next chapter by Francis Joy takes the reader to the world of cultural heritage and handicrafts. In his piece, he focuses on Sámi culture and its material level through the exploitation of traditional Sámi culture and handicrafts within the Finnish tourism industry. He explains the problematics behind the protection of Sámi culture in a profound way. For example, despite creating the Duodji trademark to protect authentic Sámi handicraft, fake artifacts are still produced and sold. The discussion on these handicrafts is naturally related to a larger discussion of cultural appropriation and colonial practices towards the Sámi people, which the chapter addresses briefly. Joy concludes the chapter by suggesting the concept of cultural sensitivity, which could offer a way forward.

Susanna Pirnes brings again a different look on the concept of resource, discussing history in Russian Arctic politics as a resource for its Arctic aspirations. Pirnes brings together the historical context of the Russian Arctic, which as a region is becoming increasingly important both globally and in the Russian context. She discusses how history is utilised in the building of the northern identity. Especially appreciated is the discussion on the meanings and differences of the concepts of Russian Arctic and the Russian North – Pirnes intelligently shows the historical and cultural roots of different concepts and how the current Russian Arctic as a megaproject is part of national identity building.

The book is concluded by a chapter by the editors.

The first part of the volume focuses more on natural resources within the Arctic context, whereas the second part expands the understanding of resources in delightful ways, challenging the dominant natural resource-centric discussion within Arctic research. The book achieves in its aim to *'illustrate different aspects of why the Arctic resource discourses and practices as they exist today are unsustainable, drawing attention to often-neglected human, social and cultural aspects of the sustainability debate'*. The volume shifts and expands the idea of the Arctic as a home only to natural resources. In addition, the work pays attention to the capabilities within the Arctic in the form of human, cultural and social issues, which are often neglected.

Throughout the book the concepts of 'sustainability' and 'sustainable development' are crucial, and the work achieves discussing them without diminishing sustainability merely to the different dimensions of development, such as economic, environmental and social. Although resources are the initial inspiration of the volume, sustainability is the foundation from which resources are approached.

The strength of this work lies within its common thread. One sees that the authors belong to the same research team and that their research topics are in discussion with one another. The work is well-aligned and only few of the chapters differ slightly from the common thread with their differing approaches and methodologies. However, this is not very disturbing. The volume is relevant for both scholars and advanced students – some of the chapters are formed more as educational chapters than others.

The book is highly recommended for scholars interested in the Arctic regions, and especially to scholars focusing on (natural) resources in the Arctic, as a way to expand and perhaps question one's own understanding of sustainability and resources.

Sohvi Kangasluoma
Aleksanteri Institute, University of Helsinki
sohvi.kangasluoma@helsinki.fi

Stephen Allen, Nigel Bankes and Øyvind Ravna (eds), *The Rights of Indigenous Peoples in Marine Areas* (Hart Publishing 2019) 432 pp. ISBN: 978-1-50992-864-4 (HB); 978-1-50992-866-8 (ePDF); 978-1-50992-865-1 (ePub).

The volume *Rights of Indigenous Peoples in Marine Areas*, edited by Allen, Bankes and Ravna, develops the study of indigenous rights and their reception within legal systems. Stephen Allen is a Senior Lecturer in Law Queen Mary, University of London and Barrister in London. Nigel Bankes is a Professor and Chair in Natural Resources Law, Faculty of Law, University of Calgary. Øyvind Ravna is a Professor of Law and Head of the Research Group for Sámi and Indigenous Law (*Same- og urfolksrett*), UiT – The Arctic University of Norway, Tromsø. The contributors' backgrounds provide an approach which looks at indigenous rights from a tripartite perspective: the international level, the country-based analysis and some interdisciplinary themes.

The editors' approach comprises four main stages of analysis, reflected in the four parts of the volume (17 chapters in total, with an Introduction by Allen, Bankes, Enyew and Ravna): I. an observation on historical aspects and relevance of the interactions (or, as called in the introduction, "encounters", p. 5) between colonisers and indigenous marine and coastal communities (Part I, chapter 1: by Robert Hamilton); II. an analysis of the international dimensions of indigenous peoples and marine areas (Part II, chapters 2–4 respectively by: 2. Endalew Lijalem Enyew; 3. Malgosia Fitzmaurice; 4. Stephen Allen); III. an overview of indigenous rights in marine areas within different jurisdictions (Part III, chapters 5–13 respectively by 5. Lee Godden; 6. Nigel Bankes; 7. Isabela Figueroa; 8. Dorothée Cambou, Jérémie Gilbert and Marlène Dégremont; 9. Øyvind Ravna and Line Kalak; 10. Andrew Erueti; 11. Jay L. Batongbacal; 12. Ekaterina Zmyvalova and Ruslan Garipov; 13. Michael C. Blumm and Olivier Jamin); IV. different perspectives on indigenous rights in marine areas (Part IV, chapters 14–17 respectively by: 14. Sue Farran; 15. Caskey Russell and X̱'unei Lance Twitchell; 16. Einar Eythórsson, Dorothee Schreiber, Camilla Brattland and Else Grete Broderstad; 17. Evelyn Pinkerton and Steve J. Langdon).

A few observations are particularly prominent in the contributions to the volume.

First, the book acknowledges the importance of a systematisation of the "shape and the content" (p. 5) of indigenous rights and the corresponding obligations for the states to protect them. It does so, by analysing the topic from an international, country-based and interdisciplinary perspective. Thus, the question addressed throughout the book is: how exactly does this interaction between levels happen? Hamilton's chapter (Part I), for example, demonstrates how legal pluralism in relation to marine space and resources can be observed in the dimension of an inter-societal system of law developed between Indigenous and European laws. Enyew, Fitzmaurice and Allen's chapters (Part II) seem to imply that an effective level interaction can only happen after the recognition of indigenous marine rights at international level.

Second, if the rights of indigenous peoples in marine areas have started to be increasingly recognised in international and national law, how can such acknowledgement be fully implemented and enforced? How does an improved implementation effectively provide a counterforce to the competition for resources triggered by the force of globalisation?

The book highlights that these questions are now recognised to be central for scholars engaged in the conversation on indigenous rights in marine areas, as well as for other practitioners and regulators. The answers, however, are still in the process of developing. Hamilton's chapter makes an interesting theoretical contribution in this respect, referring that contemporary state law will struggle to make the transition to an effective pluralism possible, if state law remains "tied to a narrow legal heritage" (p. 42), which interferes with the inter-relationship between indigenous and non-indigenous legal orders.

Part III contains cases where the recognition of indigenous rights is still in the combative phase (in Colombia, in Northern Norway and Russia, and in the Philippines, where despite the recognition of rights, the struggle for their implementation seems to be an ongoing process); cases where the cooperative and complementary phases are reaching a satisfactory level of development (in the case of aboriginal governance of Canada, Australian marine areas, New Zealand, New Caledonia and US).[1]

Part IV shows other interesting perspectives around the recognition of indigenous participatory rights: Formalising indigenous participation helps improve marine conservation governance (Farran), revives central practices like the "putting up fish" for the Tlingit Peoples (Russell and Twitchell), preserving language and cultures through generations, challenges existing power structures that inhibit indigenous stakeholders from defending their interests in natural resources against those of more powerful state or private actors

---

[1] Following the distinction of legal pluralism archetypes, drawn by Swenson (Geoffrey Swenson, Legal Pluralism in Theory and Practice, International Studies Review, Volume 20, Issue 3, September 2018, Pages 438–462, https://doi.org/10.1093/isr/vix060), there are four types of interactions between legal systems: (1) combative, (2) competitive, (3) cooperative, and (4) complementary. This book shows how often, when indigenous and traditional systems are involved, these archetypes are phases of that desirable development of inter-law interactions.

(Eythórsson et al.), and empowers and fortifies the role of collective rights (Pinkerton and Langdon).

Recognising indigenous rights does not stop at the restoration of past and present injustice, oiling of inter-societal mechanisms, protection of cultures and traditions in a way that future generations can also share. It goes beyond. Protecting indigenous and traditional communities and their rights, also implies protecting our seas.

Evaluation of the book: The collection of contributions covers a complex variety of perspectives in the panorama of indigenous rights at sea, and fills in a gap in indigenous rights research by providing a rich and unique analysis of indigenous and traditional rights in marine areas.

References and maps: All of the authors take into account the most updated literature on the topic and address it richly and appropriately. Extremely helpful is the use of maps in several contributions, that help visualising the coastal areas object of analysis and provide a geographical context for it (maps can be found at pp. 180, 213, 261, 343).

Scholarship of early career researchers and emerging scholars: One of the noteworthy merits of the book is the significant contribution of early career researchers such as Endalew Lijalem Enyew, whose work sets the tone for the following conversions and is consistently referred to as one of the major milestones in the indigenous rights discourse (among others, see the reference by Ravna and Kalak p. 219; by Farran, p. 323); Ekaterina Zmyvalova (in the Chapter co-authored with Ruslan Garipov on Marine Areas in Russia); Line Kalak (in the Chapter co-authored with Øyvind Ravna on the protection of coastal Sámi in Northern Norway).

In comparison to other works in the field, *International Law And Indigenous Peoples*, edited by Joshua Castellino and Niamh Walsh (The Raoul Wallenberg Institute Human Rights Library, Volume 20, Martinus Nijhoff, 2005) develops also the theme of indigenous rights from the perspective of international law (without focusing specifically on coastal and marine peoples). Fikret Berkes' *Coasts for Peoples Interdisciplinary Approaches to Coastal and Marine Resource Management* (Taylor and Francis, 2015), tackles the problems of environmental degradation and loss for coastal resources for indigenous peoples from the perspective of sustainability and resource management, without delving directly into the issue of indigenous peoples' rights.

The book shares also some similarities to interdisciplinary contributions from the wider field of humanities and social sciences. For instance, Hélène Artaud and Alexandre Surrallés' *The Sea Within: Marine Tenure And Cosmopolitical Debates* (International Work Group For Indigenous Affairs, 2017), focuses on different conceptions of marine resource management among indigenous and coastal people across the globe, discussing plural discourses on marine property rights of the universe, the 'pluriverse' as the authors call it. Similarly, *The Small-Scale Fisheries Guidelines: Global Implementation* edited by Svein Jentoft et al. (Springer, 2017), analyses indigenous and local customary systems of marine resource management and sheds light on the potentials for the implementation of the 2015 FAO's *Voluntary Guidelines for Securing Sustainable Small-Scale Fisheries*. This book contains in-depth case studies where authors discuss the extent to which the Guidelines can help improve the realities of small-scale fisheries, calling for a human rights-based approach to marine governance and resource management. However, while the aforementioned works mainly focus on the issue of indigenous/local governance and participation in resource management processes, *The Rights of Indigenous Peoples in Marine Areas* addresses all different substantial, cultural and procedural rights of indigenous peoples in relation to the marine space, providing a meaningful contribution to the published literature. Composed principally by legal scholars, *The Rights of Indigenous Peoples in Marine Areas* represents the first comprehensive effort to address legal discourses over indigenous rights in marine areas, focusing on their reception within diverse regional, national and transnational systems.

The book has the potential to mark a turning point in a number of ways. It is a unique multi-focal study of indigenous rights in marine areas. Legal scholars and policy-makers will gain a deeper understanding of the implications of indigenous rights recognition on legal pluralism, cultural, social and environmental preservation and protection. In addition to this, individual chapters have autonomous value and can be used in lectures, seminars, and group work on the indigenous discourse from a multidimensional perspective: for example, by looking at similarities and differences among common law jurisdictions (Australia, Canada, New Zealand and US); by exploring the interconnections between international treaty law and indigenous marine governance (e.g. Chapter 2 and Chapter 3; Chapter 4 LOSC: pp. 116–118; 131–132).

Generally, the volume opens interesting avenues for further conversations. It can be read as a call for further development of indigenous marine governance, a concept increasingly recognised as having a crucial role in marine management and conservation (Ban, Wilson and Neasloss, "Strong historical and ongoing indigenous marine governance in the northeast Pacific Ocean: a case study of the Kitasoo/Xai'xais First Nation" *Ecology and Society* 24 (2019):10). It suggests that a pluralist understanding of the relationship between indigenous peoples and sovereign states creates opportunities to resist the side effects of globalisation (such as the increased competition for resources, p. 14). The link between enabling a pluralist approach and the effective recognition of the centrality of indigenous and traditional cosmologies is not as straightforward as some of the contributions indicate (for example, in chapter 7 and in chapter 15). In this sense, the editors of the book rather propose a probably intermediate step between pluralism and recognition of indigenous cosmologies as centrally relevant for marine governance and this step consists in the recognition of the possibility for indigenous peoples to "live their lives and practice their culture, language, spirituality and deep connection with the ocean space." (p. 14) The first steps towards an effective recognition of an ocean governance that is also indigenous have been done in the volume's contributions. In our opinion, further research efforts are necessary, however, in this regard.

Margherita Paola Poto
Faculty of Law, UiT The Arctic University of Norway, Tromsø
margherita.p.poto@uit.no

Apostolos Tsiouvalas
NCLOS, The Norwegian Centre for the Law of the Sea, UiT The Arctic University of Norway, Tromsø
apostolos.tsiouvalas@uit.no

Nikolas Sellheim, *International Marine Mammal Law* (Springer 2020) 225 pp. ISBN 978-3-030-35268-4 e-book.

The book, *International Marine Mammal Law* (225 pages including references and index) is timely, written to address the misconceptions on this topical subject. There are nine chapters starting with an Introduction in Chapter 1. From Chapter 2, the chapters are followed with a short summary, concluding remarks and further readings. In Chapter 2, the author quickly introduced and familiarised the reader to basic biological aspects on the different species of whales, the species of seals and the polar bear. Chapter 3 gave an insight on the societies that rely on marine mammals, Chapter 4 considers the global and regional regimes put into the global framework for environmental and marine mammals. The next three chapters (Chapter 5, 6 and 7) considered the international legal frameworks for whales, seals and polar bears by tracing their historical backgrounds to the present. Chapter 8 attempts to link legal research with political and cultural issues that are relevant to marine mammals, while Chapter 9 summarises all preceding chapters and takes a look at the current legal regimes on the topic.

The book provides a basic overview of international conservation law as well as biological information on some marine mammal species. The book is intended for a wider audience as the author has avoided academic jargon to make it easily understandable to the audience. The author gave a good insight on the very complex relationship between the marine mammals and international law. The book does not contain footnotes or endnotes instead the reader finds a reference list at the end of each chapter. In terms of readability, this is a good read and the author's choice is consistent with the aims of the book to reach a wider audience.

As someone trained in the natural sciences, I went through the book with lots of interest and enthusiasm. The author has been very direct and pragmatic in his style of writing while addressing potential readers on these issues from a multi-disciplinary approach. This is commendable in reaching a wider audience with a simplified language to stimulate the interest of readers from different sectors and background on the topic. My approach in reviewing the book is to follow the chapters sequentially through the lens of my training, highlight some of the words of the author laced with my interpretations and identify areas that closely match food sovereignty. According to the expert panel on the State of Knowledge of Food security in Northern Canada, "Food sovereignty is based on the principle that decisions about food systems, including markets, production modes, food cultures, and environments, should be made by those who depend on them".[1]

In Chapter 3, p. 39, the author illustrates very well the different cultural environments and connotations. He mentioned that: "marine mammals have played a significant role in Inuit societies. It was regarded as an important contributor to human survival in the harsh conditions of the Arctic, it also affected social and cultural practices. It is notable that in the language of the Inuit – Inuktitut – the similarity between 'meat' and 'eating' is striking: '*niqi*' versus '*niri*'. Contrary to the English language, where there is only one word for 'fat', Inuktitut distinguishes between fat from the sea (*uksuk*) and fat from the land (*tunnuk*). When the first Europeans entered the scene in the North and started to explore and exploit the Arctic, they were quickly faced with the difficult dietary need human beings face in the cold. It soon became clear that sufficient provisions of fresh meat from seals and whales enabled overwintering and prevented the outbreak of scurvy". The above is a valid argument on the debate on why cultural preferences also matter on food security, it seems without meat, human survival would not have been possible in the Arctic. Ethnographer Franz Boas went as far as to call seals the 'staple food' of the Inuit. It underlines how vital seals were as a source of food. The dietary importance of seals is further underlined by a common depiction of the Inuit seal hunt in an extremely uncomfortable position that could last for hours, aggravated by cold winds and bad weather just to get this staple food for their survival.

In Chapter 3, p. 54, the author referred to a report by the Food and Agriculture Organization of the United Nations (FAO) on microplastics in fisheries and aquaculture exemplified in a diagram showcasing the pathways of microplastics from marine animals to the human, the depicted whale is not connected to the human. One can wonder why marine mammals was removed from any considerations as a food source. In other words, whales are not considered within contexts of food and microplastics. However, in some regions of this world, marine mammals are still sources of food. There should be a nutritional need for them, at least from the perspective of the locals in meeting their dietary preferences. The book encouraged the reader to further investigate this topic.

Henceforth, on the legal science, it is further argued by the author in Chapter 5, p. 103, where he illustrates very well the dilemma faced by nations in deciding whether the act of whaling is science or not? In order to avert any

---

[1] Council of Canadian Academies, *Aboriginal Food Security in Northern Canada: An assessment of the State of Knowledge* (Ottawa, The Expert Panel on the State of Food Security in Northern Canada, 2014).

potential future dispute over this issue, the court decided not to deal with issues related to maritime delimitation – and not to accept Japan's argument to dismiss the proceedings due to the uncertain legal situation regarding sovereignty in Antarctica – but instead to focus on the larger picture of Japanese Antarctic whaling: whether it is in contravention of the moratorium and thus whether it is "for the purposes of scientific research", as the International Convention for the Regulation of Whaling (ICRW) states. The question is "was Japanese Antarctic whaling 'science' or not?". In order to circumvent this question, the court applied extremely complex and technical reasoning and focused on the question of whether whaling operations were 'for the purposes of' science and thus not on science itself.

Usually, when marine mammals are considered, the focus has mainly been on Arctic and Antarctic waters, however the author brought in other sea areas on the seal hunting questions. In Chapter 6, p. 134, he stated: "As was common practice in the Baltic Sea, the Finnish government paid bounties to fishers in their pursuit of seals in order to protect the fisheries. This practice was also established by the Soviet government in the 1920s and the main goal of this effort was the elimination of the Ladoga ringed seal population. After all, its main forage were salmon and whitefish, which were also the main species fished by Soviet fishers. Consequently, the seal was named an 'Enemy of the fisheries' and the Soviet propaganda machinery did not spare it from depicting it as a 'harmful beast' that needed to be exterminated". This is followed on p. 135 that "the agreement, concluded in 1934, even though it was merely marginally different to its predecessor, contained a prohibition on indiscriminate hunting techniques. The 1922 agreement, on the other hand, merely referred to "authorised hunting methods" yet without further definition. Be that as it may, both agreements lasted until the outbreak of the Second World War and became obsolete with Finland's loss of its Arctic Petsamo region and the eastern parts of Karelia.

As the author discussed in Section 4.3.3, p. 142: marine mammals do play a role in the Antarctic governance, however, not directly under the purview of Antarctic institutions. The sixth Antarctic Treaty Consultative Meeting (ATCM) of 1970 opted for the second option since this would also allow non-Antarctic Treaty Consultative Parties (ATCPs) and non-Antarctic Treaty parties to enter the agreement irrespective of their ongoing research activities in Antarctica – a crucial element in the status of ATCPs. In 1972, therefore, a high-level meeting was held that discussed the draft of the convention from 1970. Ultimately, the meeting adopted the Convention for the Conservation of Antarctic Seals (CCAS). However, there is still a debacle over scientific sealing and commercial sealing as expressed by the author as follows in page 143: "At the time of adoption of the CCAS, Antarctic sealing de facto no longer played a role. Therefore, the enabling of sealing under the CCAS was rather a matter of possibility than of responding to actual commercial needs. The same can be said about the possibility to hunt seals for scientific purposes. Only on one occasion in 1986/87 did the Soviet Union make use of this provision, taking several thousand crabeater seals, around 100 Weddell seals, 1 elephant seal and an unknown number of Ross seals. While scientific sealing was permitted, the issue caused significant unrest amongst the parties of the CCAS, particularly since the Soviet Union did not act in a transparent manner. This led to a conference on the efficacy of the CCAS in 1988, which tightened the relationship between the CCAS and the ATS, particularly with regard to the adopted Convention for the Conservation of Antarctic Marine Living Resources (CAMLR) in 1980". The former Soviet Union already signalled not to conduct scientific sealing and quelled the fear of a reopening of large-scale commercial sealing.

In the same chapter on p. 145: "The large-scale hunts in Atlantic Canada were to a large degree driven by commercial incentives, meaning that it was the demand for seal products that motivated these hunts in the first place. Since seal oil was no longer of interest to the world due to the development of hydrocarbon resources. Rather, it was the fashion industry that was in high demand for seal fur, first and foremost stemming from harp and hooded seal pups".

In this chapter, the author further highlighted the role of the European Union as the forerunner of the new paradigm p. 152 and 153: "In 2015, the scope of the EU Seal Regime was altered, resulting from the proceedings before the World Trade Organization. There were two important changes in its amended version. First, the possibility to conduct non-profit trade in marine management seal products was abandoned. Second, although the Inuit exemption still persisted, new criteria required high animal welfare standards in these hunts".

The European Union was a primary market for seal products and even though Inuit were legally exempted from any trade barrier, they were de facto strongly affected by it. This stems from the closely intertwined trade pathways of both commercial seal products and seal products from subsistence hunts. There is no label to clearly distinguish commercial from subsistence seal products, this makes buyers to abstain from buying seal products altogether.

In Chapter 7, p. 157: the author reminded the readers that, the realities are far more complex as earlier discussed in Chapter 2. The Arctic Biodiversity Assessment (ABA), for instance, has found that of the 19 distinct polar bear populations all over the Arctic, seven are declining, four are stable, one is increasing, and the status of the remaining seven is unknown.

In page 162 of the same chapter, the author again highlighted the complexity on polar bears and the overall purposes of States: whether for conservation purposes; for marine management purposes to protect other living resources and provided that the products deriving therefrom were not placed on the market commercially; when polar bears are hunted by 'local people using traditional methods'; and "wherever polar bears have or might have been subject to taking by traditional means by its nationals." The latter two exceptions were inserted primarily at the behest of the United States and Canada as well as Denmark due to their respective Inuit population and their centuries-old interaction with polar bears.

In Chapter 8, p. 175: "the author argued that the main body of international law that international marine mammal law belongs to, is international environmental law as well as the law of the sea", but other branches of (international) law comprise international marine mammal law. This is well captured in the book and I agree on this position.

Essentially, this is a clarion call for the public to be aware that "the establishment of whale sanctuaries is an effective tool of advancing the conservationist agenda of the International Whaling Commission (IWC), p. 176: While the term 'sanctuary' implies that whales are free from pursuit, this does not mean that whales are free from other dangers. In other words, whale sanctuaries are merely attempting to limit or prohibit the hunt for whales in a specific area. This limitation, does not include dangers related to pollution, noise pollution, ship strikes or habitat degradation. The imposition of a zero-catch quota for specific regions is consequently merely a very limited attempt to ensure the protection of whales, either for a specific region or in the world".

"A country that is pro-whaling (or pro-sustainable use of resources) does not need to have a whaling history, but may have a whaling future. This is especially true for developing nations which might depend on whale meat as part of their overall food security in the future. It does not come as a surprise, therefore, that it has been developing nations that have put forward the link between the IWC and food security in recent IWC meetings" (p. 180).

On the future of international marine mammal law in Chapter 9, "*Be that as it may*" (a favourite quote of the author in the book), he stressed in this final chapter on p. 189: two essential facets that characterise international marine mammal law: first, it is extremely scattered; second, its controversial, adversarial nature.

Furthermore, the author identified five scenarios but my focus here will be on scenario 2 and 5. Scenario 2 – as it can be aligned to the blue economy, p. 191: "The reason is that in recent years, the IWC has seen an increasing discourse on food security. While at the time of writing no official resolution has been adopted, in light of the UN's Sustainable Development Goals that see Zero Hunger as their second goal, 1 it appears that irrespective of the commercial aspects of whaling, whales may also start to be considered as a legitimate food source by the international community. In essence, this is already occurring on the level of Aboriginal Subsistence Whaling, yet has thus far failed to enter the wider discourse on food security".

Scenario 5 as it relates to biodiversity, p. 196: in Chapter 4, the author omitted the Convention on Biological Diversity (CBD). "This was deliberate, he chose to do so since within the CBD, marine mammals play a rather non-existing role. Much more attention is paid to overall strategies for conservation and sustainable use of biodiversity instead of to specific species – after all the CBD is not species-based. Of course, marine mammals are part of this approach, yet contrary to other regimes, the CBD is significantly less confrontational, consensus based and a regime that sets international standards but does not make management decisions".

Chapter 9, p. 197: "Currently, the world appears to be at a crossroads regarding international marine mammal law. On the one hand, whales, seals and polar bears will remain iconic species that will always retain a special place in international law-making. On the other hand, the approach to environmental conservation is currently changing and more and more ecosystem-based management is appearing. the sustainability of marine mammal populations should be the highest good, rooted in the principle of precaution".

Of particular importance on the relevance of debate towards climate change, food security and sovereignty in the future are recent research which indicates that baleen and toothed whales, such as narwhals and belugas, could be susceptible to the novel coronavirus SARS-COV-2 that causes COVID-19.[2,3]

There are references missing for some authoritatively stated facts in some parts of the book – this is a shortcoming, although this was mentioned by the author in the introduction.

In summary, these nine chapters of the book is a comprehensive, introductory volume on the legal regimes governing the conservation and utilisation of marine mammals that provides an account of the legal and cultural environments of international marine mammal law. The complexity of the species of these mammals were adequately revised with biological information to bring readers up to speed. In addition, the book encourages debate and is especially

---

2   E VanWormer, et al., "Viral emergence in marine mammals in the North Pacific may be linked to Arctic sea ice reduction" *Sci Rep* 9 (2019) 15569. https://doi.org/10.1038/s41598-019-51699-4 (accessed 1 July 2020).
3   Melody Schreiber, "Narwhals and belugas may be at high risk for coronavirus infection, researchers fear" (Arctic Today, 7 May 2020), https://www.arctictoday.com/narwhals-and-belugas-may-be-at-high-risk-for-the-coronavirus-researchers-fear/ (accessed 1 July 2020).

topical as this book was written during the period when Japan announced its decision to withdraw from the International Convention for the Regulation of Whaling – and thereby from the International Whaling Commission (IWC).

All in all, this textbook meets the author's goal as a good departure for further studies on international marine mammal law for a wider audience. This book will be a good addition to the bookshelves, it provides a good material for basic courses at universities and for those outside the academic world who are working on marine mammal related issues.

Dele Raheem
Senior Researcher, Northern Institute of Environmental and Minority Law
Arctic Centre, University of Lapland
braheem@ulapland.fi

Gunhild Hoogensen Gjørv, Marc Lanteigne and Horatio Sam-Aggrey (eds),
Routledge Handbook of Arctic Security (Routledge 2020) 442 pp.

This edited book is ultimately a handbook, as the title suggests. It includes 35 chapters concerning different aspects of Arctic security, from theoretical contributions to the traditional perspectives of different states and non-traditional perspectives such as those of indigenous groups. It is a multifaceted account of the different issues that can be labelled under 'security' and of all types of governmental and non-governmental security actors in the Arctic context. The book deserves a praise for not focusing solely on perspectives from the Arctic region, but also from non-Arctic actors, such as China, Japan, the EU, NATO and the OSCE.

The volume provides a collection of studies from the field of politics and international relations, though international law also receives some attention. The editors, Gunhild Hoogensen Gjørv, Marc Lanteigne, and Horatio Sam-Aggrey, promise in their first introductory chapter that the handbook does two things: "First, based on a range of empirical data and case material, it provides a snapshot of various security perceptions about the Arctic in the second decade of the twenty first century. […] The handbook also provides insights into different security analysis tools and practices, which can help scholars reflect upon how our understanding of security – what we do to protect that which we value most, and who decides – changes over time". The first task is easy to fulfil; already the chapters dealing with each Arctic state manage to reflect different security perceptions, which are then complemented with governance, non-Arctic and human-centred perspectives.

The second task is fulfilled by Part I focused on theorising Arctic security. What can be considered praiseworthy is that the book devotes a total of ten chapters for dealing with different theoretical conceptions of security in the Arctic. What Arctic security first brings to mind is the rivalry of the Arctic states, either the Arctic Five, the littoral states surrounding the Arctic Sea (Canada, Denmark, Norway, Russia and the United States) or the Arctic Eight, the countries constituting the Arctic Council (Finland, Iceland and Sweden in addition to the above-mentioned countries). But in the Arctic, state security is often second to the everyday aspects of security, such as human and comprehensive security, indigenous security, energy security, environmental security and economic security. The Arctic Council, for example, deals with these kinds of 'soft security' issues, which is why Arctic cooperation is often cited as successful even in times of tension between the US and Russia. However, the editors challenge the view that security concerns prevailing in other parts of the world would not cover the Arctic region. The widely-held view on Arctic as a region of *asecurity* has been based on the idea of the Arctic geography being too hostile for states' security activity and of the Arctic Council focusing on mutual cooperation rather than antagonistic security issues. The editors argue, in contrast, that in addition to the various security aspects related to climate change, hard security seems to have returned to the Arctic in levels unforeseen since the end of the Cold War. This is witnessed, inter alia, in the rising military interest of Russia and the US towards the Arctic region, as well as in the attention and awareness of Arctic issues in non-Arctic states, such as China.

The theoretical part includes chapters on both conventional and novel security approaches. Even the author of Chapter 3 on conventional theoretical approaches, Barbora Padrtova, acknowledges that the concept of security from the traditional military and political fields has been widened to cover also economic, societal and environmental sectors. Furthermore, the referent object of security has been widened from the state towards issues such as civilisation, human being and the environment. She and other authors also discuss whether the Arctic could fulfil the conditions of a "regional security complex" (RSC), a concept coined by the Copenhagen School of security studies. The idea of a regional security complex is that the security of one actor cannot be analysed in isolation from the wider regional security complex, because the security of different actors and states is interdependent in such a complex. Arguments can be presented both in favour of the Arctic being a RSC and against it. The RSC theory is very state-centred, whereas the Arctic region is generally not considered to involve the entire territories of the Arctic states. What supports the definition as an RSC, in turn, is that the Arctic region can be considered an anarchic structure, as it is composed of several units that are subdivided into further units. Furthermore, the region is multipolar and includes various patterns of amity and enmity. Still, if we are to stick to the original theory of RSCs as exclusive, the Arctic could hardly constitute an RSC as the region already crosses different RSCs: the European, the post-Soviet/Russian and the North American.

Already the first theoretical chapter illustrates how difficult it is to look at Arctic security with the traditional tools focused on state-centred security, and the following nine theoretical chapters provide less-traditional aspects of security theory. They range from human and comprehensive security approaches to indigenous security theory and intersectional analysis. Most of the approaches analyse security from the more bottom-up perspective focusing on people living in the Arctic region rather than on the state security of the Arctic countries. The Arctic region indeed includes numerous special characters when thinking about security, including the rural and remote communities that prevail in the Arctic.

Part II gives a voice for all the Arctic Eight states, as Arctic cooperation remains to be led by the countries' (southern) capitals. An interesting topic in this regard is Denmark, whose mainland would geographically hardly be part of the Arctic, but which includes the island of Greenland with self-governed indigenous population inhabiting the shores of the Arctic Ocean. Greenland has been in the centre of great power interests throughout its history. A testimony of the increasing interest towards the region is the proposal of the US President Trump to buy Greenland in autumn 2019. Jan Rahbek-Clemmesen's chapter on Denmark and Greenland does not discuss this incident, but it is referred to in the concluding chapter of the book authored by Gunhild Hoogensen Gjørv and Marc Lanteigne. Trump's proposal was immediately cited as 'absurd' by the Danish Prime Minister, which caused a short diplomatic rift with Washington. The incident was telling of the Arctic power play, where big states seek to enhance their power with no interest paid towards self-determination of the inhabitants of the island.

After looking at the perspectives of the Arctic Eight, Part III addresses topics that may often remain neglected in the state-centred security discourse. These deal with security in the Arctic through governance. In addition to the Arctic Council, the chapters discuss science diplomacy, geopolitics and international law, governance, Svalbard area, the Arctic Coast Guard Forum and governance in the Russian Arctic. A particularly intriguing topic is the demilitarisation of the Norwegian Svalbard, an archipelago in the Arctic Ocean, which remains demilitarised since 1920 and despite Norway's NATO membership. Tobjørn Pedersen aptly illustrates in his chapter how Norwegian and Russian interests have sometimes collided over their utilisation of the Svalbard area.

Part IV dealing with non-Arctic actors reveals the rising interest of China in Arctic matters and the lack of interest from international and regional organisations such as the European Union. Adele Airoldi outlines in her chapter how Finland has often remained alone in pushing for Arctic and Northern perspectives in EU policy, such as the Finnish initiative of Northern Dimension (1999) that has remained marginal despite attempts to revitalise the policy. Denmark remains the only EU country with littoral territory in the Arctic Ocean, but self-governed Greenland divorced from the European Communities already in 1985. It is thus not so surprising that the EU pays little attention to what happens in the Arctic Ocean, as none of the EU countries border the ocean.

The book provides novel and intriguing insights into Arctic security throughout the book, but perhaps the most intriguing part is the concluding Part V, which is devoted to people, states and security. Three of the six chapters deal with indigenous peoples, which are numerous in the Arctic region. In addition to discussing the only indigenous people in the European Union, the Sámi living in the Northern parts of Norway, Sweden, Finland and Russia, the book unveils the numerous indigenous peoples inhabiting Northern Russia. The Arctic Council is also famous for including the indigenous voice in its operation; in addition to the eight states, six indigenous Councils have consultation rights in the Council's negotiations and decisions. Therefore, we see six indigenous representatives in the meetings of the Arctic Council alongside the leaders of the Arctic Eight. What is to be noted, however, is that indigenous people representing approximately half a million of the four million inhabitants in the (circumpolar) Arctic remain subsumed to the decision-making of the national states.

A welcome contribution is also Chapter 33 focusing on gender and intersectional approaches to security in the Arctic by Gunhild Hoogensen Gjørv, Embla Eir Oddsdóttir, and Fern Wickson. Although Nordic countries top the ranks of gender equality in the world, this does not apply to all Arctic states. What is more, given that a quarter of the Arctic inhabitants belong to an indigenous people and therefore to a minority group, gender issues intertwine with minority perspectives that are often undermined in the male-dominated sphere of traditional, military-focused security. Feminist and postcolonial perspectives are important also in the Arctic region, not least with regard to often-rejected idea of the colonial history of the Nordic countries towards the indigenous Sámi.

Another approach to security, which continues to remain under-theorised, is food security, for which the second-last chapter discusses, authored by Kamrul Hossain, Thora M. Herrmann and Dele Raheem. Food security is intimately interlinked with other security perspectives, such as environmental security and indigenous security. The possibility of indigenous peoples to continue their traditional livelihoods such as reindeer herding and fishing and prepare traditional dishes depends on the state of environment in the Arctic regions. The right to food and food sovereignty are further linked to the right to culture and to the right to land, which remain essential for continuing these traditional livelihoods.

In the end, although the governance of Arctic matters continues to be in the hands of nation-states, the book reveals the different tensions hiding underneath. Norway and Denmark have to take into account the statuses of their Arctic islands, Svalbard and Greenland, and all Arctic countries are home to indigenous people. Although capitals of course want to hold onto their power, indigenous peoples have found more influence through their transnational networks. A good example is the Saami Council established in 1956, with Sámi member organisations from Finland, Russia, Norway and Sweden. Saami Council is also the organisation that officially represents the Sámi voice in the Arctic Council. The ability to have their voices heard is not as well realised with regard to all indigenous people in the Arctic, as the book aptly illustrates.

Together with its more than 400 pages revolving around different aspects of Arctic security, the handbook offers a comprehensive view towards power play at different levels. The division into the five parts is meaningful and each part forms a coherent whole. Due to its impressive length, the book may be a bit exhausting to read from beginning to end, and its main use is definitely as a handbook where one can check topics of interest. However, even those well versed in Arctic matters can definitely find new insights in the volume. The expectations of reading a handbook may not be very high, but the book managed to surprise positively with its unexpected and novel approaches. In addition to serving as a useful and up-to-date handbook for researchers and students, the book could well be used as a course book in university courses. Compiling a coherent volume with 35 chapters is no easy task, but the editors and authors deliver what they promise; a snapshot of different security perspectives in the Arctic and insights into understanding the concept of security.

Saila Heinikoski
Senior Research Fellow, Finnish Institute of International Affairs
saila.heinikoski@fiia.fi

BOOK REVIEWS 477

Gabriella Argüello, *Marine Pollution, Shipping Waste and International Law* (Routledge 2020). ISBN: 978-0-367-18098-0, ISBN: 978-0-429-05951-3 (ebook).

Transport by sea is the lifeblood of the globalised economy. Even in times of global recession and alternative supply chains and an increasing focus on local production, the transport of goods and persons will remain relevant for the foreseeable future. Polar cruise tourism has been booming for some time and this trend is likely to continue when the global tourism industry will rebound from the economic aftershocks of the COVID-19 pandemic.

For the Arctic, the rapid loss of sea ice and the increasing availability of shipping routes in the Arctic ocean means that the effects of ship operations need to be considered in the governance of the Arctic. The central Arctic ocean, i.e., the part of the Arctic ocean in which the water is beyond the national sovereignty of the littoral States, Russia, the United States, Canada, Greenland (which still belongs to Denmark but enjoys far-reaching autonomy) and Norway, the Arctic Five (A5), is not an enclosed or semi-enclosed sea within the meaning of Article 122 of the United Nations Convention on the Law of the Sea (UNCLOS). Neither is there, yet, a regional seas programme (RSP) for the Arctic ocean. But there is a sense in the five coastal States of the Arctic of belonging together. This is reflected in the approach to Arctic marine governance which is not only shared by the A5 but by all Arctic nations, the A8, including the aforementioned countries as well as Iceland, Sweden and Finland. Together, the Arctic States have created international legal standards, utilising the framework provided by the Arctic Council (AC), the most important forum for inter-governmental cooperation in the Arctic. The international treaties which have been negotiated by the A8 under the auspices of the Arctic Council address matters of common concern which are relevant in particular to the Arctic ocean. It was also the Arctic States which have been trailblazers in protecting the biodiversity of the central Arctic ocean, for example through the Central Arctic Ocean Fisheries Agreement (CAOFA), which has been concluded by the A5, the non-Arctic nations of China, Japan, South Korea as well as Iceland the European Union, of which the remaining Arctic States, Finland and Sweden, have been members for a quarter of a century. These proactive developments in the creation of international treaty norms with relevance for the Arctic ocean, however, should not distract from the fact that key norms governing the Arctic ocean are not dependent on the will of the local States, which are arguably best suited to reflect the experiences and needs of the local communities in the Arctic (although it has to be noted that many national decisions in Arctic States continue to be made in faraway national capitals and with limited Arctic input or expertise). This regional interest in governing the Arctic ocean is contrasted with the global approach which is enabled under UNCLOS. Apart from Article 234 UNCLOS, which only applies to exclusive economic zones (EEZs), the United Nations Convention on the Law of the Sea remains silent on polar waters. Therefore, general rules under UNCLOS also apply to the Arctic ocean and the waters surrounding Antarctica. Those who are interested in protecting the marine environment of the Southern and Arctic oceans therefore have to take UNCLOS as the point of departure for any use of international law for efforts to improve the current situation. While UNCLOS provides a quasi-constitutional framework for the international law of the sea, the International Convention for the Prevention of Pollution from Ships (MARPOL) remains at the center of international regulations concerning vessel-source pollution. Together with the International Convention for the Safety of Life at Sea (SOLAS), MARPOL also provided the background to the Polar Code. The latter entered into force in 2017 after a long evolution through several soft law stages. The Polar Code is meant to enhance the protection of the marine environment of polar waters and to improve maritime safety. To do so, it addresses specific risks inherent in ship operations in polar waters. Other standards, such as MARPOL and SOLAS continue to apply, the Polar Code is merely an addition 'on top'. Among the issues regulated in the Polar Code is that of waste, in particular the discharge of wastes from ships.

One problem which has gained more attention in recent years in the context of international efforts to protect the marine environment is waste. The book discussed here therefore provides a timely contribution to an ongoing and important debate. In particular plastic waste remains a serious threat to the marine environment in many parts of the world, including in polar waters. While most marine pollution, in particular in the context of plastic waste, has its origin on land, ship operators are not blameless either. Reducing the harm caused to the marine environment, in polar waters or elsewhere, by waste pollution from ships therefore is a worthy endeavour. It is only one of the key issues that Argüello tackles in her well-written book. Gabriela Argüello, who was trained in Sweden

Three core issues form red threads which run throughout the book: the environmentally sound management (ESM) of wastes, the transboundary transport of wastes, in particular by ships and wastes generated by the operation of ships. In the context of an introduction to the work's theoretical framework and the role of public international law in the regulation of waste, the author lays the groundwork for the treatment of ESM and connects it to issues of current interest, such as sustainable development. The topic of the environmentally sound management of wastes is then expanded in the second chapter.

The author shows "that ESM is a principle that fosters cooperation between subjects of international law and prompts the development of further soft and hard law actions." Her treatment of the environmentally sound management of wastes is informed and the text is written in an informative manner which also speaks to readers who might have an interest in international environmental law but who might not yet be too familiar with ESM. This is a general characteristic of this book: the author successfully opens doors to the reader to issues which might not be familiar for all potential readers. Indeed, at times she takes a step back and allows us a view of the bigger picture, for example when placing the legal status of ESM into the wider context of customary international law and in doing so explains the relevance and functioning of customary international law. This is achieved with exactly the right amount of detail: enough to also inform readers who are not familiar with the topic, including a reference for example to key case law, but also concise enough so as not to disturb the overall flow of the text for readers who are well versed in these more general issues. This is no small achievement. While the structure of the second chapter appears somewhat unclear at first sight, with multiple "Concluding remarks", the author does a good job at explaining the locus of ESM within public international law (PIL), including its legal status in both customary and treaty law. In doing so, she does not limit her analysis to the question of the legal nature of ESM within PIL. In addition, the role of ESM as a legal framework is illuminated. ESM is described as a "principle" and the author makes sure to clarify for readers who might not be familiar with international environmental law which particular role legal principles play for international environmental law. She manages to do so in a way which is neither condescending not too much en passant, neither lost in details nor superficial. Taking a moment to enlighten readers who are new to the topic does not distract readers who may themselves be experts on a particular point. In a way, chapters 3 to 5, even though they spread over two parts (Part I, which is entitles "Preliminaries" and part II, on the regulation of transboundary movements of wastes and ship wastes) build on top of each other, dealing with waste as a legal issue (chapter 3), its transboundary movement and the international regulation thereof (chapter 4) and ship-source pollution (chapter 6). The both chapters 5 and 6 the author does not stop at public international law but specifically adds the dimension of European Union law and thereby provides a more complete picture. Particular attention is given to specific international treaties, such as MARPOL or the Basel Convention, which deal with these issues. In the context of the law of the sea dimension of chapter 3, the attempt to provide an interpretation of Article 195 UNCLOS is particularly noteworthy. Article 195 UNCLOS reads as follows: "In taking measures to prevent, reduce and control pollution of the marine environment, States shall act so as not to transfer, directly or indirectly, damage or hazards from one area to another or transform one type of pollution into another." Despite being a relatively short norm, Article 195 UNCLOS is far from clear and the author explains the difference between "transfer" and "transform" with a quality-based approach, which certainly has merit and which leads to an interpretation of Article 195 UNCLOS which appears entirely compatible with the wording of the norm. This comes after the reader has been introduced to the Basel Convention and the author then connects Article 195 UNCLOS to that international treaty. In the context of pollution from ships, the author takes not of classical case law and historical events which have shaped the development of the international law of vessel-source pollution. Here she does not limit herself to waste but takes into account the problem of oil pollution from ships, which has been a key driving force behind the development of international standards in this regard. By connecting these issues, it is shown that the treatment of waste pollution from ships does not exist in a legal vacuum but that it has to be seen in the wider context of the entirety of issues which are covered by MARPOL. The author is also cognizant of practical problems and does not limit her text to purely legal and theoretical issues. This becomes visible in her treatment of the problem of an excessive reliance on the availability and functioning of facilities for the reception of wastes in ports. She correctly identifies the lack of sufficient port reception facilities as one possible driving force behind violations of Article 195 UNCLOS.

The author returns to ESM in chapters 6 to 8, which form a key part of the book. These chapters, which make up part III build on top of the treatment of ship-source pollution. It is here that the author's expertise becomes visible most clearly. The reader is introduced to the *Probo Koala* and *Probo Emu* cases, in which large amounts of toxic waste had been dumped illegally and with severe effects on human health. In these cases, it was the management of specific wastes in a country, which had been transported by ship to a country. These cases mark the crossroads between the Basel Convention and MARPOL, as the former excludes from its scope of application wastes which are generated during regular ship operations. The author explains the limited utility of the Basel Convention with regard to wastes generated on ships, concluding that "[i]t is the very nature of shipping that precludes the applicability of the Basel Convention to ship wastes while onboard". In addition, the author connects the Basel Convention to specific concepts of the international law of the sea, such as innocent passage through the territorial sea of a State other than the flag State. Importantly, the book provides information on the question of how far ESM standards can be applied to wastes generated on ships. Overall, the author provides a fairly complete picture. Especially the part on ESM and ship wastes will be useful for legal practitioners and researchers alike.

The order in which the diverse issues are being dealt with might not be intuitive for readers with a legal background, but it serves to highlight the aforementioned core concerns of the book. In any case, does each chapter make for interesting reading on its own and the book can serve as a research resource on the diverse issues dealt within it.

In the final chapters, the author returns to more classical legal themes and addresses the issues which have been identified so far, for example the aforementioned tension between the international legal rules governing the transboundary transportation of wastes and the rules which regulate pollution from ships. Chapter 10, in particular, provides a good summary of the international legal dimension of ESM.

This book will certainly be of interest to academic researchers and should not be missing from libraries in institutions which are concerned with maritime or environmental issues, in particular, but not only, from a legal perspective. Given that it is not intended to be a research handbook per se, the among of references is sufficient and especially the jurisprudence mentioned in the text has been well chosen and encourages readers to pursue the issues covered in the text. Finally, it should not go without noting that this book not only succeeds in informing the reader – it is actually written in a manner which is accessible to readers from diverse backgrounds. It is an excellent introduction for those new to these issues but still leaves a more advanced reader with the knowledge that one has learned something new from reading this book, which is a well-written contribution and hopefully not the last monograph from this author.

Stefan Kirchner
University of Lapland
Stefan.Kirchner@ulapland.fi

Printed in the United States
By Bookmasters